batwoman

BY GREG RUCKA AND J.H. WILLIAMS III

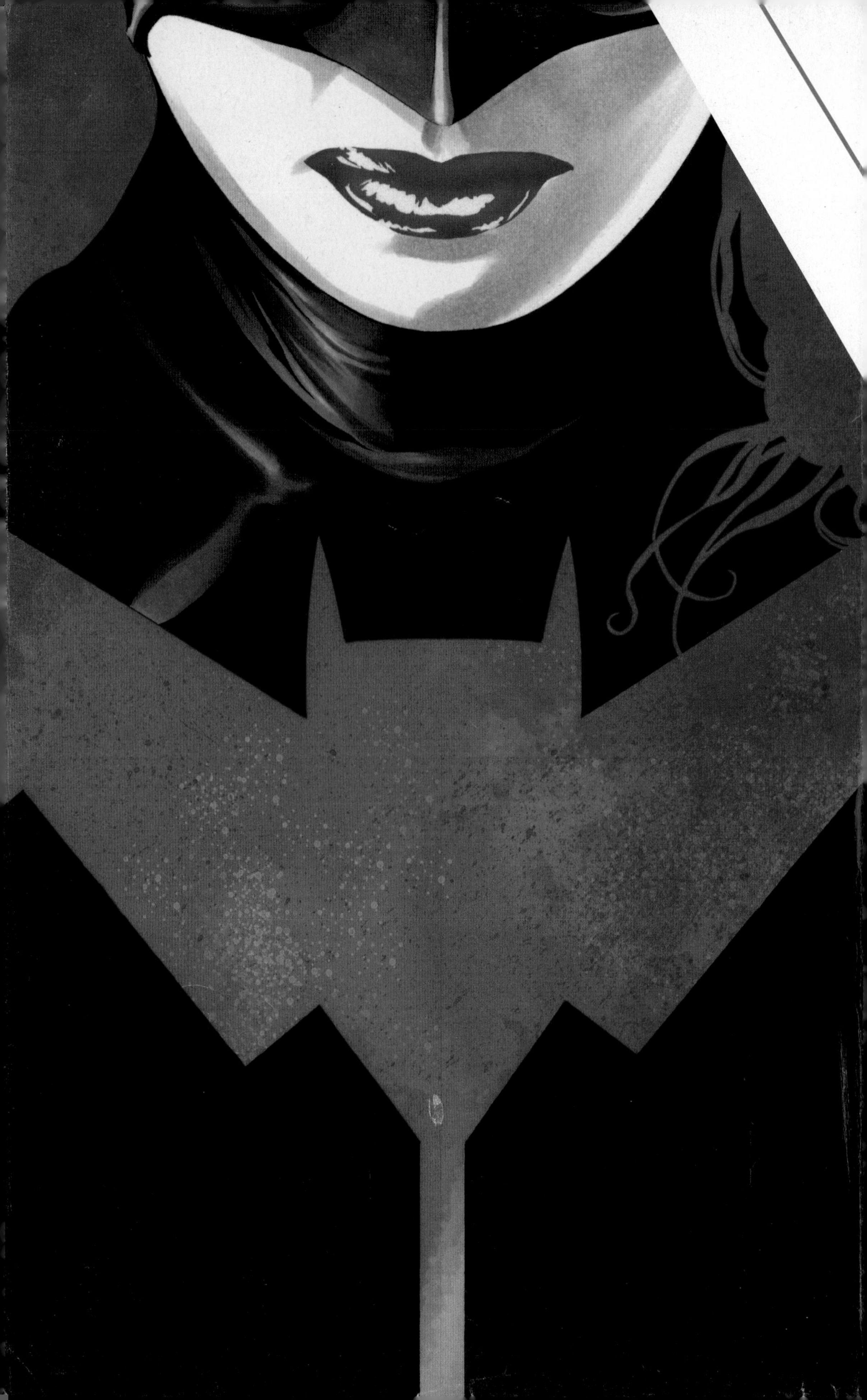

batwoman

BY GREG RUCKA AND J.H. WILLIAMS III

GREG RUCKA
WRITER

J.H. WILLIAMS III
JOCK   SCOTT KOLINS
ARTISTS

DAVE STEWART
DAVID BARON
COLORISTS

TODD KLEIN
LETTERER

J.H. WILLIAMS III
COLLECTION COVER ARTIST

BATMAN CREATED BY BOB KANE WITH BILL FINGER

MICHAEL SIGLAIN EDITOR – ORIGINAL SERIES
HARVEY RICHARDS ASSISTANT EDITOR – ORIGINAL SERIES
JEB WOODARD GROUP EDITOR – COLLECTED EDITIONS
ROBIN WILDMAN EDITOR – COLLECTED EDITIONS
STEVE COOK DESIGN DIRECTOR – BOOKS
BOB HARRAS SENIOR VP – EDITOR-IN-CHIEF, DC COMICS
MONIQUE GRUSPE PUBLICATION DESIGN

DIANE NELSON PRESIDENT
DAN DIDIO PUBLISHER
JIM LEE PUBLISHER
GEOFF JOHNS PRESIDENT & CHIEF CREATIVE OFFICER
AMIT DESAI EXECUTIVE VP – BUSINESS & MARKETING STRATEGY, DIRECT TO CONSUMER
& GLOBAL FRANCHISE MANAGEMENT
SAM ADES SENIOR VP – DIRECT TO CONSUMER
BOBBIE CHASE VP – TALENT DEVELOPMENT
MARK CHIARELLO SENIOR VP – ART, DESIGN & COLLECTED EDITIONS
JOHN CUNNINGHAM SENIOR VP – SALES & TRADE MARKETING
ANNE DePIES SENIOR VP – BUSINESS STRATEGY, FINANCE & ADMINISTRATION
DON FALLETTI VP – MANUFACTURING OPERATIONS
LAWRENCE GANEM VP – EDITORIAL ADMINISTRATION & TALENT RELATIONS
ALISON GILL SENIOR VP – MANUFACTURING & OPERATIONS
HANK KANALZ SENIOR VP – EDITORIAL STRATEGY & ADMINISTRATION
JAY KOGAN VP – LEGAL AFFAIRS
THOMAS LOFTUS VP – BUSINESS AFFAIRS
JACK MAHAN VP – BUSINESS AFFAIRS
NICK J. NAPOLITANO VP – MANUFACTURING ADMINISTRATION
EDDIE SCANNELL VP – CONSUMER MARKETING
COURTNEY SIMMONS SENIOR VP – PUBLICITY & COMMUNICATIONS
JIM (SKI) SOKOLOWSKI VP – COMIC BOOK SPECIALTY SALES & TRADE MARKETING
NANCY SPEARS VP – MASS, BOOK, DIGITAL SALES & TRADE MARKETING

BATWOMAN BY GREG RUCKA AND J.H. WILLIAMS III

Published by DC Comics. Compilation and all new material Copyright © 2017 DC Comics.
All Rights Reserved. Originally published in single magazine form in DETECTIVE COMICS 854-863.
Copyright © 2009, 2010 DC Comics. All Rights Reserved. All characters, their distinctive likenesses and
related elements featured in this publication are trademarks of DC Comics.
The stories, characters and incidents featured in this publication are entirely fictional.
DC Comics does not read or accept unsolicited submissions of ideas, stories or artwork.

DC Comics, 2900 West Alameda Ave., Burbank, CA 91505
Printed by Solisco Printers, Scott, QC, Canada. 5/12/17. First Printing.
ISBN: 978-1-4012-7413-9

Library of Congress Cataloging-in-Publication Data is available.

INTRODUCTION BY RACHEL MADDOW

I confess to once giving a copy of Greg Rucka's *Queen and Country: Operation Broken Ground* to a member of the Senate Intelligence Committee, because I thought it might be helpful to the Senator. It's not as crazy as it sounds: get to know Rucka's character Tara Chase and then Google the real modern American spook Dusty Foggo, and see which one you find more edifying.

In *Batwoman*, Katherine Rebecca Kane is another character written by Rucka that you can't quite believe doesn't exist in the real world. Her recitation of West Point's honor code—"A cadet shall not lie, cheat or steal, nor suffer others to do so"—rings in my ears like Lieutenant Dan Choi reciting the same code to me on television in March 2009, proving that the "Don't Ask, Don't Tell" policy forced him to lie as a condition of his military service.

In Kate Kane's quiet but life-defining drive to serve, there's the veterans of my generation who in the absence of a draft but through nine straight years of war, have done three, four, five combat tours, to come home to a nation that doesn't always quite remember we're at war.

"When you act wrongly, you have to answer for it. Without hiding, without complaint... That's integrity, and it is the foundation of honor." That's the moral spine on which Kate Kane's battered frame is hung. She is brave and surly and hurt and strong and always on the Batman rule. For all the brilliant literary allusion, mystery and trademark Rucka attention to detail, what you won't be able to shake when you're done here is that damn compelling lead character.

Well, maybe that and the art.

In a single, wordless panel showing Kate's father's reaction after she tells him why she's been separated from the Army, artist J.H. Williams III captures both a turning point between characters, and a nation's point of decision. It actually feels, right now, in America, the way Colonel Kane looks in that panel, hurt by the plain open ask of his daughter's green eyes.

Yes, cyanogen chloride is a real thing. No, "Southern Misunderstandistan" is not a real place, but you can bet I'll steal it for commenting on our wars, if I haven't done so already by the time you read this. Yes, some of the baddies in the true religion of crime are super genderqueer and yes, guns mix with magic. Get over it. It's all true, it's all gut-wrenching and you love it.

I won't lie to you: I would read anything Greg Rucka wrote. I would read Greg Rucka's grocery lists. I would read Greg Rucka's discarded edits. I would read a Greg Rucka forty-volume soft-hearted navel-gazer about characters I couldn't care less about, if he was capable of writing such a thing, and if he did I'd probably read it out loud to my friends and exclaim and swear about how he made me care.

Batwoman's in good hands here. You'll see.

RACHEL MADDOW
MARCH 2010

RACHEL MADDOW IS A POLITICAL COMMENTATOR AND TELEVISION HOST. SHE HAS BEEN THE HOST OF SEVERAL SYNDICATED TALK RADIO PROGRAMS, AND IS CURRENTLY THE HOST OF THE NIGHTLY TELEVISION PROGRAM THE RACHEL MADDOW SHOW ON MSNBC.

THERE WAS A YEAR, NOT SO VERY LONG PAST, WHERE THE WORLD TURNED WITHOUT THE EYES OF ITS THREE GREATEST HEROES LOOKING UPON IT, WHEN BATMAN, SUPERMAN AND WONDER WOMAN STEPPED BACK FROM THEIR ROLES.

IT WAS IN GOTHAM CITY, THEN, THAT THE SYMBOL OF THE RED BAT WAS FIRST TRULY NOTED, THOUGH SOME HAVE SPECULATED THAT BOTH IT AND ITS WEARER HAD BEEN THERE FOR QUITE SOME TIME ALREADY, WATCHING AND WAITING. BUT IT WAS NOT UNTIL THE DARK KNIGHT'S ABSENCE THAT THIS NEW PRESENCE BECAME TRULY KNOWN.

THIS NEW HERO WAS, IN MANY WAYS, A REFLECTION OF THE BATMAN—THE SAME RUTHLESS PURSUIT OF JUSTICE; THE SAME SAVAGE NEED TO DEFEND THE INNOCENT. BUT THIS WAS NOT SOME ROBIN ALL GROWN UP, NOR WAS IT SOME BOY RAISED TO FIT BOOTS HE HAD NO HOPE OF BEING ABLE TO FILL.

THIS WAS A WOMAN, THE *BATWOMAN*, AND WHILE THERE WAS, INDEED, A REFLECTION, IT WAS CLEAR TO ALL WHO SAW HER THAT THIS WAS SOMETHING DIFFERENT. THIS WAS NOT ANOTHER DEVOTEE OF THE DARK KNIGHT. THIS WOMAN WENT HER OWN WAY.

AT THE END OF THIS YEAR, THE BATWOMAN FELL, CAPTURED BY A CULT DEVOTED TO EVIL, A CULT THAT SAW, IN HER, THE FULFILLMENT OF ITS DARK DESTINY. IT WAS THE HAND OF THE CULT'S LEADER, THE HIGH MADAME OF THE RELIGION OF CRIME, THAT DROVE A KNIFE INTO THE HEART OF BATWOMAN.

SHE SHOULD HAVE DIED. SHE NEARLY DID. INSTEAD, IT WAS THE HIGH MADAME WHO FELL, AND THE BATWOMAN WHO SURVIVED. BUT A WOUND TO THE HEART IS NOT ONE EASILY HEALED.

IT HAS BEEN A LONG ROAD BACK, AND NOW THE BATWOMAN HEARS WHISPERS IN THE NIGHT: A NEW HIGH MADAME IS COMING TO GOTHAM.

THE BATWOMAN IS LOOKING FORWARD TO MEETING HER...

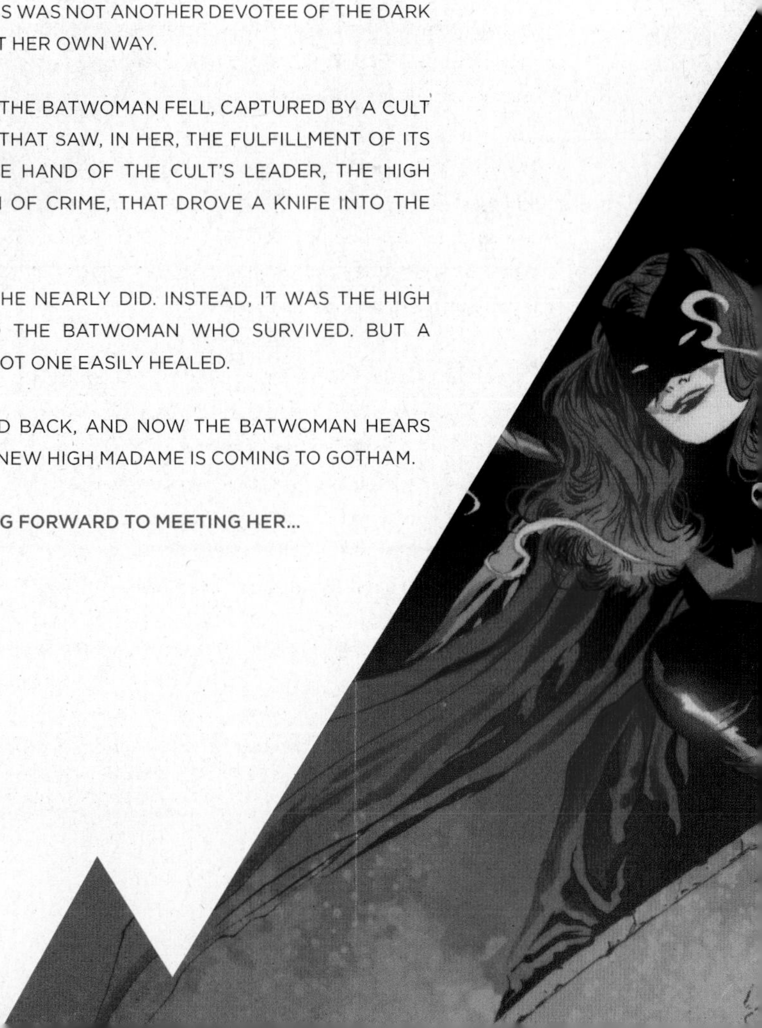

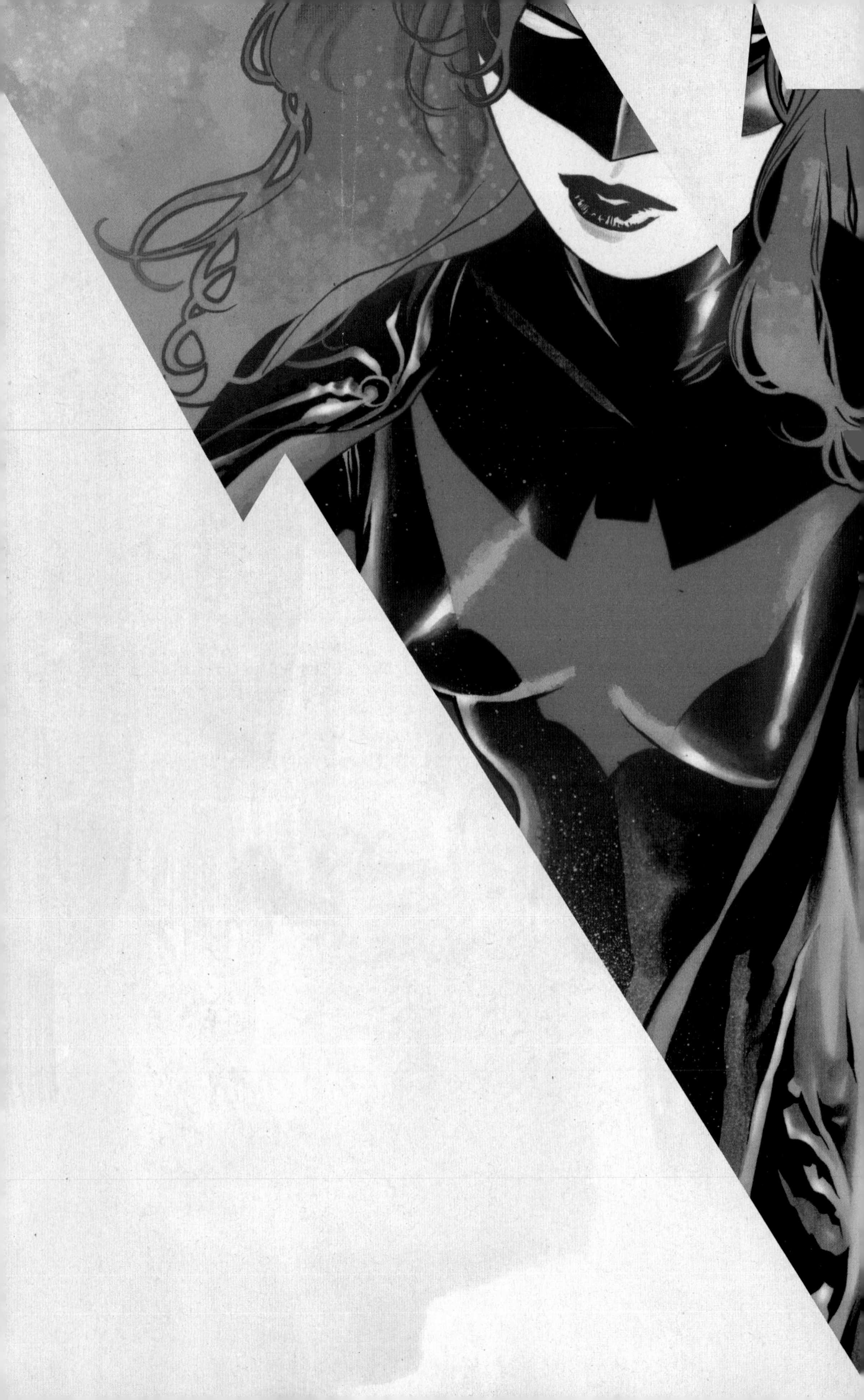

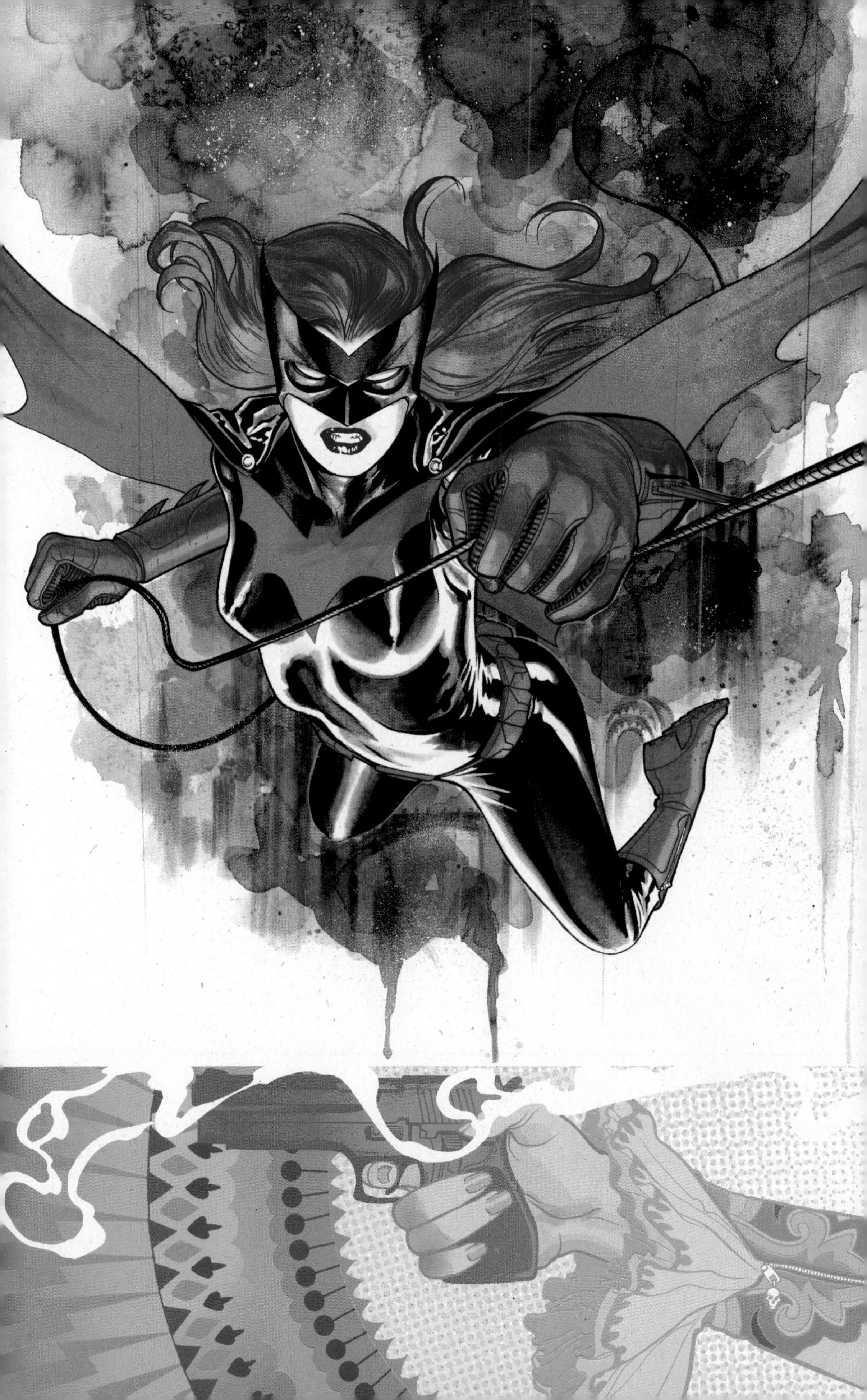

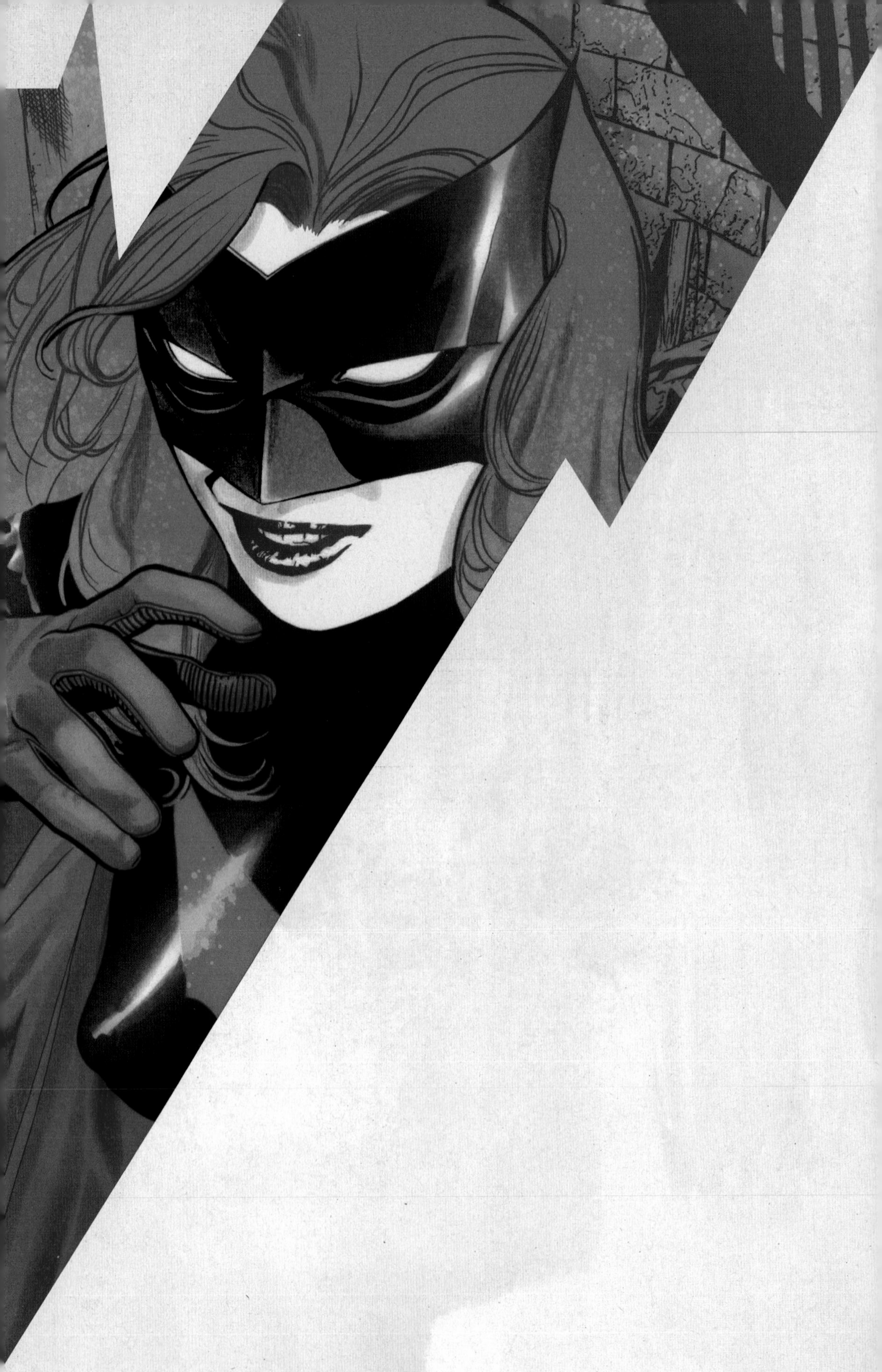

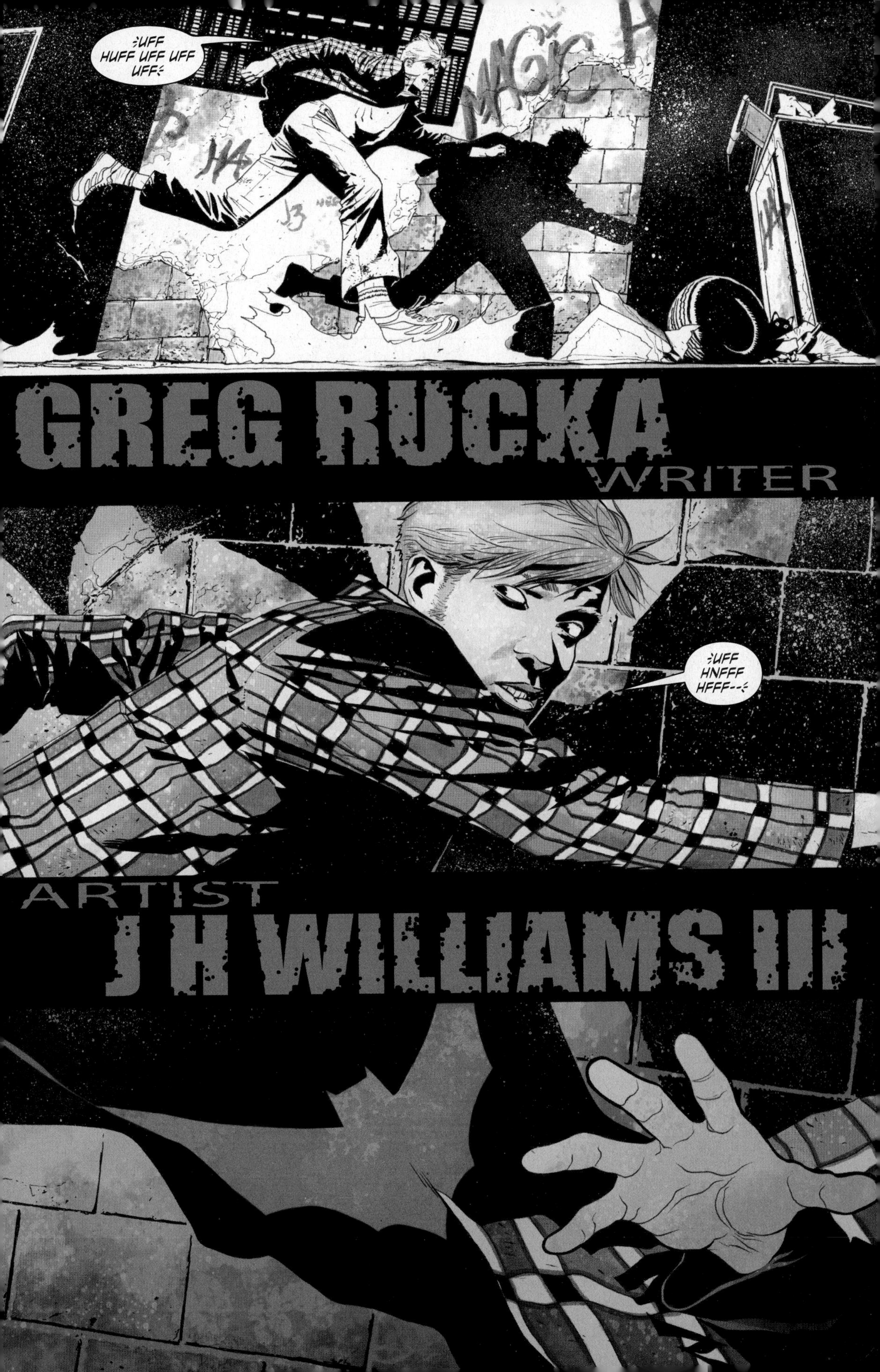

UFF HUFF UFF UFF UFF
GREG RUCKA
WRITER
UFF HNFFF HFFF--
ARTIST
J H WILLIAMS III

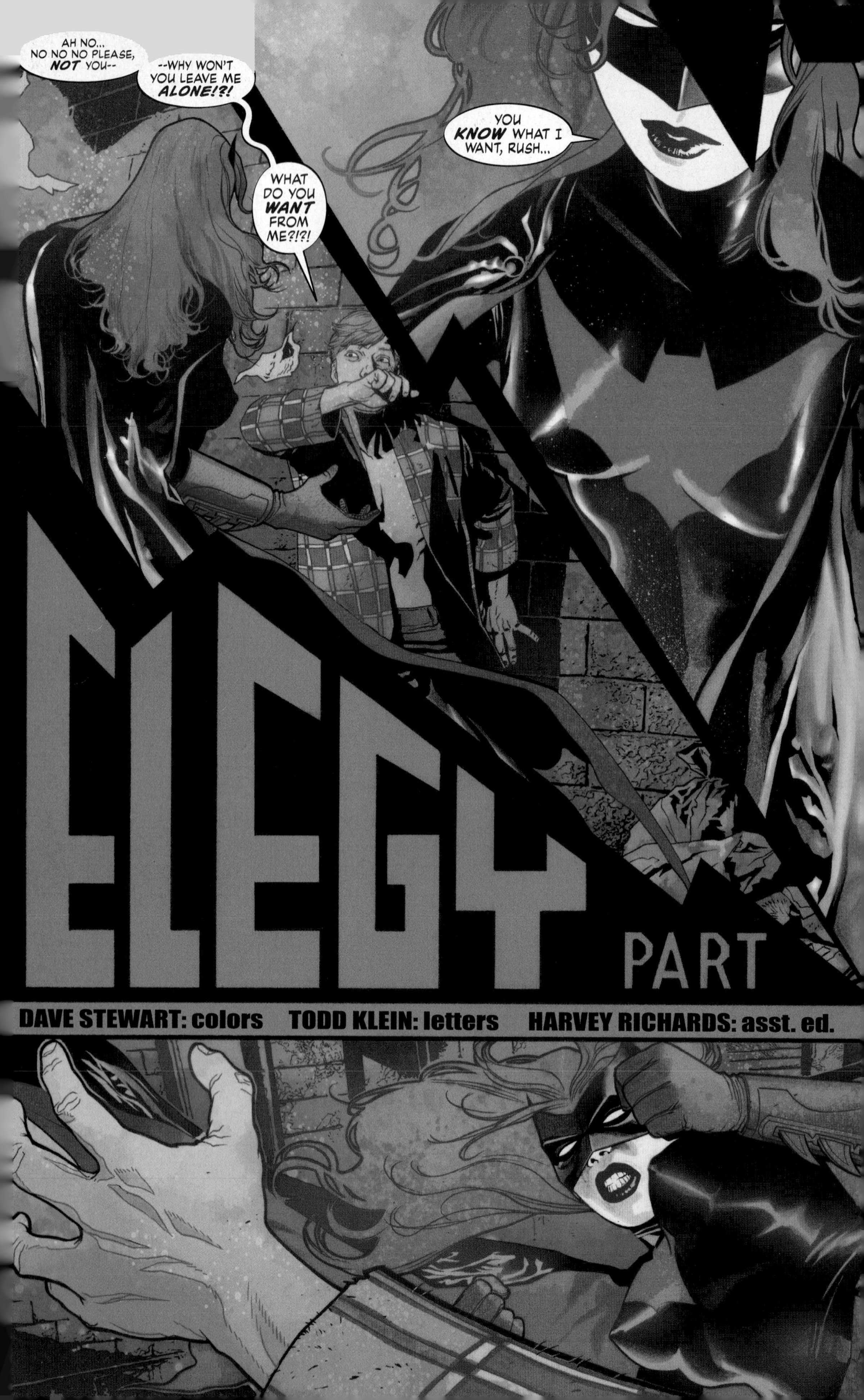
AH NO... NO NO NO PLEASE, NOT YOU--
--WHY WON'T YOU LEAVE ME ALONE!?!
WHAT DO YOU WANT FROM ME?!?!
YOU KNOW WHAT I WANT, RUSH...
ELEGY PART
DAVE STEWART: colors TODD KLEIN: letters HARVEY RICHARDS: asst. ed.

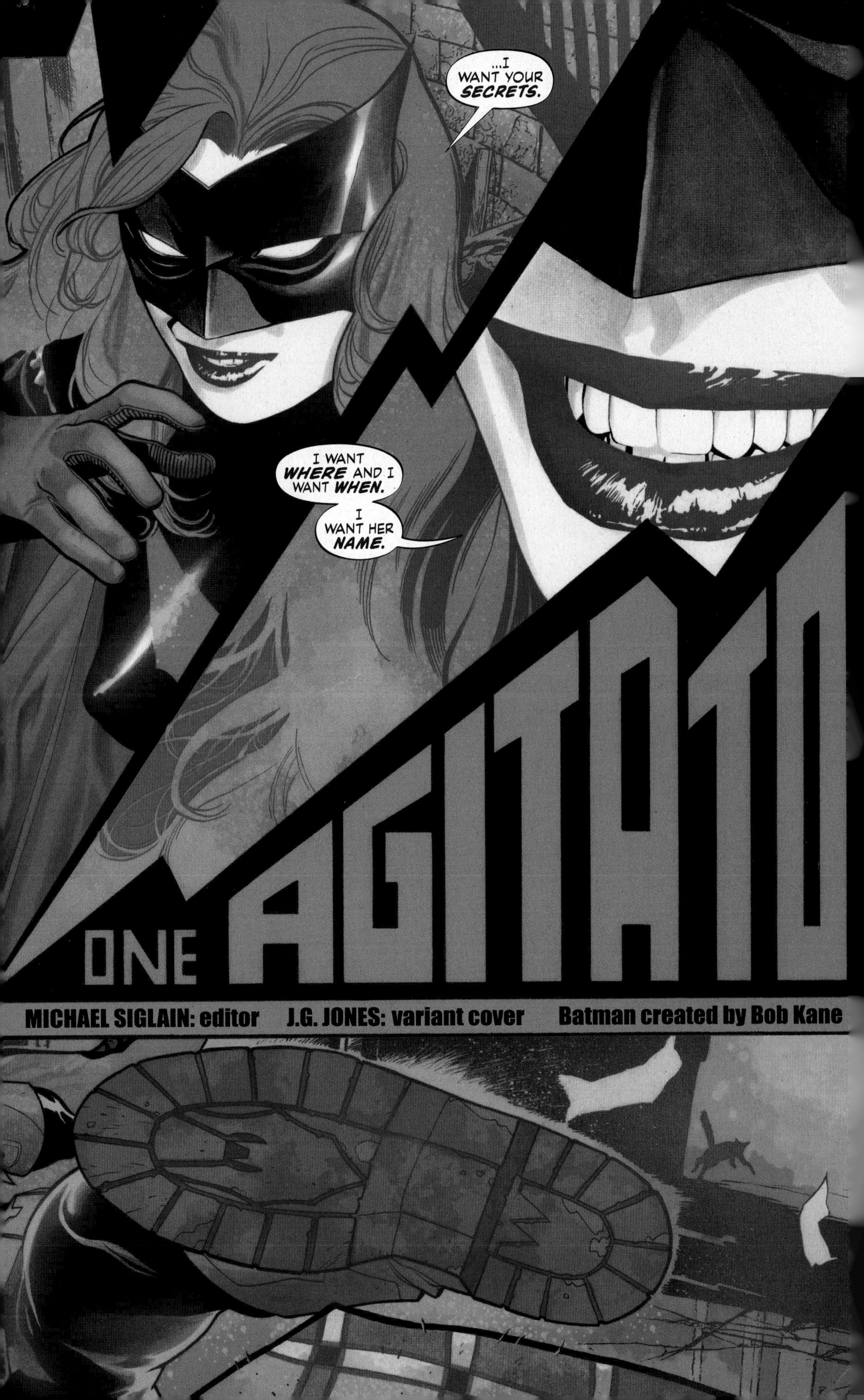
...I WANT YOUR SECRETS.
I WANT WHERE AND I WANT WHEN.
I WANT HER NAME.
ONE AGITATO
MICHAEL SIGLAIN: editor J.G. JONES: variant cover Batman created by Bob Kane

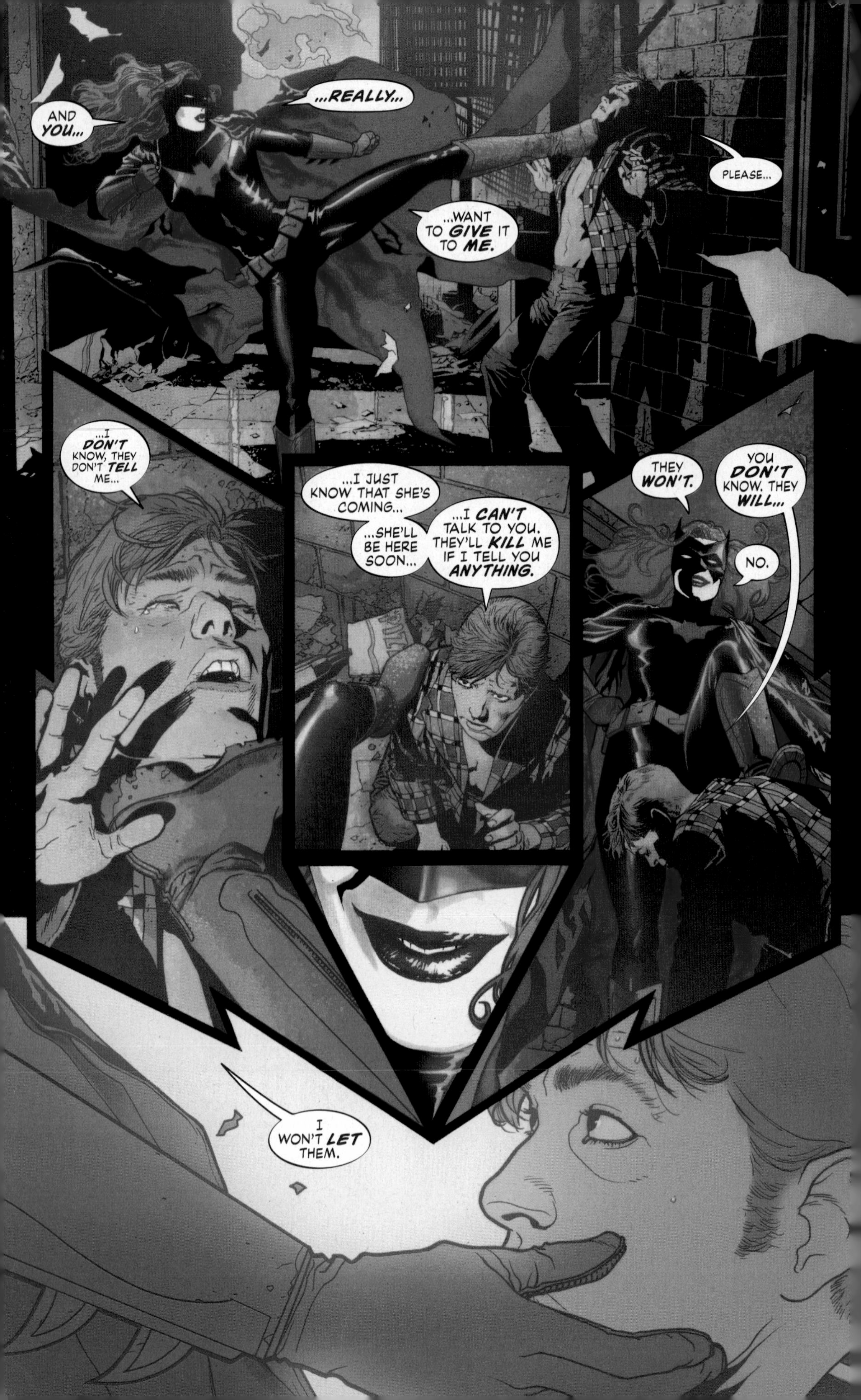
AND YOU...
...REALLY...
...WANT TO GIVE IT TO ME.
PLEASE...
...I DON'T KNOW, THEY DON'T TELL ME...
...I JUST KNOW THAT SHE'S COMING...
...SHE'LL BE HERE SOON...
...I CAN'T TALK TO YOU. THEY'LL KILL ME IF I TELL YOU ANYTHING.
THEY WON'T.
YOU DON'T KNOW. THEY WILL...
NO.
I WON'T LET THEM.

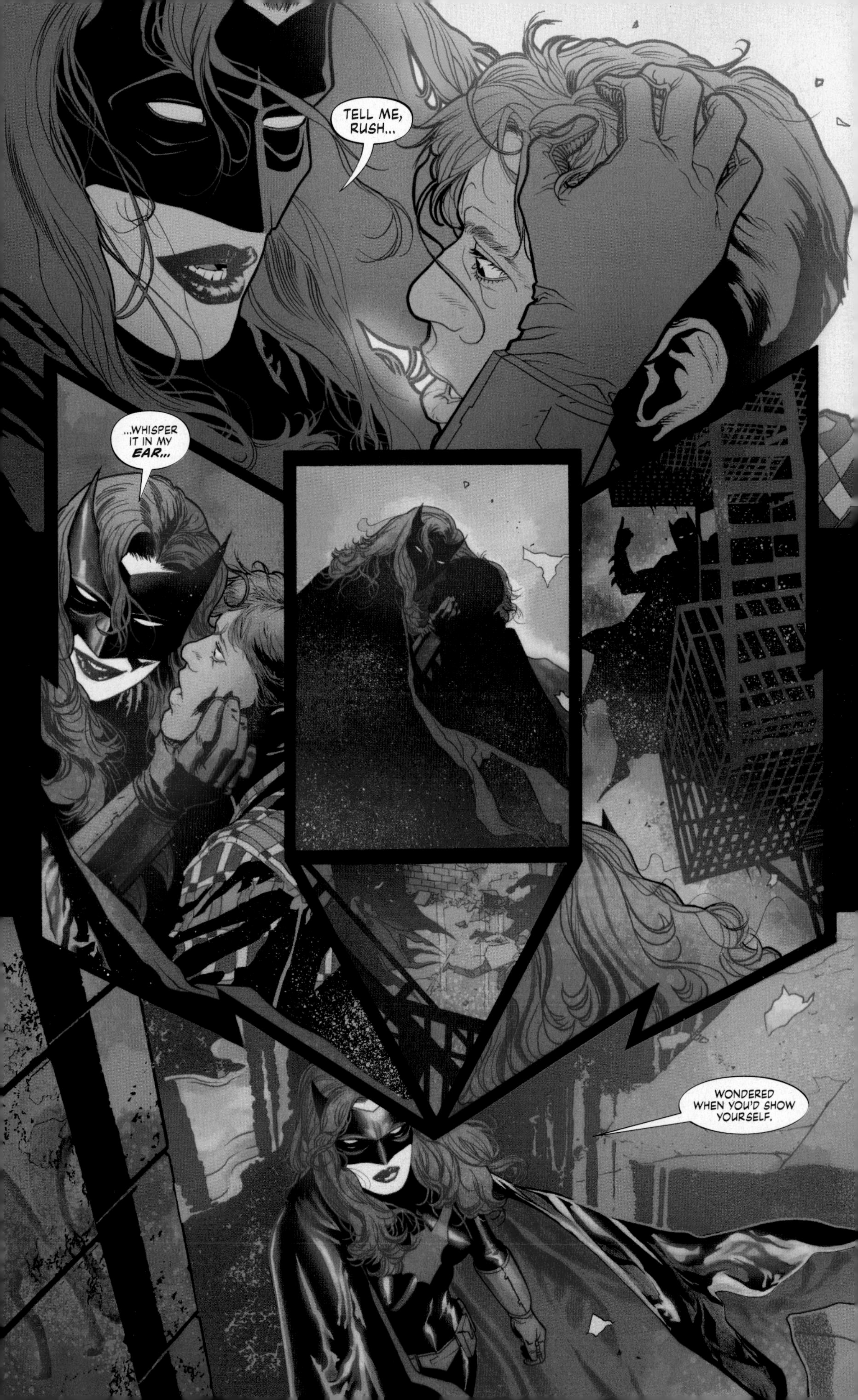
TELL ME, RUSH...
...WHISPER IT IN MY EAR...
WONDERED WHEN YOU'D SHOW YOURSELF.

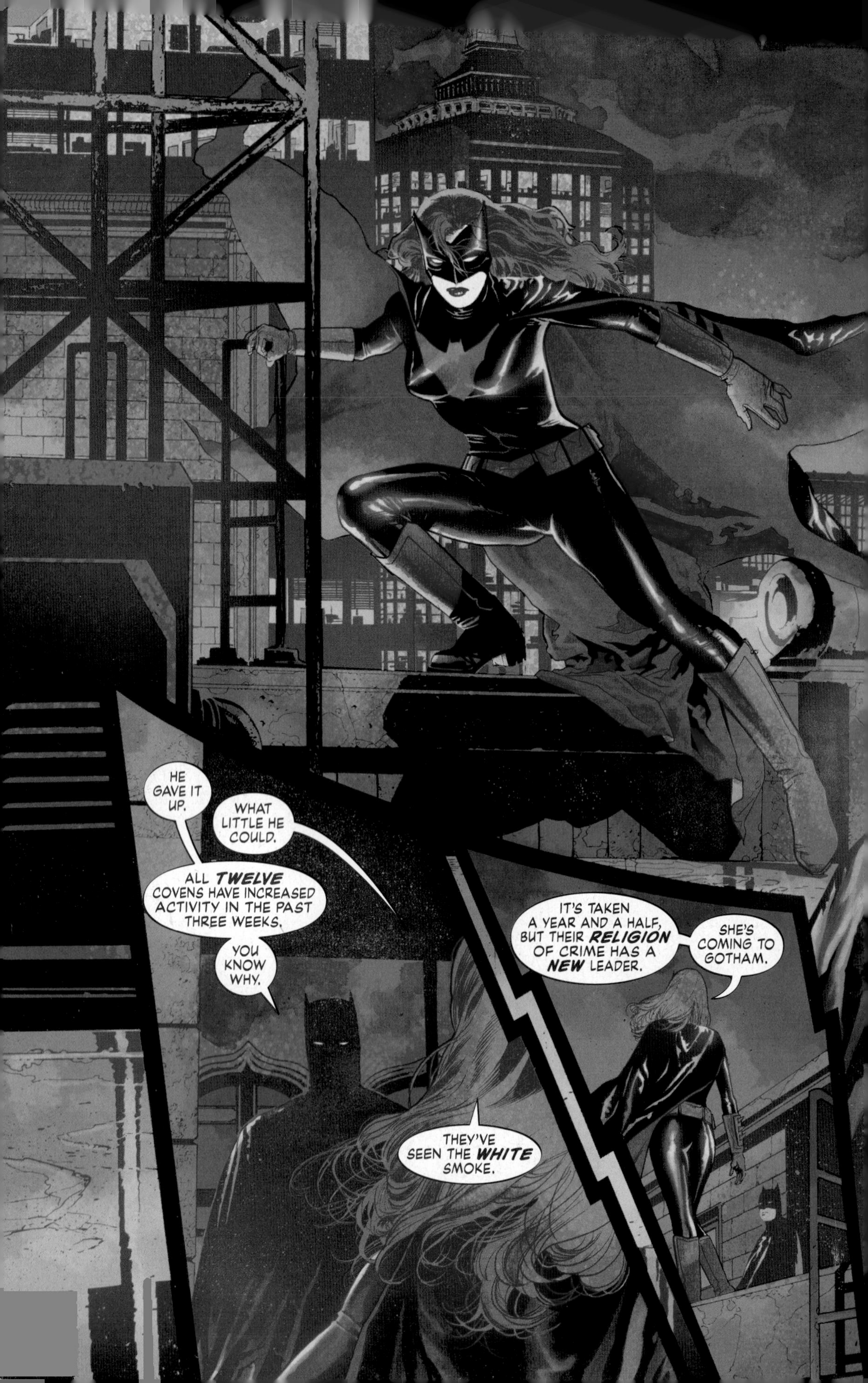
HE GAVE IT UP.
WHAT LITTLE HE COULD.
ALL TWELVE COVENS HAVE INCREASED ACTIVITY IN THE PAST THREE WEEKS.
YOU KNOW WHY.
THEY'VE SEEN THE WHITE SMOKE.
IT'S TAKEN A YEAR AND A HALF, BUT THEIR RELIGION OF CRIME HAS A NEW LEADER.
SHE'S COMING TO GOTHAM.

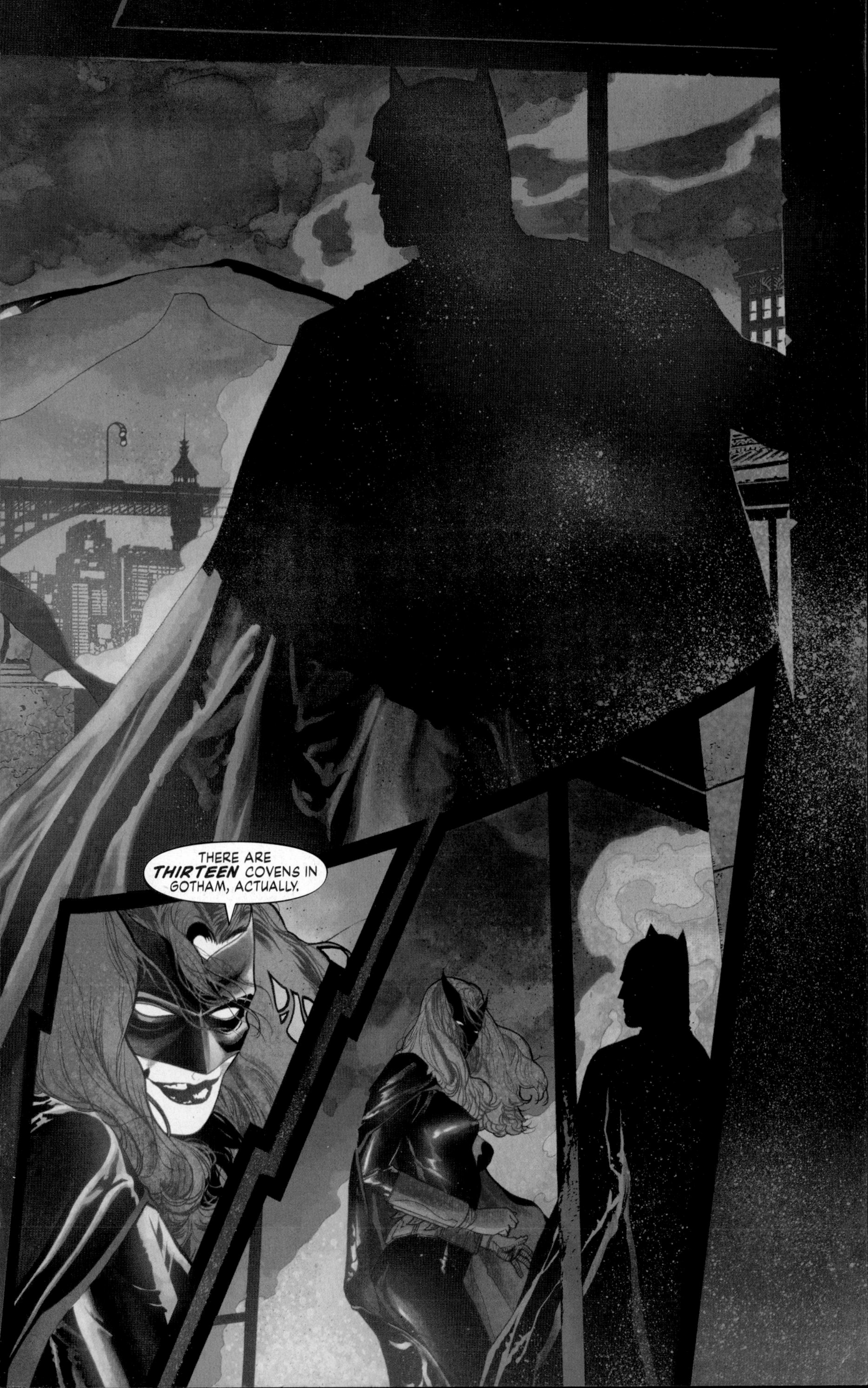
THERE ARE THIRTEEN COVENS IN GOTHAM, ACTUALLY.

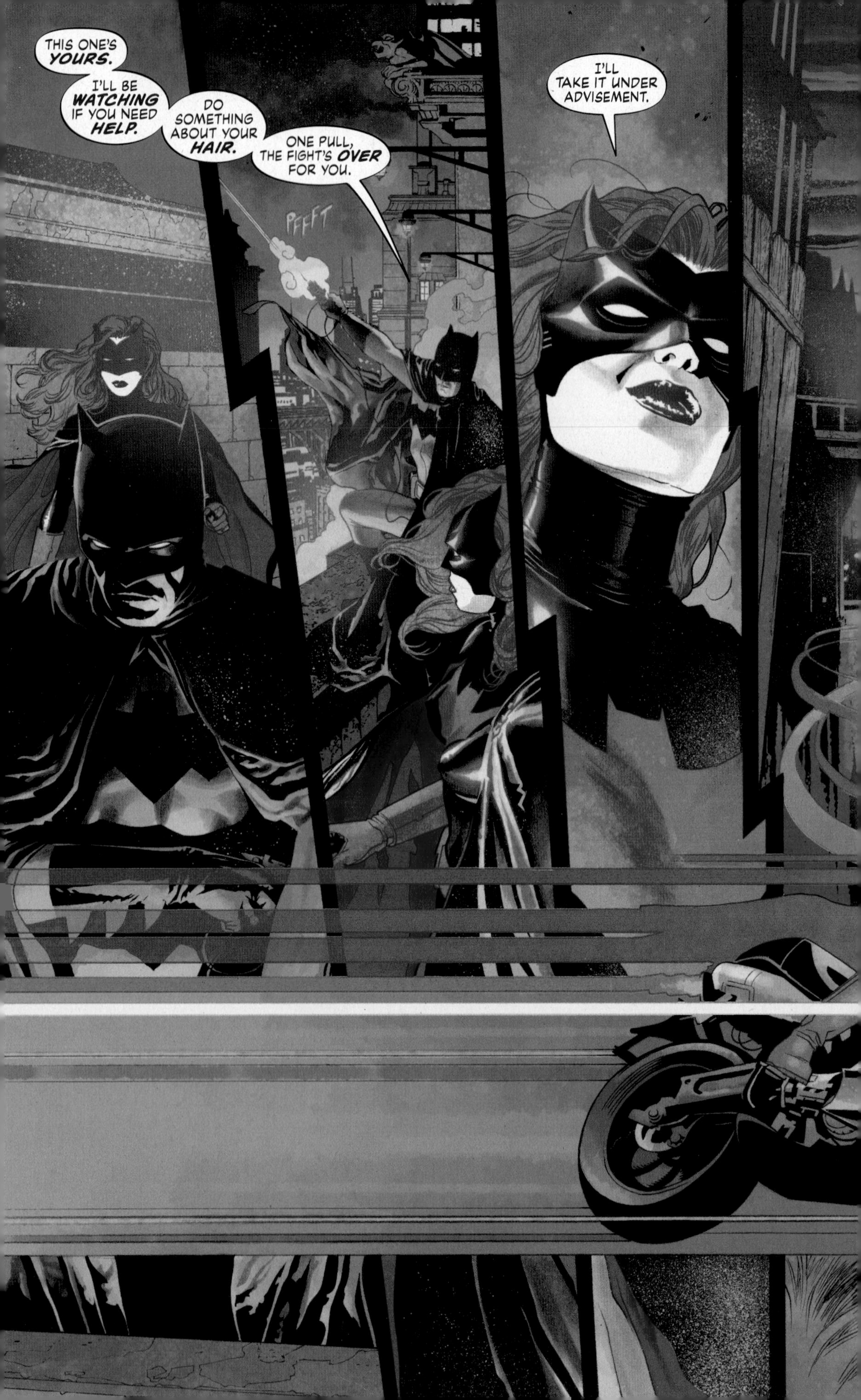
THIS ONE'S YOURS.
I'LL BE WATCHING IF YOU NEED HELP.
DO SOMETHING ABOUT YOUR HAIR.
ONE PULL, THE FIGHT'S OVER FOR YOU.
PFFFT
I'LL TAKE IT UNDER ADVISEMENT.

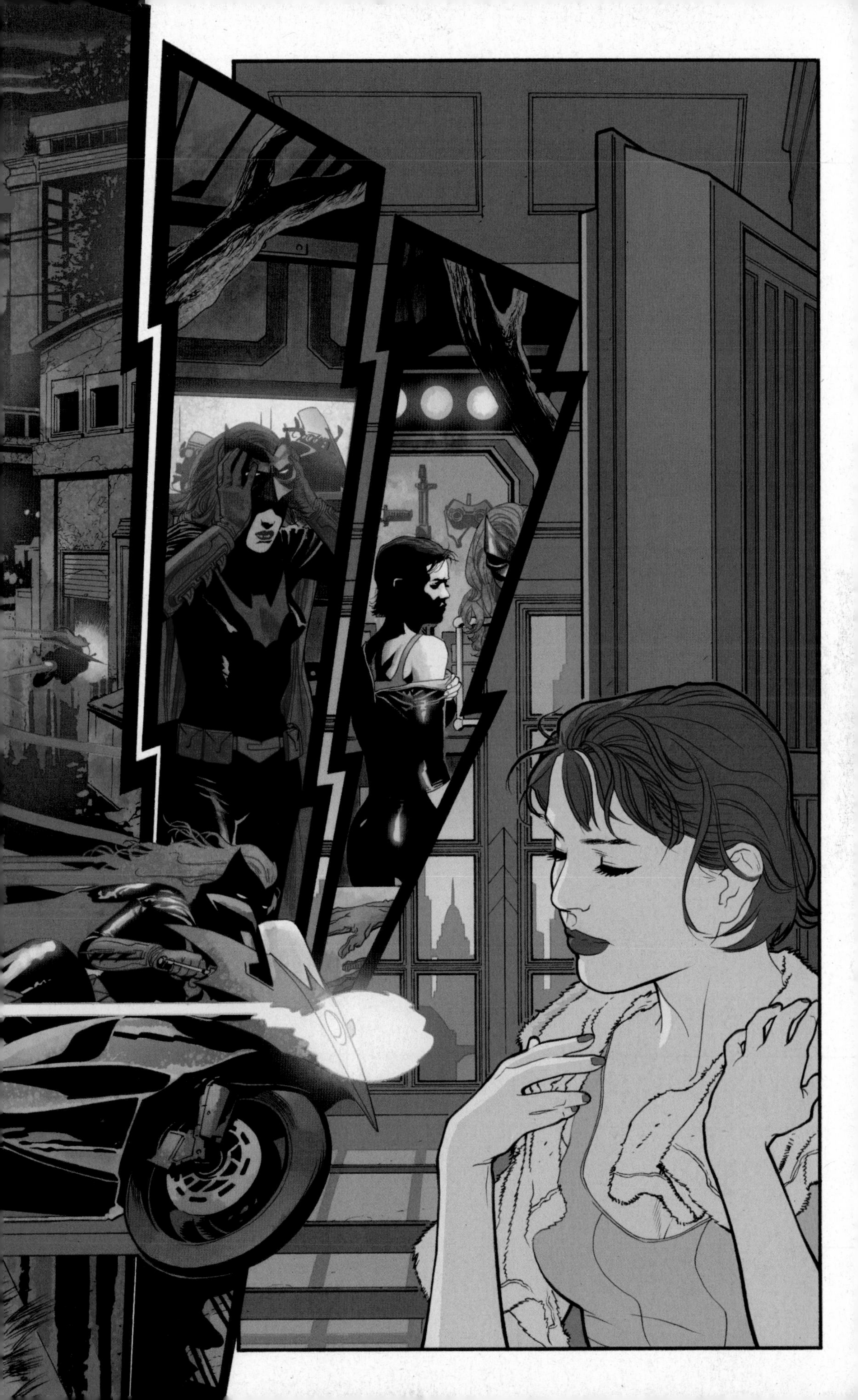

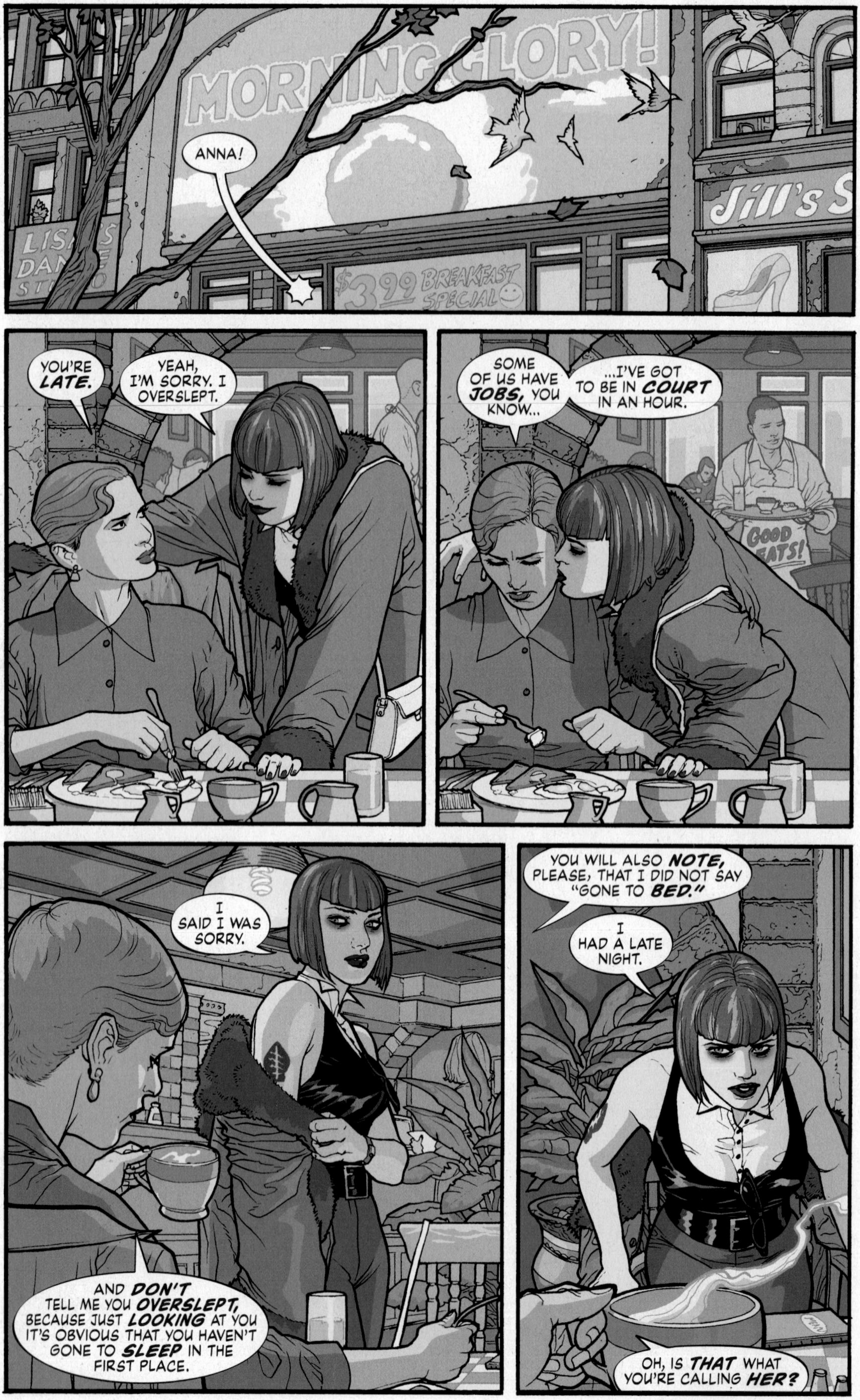
MORNING GLORY!
ANNA!
$3.99 BREAKFAST SPECIAL
YOU'RE **LATE.**
YEAH, I'M SORRY. I OVERSLEPT.
SOME OF US HAVE **JOBS,** YOU KNOW...
...I'VE GOT TO BE IN **COURT** IN AN HOUR.
GOOD EATS!
I SAID I WAS SORRY.
AND **DON'T** TELL ME YOU **OVERSLEPT,** BECAUSE JUST **LOOKING** AT YOU IT'S OBVIOUS THAT YOU HAVEN'T GONE TO **SLEEP** IN THE FIRST PLACE.
YOU WILL ALSO **NOTE,** PLEASE, THAT I DID NOT SAY "GONE TO **BED.**"
I HAD A LATE NIGHT.
OH, IS **THAT** WHAT YOU'RE CALLING **HER?**

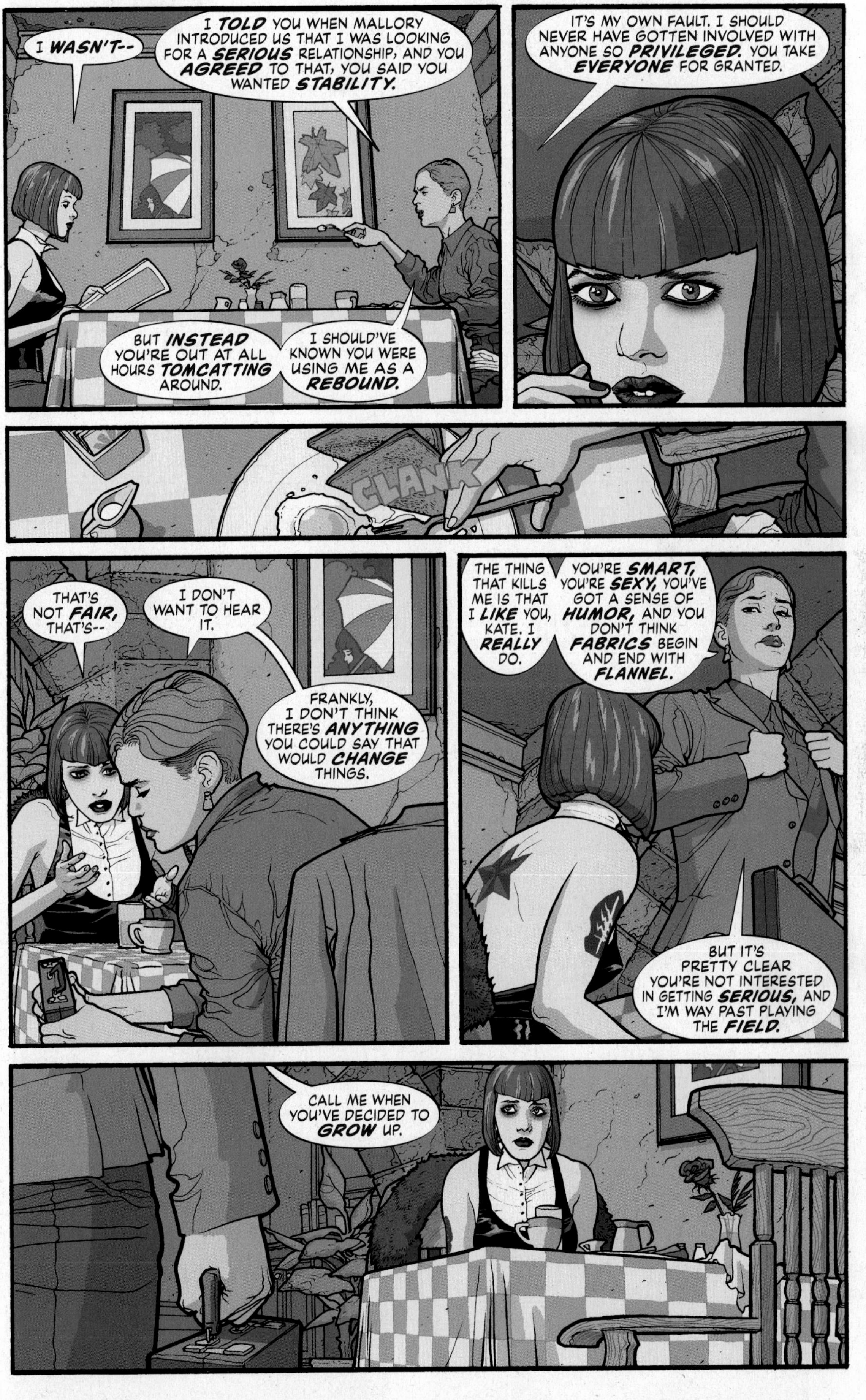

I WASN'T--
I TOLD YOU WHEN MALLORY INTRODUCED US THAT I WAS LOOKING FOR A SERIOUS RELATIONSHIP, AND YOU AGREED TO THAT, YOU SAID YOU WANTED STABILITY.
BUT INSTEAD YOU'RE OUT AT ALL HOURS TOMCATTING AROUND.
I SHOULD'VE KNOWN YOU WERE USING ME AS A REBOUND.
IT'S MY OWN FAULT. I SHOULD NEVER HAVE GOTTEN INVOLVED WITH ANYONE SO PRIVILEGED. YOU TAKE EVERYONE FOR GRANTED.
CLANK
THAT'S NOT FAIR, THAT'S--
I DON'T WANT TO HEAR IT.
FRANKLY, I DON'T THINK THERE'S ANYTHING YOU COULD SAY THAT WOULD CHANGE THINGS.
THE THING THAT KILLS ME IS THAT I LIKE YOU, KATE. I REALLY DO.
YOU'RE SMART, YOU'RE SEXY, YOU'VE GOT A SENSE OF HUMOR, AND YOU DON'T THINK FABRICS BEGIN AND END WITH FLANNEL.
BUT IT'S PRETTY CLEAR YOU'RE NOT INTERESTED IN GETTING SERIOUS, AND I'M WAY PAST PLAYING THE FIELD.
CALL ME WHEN YOU'VE DECIDED TO GROW UP.

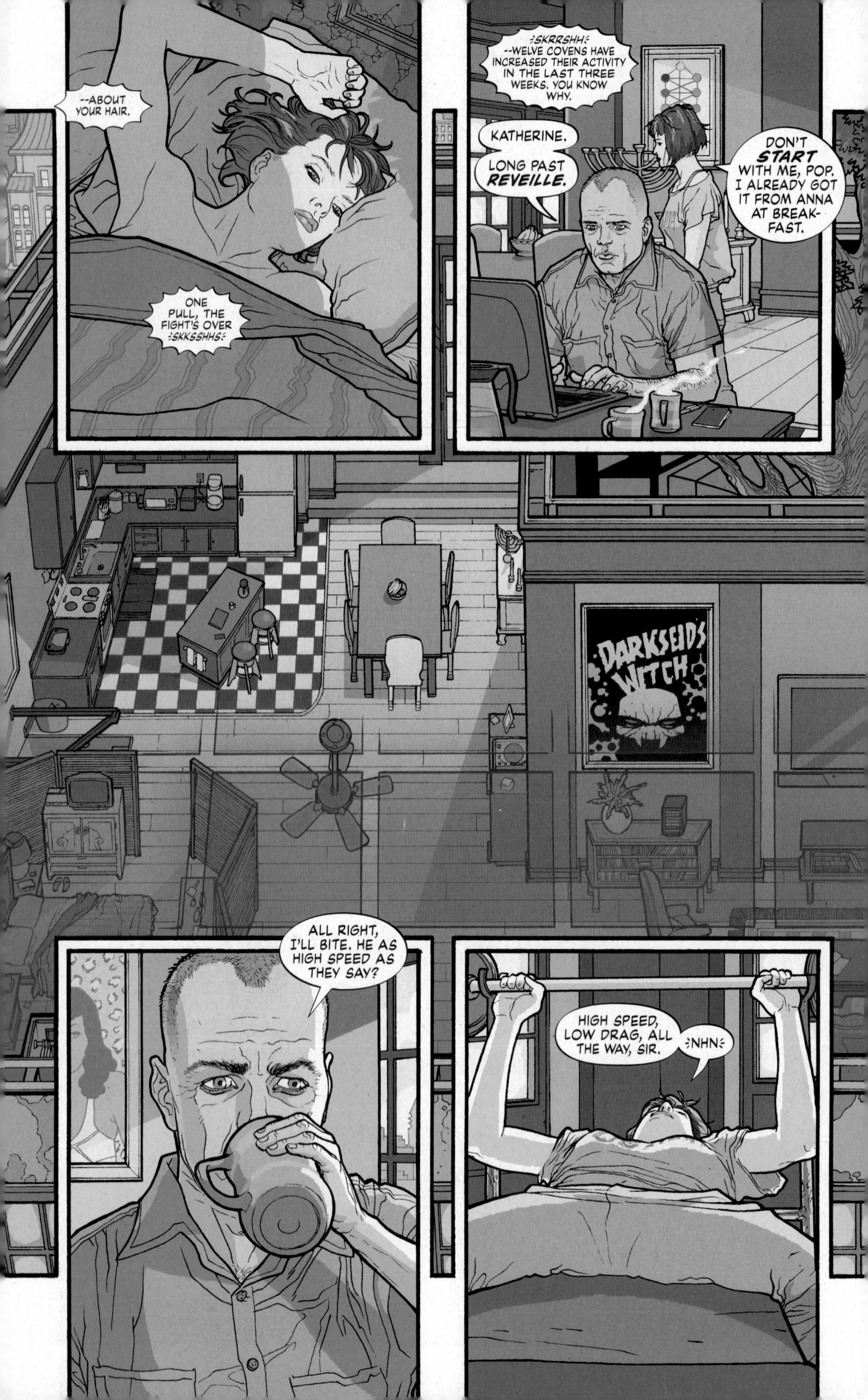
--ABOUT YOUR HAIR.
ONE PULL, THE FIGHT'S OVER
SKKSSHHS
SKRRSHH
--WELVE COVENS HAVE INCREASED THEIR ACTIVITY IN THE LAST THREE WEEKS. YOU KNOW WHY.
KATHERINE.
LONG PAST REVEILLE.
DON'T START WITH ME, POP. I ALREADY GOT IT FROM ANNA AT BREAK-FAST.
DARKSEID'S WITCH
ALL RIGHT, I'LL BITE. HE AS HIGH SPEED AS THEY SAY?
HIGH SPEED, LOW DRAG, ALL THE WAY, SIR.
NHN

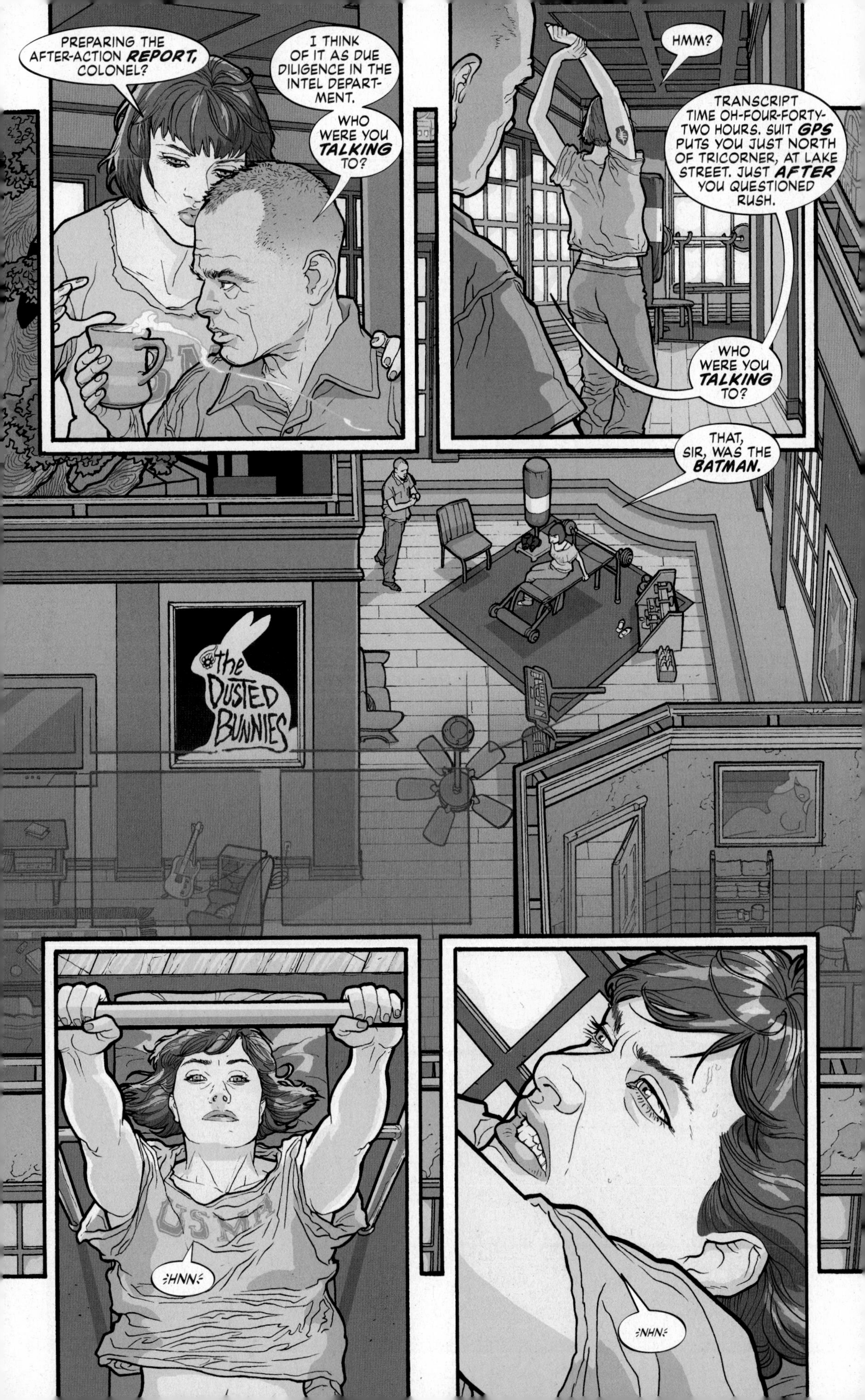

PREPARING THE AFTER-ACTION REPORT, COLONEL?
I THINK OF IT AS DUE DILIGENCE IN THE INTEL DEPARTMENT.
WHO WERE YOU TALKING TO?
HMM?
TRANSCRIPT TIME OH-FOUR-FORTY-TWO HOURS. SUIT GPS PUTS YOU JUST NORTH OF TRICORNER, AT LAKE STREET. JUST AFTER YOU QUESTIONED RUSH.
WHO WERE YOU TALKING TO?
THAT, SIR, WAS THE BATMAN.
the DUSTED BUNNIES
USMA
HNN
NHN

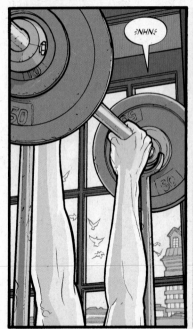

YOU ALL RIGHT?

JUST *MINOR* DISCOMFORT...

...NOTHING I CAN'T TAKE.

YOU KEEP PUSHING, YOU'RE GOING TO *HURT* YOURSELF AGAIN.

MAYBE BAD ENOUGH THAT THIS TIME YOU *DON'T* RECOVER FROM IT.

HELL, YOU'RE NOT COMPLETELY RECOVERED *NOW.* YOU'RE NEVER *GOING* TO BE.

I'M DOING WHAT *YOU* TAUGHT ME.

I'M *SOLDIERING* ON.

YOU WERE *STABBED* THROUGH THE *HEART,* KATE!

IT'S A *MIRACLE* YOU'RE STILL ALIVE!

DO YOU THINK I'VE *FORGOTTEN?*

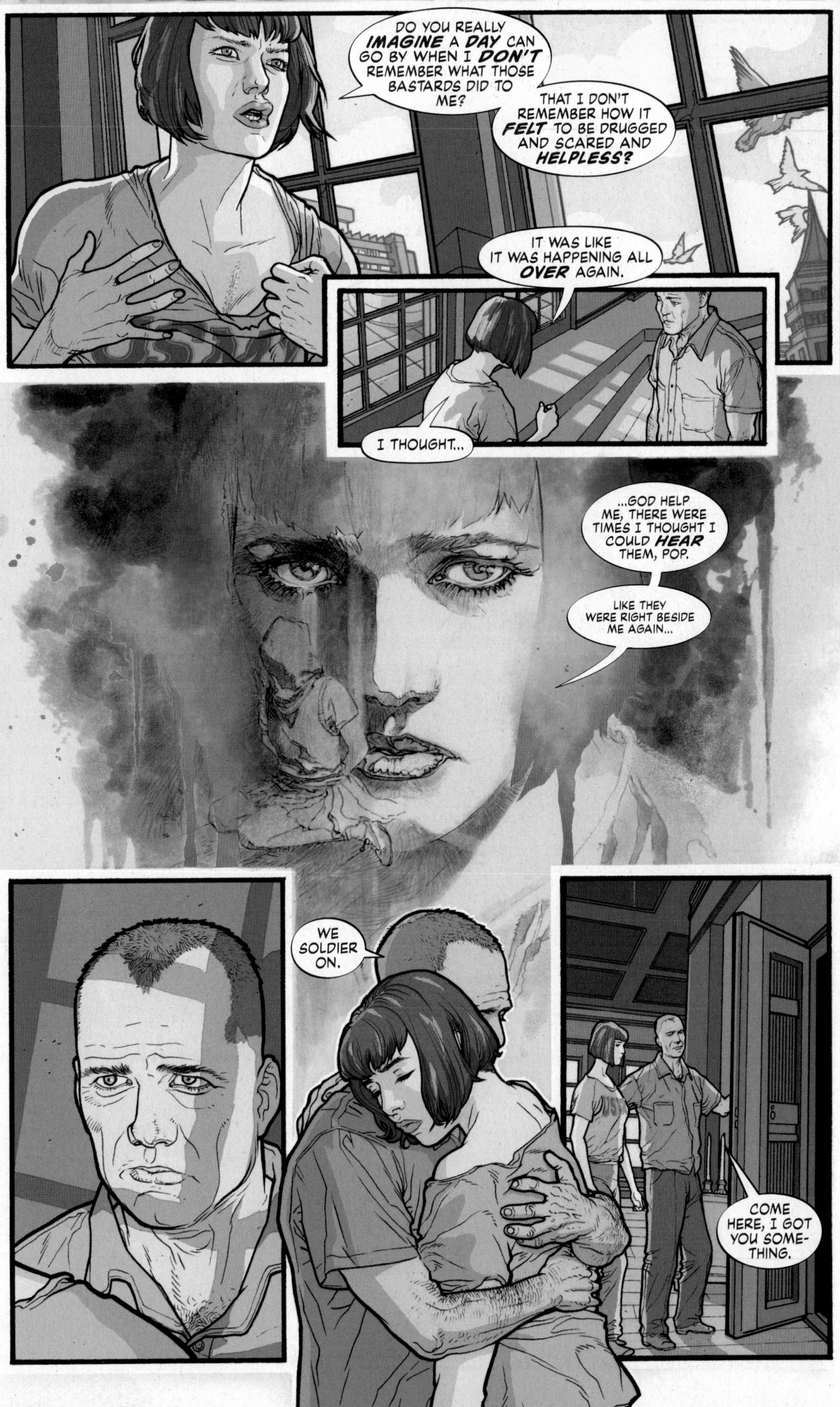
DO YOU REALLY IMAGINE A DAY CAN GO BY WHEN I DON'T REMEMBER WHAT THOSE BASTARDS DID TO ME?
THAT I DON'T REMEMBER HOW IT FELT TO BE DRUGGED AND SCARED AND HELPLESS?
IT WAS LIKE IT WAS HAPPENING ALL OVER AGAIN.
I THOUGHT...
...GOD HELP ME, THERE WERE TIMES I THOUGHT I COULD HEAR THEM, POP.
LIKE THEY WERE RIGHT BESIDE ME AGAIN...
WE SOLDIER ON.
COME HERE, I GOT YOU SOME-THING.

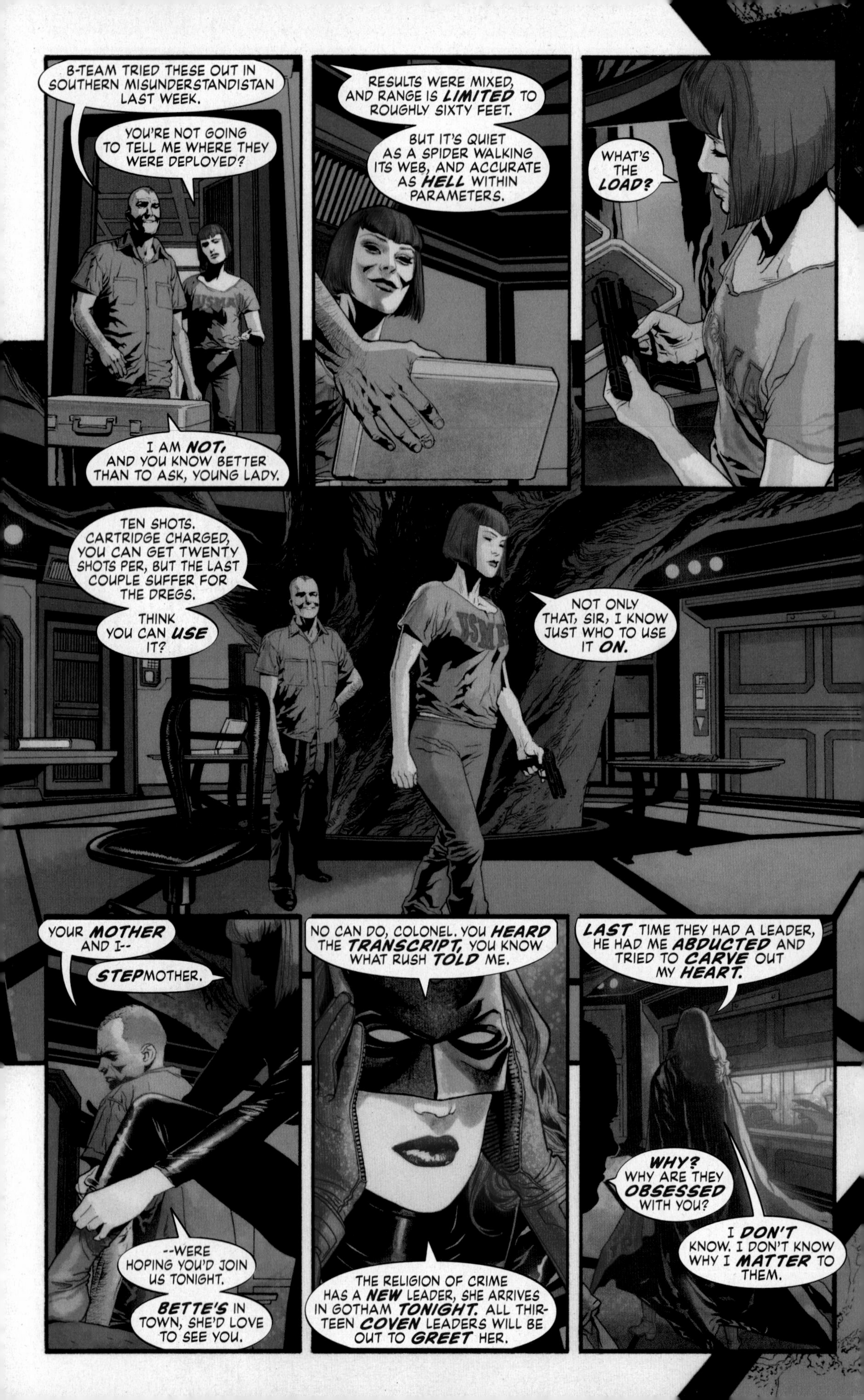
B-TEAM TRIED THESE OUT IN SOUTHERN MISUNDERSTANDISTAN LAST WEEK.
YOU'RE NOT GOING TO TELL ME WHERE THEY WERE DEPLOYED?
I AM NOT, AND YOU KNOW BETTER THAN TO ASK, YOUNG LADY.
RESULTS WERE MIXED, AND RANGE IS LIMITED TO ROUGHLY SIXTY FEET.
BUT IT'S QUIET AS A SPIDER WALKING ITS WEB, AND ACCURATE AS HELL WITHIN PARAMETERS.
WHAT'S THE LOAD?
TEN SHOTS. CARTRIDGE CHARGED, YOU CAN GET TWENTY SHOTS PER, BUT THE LAST COUPLE SUFFER FOR THE DREGS.
THINK YOU CAN USE IT?
NOT ONLY THAT, SIR, I KNOW JUST WHO TO USE IT ON.
YOUR MOTHER AND I--
STEPMOTHER.
--WERE HOPING YOU'D JOIN US TONIGHT.
BETTE'S IN TOWN, SHE'D LOVE TO SEE YOU.
NO CAN DO, COLONEL. YOU HEARD THE TRANSCRIPT, YOU KNOW WHAT RUSH TOLD ME.
THE RELIGION OF CRIME HAS A NEW LEADER, SHE ARRIVES IN GOTHAM TONIGHT. ALL THIRTEEN COVEN LEADERS WILL BE OUT TO GREET HER.
LAST TIME THEY HAD A LEADER, HE HAD ME ABDUCTED AND TRIED TO CARVE OUT MY HEART.
WHY? WHY ARE THEY OBSESSED WITH YOU?
I DON'T KNOW. I DON'T KNOW WHY I MATTER TO THEM.

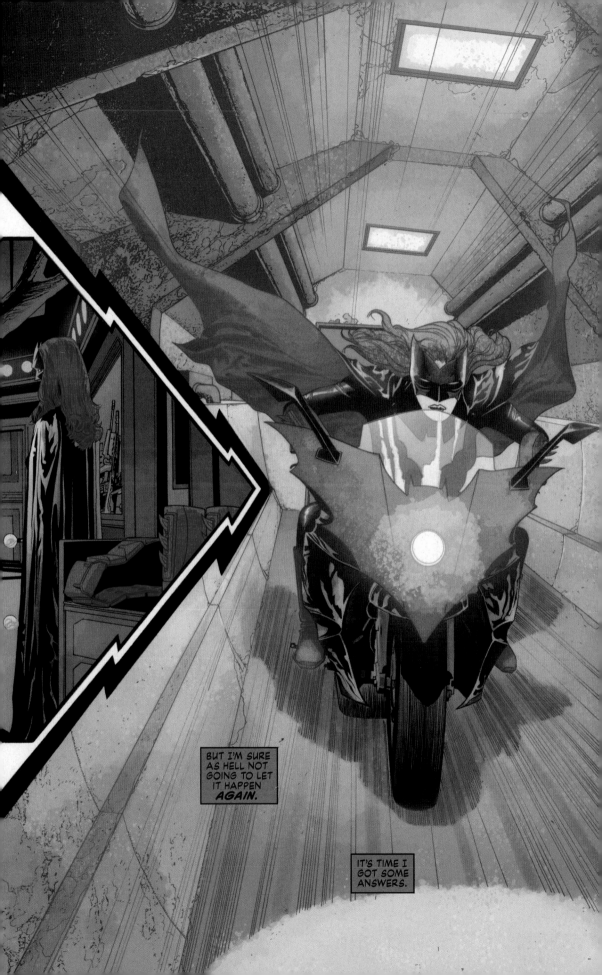

BUT I'M SURE AS HELL NOT GOING TO LET IT HAPPEN *AGAIN.*

IT'S TIME I GOT SOME ANSWERS.

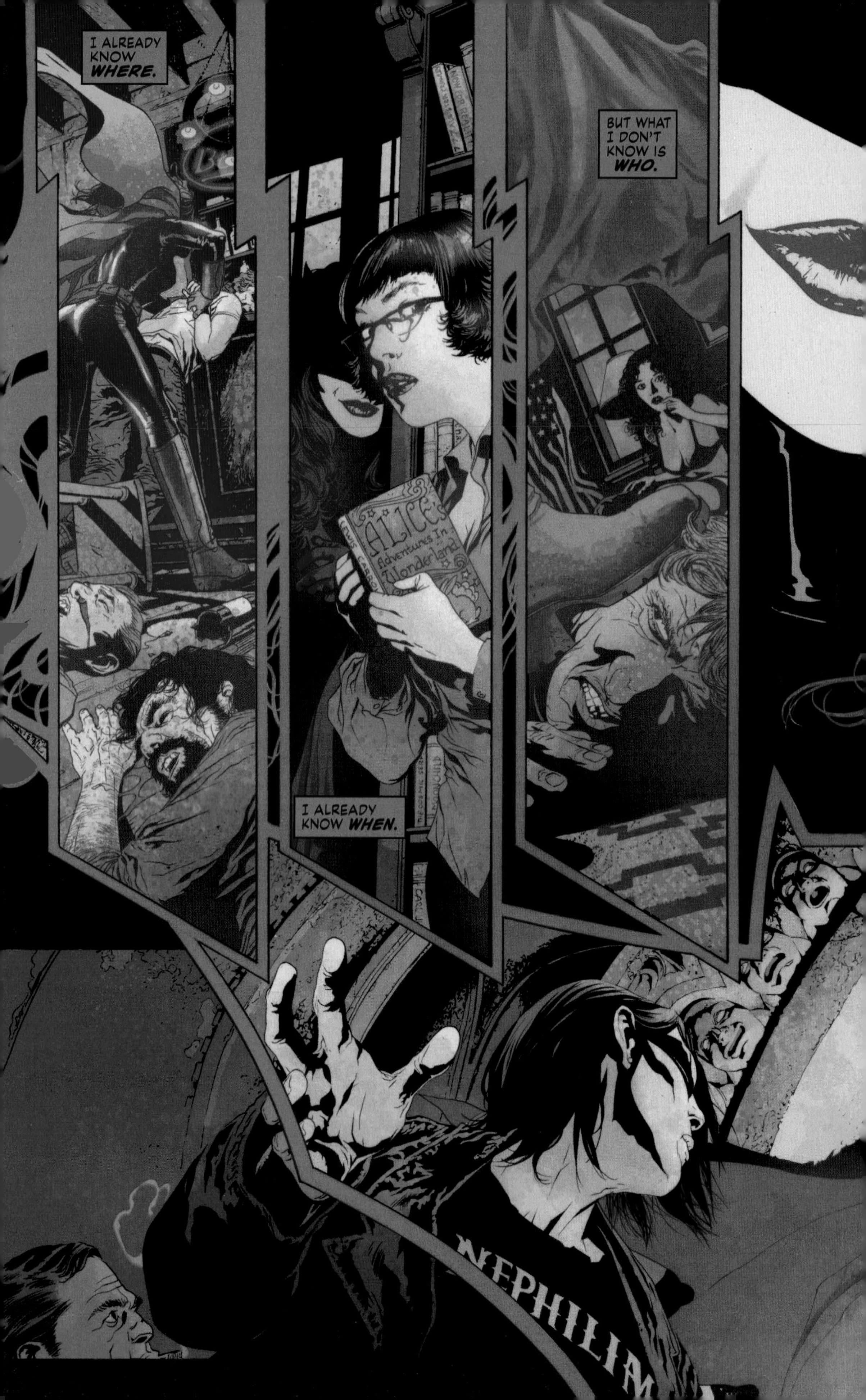
I ALREADY KNOW *WHERE.*
I ALREADY KNOW *WHEN.*
BUT WHAT I DON'T KNOW IS *WHO.*
ALICE'S Adventures In Wonderland
NEPHILIM

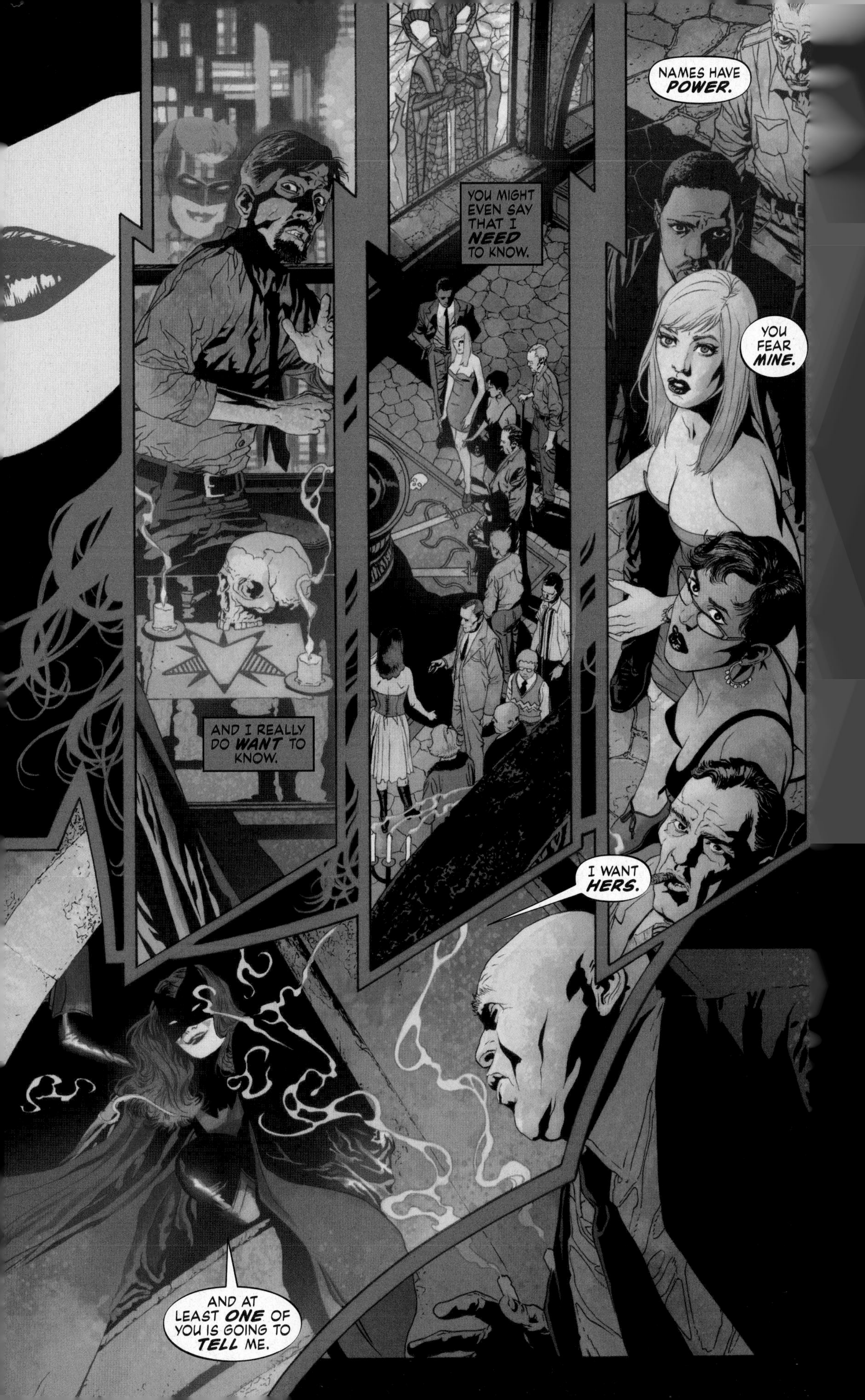

YOU MIGHT EVEN SAY THAT I NEED TO KNOW.
AND I REALLY DO WANT TO KNOW.
NAMES HAVE POWER.
YOU FEAR MINE.
I WANT HERS.
AND AT LEAST ONE OF YOU IS GOING TO TELL ME.

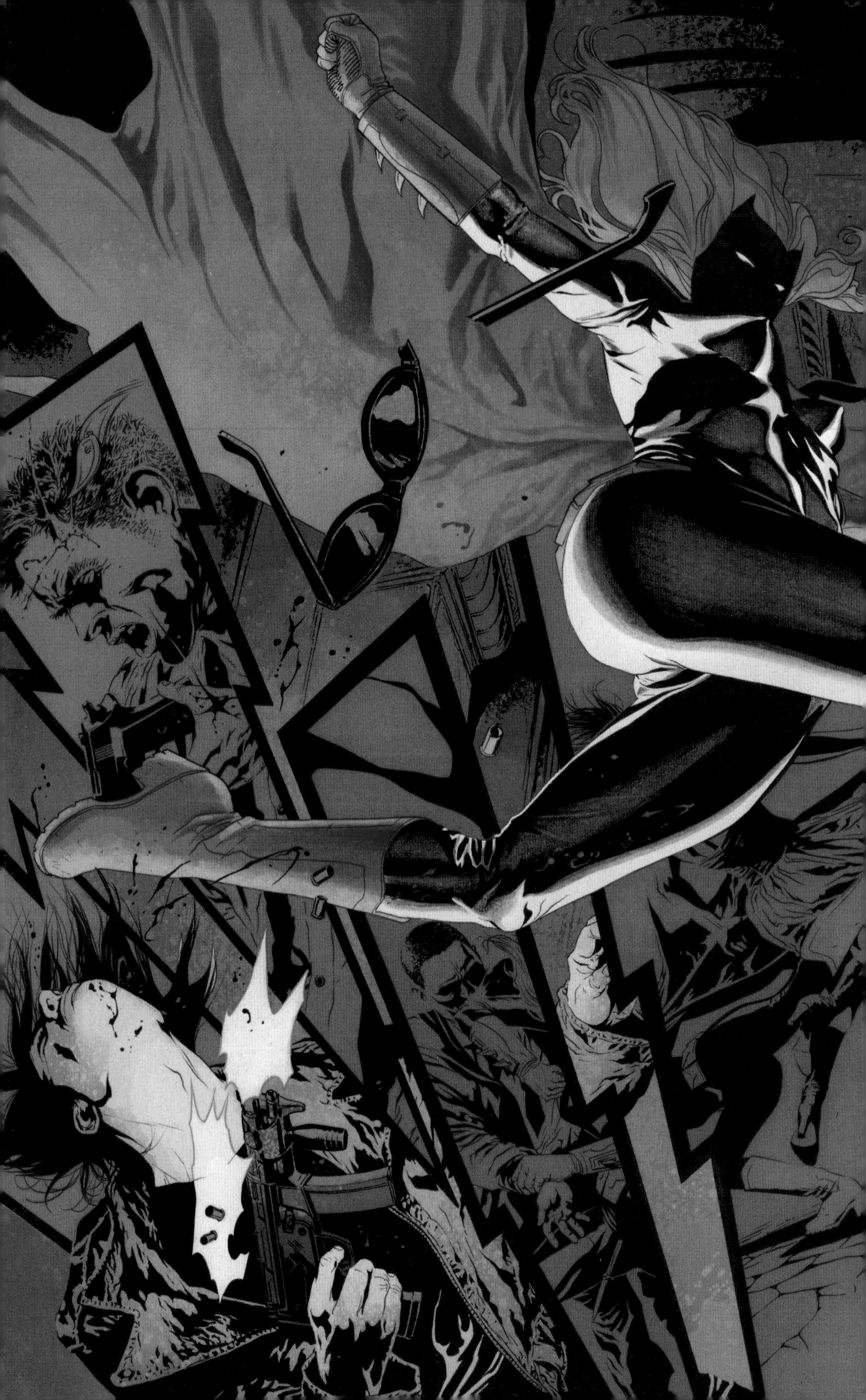

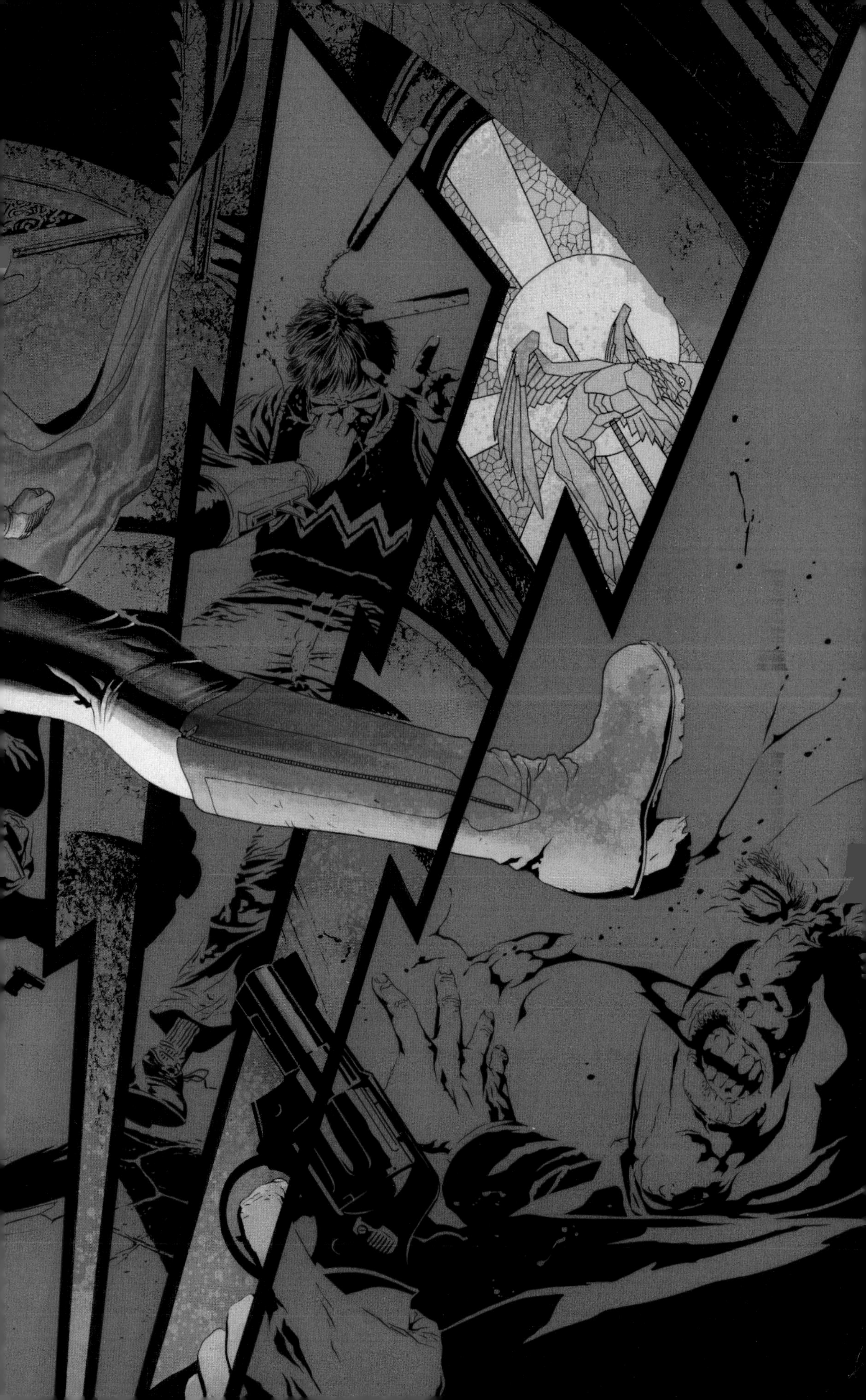

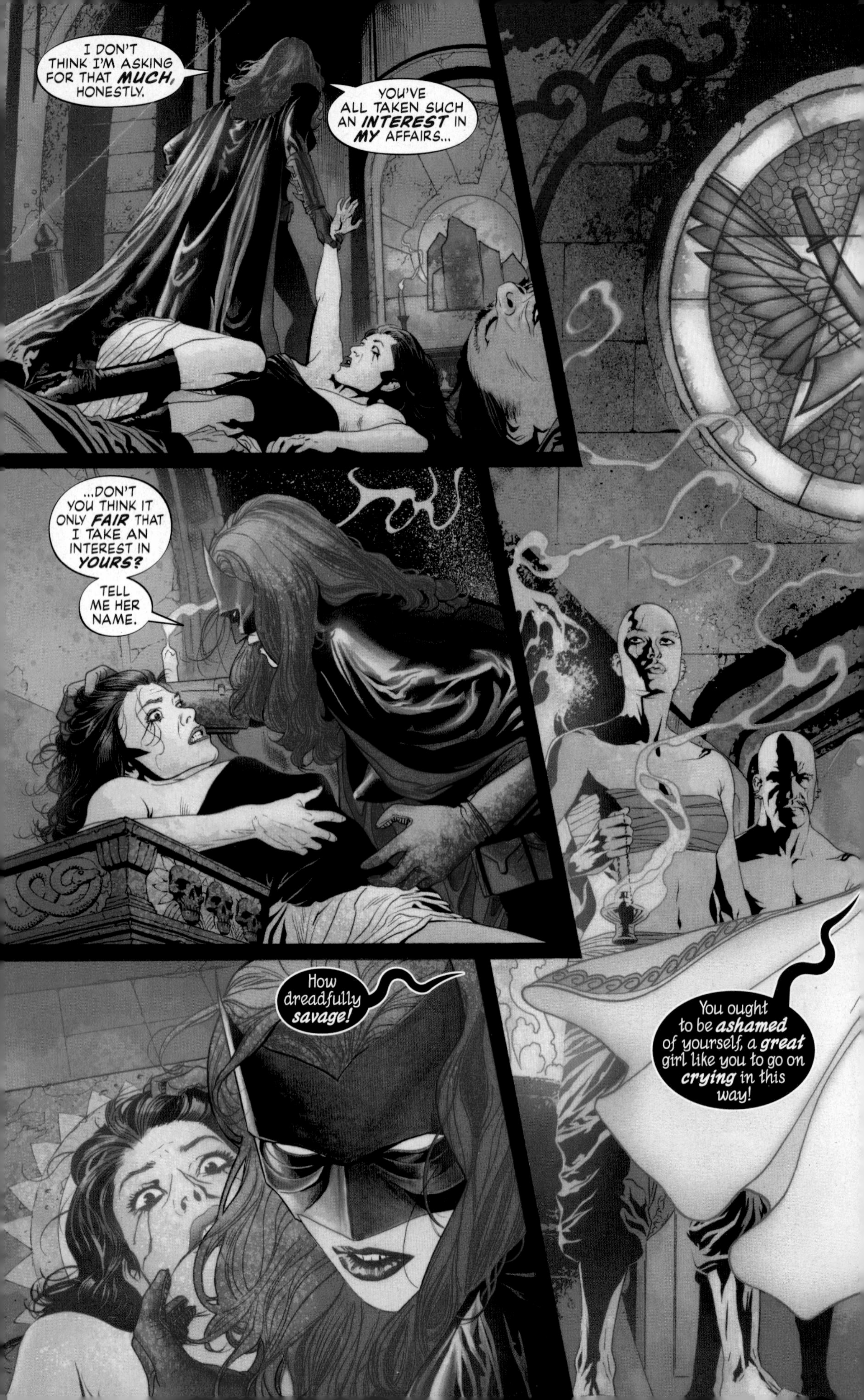
I DON'T THINK I'M ASKING FOR THAT MUCH, HONESTLY.
YOU'VE ALL TAKEN SUCH AN INTEREST IN MY AFFAIRS...
...DON'T YOU THINK IT ONLY FAIR THAT I TAKE AN INTEREST IN YOURS?
TELL ME HER NAME.
How dreadfully savage!
You ought to be ashamed of yourself, a great girl like you to go on crying in this way!

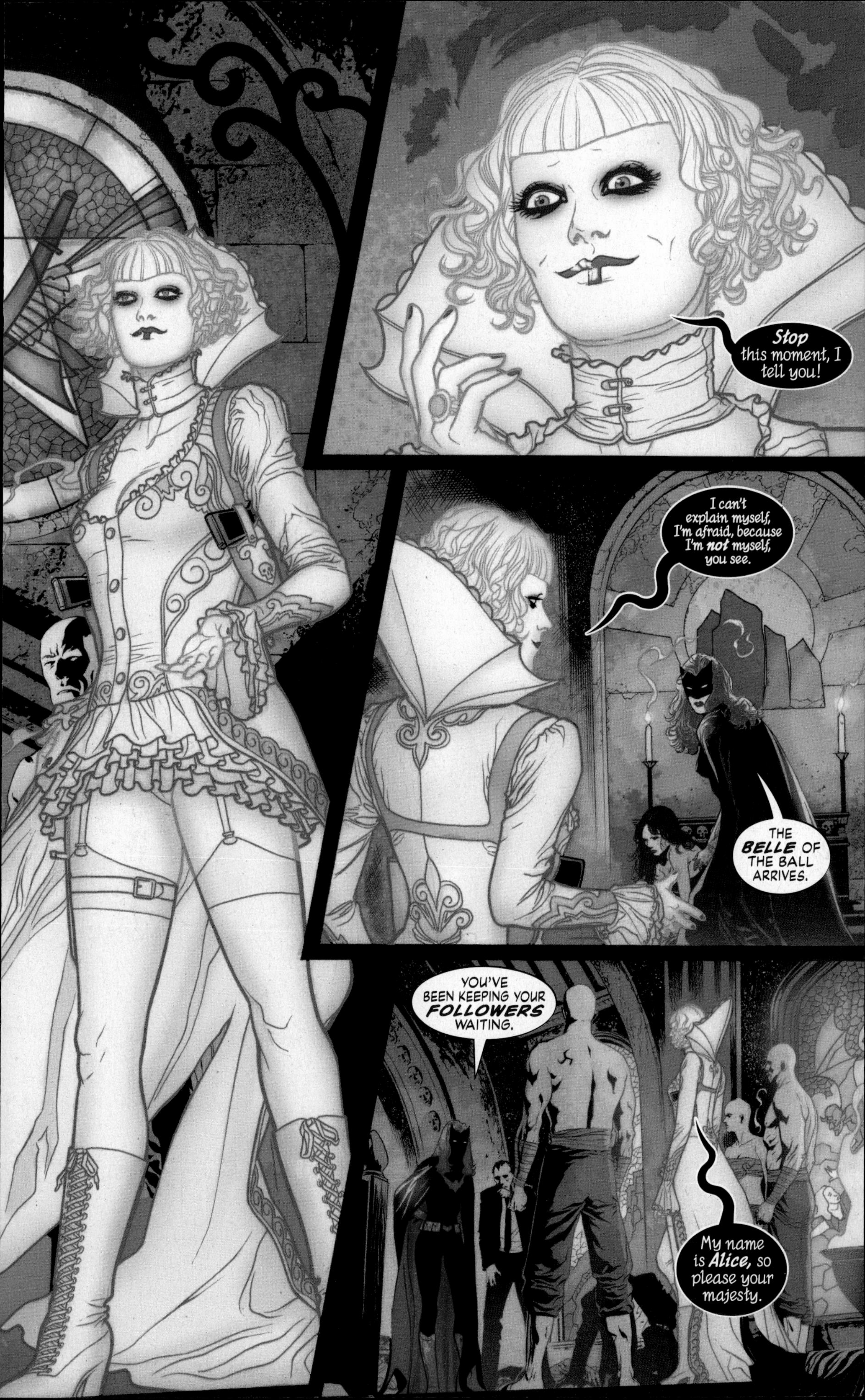
Stop this moment, I tell you!
I can't explain myself, I'm afraid, because I'm not myself, you see.
THE BELLE OF THE BALL ARRIVES.
YOU'VE BEEN KEEPING YOUR FOLLOWERS WAITING.
My name is Alice, so please your majesty.

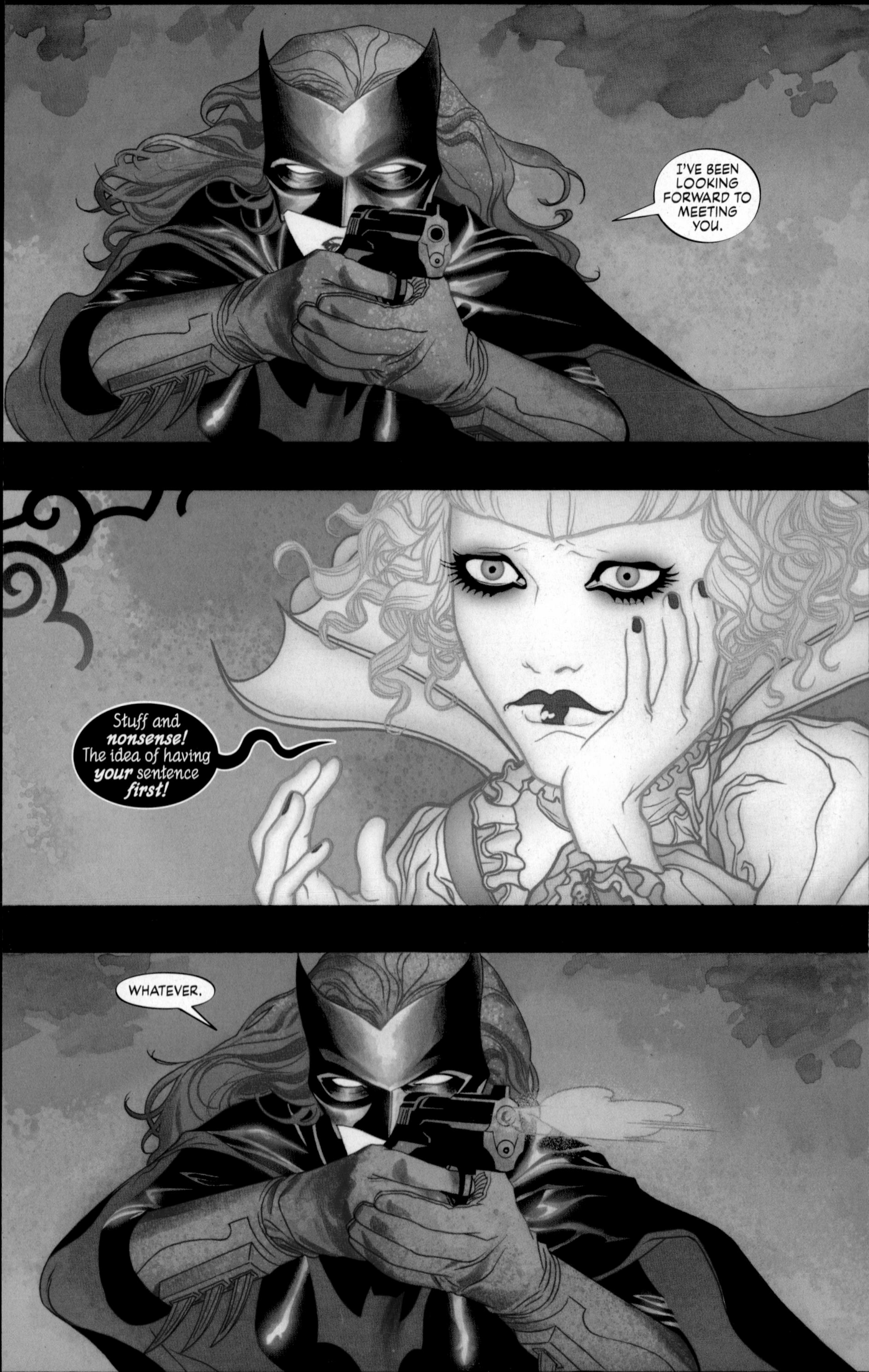
I'VE BEEN LOOKING FORWARD TO MEETING YOU.
Stuff and nonsense! The idea of having your sentence first!
WHATEVER.

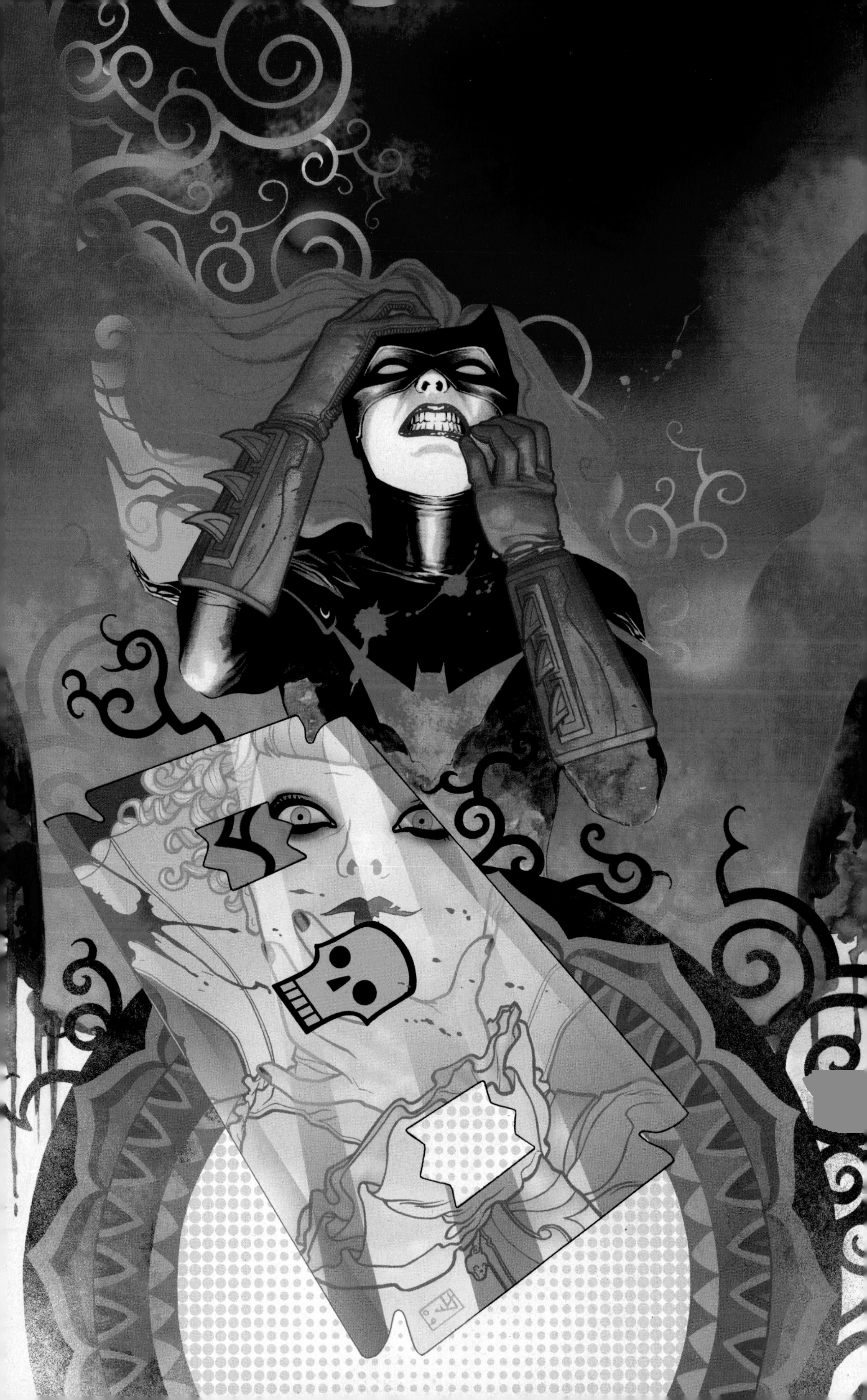

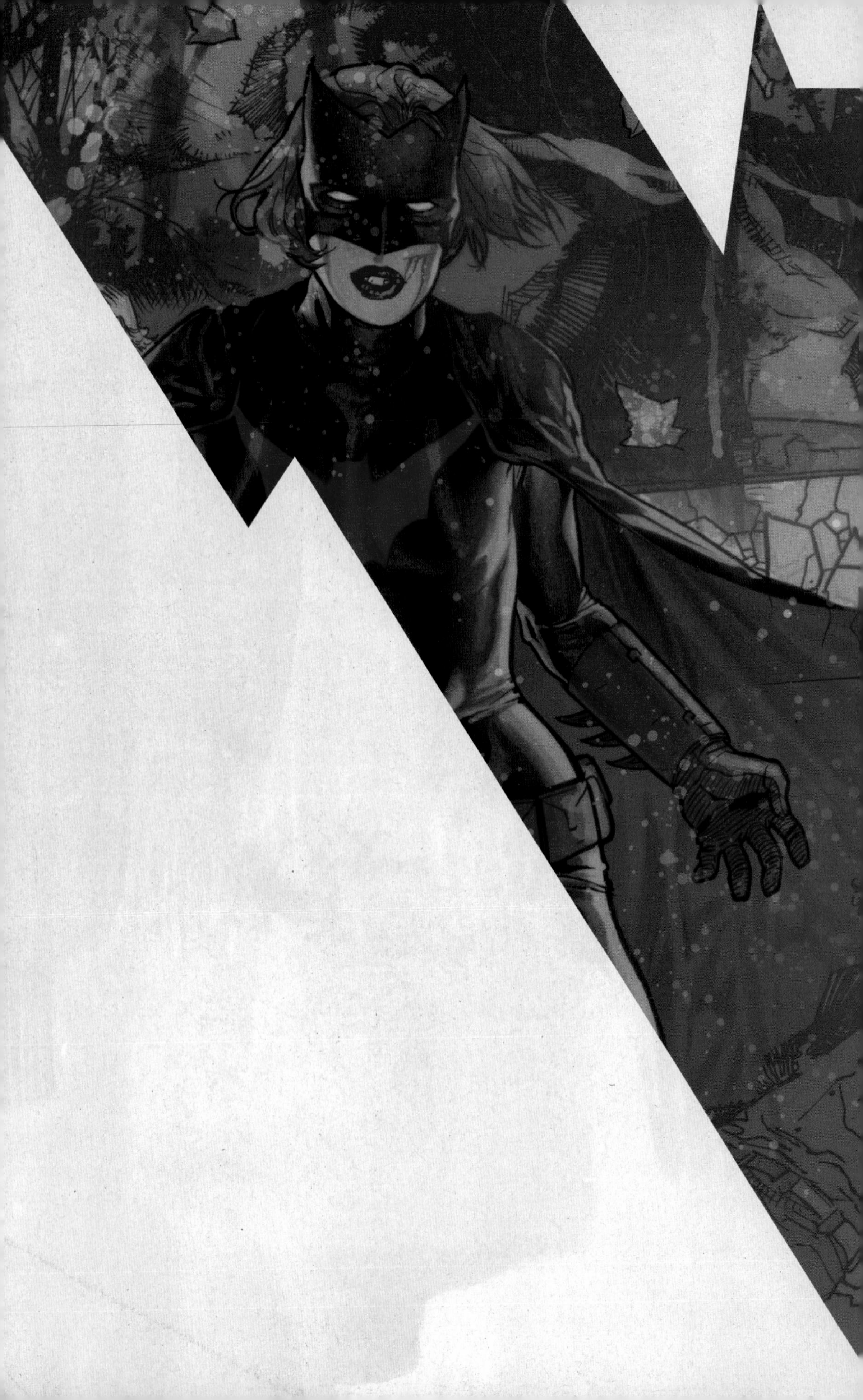

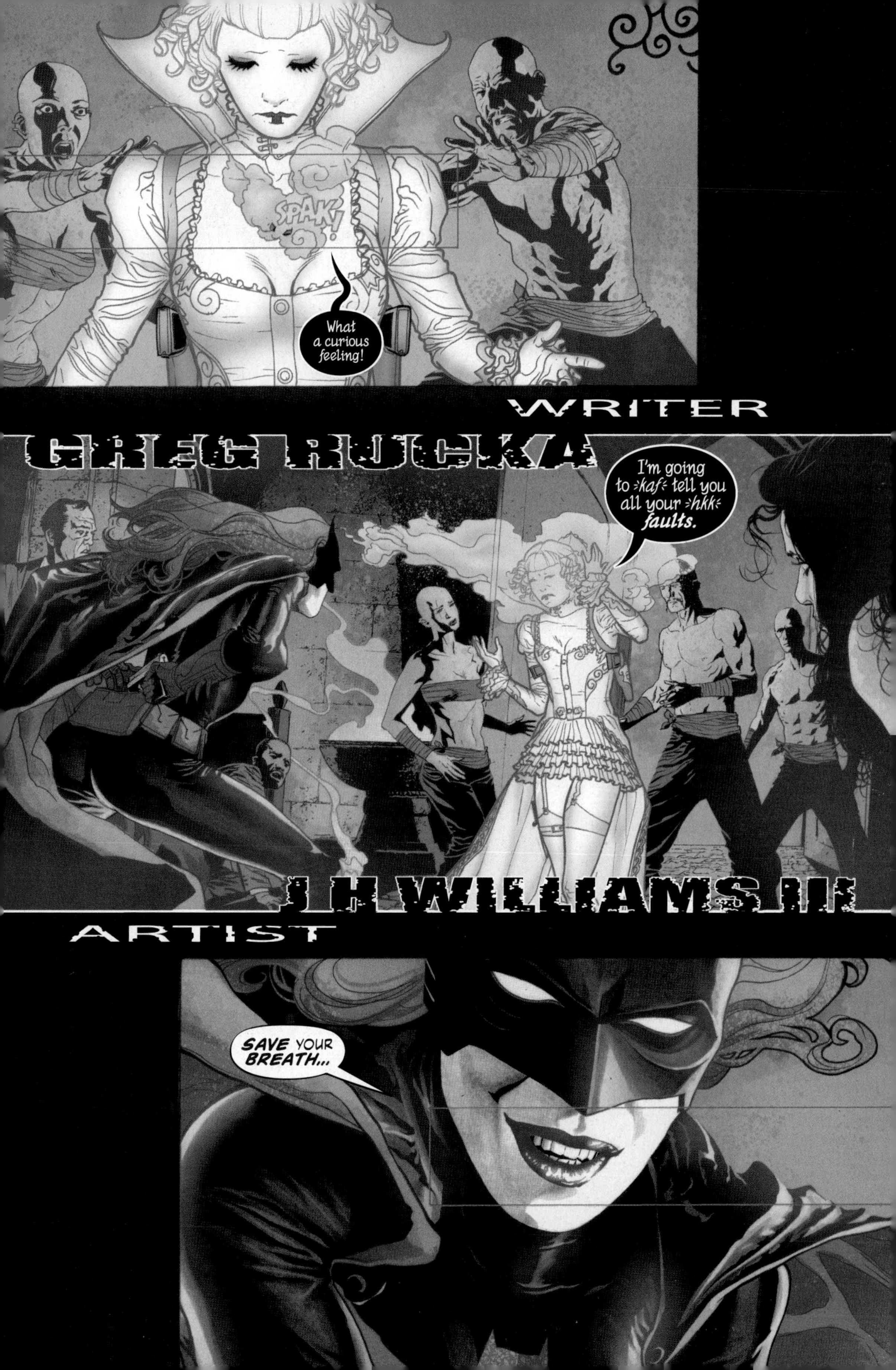

SPAK!
What a curious feeling!
WRITER
GREG RUCKA
I'm going to =kaf= tell you all your =hkk= faults.
J H WILLIAMS III
ARTIST
SAVE YOUR BREATH...

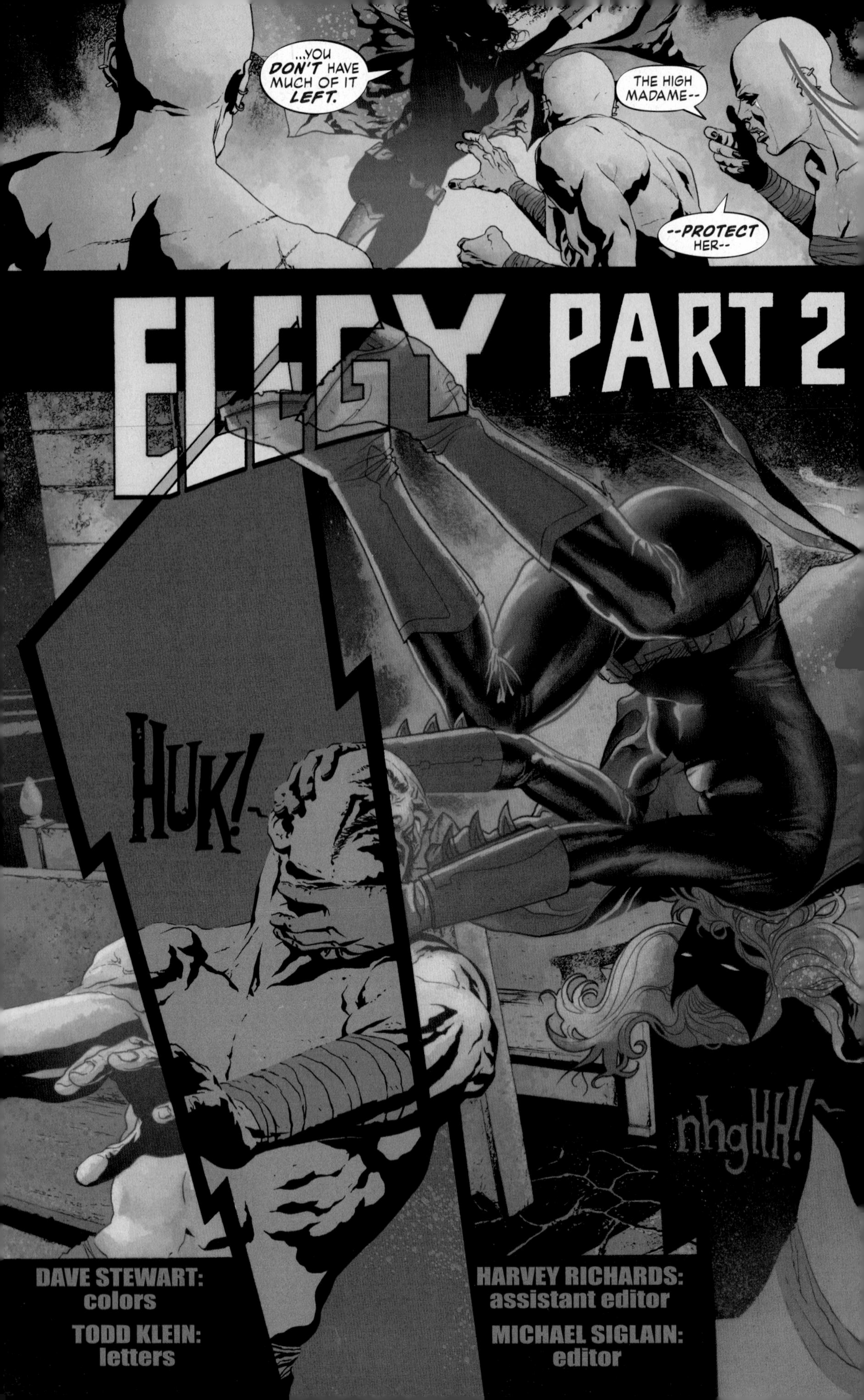
...YOU DON'T HAVE MUCH OF IT LEFT.
THE HIGH MADAME--
--PROTECT HER--
ELEGY PART 2
HUK!
nhgHH!
DAVE STEWART: colors
TODD KLEIN: letters
HARVEY RICHARDS: assistant editor
MICHAEL SIGLAIN: editor

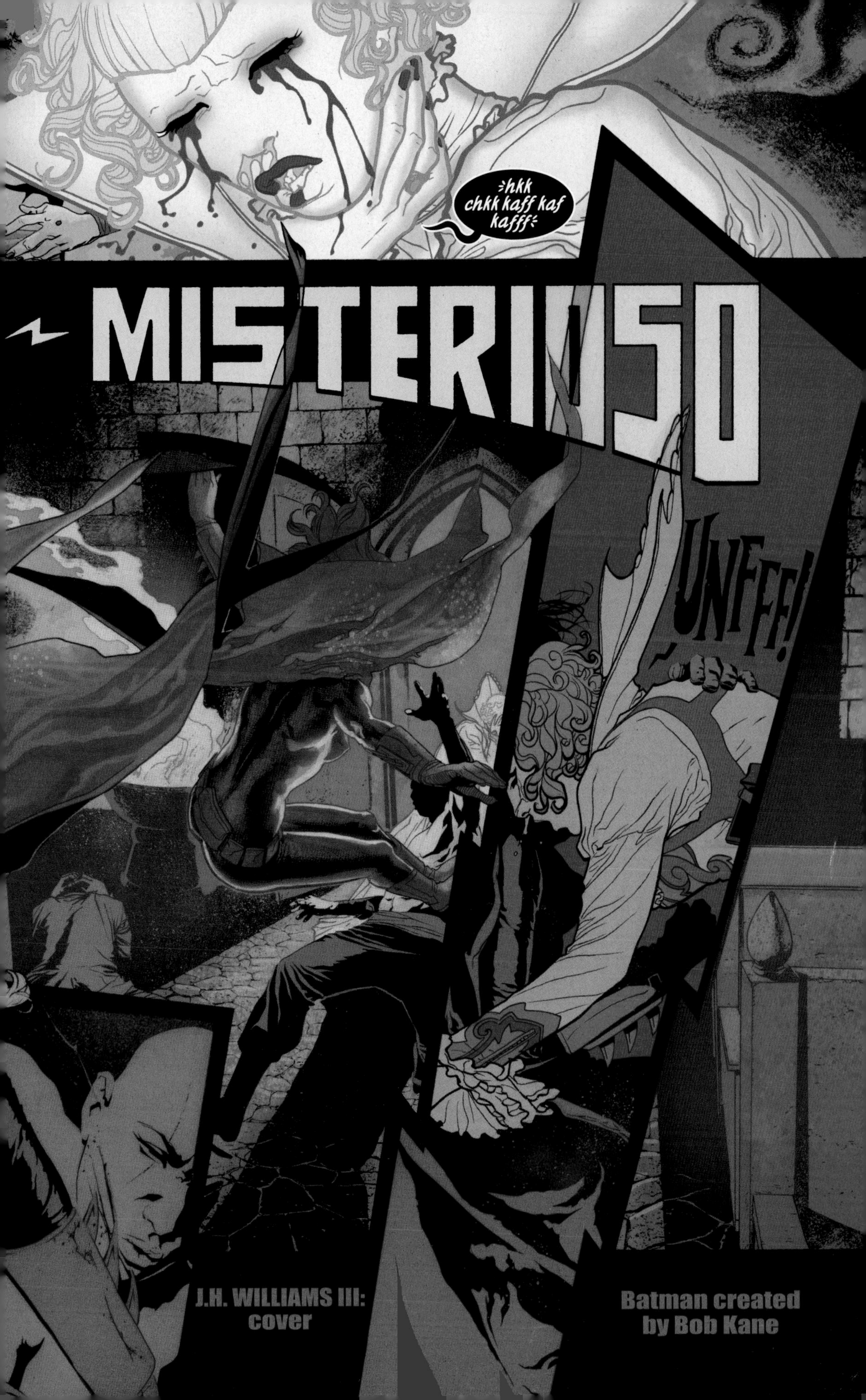

hkk chkk kaff kaf kafff
MISTERIOSO
UNFFF!
J.H. WILLIAMS III: cover
Batman created by Bob Kane

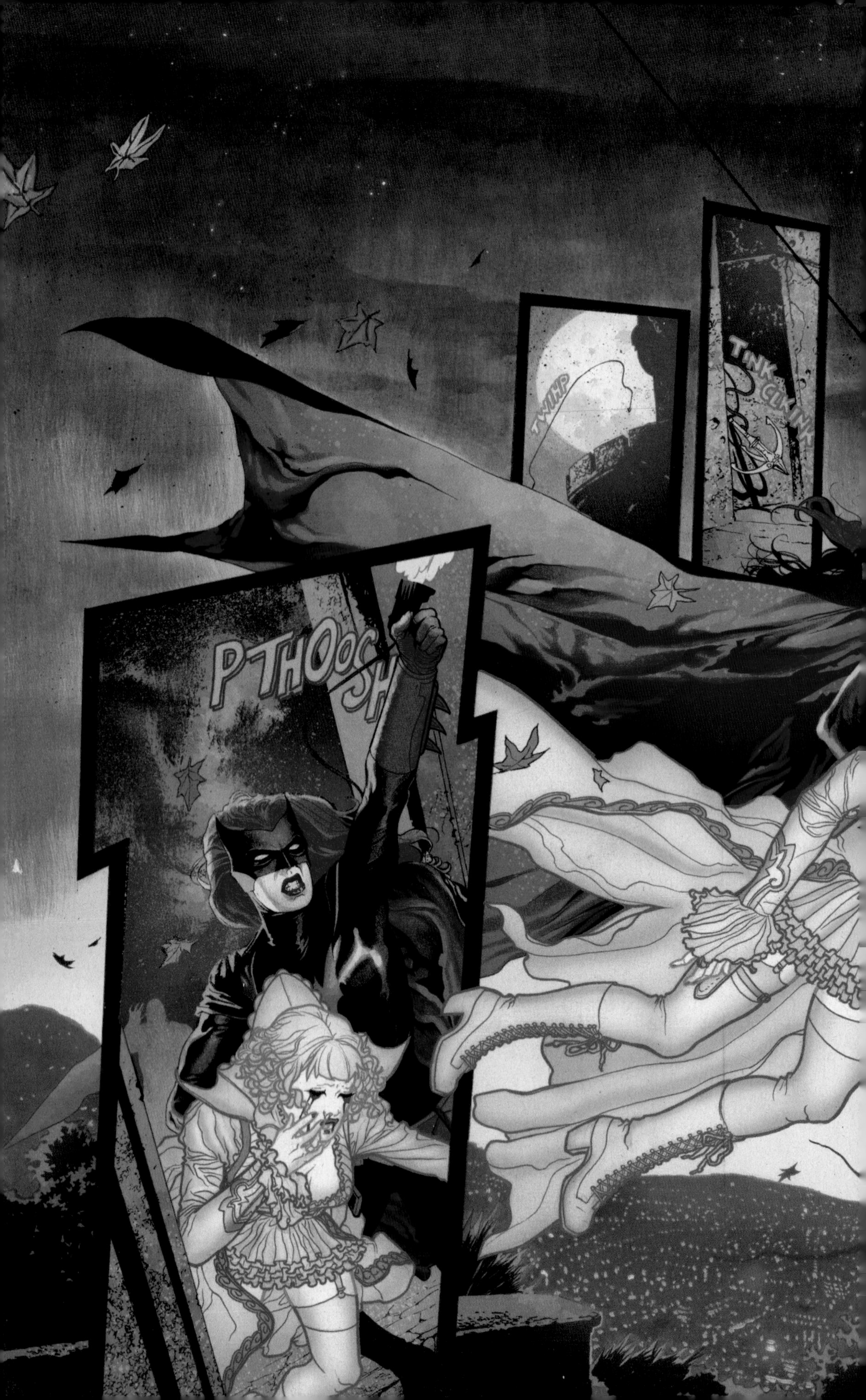
TWIHP
TINK CLIK INK
PTHOOSH

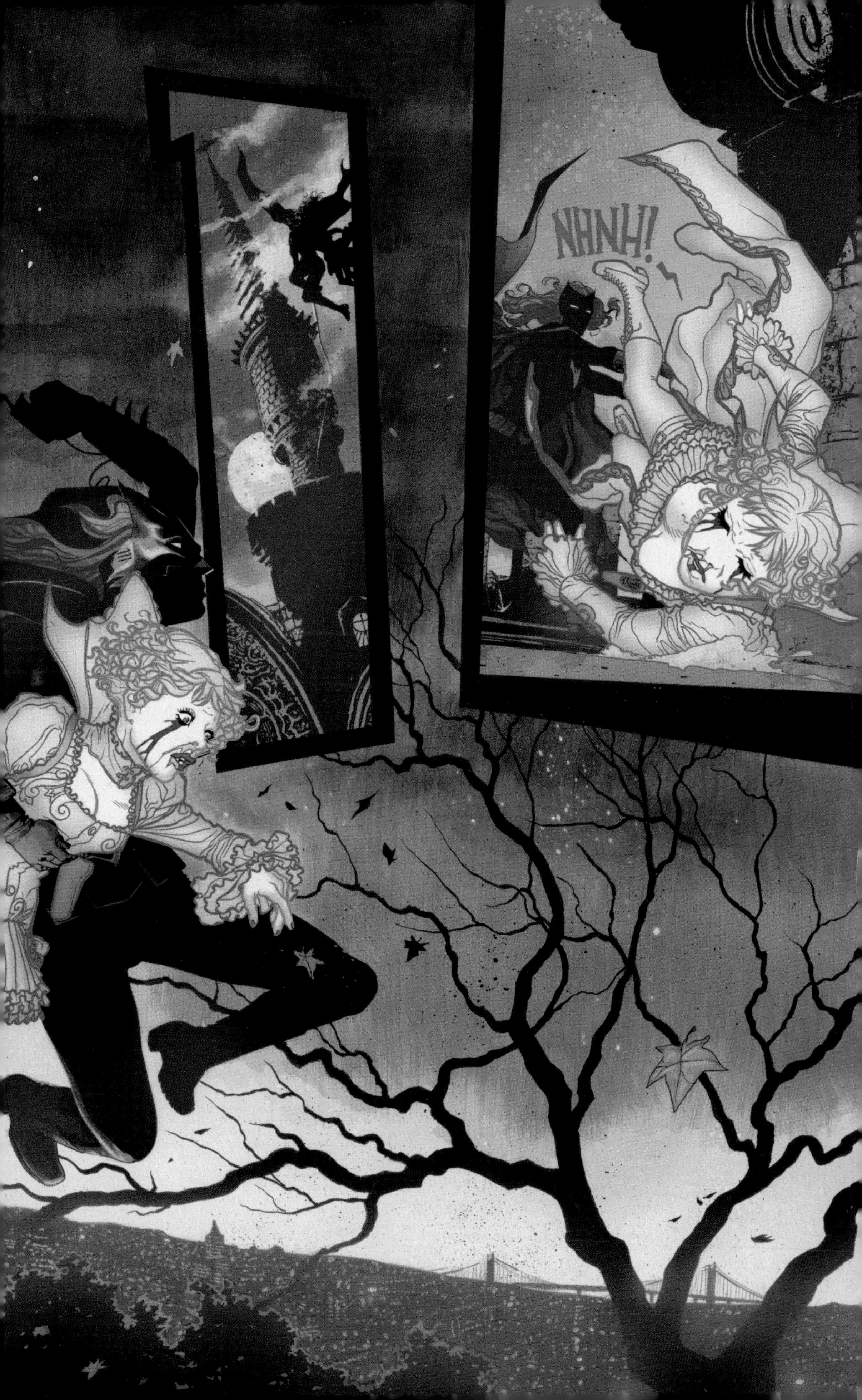
NHNH!

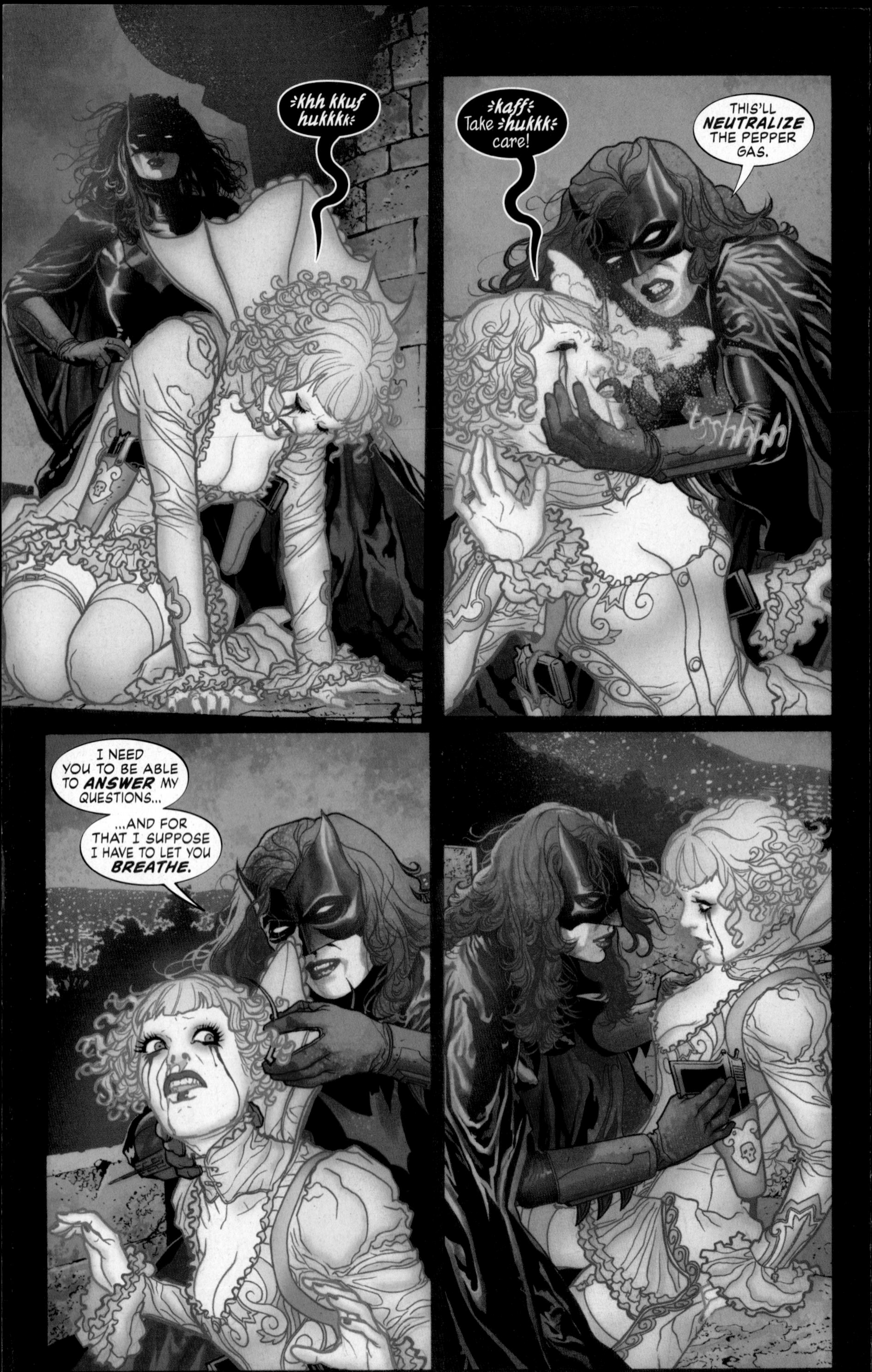

khh kkuf hukkkk
kaff Take hukkk care!
THIS'LL NEUTRALIZE THE PEPPER GAS.
tsshhhh
I NEED YOU TO BE ABLE TO ANSWER MY QUESTIONS...
...AND FOR THAT I SUPPOSE I HAVE TO LET YOU BREATHE.

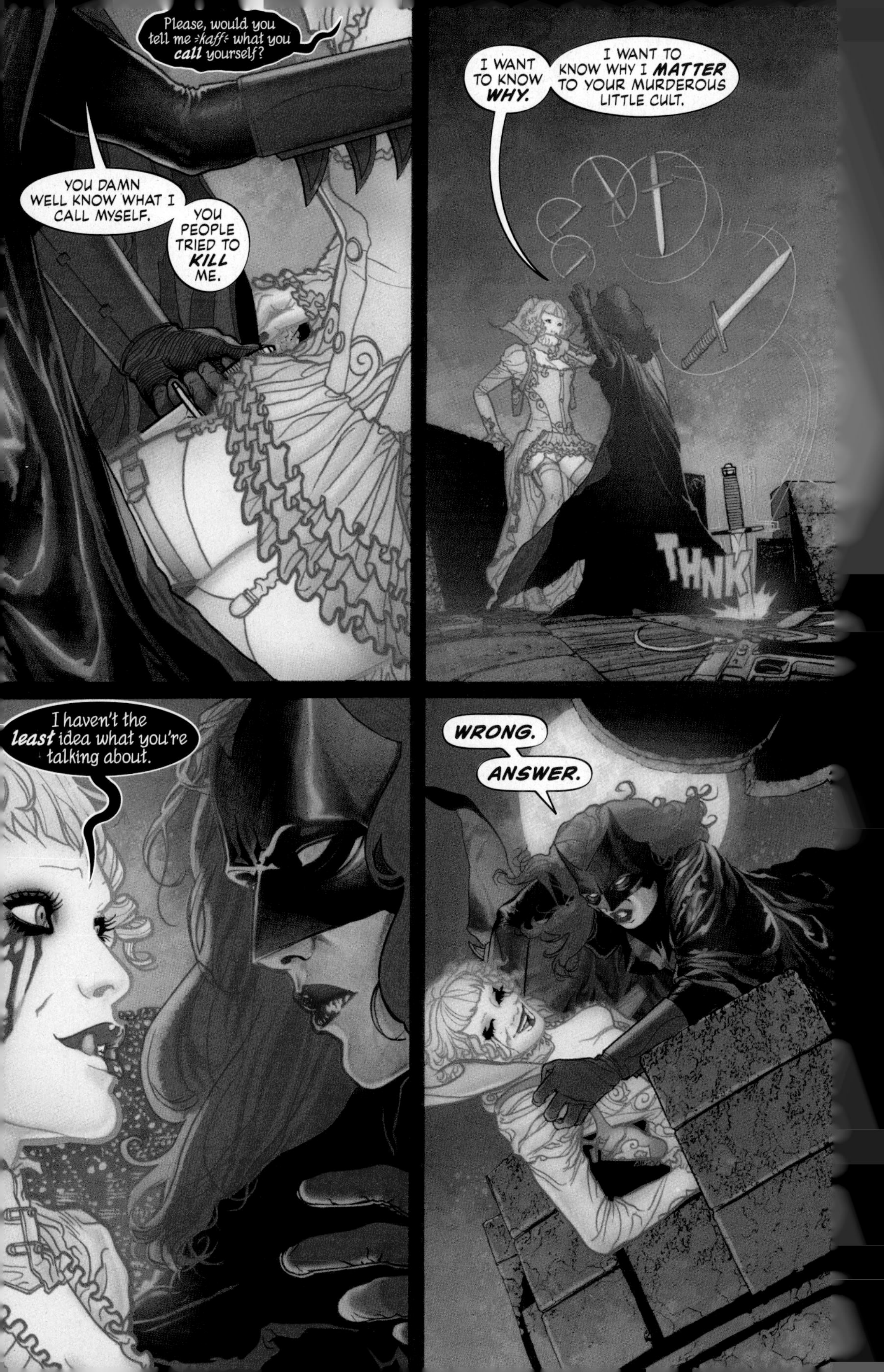
Please, would you tell me ≥kaff≤ what you **call** yourself?
YOU DAMN WELL KNOW WHAT I CALL MYSELF.
YOU PEOPLE TRIED TO **KILL** ME.
I WANT TO KNOW **WHY.**
I WANT TO KNOW WHY I **MATTER** TO YOUR MURDEROUS LITTLE CULT.
THNK
I haven't the **least** idea what you're talking about.
WRONG.
ANSWER.

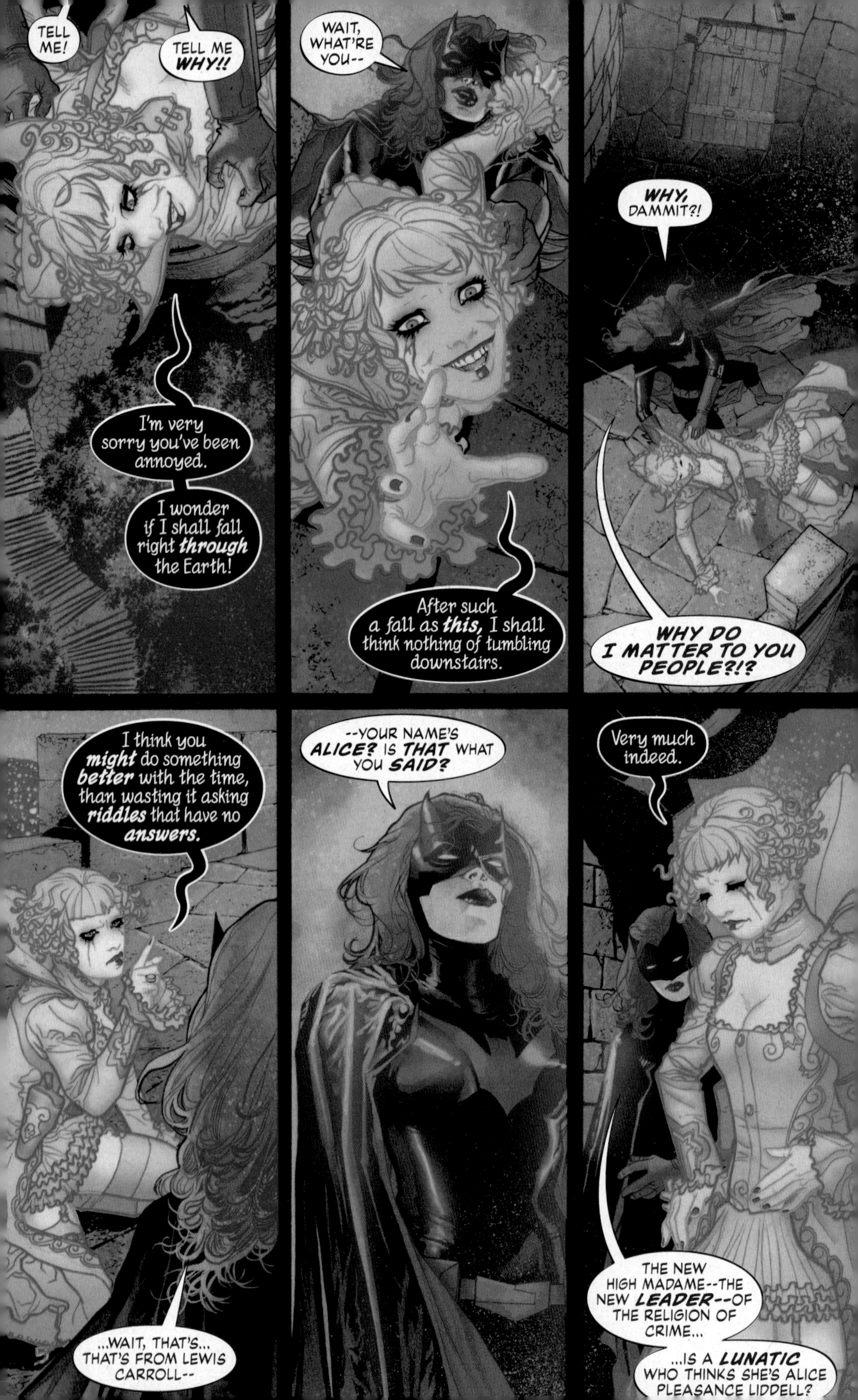

TELL ME!
TELL ME WHY!!
I'm very sorry you've been annoyed.
I wonder if I shall fall right through the Earth!
WAIT, WHAT'RE YOU--
After such a fall as this, I shall think nothing of tumbling downstairs.
WHY, DAMMIT?!
WHY DO I MATTER TO YOU PEOPLE?!?
I think you might do something better with the time, than wasting it asking riddles that have no answers.
...WAIT, THAT'S... THAT'S FROM LEWIS CARROLL--
--YOUR NAME'S ALICE? IS THAT WHAT YOU SAID?
Very much indeed.
THE NEW HIGH MADAME--THE NEW LEADER--OF THE RELIGION OF CRIME...
...IS A LUNATIC WHO THINKS SHE'S ALICE PLEASANCE LIDDELL?

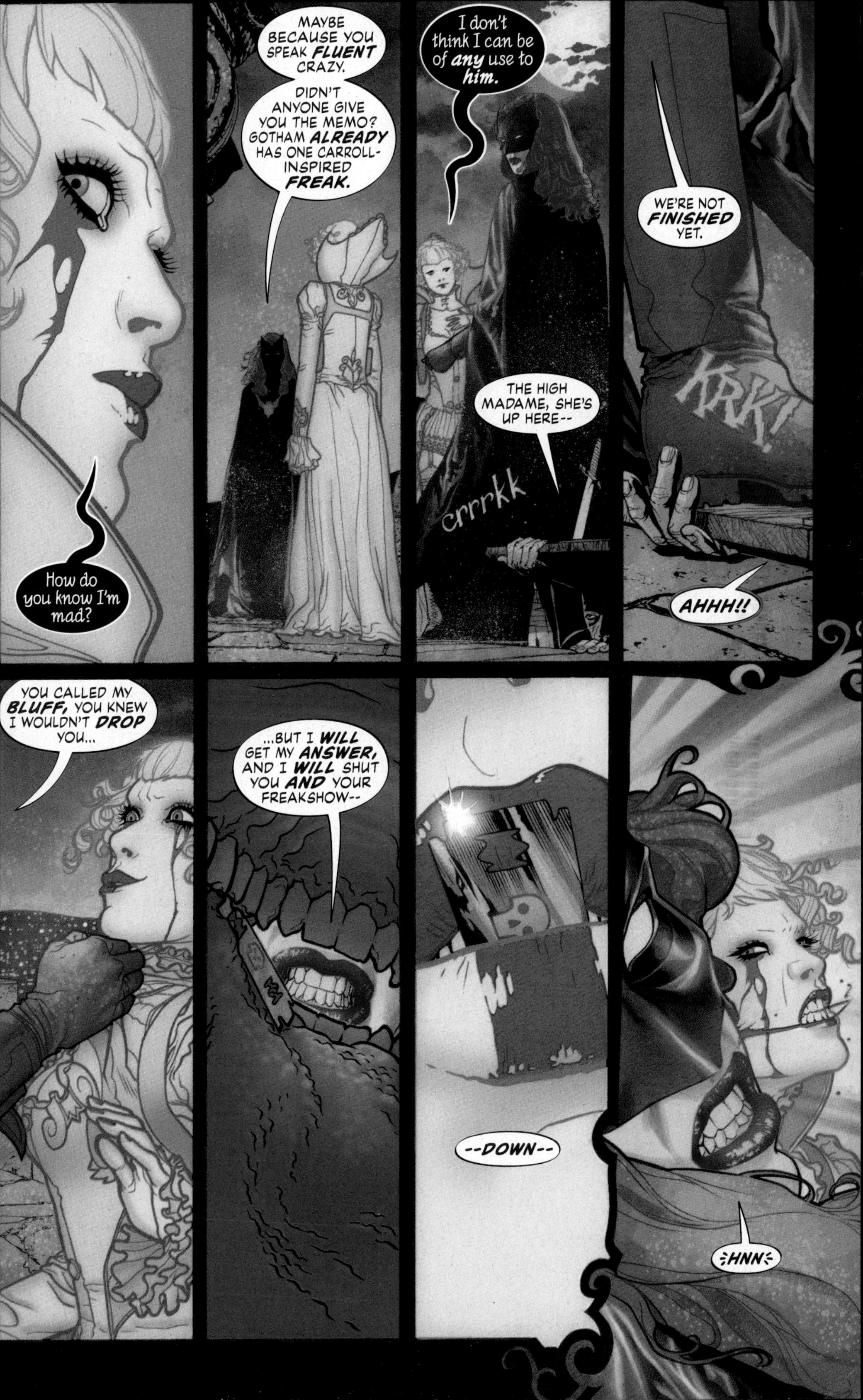
How do you know I'm mad?
MAYBE BECAUSE YOU SPEAK FLUENT CRAZY.
DIDN'T ANYONE GIVE YOU THE MEMO? GOTHAM ALREADY HAS ONE CARROLL-INSPIRED FREAK.
I don't think I can be of any use to him.
THE HIGH MADAME, SHE'S UP HERE--
crrrkk
WE'RE NOT FINISHED YET.
KRK!
AHHH!!
YOU CALLED MY BLUFF, YOU KNEW I WOULDN'T DROP YOU...
...BUT I WILL GET MY ANSWER, AND I WILL SHUT YOU AND YOUR FREAKSHOW--
--DOWN--
HNN

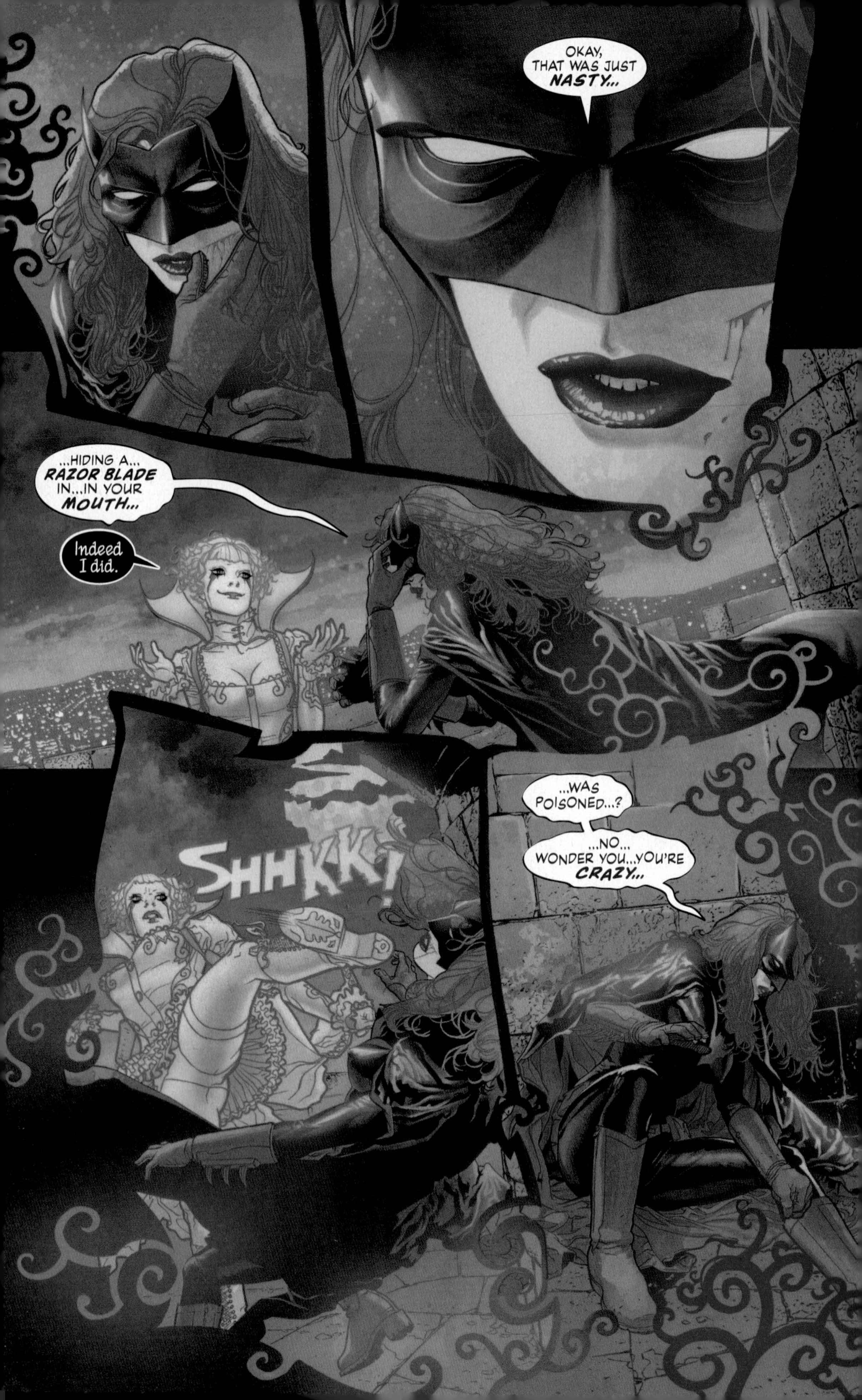
OKAY, THAT WAS JUST NASTY...
...HIDING A... RAZOR BLADE IN...IN YOUR MOUTH...
Indeed I did.
SHHKK!
...WAS POISONED...?
...NO... WONDER YOU...YOU'RE CRAZY...

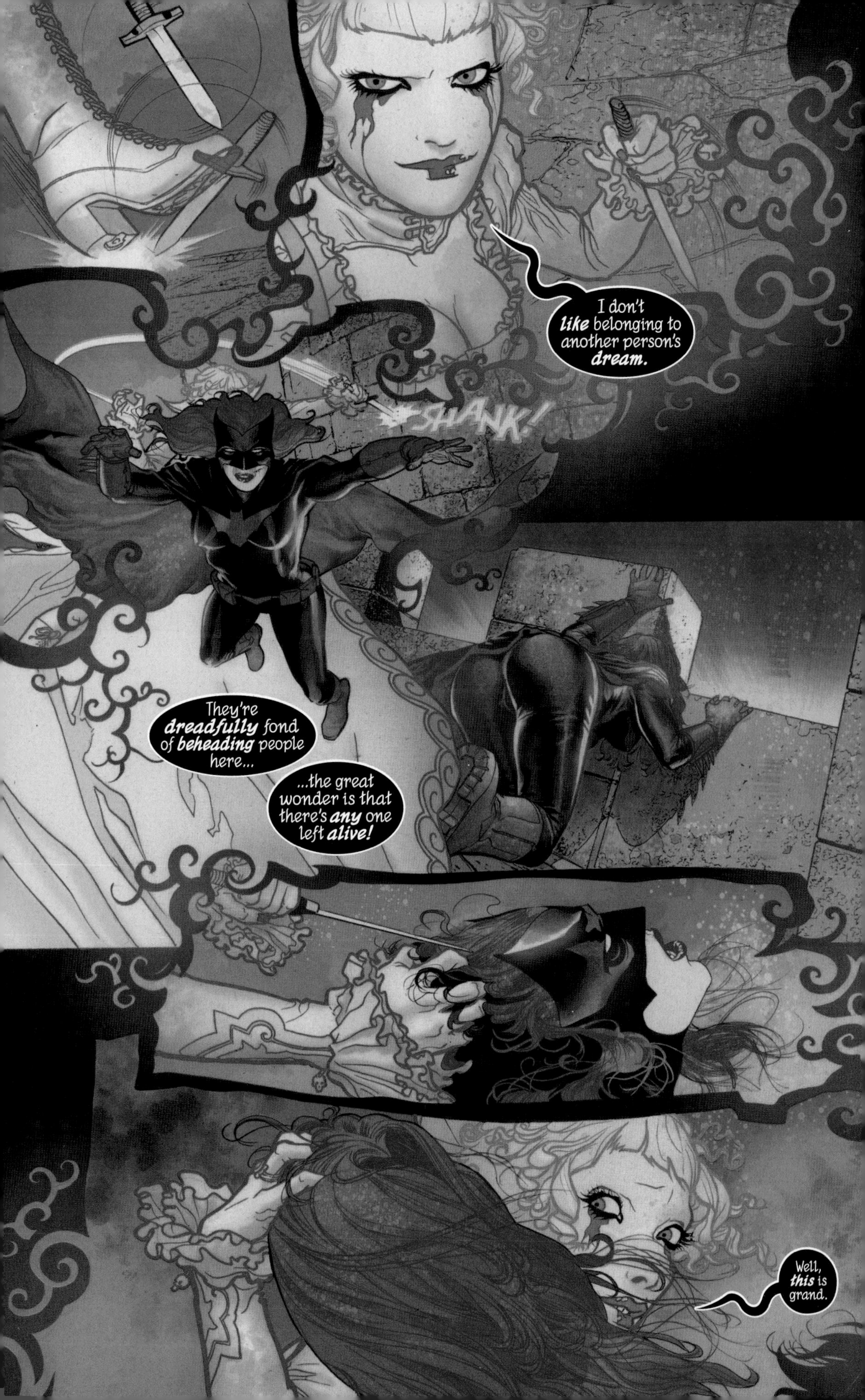
I don't **like** belonging to another person's **dream.**
SHANK!
They're **dreadfully** fond of **beheading** people here...
...the great wonder is that there's **any** one left **alive!**
Well, **this** is grand.

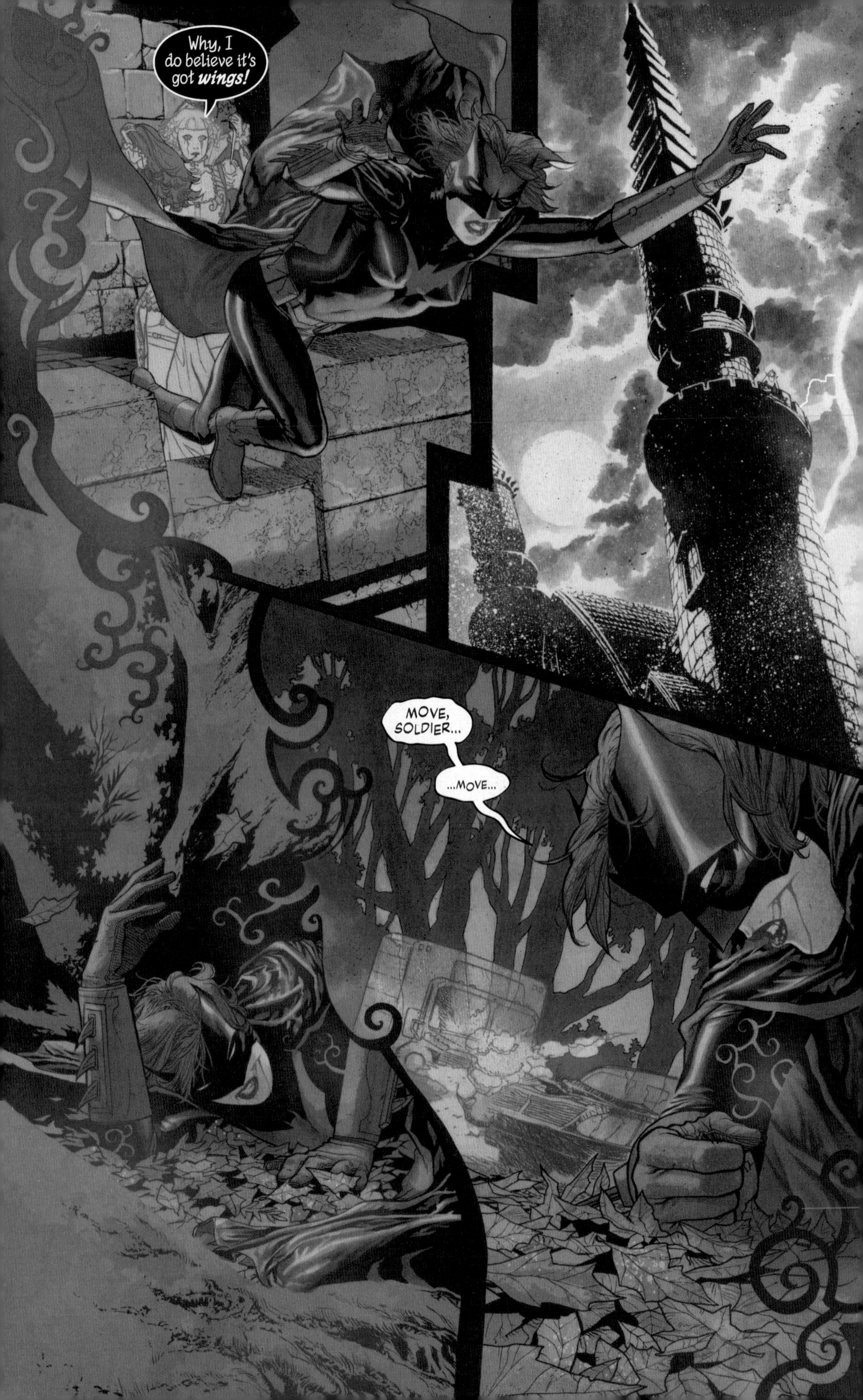
Why, I do believe it's got *wings!*
MOVE, SOLDIER...
...MOVE...

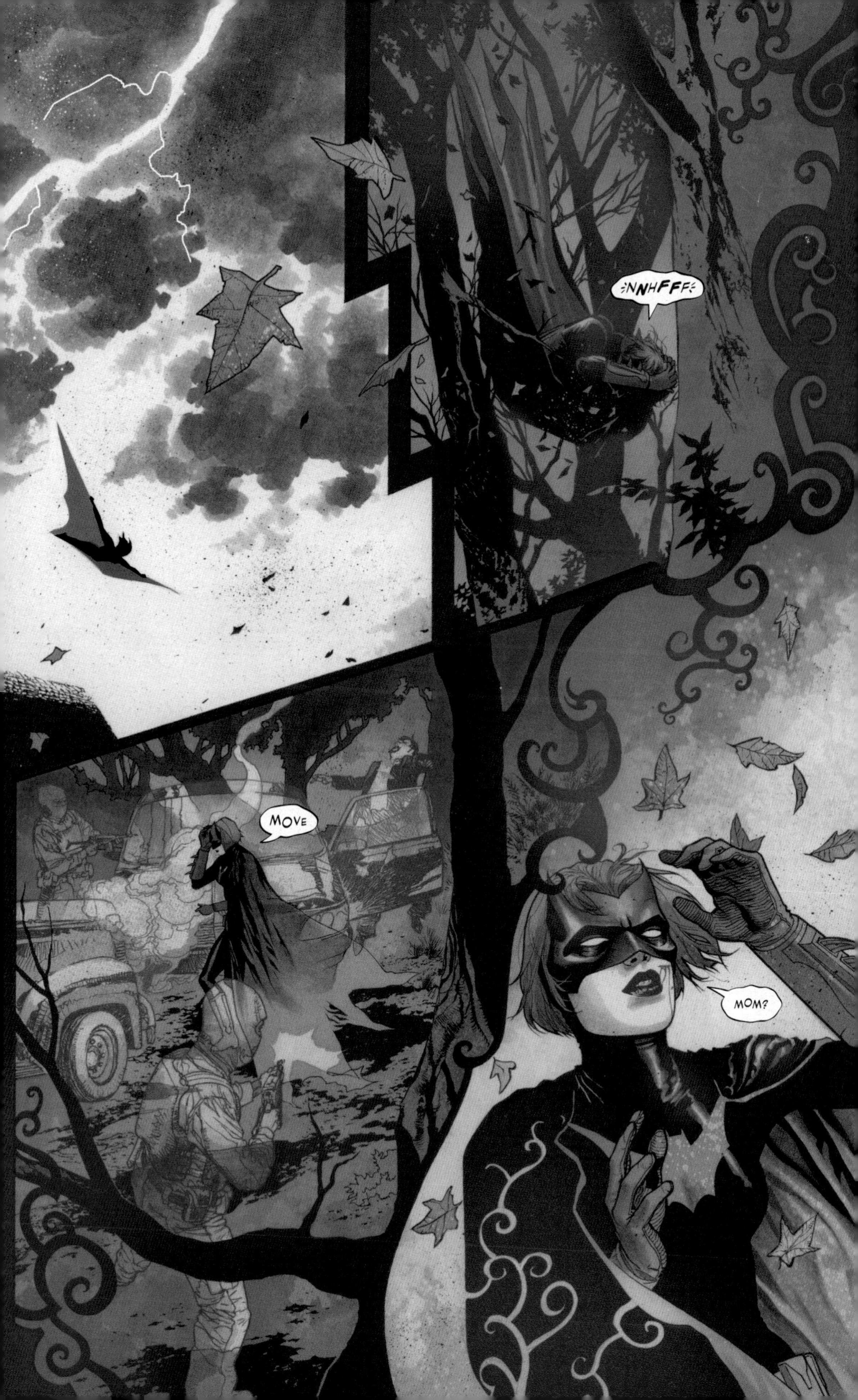
NNHFFF
MOVE
MOM?

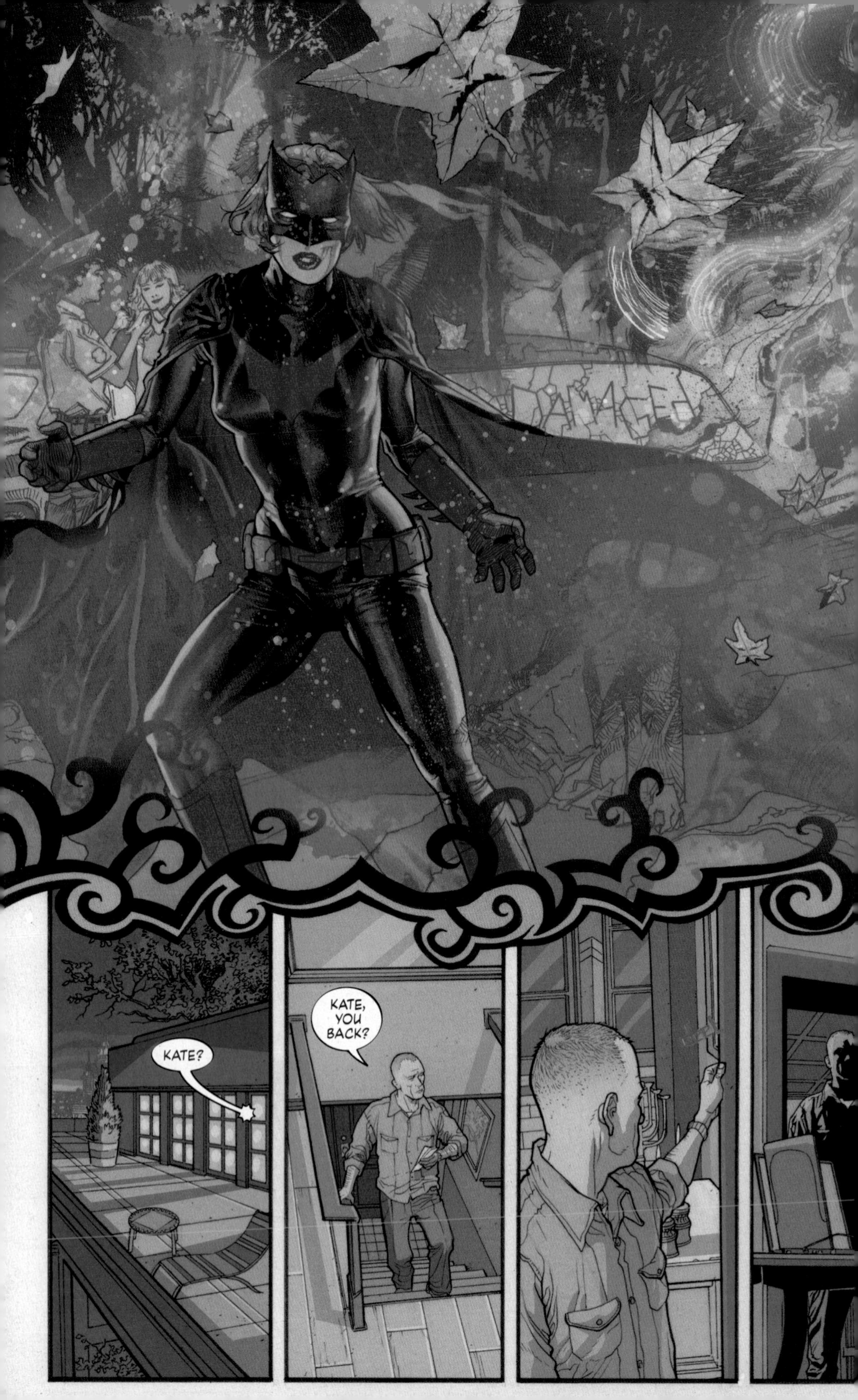
DAMAGE
KATE?
KATE, YOU BACK?

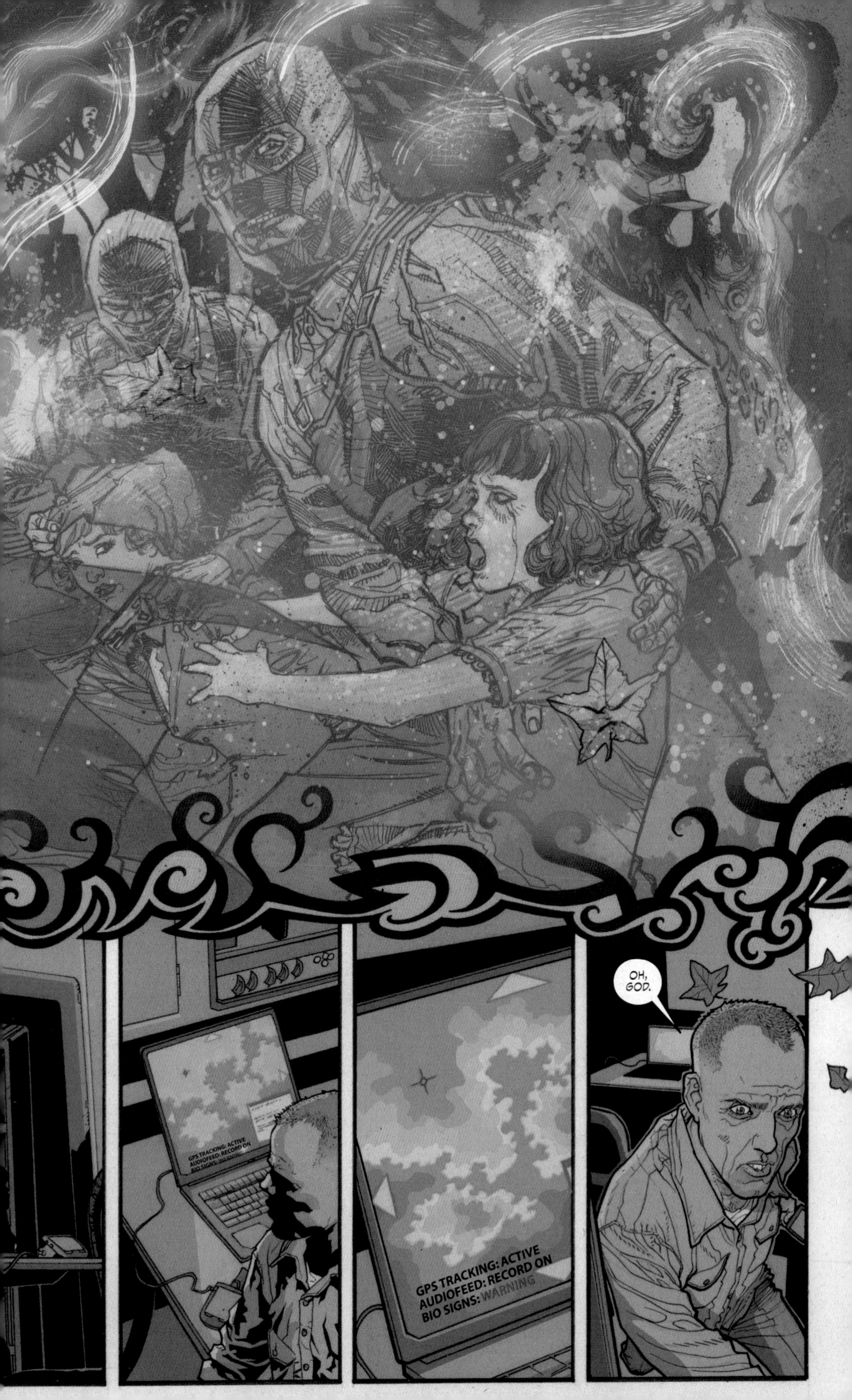
GPS TRACKING: ACTIVE
AUDIOFEED: RECORD ON
BIO SIGNS: WARNING
GPS TRACKING: ACTIVE
AUDIOFEED: RECORD ON
BIO SIGNS: WARNING
OH, GOD.

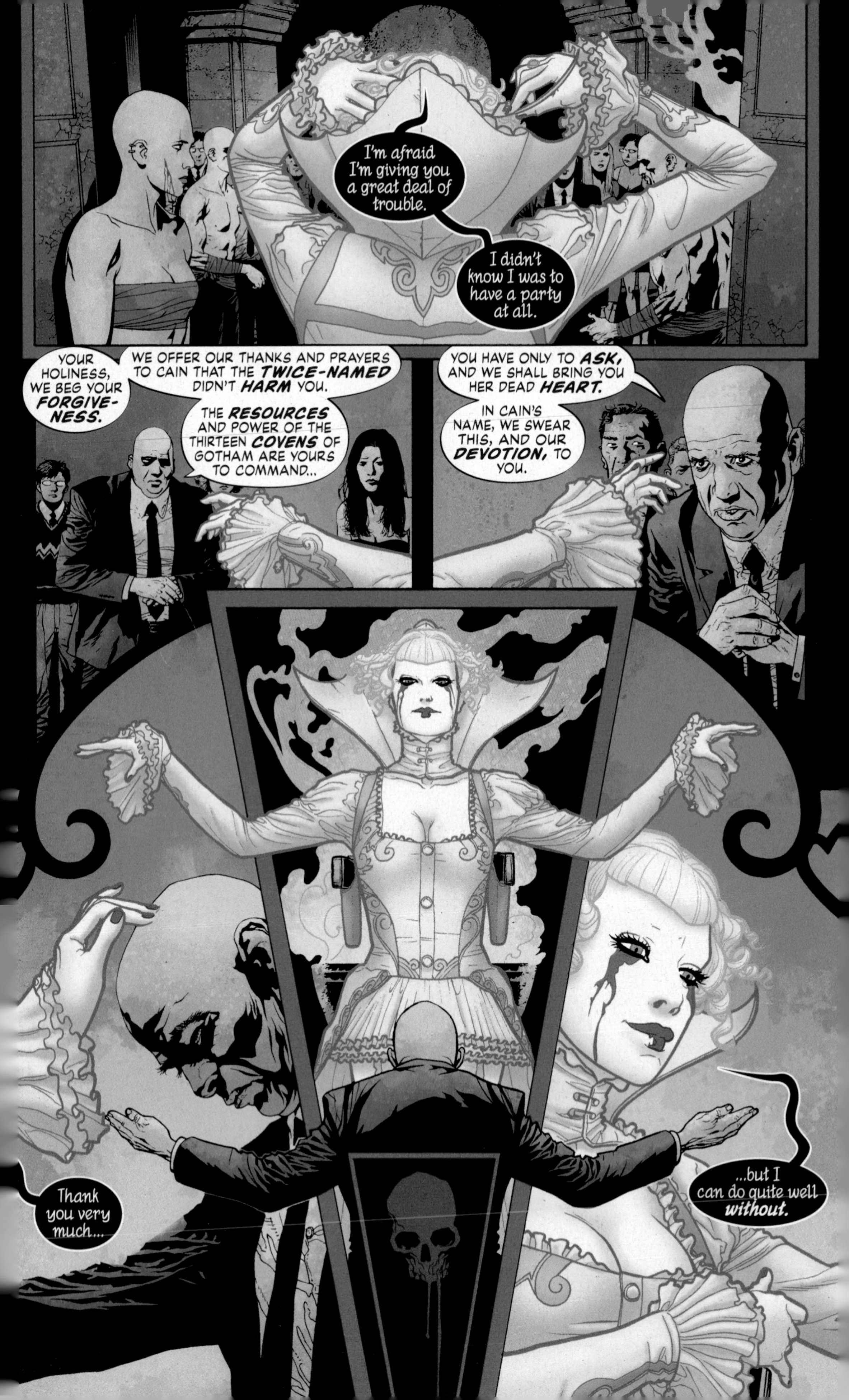
I'm afraid I'm giving you a great deal of trouble.
I didn't know I was to have a party at all.
YOUR HOLINESS, WE BEG YOUR FORGIVE-NESS.
WE OFFER OUR THANKS AND PRAYERS TO CAIN THAT THE TWICE-NAMED DIDN'T HARM YOU.
THE RESOURCES AND POWER OF THE THIRTEEN COVENS OF GOTHAM ARE YOURS TO COMMAND...
YOU HAVE ONLY TO ASK, AND WE SHALL BRING YOU HER DEAD HEART.
IN CAIN'S NAME, WE SWEAR THIS, AND OUR DEVOTION, TO YOU.
Thank you very much...
...but I can do quite well without.

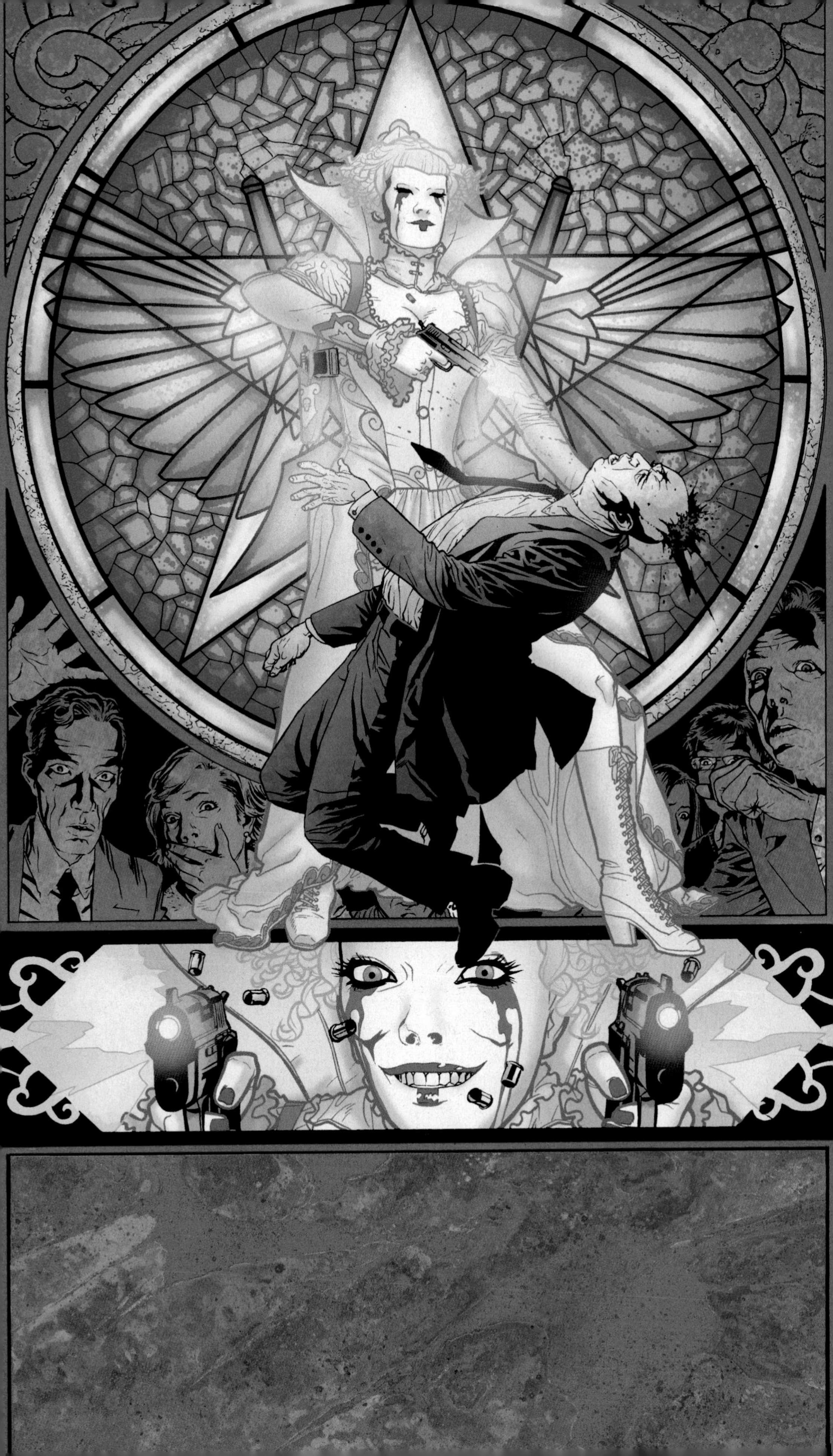

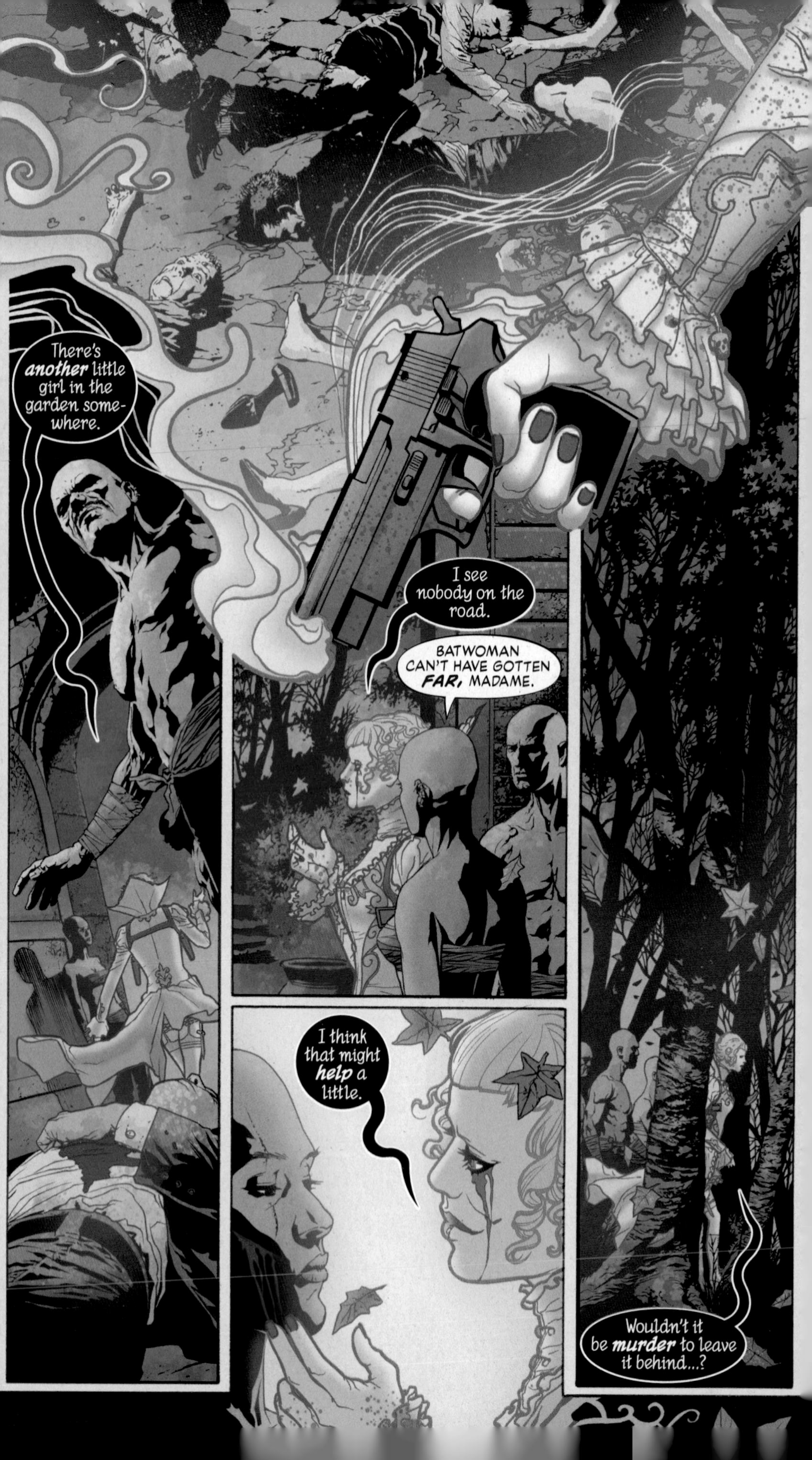
There's **another** little girl in the garden some-where.
I see nobody on the road.
BATWOMAN CAN'T HAVE GOTTEN **FAR,** MADAME.
I think that might **help** a little.
Wouldn't it be **murder** to leave it behind...?

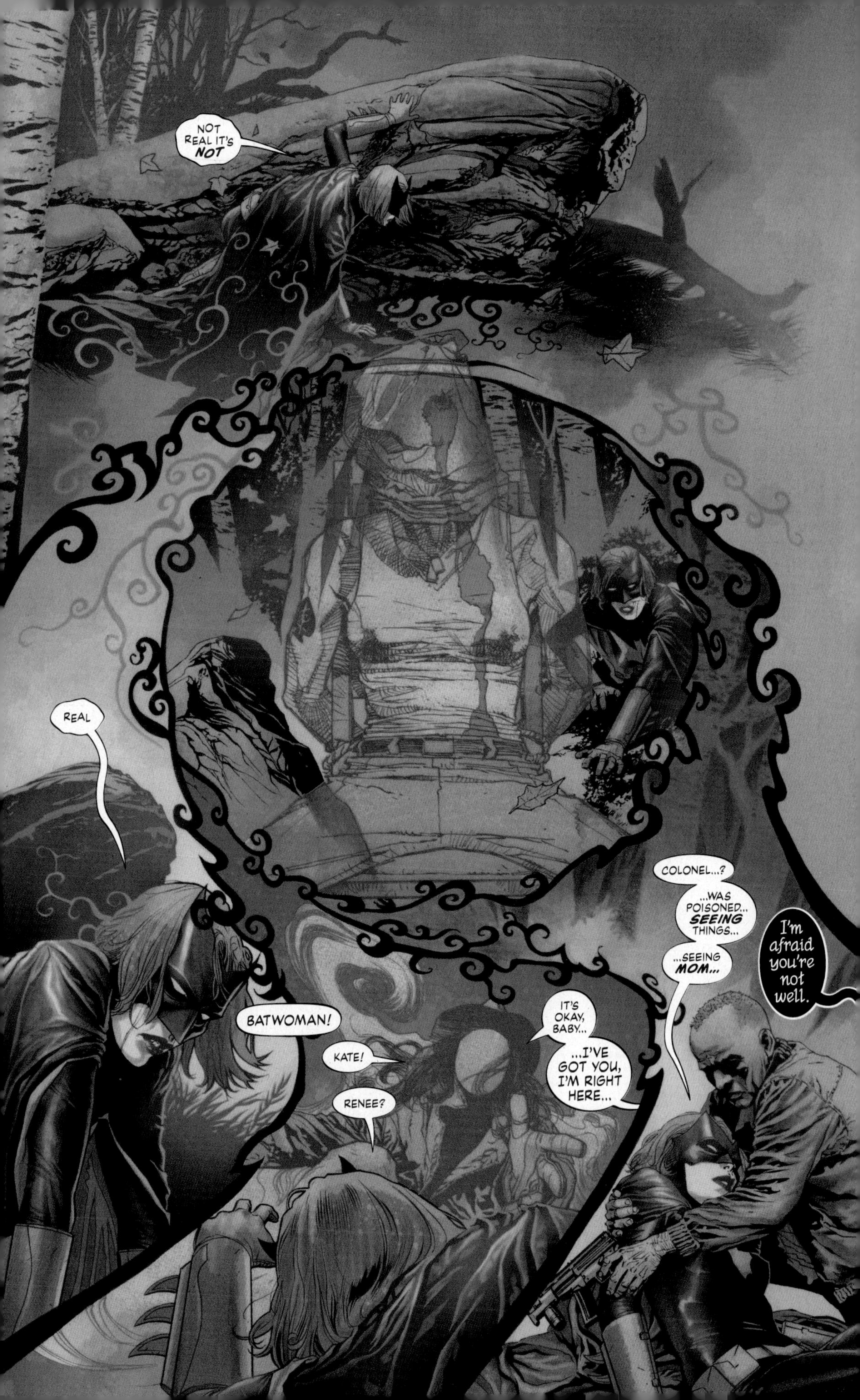
NOT REAL IT'S NOT
REAL
BATWOMAN!
KATE!
RENEE?
IT'S OKAY, BABY...
...I'VE GOT YOU, I'M RIGHT HERE...
COLONEL...?
...WAS POISONED... SEEING THINGS...
...SEEING MOM...
I'm afraid you're not well.

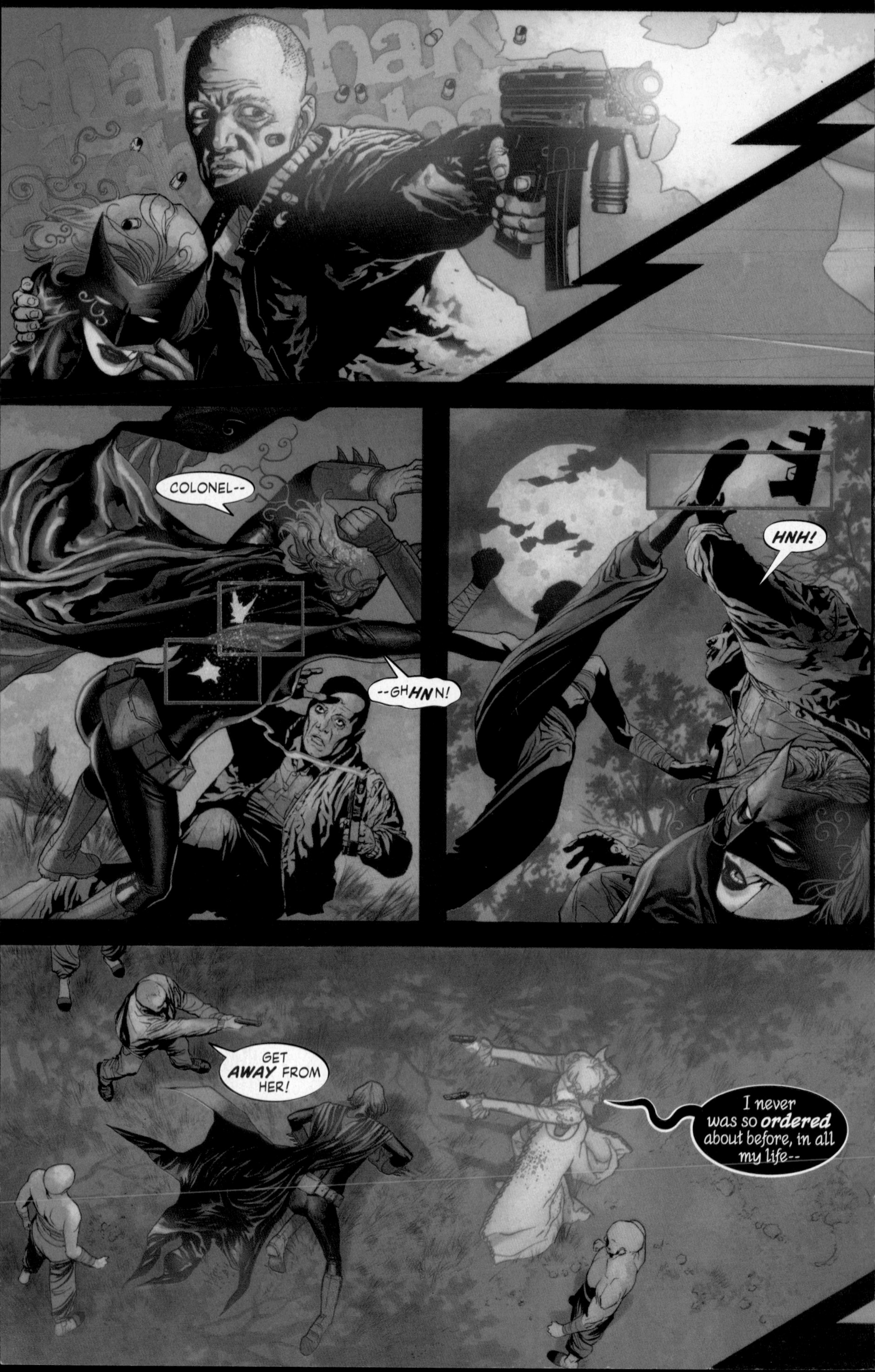
COLONEL--
--GHHNN!
HNH!
GET AWAY FROM HER!
I never was so **ordered** about before, in all my life--

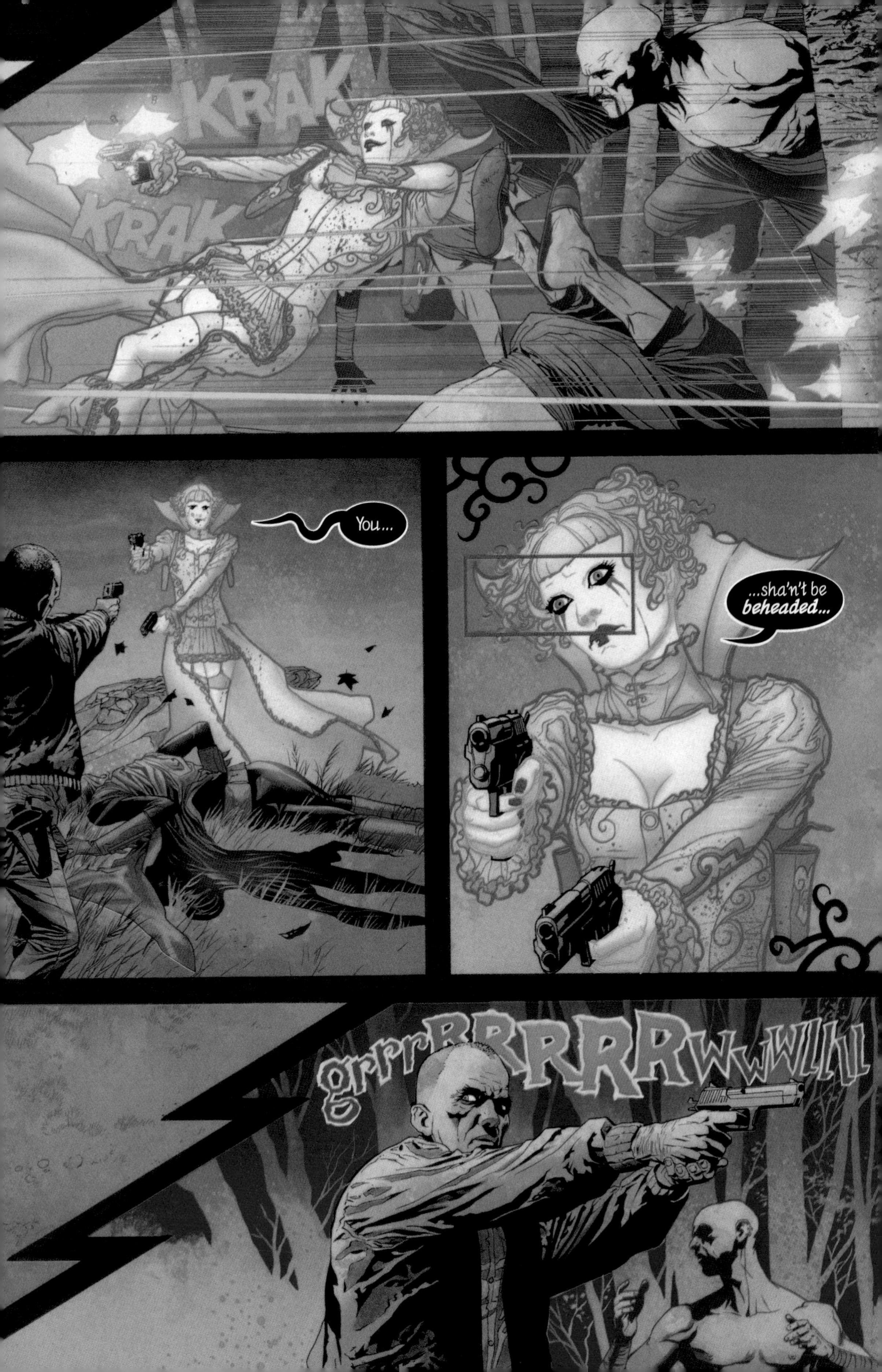
KRAK
KRAK
You...
...sha'n't be *beheaded*...
grrrRRRRRRwwWllll

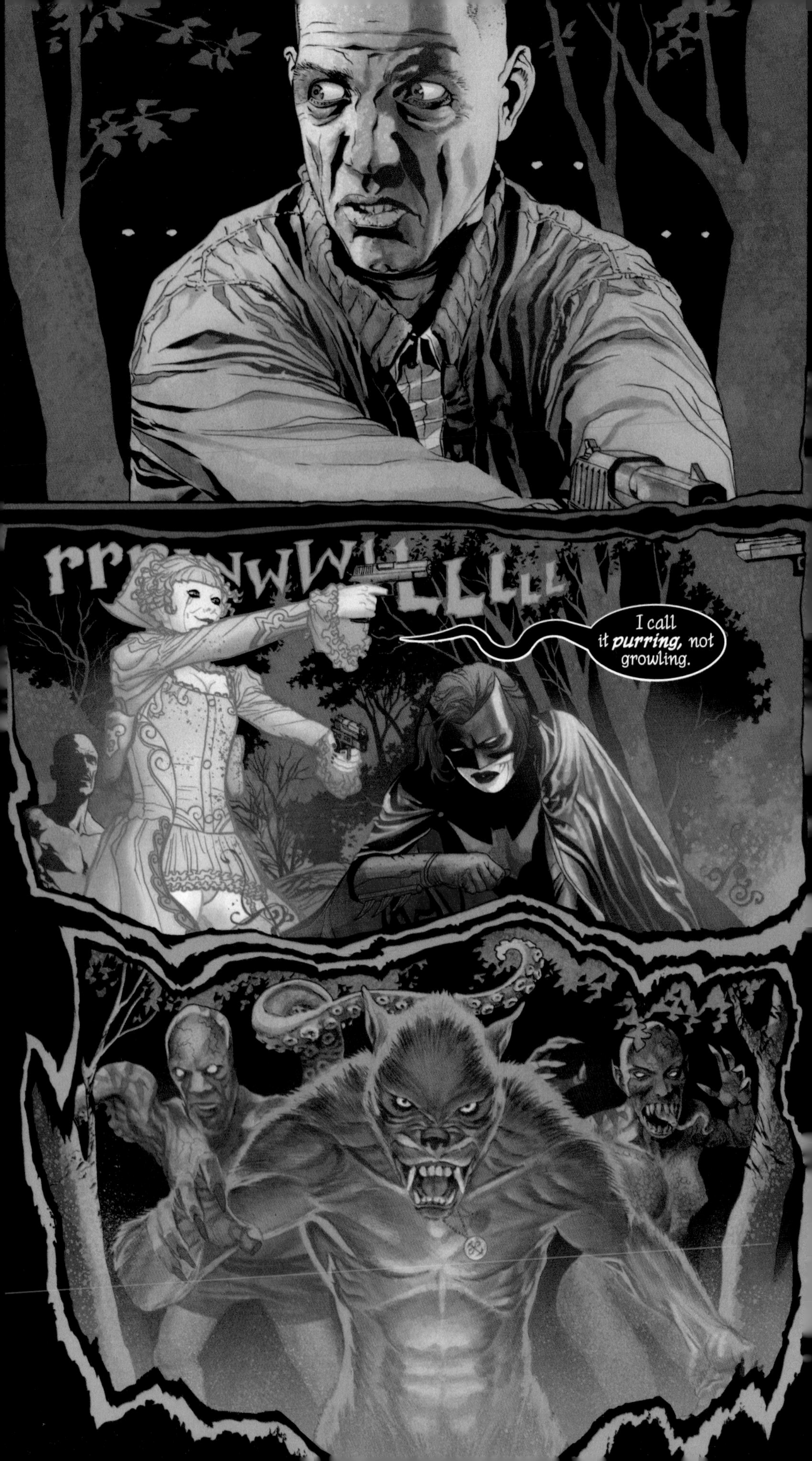
I call it **purring,** not growling.

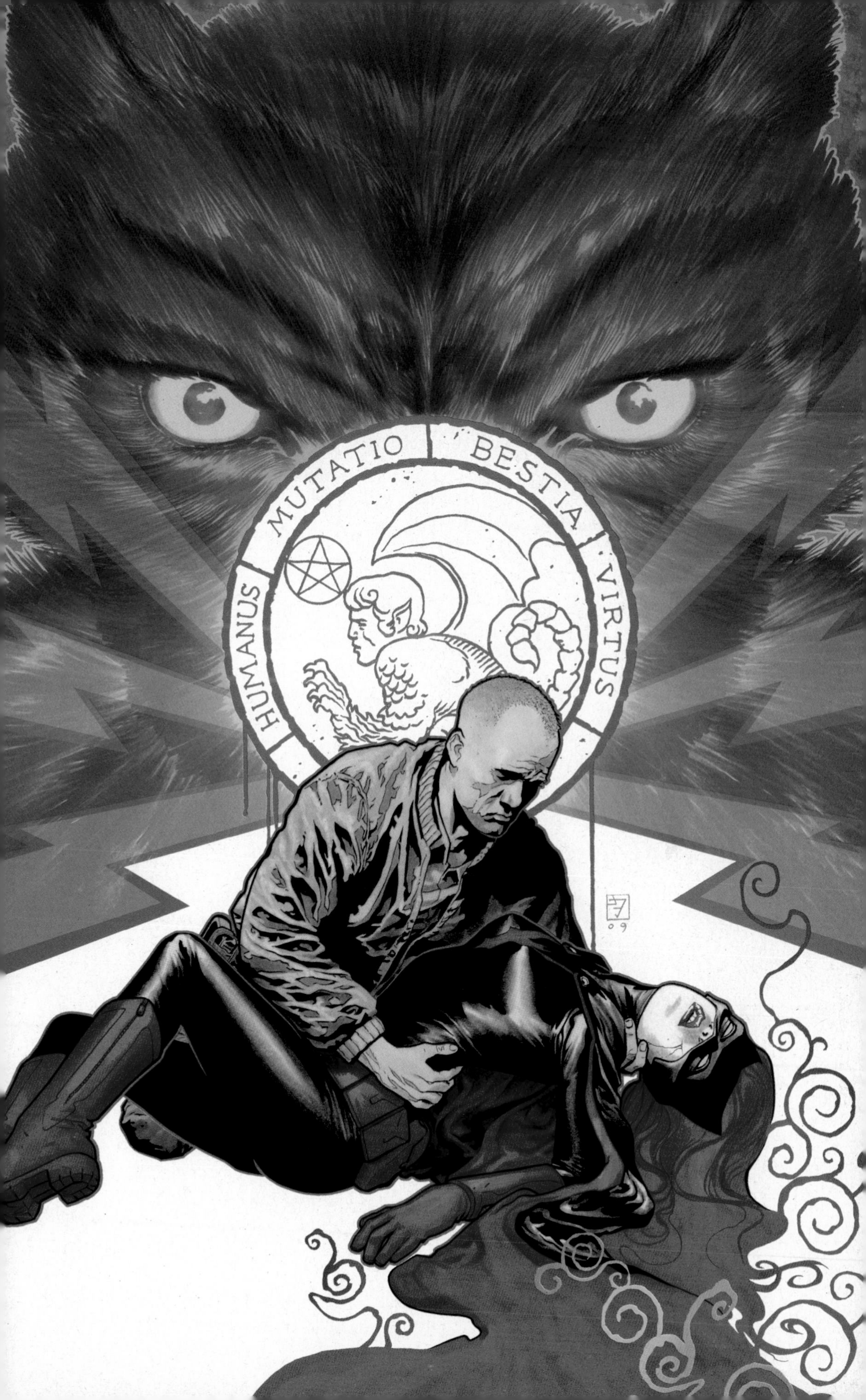
MUTATIO
BESTIA
HUMANUS
VIRTUS

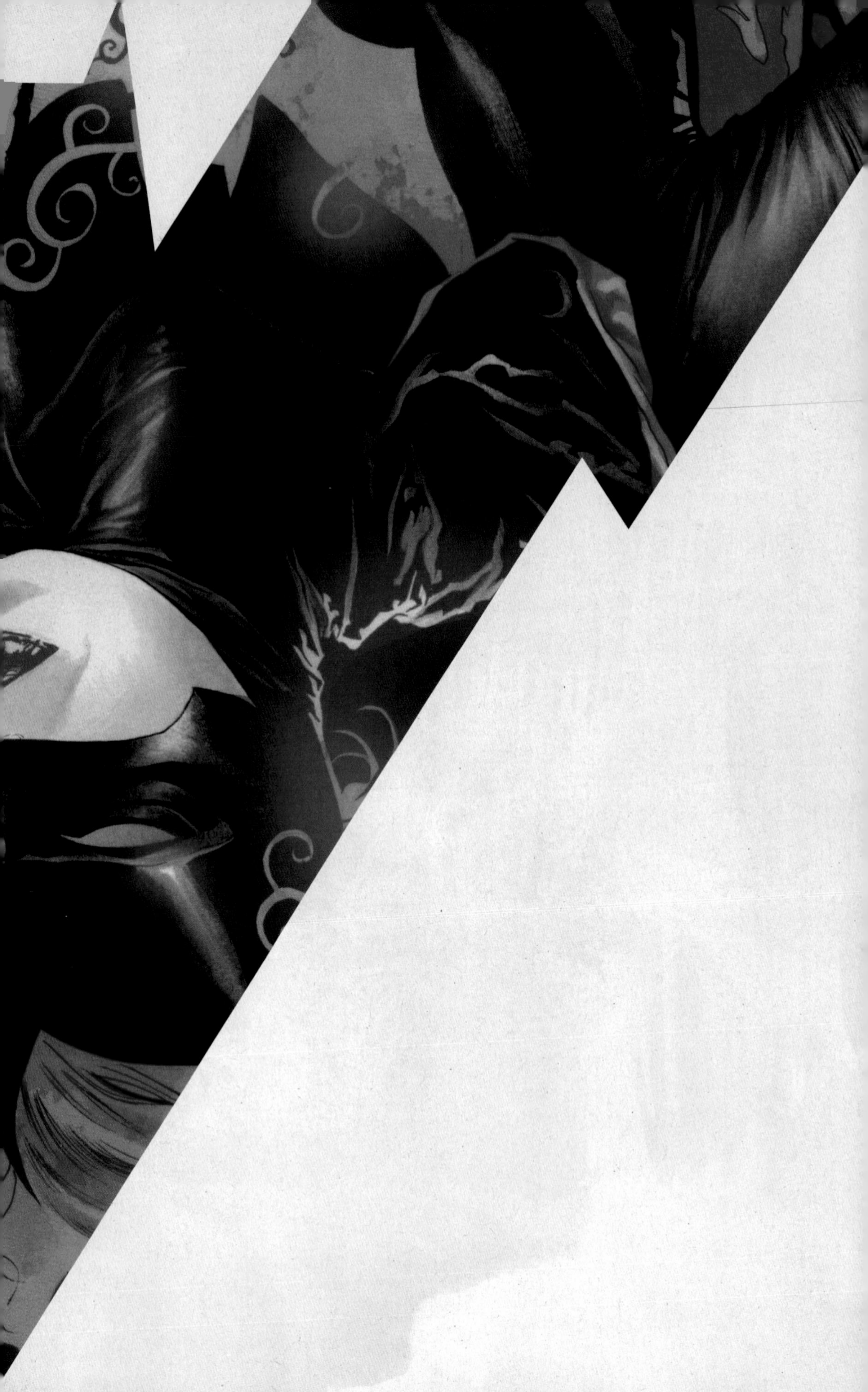

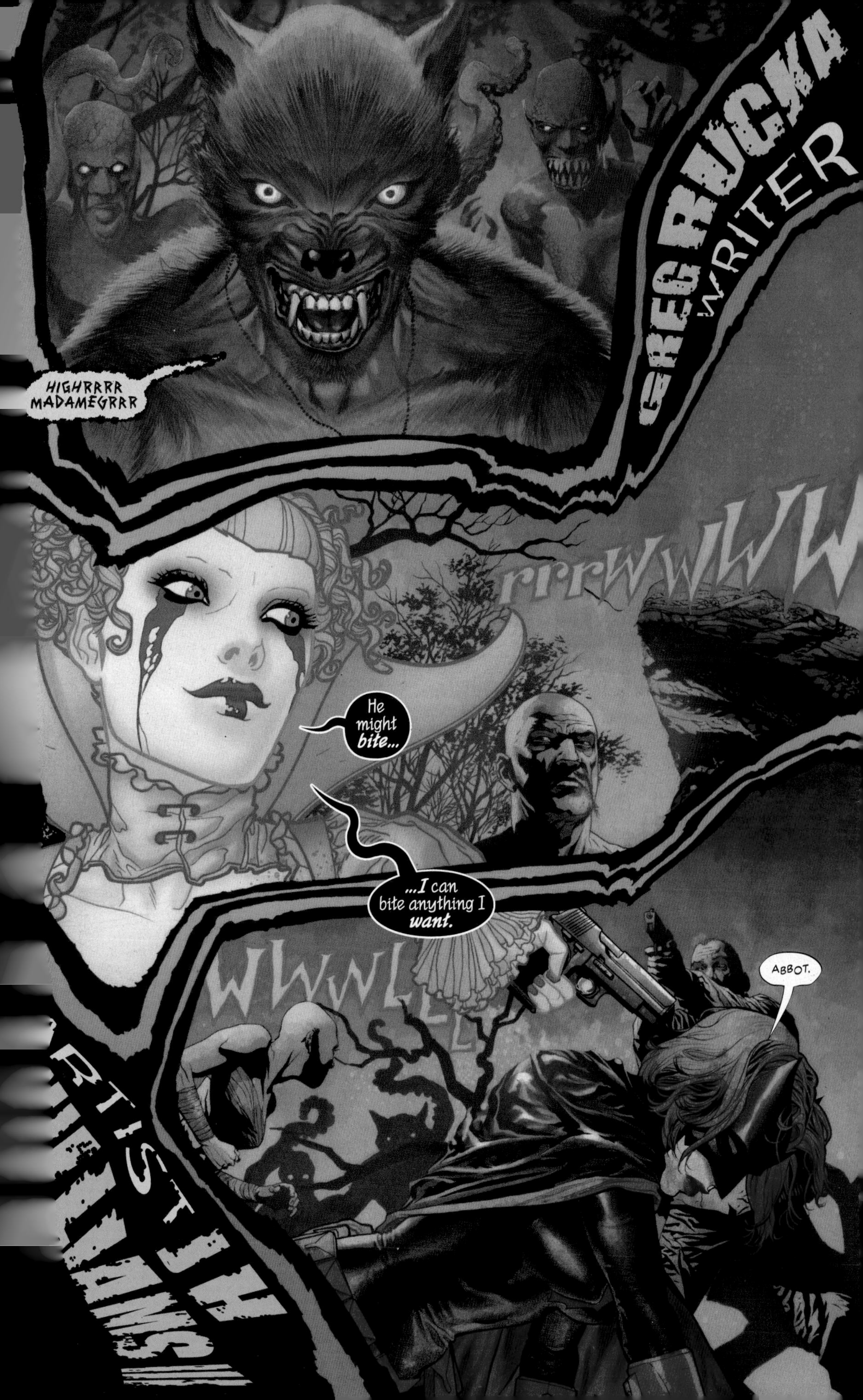
GREG RUCKA
WRITER
HIGHRRRR MADAMEGRRR
rrrWWWW
He might *bite*...
...*I* can bite anything I ***want.***
WWWLLL
ABBOT.

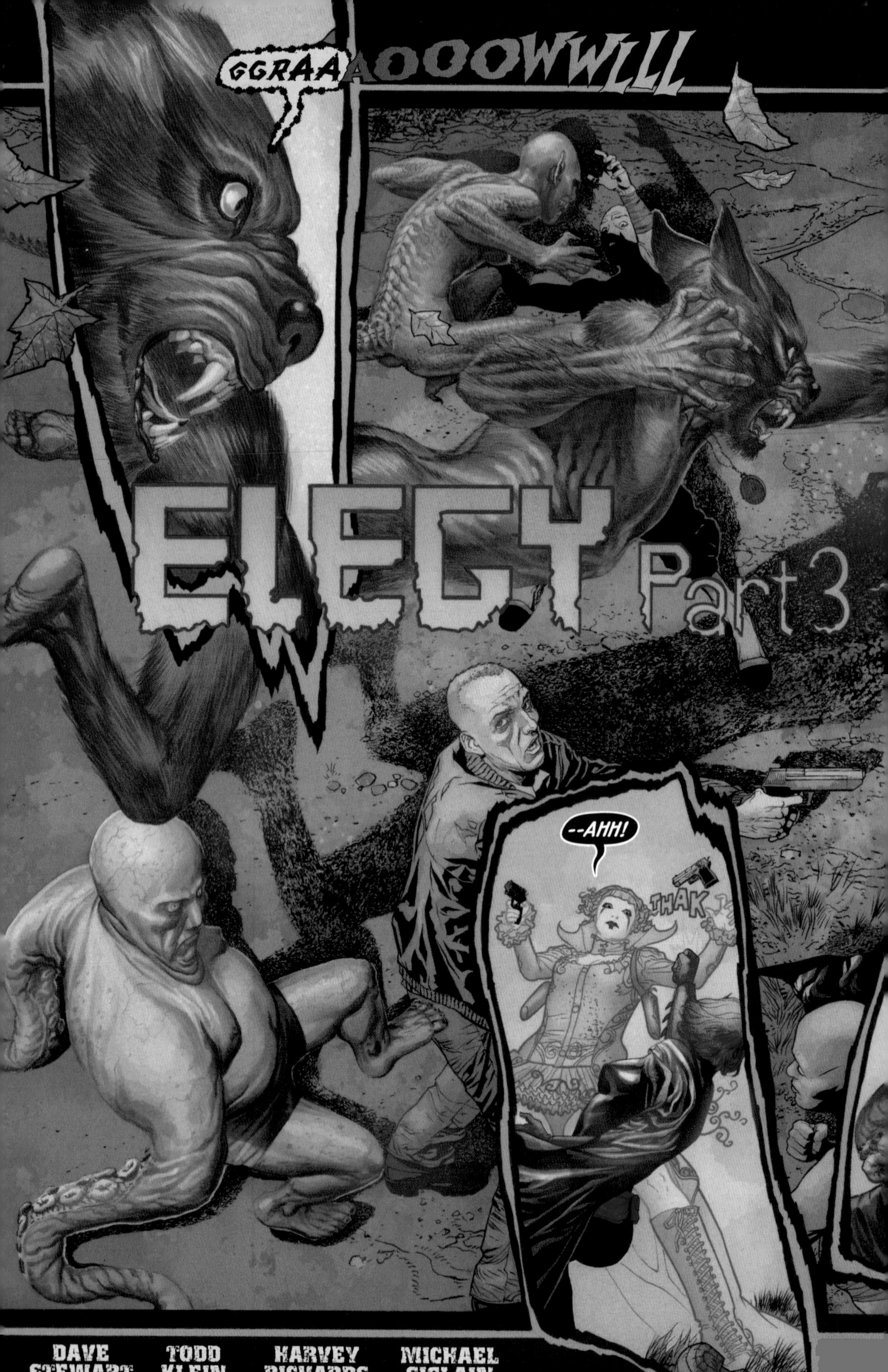
GGRAAAOOOOWWLLL
ELEGY Part3
--AHH!
THAK

DAVE STEWART colors

TODD KLEIN letters

HARVEY RICHARDS asst. ed.

MICHAEL SIGLAIN editor

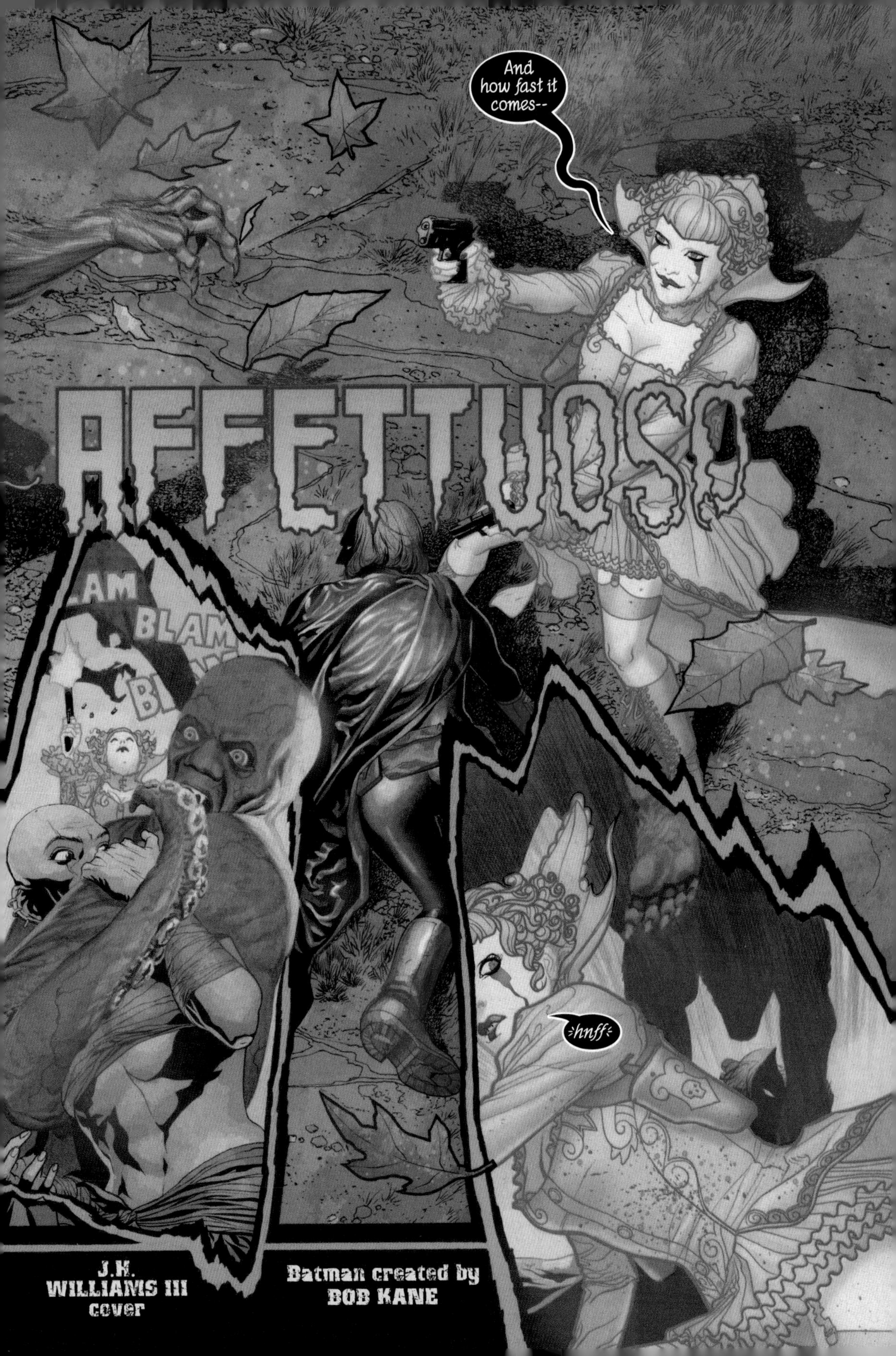
And how fast it comes--
AFFETTUOSO
BLAM
hnff
J.H. WILLIAMS III cover
Batman created by BOB KANE

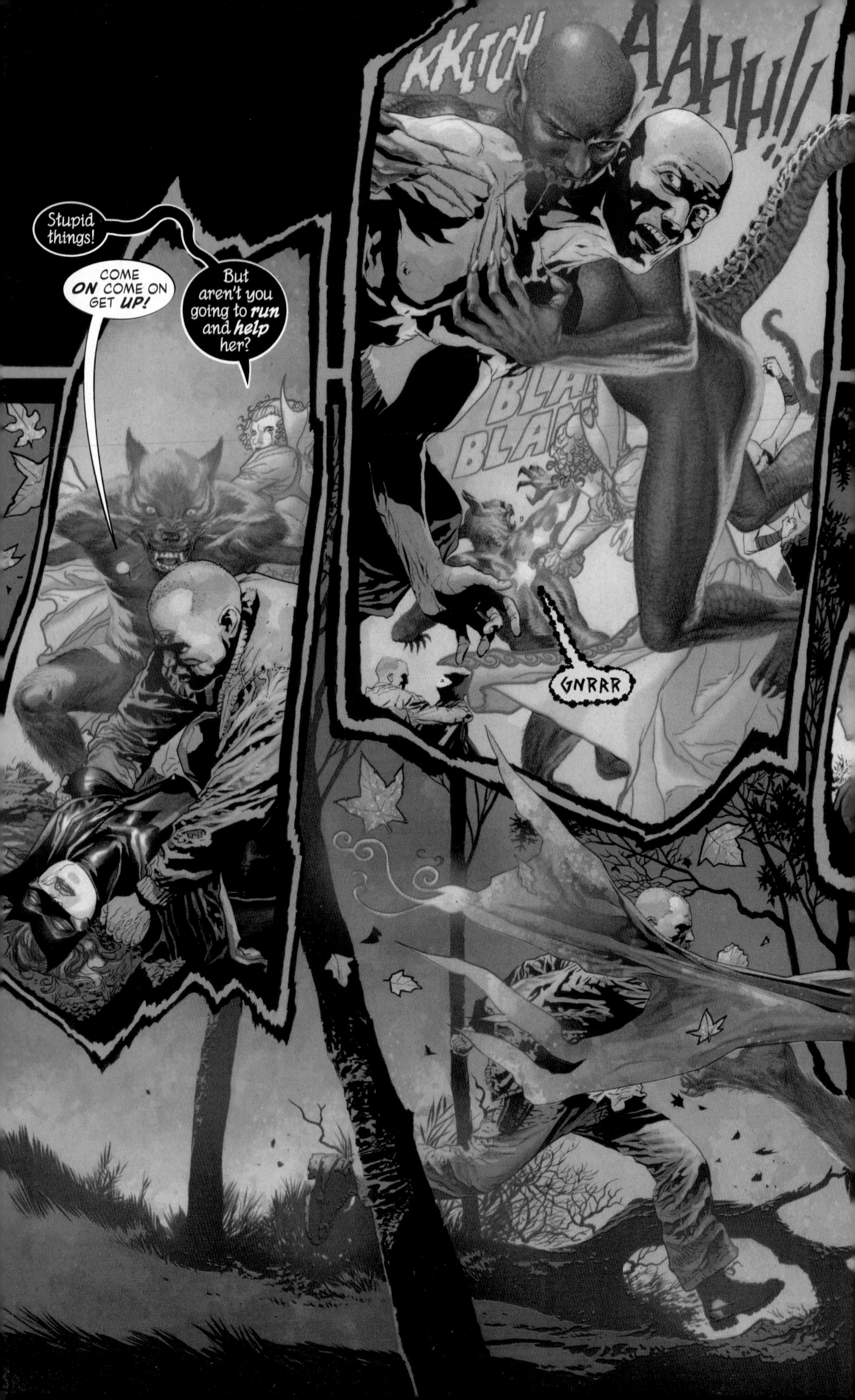
KKLITCH
AAHH!!!
Stupid things!
COME ON COME ON GET UP!
But aren't you going to run and help her?
BLAM BLAM
GNRRR

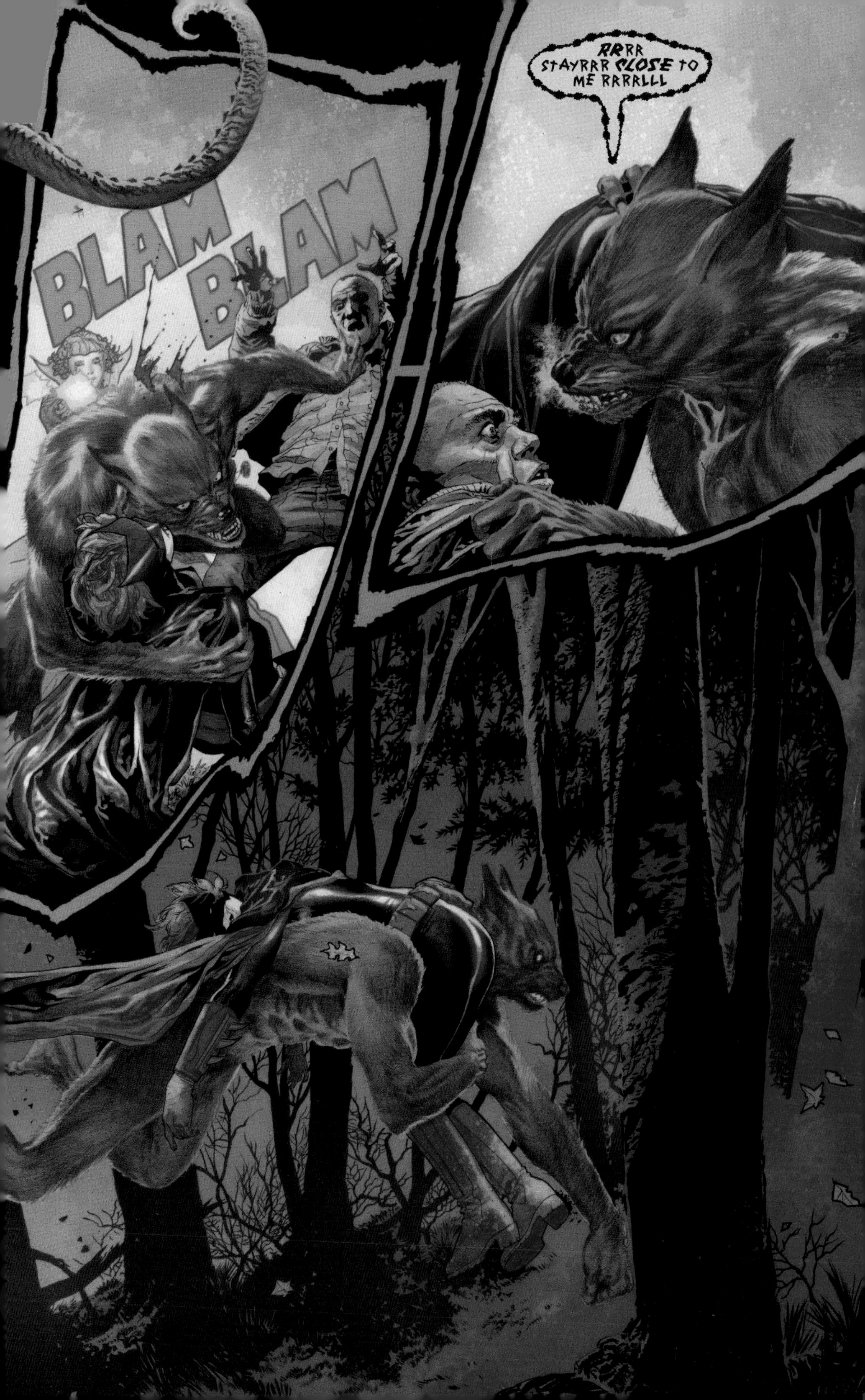
BLAM
BLAM
RRRR STAYRRR CLOSE TO ME RRRRLLL

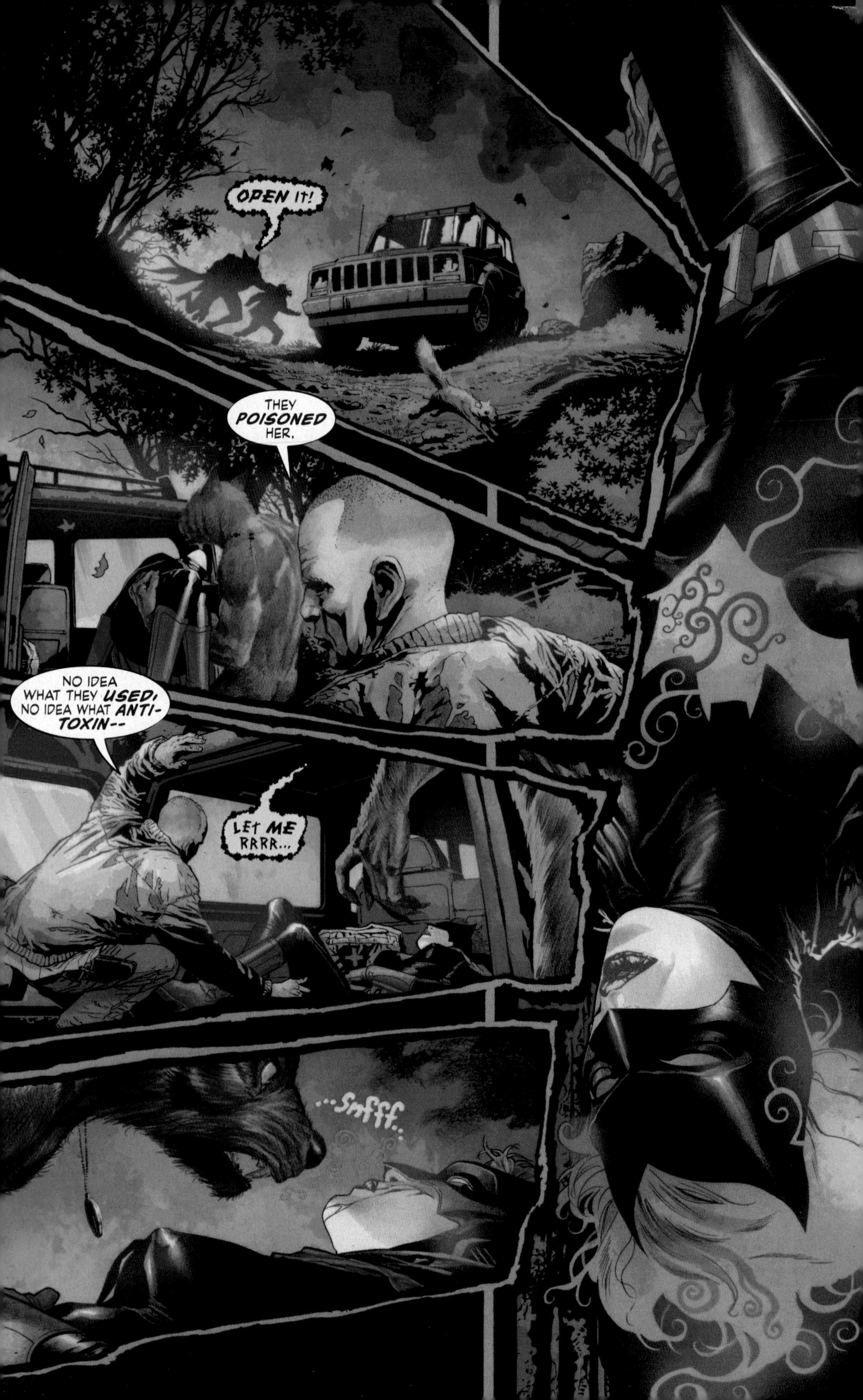
OPEN IT!
THEY POISONED HER.
NO IDEA WHAT THEY USED, NO IDEA WHAT ANTI-TOXIN--
LET ME RRRR...
..Snfff..

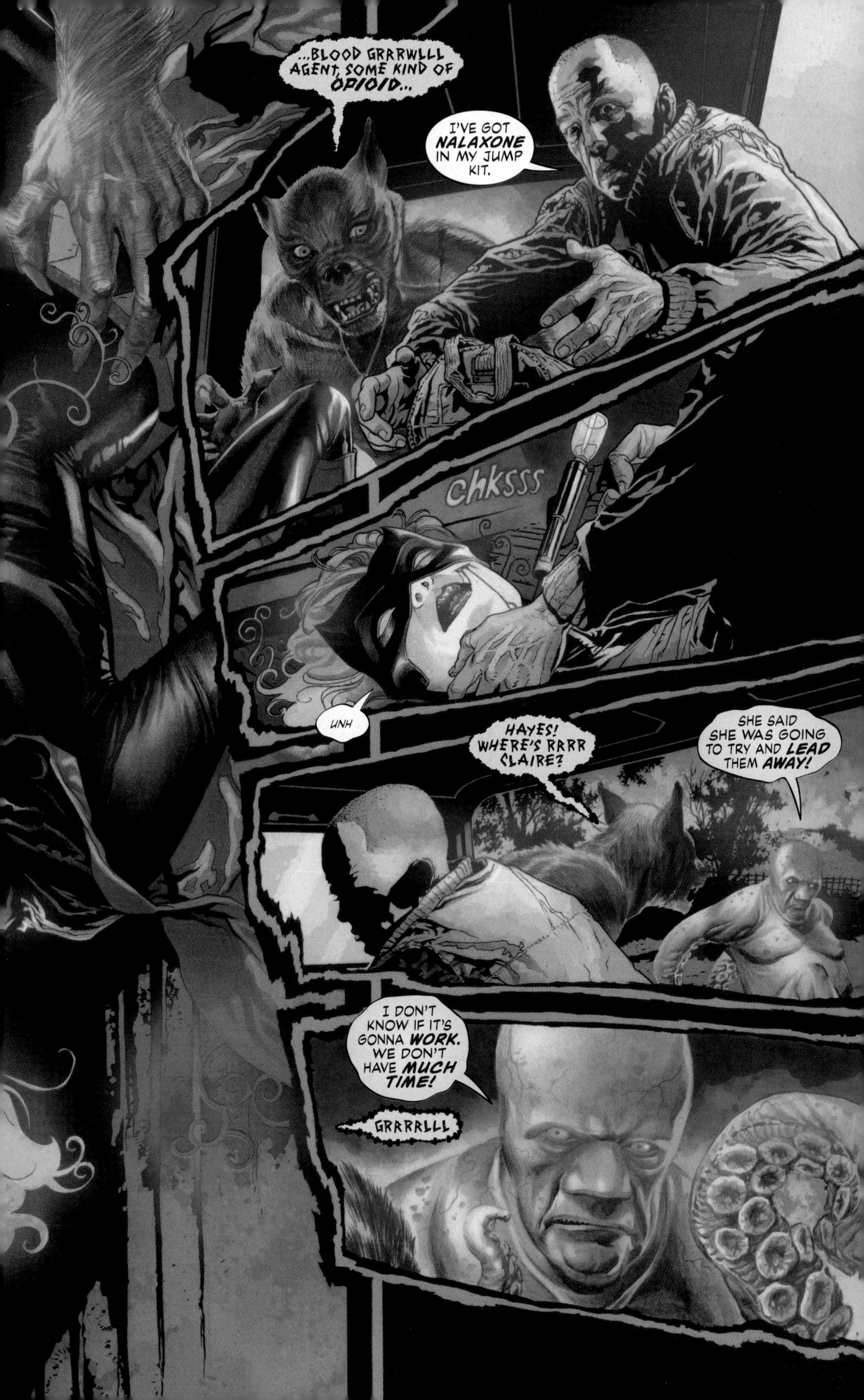
...BLOOD GRRRWLLL AGENT, SOME KIND OF OPIOID...
I'VE GOT NALAXONE IN MY JUMP KIT.
chksss
UNH
HAYES! WHERE'S RRRR CLAIRE?
SHE SAID SHE WAS GOING TO TRY AND LEAD THEM AWAY!
I DON'T KNOW IF IT'S GONNA WORK. WE DON'T HAVE MUCH TIME!
GRRRRLLL

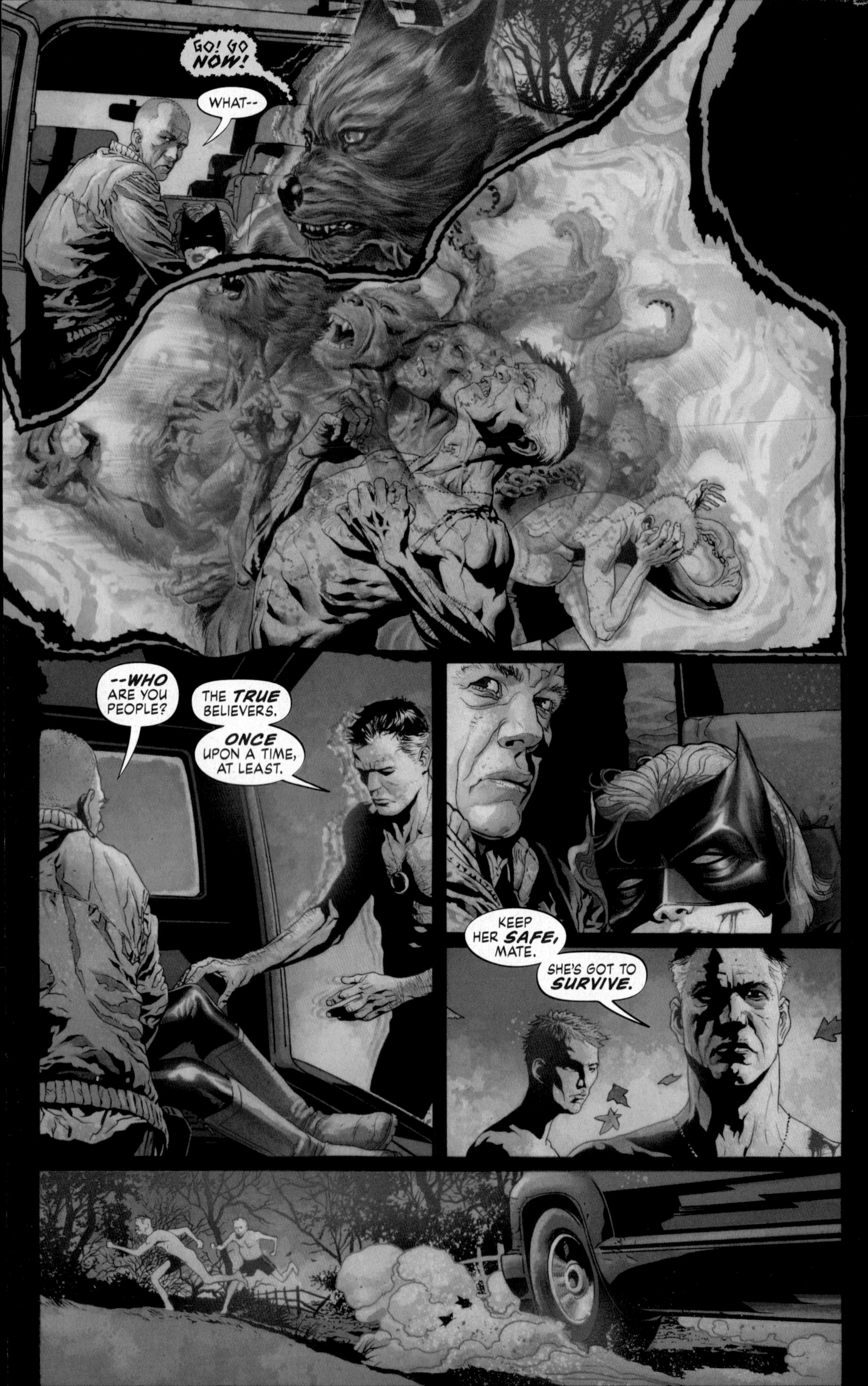
GO! GO NOW!
WHAT--
--WHO ARE YOU PEOPLE?
THE TRUE BELIEVERS.
ONCE UPON A TIME, AT LEAST.
KEEP HER SAFE, MATE.
SHE'S GOT TO SURVIVE.

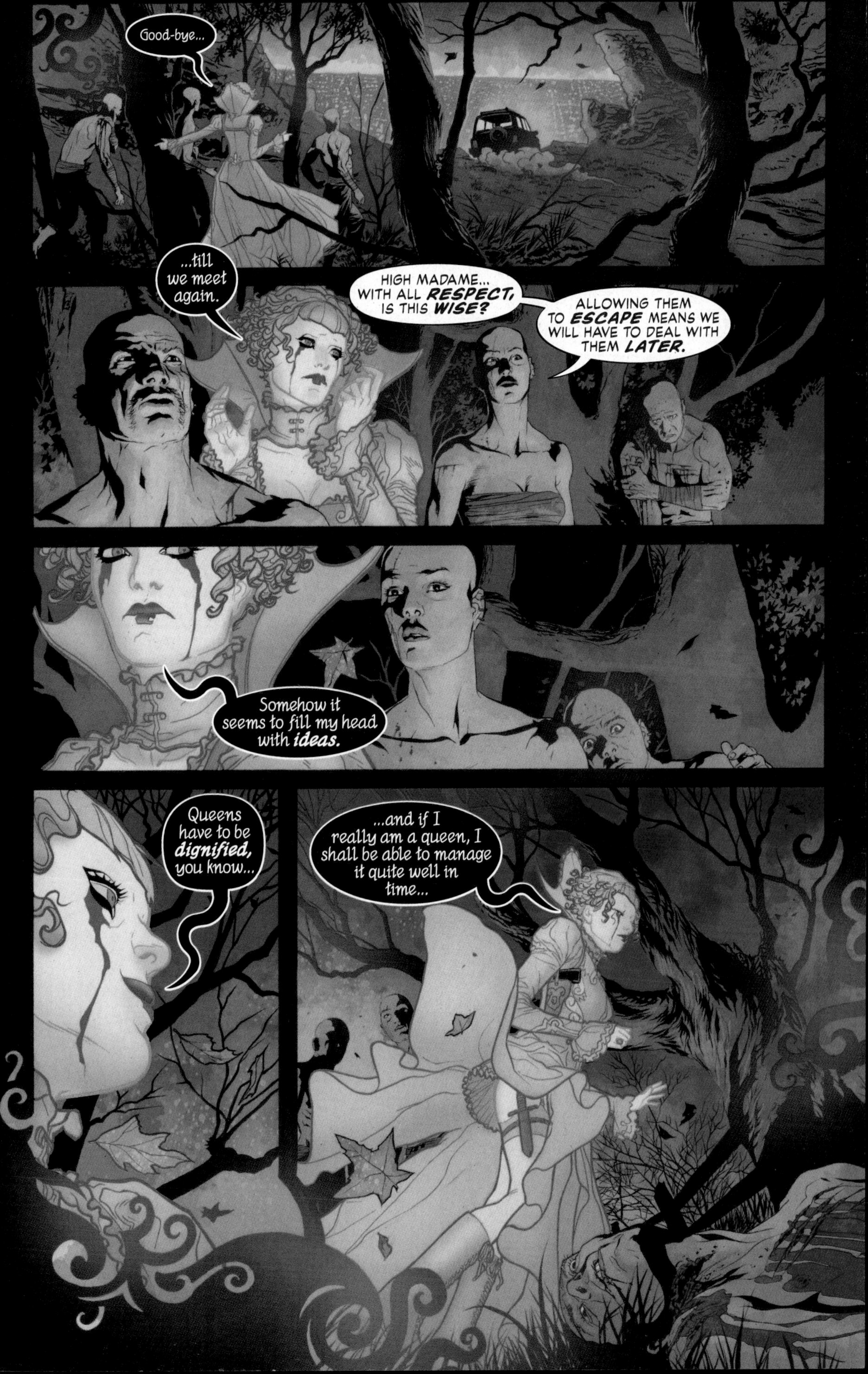
Good-bye...
...till we meet again.
HIGH MADAME... WITH ALL RESPECT, IS THIS WISE?
ALLOWING THEM TO ESCAPE MEANS WE WILL HAVE TO DEAL WITH THEM LATER.
Somehow it seems to fill my head with ideas.
Queens have to be dignified, you know...
...and if I really am a queen, I shall be able to manage it quite well in time...

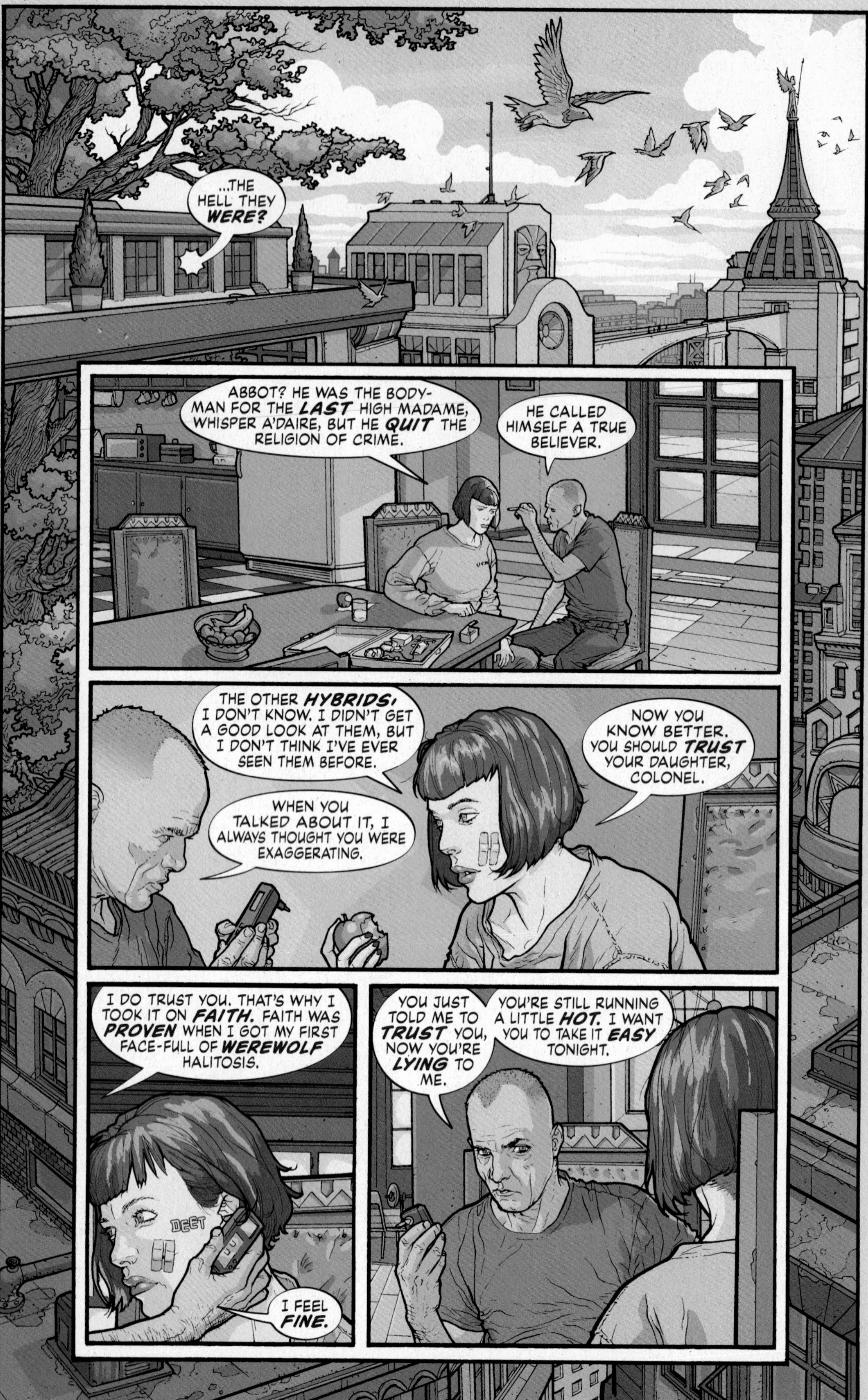
...THE HELL THEY WERE?
ABBOT? HE WAS THE BODY-MAN FOR THE LAST HIGH MADAME, WHISPER A'DAIRE, BUT HE QUIT THE RELIGION OF CRIME.
HE CALLED HIMSELF A TRUE BELIEVER.
THE OTHER HYBRIDS, I DON'T KNOW. I DIDN'T GET A GOOD LOOK AT THEM, BUT I DON'T THINK I'VE EVER SEEN THEM BEFORE.
WHEN YOU TALKED ABOUT IT, I ALWAYS THOUGHT YOU WERE EXAGGERATING.
NOW YOU KNOW BETTER. YOU SHOULD TRUST YOUR DAUGHTER, COLONEL.
I DO TRUST YOU. THAT'S WHY I TOOK IT ON FAITH. FAITH WAS PROVEN WHEN I GOT MY FIRST FACE-FULL OF WEREWOLF HALITOSIS.
I FEEL FINE.
YOU JUST TOLD ME TO TRUST YOU, NOW YOU'RE LYING TO ME.
YOU'RE STILL RUNNING A LITTLE HOT. I WANT YOU TO TAKE IT EASY TONIGHT.

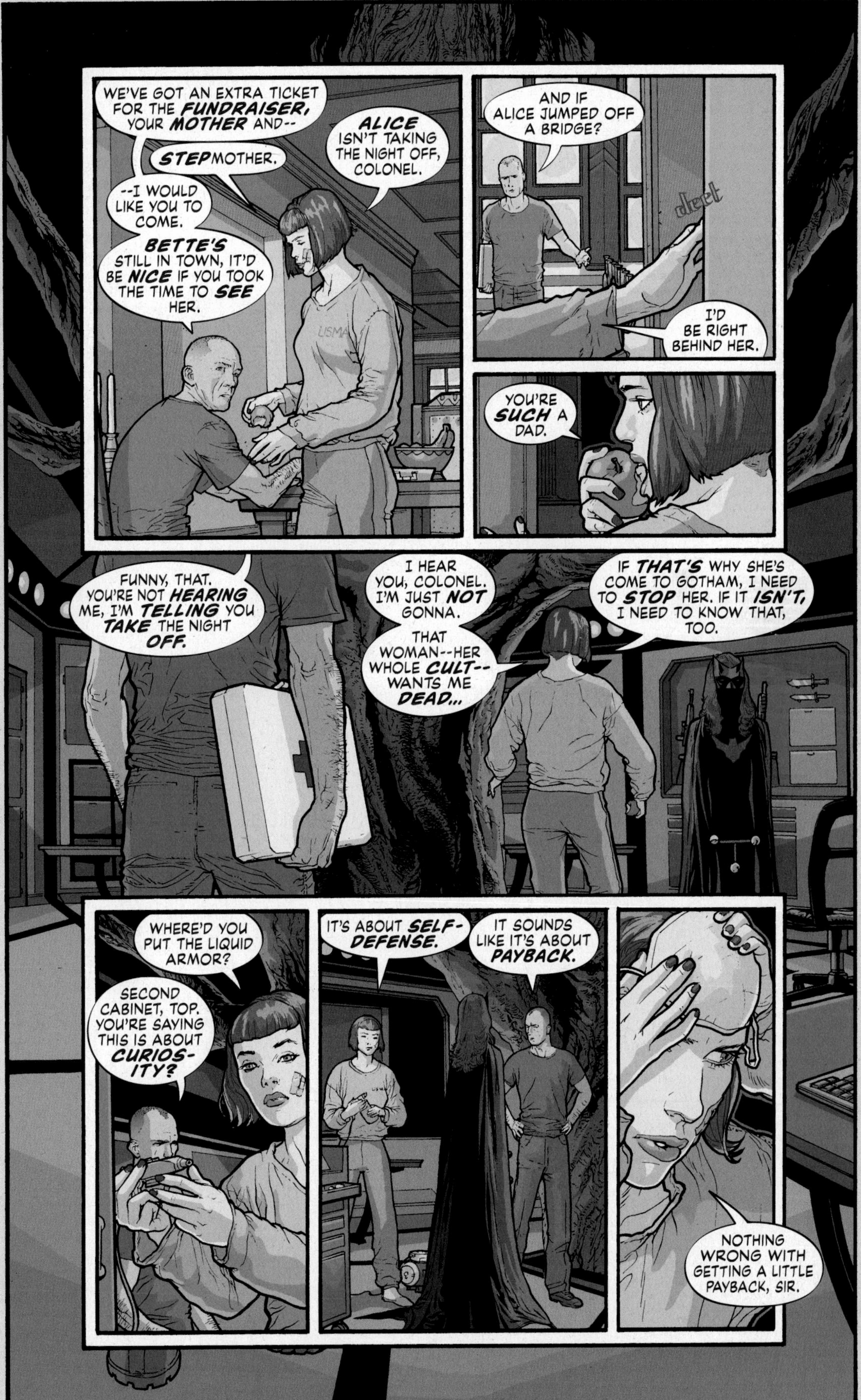
WE'VE GOT AN EXTRA TICKET FOR THE FUNDRAISER, YOUR MOTHER AND--
STEPMOTHER.
--I WOULD LIKE YOU TO COME.
BETTE'S STILL IN TOWN, IT'D BE NICE IF YOU TOOK THE TIME TO SEE HER.
ALICE ISN'T TAKING THE NIGHT OFF, COLONEL.
AND IF ALICE JUMPED OFF A BRIDGE?
dleet
I'D BE RIGHT BEHIND HER.
YOU'RE SUCH A DAD.
FUNNY, THAT. YOU'RE NOT HEARING ME, I'M TELLING YOU TAKE THE NIGHT OFF.
I HEAR YOU, COLONEL. I'M JUST NOT GONNA.
THAT WOMAN--HER WHOLE CULT--WANTS ME DEAD...
IF THAT'S WHY SHE'S COME TO GOTHAM, I NEED TO STOP HER. IF IT ISN'T, I NEED TO KNOW THAT, TOO.
WHERE'D YOU PUT THE LIQUID ARMOR?
SECOND CABINET, TOP. YOU'RE SAYING THIS IS ABOUT CURIOSITY?
IT'S ABOUT SELF-DEFENSE.
IT SOUNDS LIKE IT'S ABOUT PAYBACK.
NOTHING WRONG WITH GETTING A LITTLE PAYBACK, SIR.

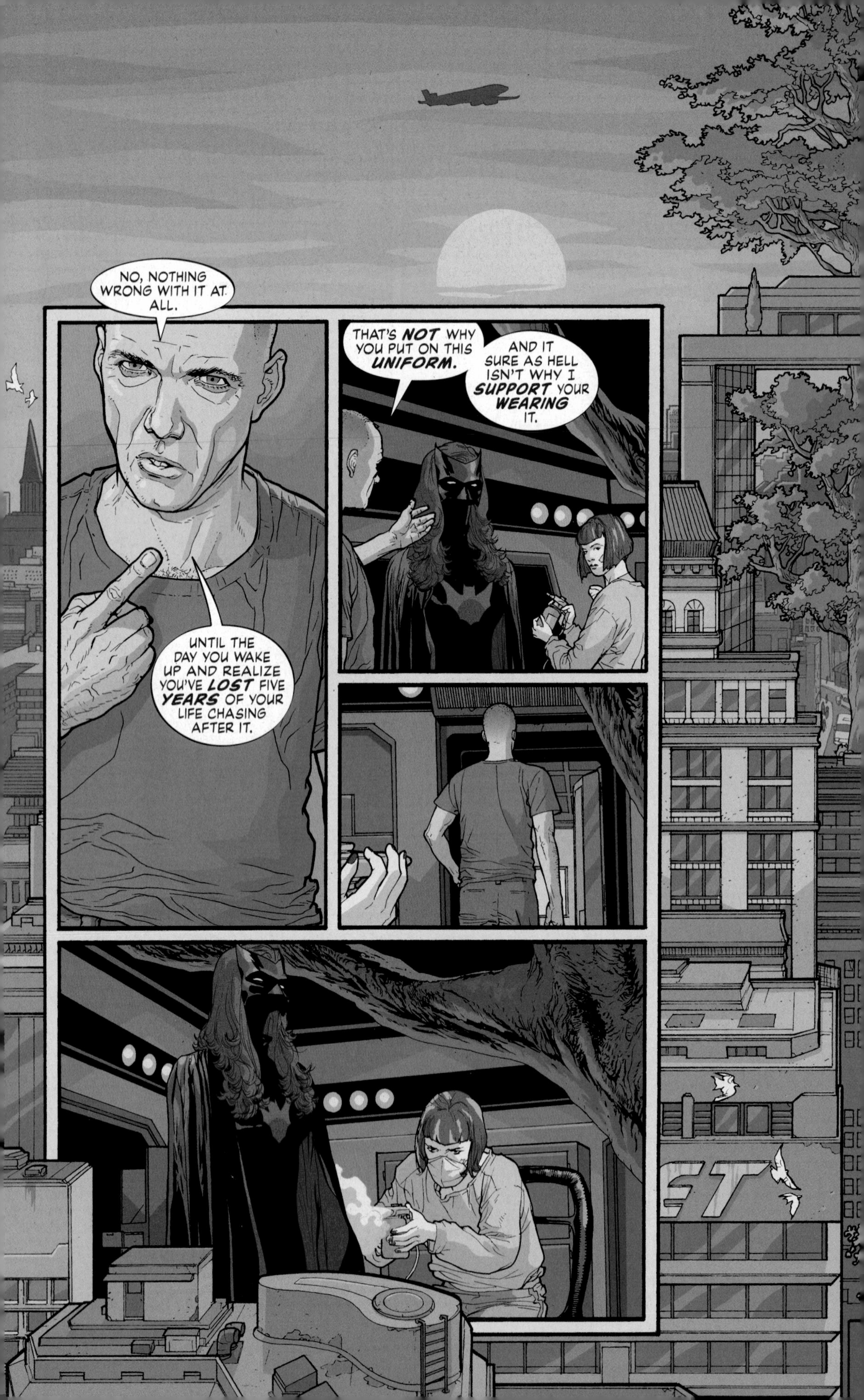
NO, NOTHING WRONG WITH IT AT ALL.
UNTIL THE DAY YOU WAKE UP AND REALIZE YOU'VE LOST FIVE YEARS OF YOUR LIFE CHASING AFTER IT.
THAT'S NOT WHY YOU PUT ON THIS UNIFORM.
AND IT SURE AS HELL ISN'T WHY I SUPPORT YOUR WEARING IT.

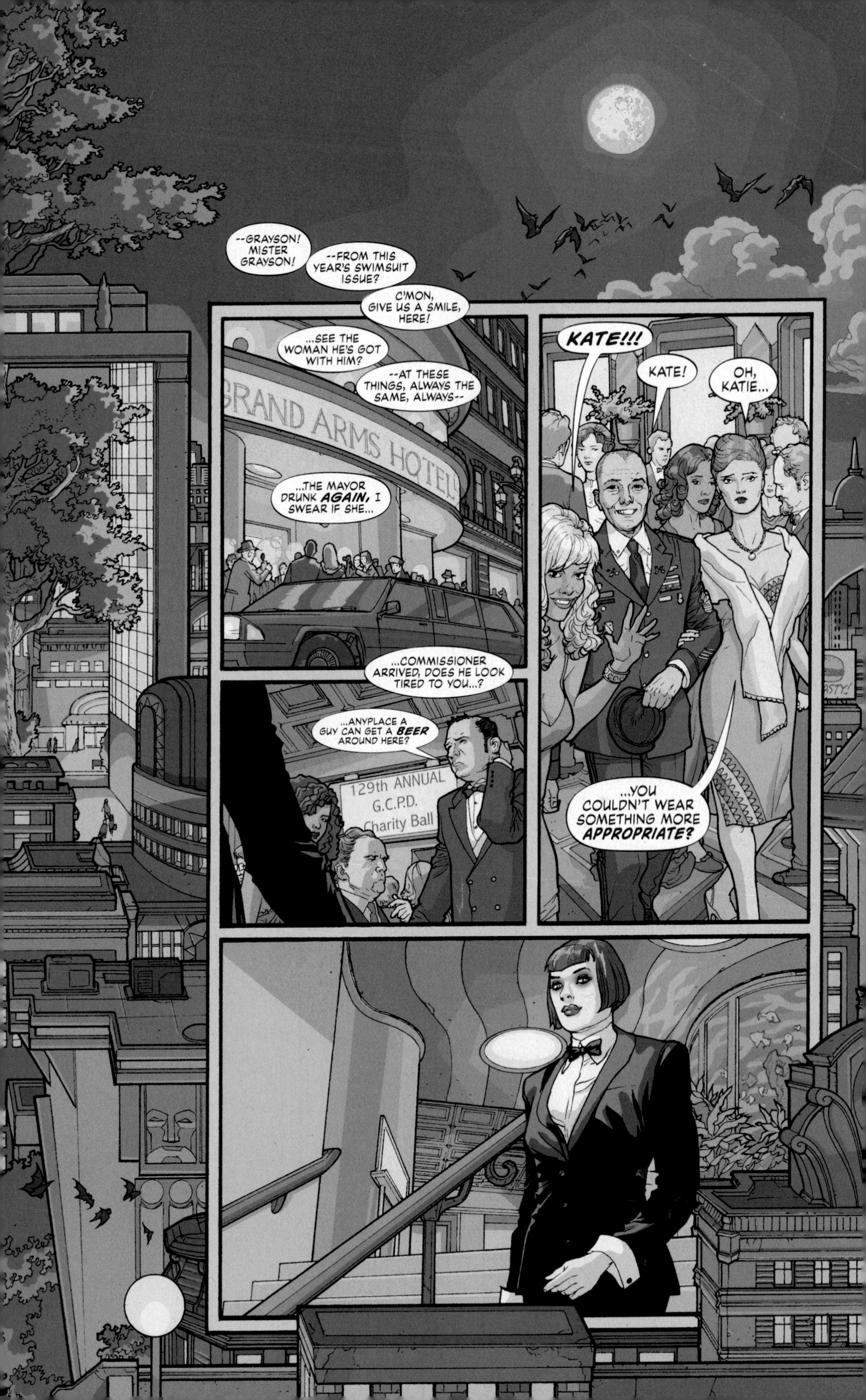
--GRAYSON! MISTER GRAYSON!
--FROM THIS YEAR'S SWIMSUIT ISSUE?
C'MON, GIVE US A SMILE, HERE!
...SEE THE WOMAN HE'S GOT WITH HIM?
--AT THESE THINGS, ALWAYS THE SAME, ALWAYS--
GRAND ARMS HOTEL
...THE MAYOR DRUNK AGAIN, I SWEAR IF SHE...
...COMMISSIONER ARRIVED, DOES HE LOOK TIRED TO YOU...?
...ANYPLACE A GUY CAN GET A BEER AROUND HERE?
129th ANNUAL
G.C.P.D.
Charity Ball
KATE!!!
KATE!
OH, KATIE...
...YOU COULDN'T WEAR SOMETHING MORE APPROPRIATE?

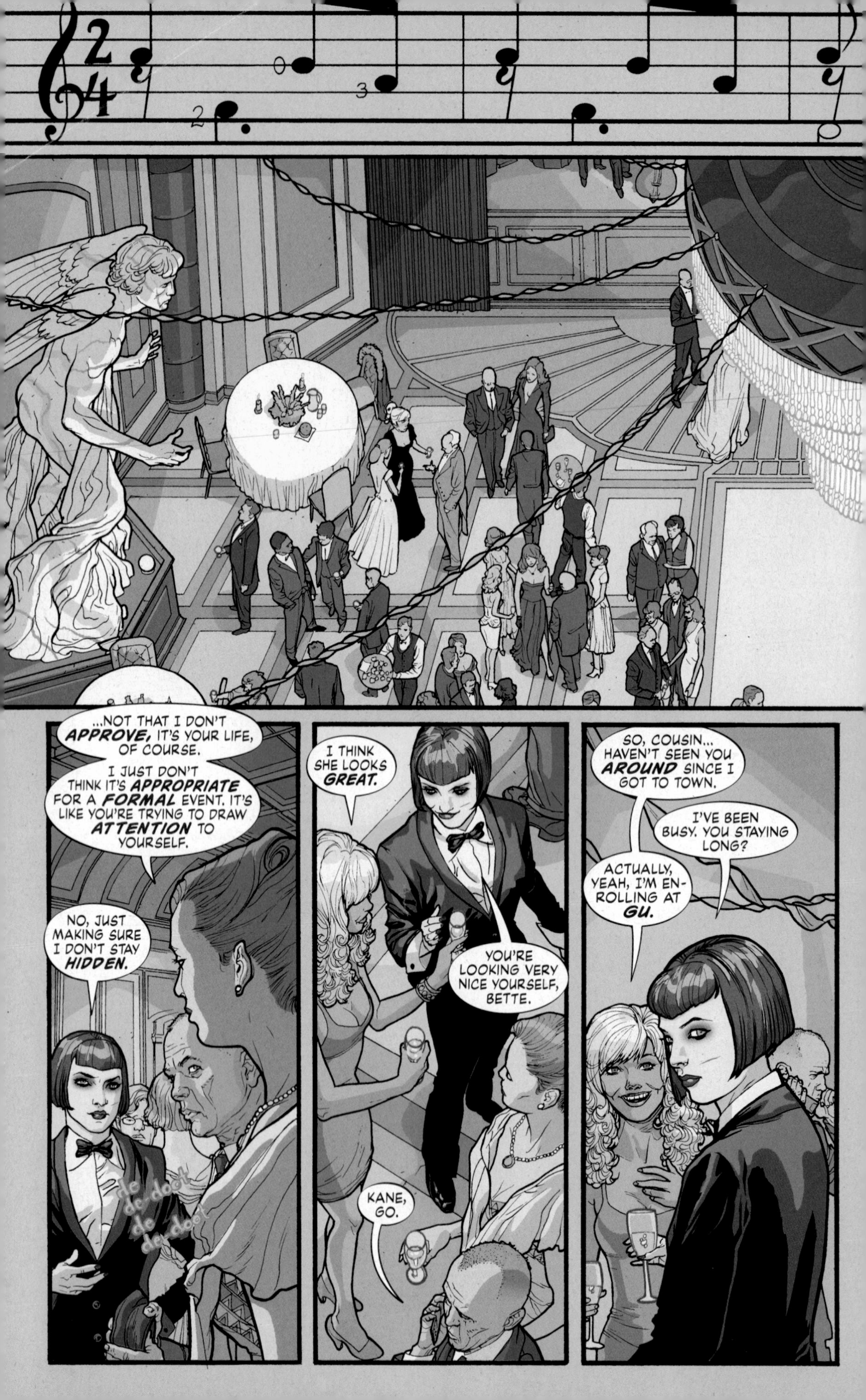
...NOT THAT I DON'T APPROVE, IT'S YOUR LIFE, OF COURSE.
I JUST DON'T THINK IT'S APPROPRIATE FOR A FORMAL EVENT. IT'S LIKE YOU'RE TRYING TO DRAW ATTENTION TO YOURSELF.
NO, JUST MAKING SURE I DON'T STAY HIDDEN.
de doot de-doot de de-doot
I THINK SHE LOOKS GREAT.
YOU'RE LOOKING VERY NICE YOURSELF, BETTE.
KANE, GO.
SO, COUSIN... HAVEN'T SEEN YOU AROUND SINCE I GOT TO TOWN.
I'VE BEEN BUSY. YOU STAYING LONG?
ACTUALLY, YEAH, I'M EN-ROLLING AT GU.

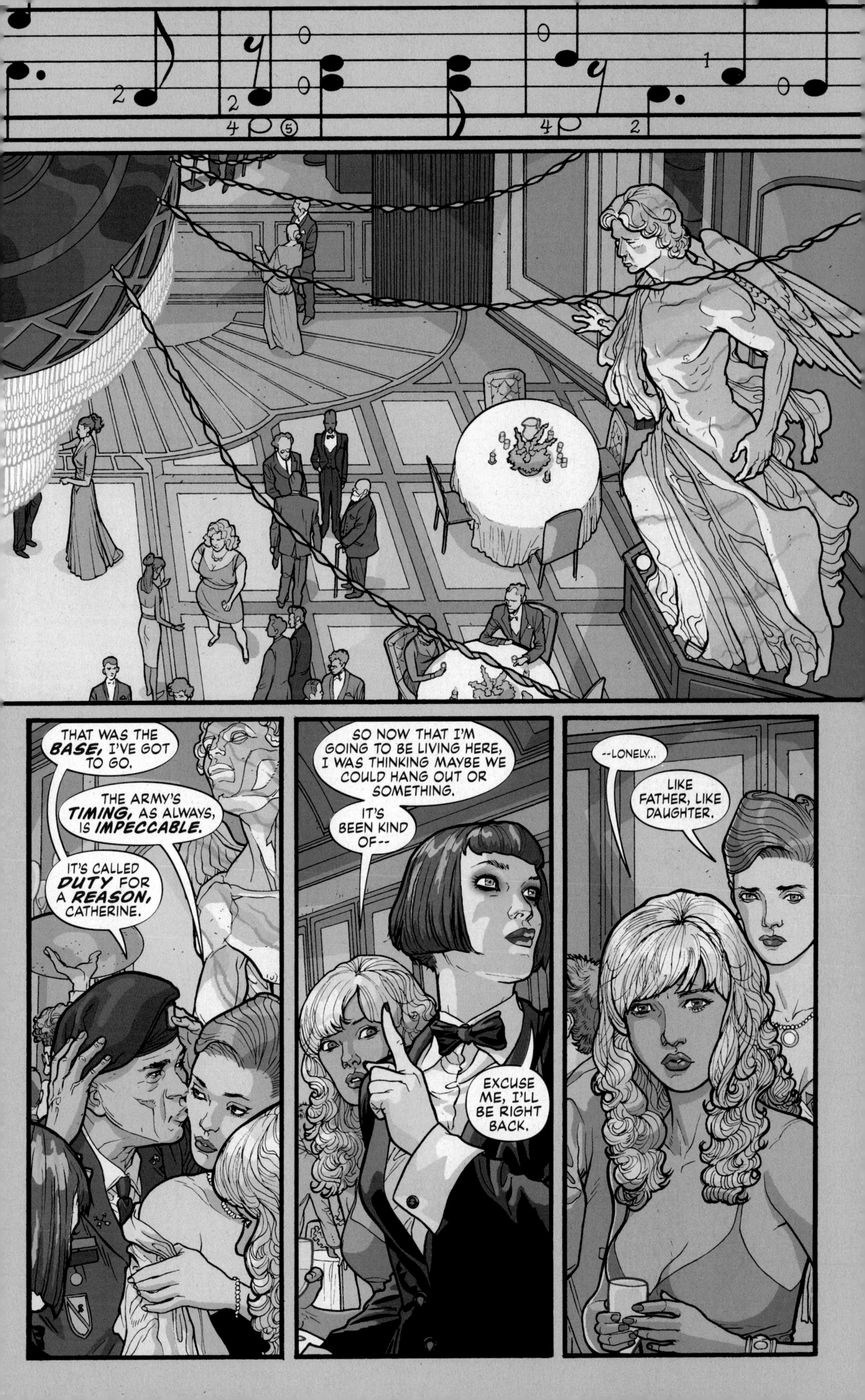
4
5
4
2
2
2
1
THAT WAS THE BASE, I'VE GOT TO GO.
THE ARMY'S TIMING, AS ALWAYS, IS IMPECCABLE.
IT'S CALLED DUTY FOR A REASON, CATHERINE.
SO NOW THAT I'M GOING TO BE LIVING HERE, I WAS THINKING MAYBE WE COULD HANG OUT OR SOMETHING.
IT'S BEEN KIND OF--
EXCUSE ME, I'LL BE RIGHT BACK.
--LONELY...
LIKE FATHER, LIKE DAUGHTER.

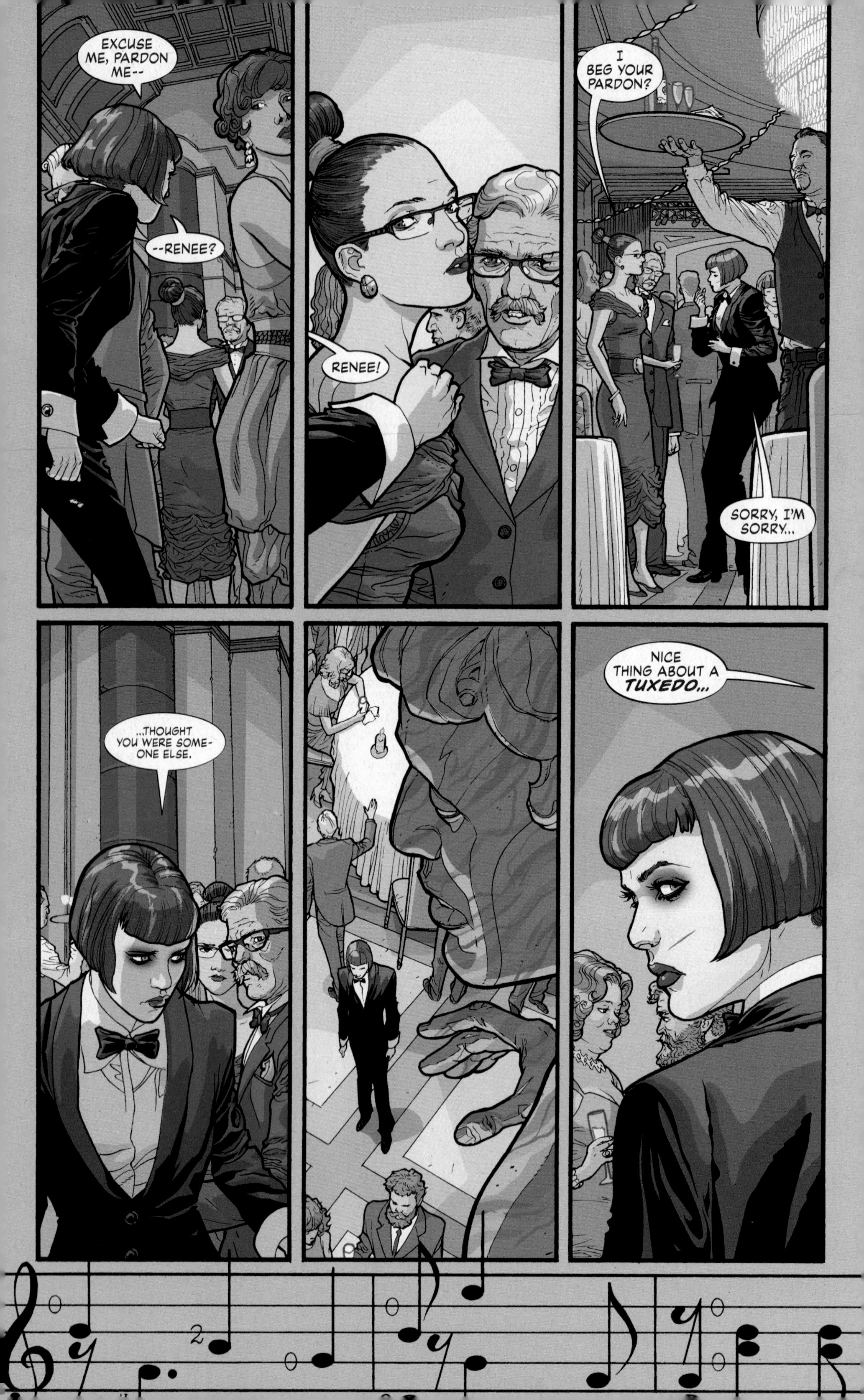
EXCUSE ME, PARDON ME--
--RENEE?
RENEE!
I BEG YOUR PARDON?
SORRY, I'M SORRY...
...THOUGHT YOU WERE SOME-ONE ELSE.
NICE THING ABOUT A *TUXEDO*...

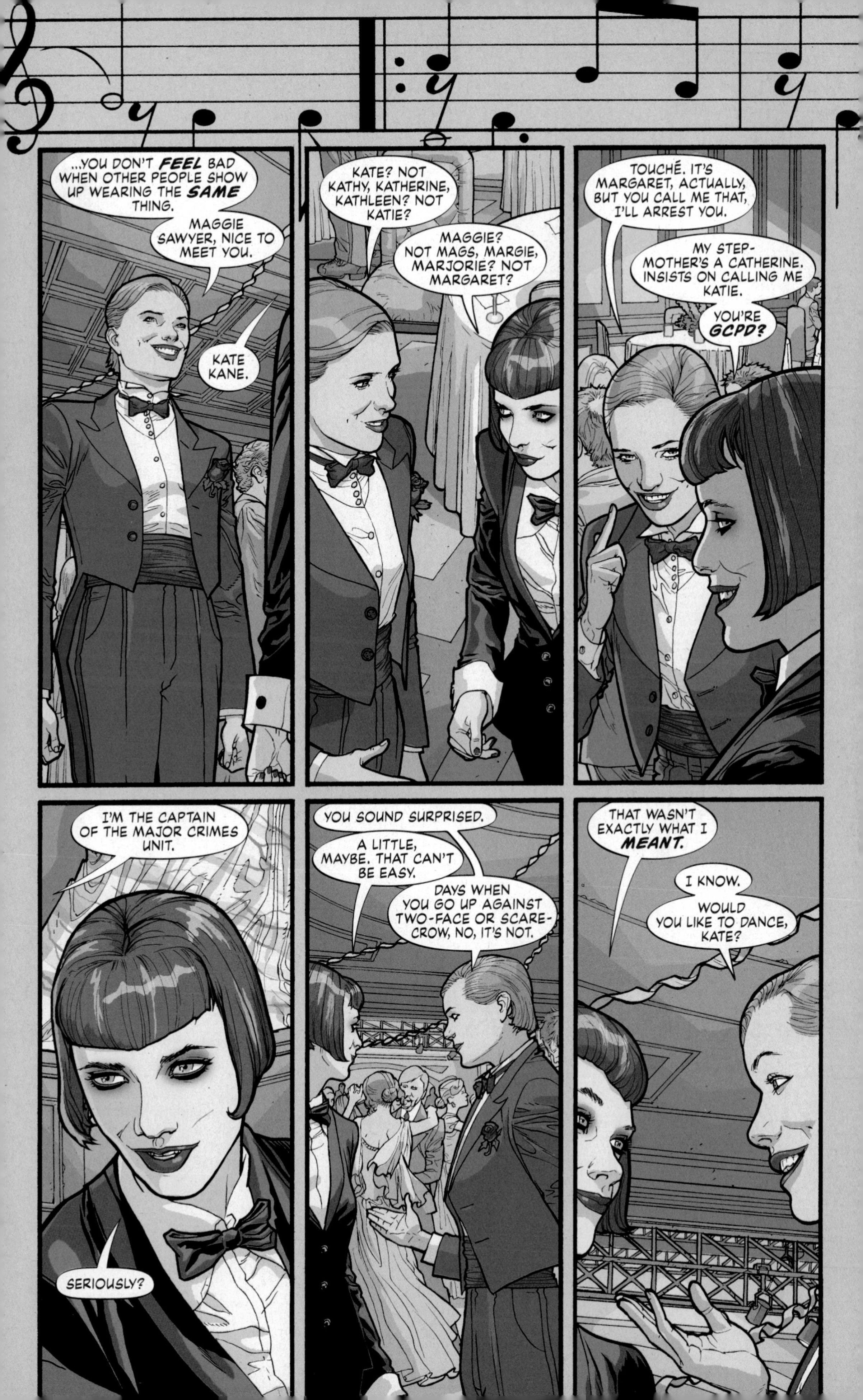
...YOU DON'T FEEL BAD WHEN OTHER PEOPLE SHOW UP WEARING THE SAME THING.
MAGGIE SAWYER, NICE TO MEET YOU.
KATE KANE.
KATE? NOT KATHY, KATHERINE, KATHLEEN? NOT KATIE?
MAGGIE? NOT MAGS, MARGIE, MARJORIE? NOT MARGARET?
TOUCHÉ. IT'S MARGARET, ACTUALLY, BUT YOU CALL ME THAT, I'LL ARREST YOU.
MY STEP-MOTHER'S A CATHERINE. INSISTS ON CALLING ME KATIE.
YOU'RE GCPD?
I'M THE CAPTAIN OF THE MAJOR CRIMES UNIT.
SERIOUSLY?
YOU SOUND SURPRISED.
A LITTLE, MAYBE. THAT CAN'T BE EASY.
DAYS WHEN YOU GO UP AGAINST TWO-FACE OR SCARE-CROW, NO, IT'S NOT.
THAT WASN'T EXACTLY WHAT I MEANT.
I KNOW.
WOULD YOU LIKE TO DANCE, KATE?

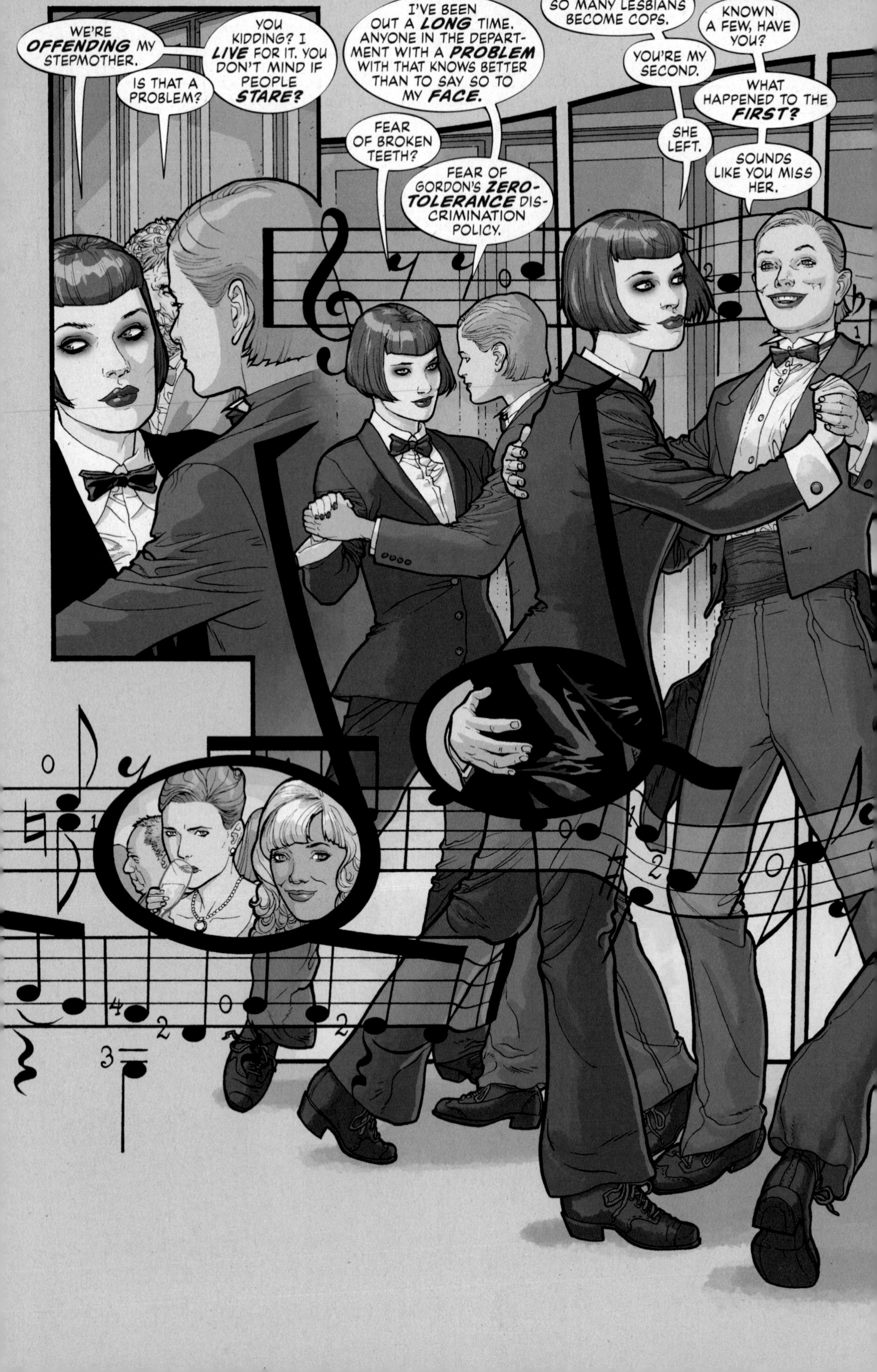
WE'RE OFFENDING MY STEPMOTHER.
IS THAT A PROBLEM?
YOU KIDDING? I LIVE FOR IT. YOU DON'T MIND IF PEOPLE STARE?
I'VE BEEN OUT A LONG TIME. ANYONE IN THE DEPARTMENT WITH A PROBLEM WITH THAT KNOWS BETTER THAN TO SAY SO TO MY FACE.
FEAR OF BROKEN TEETH?
FEAR OF GORDON'S ZERO-TOLERANCE DISCRIMINATION POLICY.
NO WONDER SO MANY LESBIANS BECOME COPS.
YOU'RE MY SECOND.
SHE LEFT.
KNOWN A FEW, HAVE YOU?
WHAT HAPPENED TO THE FIRST?
SOUNDS LIKE YOU MISS HER.

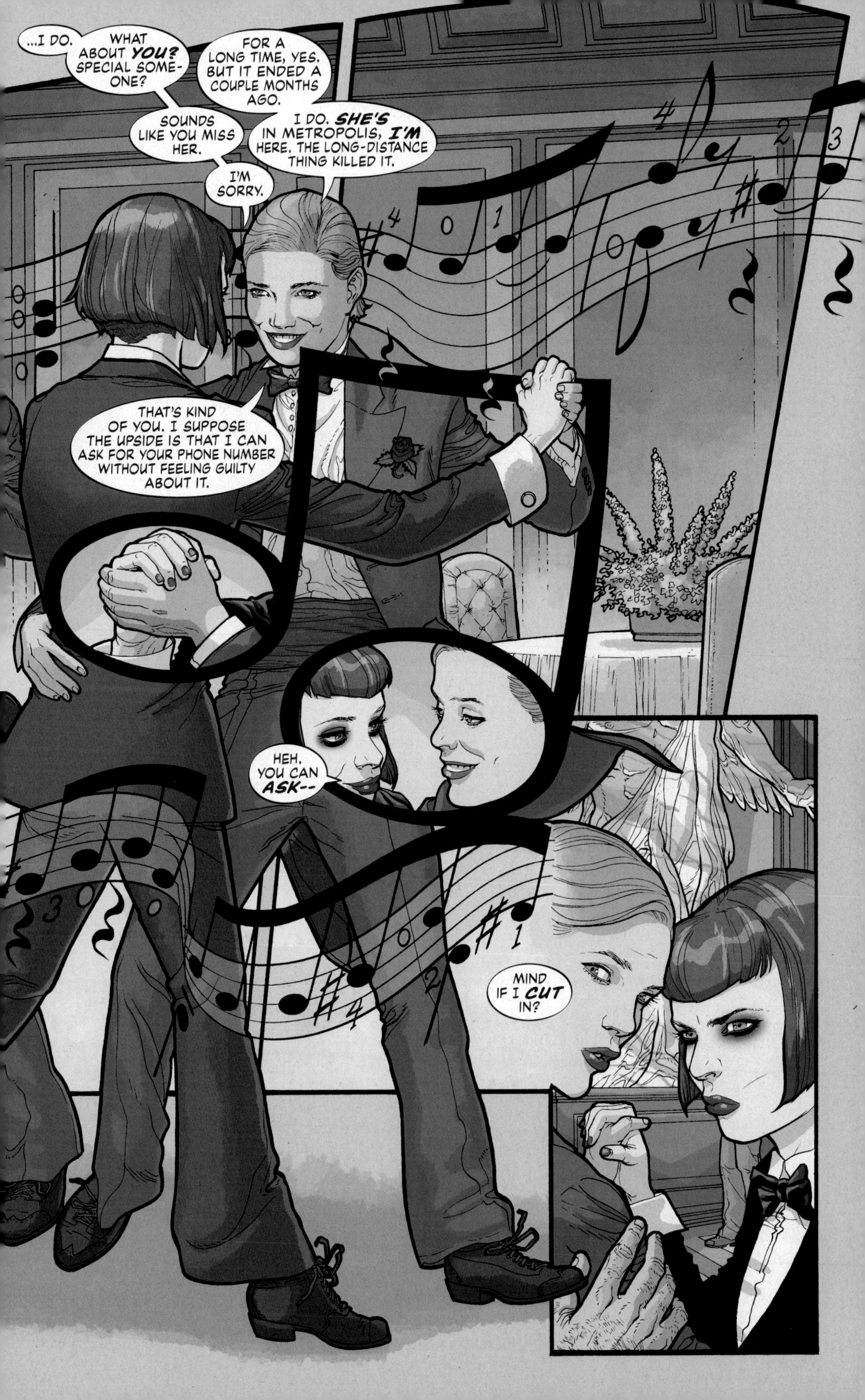
...I DO.
WHAT ABOUT YOU? SPECIAL SOME-ONE?
FOR A LONG TIME, YES. BUT IT ENDED A COUPLE MONTHS AGO.
SOUNDS LIKE YOU MISS HER.
I DO. SHE'S IN METROPOLIS, I'M HERE. THE LONG-DISTANCE THING KILLED IT.
I'M SORRY.
THAT'S KIND OF YOU. I SUPPOSE THE UPSIDE IS THAT I CAN ASK FOR YOUR PHONE NUMBER WITHOUT FEELING GUILTY ABOUT IT.
HEH. YOU CAN ASK--
MIND IF I CUT IN?

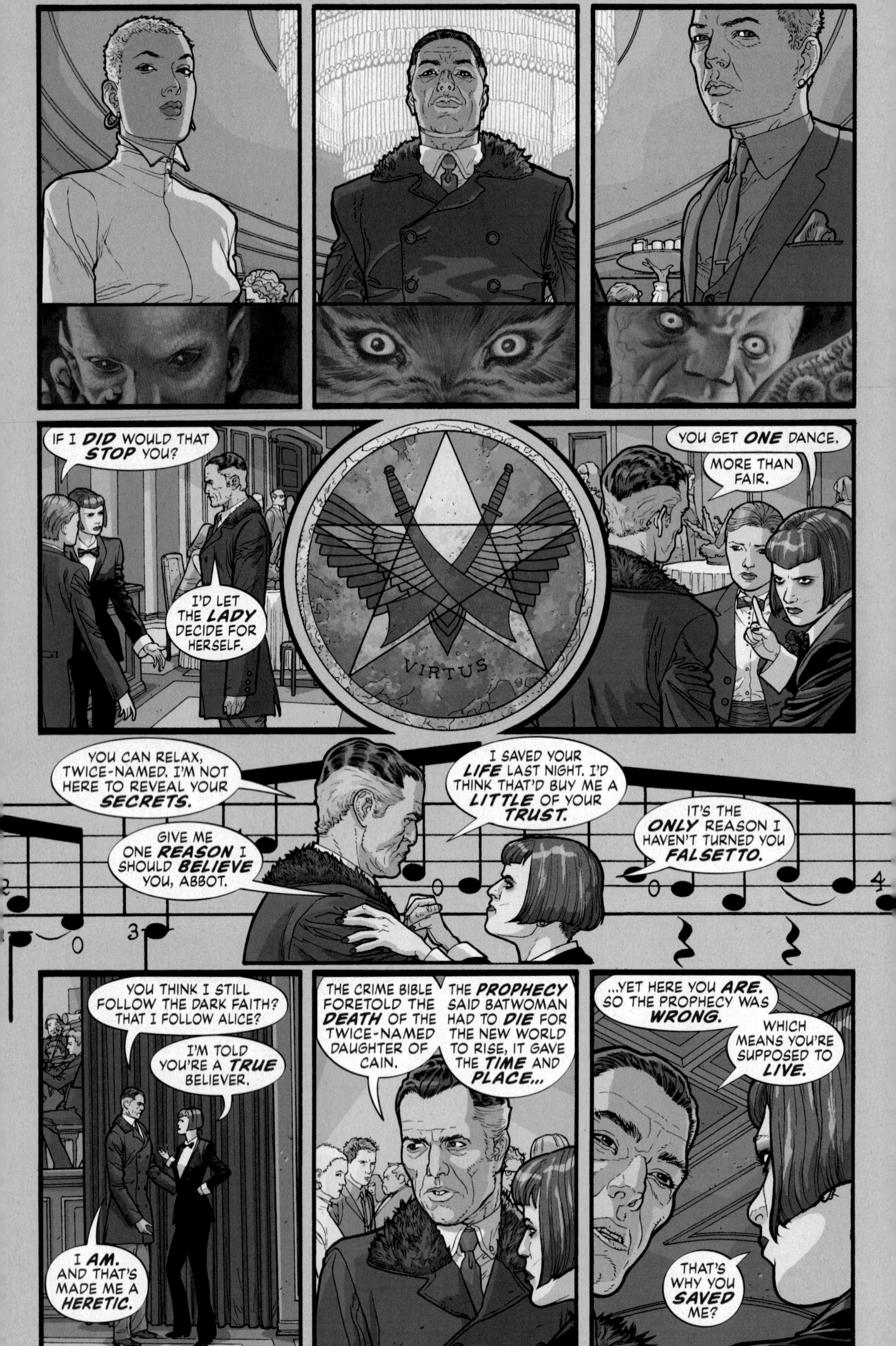

IF I DID WOULD THAT STOP YOU?
I'D LET THE LADY DECIDE FOR HERSELF.
VIRTUS
YOU GET ONE DANCE.
MORE THAN FAIR.
YOU CAN RELAX, TWICE-NAMED. I'M NOT HERE TO REVEAL YOUR SECRETS.
GIVE ME ONE REASON I SHOULD BELIEVE YOU, ABBOT.
I SAVED YOUR LIFE LAST NIGHT. I'D THINK THAT'D BUY ME A LITTLE OF YOUR TRUST.
IT'S THE ONLY REASON I HAVEN'T TURNED YOU FALSETTO.
YOU THINK I STILL FOLLOW THE DARK FAITH? THAT I FOLLOW ALICE?
I'M TOLD YOU'RE A TRUE BELIEVER.
I AM. AND THAT'S MADE ME A HERETIC.
THE CRIME BIBLE FORETOLD THE DEATH OF THE TWICE-NAMED DAUGHTER OF CAIN.
THE PROPHECY SAID BATWOMAN HAD TO DIE FOR THE NEW WORLD TO RISE, IT GAVE THE TIME AND PLACE...
...YET HERE YOU ARE. SO THE PROPHECY WAS WRONG.
WHICH MEANS YOU'RE SUPPOSED TO LIVE.
THAT'S WHY YOU SAVED ME?

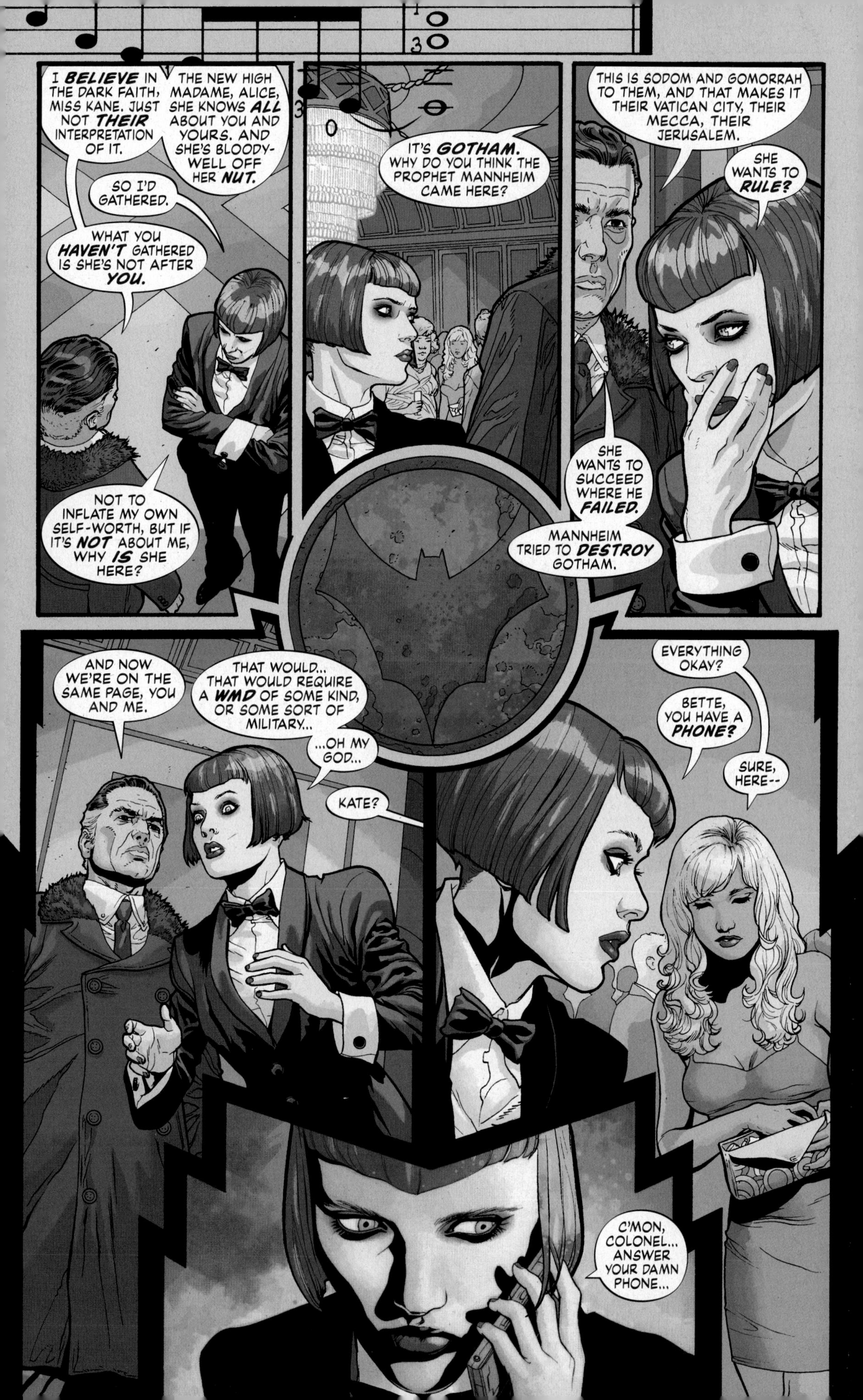
I BELIEVE IN THE DARK FAITH, MISS KANE. JUST NOT THEIR INTERPRETATION OF IT.
THE NEW HIGH MADAME, ALICE, SHE KNOWS ALL ABOUT YOU AND YOURS. AND SHE'S BLOODY-WELL OFF HER NUT.
SO I'D GATHERED.
WHAT YOU HAVEN'T GATHERED IS SHE'S NOT AFTER YOU.
NOT TO INFLATE MY OWN SELF-WORTH, BUT IF IT'S NOT ABOUT ME, WHY IS SHE HERE?
IT'S GOTHAM. WHY DO YOU THINK THE PROPHET MANNHEIM CAME HERE?
THIS IS SODOM AND GOMORRAH TO THEM, AND THAT MAKES IT THEIR VATICAN CITY, THEIR MECCA, THEIR JERUSALEM.
SHE WANTS TO RULE?
SHE WANTS TO SUCCEED WHERE HE FAILED.
MANNHEIM TRIED TO DESTROY GOTHAM.
AND NOW WE'RE ON THE SAME PAGE, YOU AND ME.
THAT WOULD... THAT WOULD REQUIRE A WMD OF SOME KIND, OR SOME SORT OF MILITARY...
...OH MY GOD...
KATE?
EVERYTHING OKAY?
BETTE, YOU HAVE A PHONE?
SURE, HERE--
C'MON, COLONEL... ANSWER YOUR DAMN PHONE...

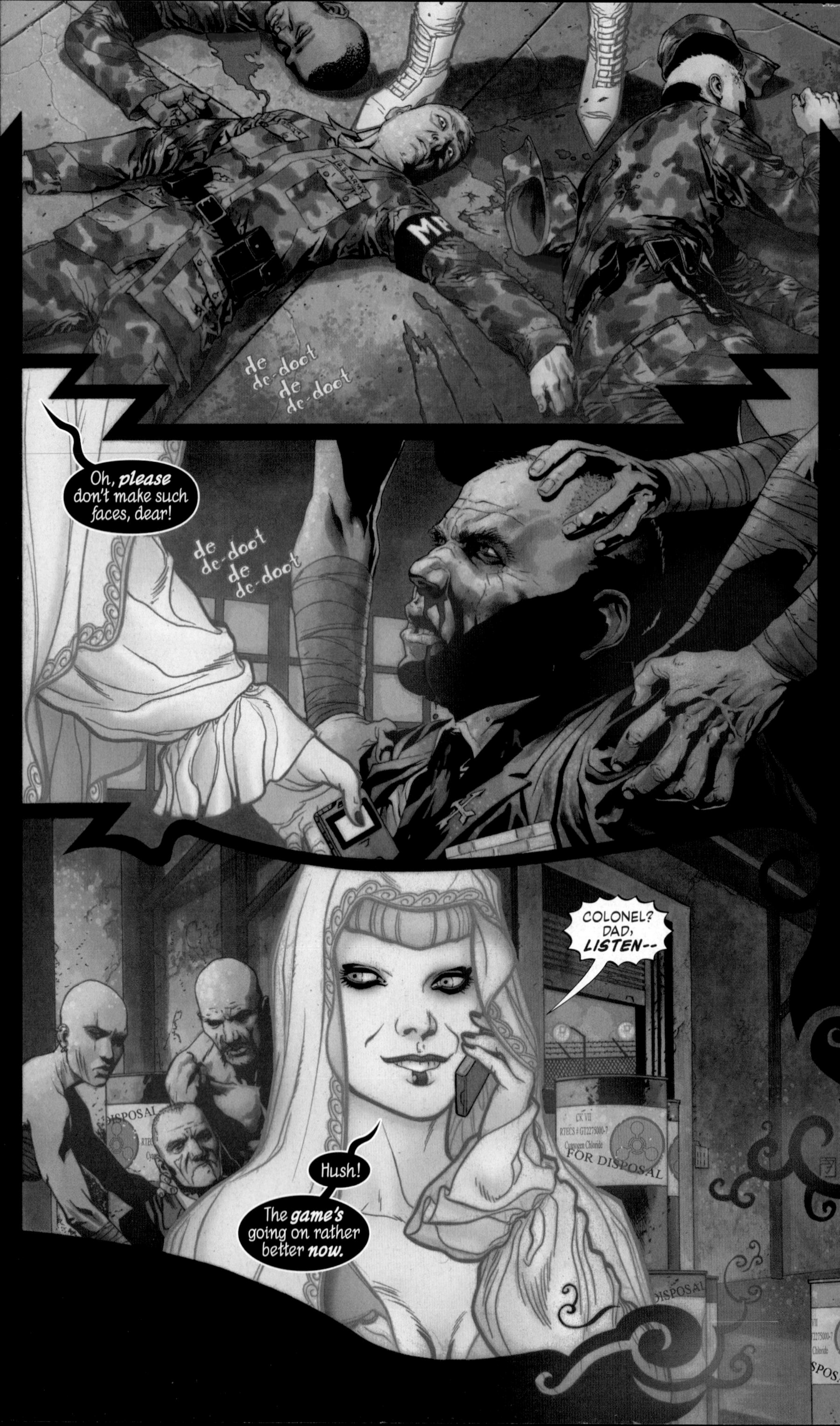
de-doot
de-doot
de
de-doot
Oh, please don't make such faces, dear!
de-doot
de-doot
de
de-doot
COLONEL? DAD, LISTEN--
Hush!
The game's going on rather better now.
FOR DISPOSAL

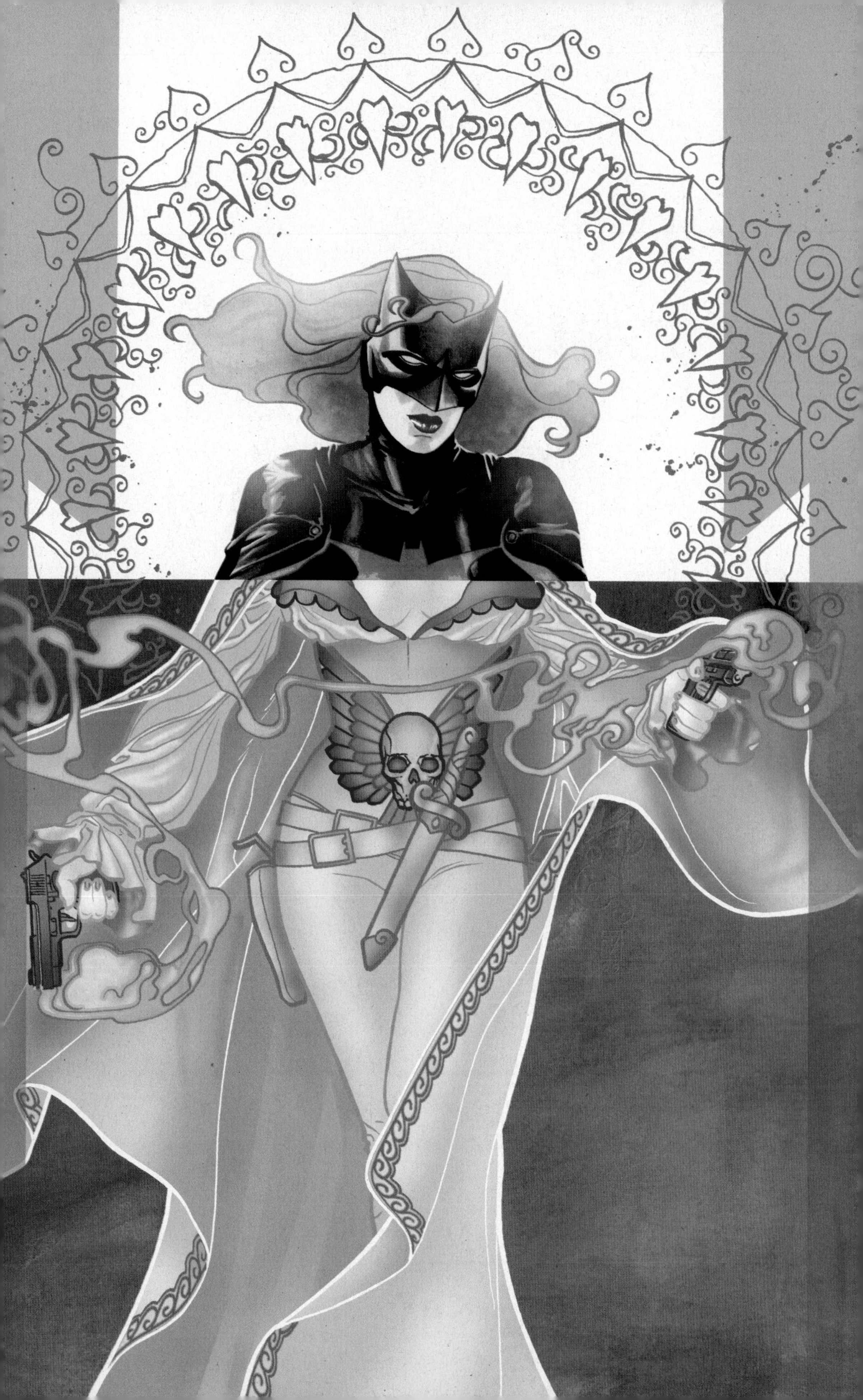

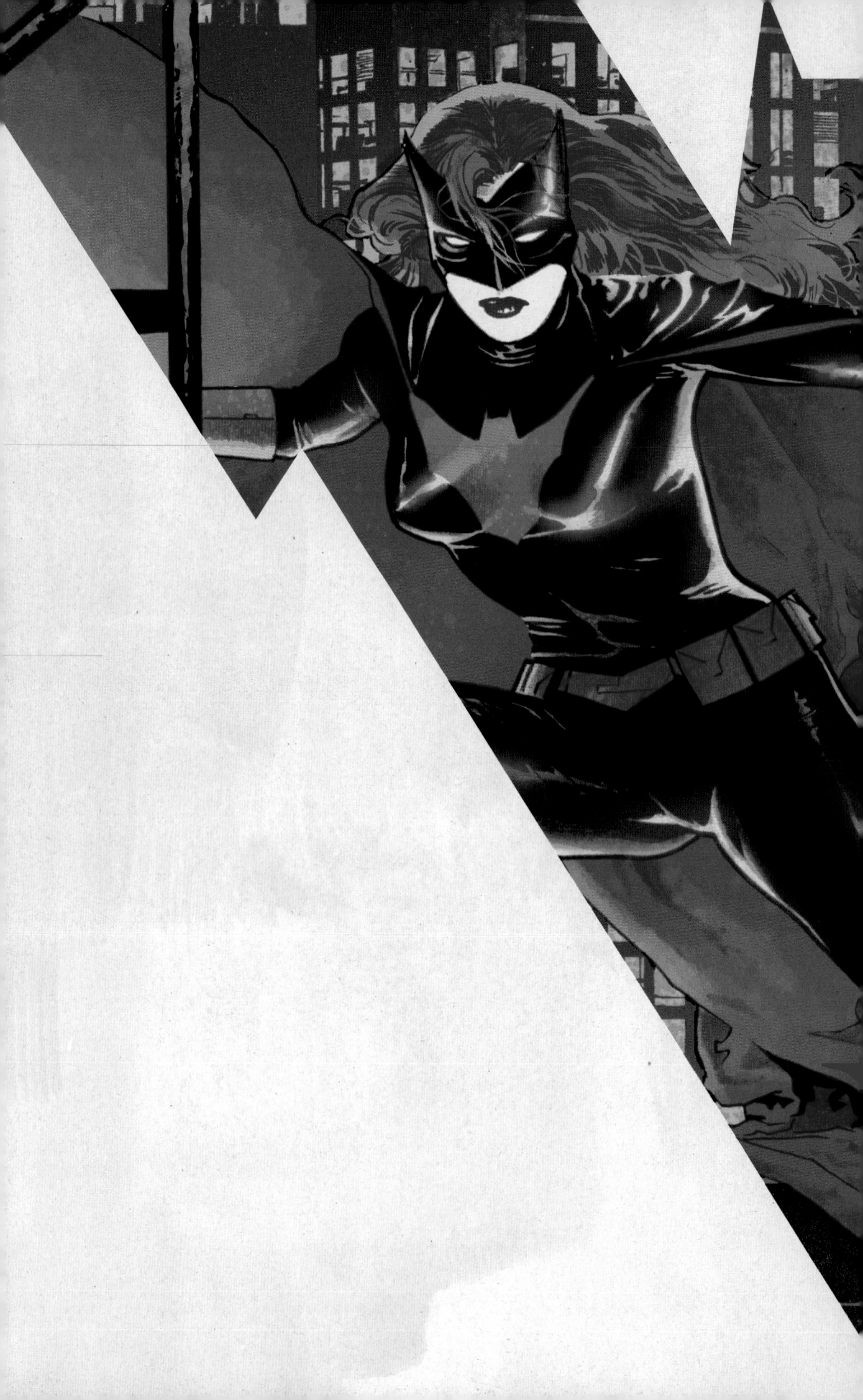

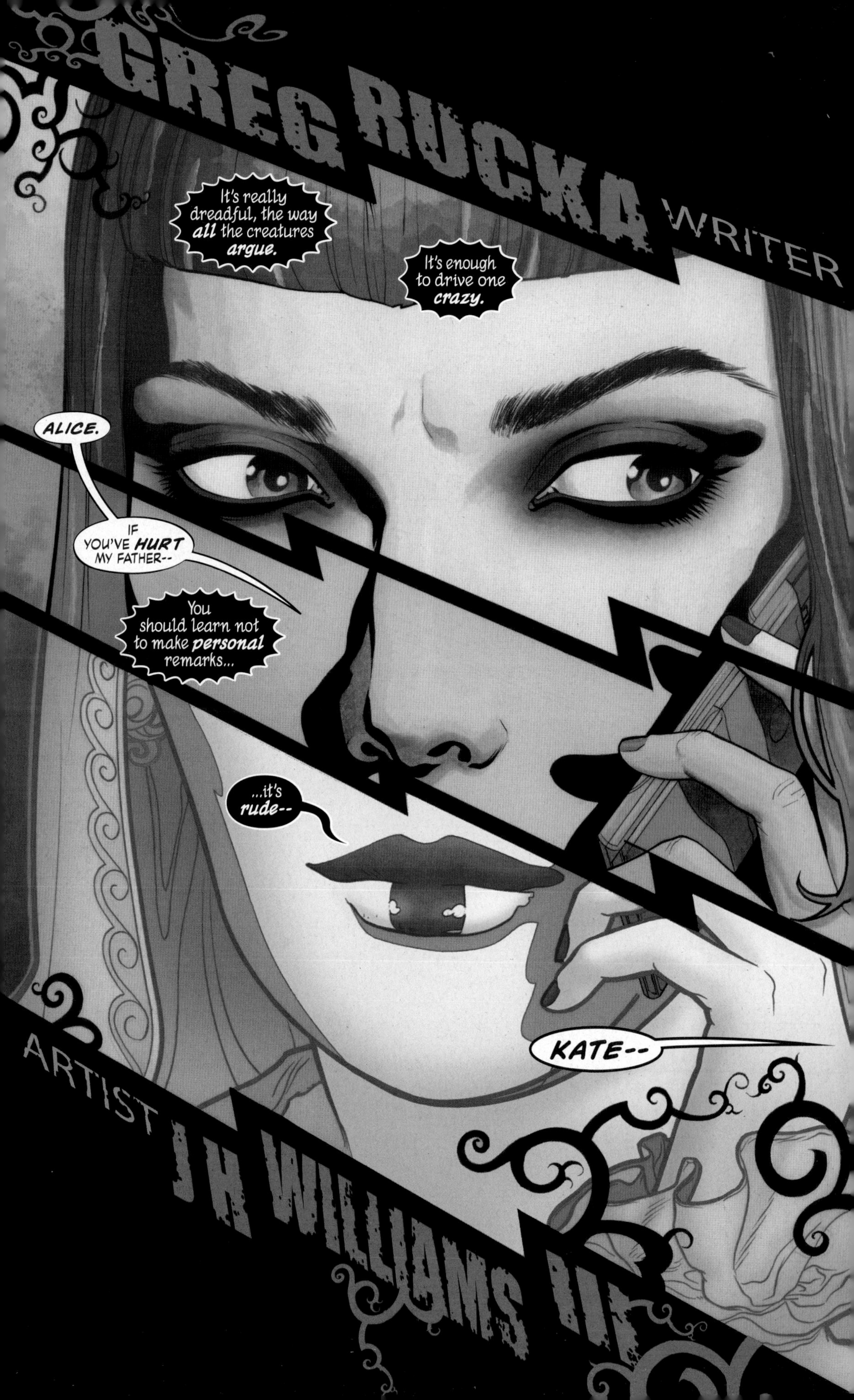

GREG RUCKA WRITER
It's really dreadful, the way all the creatures argue.
It's enough to drive one crazy.
ALICE.
IF YOU'VE HURT MY FATHER--
You should learn not to make personal remarks...
...it's rude--
KATE--
ARTIST J H WILLIAMS III

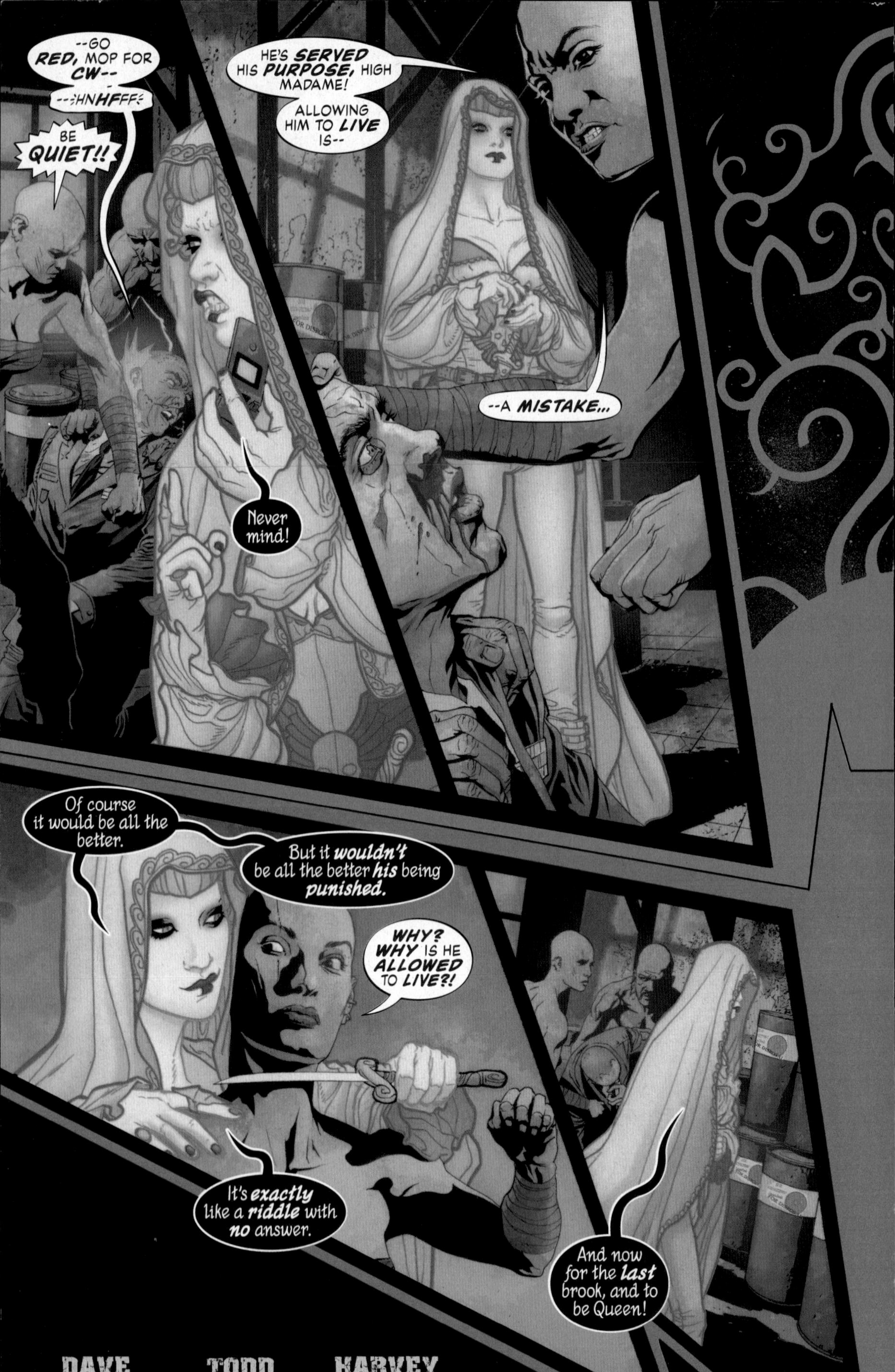
--GO RED, MOP FOR CW--
--HNHFFF--
BE QUIET!!
HE'S SERVED HIS PURPOSE, HIGH MADAME!
ALLOWING HIM TO LIVE IS--
--A MISTAKE...
Never mind!
Of course it would be all the better.
But it wouldn't be all the better his being punished.
WHY? WHY IS HE ALLOWED TO LIVE?!
It's exactly like a riddle with no answer.
And now for the last brook, and to be Queen!

DAVE STEWART colors

TODD KLEIN letters

HARVEY RICHARDS asst. ed.

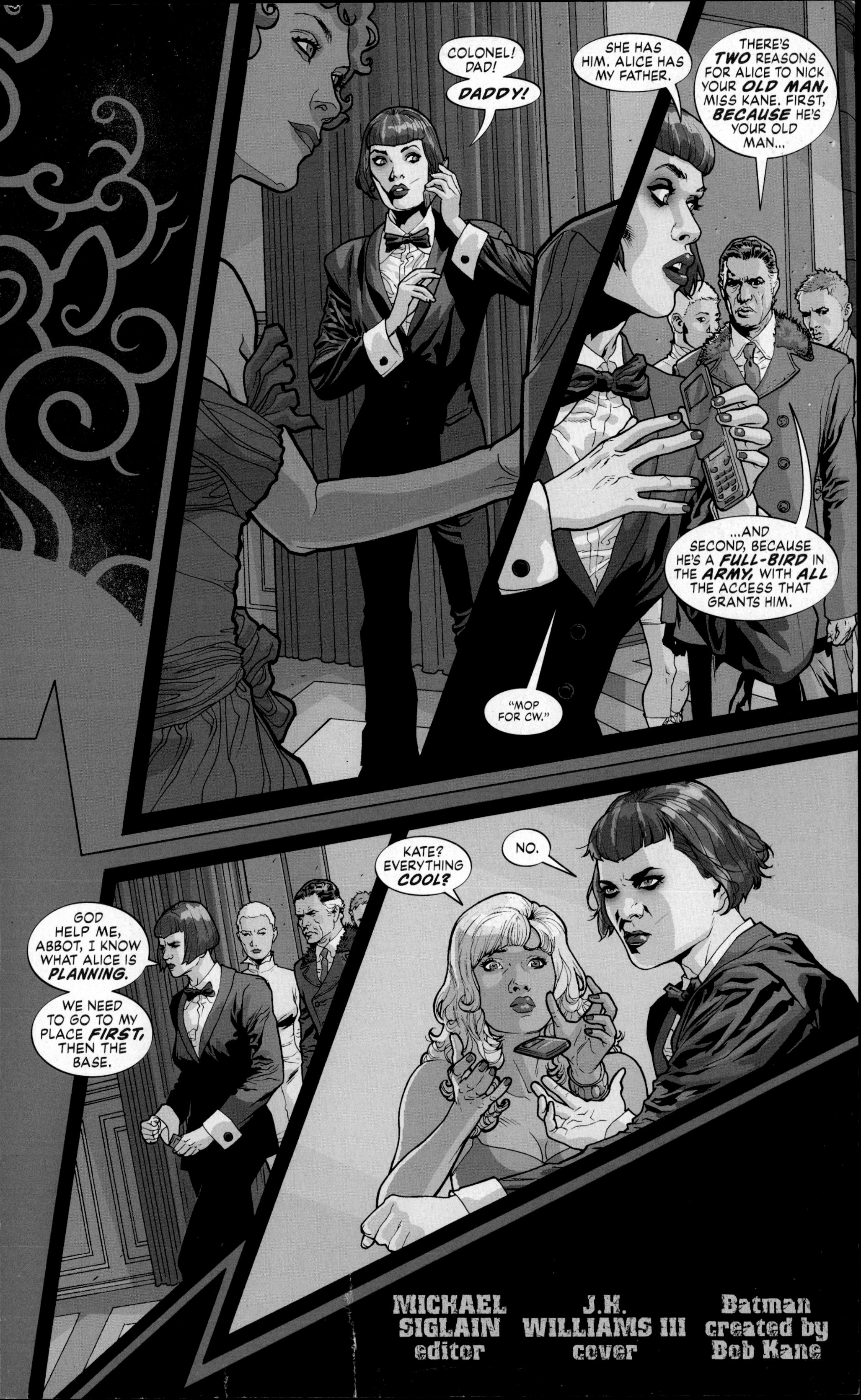
COLONEL! DAD! DADDY!
SHE HAS HIM. ALICE HAS MY FATHER.
THERE'S TWO REASONS FOR ALICE TO NICK YOUR OLD MAN, MISS KANE. FIRST, BECAUSE HE'S YOUR OLD MAN...
...AND SECOND, BECAUSE HE'S A FULL-BIRD IN THE ARMY, WITH ALL THE ACCESS THAT GRANTS HIM.
"MOP FOR CW."
KATE? EVERYTHING COOL?
NO.
GOD HELP ME, ABBOT, I KNOW WHAT ALICE IS PLANNING.
WE NEED TO GO TO MY PLACE FIRST, THEN THE BASE.
MICHAEL SIGLAIN editor
J.H. WILLIAMS III cover
Batman created by Bob Kane

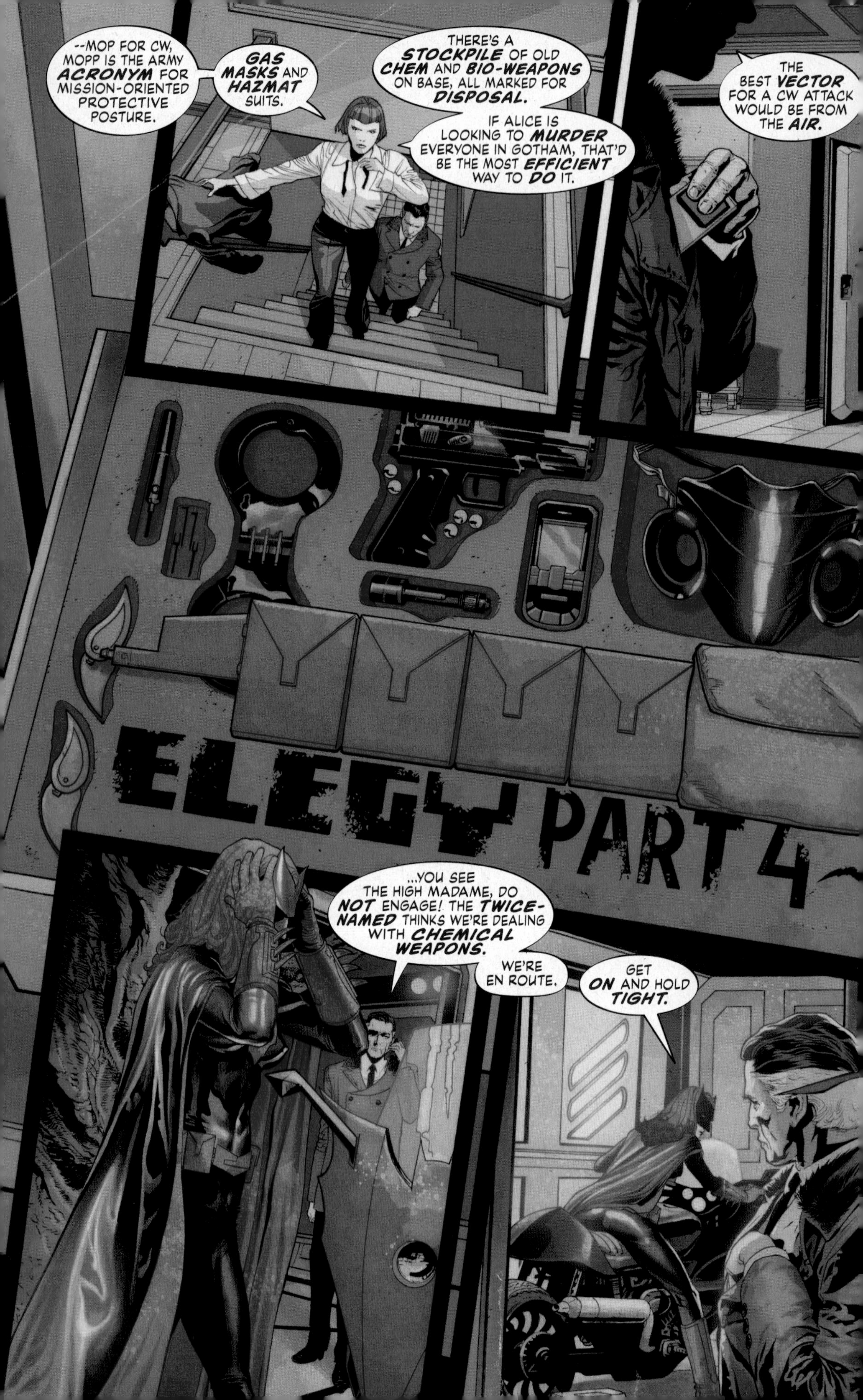
--MOP FOR CW, MOPP IS THE ARMY ACRONYM FOR MISSION-ORIENTED PROTECTIVE POSTURE.
GAS MASKS AND HAZMAT SUITS.
THERE'S A STOCKPILE OF OLD CHEM AND BIO-WEAPONS ON BASE, ALL MARKED FOR DISPOSAL.
IF ALICE IS LOOKING TO MURDER EVERYONE IN GOTHAM, THAT'D BE THE MOST EFFICIENT WAY TO DO IT.
THE BEST VECTOR FOR A CW ATTACK WOULD BE FROM THE AIR.
ELEGY PART 4
...YOU SEE THE HIGH MADAME, DO NOT ENGAGE! THE TWICE-NAMED THINKS WE'RE DEALING WITH CHEMICAL WEAPONS.
WE'RE EN ROUTE.
GET ON AND HOLD TIGHT.

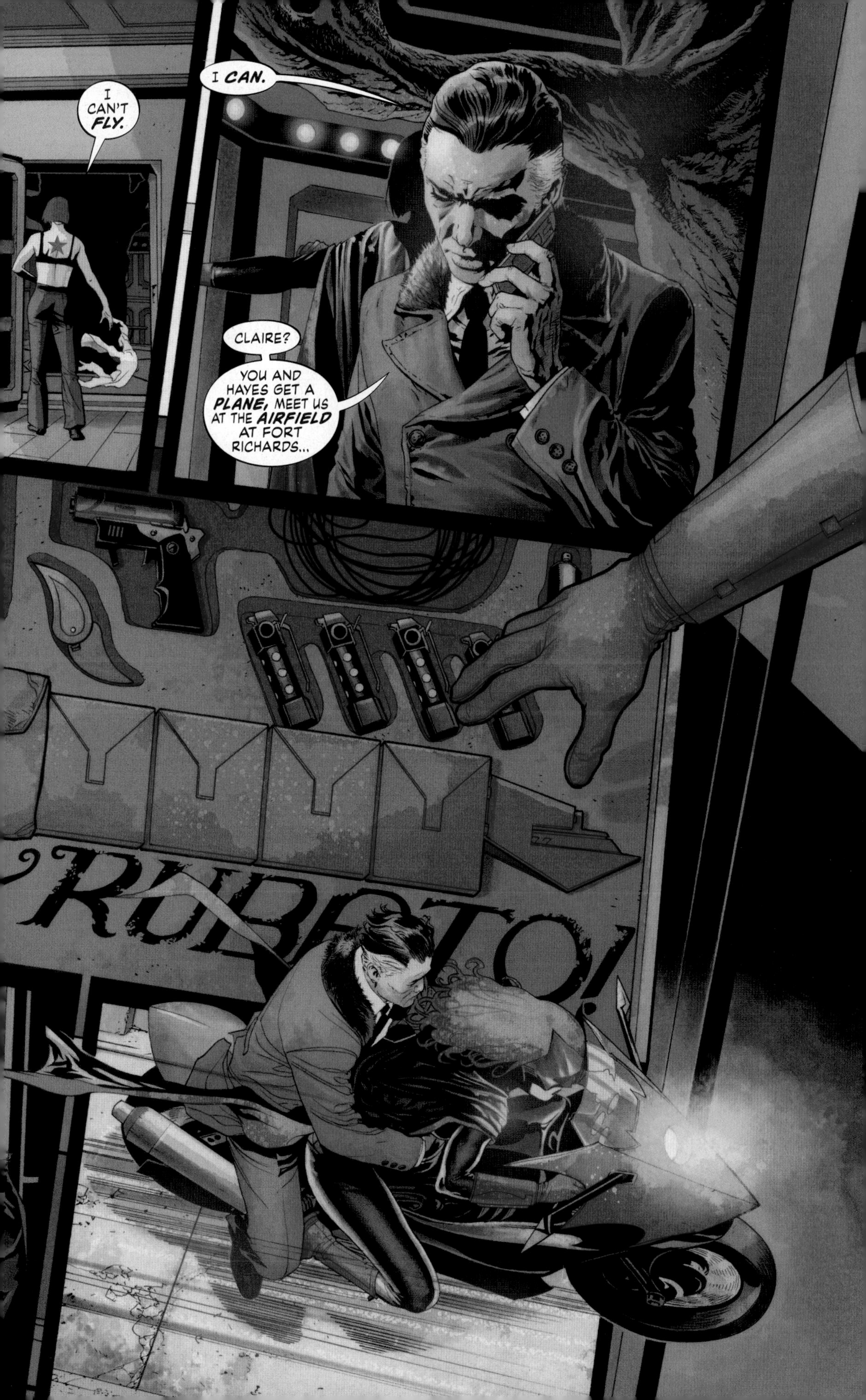
I CAN'T FLY.
I CAN.
CLAIRE?
YOU AND HAYES GET A PLANE, MEET US AT THE AIRFIELD AT FORT RICHARDS...
RUBATO!

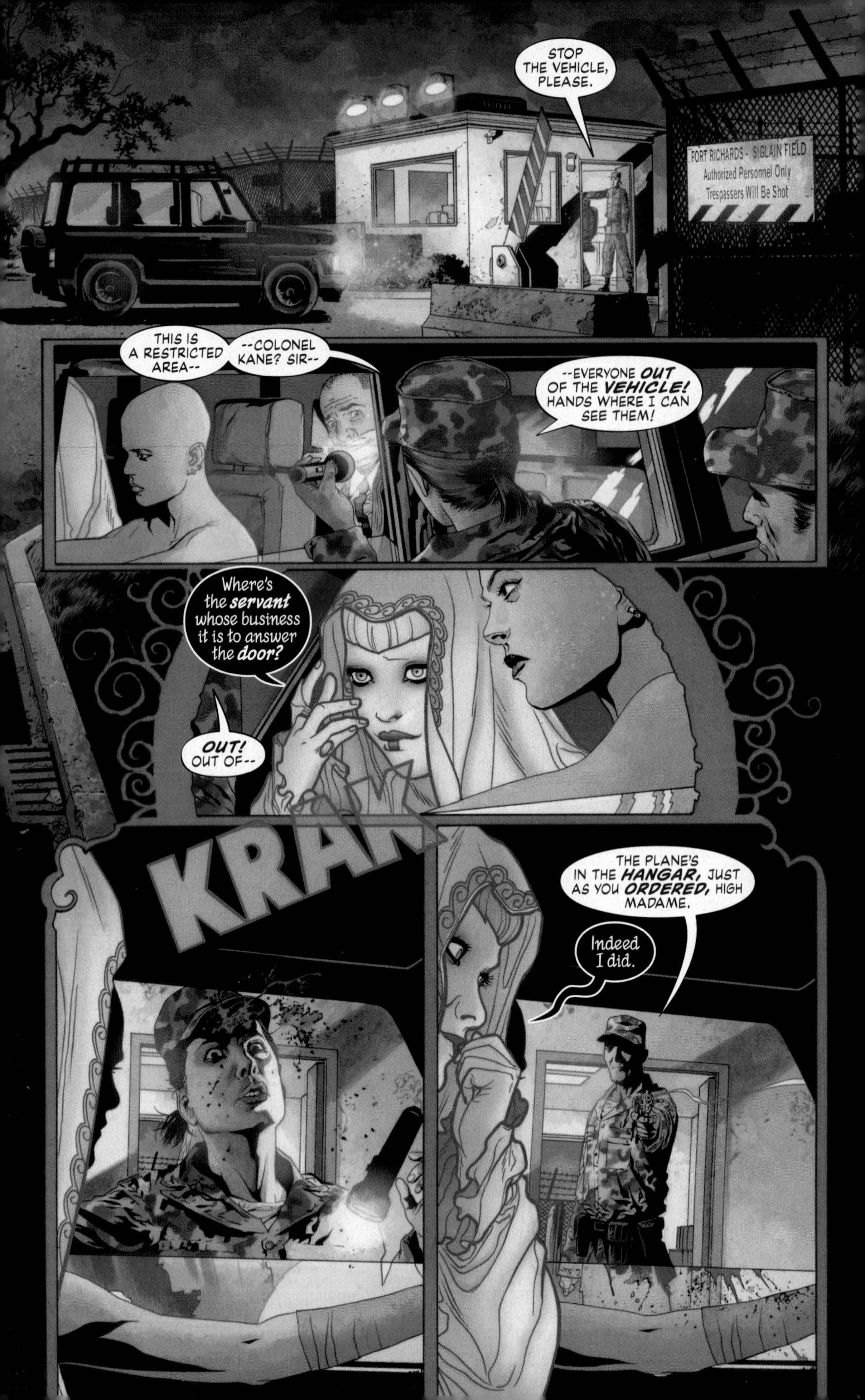
STOP THE VEHICLE, PLEASE.
FORT RICHARDS - SIGLAIN FIELD
Authorized Personnel Only
Trespassers Will Be Shot
THIS IS A RESTRICTED AREA--
--COLONEL KANE? SIR--
--EVERYONE OUT OF THE VEHICLE! HANDS WHERE I CAN SEE THEM!
Where's the servant whose business it is to answer the door?
OUT! OUT OF--
KRAM
THE PLANE'S IN THE HANGAR, JUST AS YOU ORDERED, HIGH MADAME.
Indeed I did.

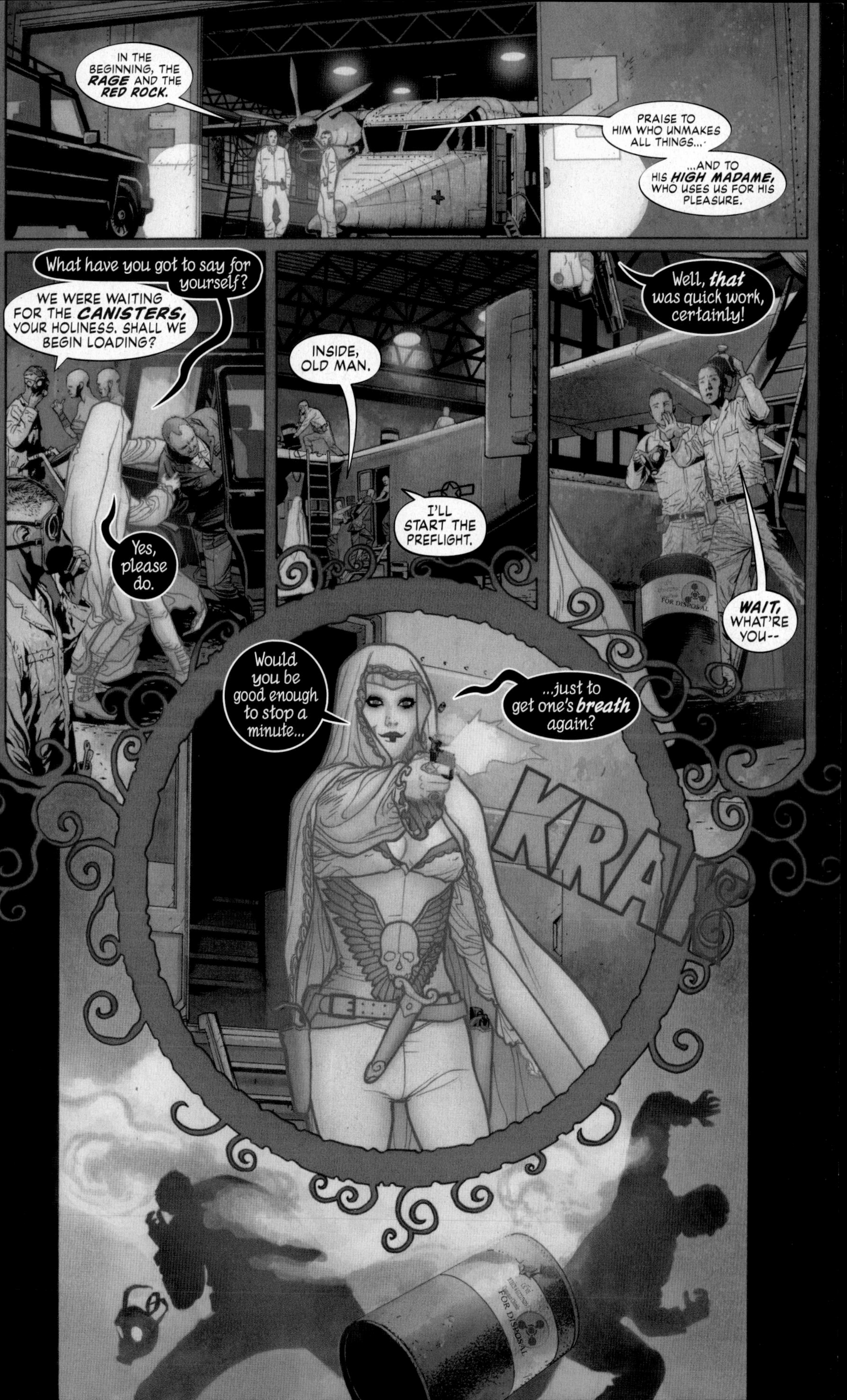
IN THE BEGINNING, THE RAGE AND THE RED ROCK.
PRAISE TO HIM WHO UNMAKES ALL THINGS...
...AND TO HIS HIGH MADAME, WHO USES US FOR HIS PLEASURE.
What have you got to say for yourself?
WE WERE WAITING FOR THE CANISTERS, YOUR HOLINESS. SHALL WE BEGIN LOADING?
Yes, please do.
INSIDE, OLD MAN.
I'LL START THE PREFLIGHT.
Well, that was quick work, certainly!
WAIT, WHAT'RE YOU--
FOR DISPOSAL
Would you be good enough to stop a minute...
...just to get one's breath again?
KRAK
FOR DISPOSAL

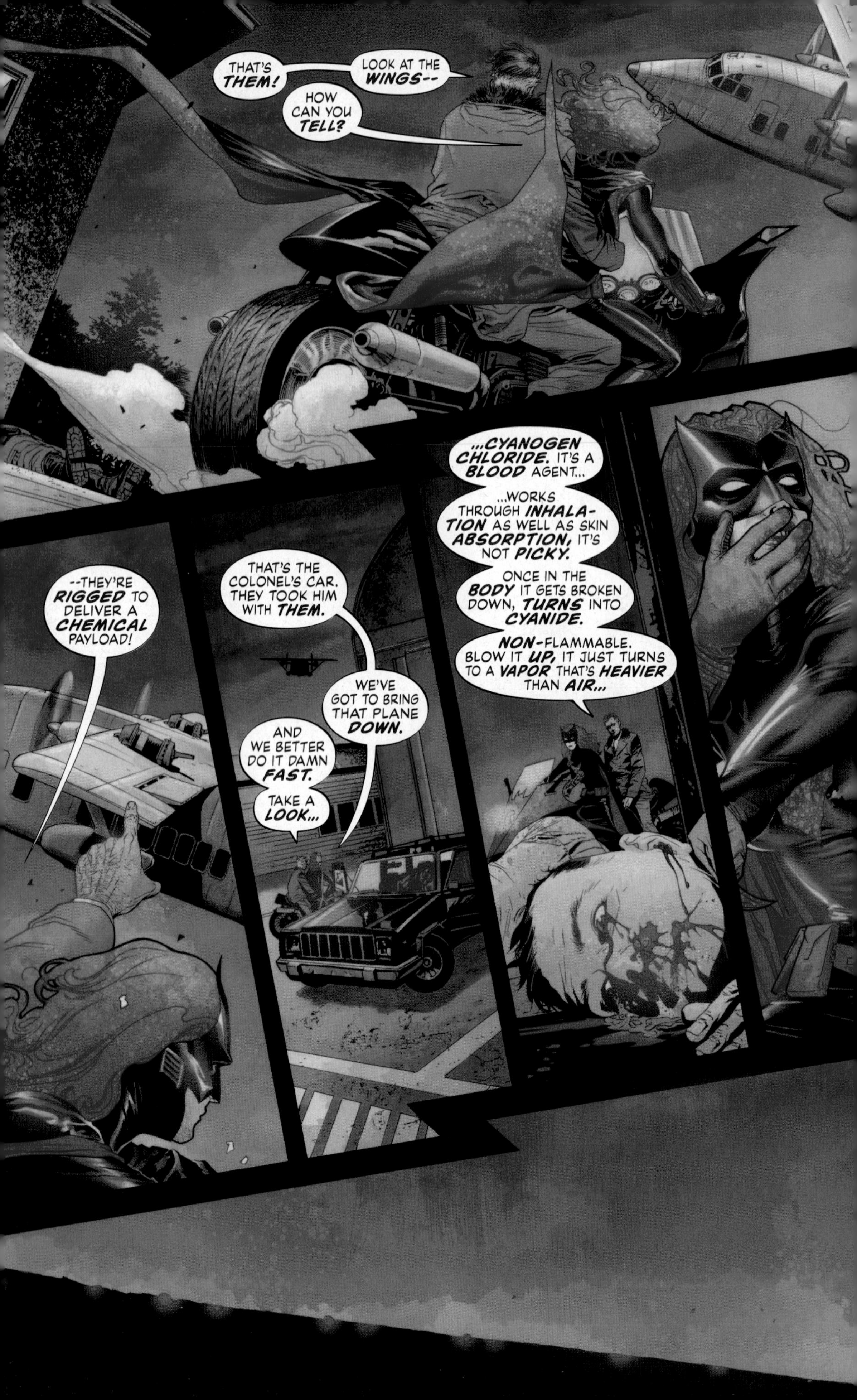
THAT'S THEM!
LOOK AT THE WINGS--
HOW CAN YOU TELL?
--THEY'RE RIGGED TO DELIVER A CHEMICAL PAYLOAD!
THAT'S THE COLONEL'S CAR. THEY TOOK HIM WITH THEM.
WE'VE GOT TO BRING THAT PLANE DOWN.
AND WE BETTER DO IT DAMN FAST.
TAKE A LOOK...
...CYANOGEN CHLORIDE. IT'S A BLOOD AGENT...
...WORKS THROUGH INHALATION AS WELL AS SKIN ABSORPTION, IT'S NOT PICKY.
ONCE IN THE BODY IT GETS BROKEN DOWN, TURNS INTO CYANIDE.
NON-FLAMMABLE. BLOW IT UP, IT JUST TURNS TO A VAPOR THAT'S HEAVIER THAN AIR...

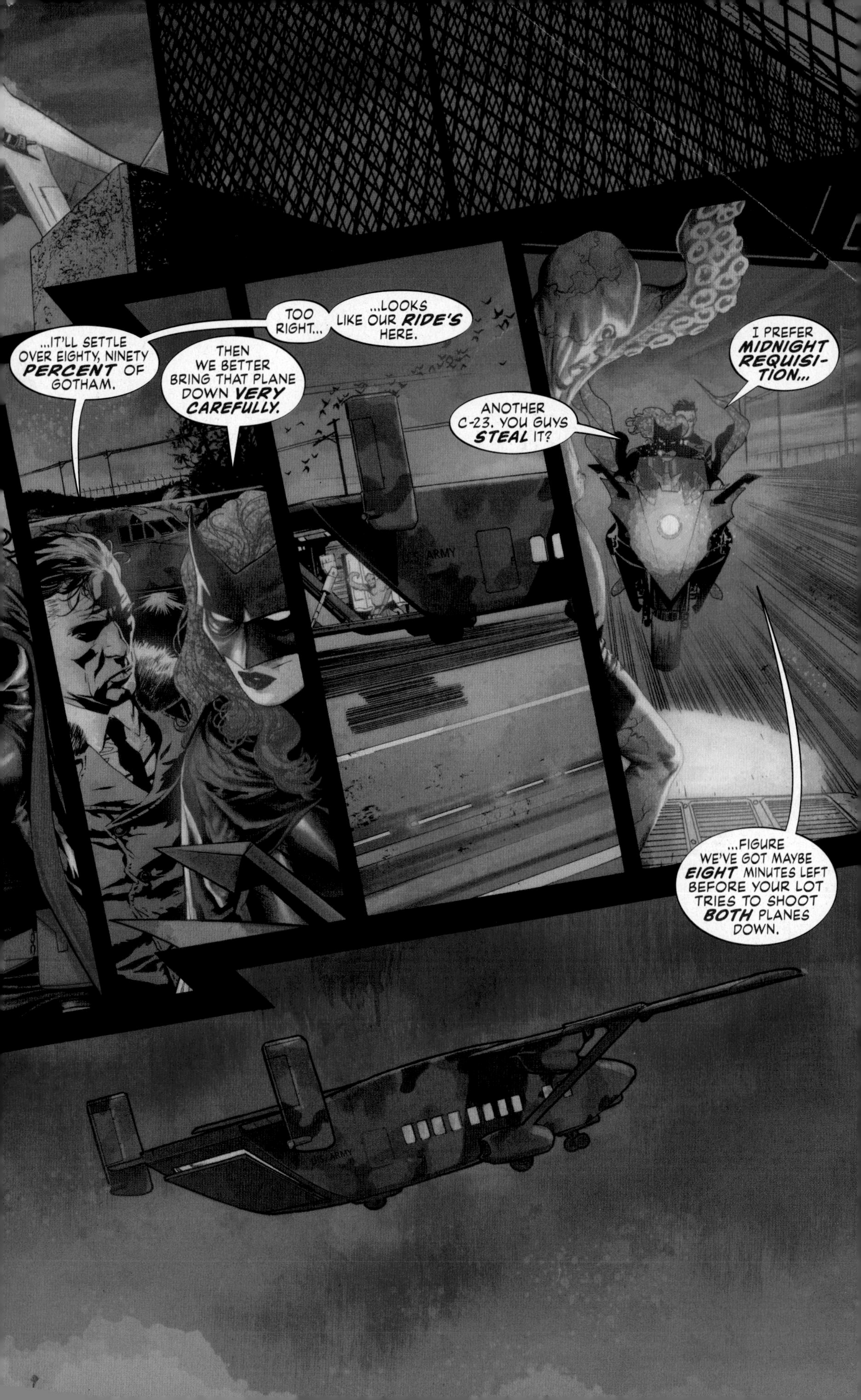
...IT'LL SETTLE OVER EIGHTY, NINETY PERCENT OF GOTHAM.
THEN WE BETTER BRING THAT PLANE DOWN VERY CAREFULLY.
TOO RIGHT...
...LOOKS LIKE OUR RIDE'S HERE.
ANOTHER C-23. YOU GUYS STEAL IT?
I PREFER MIDNIGHT REQUISITION...
...FIGURE WE'VE GOT MAYBE EIGHT MINUTES LEFT BEFORE YOUR LOT TRIES TO SHOOT BOTH PLANES DOWN.
ARMY
U.S. ARMY

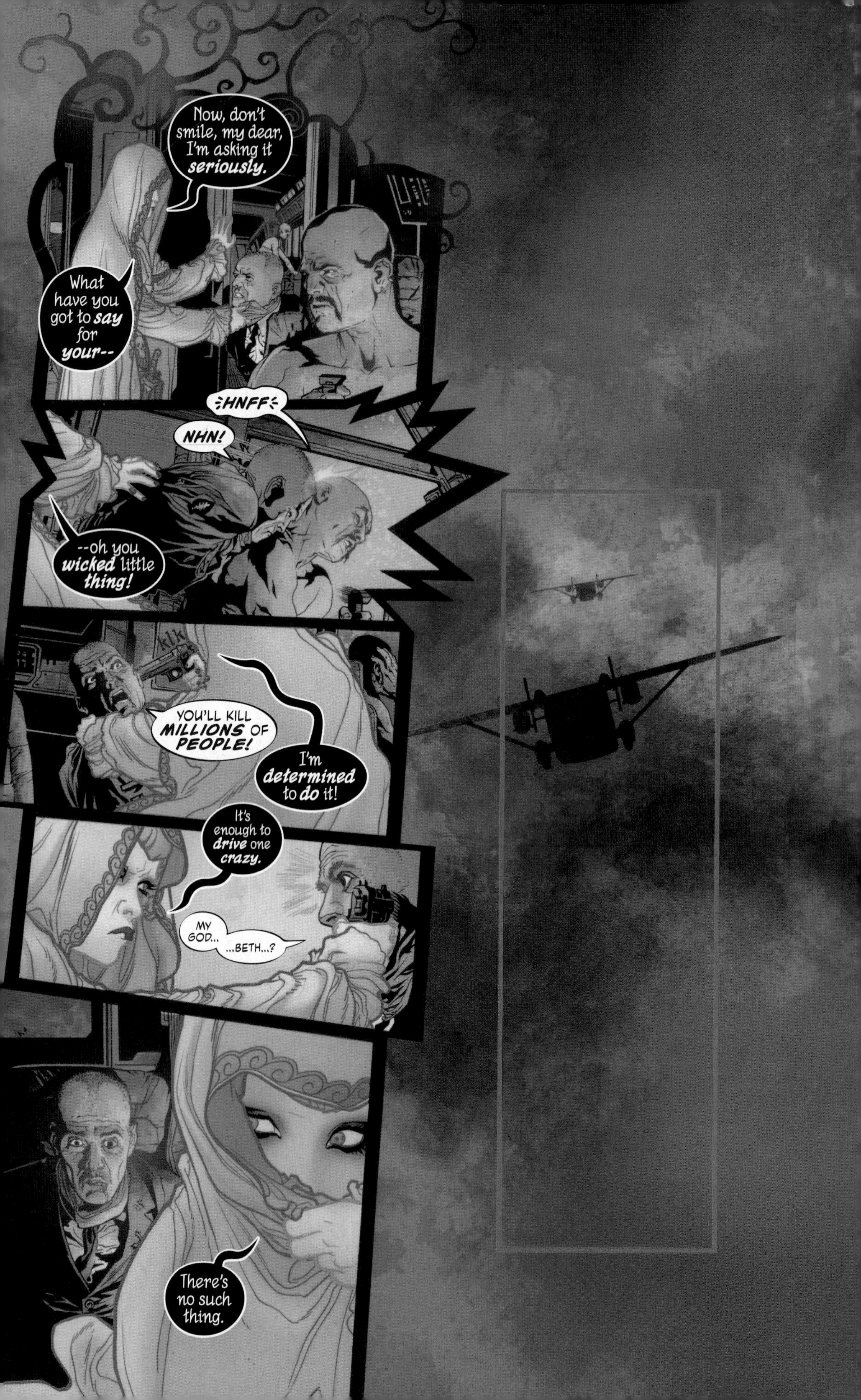

Now, don't smile, my dear, I'm asking it seriously.
What have you got to say for your--
HNFF
NHN!
--oh you wicked little thing!
klk
YOU'LL KILL MILLIONS OF PEOPLE!
I'm determined to do it!
It's enough to drive one crazy.
MY GOD...
...BETH...?
There's no such thing.

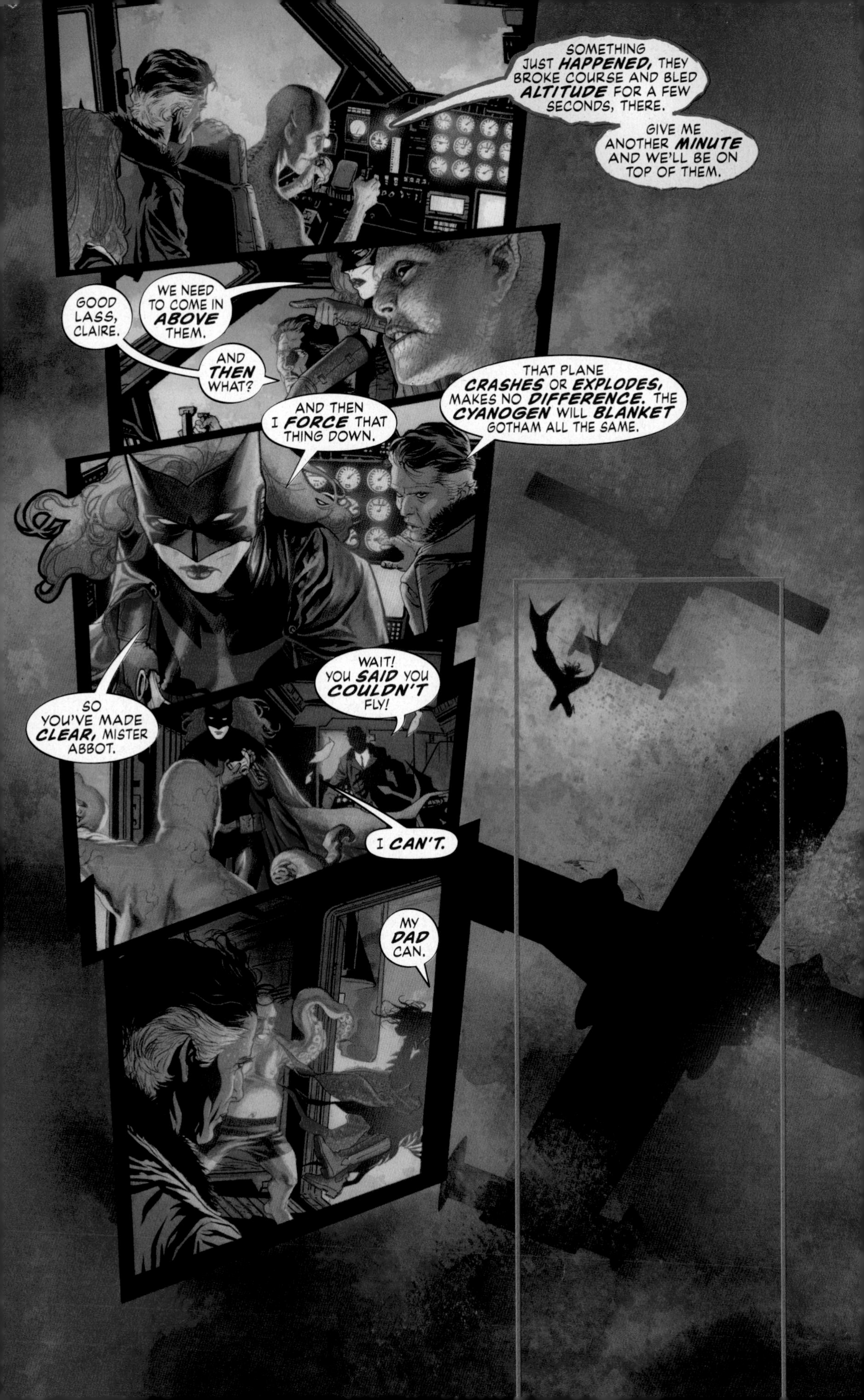
SOMETHING JUST HAPPENED, THEY BROKE COURSE AND BLED ALTITUDE FOR A FEW SECONDS, THERE.
GIVE ME ANOTHER MINUTE AND WE'LL BE ON TOP OF THEM.
WE NEED TO COME IN ABOVE THEM.
GOOD LASS, CLAIRE.
AND THEN WHAT?
AND THEN I FORCE THAT THING DOWN.
THAT PLANE CRASHES OR EXPLODES, MAKES NO DIFFERENCE. THE CYANOGEN WILL BLANKET GOTHAM ALL THE SAME.
SO YOU'VE MADE CLEAR, MISTER ABBOT.
WAIT! YOU SAID YOU COULDN'T FLY!
I CAN'T.
MY DAD CAN.

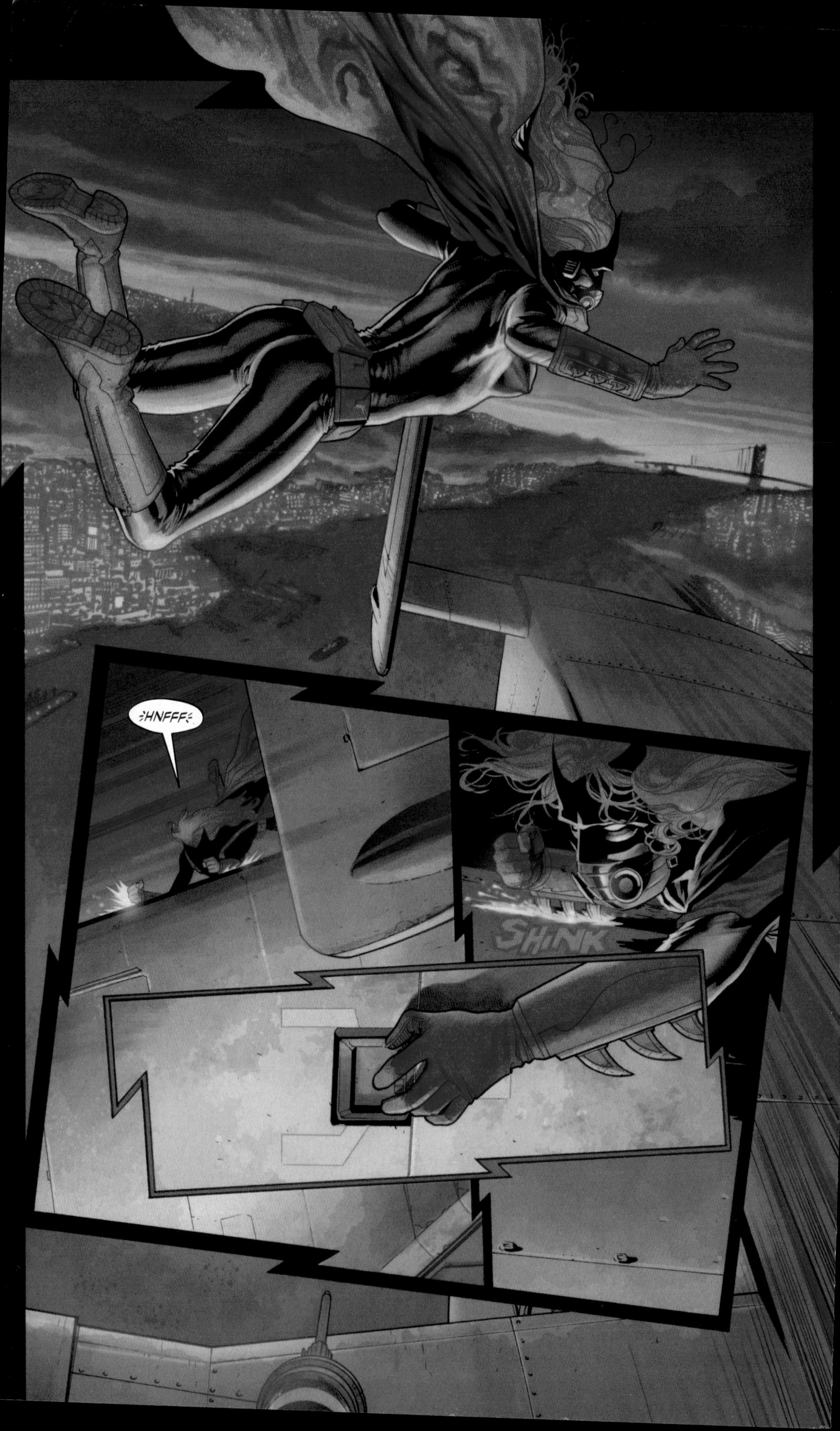

HNFFF
SHINK

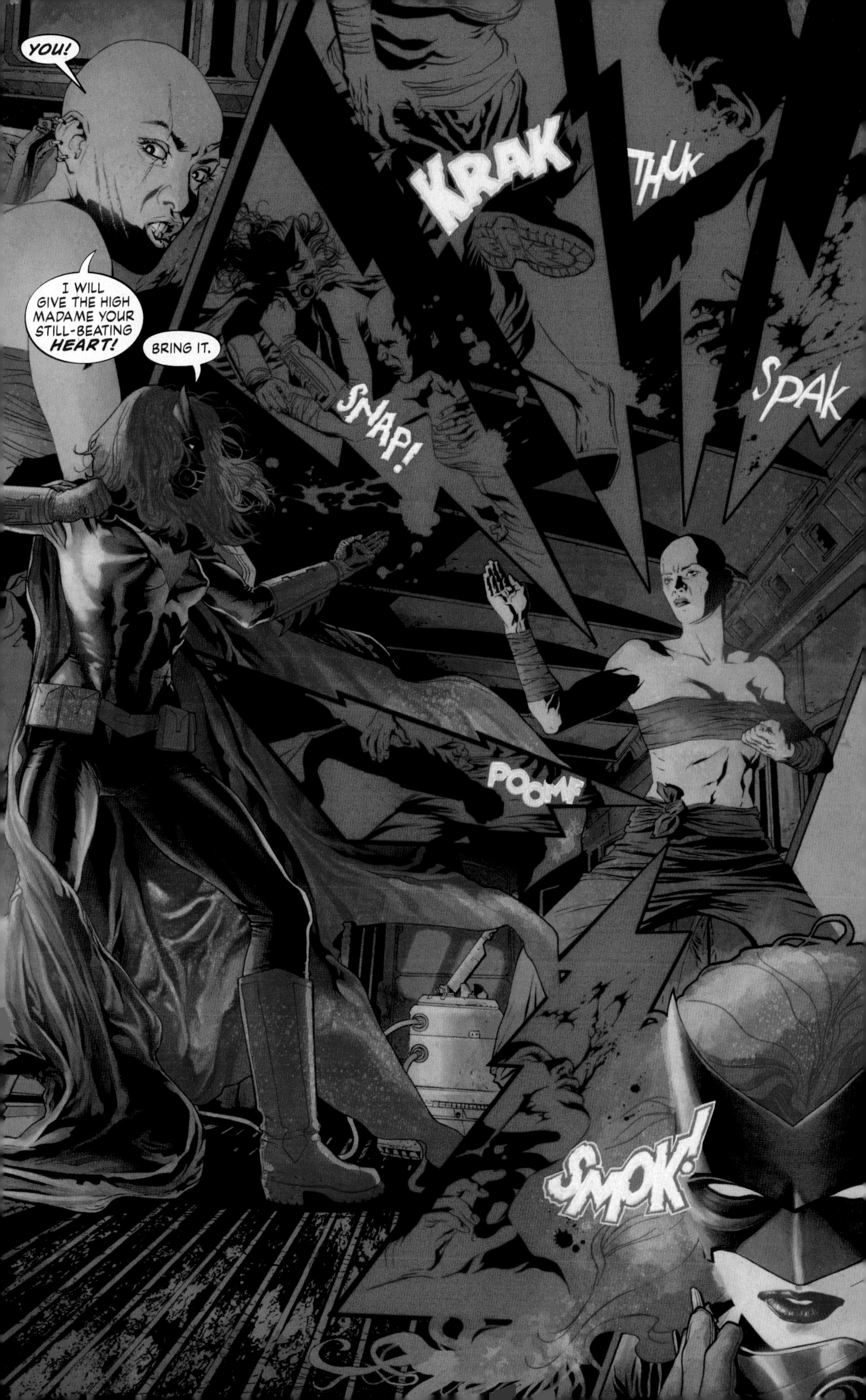
YOU!
KRAK
THUK
I WILL GIVE THE HIGH MADAME YOUR STILL-BEATING HEART!
BRING IT.
SNAP!
SPAK
POOMF
SMOK!

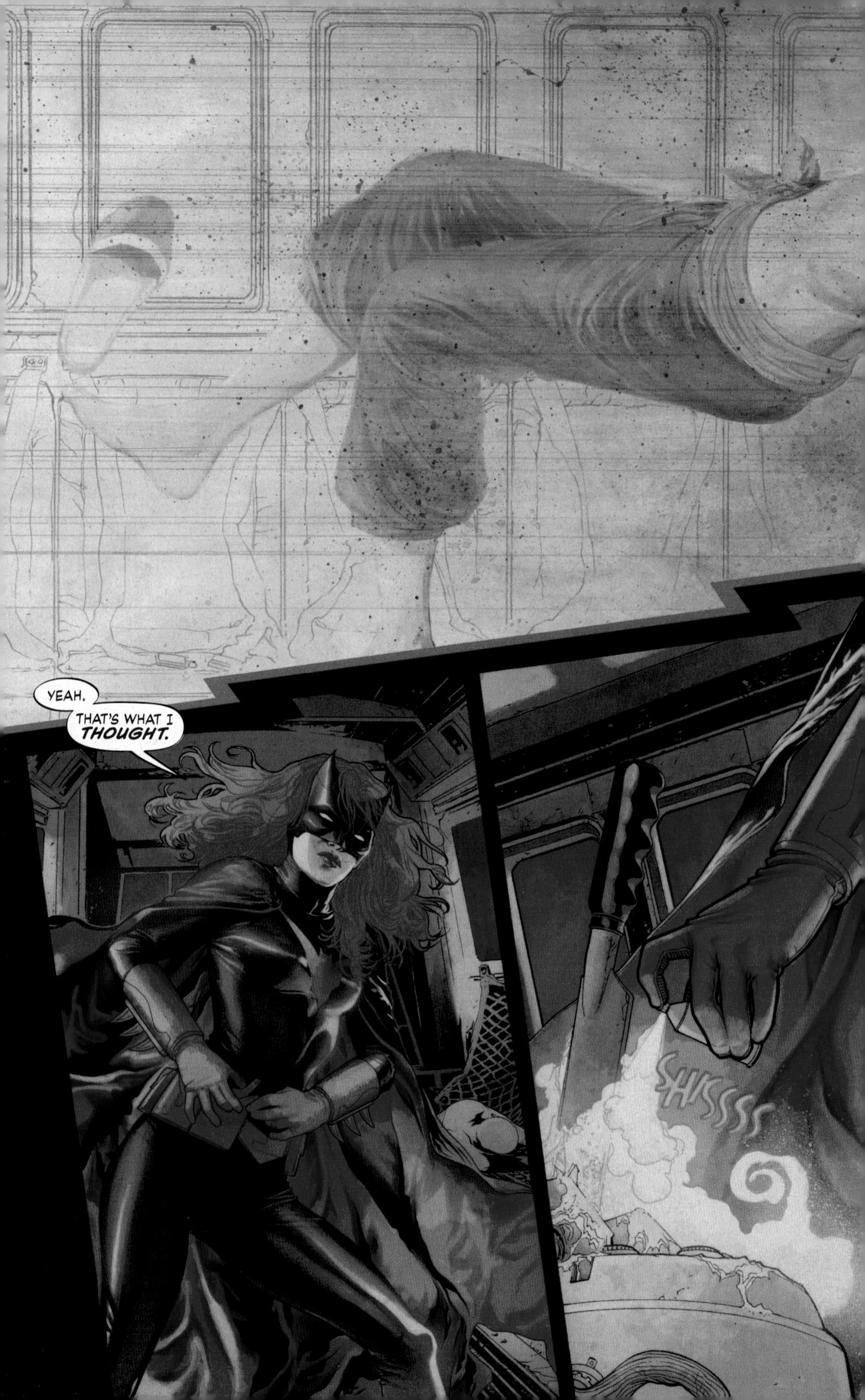
YEAH.
THAT'S WHAT I *THOUGHT.*
SHSSSS

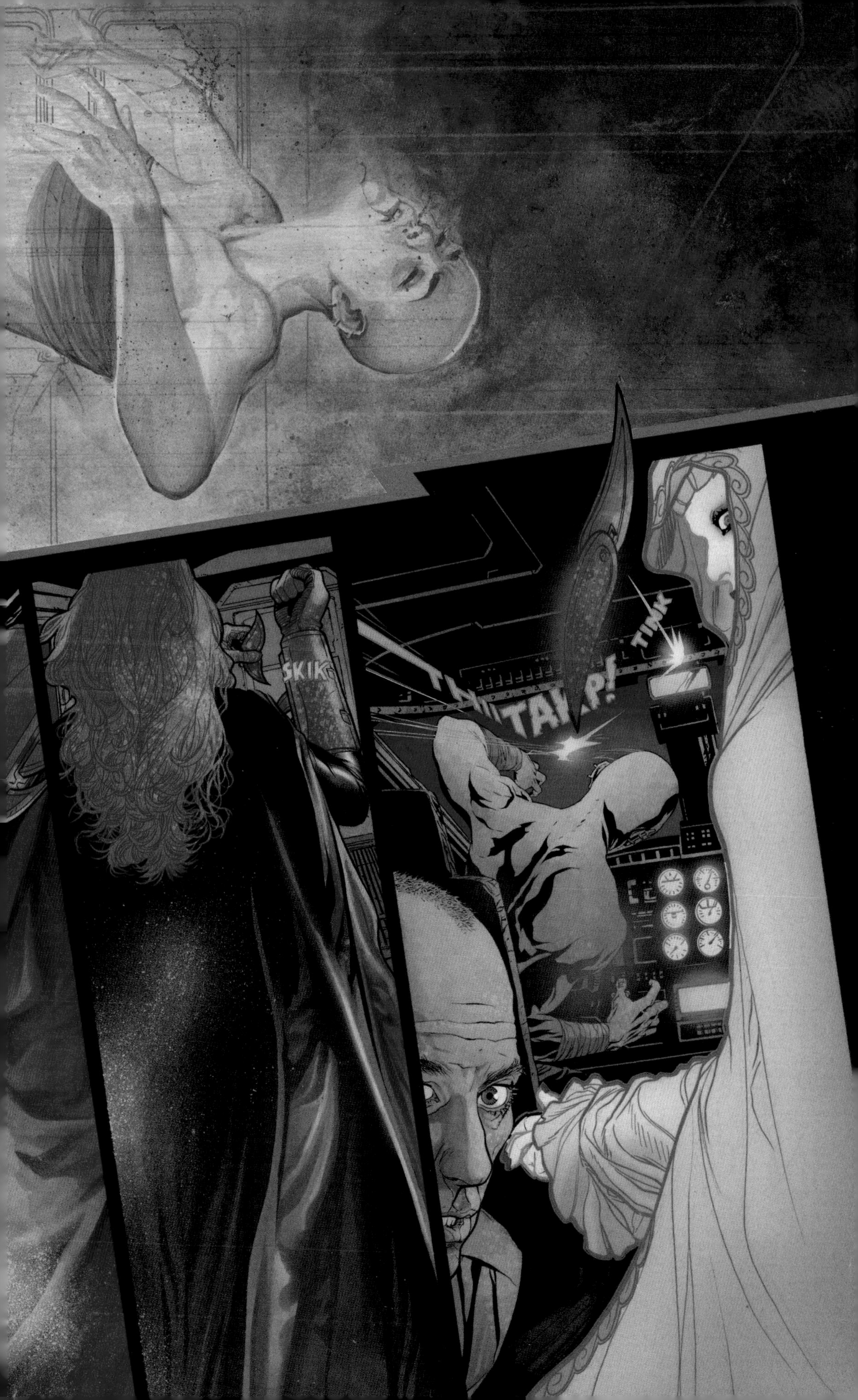
SKIK
TINK

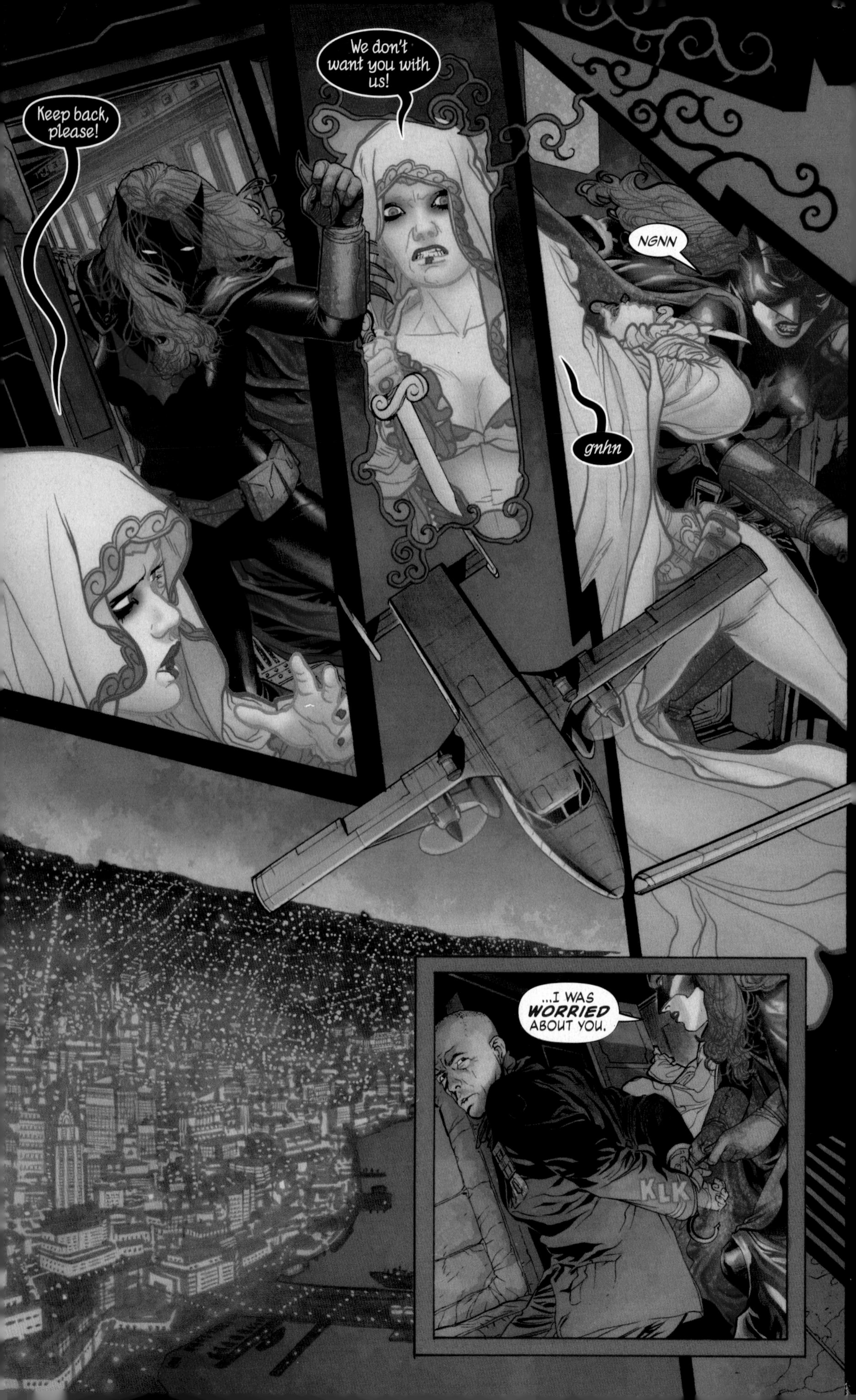
Keep back, please!
We don't want you with us!
NGNN
gnhn
...I WAS WORRIED ABOUT YOU.
KLK

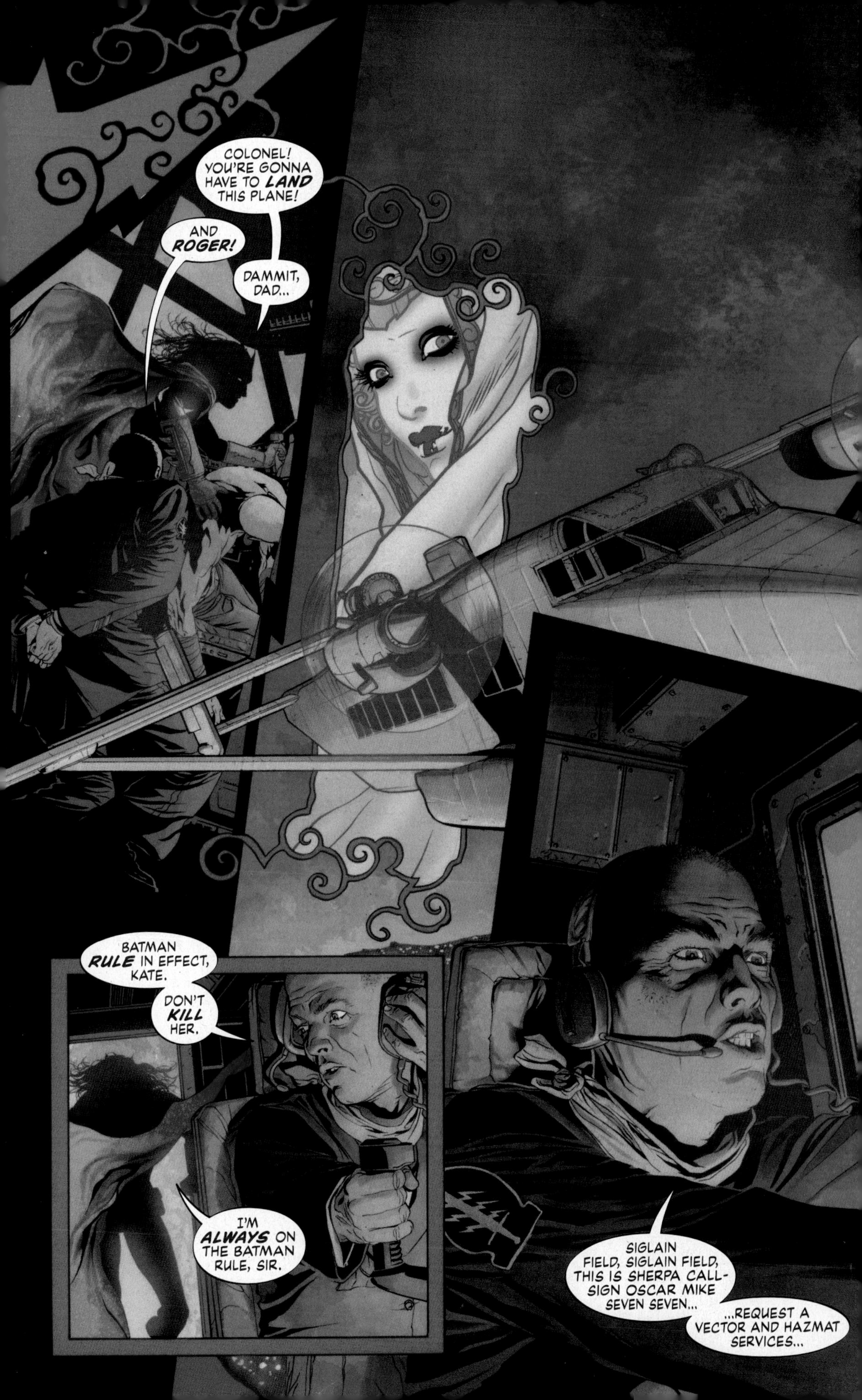
COLONEL! YOU'RE GONNA HAVE TO LAND THIS PLANE!
AND ROGER!
DAMMIT, DAD...
BATMAN RULE IN EFFECT, KATE.
DON'T KILL HER.
I'M ALWAYS ON THE BATMAN RULE, SIR.
SIGLAIN FIELD, SIGLAIN FIELD, THIS IS SHERPA CALL-SIGN OSCAR MIKE SEVEN SEVEN...
...REQUEST A VECTOR AND HAZMAT SERVICES...

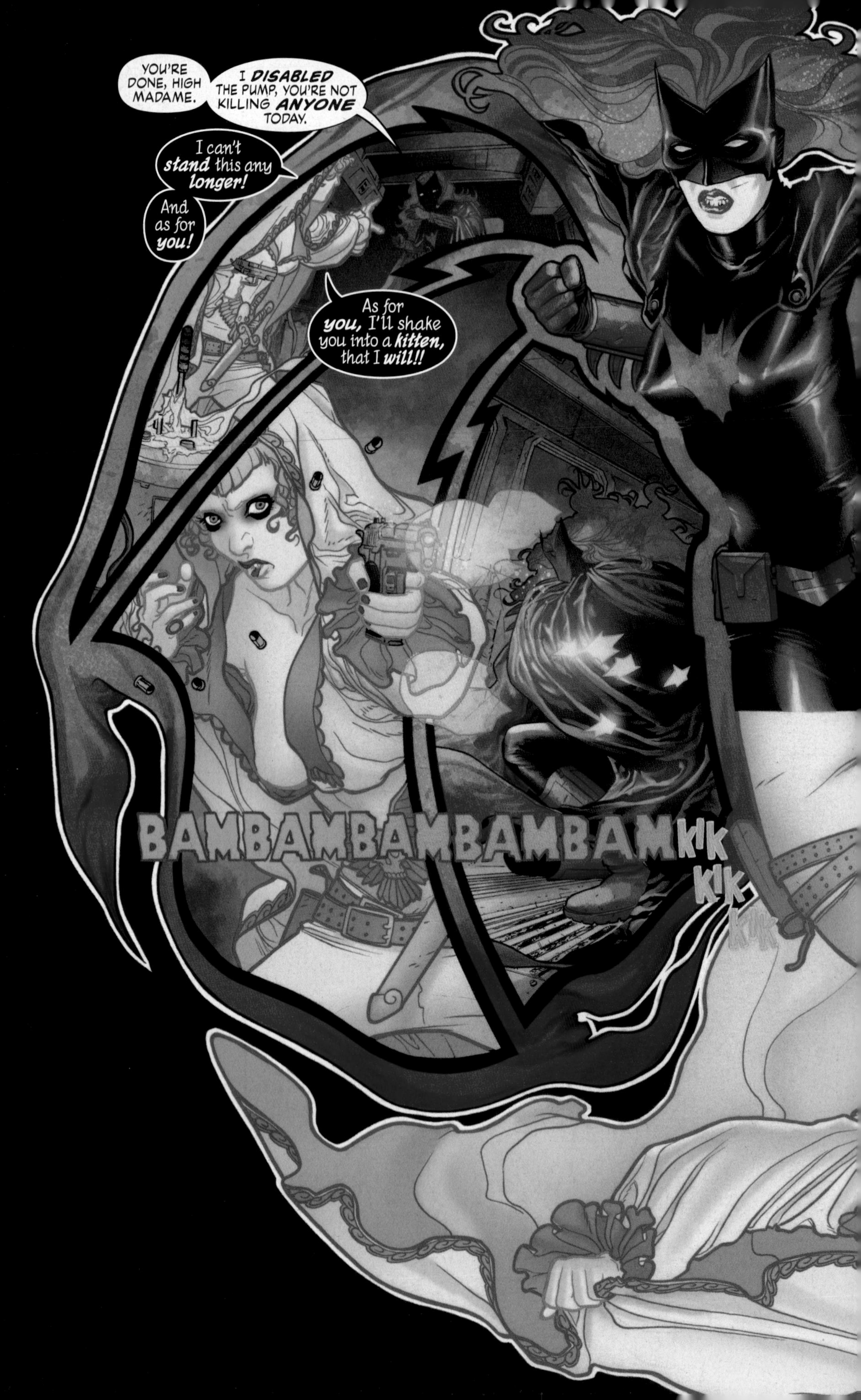
YOU'RE DONE, HIGH MADAME.
I DISABLED THE PUMP, YOU'RE NOT KILLING ANYONE TODAY.
I can't stand this any longer!
And as for you!
As for you, I'll shake you into a kitten, that I will!!
BAMBAMBAMBAMBAM
KIK KIK KIK

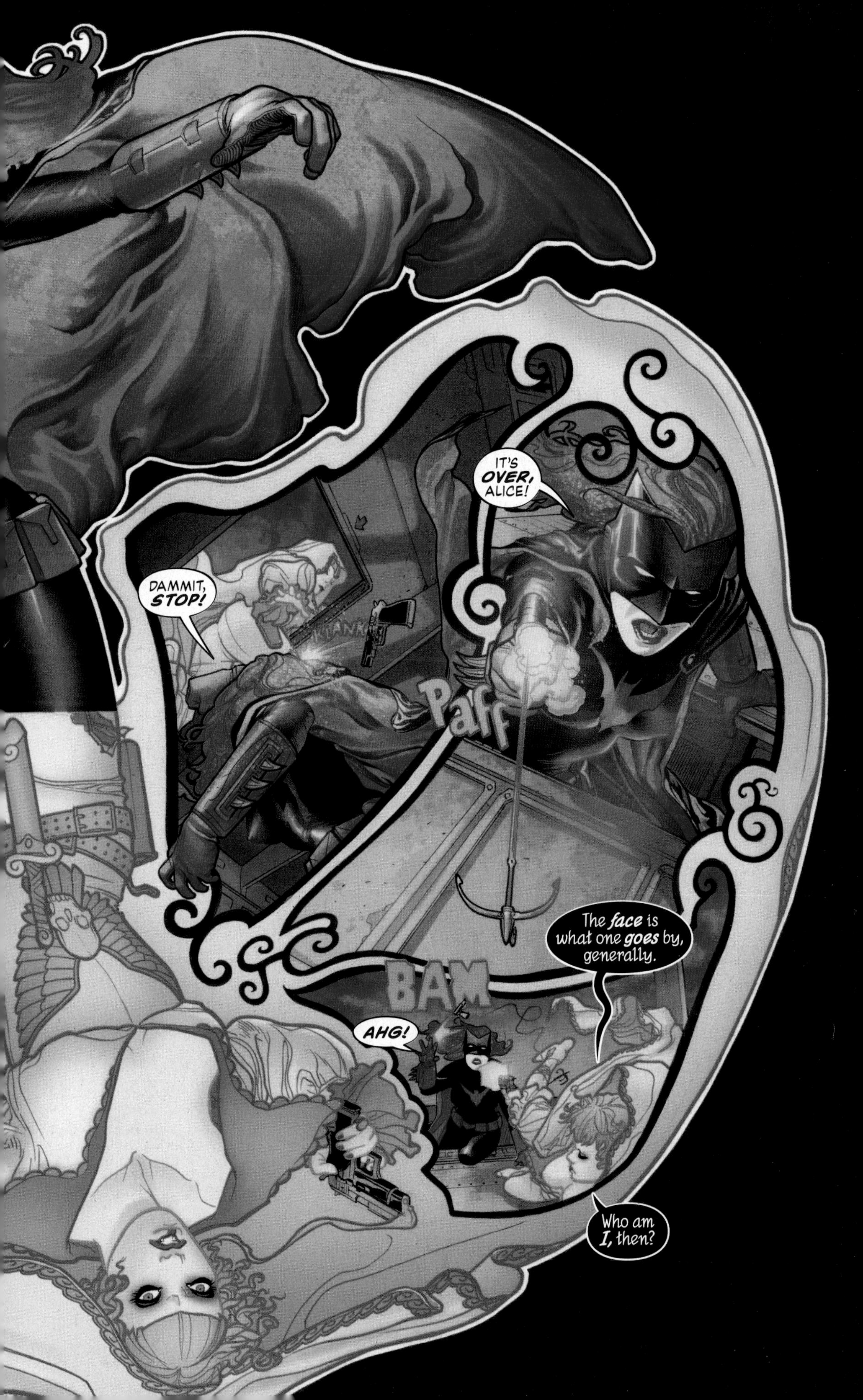

IT'S OVER, ALICE!
DAMMIT, STOP!
PAFF
The face is what one goes by, generally.
BAM
AHG!
Who am I, then?

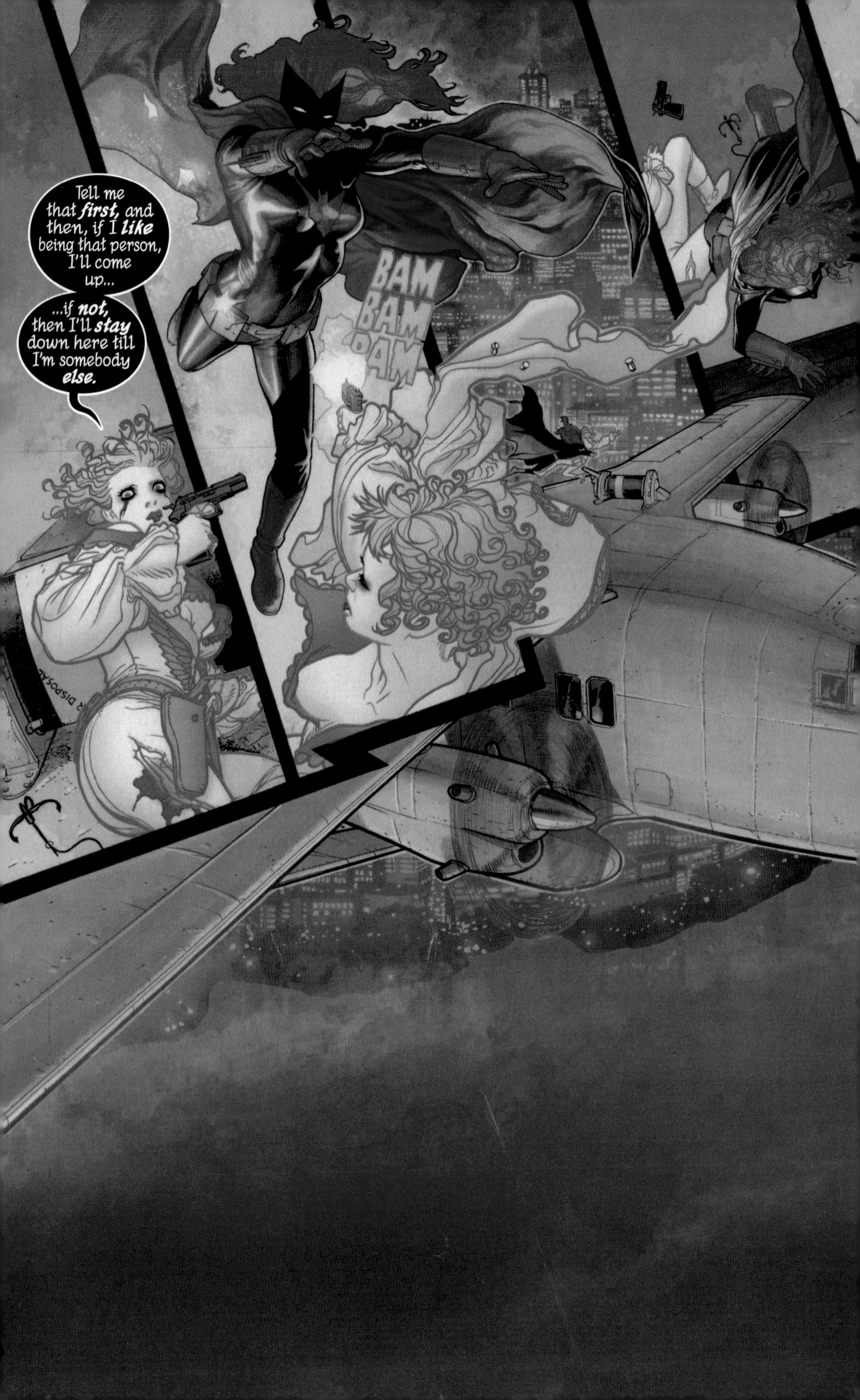
Tell me that *first,* and then, if I *like* being that person, I'll come up...
...if *not,* then I'll *stay* down here till I'm somebody *else.*
BAM BAM BAM

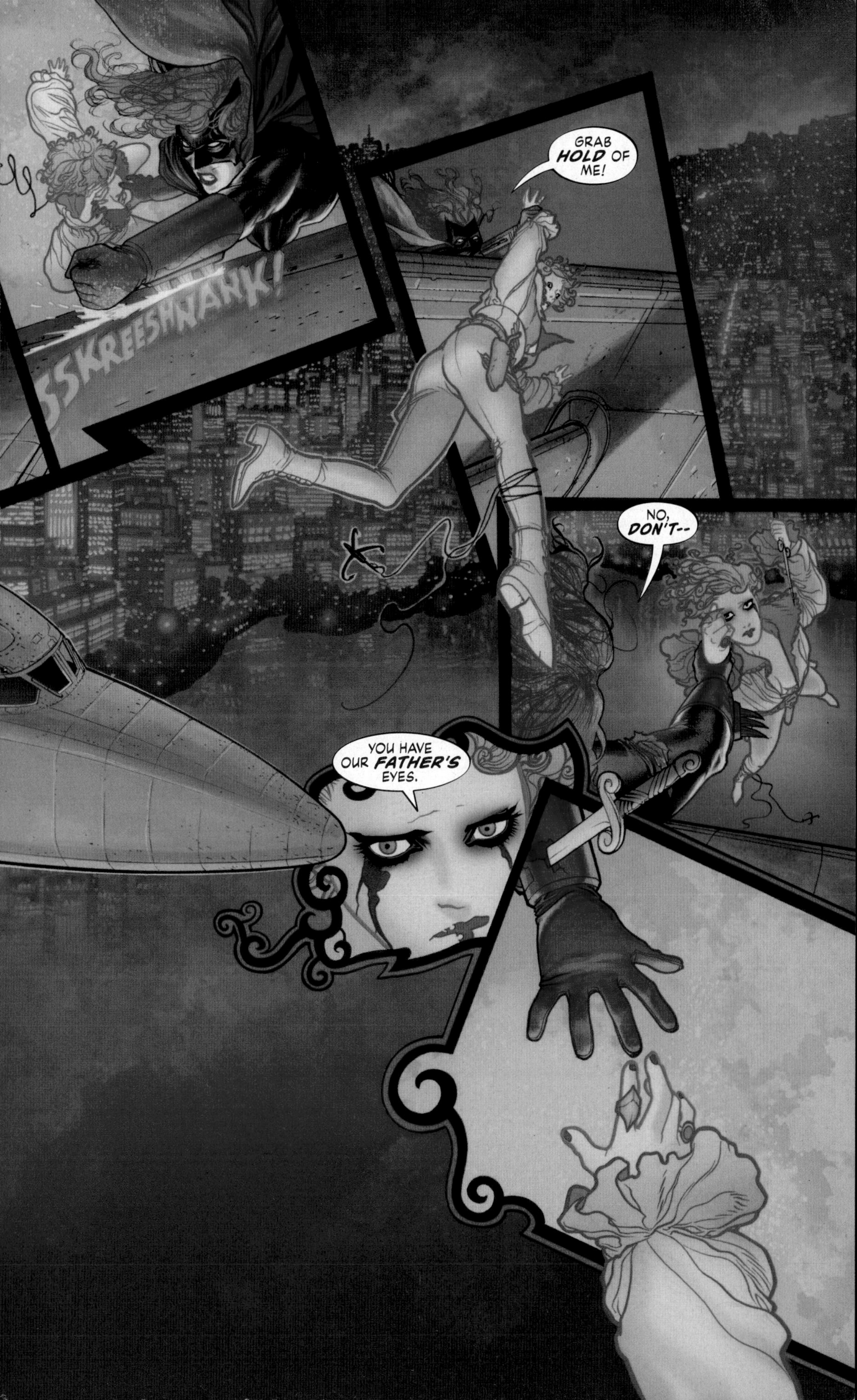
SSKREESHNAHK!
GRAB HOLD OF ME!
NO, DON'T--
YOU HAVE OUR FATHER'S EYES.

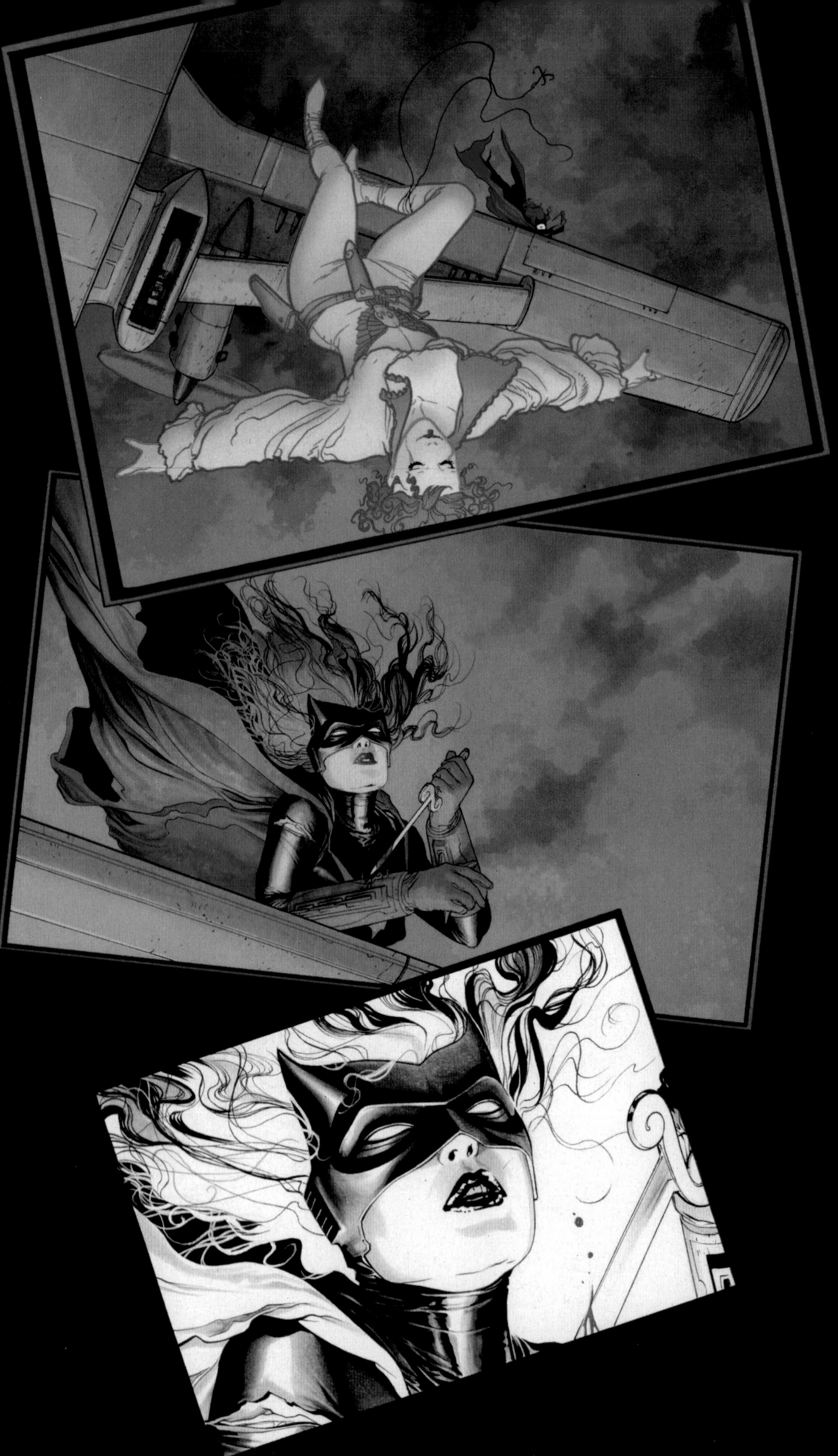

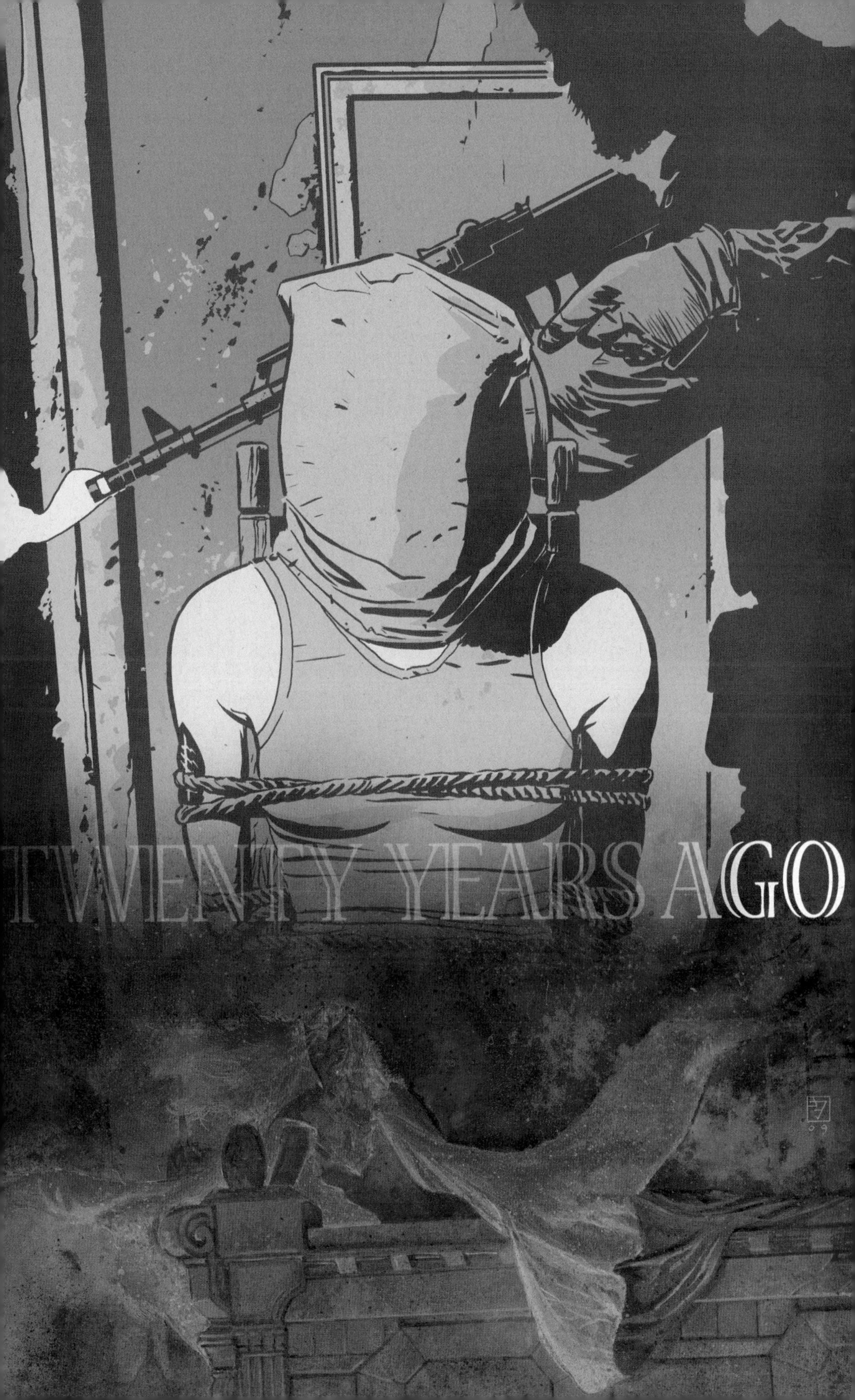
TWENTY YEARS AGO

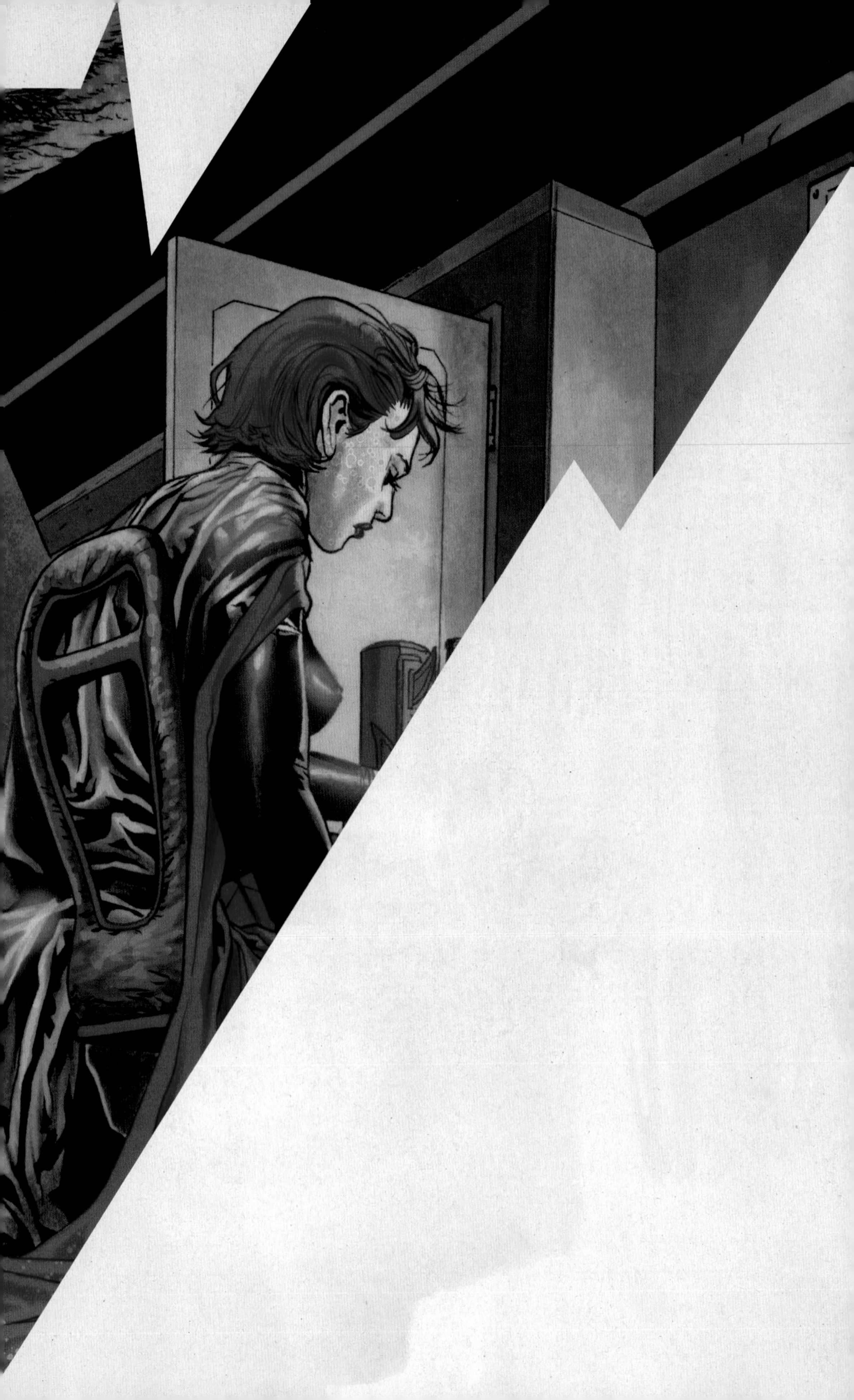

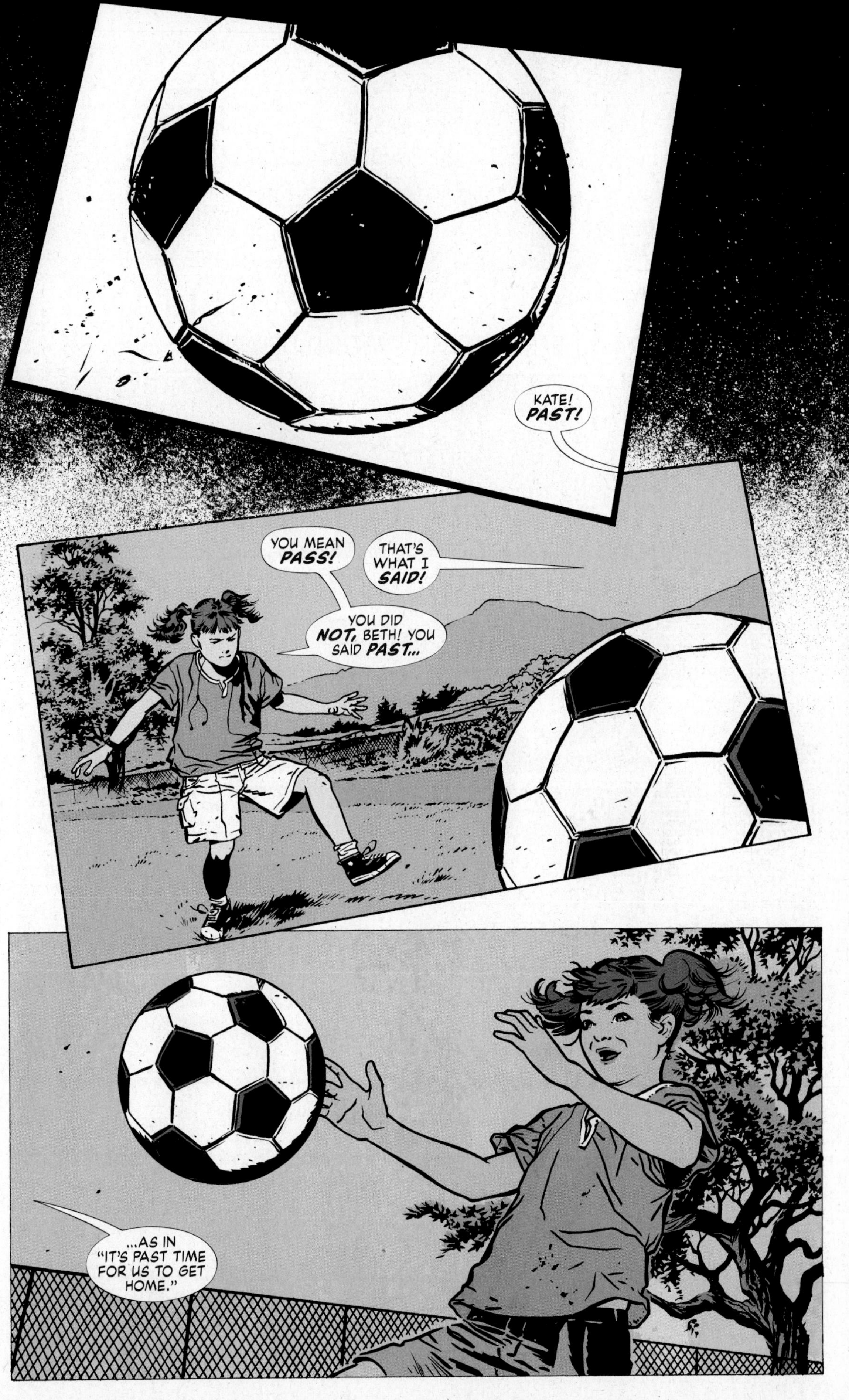
KATE! PAST!
YOU MEAN PASS!
THAT'S WHAT I SAID!
YOU DID NOT, BETH! YOU SAID PAST...
...AS IN "IT'S PAST TIME FOR US TO GET HOME."

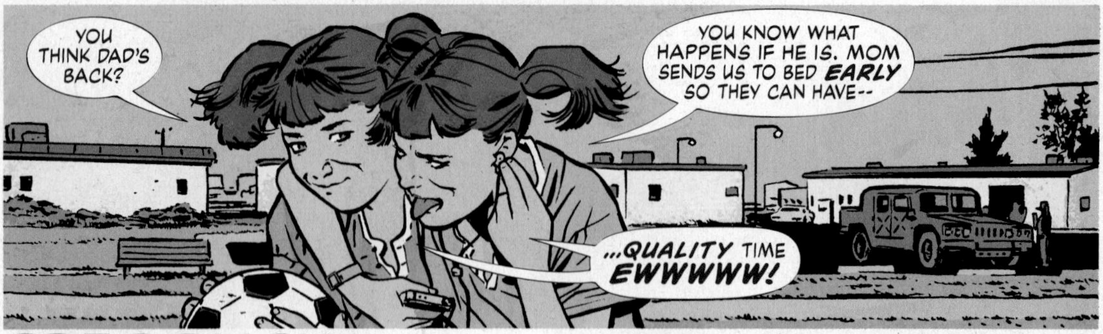

YOU THINK DAD'S BACK?
YOU KNOW WHAT HAPPENS IF HE IS. MOM SENDS US TO BED EARLY SO THEY CAN HAVE--
...QUALITY TIME EWWWWW!

GREG RUCKA
WRITER

J.H. WILLIAMS III
ARTIST/COVER

DAVE STEWART
COLORS

TODD KLEIN
LETTERS

HARVEY RICHARDS
ASST. EDITOR

MICHAEL SIGLAIN
EDITOR

ADAM HUGHES
VARIANT COVER

BATMAN CREATED BY BOB KANE

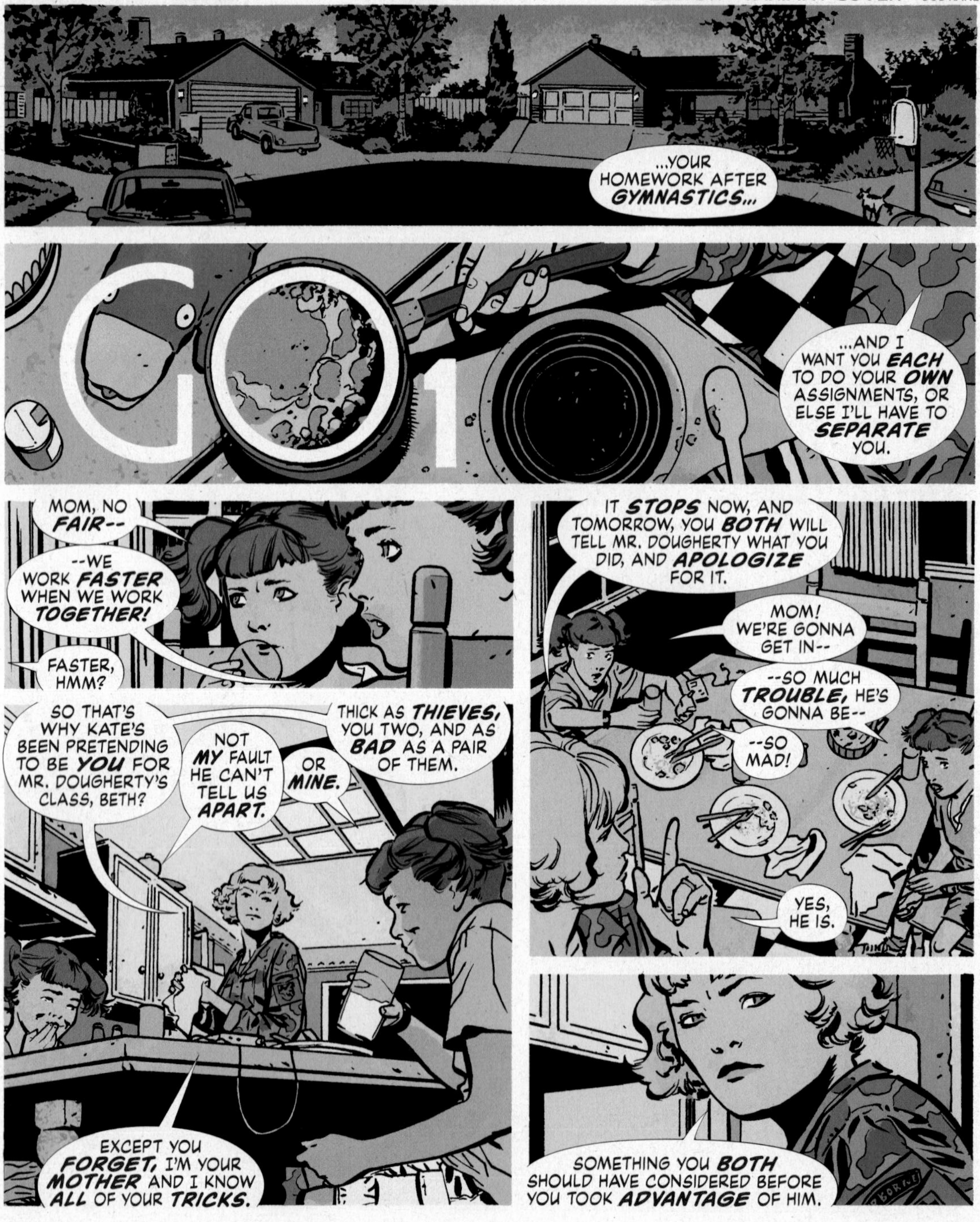

...YOUR HOMEWORK AFTER GYMNASTICS...
...AND I WANT YOU EACH TO DO YOUR OWN ASSIGNMENTS, OR ELSE I'LL HAVE TO SEPARATE YOU.
MOM, NO FAIR--
--WE WORK FASTER WHEN WE WORK TOGETHER!
FASTER, HMM?
SO THAT'S WHY KATE'S BEEN PRETENDING TO BE YOU FOR MR. DOUGHERTY'S CLASS, BETH?
NOT MY FAULT HE CAN'T TELL US APART.
OR MINE.
THICK AS THIEVES, YOU TWO, AND AS BAD AS A PAIR OF THEM.
EXCEPT YOU FORGET, I'M YOUR MOTHER AND I KNOW ALL OF YOUR TRICKS.
IT STOPS NOW, AND TOMORROW, YOU BOTH WILL TELL MR. DOUGHERTY WHAT YOU DID, AND APOLOGIZE FOR IT.
MOM! WE'RE GONNA GET IN--
--SO MUCH TROUBLE, HE'S GONNA BE--
--SO MAD!
YES, HE IS.
SOMETHING YOU BOTH SHOULD HAVE CONSIDERED BEFORE YOU TOOK ADVANTAGE OF HIM.

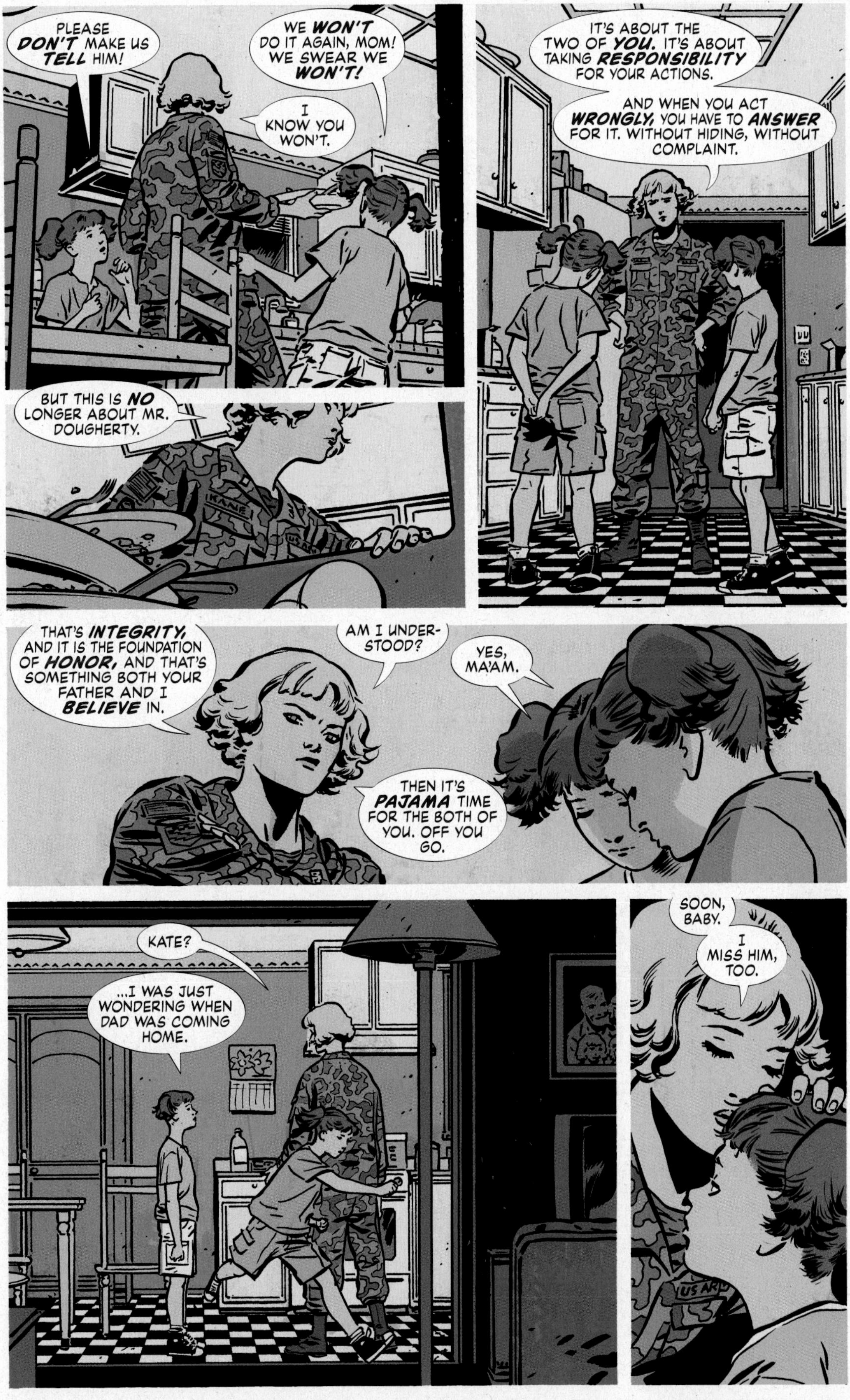
PLEASE DON'T MAKE US TELL HIM!
WE WON'T DO IT AGAIN, MOM! WE SWEAR WE WON'T!
I KNOW YOU WON'T.
BUT THIS IS NO LONGER ABOUT MR. DOUGHERTY.
IT'S ABOUT THE TWO OF YOU. IT'S ABOUT TAKING RESPONSIBILITY FOR YOUR ACTIONS.
AND WHEN YOU ACT WRONGLY, YOU HAVE TO ANSWER FOR IT. WITHOUT HIDING, WITHOUT COMPLAINT.
KANE
THAT'S INTEGRITY, AND IT IS THE FOUNDATION OF HONOR, AND THAT'S SOMETHING BOTH YOUR FATHER AND I BELIEVE IN.
AM I UNDERSTOOD?
YES, MA'AM.
THEN IT'S PAJAMA TIME FOR THE BOTH OF YOU. OFF YOU GO.
KATE?
...I WAS JUST WONDERING WHEN DAD WAS COMING HOME.
SOON, BABY.
I MISS HIM, TOO.

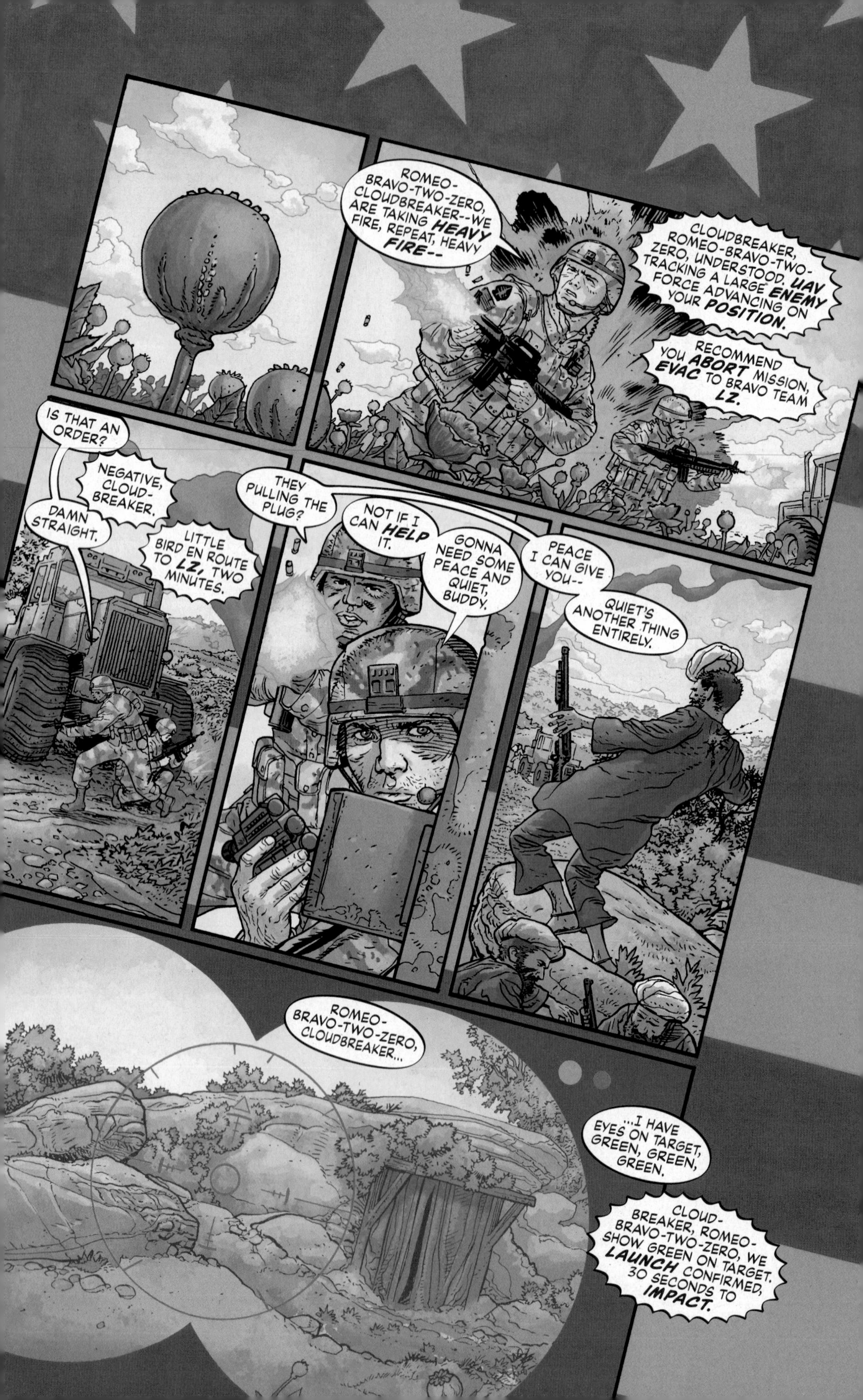
ROMEO-BRAVO-TWO-ZERO, CLOUDBREAKER--WE ARE TAKING HEAVY FIRE, REPEAT, HEAVY FIRE--
CLOUDBREAKER, ROMEO-BRAVO-TWO-ZERO, UNDERSTOOD. UAV TRACKING A LARGE ENEMY FORCE ADVANCING ON YOUR POSITION.
RECOMMEND YOU ABORT MISSION, EVAC TO BRAVO TEAM LZ.
IS THAT AN ORDER?
NEGATIVE, CLOUD-BREAKER.
DAMN STRAIGHT.
LITTLE BIRD EN ROUTE TO LZ, TWO MINUTES.
THEY PULLING THE PLUG?
NOT IF I CAN HELP IT.
GONNA NEED SOME PEACE AND QUIET, BUDDY.
PEACE I CAN GIVE YOU--
QUIET'S ANOTHER THING ENTIRELY.
ROMEO-BRAVO-TWO-ZERO, CLOUDBREAKER...
...I HAVE EYES ON TARGET. GREEN, GREEN, GREEN.
CLOUD-BREAKER, ROMEO-BRAVO-TWO-ZERO, WE SHOW GREEN ON TARGET. LAUNCH CONFIRMED, 30 SECONDS TO IMPACT.

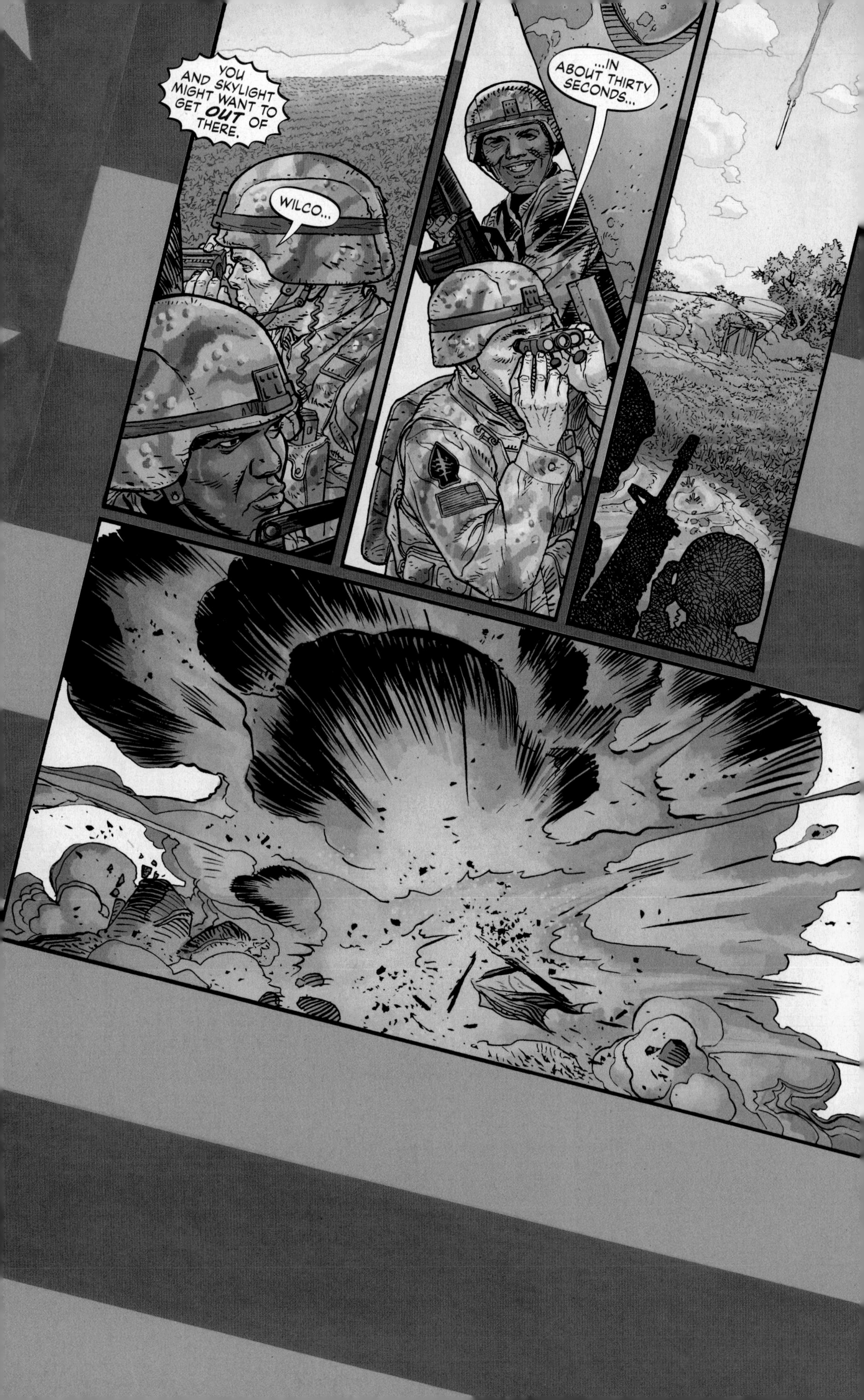
YOU AND SKYLIGHT MIGHT WANT TO GET OUT OF THERE.
WILCO...
...IN ABOUT THIRTY SECONDS...

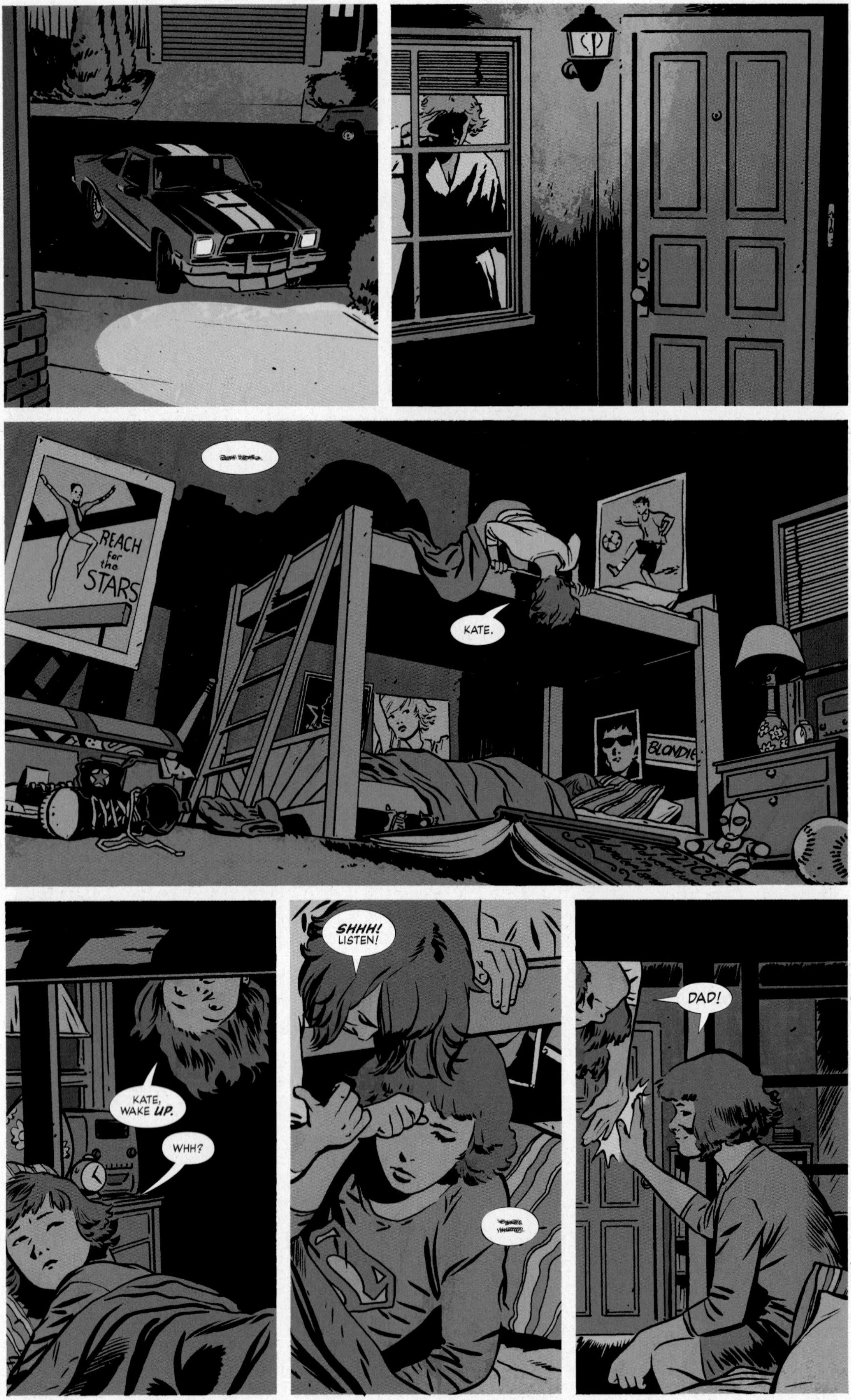
REACH for the STARS
KATE.
BLONDIE
KATE, WAKE UP.
WHH?
SHHH! LISTEN!
DAD!

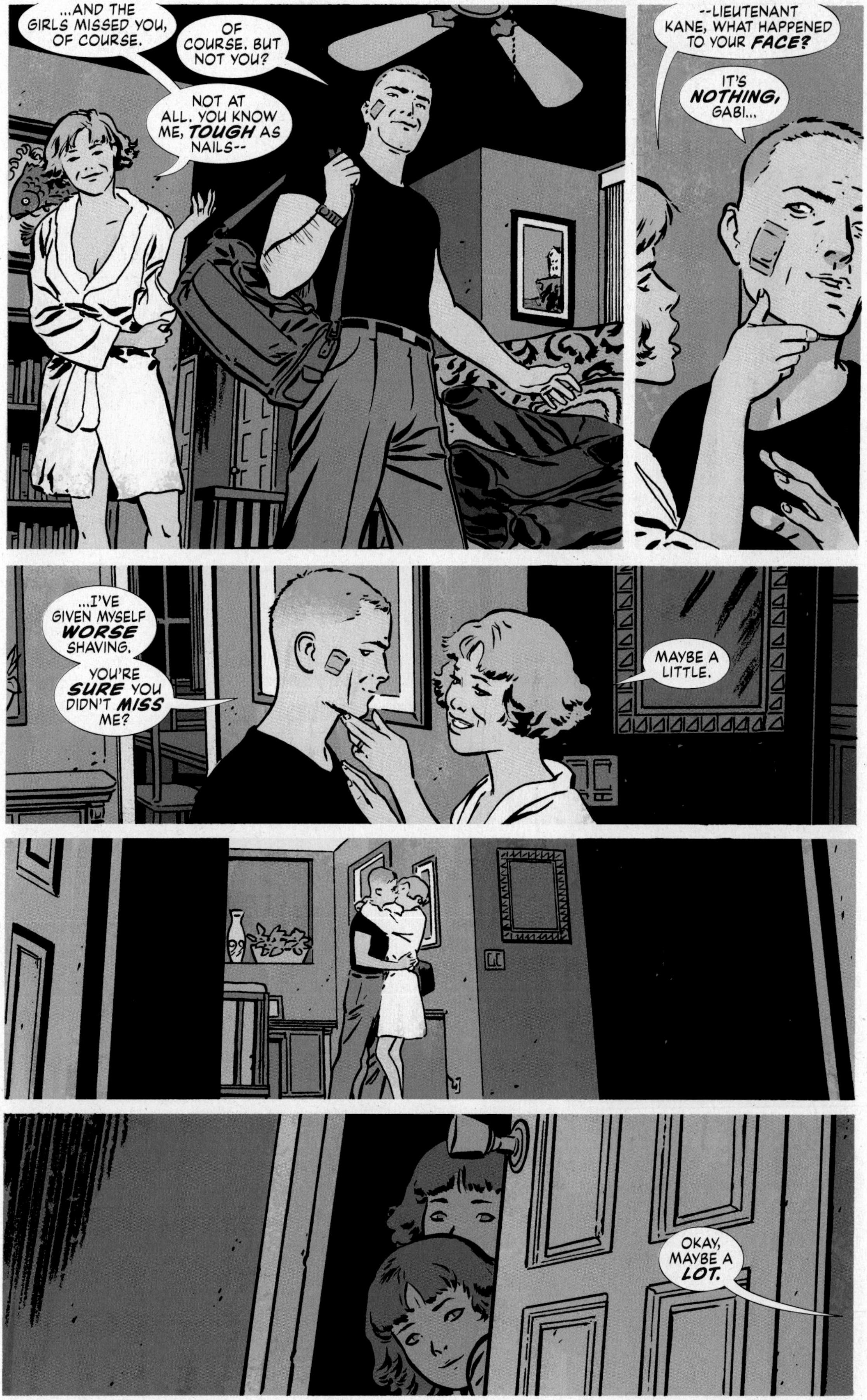
...AND THE GIRLS MISSED YOU, OF COURSE.
OF COURSE. BUT NOT YOU?
NOT AT ALL. YOU KNOW ME, TOUGH AS NAILS--
--LIEUTENANT KANE, WHAT HAPPENED TO YOUR FACE?
IT'S NOTHING, GABI...
...I'VE GIVEN MYSELF WORSE SHAVING.
YOU'RE SURE YOU DIDN'T MISS ME?
MAYBE A LITTLE.
OKAY, MAYBE A LOT.

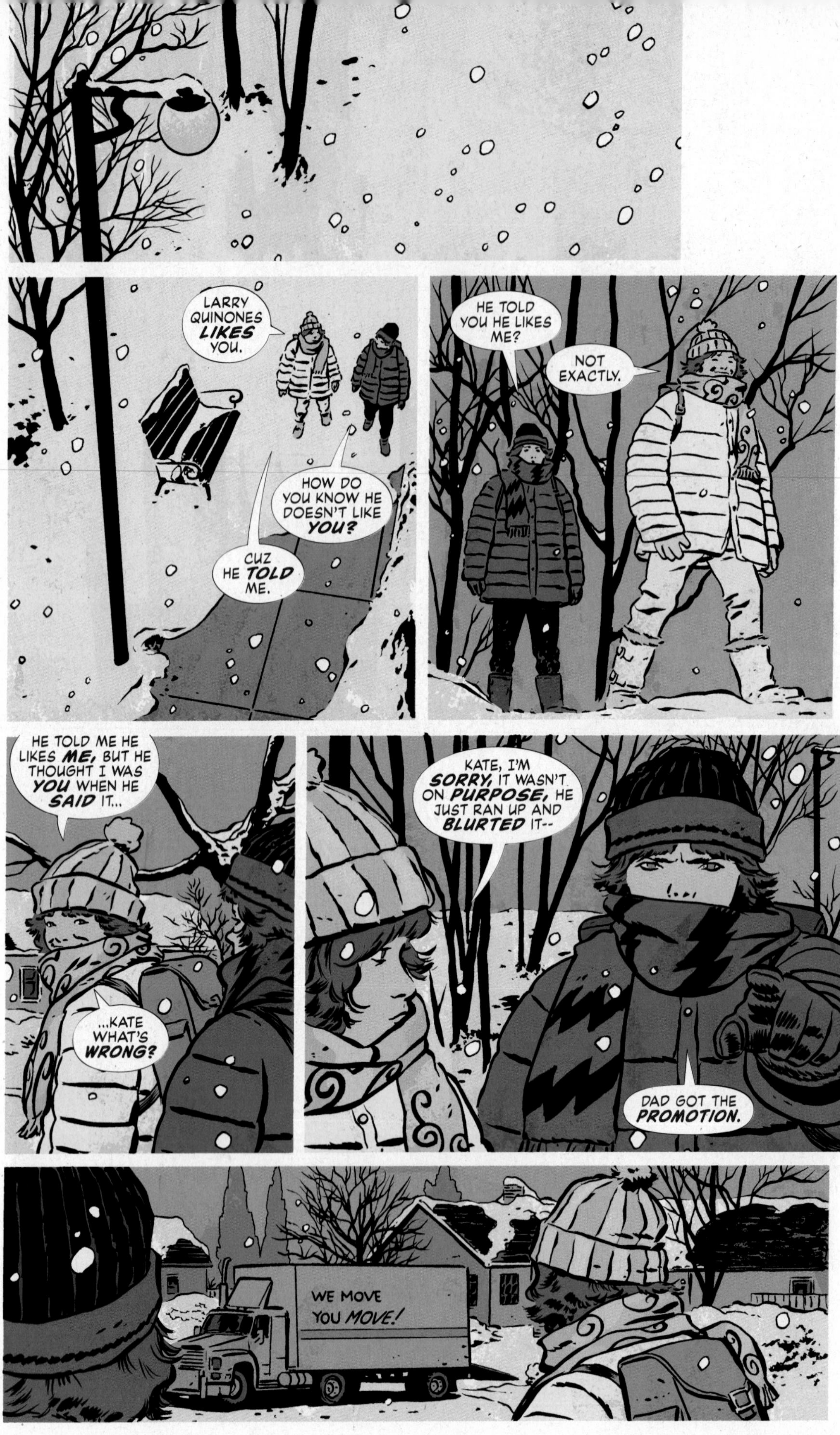
LARRY QUINONES LIKES YOU.
HOW DO YOU KNOW HE DOESN'T LIKE YOU?
CUZ HE TOLD ME.
HE TOLD YOU HE LIKES ME?
NOT EXACTLY.
HE TOLD ME HE LIKES ME, BUT HE THOUGHT I WAS YOU WHEN HE SAID IT...
...KATE WHAT'S WRONG?
KATE, I'M SORRY, IT WASN'T ON PURPOSE, HE JUST RAN UP AND BLURTED IT--
DAD GOT THE PROMOTION.
WE MOVE YOU MOVE!

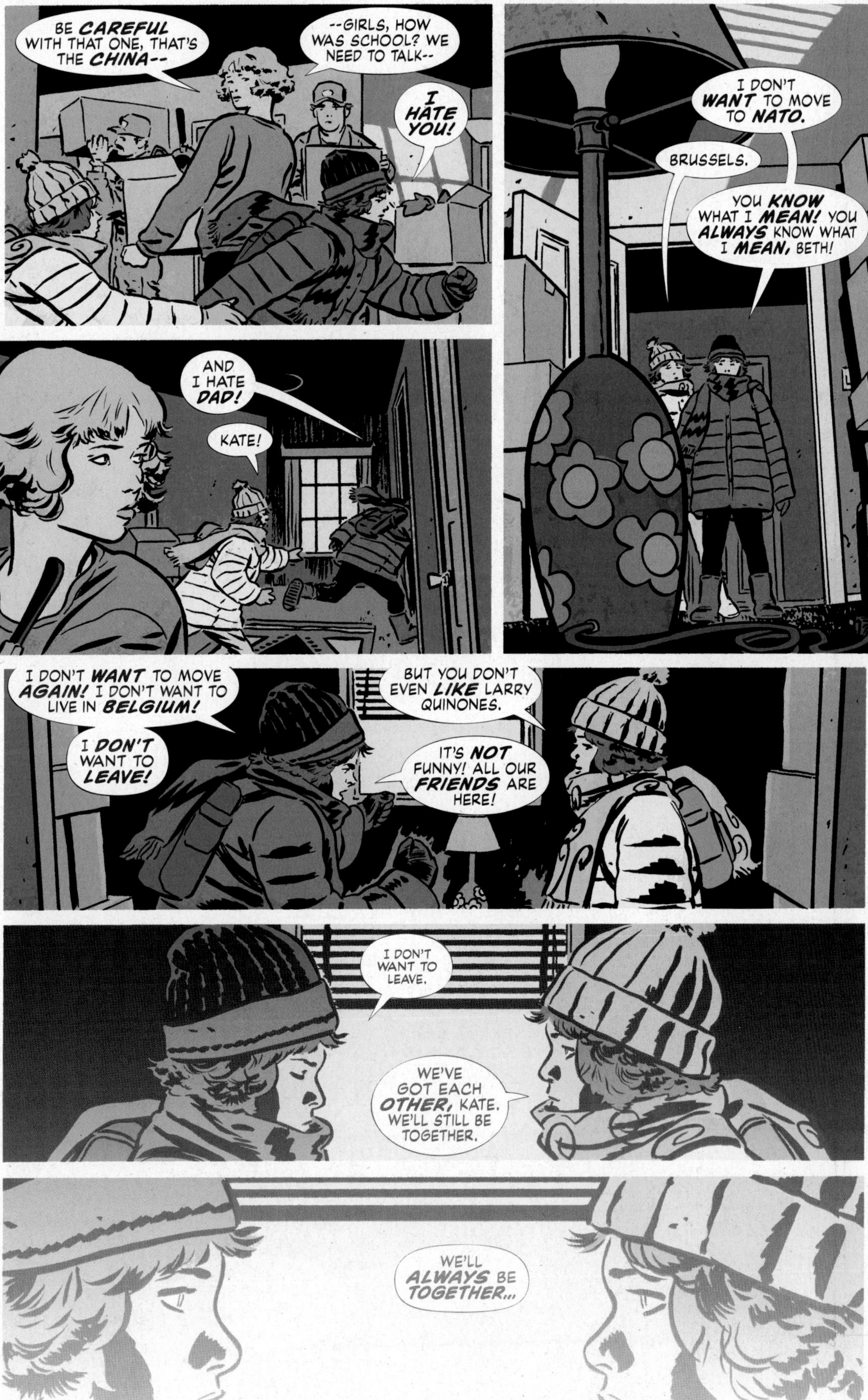
BE CAREFUL WITH THAT ONE, THAT'S THE CHINA--
--GIRLS, HOW WAS SCHOOL? WE NEED TO TALK--
I HATE YOU!
AND I HATE DAD!
KATE!
I DON'T WANT TO MOVE TO NATO.
BRUSSELS.
YOU KNOW WHAT I MEAN! YOU ALWAYS KNOW WHAT I MEAN, BETH!
I DON'T WANT TO MOVE AGAIN! I DON'T WANT TO LIVE IN BELGIUM!
I DON'T WANT TO LEAVE!
BUT YOU DON'T EVEN LIKE LARRY QUINONES.
IT'S NOT FUNNY! ALL OUR FRIENDS ARE HERE!
I DON'T WANT TO LEAVE.
WE'VE GOT EACH OTHER, KATE. WE'LL STILL BE TOGETHER.
WE'LL ALWAYS BE TOGETHER...

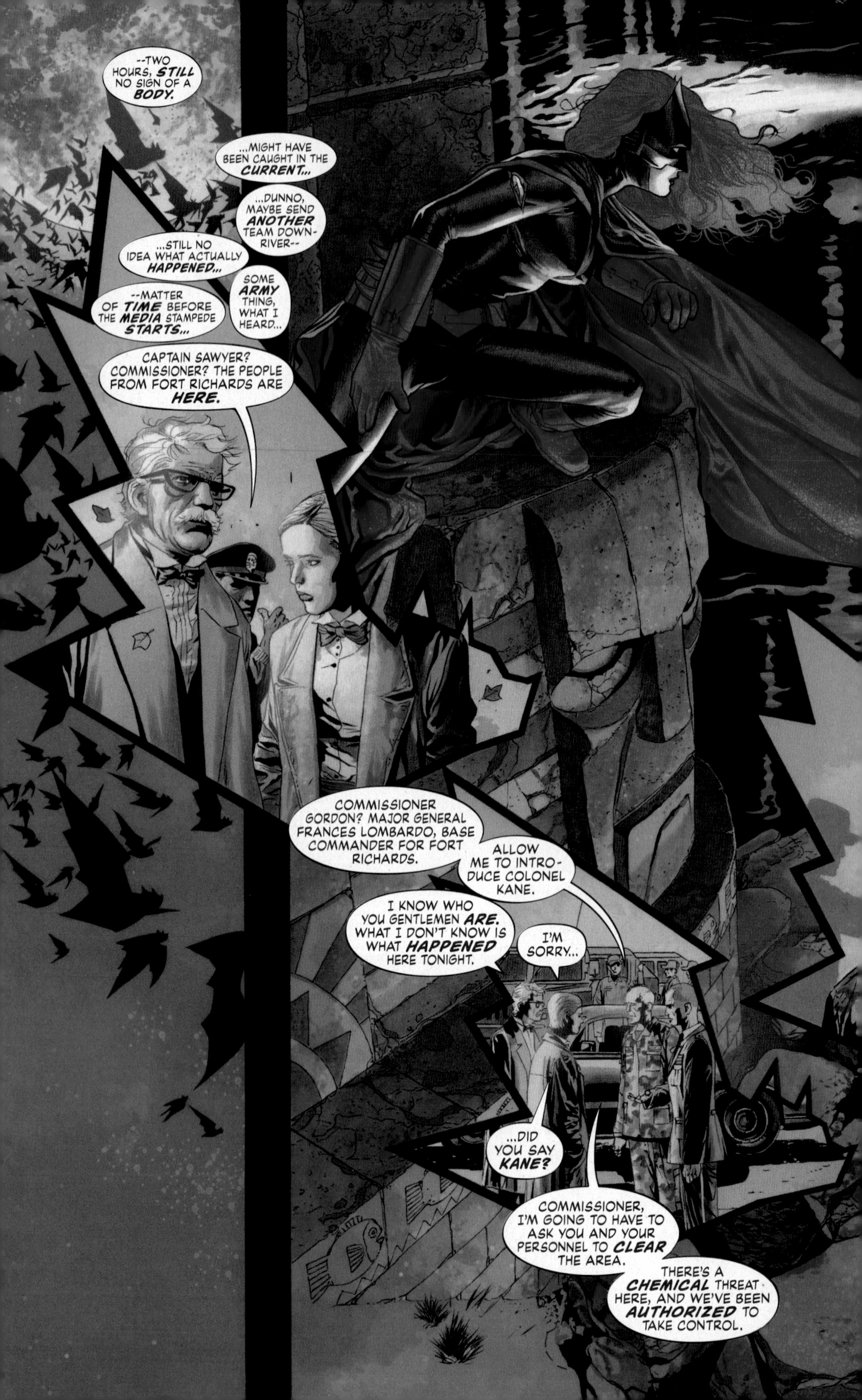
--TWO HOURS, STILL NO SIGN OF A BODY.
...MIGHT HAVE BEEN CAUGHT IN THE CURRENT...
...DUNNO, MAYBE SEND ANOTHER TEAM DOWN-RIVER--
...STILL NO IDEA WHAT ACTUALLY HAPPENED...
SOME ARMY THING, WHAT I HEARD...
--MATTER OF TIME BEFORE THE MEDIA STAMPEDE STARTS...
CAPTAIN SAWYER? COMMISSIONER? THE PEOPLE FROM FORT RICHARDS ARE HERE.
COMMISSIONER GORDON? MAJOR GENERAL FRANCES LOMBARDO, BASE COMMANDER FOR FORT RICHARDS.
ALLOW ME TO INTRO-DUCE COLONEL KANE.
I KNOW WHO YOU GENTLEMEN ARE. WHAT I DON'T KNOW IS WHAT HAPPENED HERE TONIGHT.
I'M SORRY...
...DID YOU SAY KANE?
COMMISSIONER, I'M GOING TO HAVE TO ASK YOU AND YOUR PERSONNEL TO CLEAR THE AREA.
THERE'S A CHEMICAL THREAT HERE, AND WE'VE BEEN AUTHORIZED TO TAKE CONTROL.

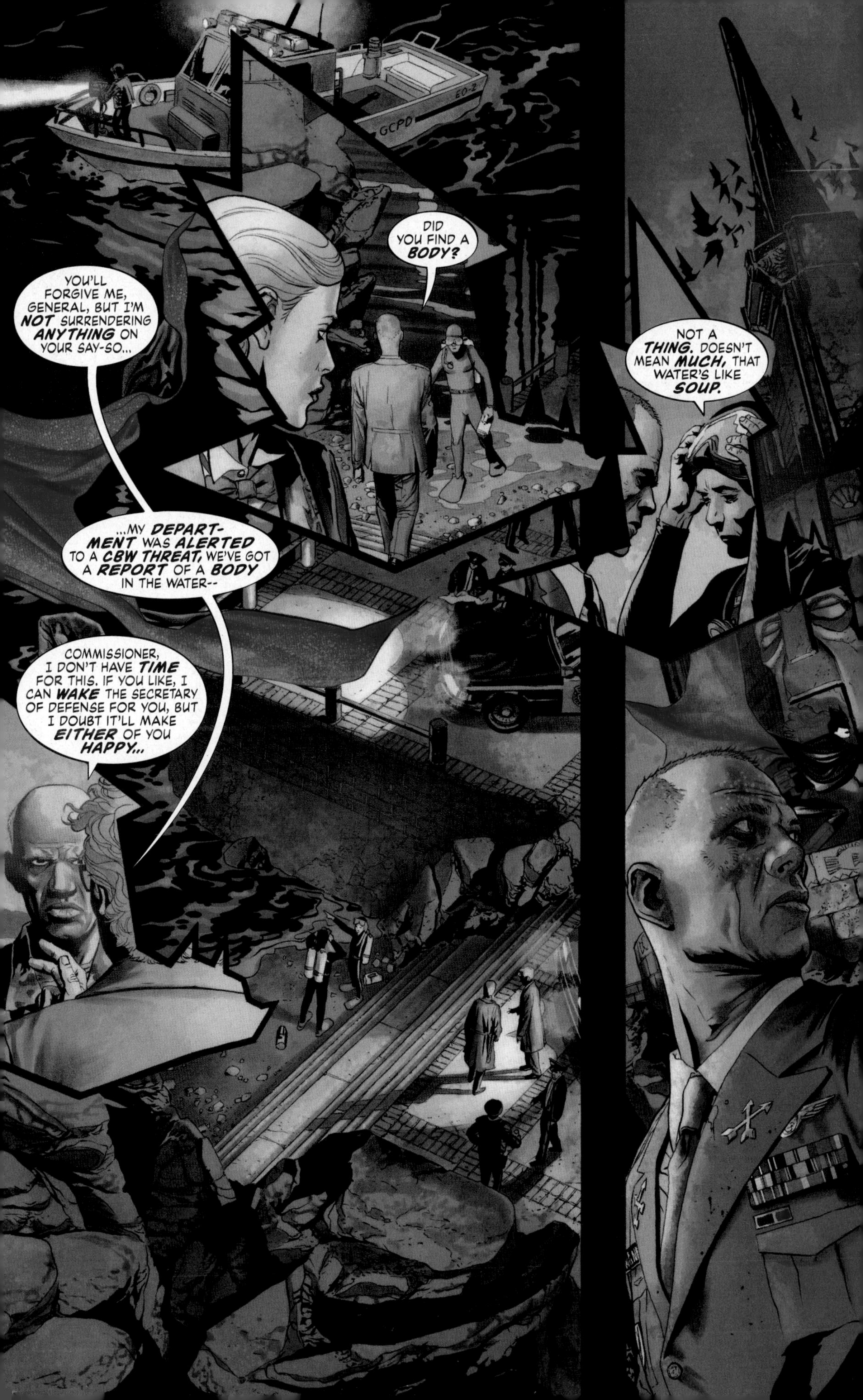

DID YOU FIND A BODY?
NOT A THING. DOESN'T MEAN MUCH, THAT WATER'S LIKE SOUP.
YOU'LL FORGIVE ME, GENERAL, BUT I'M NOT SURRENDERING ANYTHING ON YOUR SAY-SO...
...MY DEPART-MENT WAS ALERTED TO A CBW THREAT, WE'VE GOT A REPORT OF A BODY IN THE WATER--
COMMISSIONER, I DON'T HAVE TIME FOR THIS. IF YOU LIKE, I CAN WAKE THE SECRETARY OF DEFENSE FOR YOU, BUT I DOUBT IT'LL MAKE EITHER OF YOU HAPPY...
GCPD
EO-2

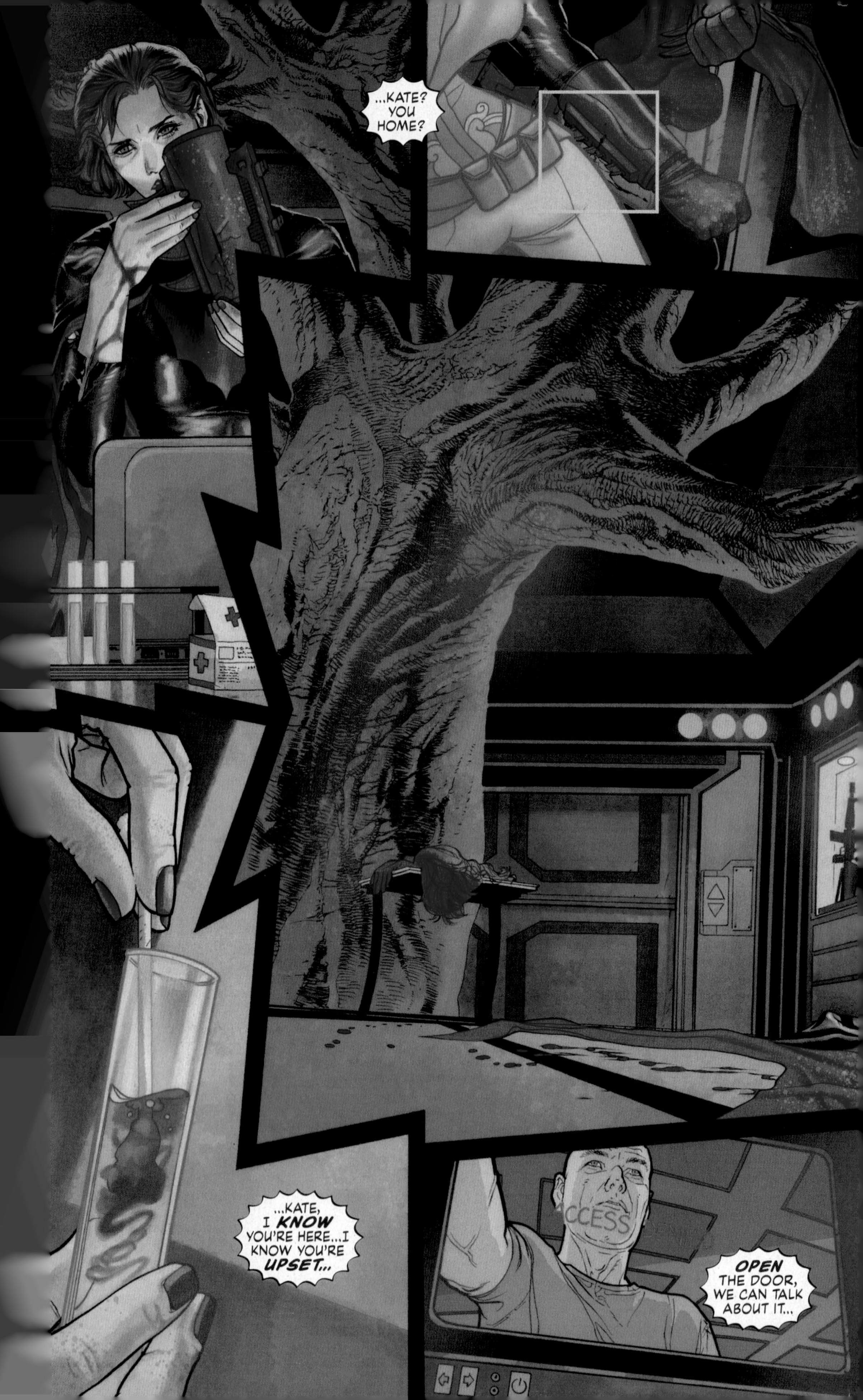
...KATE? YOU HOME?
...KATE, I KNOW YOU'RE HERE...I KNOW YOU'RE UPSET...
CCESS
OPEN THE DOOR, WE CAN TALK ABOUT IT...

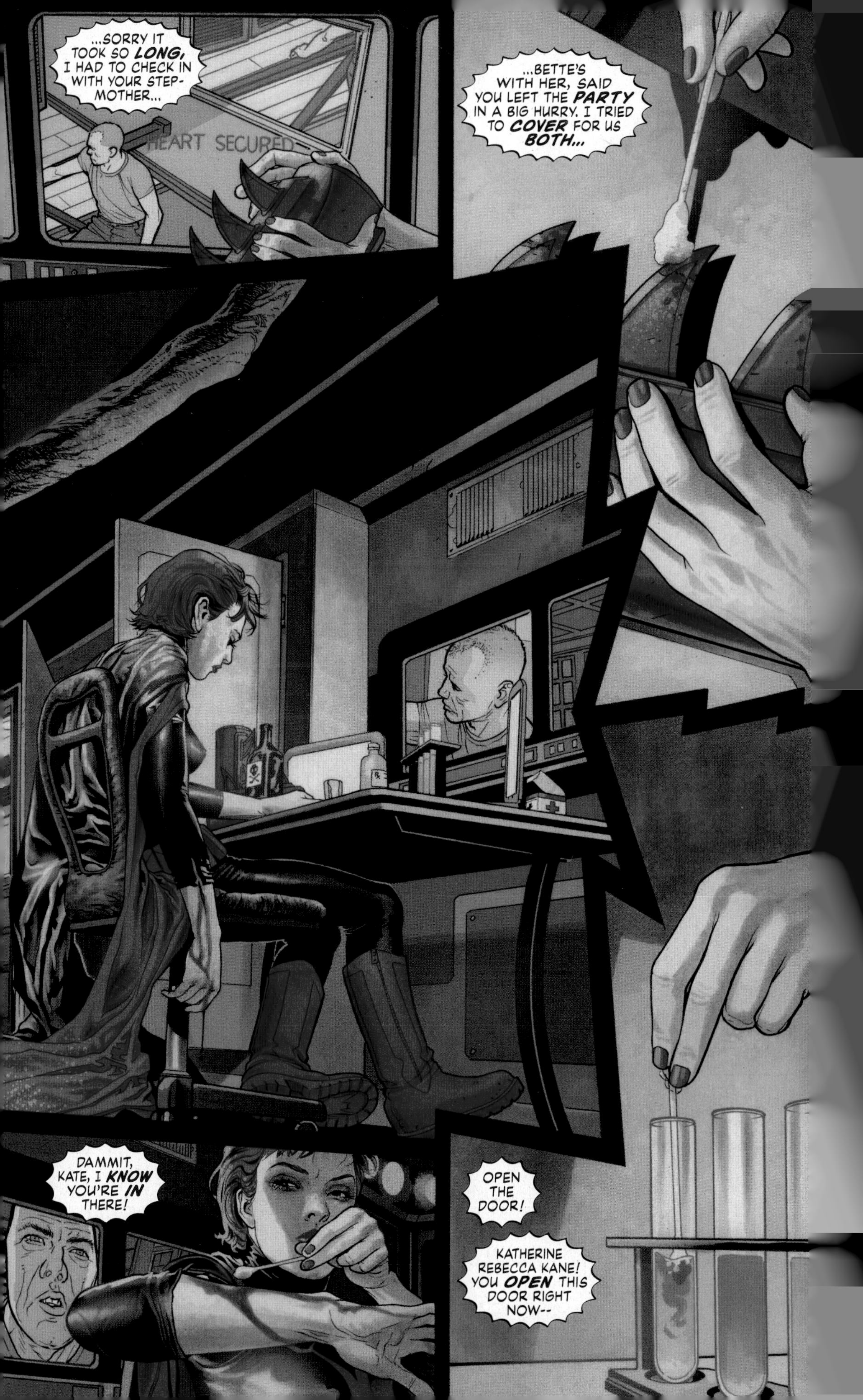
...SORRY IT TOOK SO LONG, I HAD TO CHECK IN WITH YOUR STEP-MOTHER...
HEART SECURED
...BETTE'S WITH HER, SAID YOU LEFT THE PARTY IN A BIG HURRY. I TRIED TO COVER FOR US BOTH...
DAMMIT, KATE, I KNOW YOU'RE IN THERE!
OPEN THE DOOR!
KATHERINE REBECCA KANE! YOU OPEN THIS DOOR RIGHT NOW--

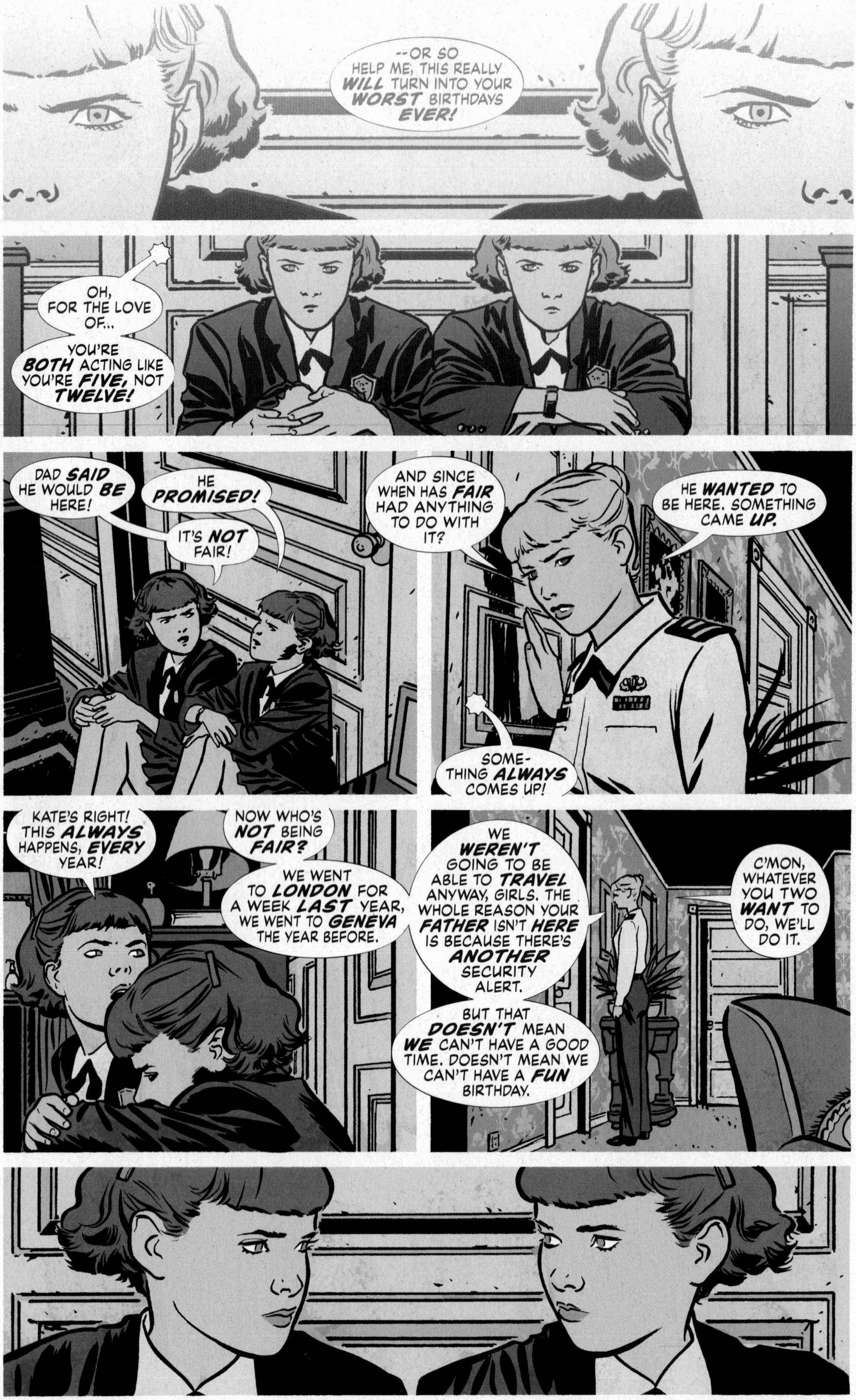
--OR SO HELP ME, THIS REALLY WILL TURN INTO YOUR WORST BIRTHDAYS EVER!
OH, FOR THE LOVE OF...
YOU'RE BOTH ACTING LIKE YOU'RE FIVE, NOT TWELVE!
DAD SAID HE WOULD BE HERE!
HE PROMISED!
IT'S NOT FAIR!
AND SINCE WHEN HAS FAIR HAD ANYTHING TO DO WITH IT?
HE WANTED TO BE HERE. SOMETHING CAME UP.
SOME-THING ALWAYS COMES UP!
KATE'S RIGHT! THIS ALWAYS HAPPENS, EVERY YEAR!
NOW WHO'S NOT BEING FAIR?
WE WENT TO LONDON FOR A WEEK LAST YEAR, WE WENT TO GENEVA THE YEAR BEFORE.
WE WEREN'T GOING TO BE ABLE TO TRAVEL ANYWAY, GIRLS. THE WHOLE REASON YOUR FATHER ISN'T HERE IS BECAUSE THERE'S ANOTHER SECURITY ALERT.
BUT THAT DOESN'T MEAN WE CAN'T HAVE A GOOD TIME. DOESN'T MEAN WE CAN'T HAVE A FUN BIRTHDAY.
C'MON, WHATEVER YOU TWO WANT TO DO, WE'LL DO IT.

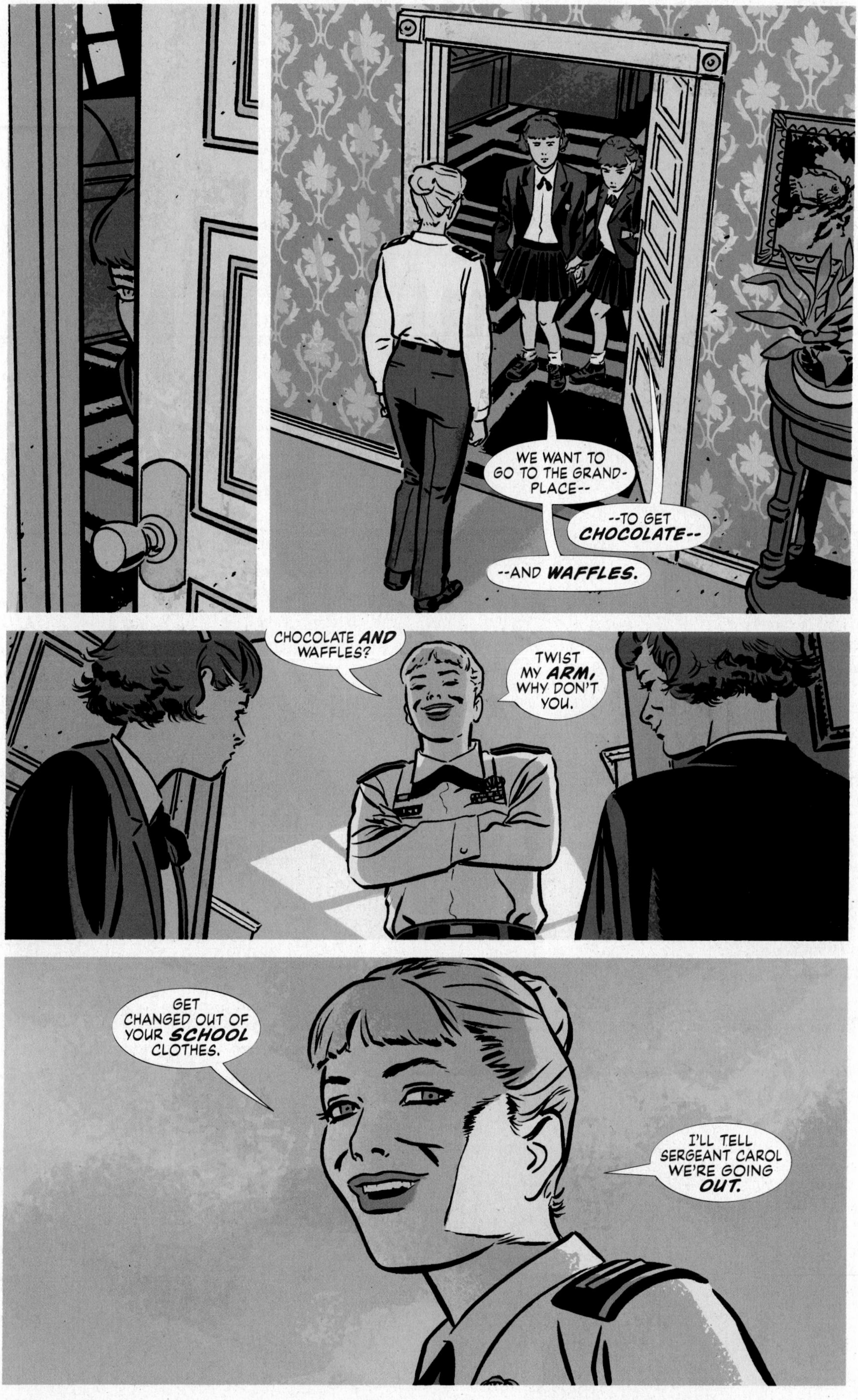
WE WANT TO GO TO THE GRAND-PLACE--
--TO GET CHOCOLATE--
--AND WAFFLES.
CHOCOLATE AND WAFFLES?
TWIST MY ARM, WHY DON'T YOU.
GET CHANGED OUT OF YOUR SCHOOL CLOTHES.
I'LL TELL SERGEANT CAROL WE'RE GOING OUT.

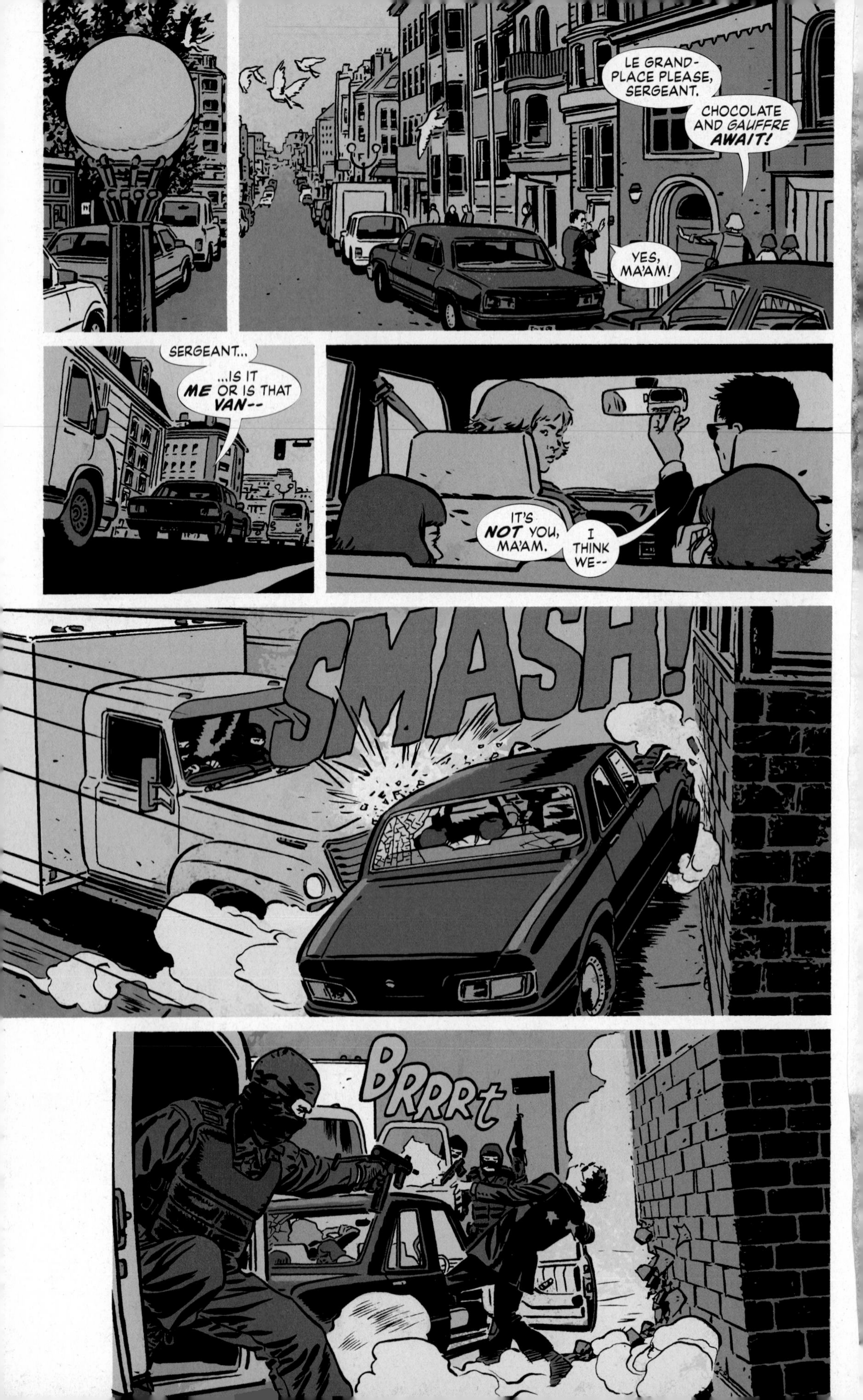
LE GRAND-PLACE PLEASE, SERGEANT.
CHOCOLATE AND GAUFFRE AWAIT!
YES, MA'AM!
SERGEANT...
...IS IT ME OR IS THAT VAN--
IT'S NOT YOU, MA'AM.
I THINK WE--
SMASH!
BRRRt

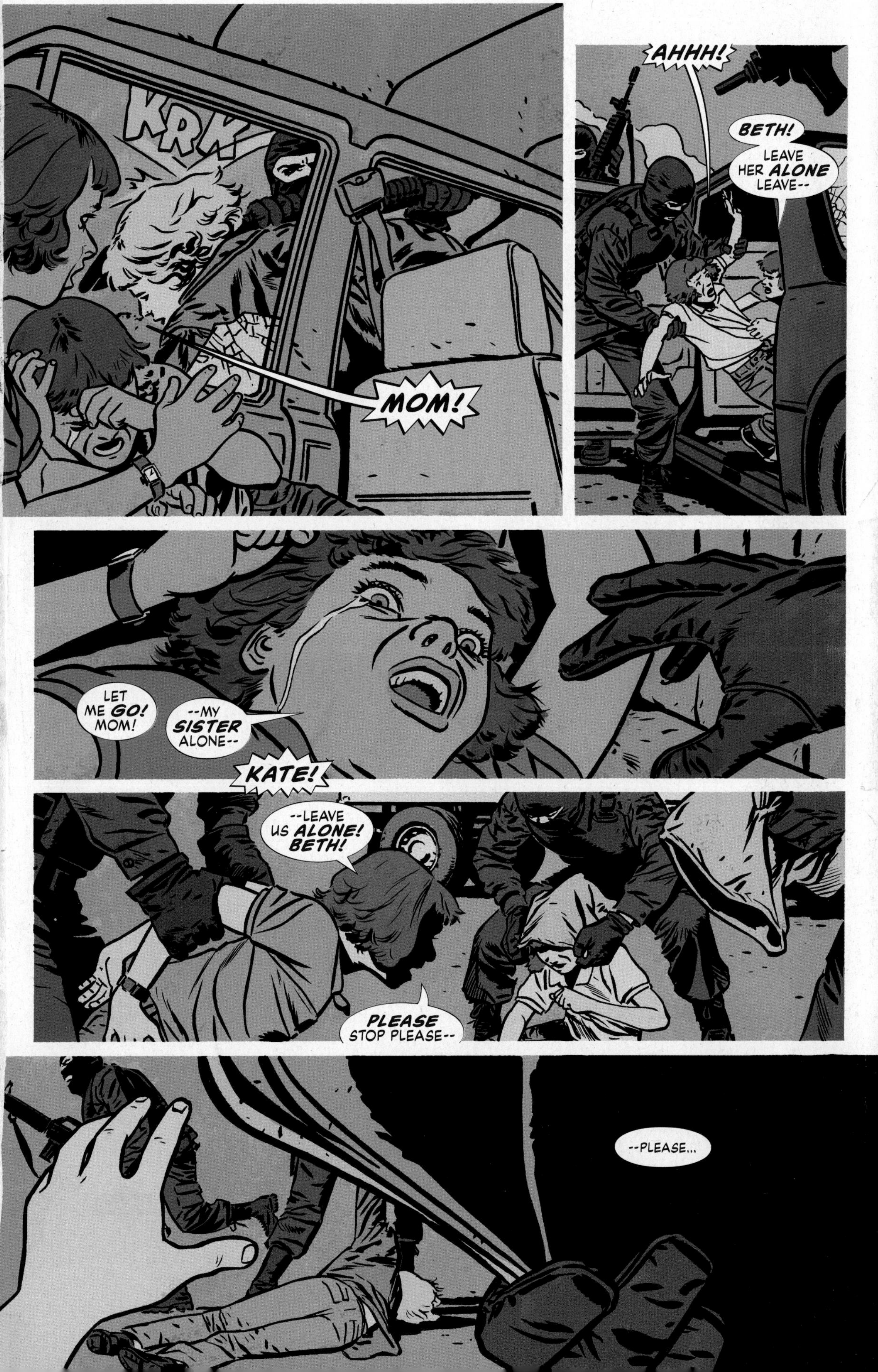
KRK
MOM!
AHHH!
BETH!
LEAVE HER ALONE LEAVE--
LET ME GO! MOM!
--MY SISTER ALONE--
KATE!
--LEAVE US ALONE! BETH!
PLEASE STOP PLEASE--
--PLEASE...

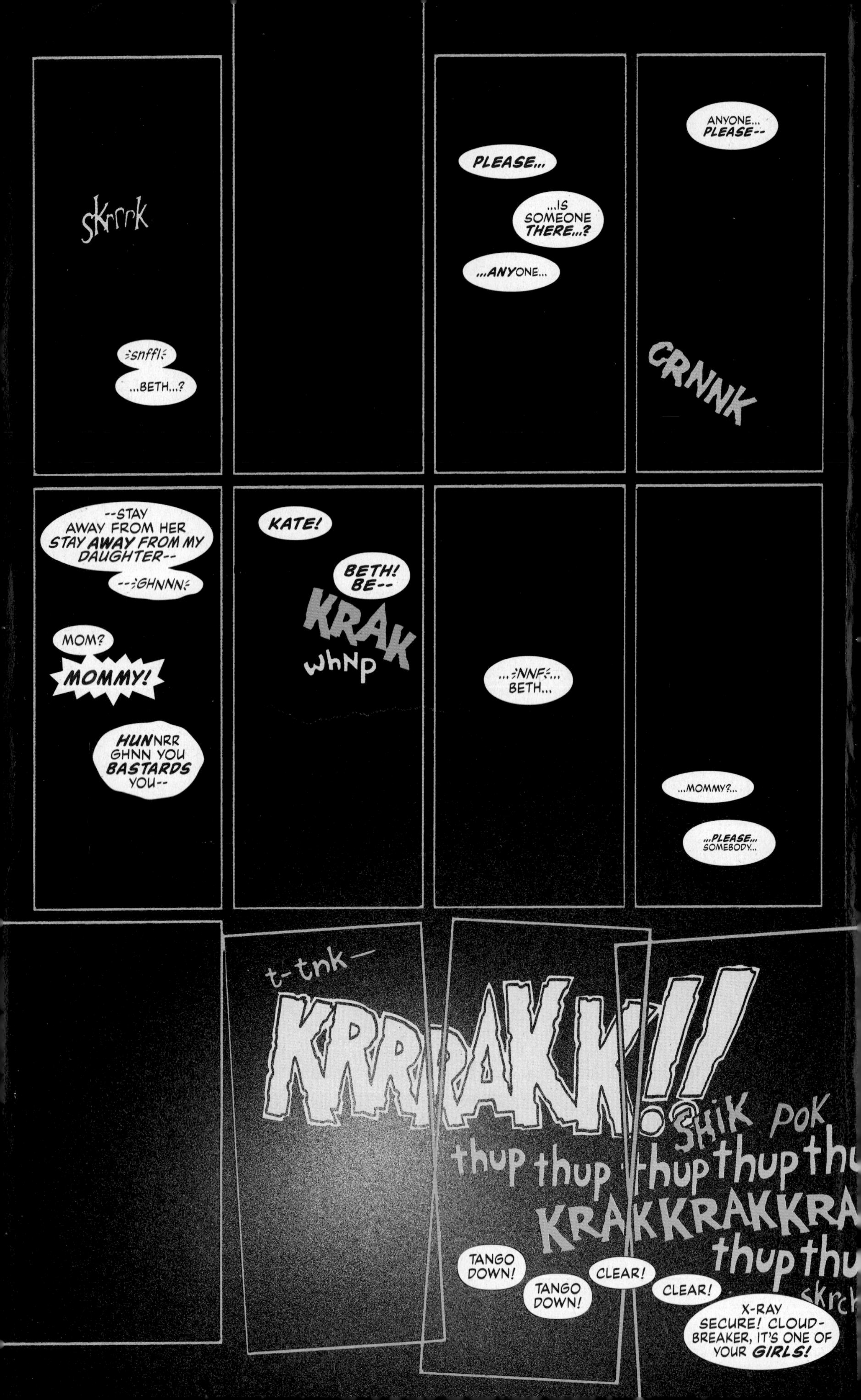

sKrrrk
snffl
...BETH...?
PLEASE...
...IS SOMEONE THERE...?
...ANYONE...
ANYONE... PLEASE--
CRNNK
--STAY AWAY FROM HER STAY AWAY FROM MY DAUGHTER--
--GHNNN
MOM?
MOMMY!
HUNNRR GHNN YOU BASTARDS YOU--
KATE!
BETH! BE--
KRAK
whNp
...NNF... BETH...
...MOMMY?...
...PLEASE... SOMEBODY...
t-tnk—
KRRRAKK!!
SHIK POK
thup thup thup thup thu
KRAKKRAKKRA
thup thu
TANGO DOWN!
TANGO DOWN!
CLEAR!
CLEAR!
X-RAY SECURE! CLOUDBREAKER, IT'S ONE OF YOUR GIRLS!

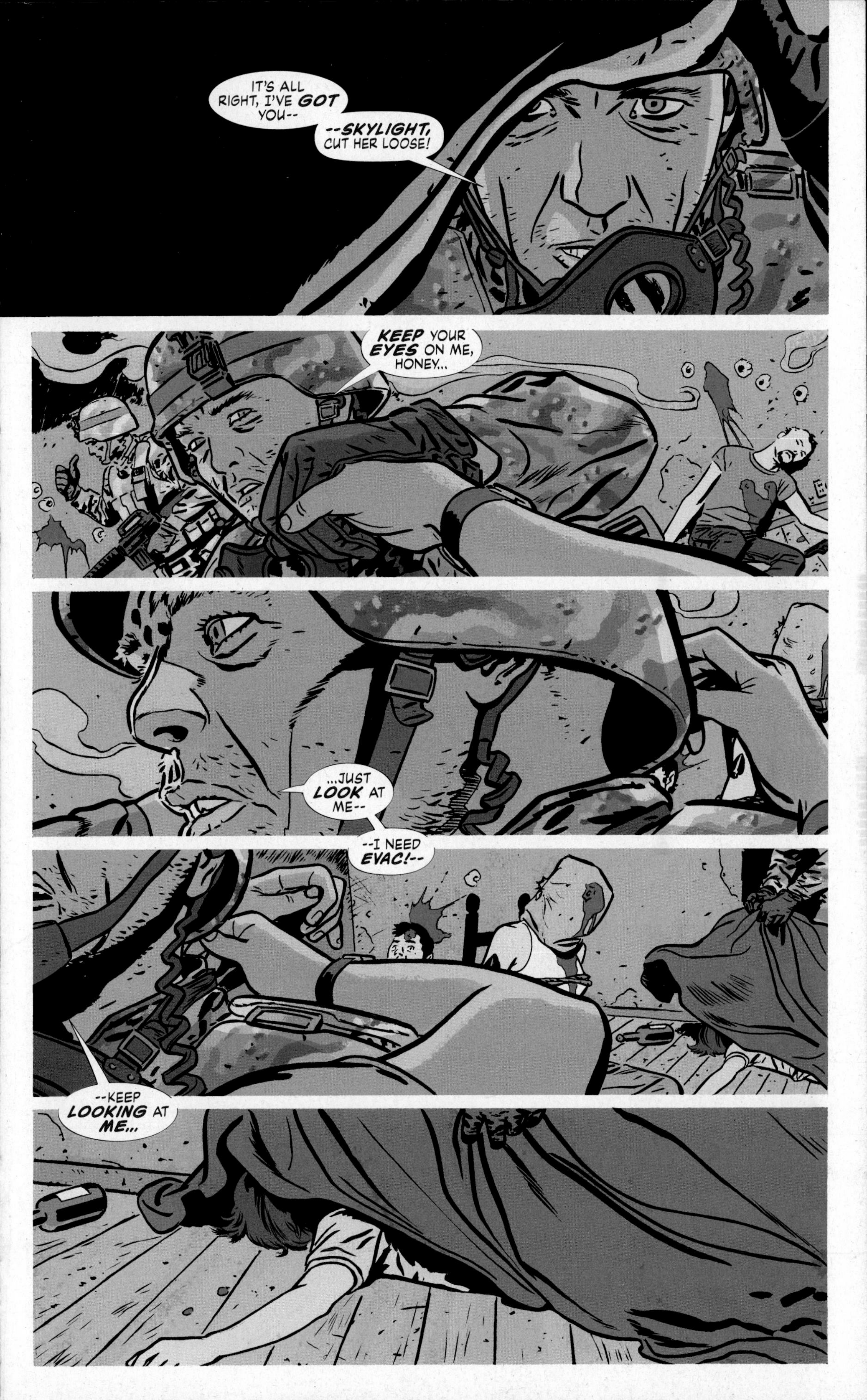
IT'S ALL RIGHT, I'VE GOT YOU--
--SKYLIGHT, CUT HER LOOSE!
KEEP YOUR EYES ON ME, HONEY...
...JUST LOOK AT ME--
--I NEED EVAC!--
--KEEP LOOKING AT ME...

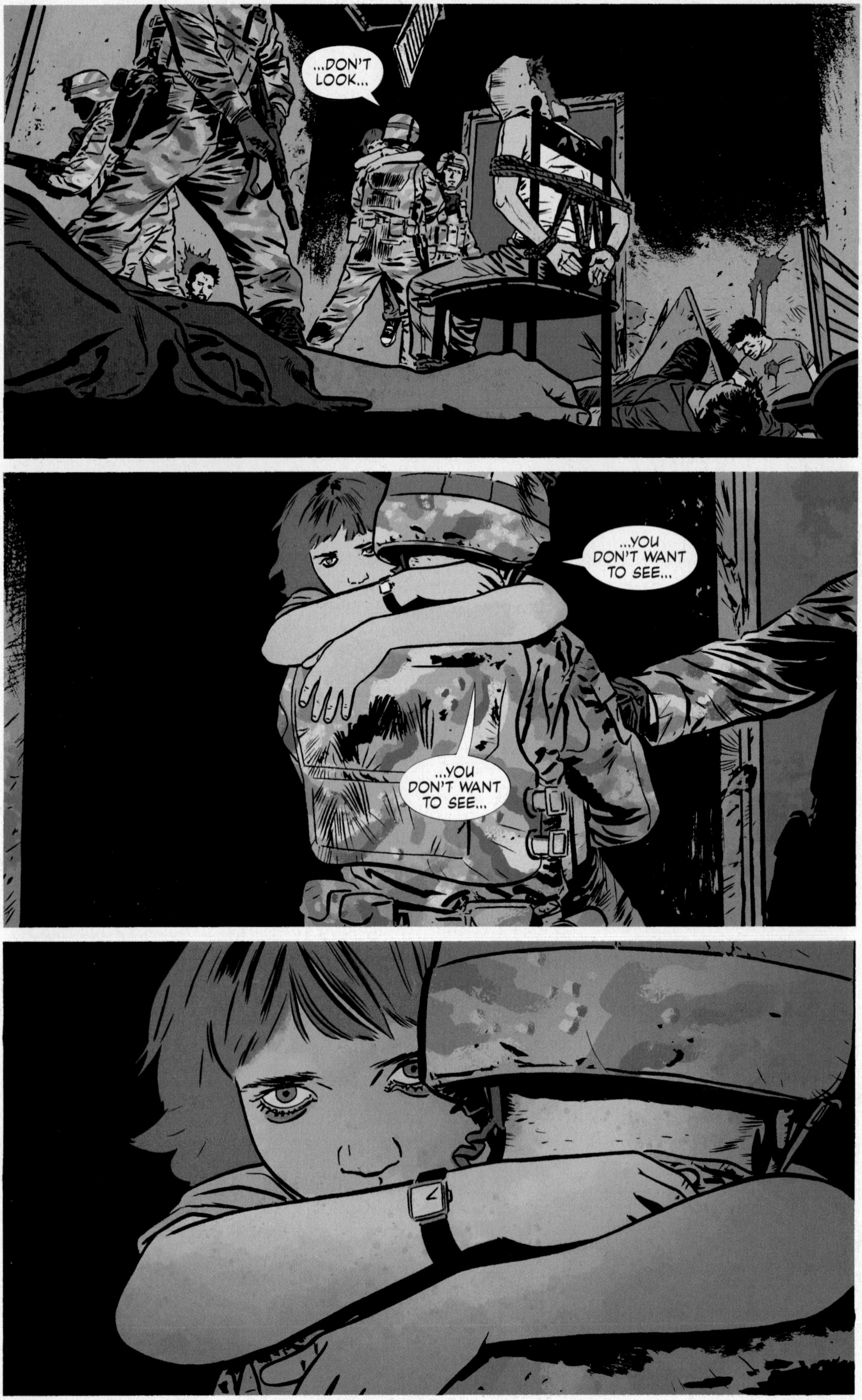
...DON'T LOOK...
...YOU DON'T WANT TO SEE...
...YOU DON'T WANT TO SEE...

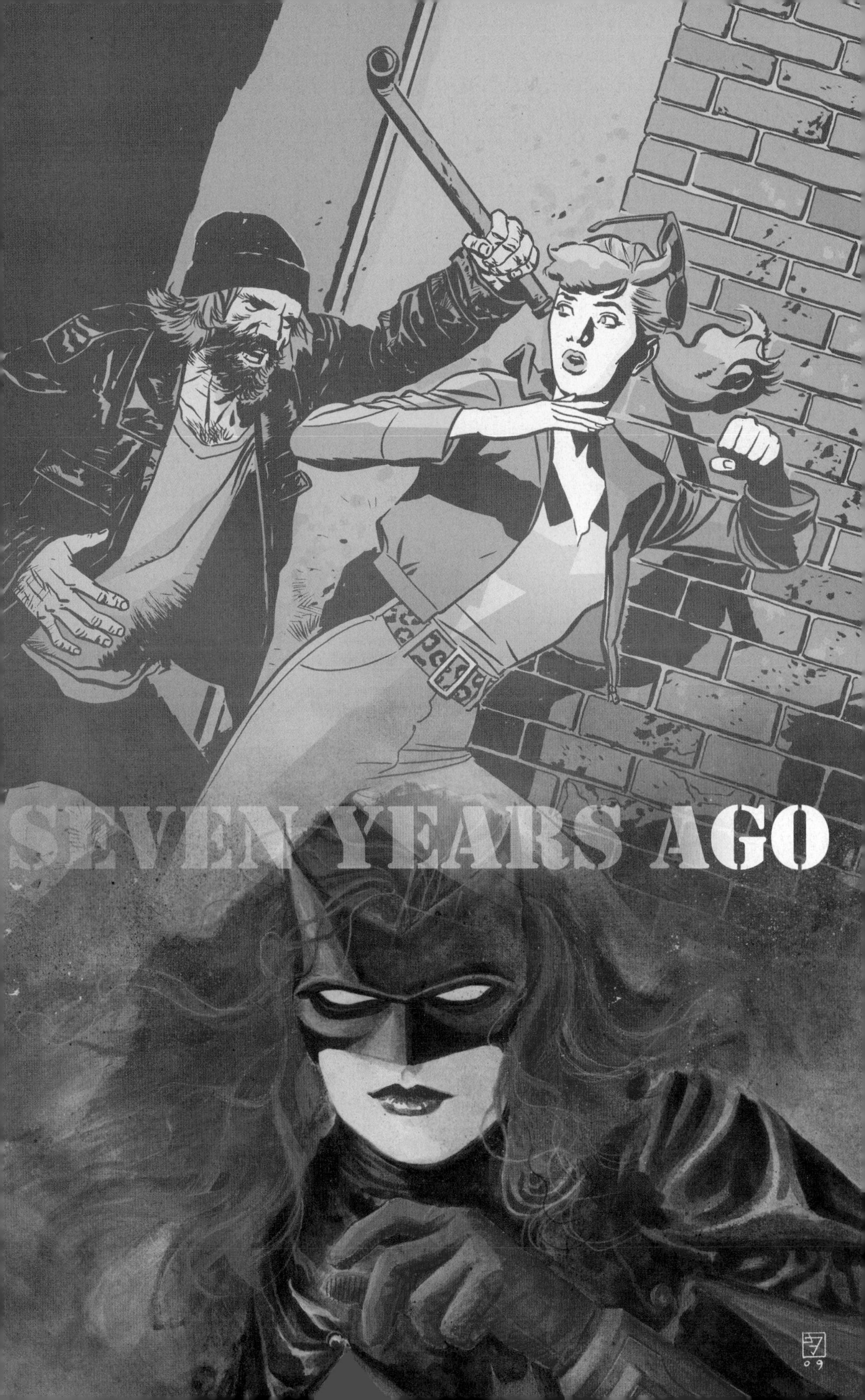
SEVEN YEARS AGO

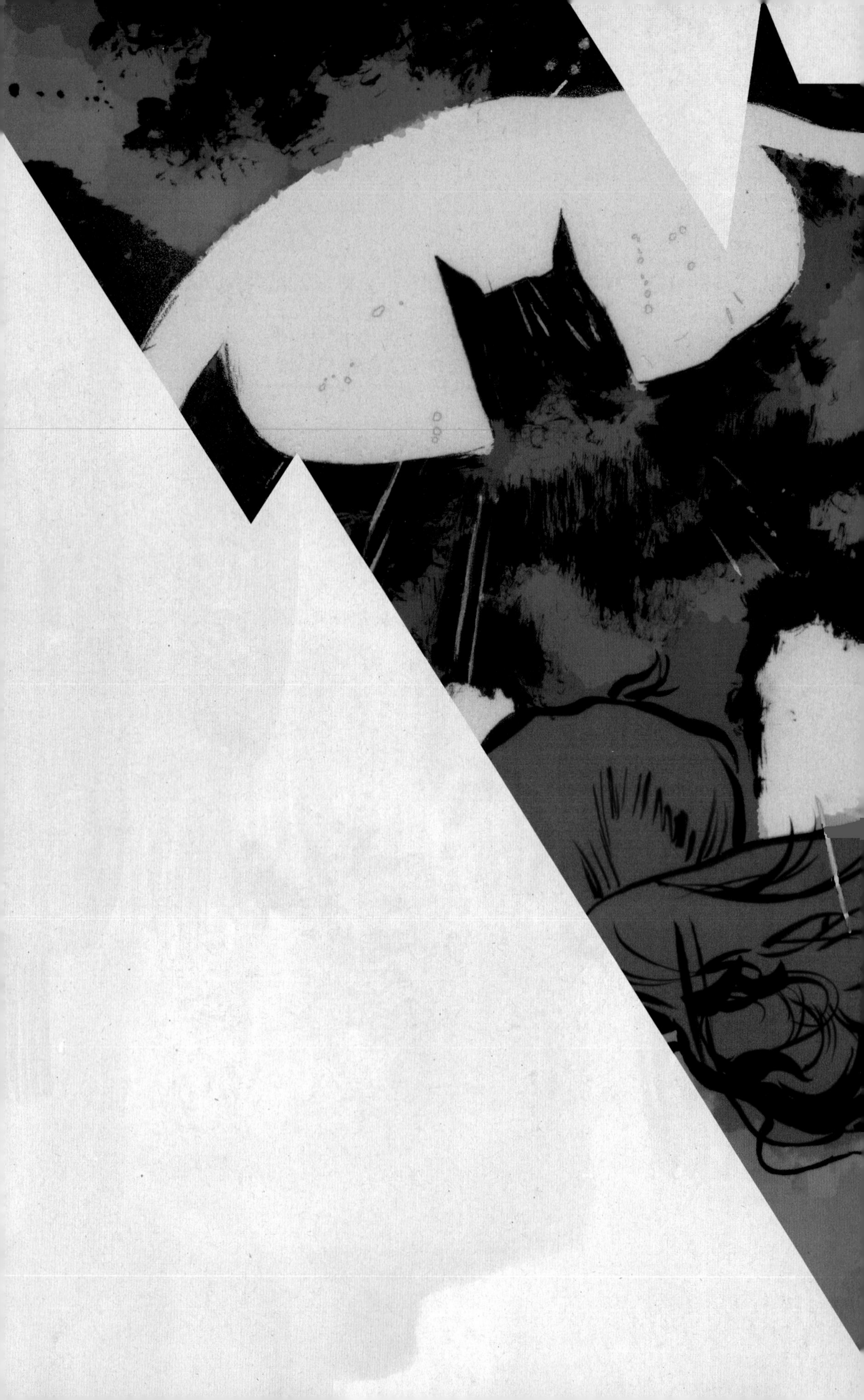

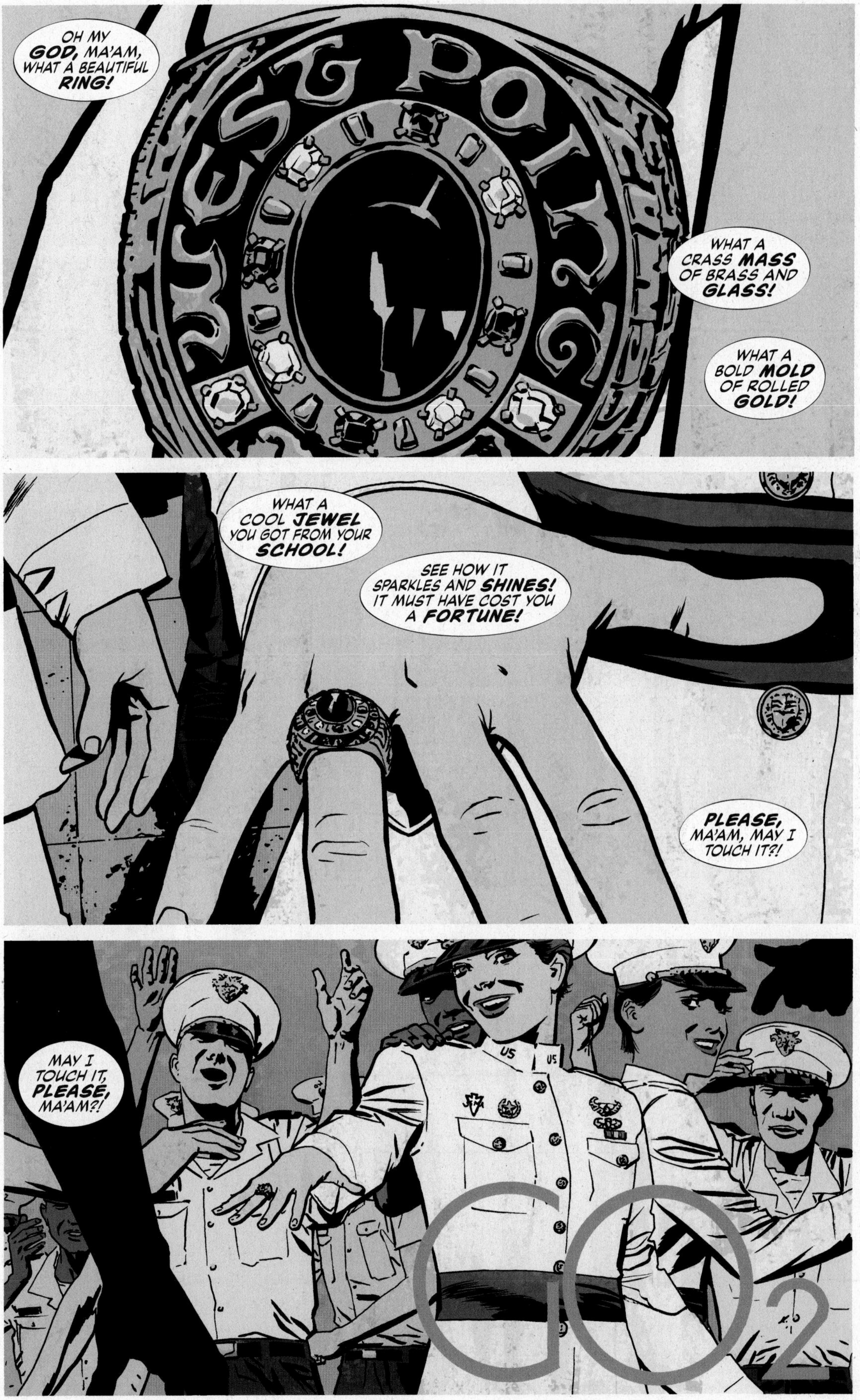

OH MY GOD, MA'AM, WHAT A BEAUTIFUL RING!
WHAT A CRASS MASS OF BRASS AND GLASS!
WHAT A BOLD MOLD OF ROLLED GOLD!
WHAT A COOL JEWEL YOU GOT FROM YOUR SCHOOL!
SEE HOW IT SPARKLES AND SHINES! IT MUST HAVE COST YOU A FORTUNE!
PLEASE, MA'AM, MAY I TOUCH IT?!
MAY I TOUCH IT, PLEASE, MA'AM?!
GO2

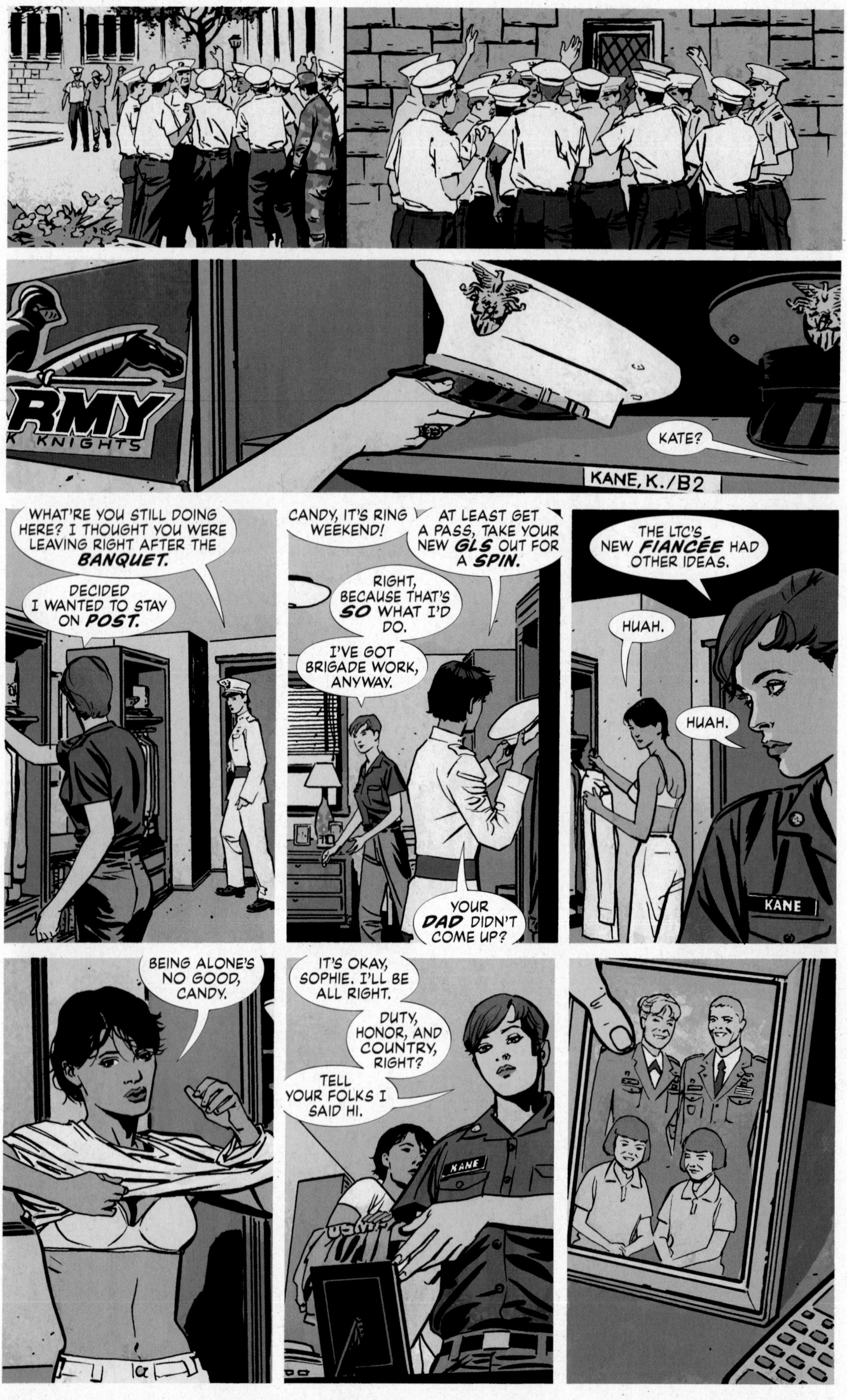

RMY
K KNIGHTS
KATE?
KANE, K./B2
WHAT'RE YOU STILL DOING HERE? I THOUGHT YOU WERE LEAVING RIGHT AFTER THE **BANQUET.**
DECIDED I WANTED TO STAY ON **POST.**
CANDY, IT'S RING WEEKEND!
AT LEAST GET A PASS, TAKE YOUR NEW **GLS** OUT FOR A **SPIN.**
RIGHT, BECAUSE THAT'S **SO** WHAT I'D DO.
I'VE GOT BRIGADE WORK, ANYWAY.
YOUR **DAD** DIDN'T COME UP?
THE LTC'S NEW **FIANCÉE** HAD OTHER IDEAS.
HUAH.
HUAH.
KANE
BEING ALONE'S NO GOOD, CANDY.
IT'S OKAY, SOPHIE. I'LL BE ALL RIGHT.
DUTY, HONOR, AND COUNTRY, RIGHT?
TELL YOUR FOLKS I SAID HI.
KANE

GREG RUCKA
WRITER

J.H. WILLIAMS III
ARTIST/COVER

DAVE STEWART
COLORS

TODD KLEIN
LETTERS

HARVEY RICHARDS
ASST. EDITOR

MICHAEL SIGLAIN
LETTERS

ALEX ROSS: VARIANT COVER

BATMAN CREATED BY BOB KANE

SPECIAL THANKS TO 1LT DANIEL CHOI (USMA 2003) FOR HIS GENEROUS ASSISTANCE IN RESEARCH FOR THIS ISSUE

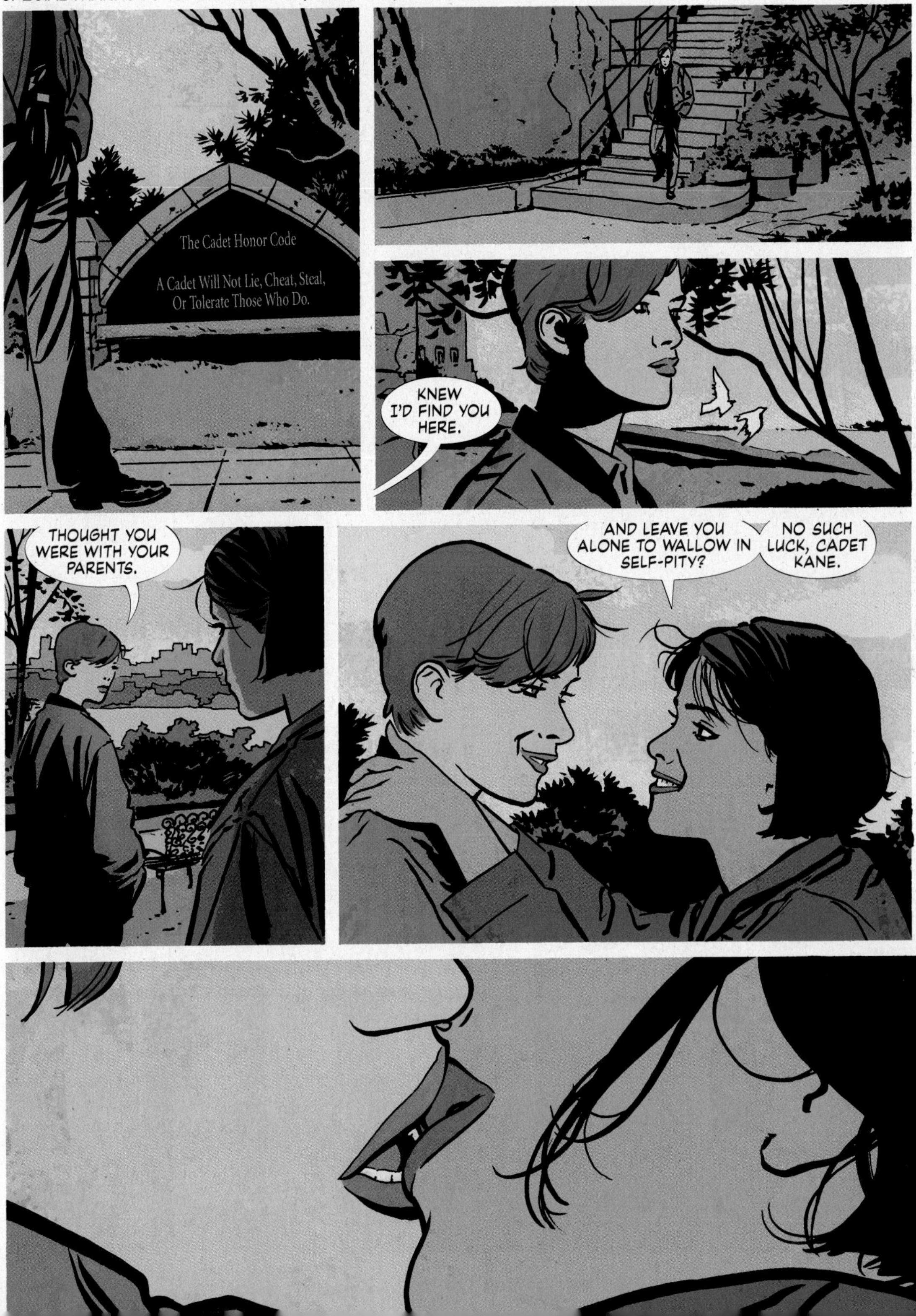

The Cadet Honor Code
A Cadet Will Not Lie, Cheat, Steal, Or Tolerate Those Who Do.
KNEW I'D FIND YOU HERE.
THOUGHT YOU WERE WITH YOUR PARENTS.
AND LEAVE YOU ALONE TO WALLOW IN SELF-PITY?
NO SUCH LUCK, CADET KANE.

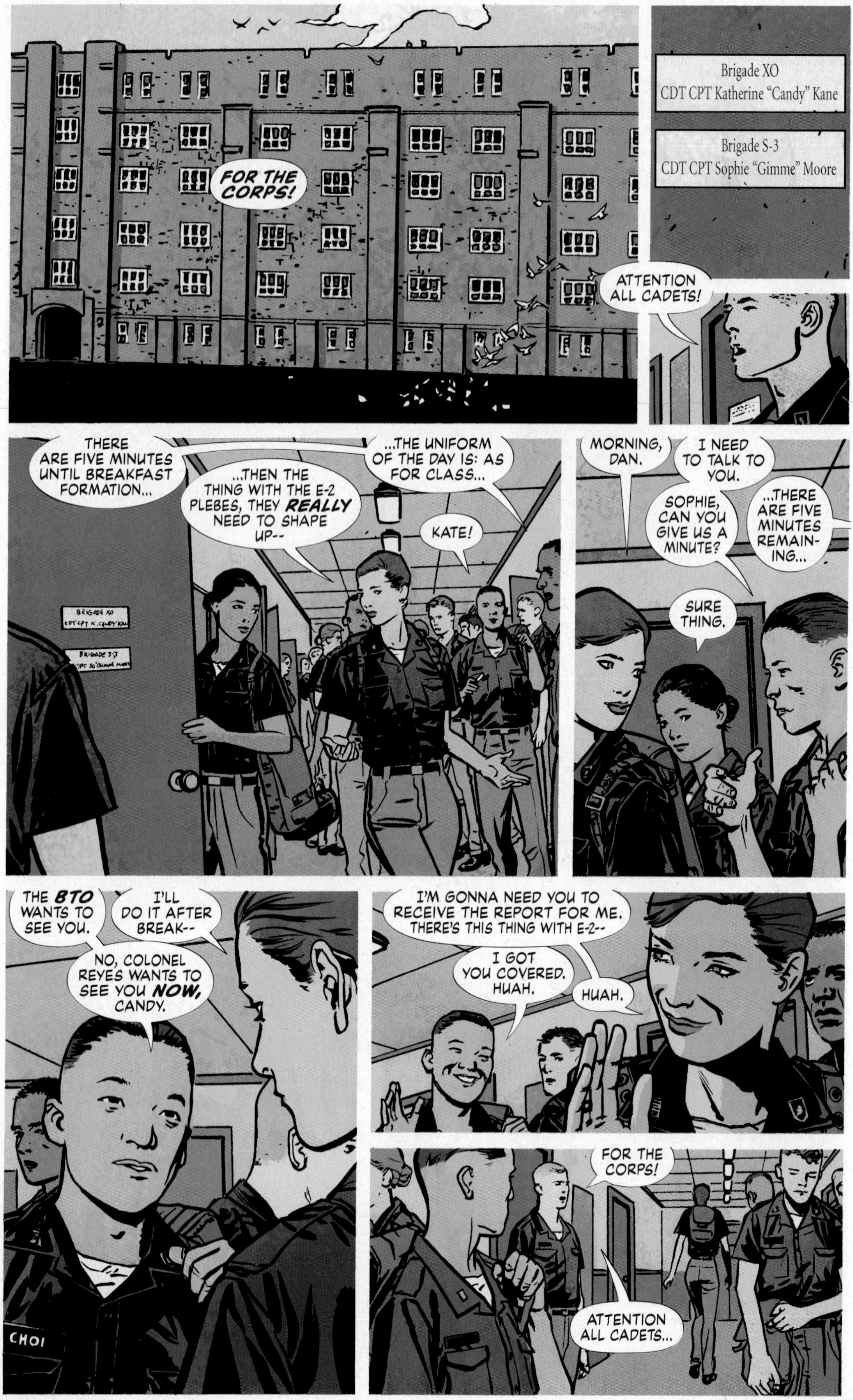
FOR THE CORPS!
Brigade XO
CDT CPT Katherine "Candy" Kane
Brigade S-3
CDT CPT Sophie "Gimme" Moore
ATTENTION ALL CADETS!
THERE ARE FIVE MINUTES UNTIL BREAKFAST FORMATION...
...THE UNIFORM OF THE DAY IS: AS FOR CLASS...
...THEN THE THING WITH THE E-2 PLEBES, THEY REALLY NEED TO SHAPE UP--
KATE!
MORNING, DAN.
I NEED TO TALK TO YOU.
SOPHIE, CAN YOU GIVE US A MINUTE?
...THERE ARE FIVE MINUTES REMAIN-ING...
SURE THING.
THE BTO WANTS TO SEE YOU.
I'LL DO IT AFTER BREAK--
NO, COLONEL REYES WANTS TO SEE YOU NOW, CANDY.
CHOI
I'M GONNA NEED YOU TO RECEIVE THE REPORT FOR ME. THERE'S THIS THING WITH E-2--
I GOT YOU COVERED. HUAH.
HUAH.
FOR THE CORPS!
ATTENTION ALL CADETS...

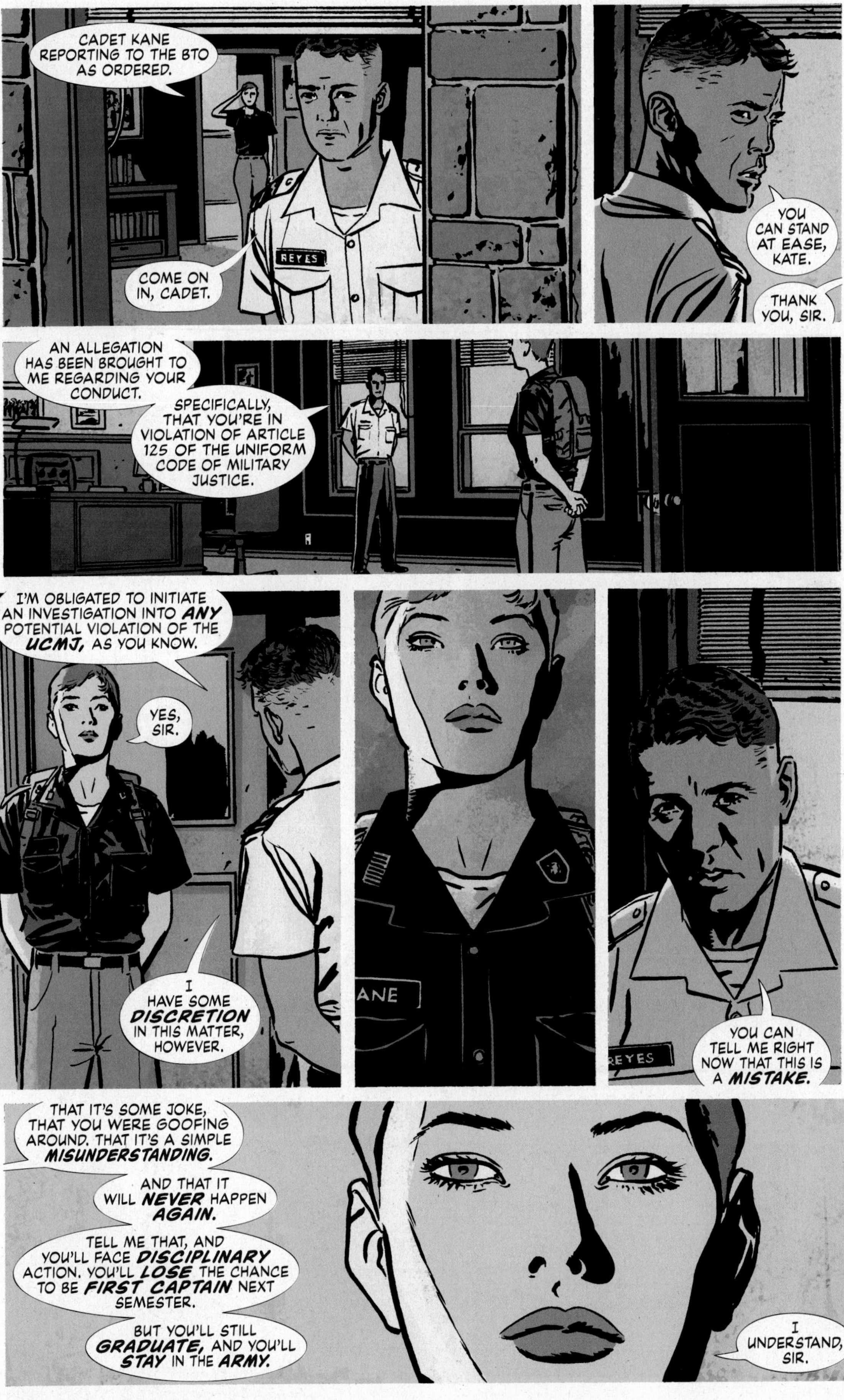
CADET KANE REPORTING TO THE BTO AS ORDERED.
COME ON IN, CADET.
REYES
YOU CAN STAND AT EASE, KATE.
THANK YOU, SIR.
AN ALLEGATION HAS BEEN BROUGHT TO ME REGARDING YOUR CONDUCT.
SPECIFICALLY, THAT YOU'RE IN VIOLATION OF ARTICLE 125 OF THE UNIFORM CODE OF MILITARY JUSTICE.
I'M OBLIGATED TO INITIATE AN INVESTIGATION INTO ANY POTENTIAL VIOLATION OF THE UCMJ, AS YOU KNOW.
YES, SIR.
I HAVE SOME DISCRETION IN THIS MATTER, HOWEVER.
ANE
REYES
YOU CAN TELL ME RIGHT NOW THAT THIS IS A MISTAKE.
THAT IT'S SOME JOKE, THAT YOU WERE GOOFING AROUND. THAT IT'S A SIMPLE MISUNDERSTANDING.
AND THAT IT WILL NEVER HAPPEN AGAIN.
TELL ME THAT, AND YOU'LL FACE DISCIPLINARY ACTION. YOU'LL LOSE THE CHANCE TO BE FIRST CAPTAIN NEXT SEMESTER.
BUT YOU'LL STILL GRADUATE, AND YOU'LL STAY IN THE ARMY.
I UNDERSTAND, SIR.

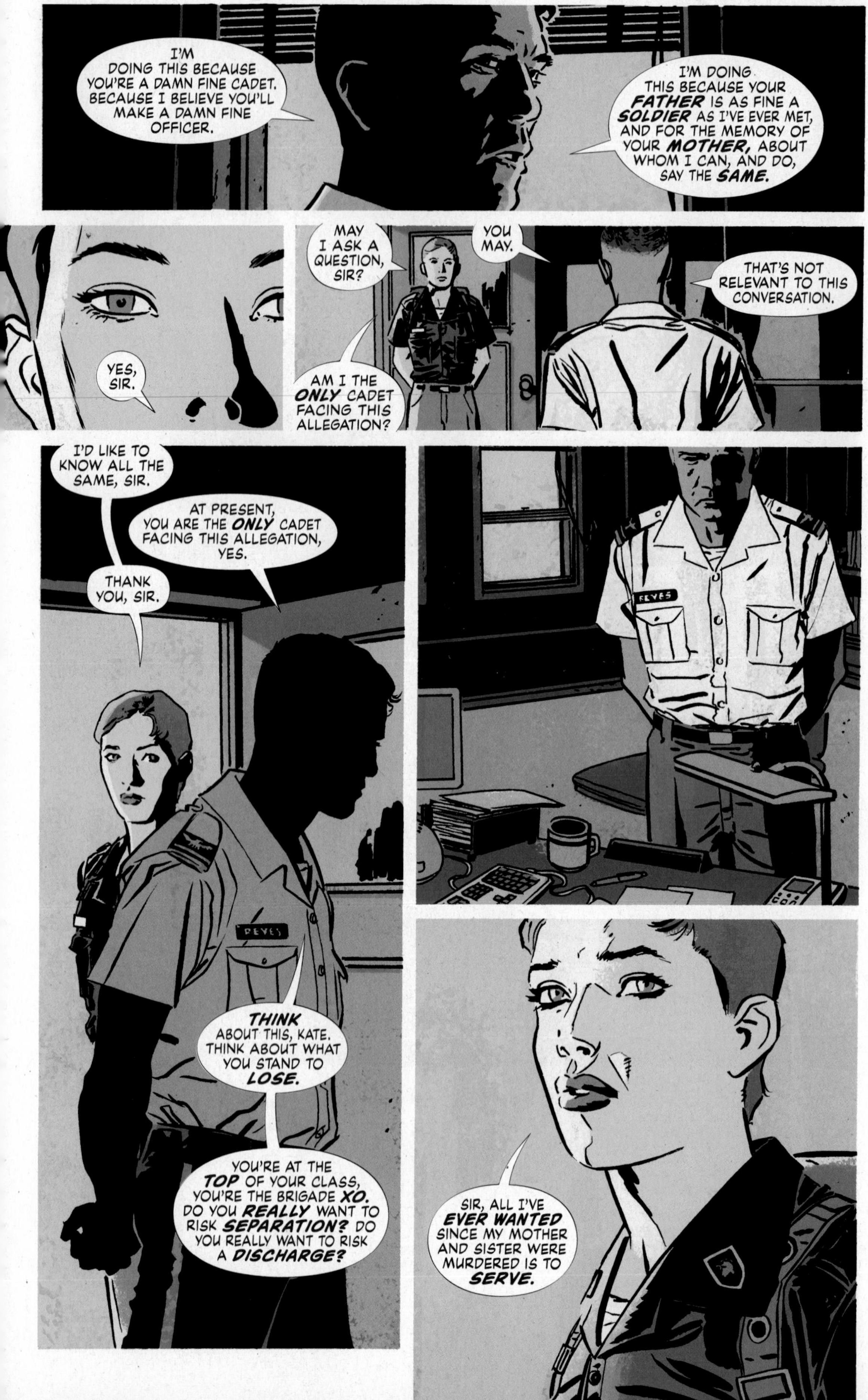
I'M DOING THIS BECAUSE YOU'RE A DAMN FINE CADET. BECAUSE I BELIEVE YOU'LL MAKE A DAMN FINE OFFICER.
I'M DOING THIS BECAUSE YOUR FATHER IS AS FINE A SOLDIER AS I'VE EVER MET, AND FOR THE MEMORY OF YOUR MOTHER, ABOUT WHOM I CAN, AND DO, SAY THE SAME.
YES, SIR.
MAY I ASK A QUESTION, SIR?
YOU MAY.
AM I THE ONLY CADET FACING THIS ALLEGATION?
THAT'S NOT RELEVANT TO THIS CONVERSATION.
I'D LIKE TO KNOW ALL THE SAME, SIR.
AT PRESENT, YOU ARE THE ONLY CADET FACING THIS ALLEGATION, YES.
THANK YOU, SIR.
REYES
THINK ABOUT THIS, KATE. THINK ABOUT WHAT YOU STAND TO LOSE.
YOU'RE AT THE TOP OF YOUR CLASS, YOU'RE THE BRIGADE XO. DO YOU REALLY WANT TO RISK SEPARATION? DO YOU REALLY WANT TO RISK A DISCHARGE?
REYES
SIR, ALL I'VE EVER WANTED SINCE MY MOTHER AND SISTER WERE MURDERED IS TO SERVE.

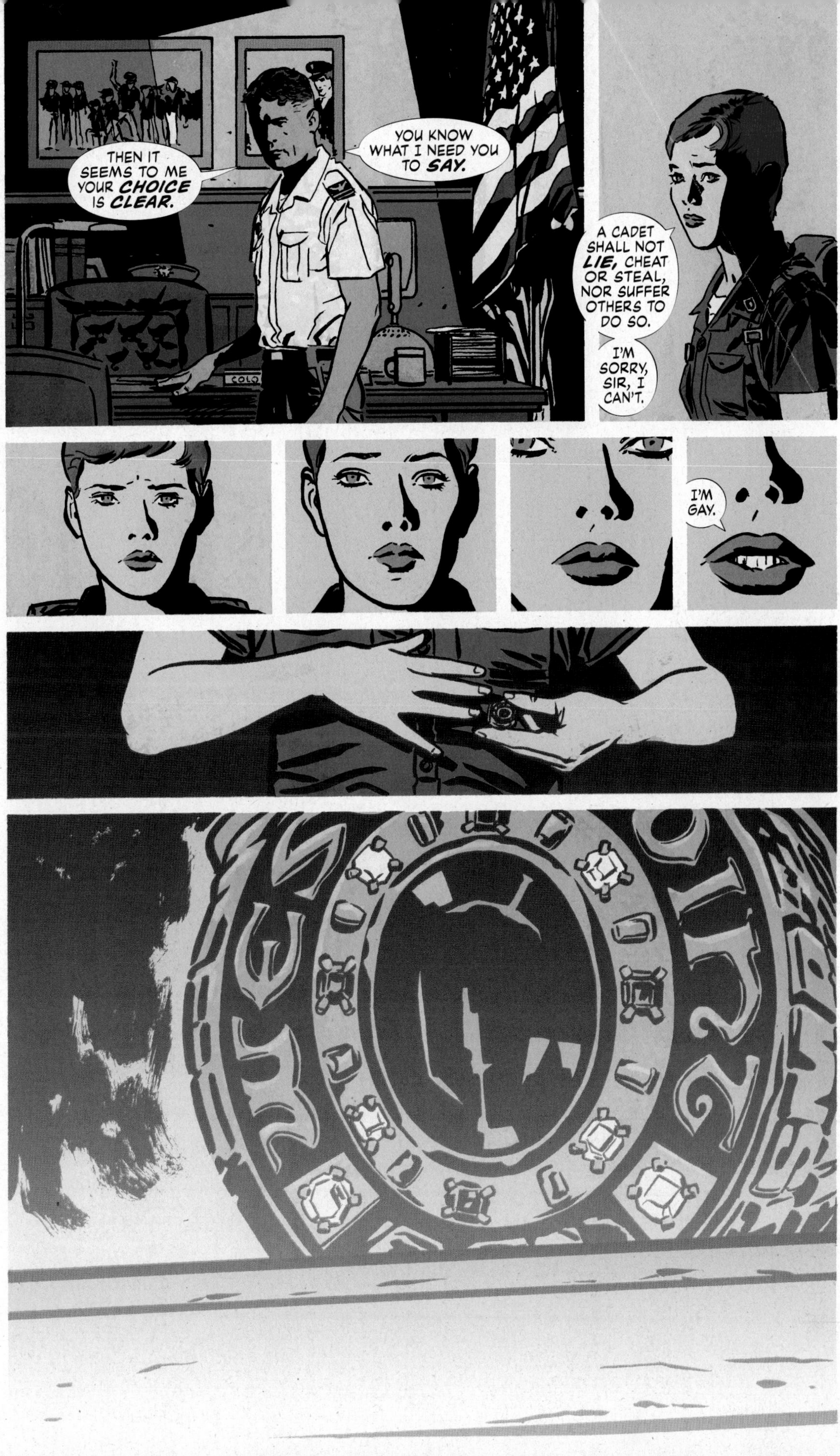
THEN IT SEEMS TO ME YOUR CHOICE IS CLEAR.
YOU KNOW WHAT I NEED YOU TO SAY.
A CADET SHALL NOT LIE, CHEAT OR STEAL, NOR SUFFER OTHERS TO DO SO.
I'M SORRY, SIR, I CAN'T.
I'M GAY.

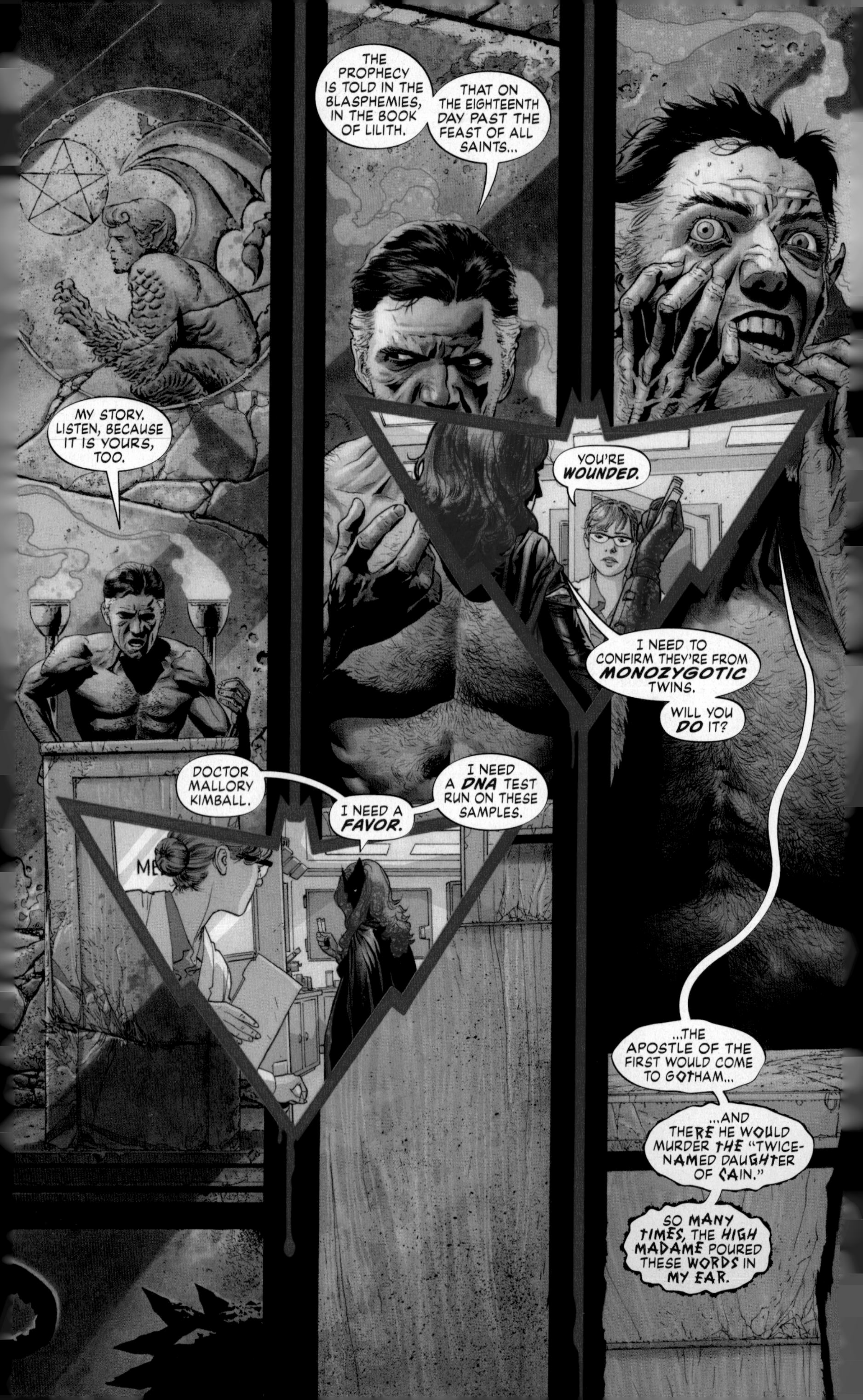

MY STORY. LISTEN, BECAUSE IT IS YOURS, TOO.
THE PROPHECY IS TOLD IN THE BLASPHEMIES, IN THE BOOK OF LILITH.
THAT ON THE EIGHTEENTH DAY PAST THE FEAST OF ALL SAINTS...
DOCTOR MALLORY KIMBALL.
I NEED A FAVOR.
I NEED A DNA TEST RUN ON THESE SAMPLES.
YOU'RE WOUNDED.
I NEED TO CONFIRM THEY'RE FROM MONOZYGOTIC TWINS.
WILL YOU DO IT?
...THE APOSTLE OF THE FIRST WOULD COME TO GOTHAM...
...AND THERE HE WOULD MURDER THE "TWICE-NAMED DAUGHTER OF CAIN."
SO MANY TIMES, THE HIGH MADAME POURED THESE WORDS IN MY EAR.

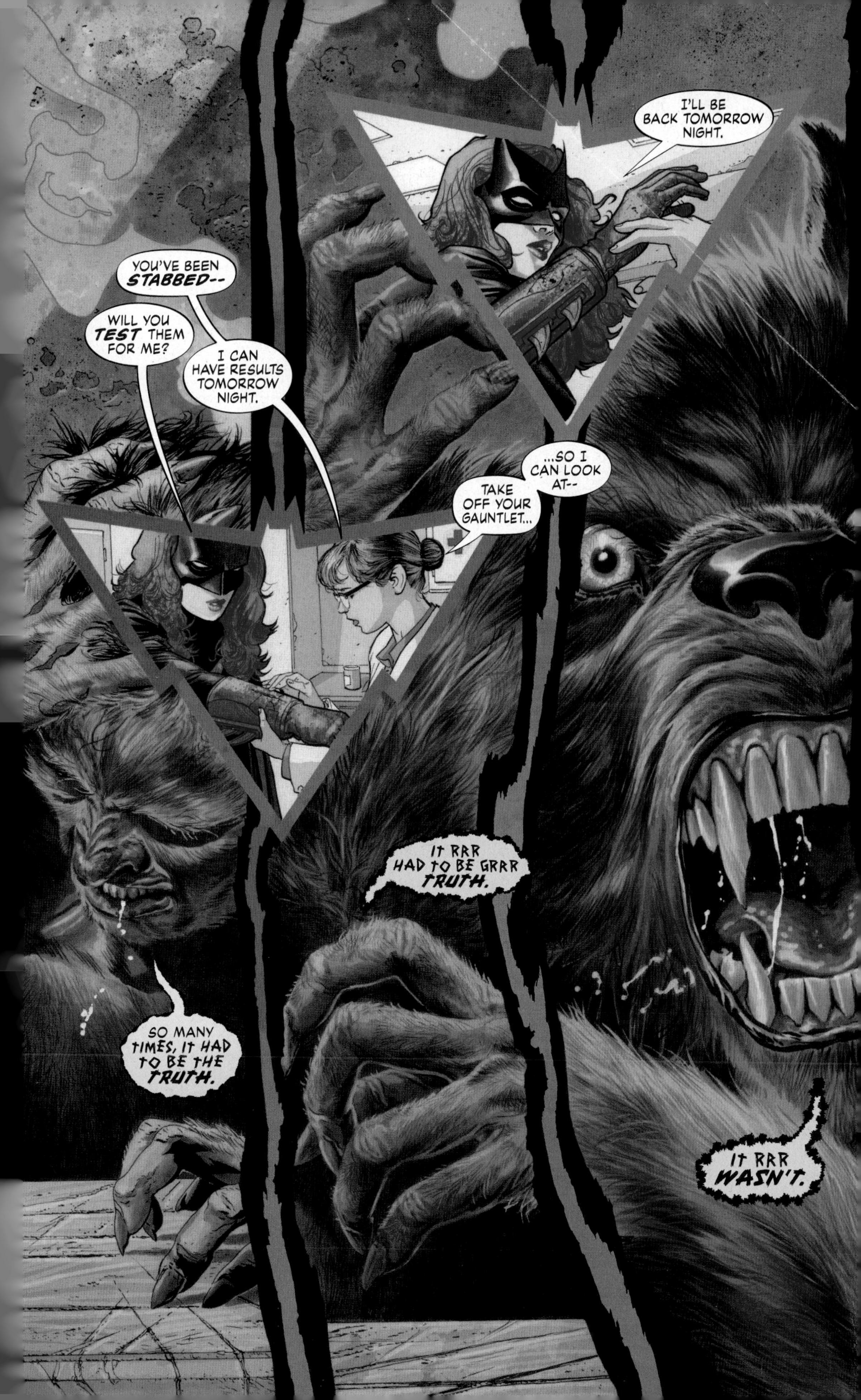
I'LL BE BACK TOMORROW NIGHT.
YOU'VE BEEN STABBED--
I CAN HAVE RESULTS TOMORROW NIGHT.
WILL YOU TEST THEM FOR ME?
TAKE OFF YOUR GAUNTLET...
...SO I CAN LOOK AT--
IT RRR HAD TO BE GRRR TRUTH.
SO MANY TIMES, IT HAD TO BE THE TRUTH.
IT RRR WASN'T.

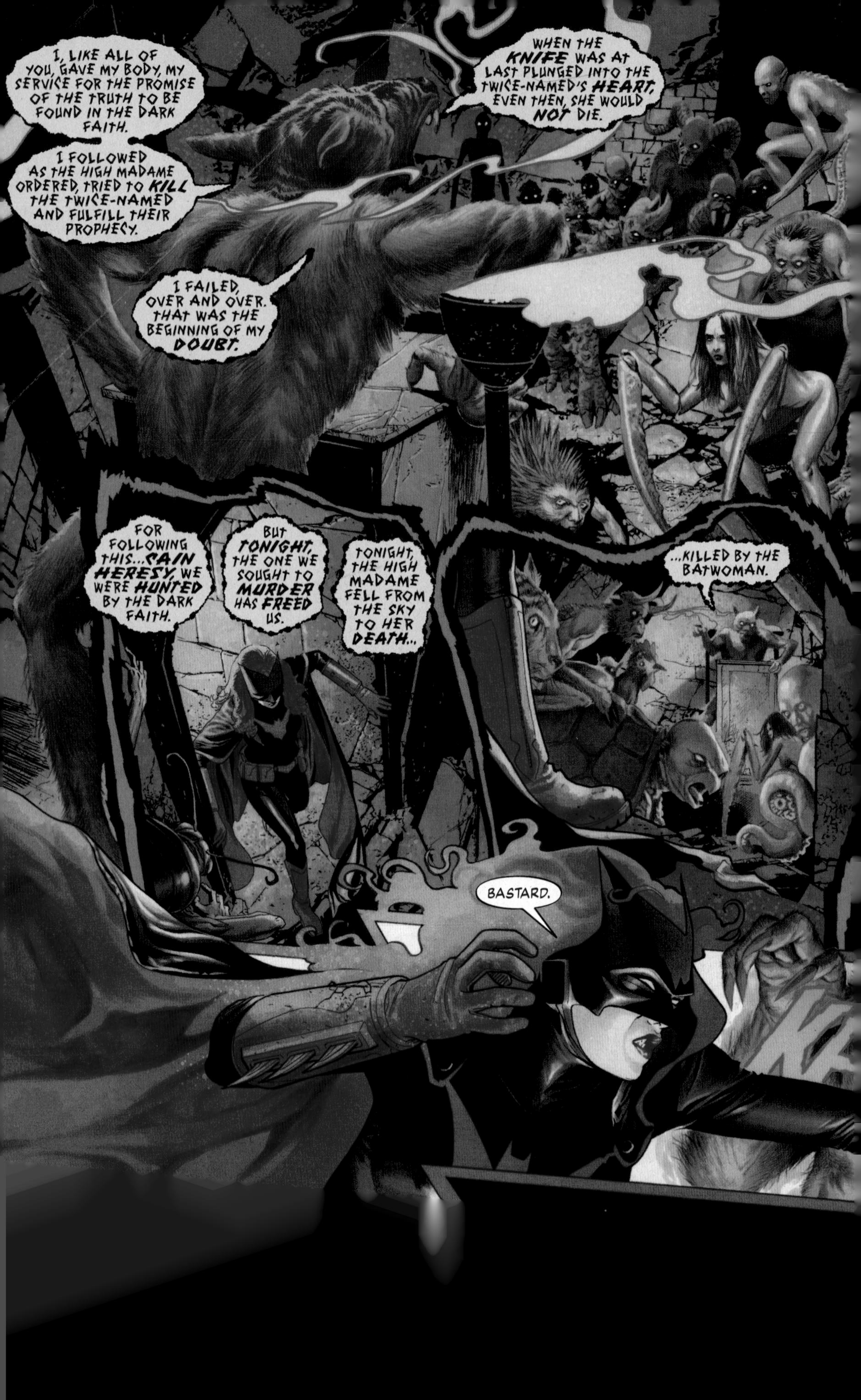
I, LIKE ALL OF YOU, GAVE MY BODY, MY SERVICE FOR THE PROMISE OF THE TRUTH TO BE FOUND IN THE DARK FAITH.
I FOLLOWED AS THE HIGH MADAME ORDERED, TRIED TO KILL THE TWICE-NAMED AND FULFILL THEIR PROPHECY.
WHEN THE KNIFE WAS AT LAST PLUNGED INTO THE TWICE-NAMED'S HEART, EVEN THEN, SHE WOULD NOT DIE.
I FAILED, OVER AND OVER. THAT WAS THE BEGINNING OF MY DOUBT.
FOR FOLLOWING THIS...CAIN HERESY, WE WERE HUNTED BY THE DARK FAITH.
BUT TONIGHT, THE ONE WE SOUGHT TO MURDER HAS FREED US.
TONIGHT, THE HIGH MADAME FELL FROM THE SKY TO HER DEATH...
...KILLED BY THE BATWOMAN.
BASTARD.

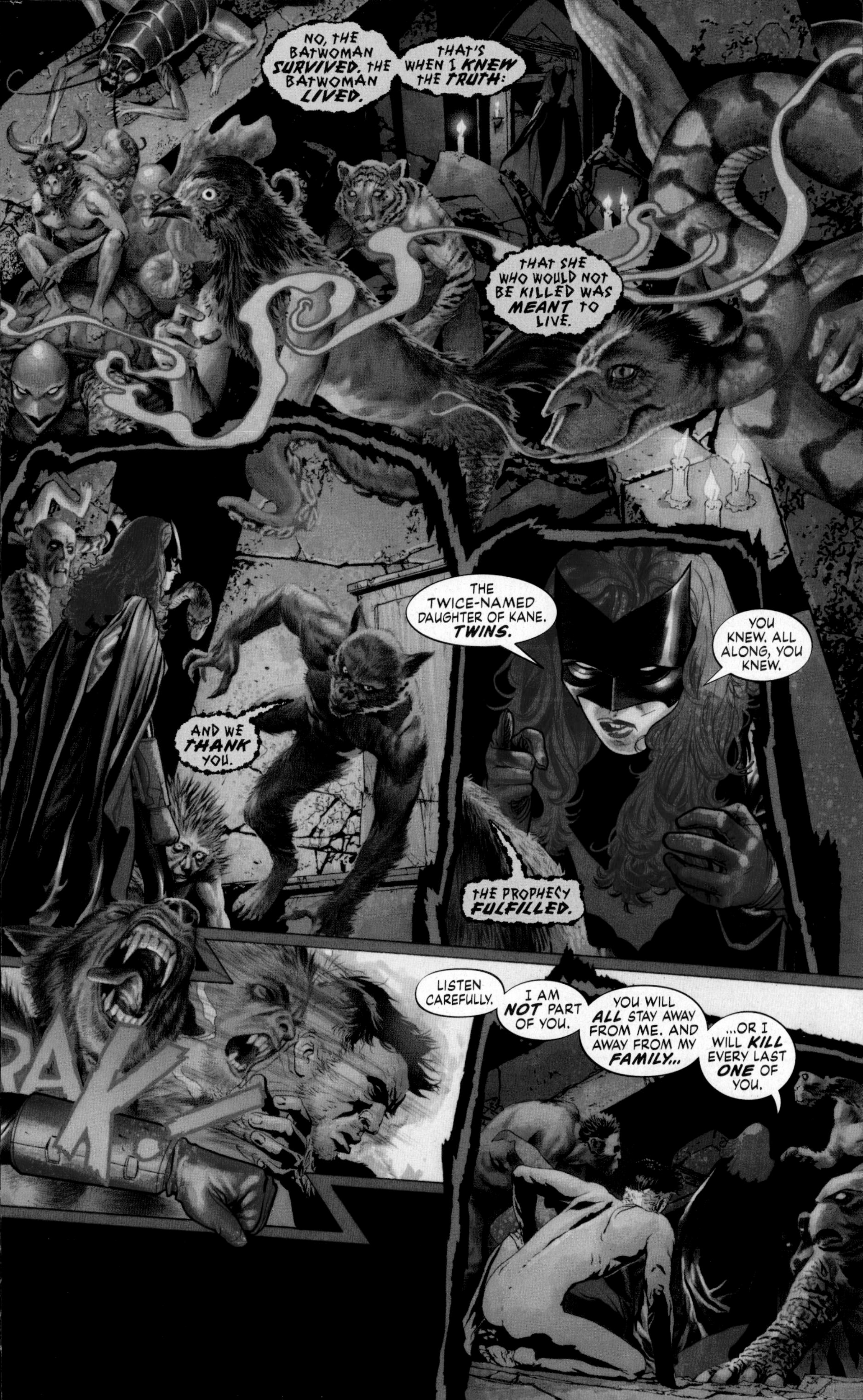
NO, THE BATWOMAN SURVIVED. THE BATWOMAN LIVED.
THAT'S WHEN I KNEW THE TRUTH:
THAT SHE WHO WOULD NOT BE KILLED WAS MEANT TO LIVE.
AND WE THANK YOU.
THE TWICE-NAMED DAUGHTER OF KANE. TWINS.
THE PROPHECY FULFILLED.
YOU KNEW. ALL ALONG, YOU KNEW.
RAK
LISTEN CAREFULLY.
I AM NOT PART OF YOU.
YOU WILL ALL STAY AWAY FROM ME. AND AWAY FROM MY FAMILY...
...OR I WILL KILL EVERY LAST ONE OF YOU.

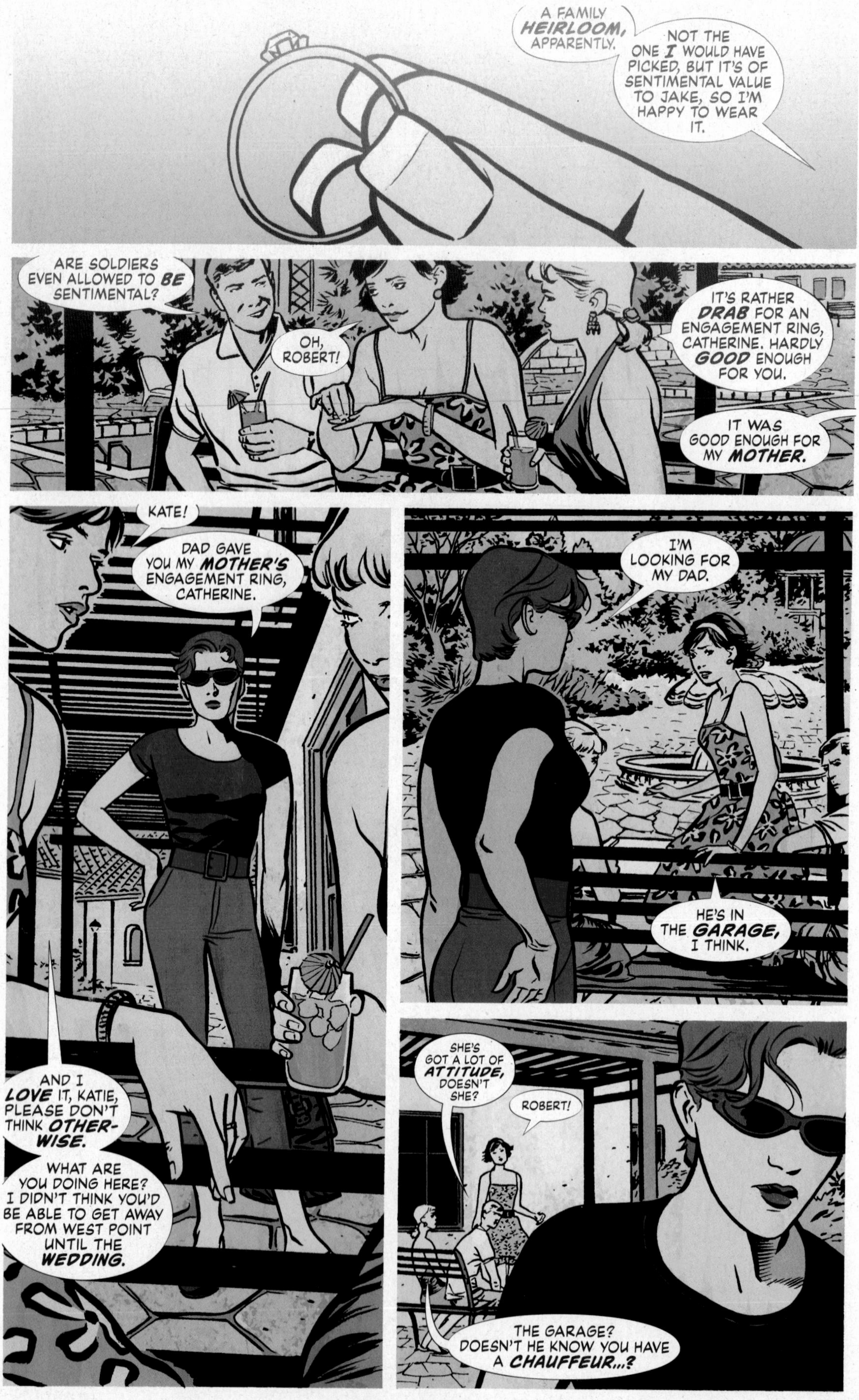
A FAMILY HEIRLOOM, APPARENTLY.
NOT THE ONE I WOULD HAVE PICKED, BUT IT'S OF SENTIMENTAL VALUE TO JAKE, SO I'M HAPPY TO WEAR IT.
ARE SOLDIERS EVEN ALLOWED TO BE SENTIMENTAL?
OH, ROBERT!
IT'S RATHER DRAB FOR AN ENGAGEMENT RING, CATHERINE. HARDLY GOOD ENOUGH FOR YOU.
IT WAS GOOD ENOUGH FOR MY MOTHER.
KATE!
DAD GAVE YOU MY MOTHER'S ENGAGEMENT RING, CATHERINE.
AND I LOVE IT, KATIE, PLEASE DON'T THINK OTHER-WISE.
WHAT ARE YOU DOING HERE? I DIDN'T THINK YOU'D BE ABLE TO GET AWAY FROM WEST POINT UNTIL THE WEDDING.
I'M LOOKING FOR MY DAD.
HE'S IN THE GARAGE, I THINK.
SHE'S GOT A LOT OF ATTITUDE, DOESN'T SHE?
ROBERT!
THE GARAGE? DOESN'T HE KNOW YOU HAVE A CHAUFFEUR...?

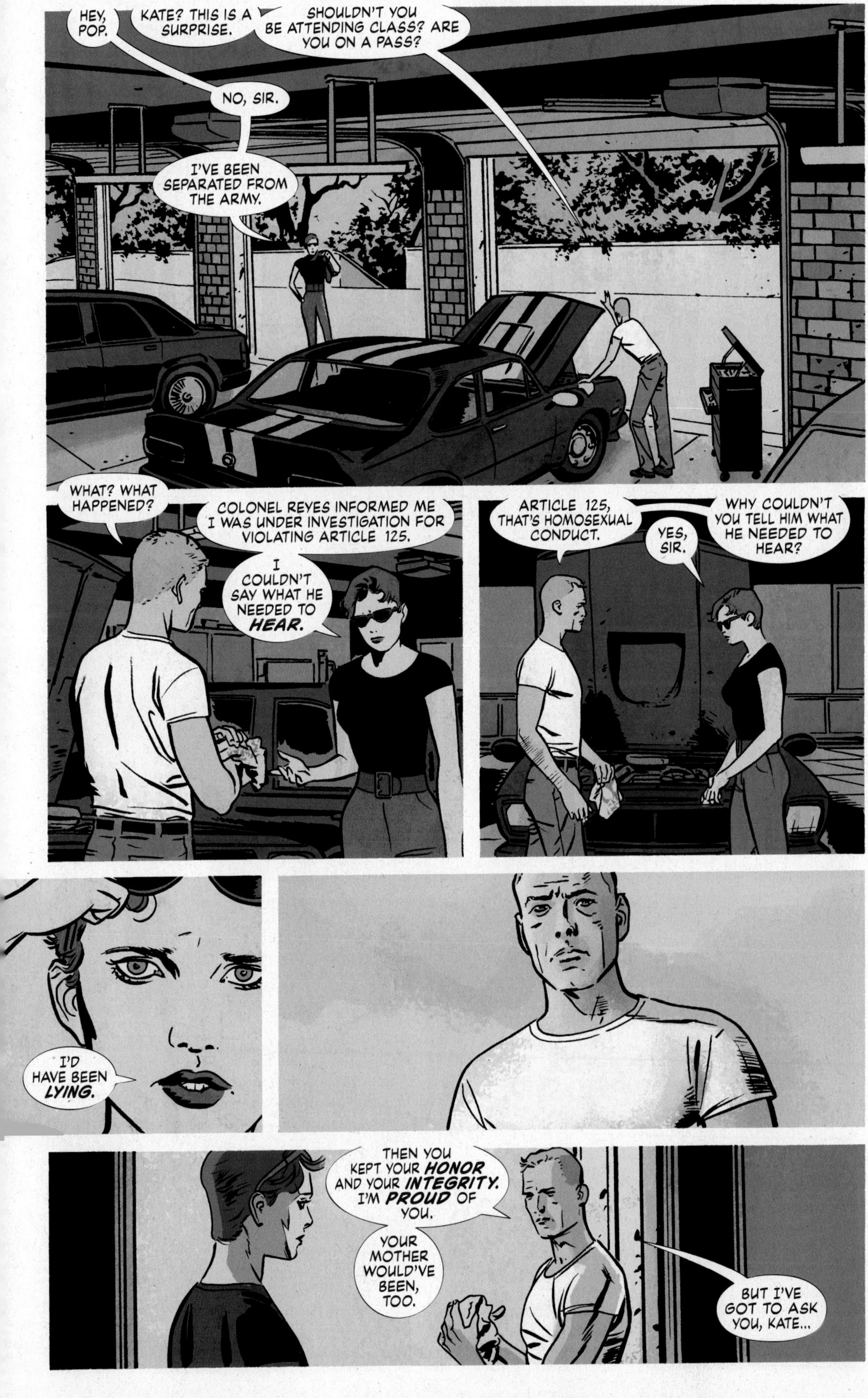

HEY, POP.
KATE? THIS IS A SURPRISE.
SHOULDN'T YOU BE ATTENDING CLASS? ARE YOU ON A PASS?
NO, SIR.
I'VE BEEN SEPARATED FROM THE ARMY.
WHAT? WHAT HAPPENED?
COLONEL REYES INFORMED ME I WAS UNDER INVESTIGATION FOR VIOLATING ARTICLE 125.
I COULDN'T SAY WHAT HE NEEDED TO HEAR.
ARTICLE 125, THAT'S HOMOSEXUAL CONDUCT.
YES, SIR.
WHY COULDN'T YOU TELL HIM WHAT HE NEEDED TO HEAR?
I'D HAVE BEEN LYING.
THEN YOU KEPT YOUR HONOR AND YOUR INTEGRITY. I'M PROUD OF YOU.
YOUR MOTHER WOULD'VE BEEN, TOO.
BUT I'VE GOT TO ASK YOU, KATE...

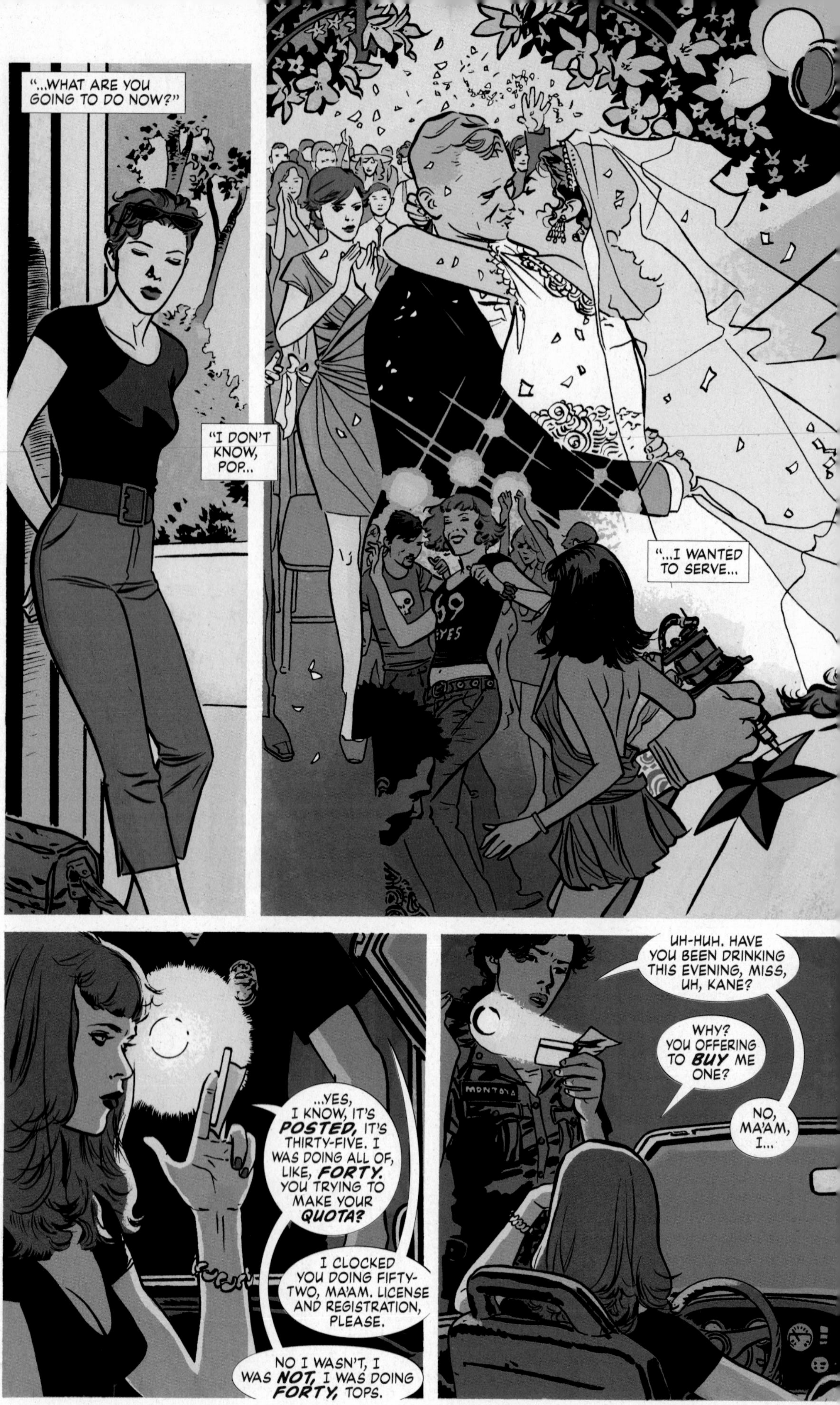
"...WHAT ARE YOU GOING TO DO NOW?"
"I DON'T KNOW, POP...
"...I WANTED TO SERVE...
...YES, I KNOW, IT'S POSTED, IT'S THIRTY-FIVE. I WAS DOING ALL OF, LIKE, FORTY. YOU TRYING TO MAKE YOUR QUOTA?
I CLOCKED YOU DOING FIFTY-TWO, MA'AM. LICENSE AND REGISTRATION, PLEASE.
NO I WASN'T, I WAS NOT, I WAS DOING FORTY, TOPS.
UH-HUH. HAVE YOU BEEN DRINKING THIS EVENING, MISS, UH, KANE?
WHY? YOU OFFERING TO BUY ME ONE?
NO, MA'AM, I...

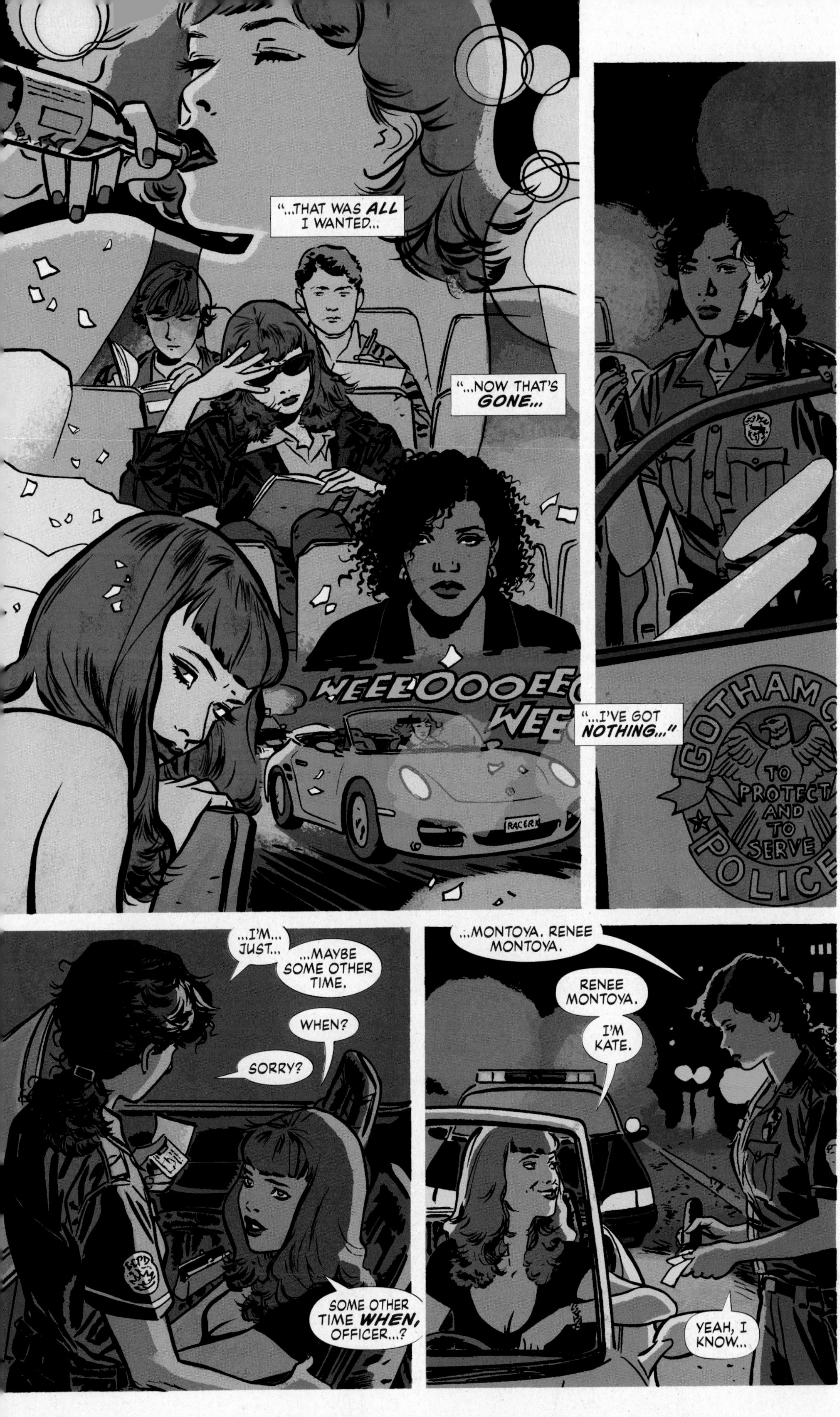
"...THAT WAS ALL I WANTED...
"...NOW THAT'S GONE...
WEEEOOOOEE
WEE
"...I'VE GOT NOTHING..."
GOTHAM
TO PROTECT AND TO SERVE
POLICE
RACER
...I'M... JUST...
...MAYBE SOME OTHER TIME.
WHEN?
SORRY?
SOME OTHER TIME WHEN, OFFICER...?
...MONTOYA. RENEE MONTOYA.
RENEE MONTOYA.
I'M KATE.
YEAH, I KNOW...

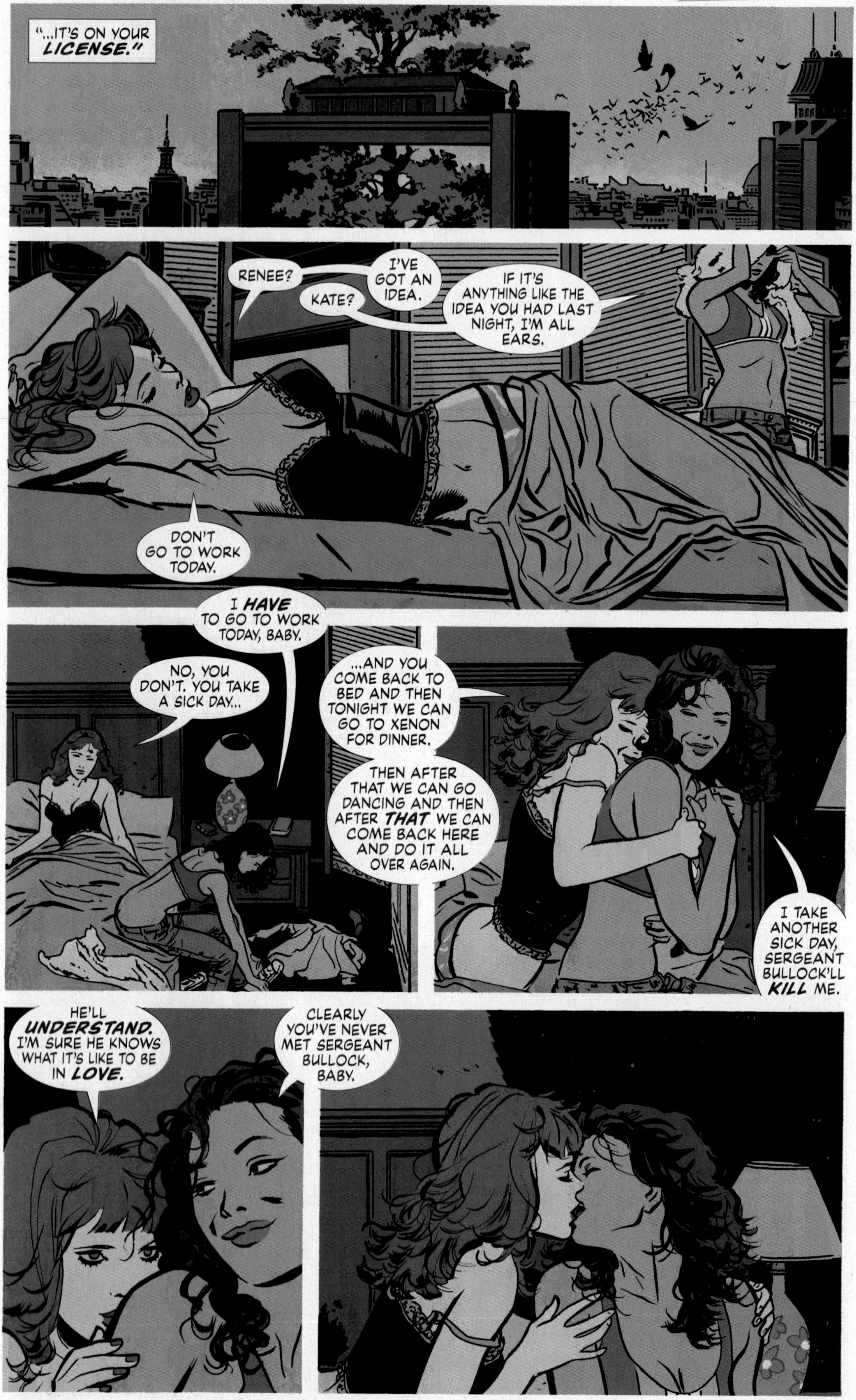
"...IT'S ON YOUR LICENSE."
RENEE?
I'VE GOT AN IDEA.
KATE?
IF IT'S ANYTHING LIKE THE IDEA YOU HAD LAST NIGHT, I'M ALL EARS.
DON'T GO TO WORK TODAY.
I HAVE TO GO TO WORK TODAY, BABY.
NO, YOU DON'T. YOU TAKE A SICK DAY...
...AND YOU COME BACK TO BED AND THEN TONIGHT WE CAN GO TO XENON FOR DINNER.
THEN AFTER THAT WE CAN GO DANCING AND THEN AFTER THAT WE CAN COME BACK HERE AND DO IT ALL OVER AGAIN.
I TAKE ANOTHER SICK DAY, SERGEANT BULLOCK'LL KILL ME.
HE'LL UNDERSTAND. I'M SURE HE KNOWS WHAT IT'S LIKE TO BE IN LOVE.
CLEARLY YOU'VE NEVER MET SERGEANT BULLOCK, BABY.

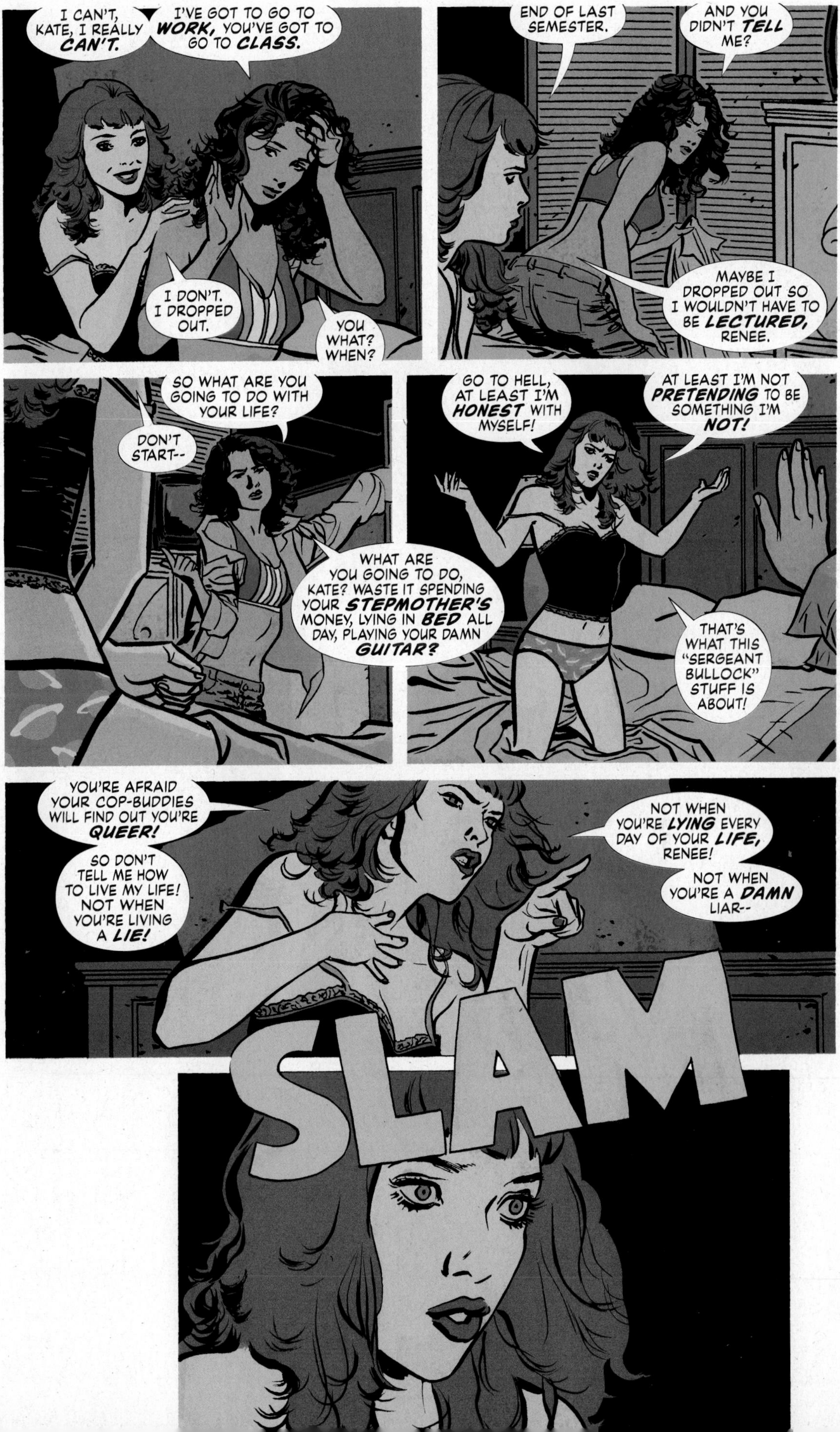
I CAN'T, KATE, I REALLY CAN'T.
I'VE GOT TO GO TO WORK, YOU'VE GOT TO GO TO CLASS.
I DON'T. I DROPPED OUT.
YOU WHAT? WHEN?
END OF LAST SEMESTER.
AND YOU DIDN'T TELL ME?
MAYBE I DROPPED OUT SO I WOULDN'T HAVE TO BE LECTURED, RENEE.
DON'T START--
SO WHAT ARE YOU GOING TO DO WITH YOUR LIFE?
WHAT ARE YOU GOING TO DO, KATE? WASTE IT SPENDING YOUR STEPMOTHER'S MONEY, LYING IN BED ALL DAY, PLAYING YOUR DAMN GUITAR?
GO TO HELL, AT LEAST I'M HONEST WITH MYSELF!
AT LEAST I'M NOT PRETENDING TO BE SOMETHING I'M NOT!
THAT'S WHAT THIS "SERGEANT BULLOCK" STUFF IS ABOUT!
YOU'RE AFRAID YOUR COP-BUDDIES WILL FIND OUT YOU'RE QUEER!
SO DON'T TELL ME HOW TO LIVE MY LIFE! NOT WHEN YOU'RE LIVING A LIE!
NOT WHEN YOU'RE LYING EVERY DAY OF YOUR LIFE, RENEE!
NOT WHEN YOU'RE A DAMN LIAR--
SLAM

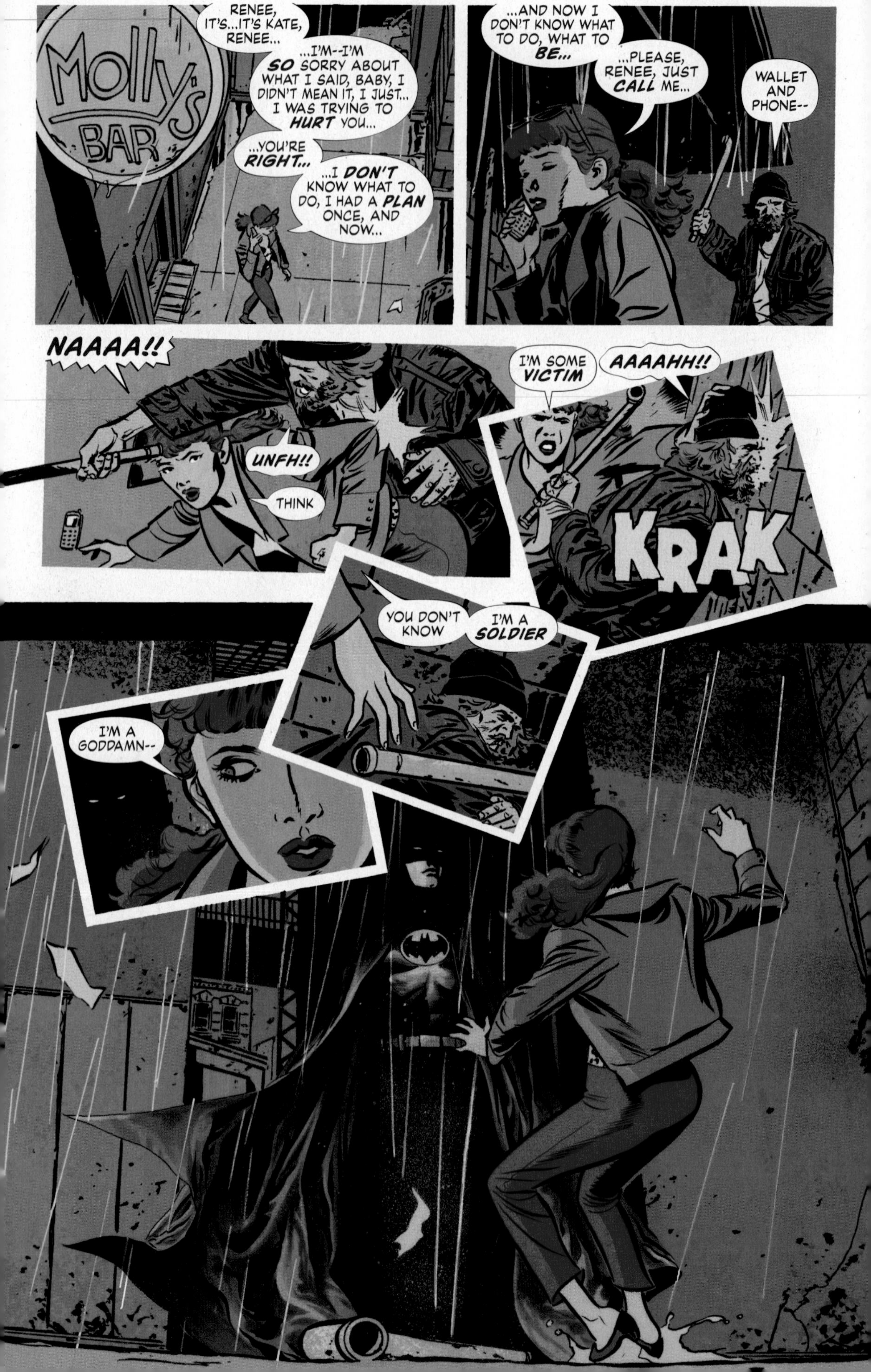
Molly's BAR
RENEE, IT'S...IT'S KATE, RENEE...
...I'M--I'M SO SORRY ABOUT WHAT I SAID, BABY, I DIDN'T MEAN IT, I JUST... I WAS TRYING TO HURT YOU...
...YOU'RE RIGHT...
...I DON'T KNOW WHAT TO DO, I HAD A PLAN ONCE, AND NOW...
...AND NOW I DON'T KNOW WHAT TO DO, WHAT TO BE...
...PLEASE, RENEE, JUST CALL ME...
WALLET AND PHONE--
NAAAA!!
UNFH!!
THINK
I'M SOME VICTIM
AAAAHH!!
KRAK
YOU DON'T KNOW
I'M A SOLDIER
I'M A GODDAMN--

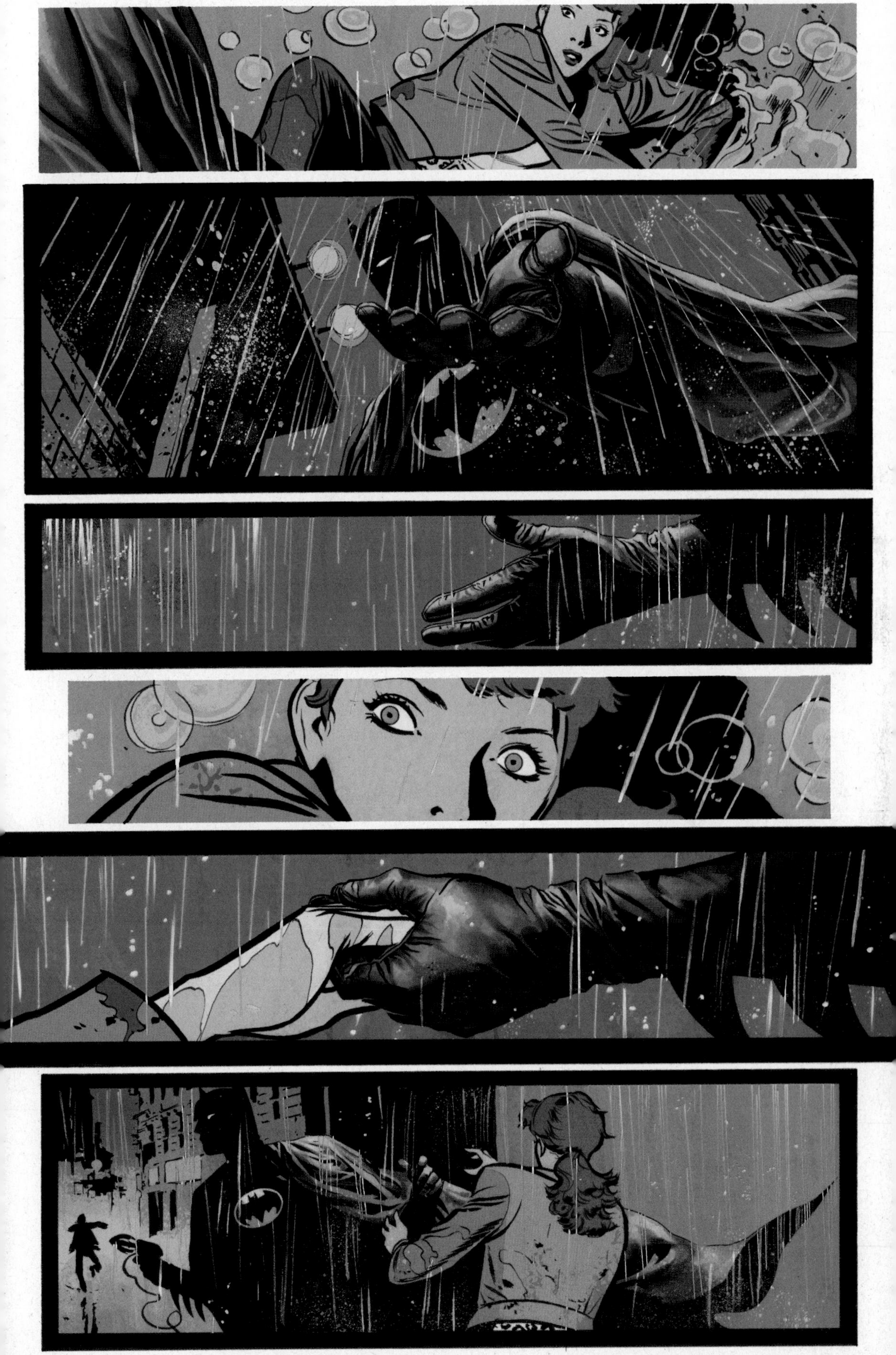

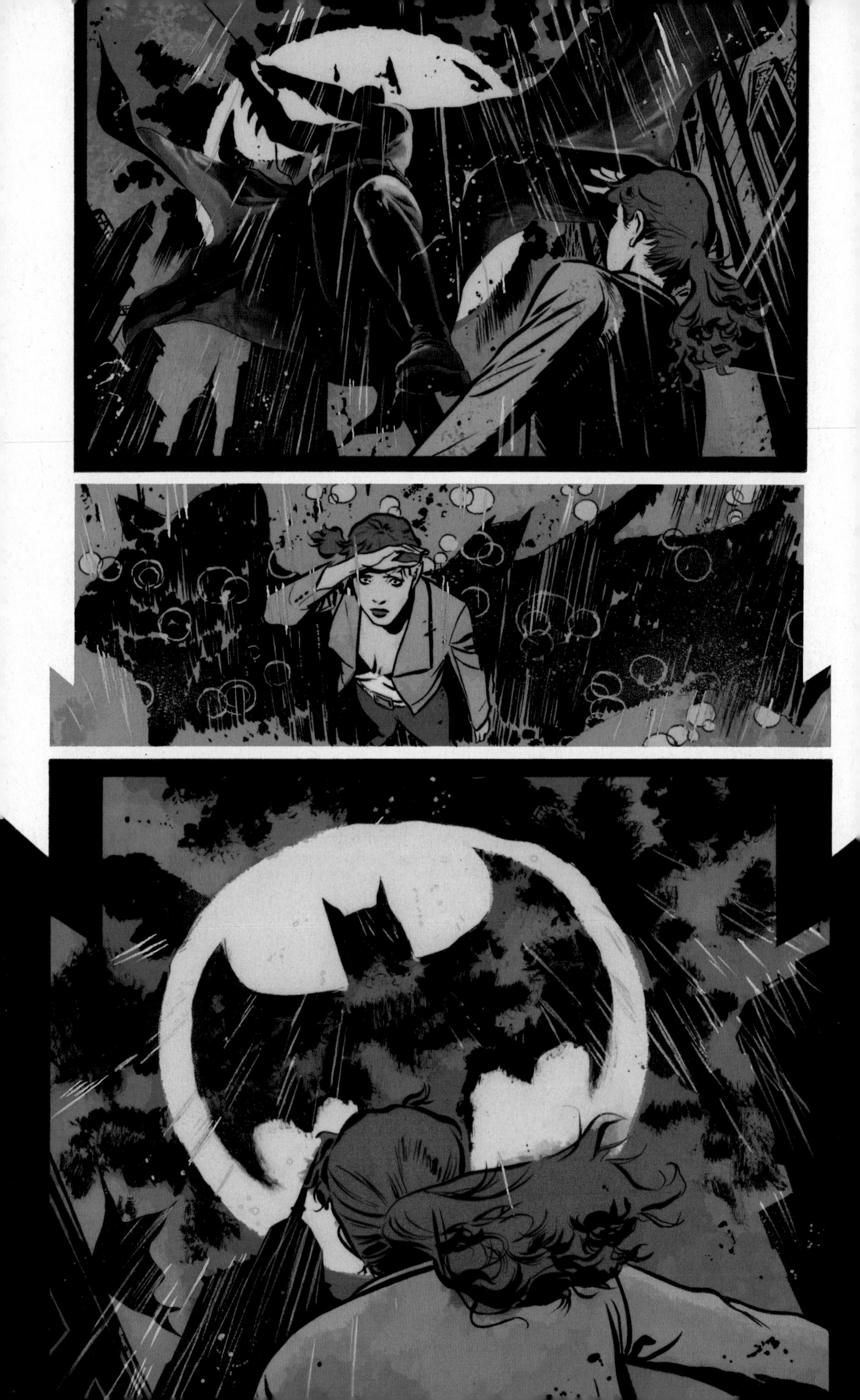

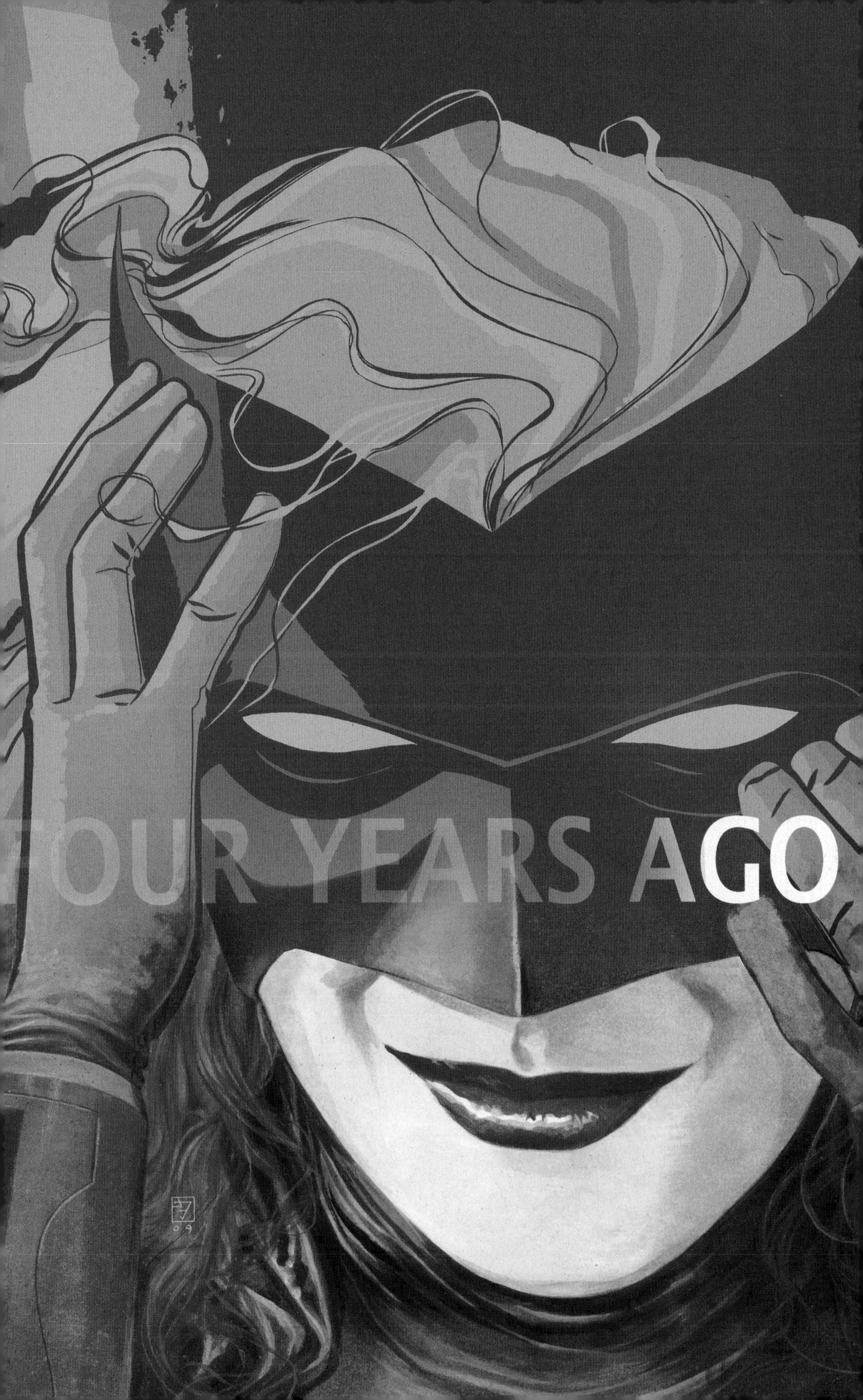
FOUR YEARS AGO

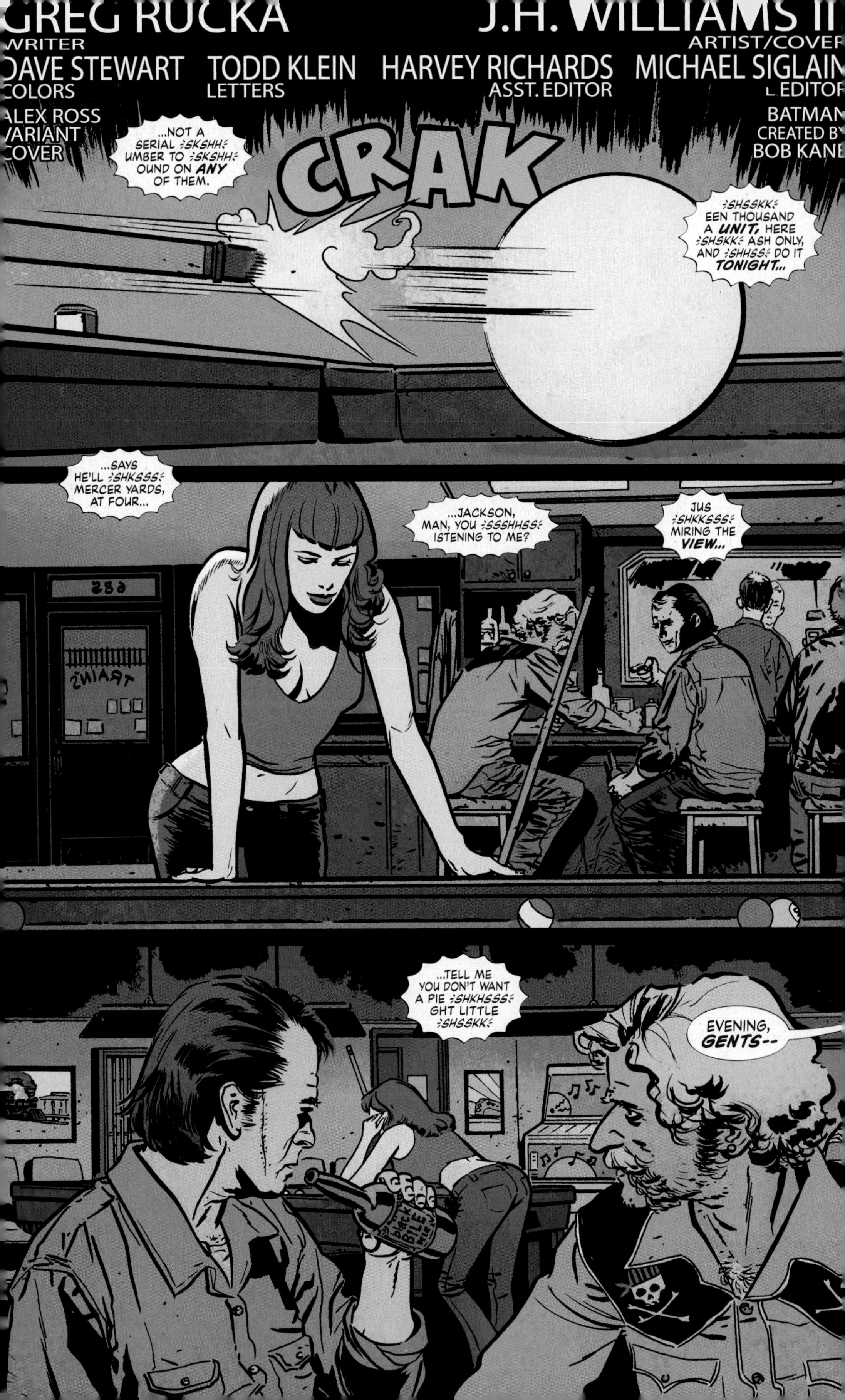
GREG RUCKA
WRITER
J.H. WILLIAMS III
ARTIST/COVER
DAVE STEWART
COLORS
TODD KLEIN
LETTERS
HARVEY RICHARDS
ASST. EDITOR
MICHAEL SIGLAIN
EDITOR
ALEX ROSS
VARIANT
COVER
BATMAN
CREATED BY
BOB KANE
...NOT A SERIAL ⚡SKSHH⚡ UMBER TO ⚡SKSHH⚡ OUND ON ANY OF THEM.
CRAK
⚡SHSSKK⚡ EEN THOUSAND A UNIT, HERE ⚡SHSKK⚡ ASH ONLY, AND ⚡SHHSS⚡ DO IT TONIGHT...
...SAYS HE'LL ⚡SHKSSS⚡ MERCER YARDS, AT FOUR...
...JACKSON, MAN, YOU ⚡SSSHHSS⚡ ISTENING TO ME?
JUS ⚡SHKKSSS⚡ MIRING THE VIEW...
TRAINS
...TELL ME YOU DON'T WANT A PIE ⚡SHKHSSS⚡ GHT LITTLE ⚡SHSSKK⚡
EVENING, GENTS--
BLACK BILE BEER

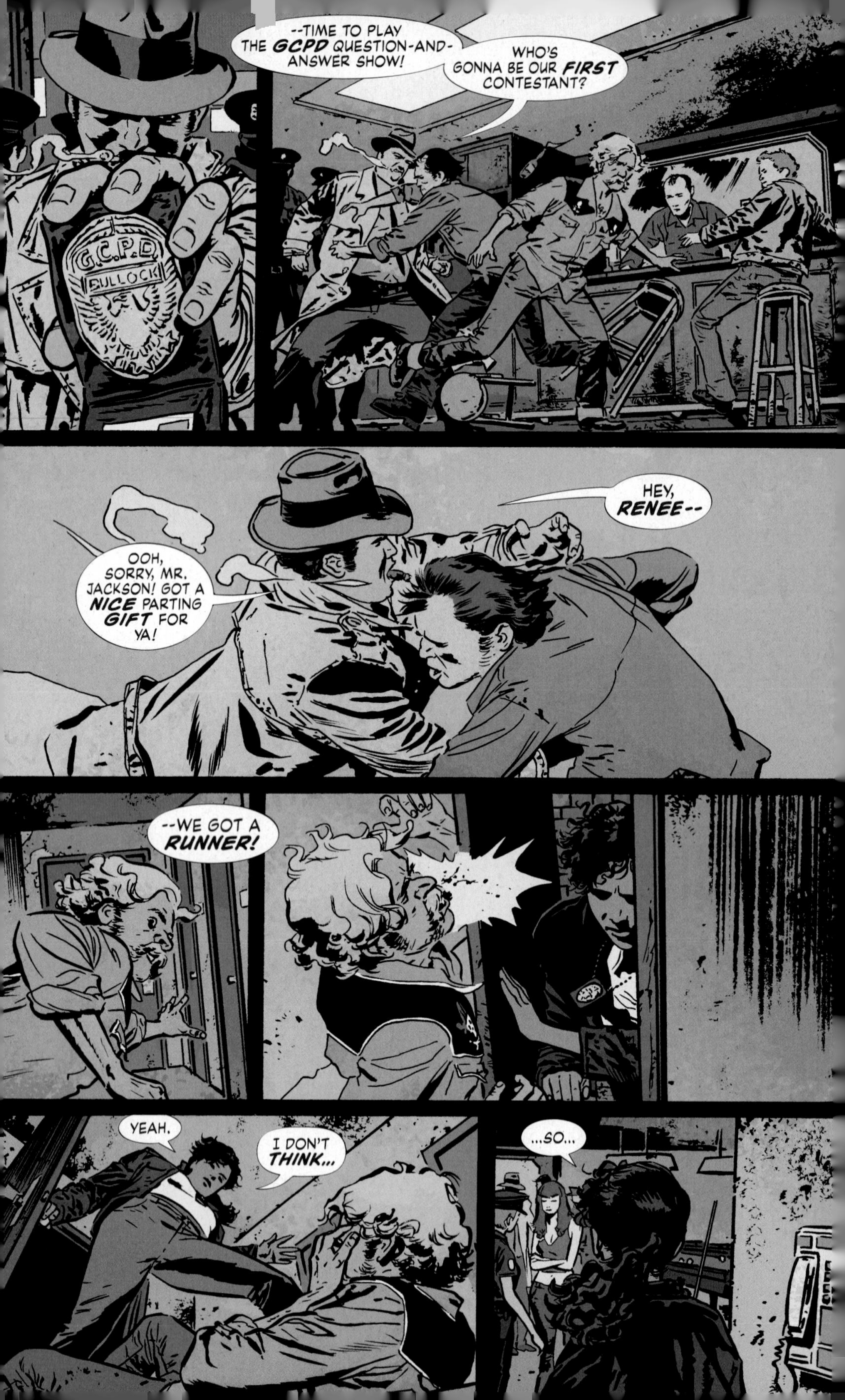

--TIME TO PLAY THE GCPD QUESTION-AND-ANSWER SHOW!
WHO'S GONNA BE OUR FIRST CONTESTANT?
G.C.P.D. BULLOCK
HEY, RENEE--
OOH, SORRY, MR. JACKSON! GOT A NICE PARTING GIFT FOR YA!
--WE GOT A RUNNER!
YEAH.
I DON'T THINK...
...SO...

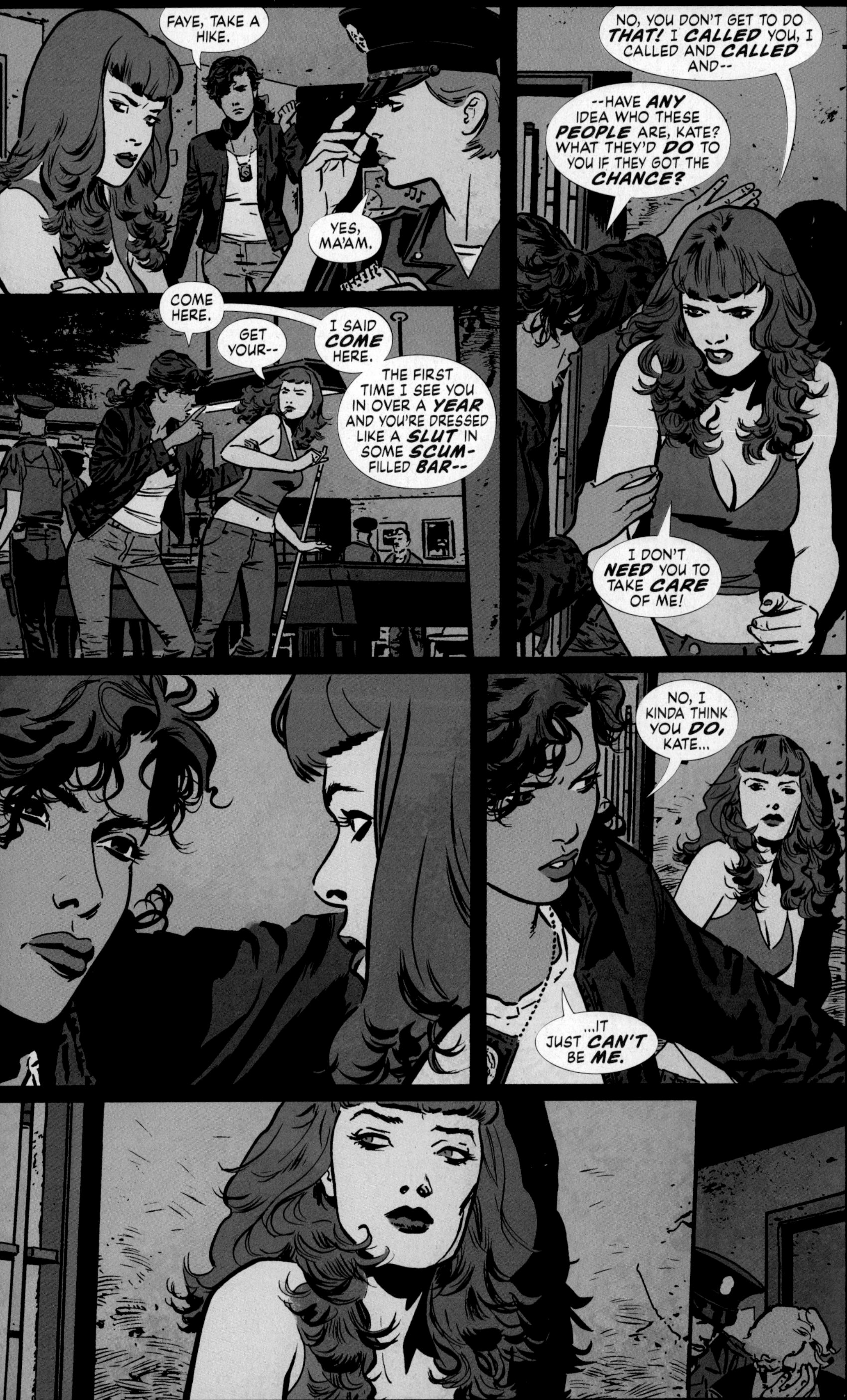
FAYE, TAKE A HIKE.
YES, MA'AM.
NO, YOU DON'T GET TO DO THAT! I CALLED YOU, I CALLED AND CALLED AND--
--HAVE ANY IDEA WHO THESE PEOPLE ARE, KATE? WHAT THEY'D DO TO YOU IF THEY GOT THE CHANCE?
COME HERE.
GET YOUR--
I SAID COME HERE.
THE FIRST TIME I SEE YOU IN OVER A YEAR AND YOU'RE DRESSED LIKE A SLUT IN SOME SCUM-FILLED BAR--
I DON'T NEED YOU TO TAKE CARE OF ME!
NO, I KINDA THINK YOU DO, KATE...
...IT JUST CAN'T BE ME.

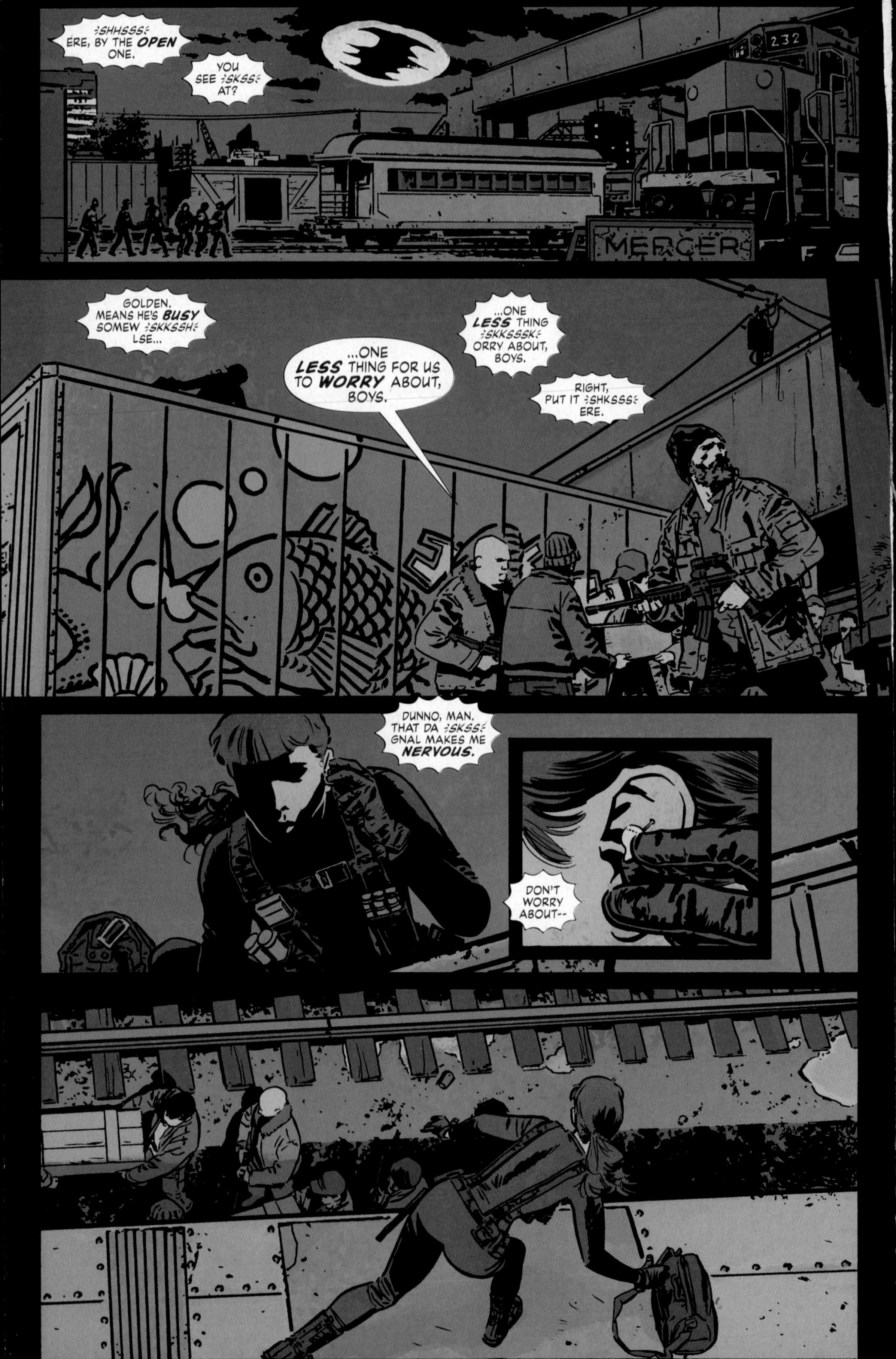
⚡SHHSSS⚡ ERE, BY THE **OPEN** ONE.
YOU SEE ⚡SKSS⚡ AT?
GOLDEN. MEANS HE'S **BUSY** SOMEW ⚡SKKSSH⚡ LSE...
...ONE **LESS** THING FOR US TO **WORRY** ABOUT, BOYS.
...ONE **LESS** THING ⚡SKKSSSK⚡ ORRY ABOUT, BOYS.
RIGHT, PUT IT ⚡SHKSSS⚡ ERE.
DUNNO, MAN. THAT DA ⚡SKSS⚡ GNAL MAKES ME **NERVOUS**.
DON'T WORRY ABOUT--

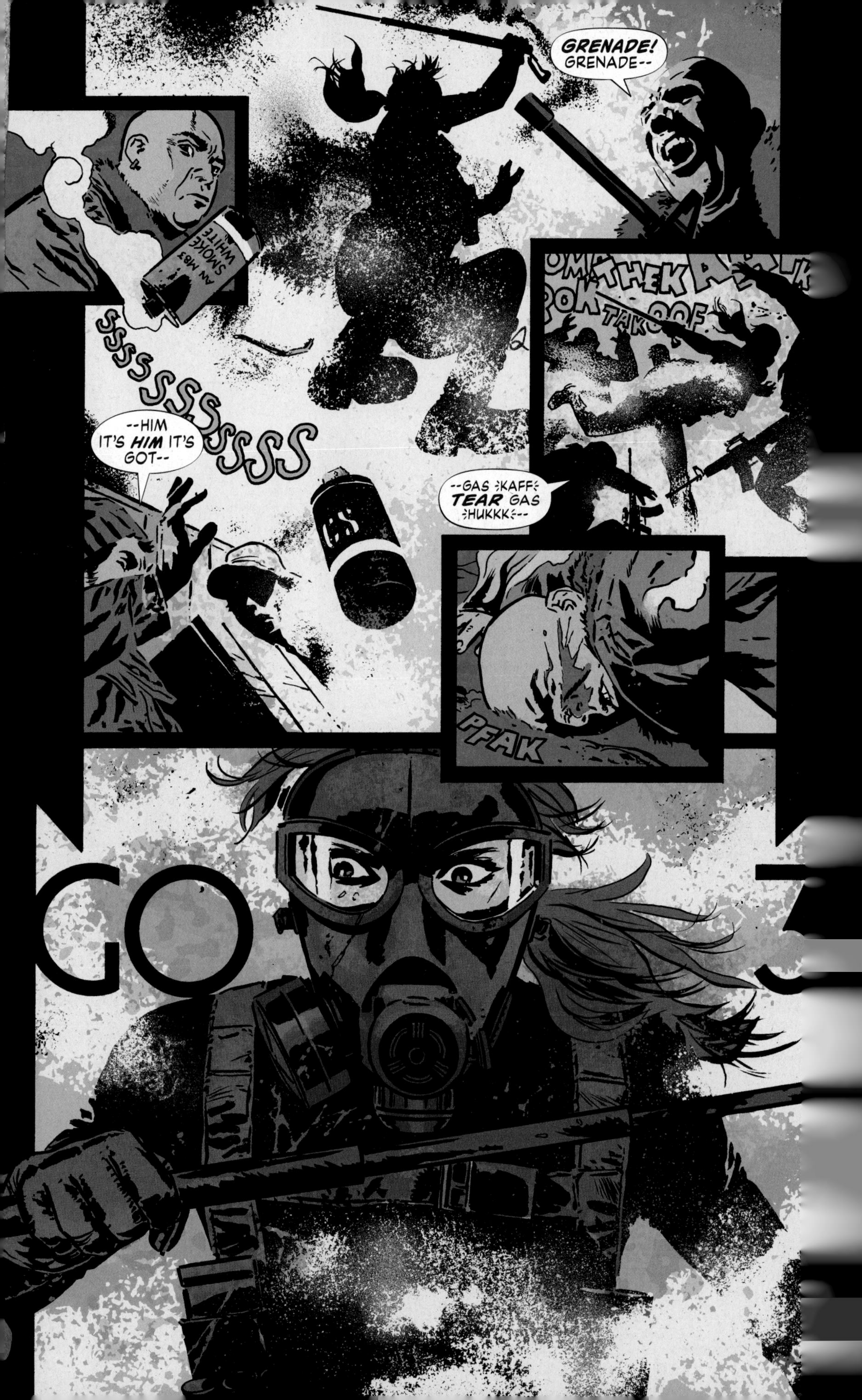
GRENADE! GRENADE--
AN M83 SMOKE WHITE
SSSSSSSSSSSSS
--HIM IT'S HIM IT'S GOT--
CS
THEK
TAK
OOF
--GAS KAFF TEAR GAS HUKKK--
PFAK
GO

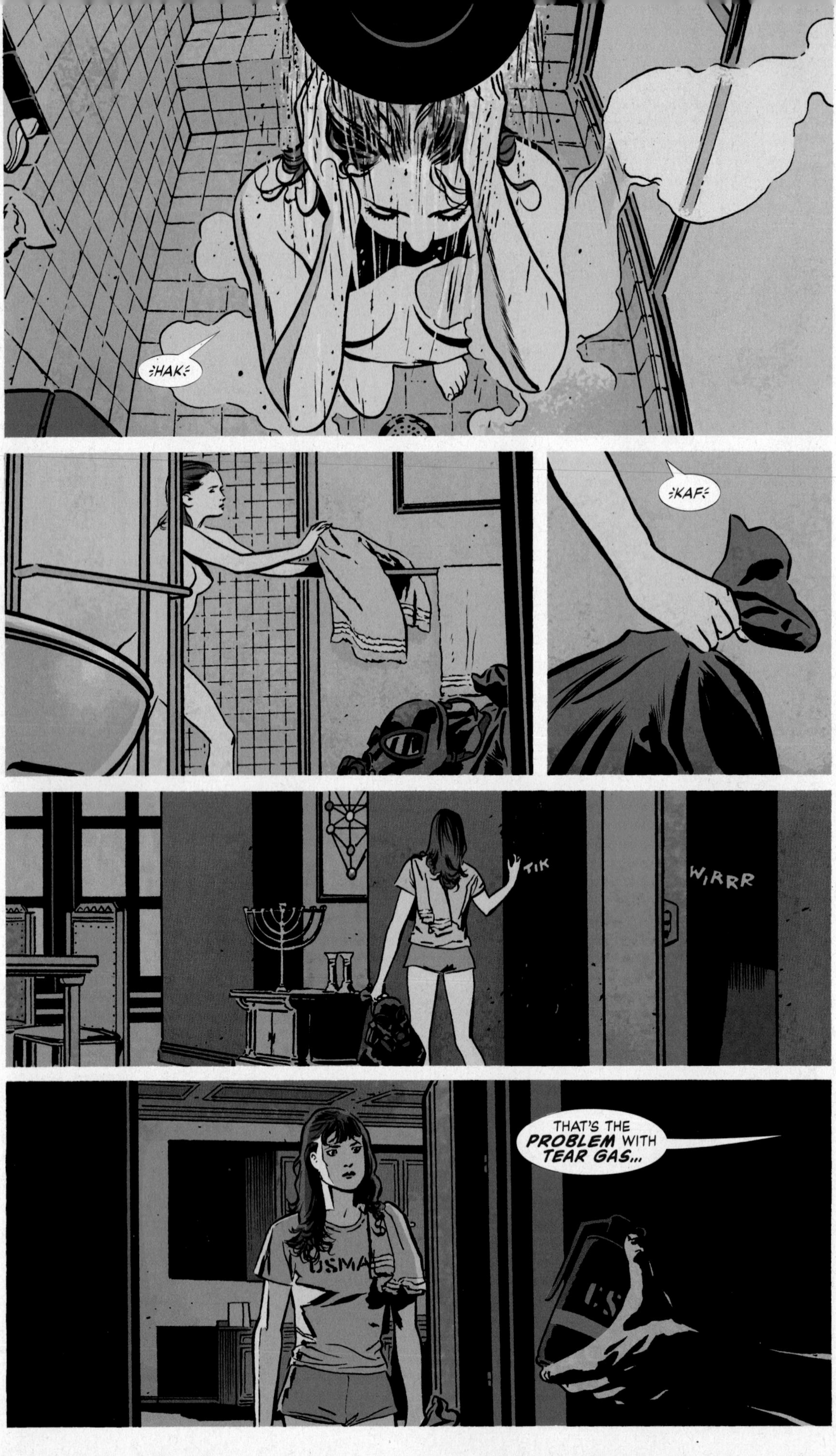
HAK
KAF
TIK
WIRRR
THAT'S THE PROBLEM WITH TEAR GAS...

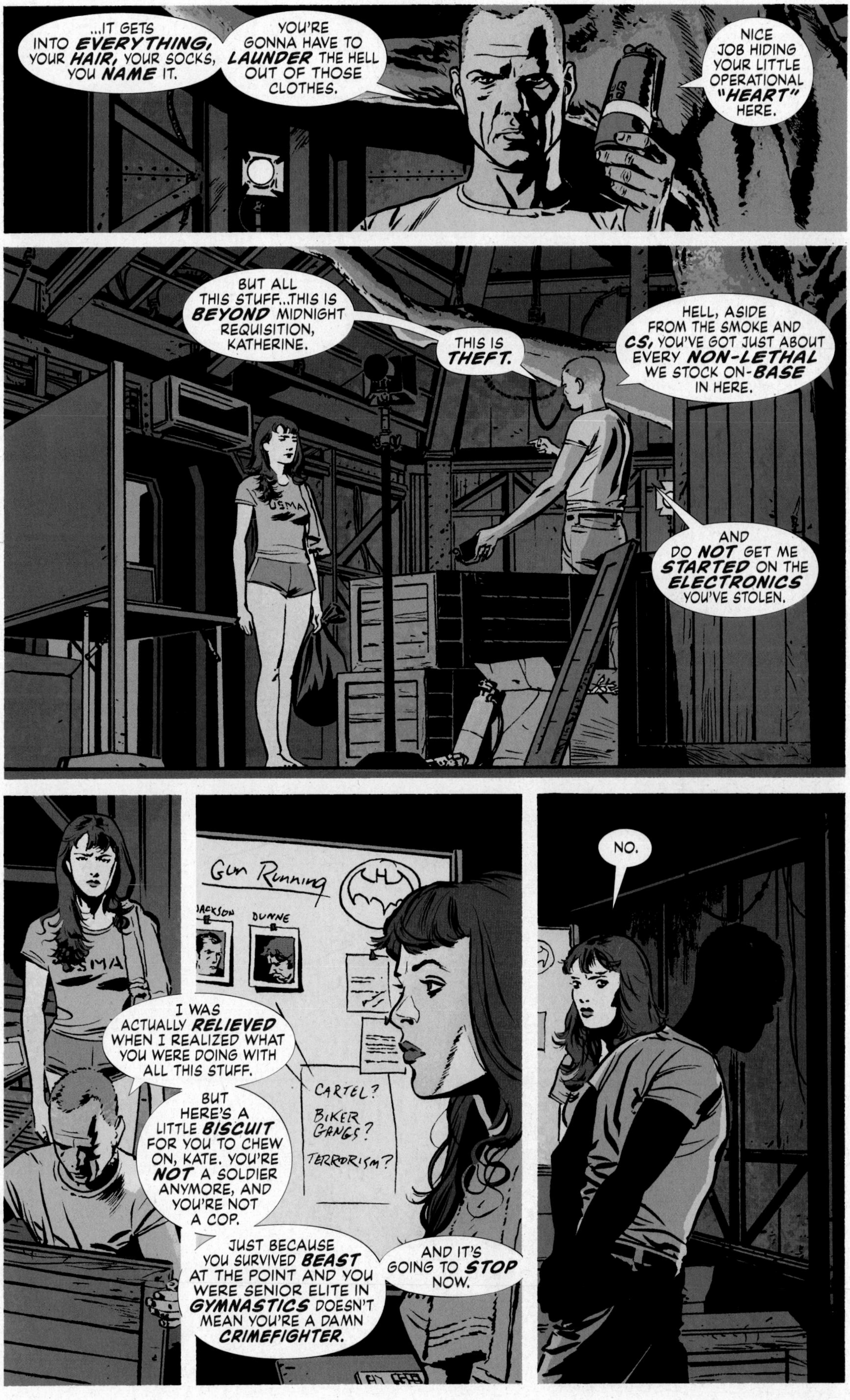
...IT GETS INTO EVERYTHING, YOUR HAIR, YOUR SOCKS, YOU NAME IT.
YOU'RE GONNA HAVE TO LAUNDER THE HELL OUT OF THOSE CLOTHES.
NICE JOB HIDING YOUR LITTLE OPERATIONAL "HEART" HERE.
BUT ALL THIS STUFF...THIS IS BEYOND MIDNIGHT REQUISITION, KATHERINE.
THIS IS THEFT.
HELL, ASIDE FROM THE SMOKE AND CS, YOU'VE GOT JUST ABOUT EVERY NON-LETHAL WE STOCK ON-BASE IN HERE.
AND DO NOT GET ME STARTED ON THE ELECTRONICS YOU'VE STOLEN.
Gun Running
JACKSON
DUNNE
I WAS ACTUALLY RELIEVED WHEN I REALIZED WHAT YOU WERE DOING WITH ALL THIS STUFF.
BUT HERE'S A LITTLE BISCUIT FOR YOU TO CHEW ON, KATE. YOU'RE NOT A SOLDIER ANYMORE, AND YOU'RE NOT A COP.
CARTEL?
BIKER GANGS?
TERRORISM?
JUST BECAUSE YOU SURVIVED BEAST AT THE POINT AND YOU WERE SENIOR ELITE IN GYMNASTICS DOESN'T MEAN YOU'RE A DAMN CRIMEFIGHTER.
AND IT'S GOING TO STOP NOW.
NO.

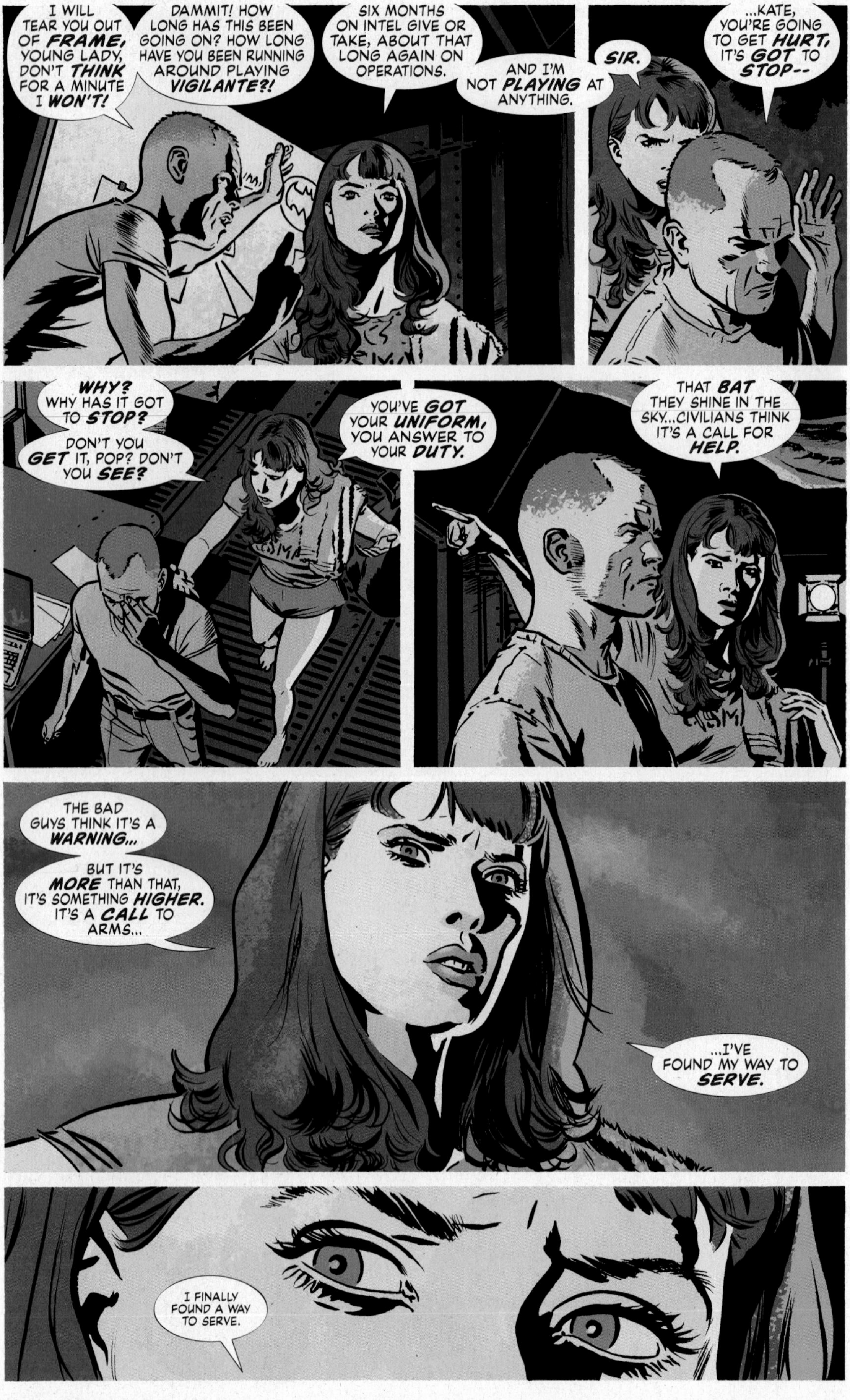
I WILL TEAR YOU OUT OF FRAME, YOUNG LADY, DON'T THINK FOR A MINUTE I WON'T!
DAMMIT! HOW LONG HAS THIS BEEN GOING ON? HOW LONG HAVE YOU BEEN RUNNING AROUND PLAYING VIGILANTE?!
SIX MONTHS ON INTEL GIVE OR TAKE, ABOUT THAT LONG AGAIN ON OPERATIONS.
AND I'M NOT PLAYING AT ANYTHING.
SIR.
...KATE, YOU'RE GOING TO GET HURT, IT'S GOT TO STOP--
WHY? WHY HAS IT GOT TO STOP?
DON'T YOU GET IT, POP? DON'T YOU SEE?
YOU'VE GOT YOUR UNIFORM, YOU ANSWER TO YOUR DUTY.
THAT BAT THEY SHINE IN THE SKY...CIVILIANS THINK IT'S A CALL FOR HELP.
THE BAD GUYS THINK IT'S A WARNING...
BUT IT'S MORE THAN THAT, IT'S SOMETHING HIGHER. IT'S A CALL TO ARMS...
...I'VE FOUND MY WAY TO SERVE.
I FINALLY FOUND A WAY TO SERVE.

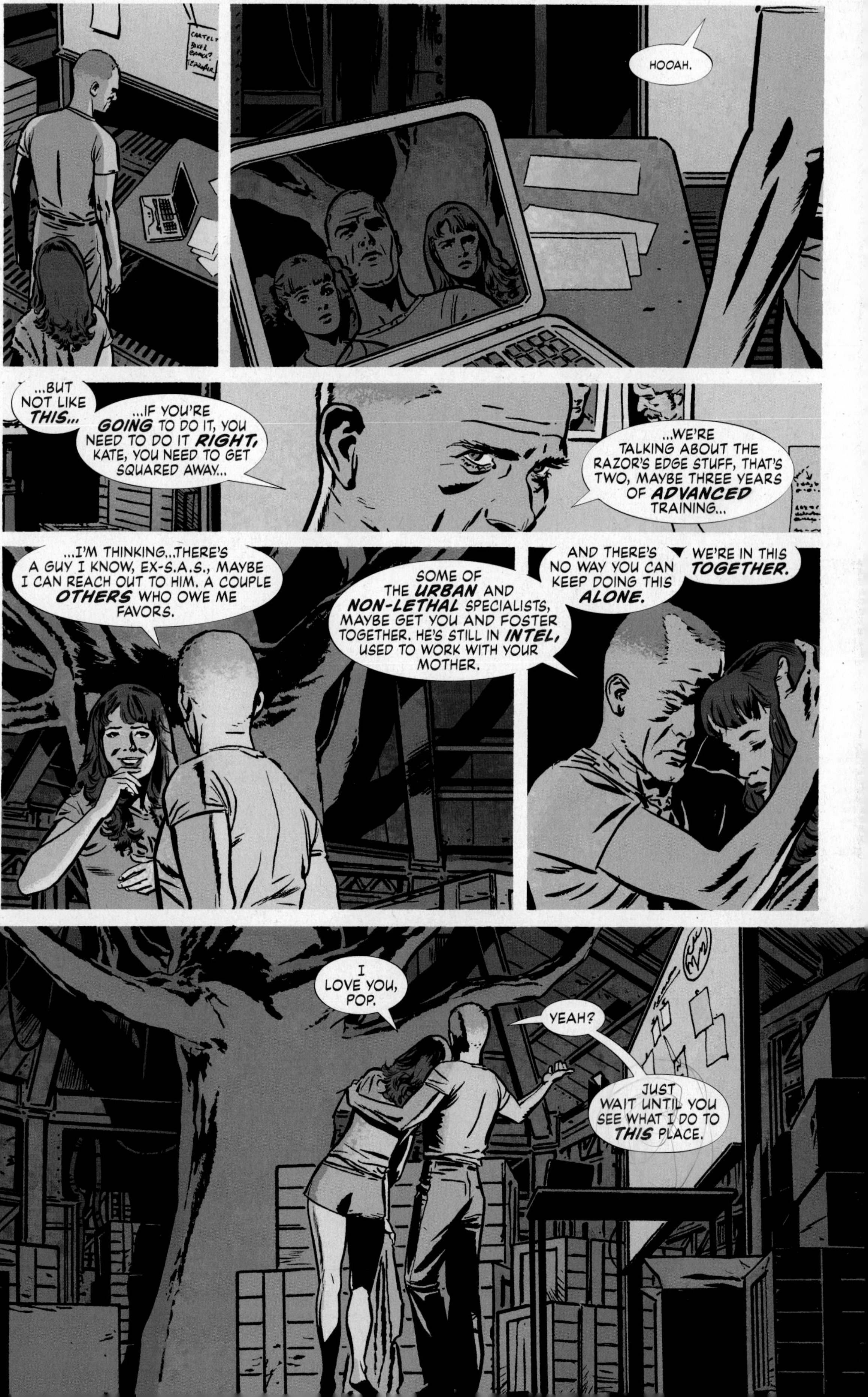
HOOAH.
...BUT NOT LIKE THIS...
...IF YOU'RE GOING TO DO IT, YOU NEED TO DO IT RIGHT, KATE, YOU NEED TO GET SQUARED AWAY...
...WE'RE TALKING ABOUT THE RAZOR'S EDGE STUFF, THAT'S TWO, MAYBE THREE YEARS OF ADVANCED TRAINING...
...I'M THINKING...THERE'S A GUY I KNOW, EX-S.A.S., MAYBE I CAN REACH OUT TO HIM. A COUPLE OTHERS WHO OWE ME FAVORS.
SOME OF THE URBAN AND NON-LETHAL SPECIALISTS, MAYBE GET YOU AND FOSTER TOGETHER. HE'S STILL IN INTEL, USED TO WORK WITH YOUR MOTHER.
AND THERE'S NO WAY YOU CAN KEEP DOING THIS ALONE.
WE'RE IN THIS TOGETHER.
I LOVE YOU, POP.
YEAH?
JUST WAIT UNTIL YOU SEE WHAT I DO TO THIS PLACE.

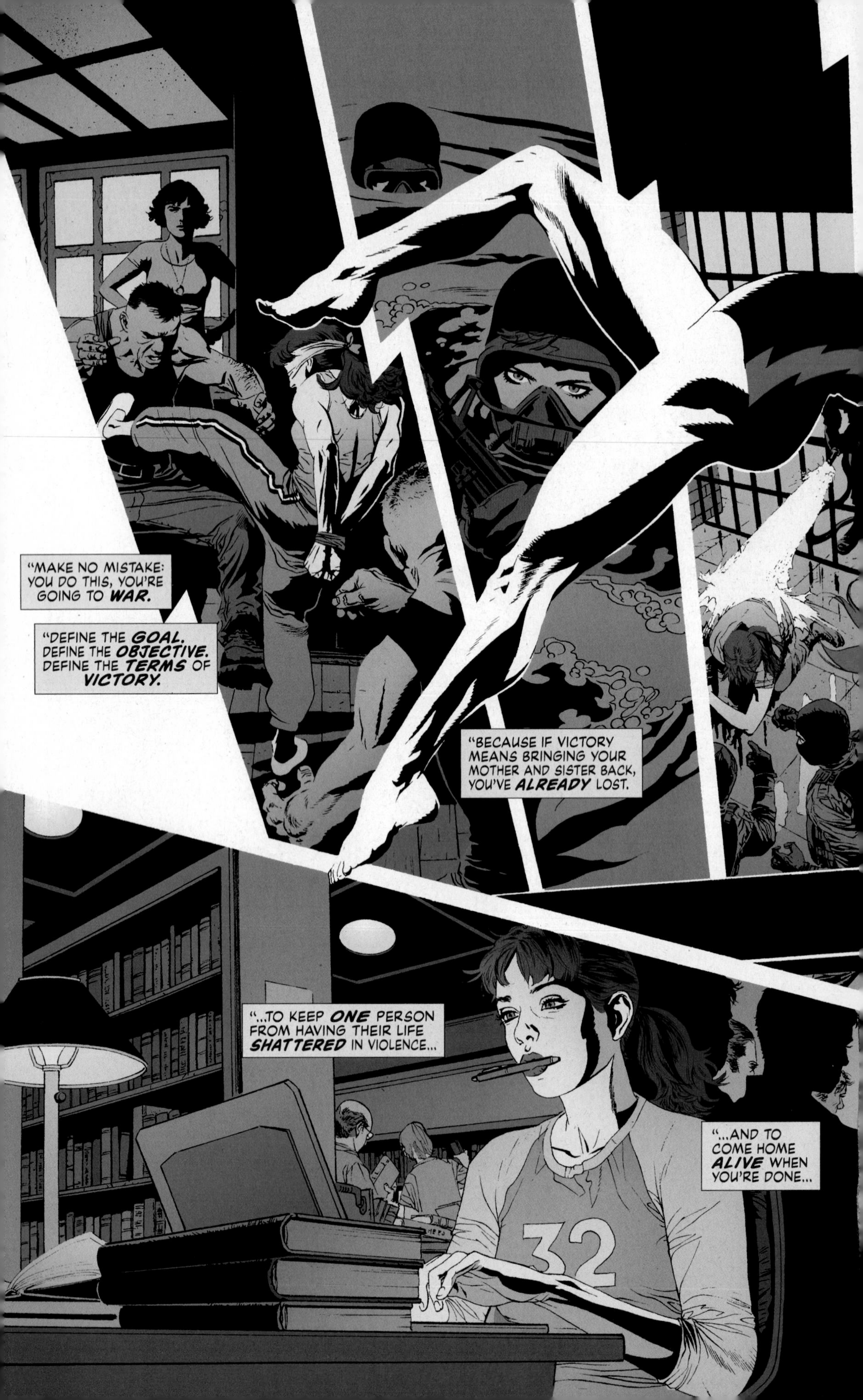
"MAKE NO MISTAKE: YOU DO THIS, YOU'RE GOING TO WAR.
"DEFINE THE GOAL. DEFINE THE OBJECTIVE. DEFINE THE TERMS OF VICTORY.
"BECAUSE IF VICTORY MEANS BRINGING YOUR MOTHER AND SISTER BACK, YOU'VE ALREADY LOST.
"...TO KEEP ONE PERSON FROM HAVING THEIR LIFE SHATTERED IN VIOLENCE...
"...AND TO COME HOME ALIVE WHEN YOU'RE DONE...

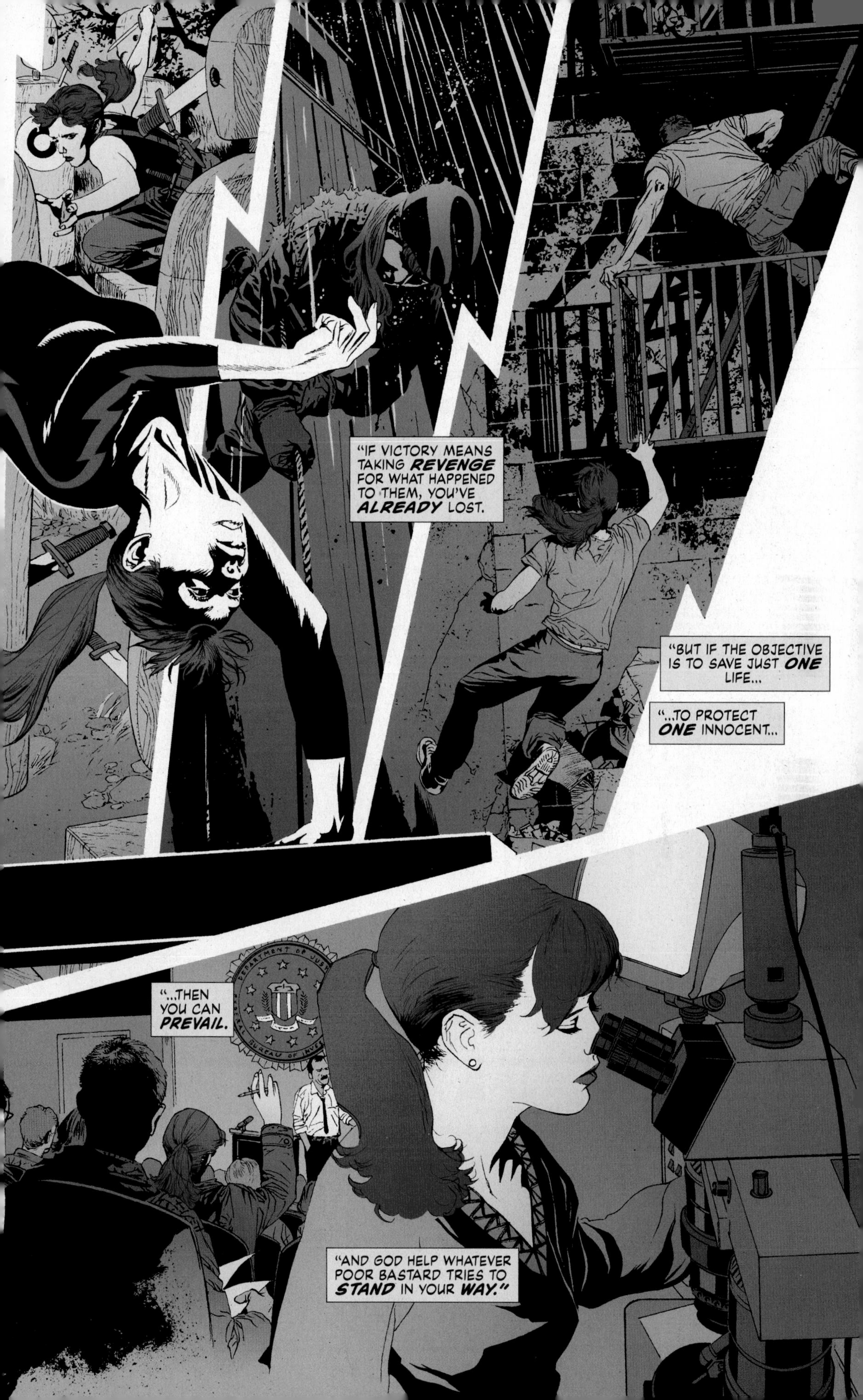
"IF VICTORY MEANS TAKING REVENGE FOR WHAT HAPPENED TO THEM, YOU'VE ALREADY LOST.
"BUT IF THE OBJECTIVE IS TO SAVE JUST ONE LIFE...
"...TO PROTECT ONE INNOCENT...
"...THEN YOU CAN PREVAIL.
"AND GOD HELP WHATEVER POOR BASTARD TRIES TO STAND IN YOUR WAY."

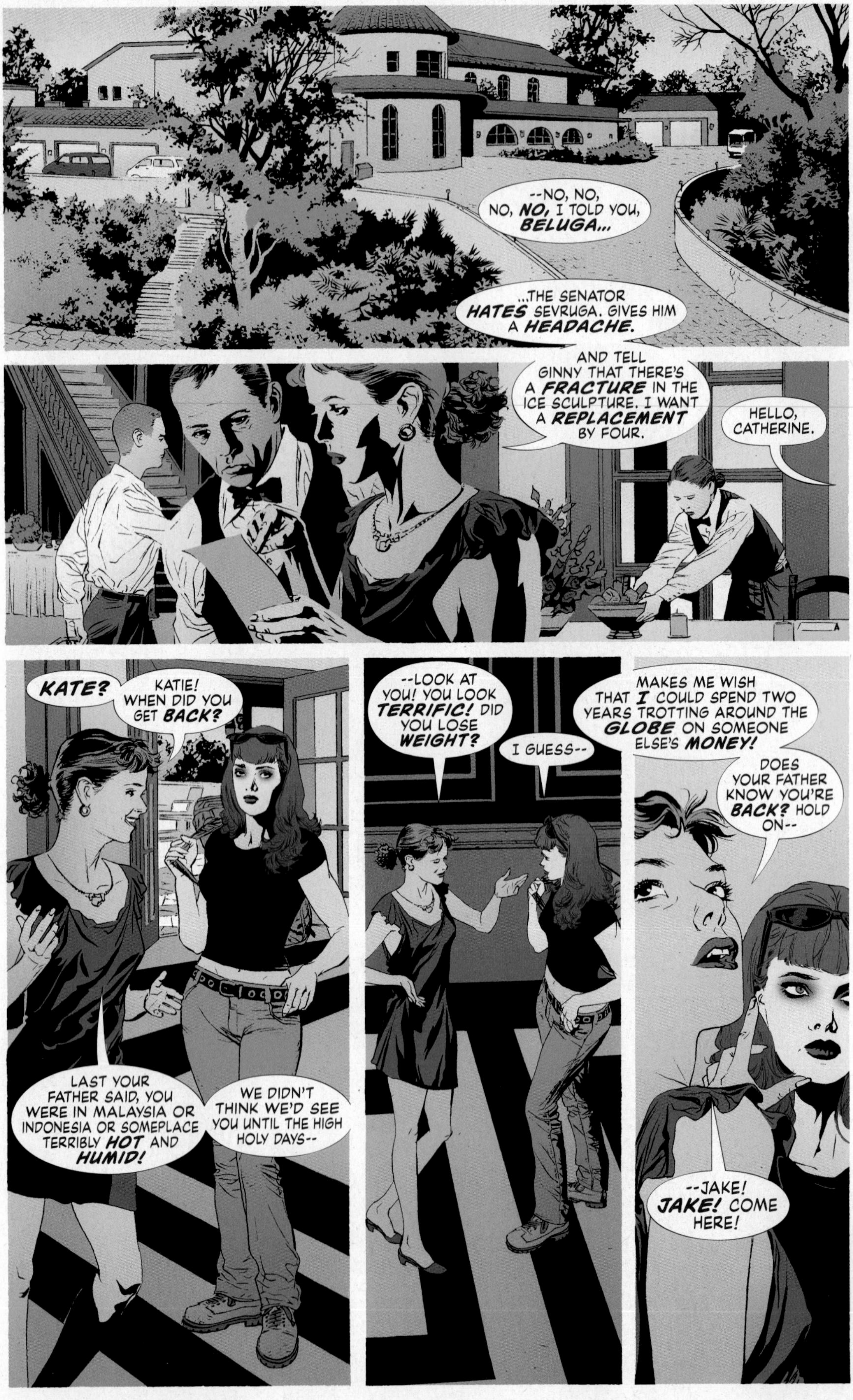
--NO, NO, NO, NO, I TOLD YOU, BELUGA...
...THE SENATOR HATES SEVRUGA. GIVES HIM A HEADACHE.
AND TELL GINNY THAT THERE'S A FRACTURE IN THE ICE SCULPTURE. I WANT A REPLACEMENT BY FOUR.
HELLO, CATHERINE.
KATE?
KATIE! WHEN DID YOU GET BACK?
LAST YOUR FATHER SAID, YOU WERE IN MALAYSIA OR INDONESIA OR SOMEPLACE TERRIBLY HOT AND HUMID!
WE DIDN'T THINK WE'D SEE YOU UNTIL THE HIGH HOLY DAYS--
--LOOK AT YOU! YOU LOOK TERRIFIC! DID YOU LOSE WEIGHT?
I GUESS--
MAKES ME WISH THAT I COULD SPEND TWO YEARS TROTTING AROUND THE GLOBE ON SOMEONE ELSE'S MONEY!
DOES YOUR FATHER KNOW YOU'RE BACK? HOLD ON--
--JAKE! JAKE! COME HERE!

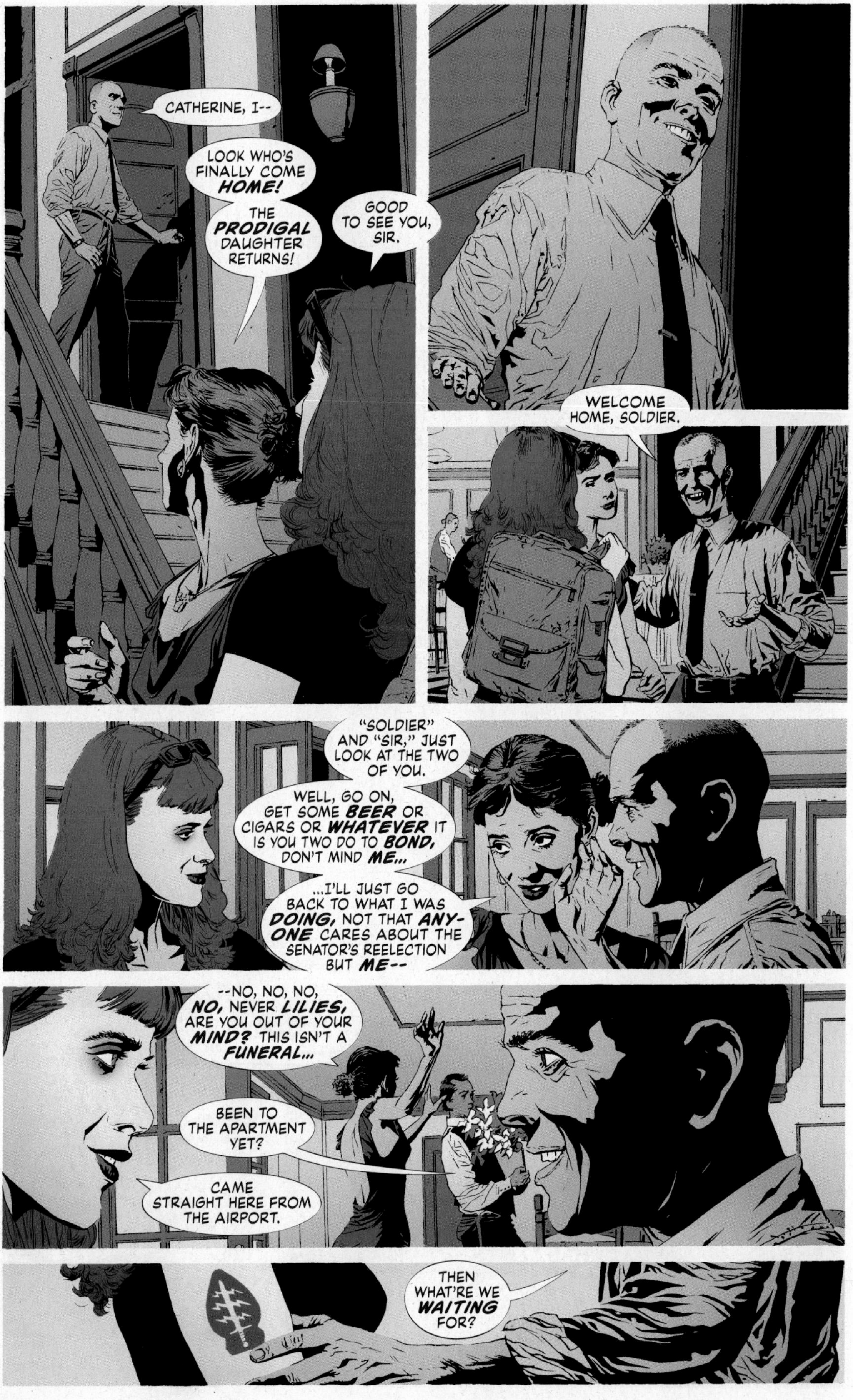
CATHERINE, I--
LOOK WHO'S FINALLY COME HOME!
THE PRODIGAL DAUGHTER RETURNS!
GOOD TO SEE YOU, SIR.
WELCOME HOME, SOLDIER.
"SOLDIER" AND "SIR," JUST LOOK AT THE TWO OF YOU.
WELL, GO ON, GET SOME BEER OR CIGARS OR WHATEVER IT IS YOU TWO DO TO BOND, DON'T MIND ME...
...I'LL JUST GO BACK TO WHAT I WAS DOING, NOT THAT ANYONE CARES ABOUT THE SENATOR'S REELECTION BUT ME--
--NO, NO, NO, NO, NEVER LILIES, ARE YOU OUT OF YOUR MIND? THIS ISN'T A FUNERAL...
BEEN TO THE APARTMENT YET?
CAME STRAIGHT HERE FROM THE AIRPORT.
THEN WHAT'RE WE WAITING FOR?

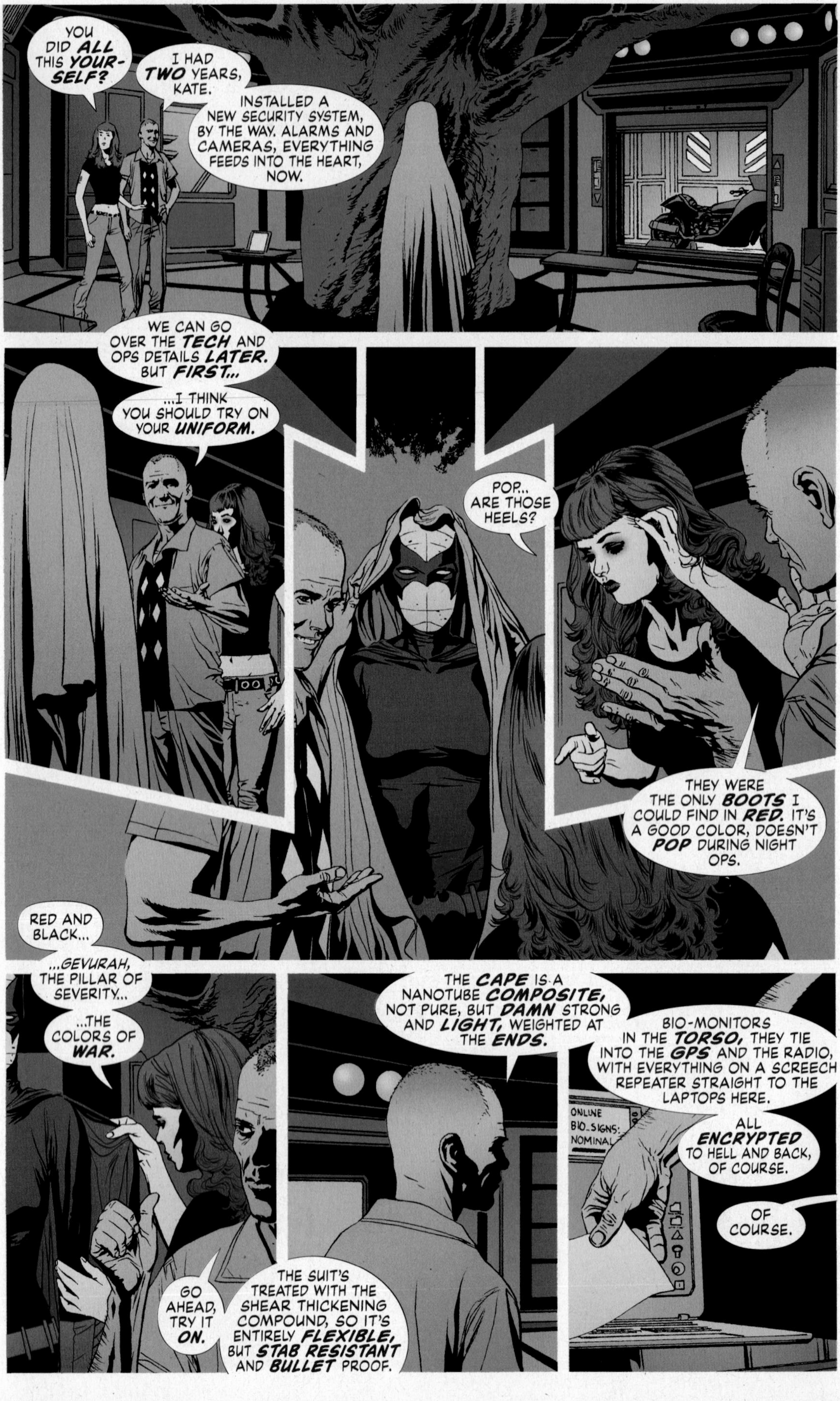
YOU DID ALL THIS YOURSELF?
I HAD TWO YEARS, KATE.
INSTALLED A NEW SECURITY SYSTEM, BY THE WAY. ALARMS AND CAMERAS, EVERYTHING FEEDS INTO THE HEART, NOW.
WE CAN GO OVER THE TECH AND OPS DETAILS LATER. BUT FIRST...
...I THINK YOU SHOULD TRY ON YOUR UNIFORM.
POP.. ARE THOSE HEELS?
THEY WERE THE ONLY BOOTS I COULD FIND IN RED. IT'S A GOOD COLOR, DOESN'T POP DURING NIGHT OPS.
RED AND BLACK...
...GEVURAH, THE PILLAR OF SEVERITY...
...THE COLORS OF WAR.
GO AHEAD, TRY IT ON.
THE SUIT'S TREATED WITH THE SHEAR THICKENING COMPOUND, SO IT'S ENTIRELY FLEXIBLE, BUT STAB RESISTANT AND BULLET PROOF.
THE CAPE IS A NANOTUBE COMPOSITE, NOT PURE, BUT DAMN STRONG AND LIGHT, WEIGHTED AT THE ENDS.
BIO-MONITORS IN THE TORSO, THEY TIE INTO THE GPS AND THE RADIO, WITH EVERYTHING ON A SCREECH REPEATER STRAIGHT TO THE LAPTOPS HERE.
ONLINE
BIO_SIGNS: NOMINAL
ALL ENCRYPTED TO HELL AND BACK, OF COURSE.
OF COURSE.

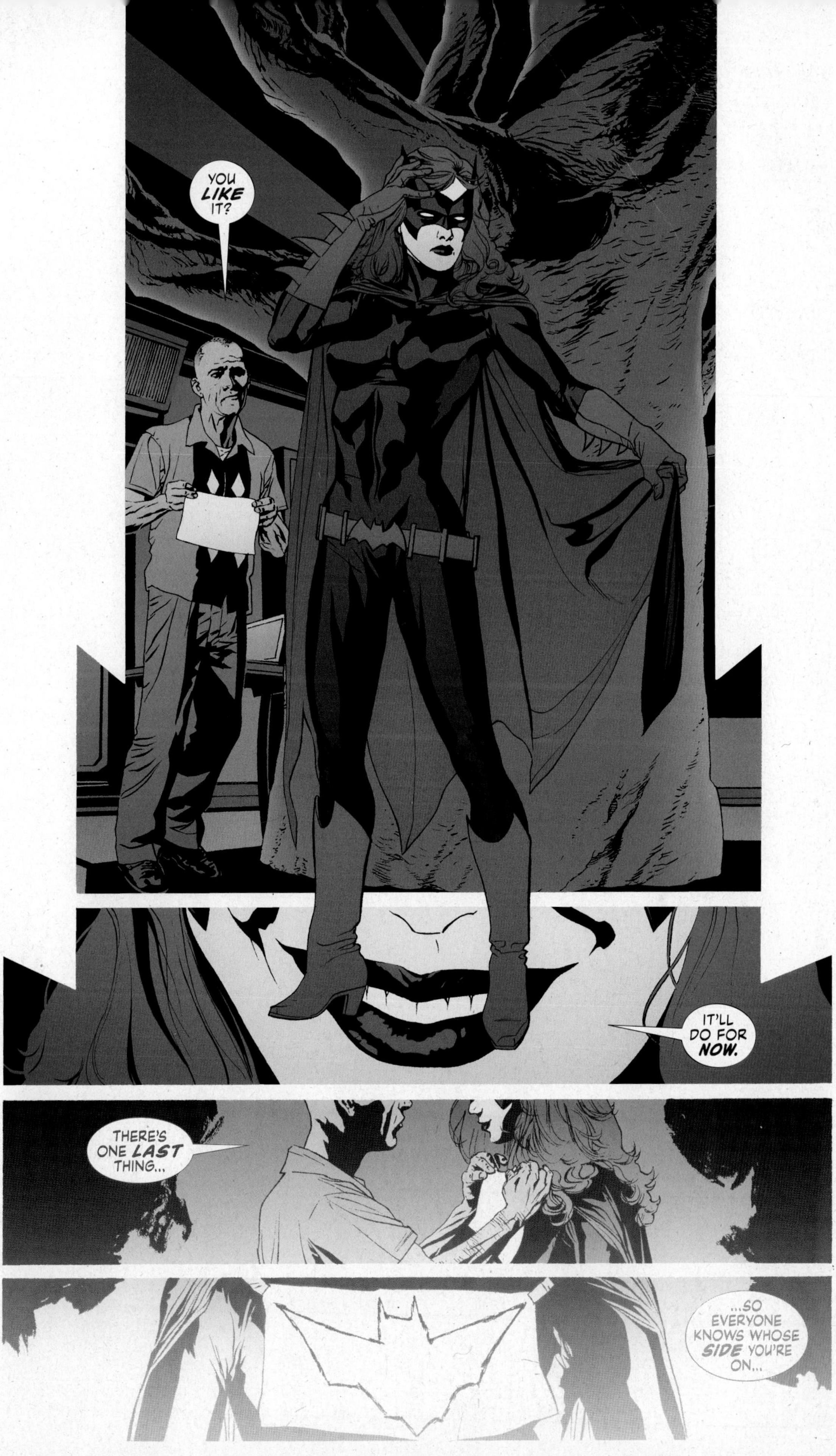
YOU LIKE IT?
IT'LL DO FOR NOW.
THERE'S ONE LAST THING...
...SO EVERYONE KNOWS WHOSE SIDE YOU'RE ON...

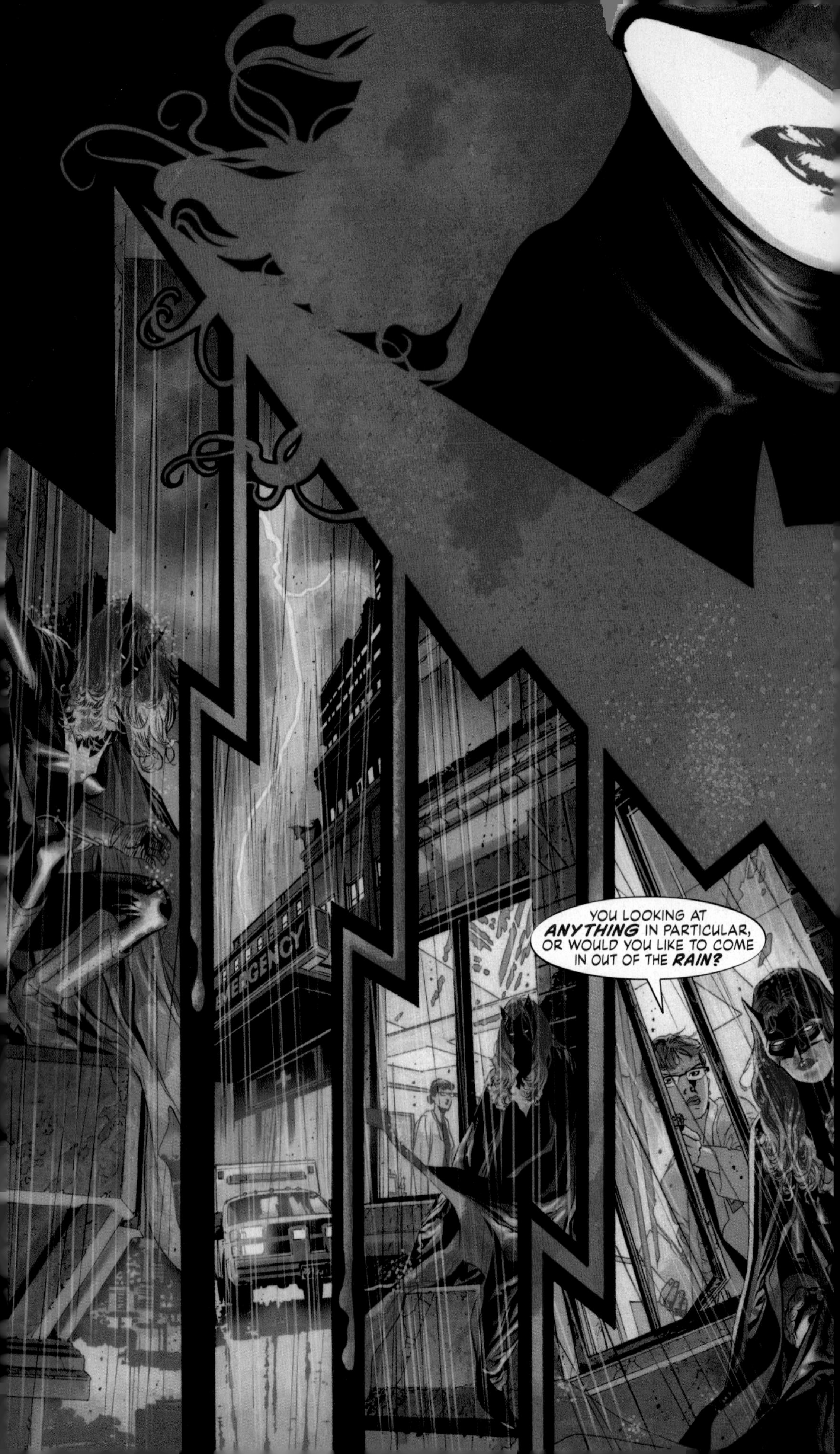
YOU LOOKING AT ANYTHING IN PARTICULAR, OR WOULD YOU LIKE TO COME IN OUT OF THE RAIN?

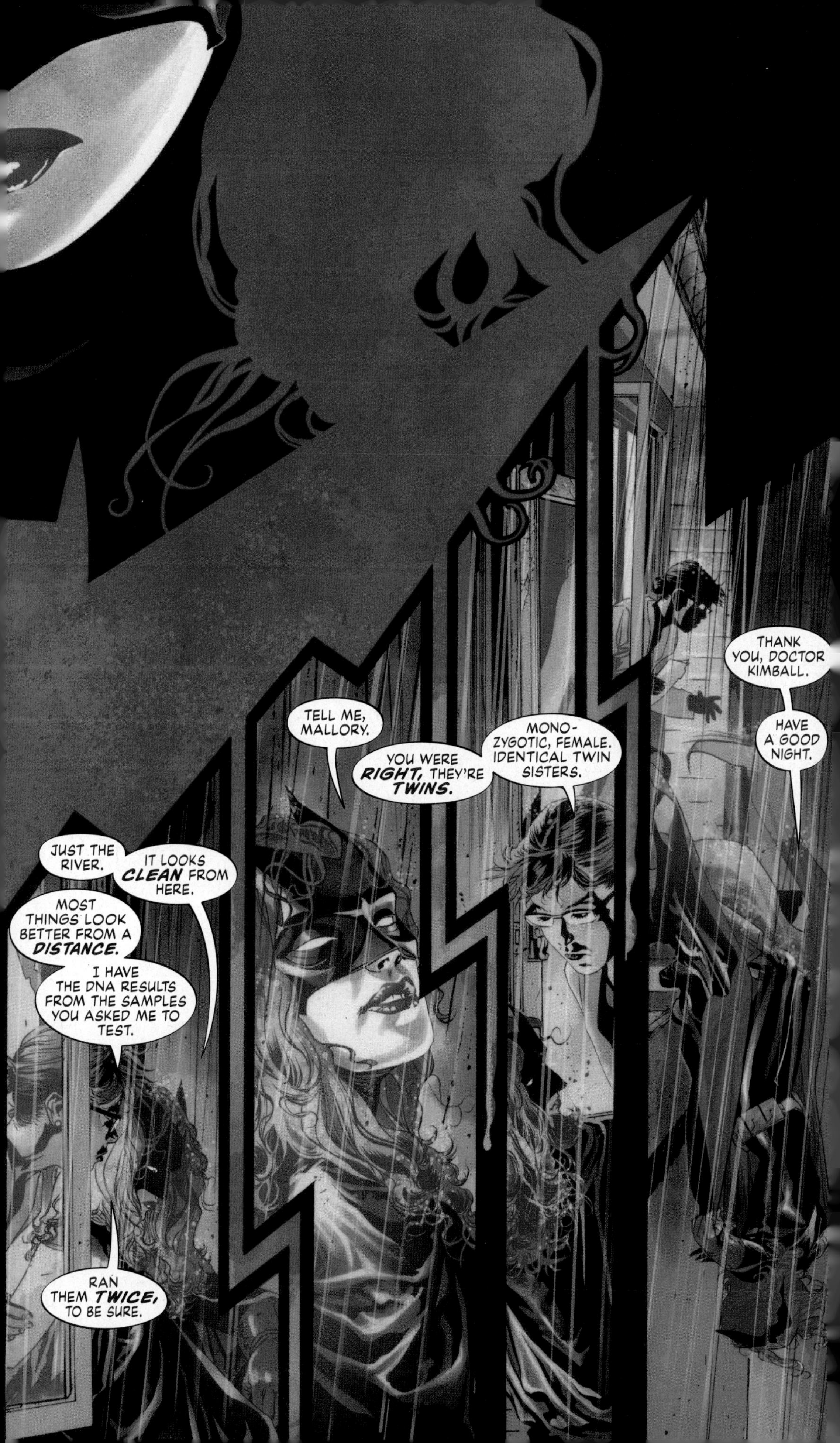
JUST THE RIVER.
IT LOOKS CLEAN FROM HERE.
MOST THINGS LOOK BETTER FROM A DISTANCE.
I HAVE THE DNA RESULTS FROM THE SAMPLES YOU ASKED ME TO TEST.
RAN THEM TWICE, TO BE SURE.
TELL ME, MALLORY.
YOU WERE RIGHT, THEY'RE TWINS.
MONO-ZYGOTIC, FEMALE. IDENTICAL TWIN SISTERS.
THANK YOU, DOCTOR KIMBALL.
HAVE A GOOD NIGHT.

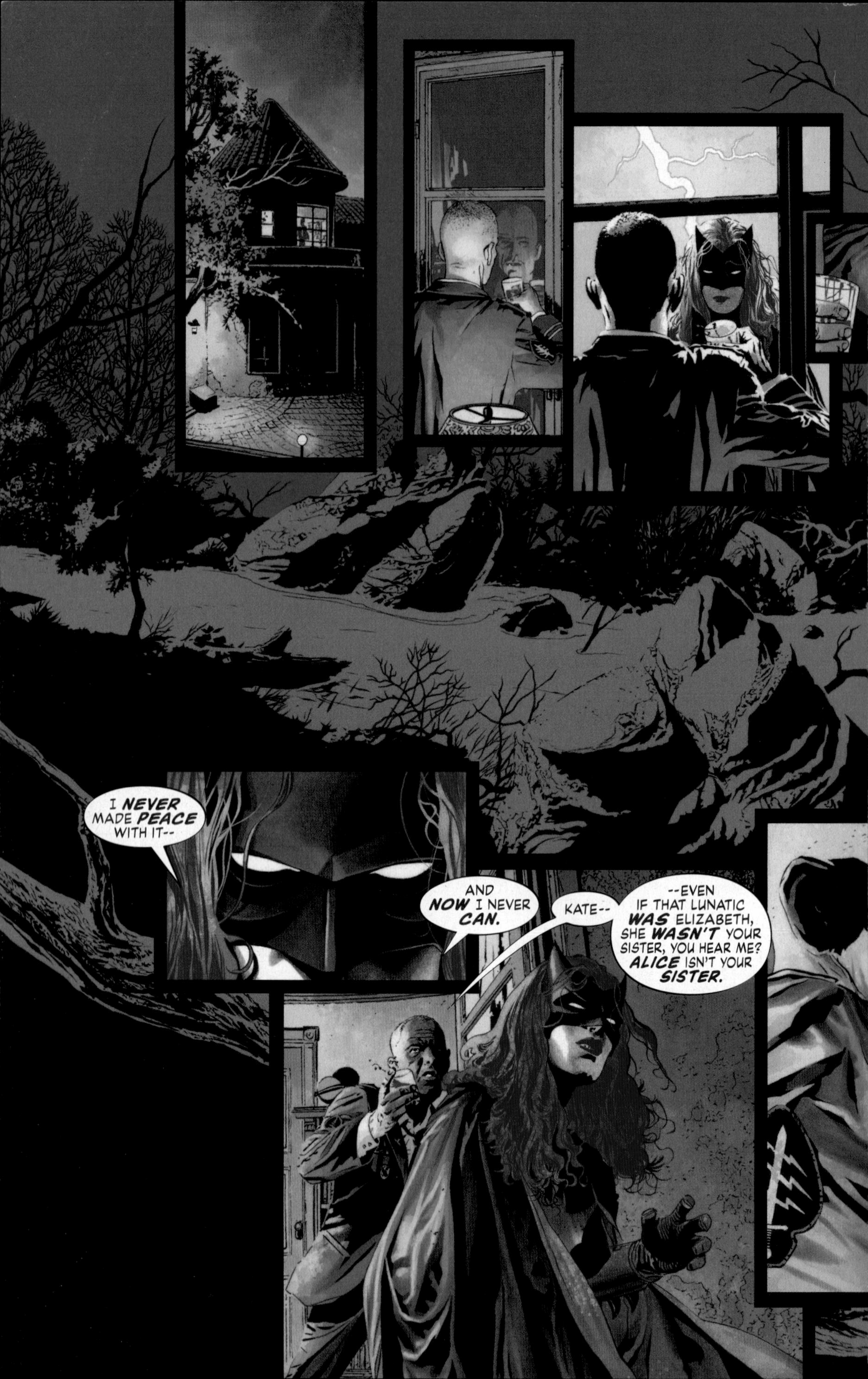
I NEVER MADE PEACE WITH IT--
AND NOW I NEVER CAN.
KATE--
--EVEN IF THAT LUNATIC WAS ELIZABETH, SHE WASN'T YOUR SISTER, YOU HEAR ME? ALICE ISN'T YOUR SISTER.

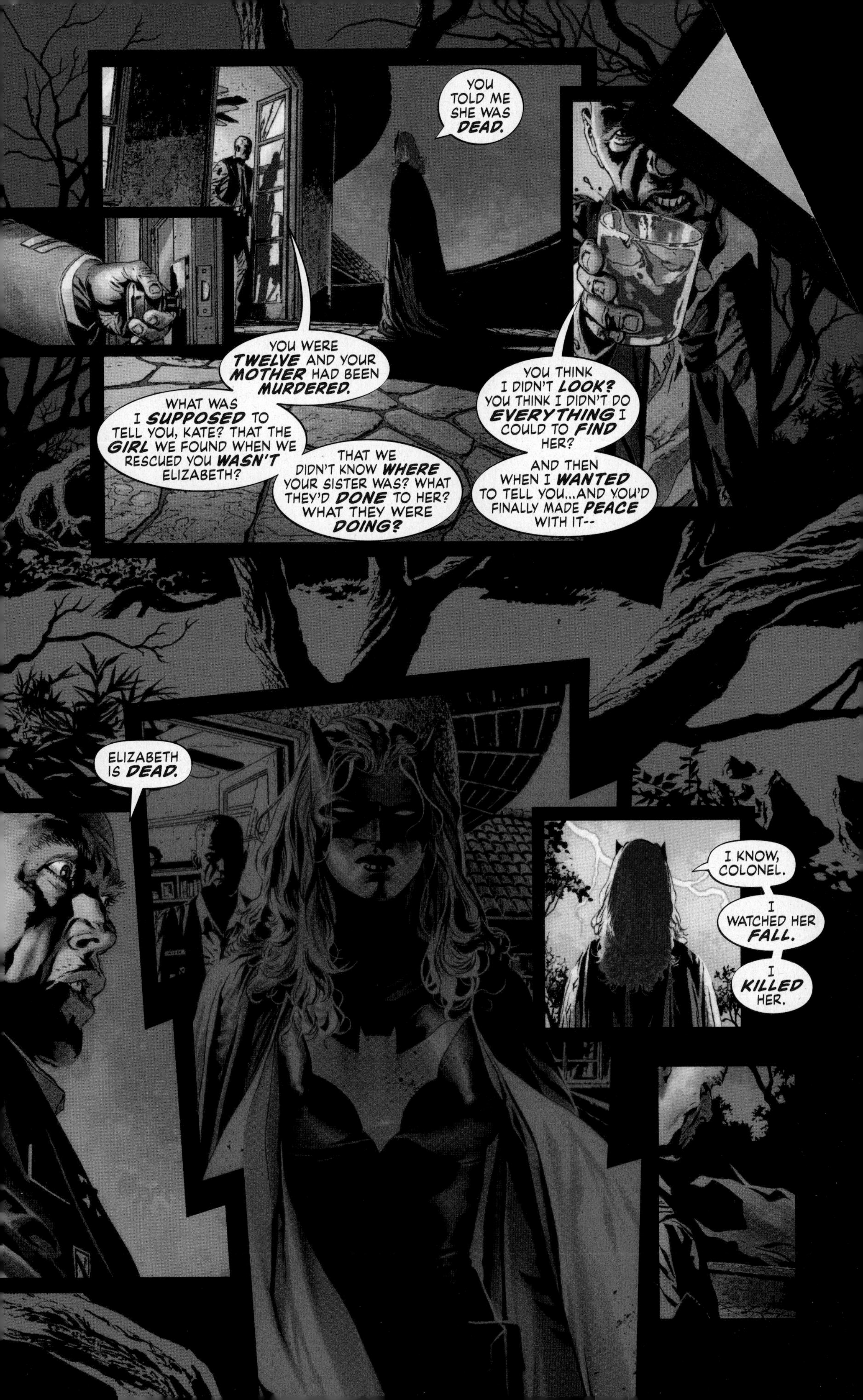
YOU TOLD ME SHE WAS DEAD.
YOU WERE TWELVE AND YOUR MOTHER HAD BEEN MURDERED.
WHAT WAS I SUPPOSED TO TELL YOU, KATE? THAT THE GIRL WE FOUND WHEN WE RESCUED YOU WASN'T ELIZABETH?
THAT WE DIDN'T KNOW WHERE YOUR SISTER WAS? WHAT THEY'D DONE TO HER? WHAT THEY WERE DOING?
YOU THINK I DIDN'T LOOK? YOU THINK I DIDN'T DO EVERYTHING I COULD TO FIND HER?
AND THEN WHEN I WANTED TO TELL YOU...AND YOU'D FINALLY MADE PEACE WITH IT--
ELIZABETH IS DEAD.
I KNOW, COLONEL.
I WATCHED HER FALL.
I KILLED HER.

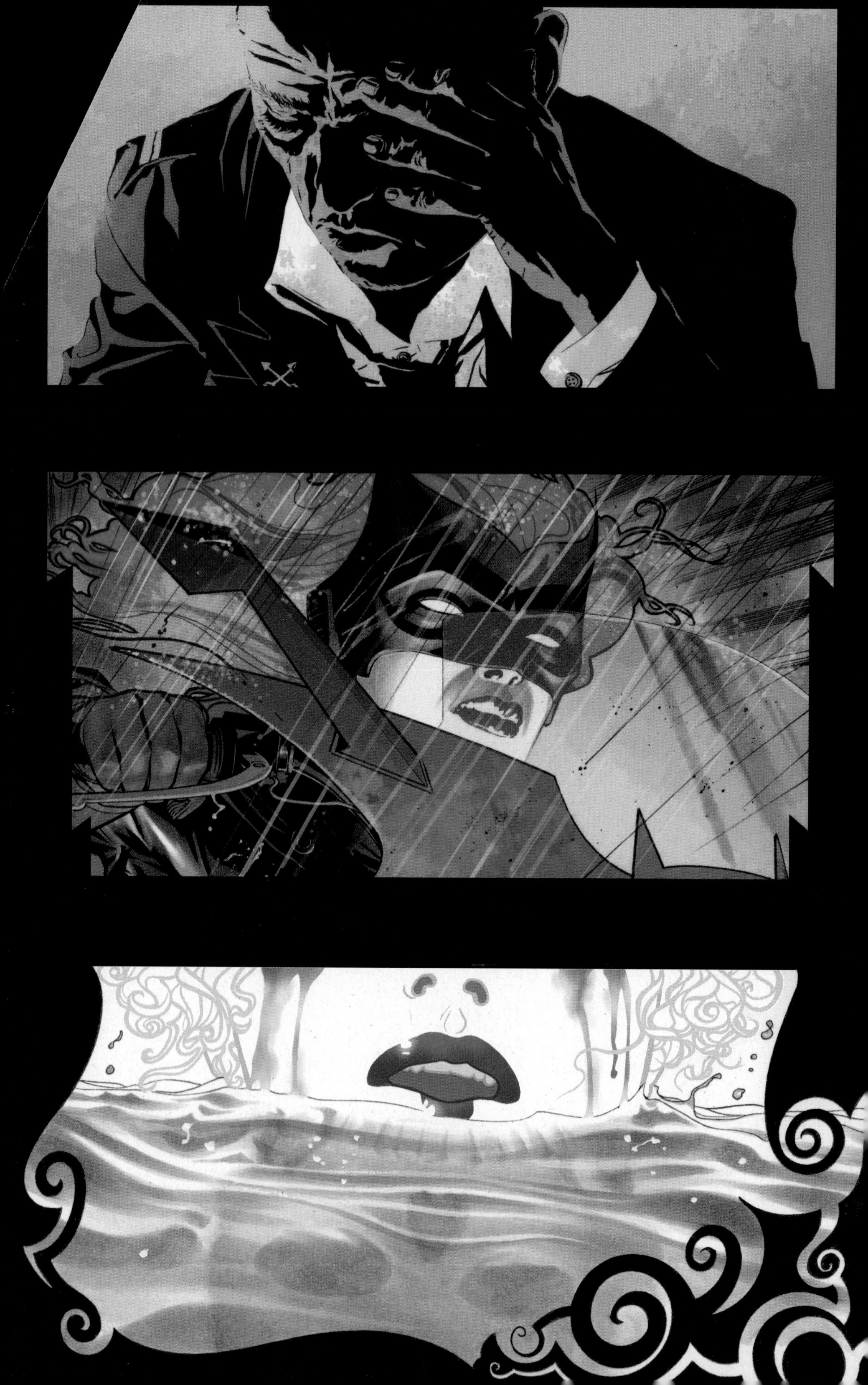

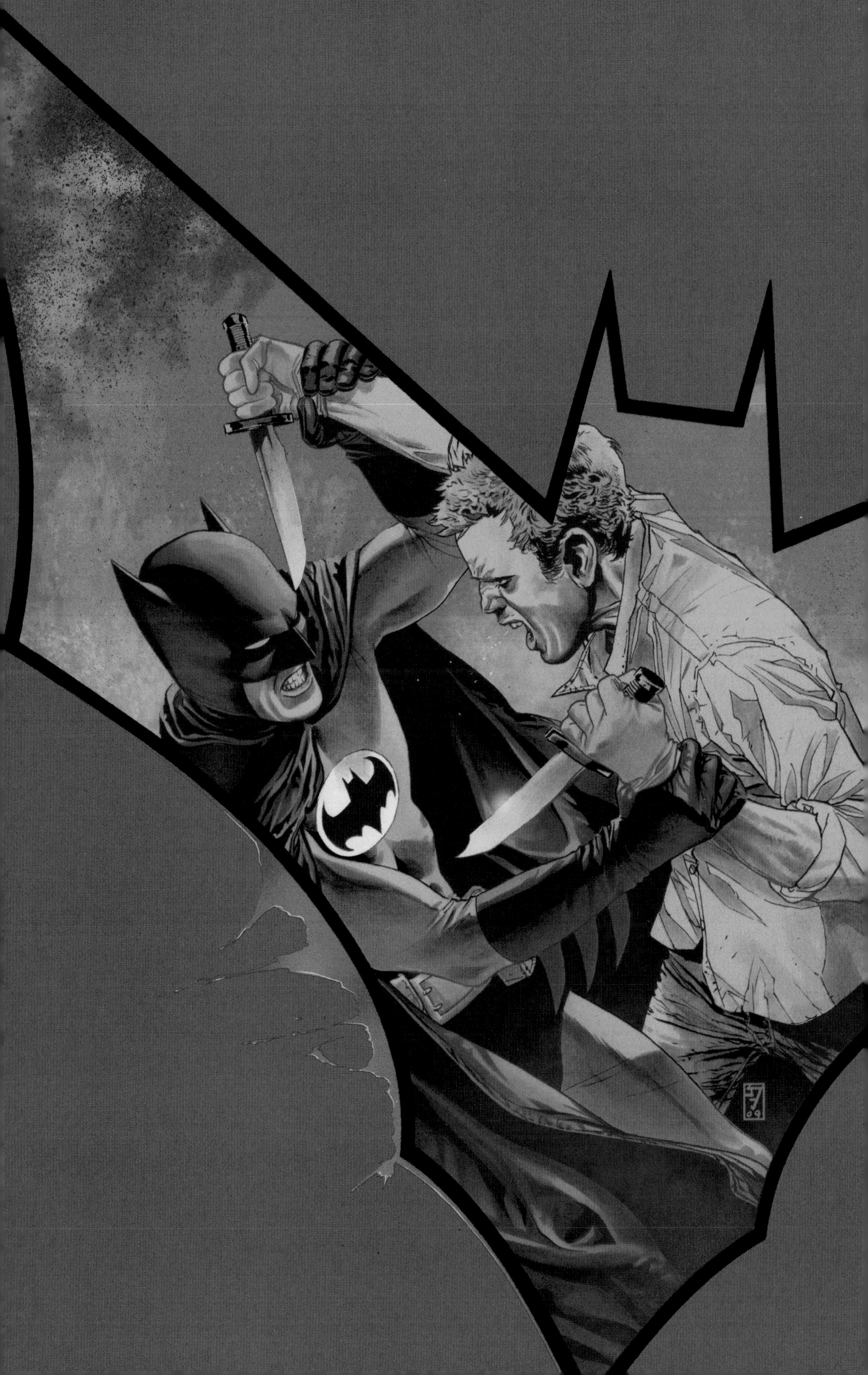

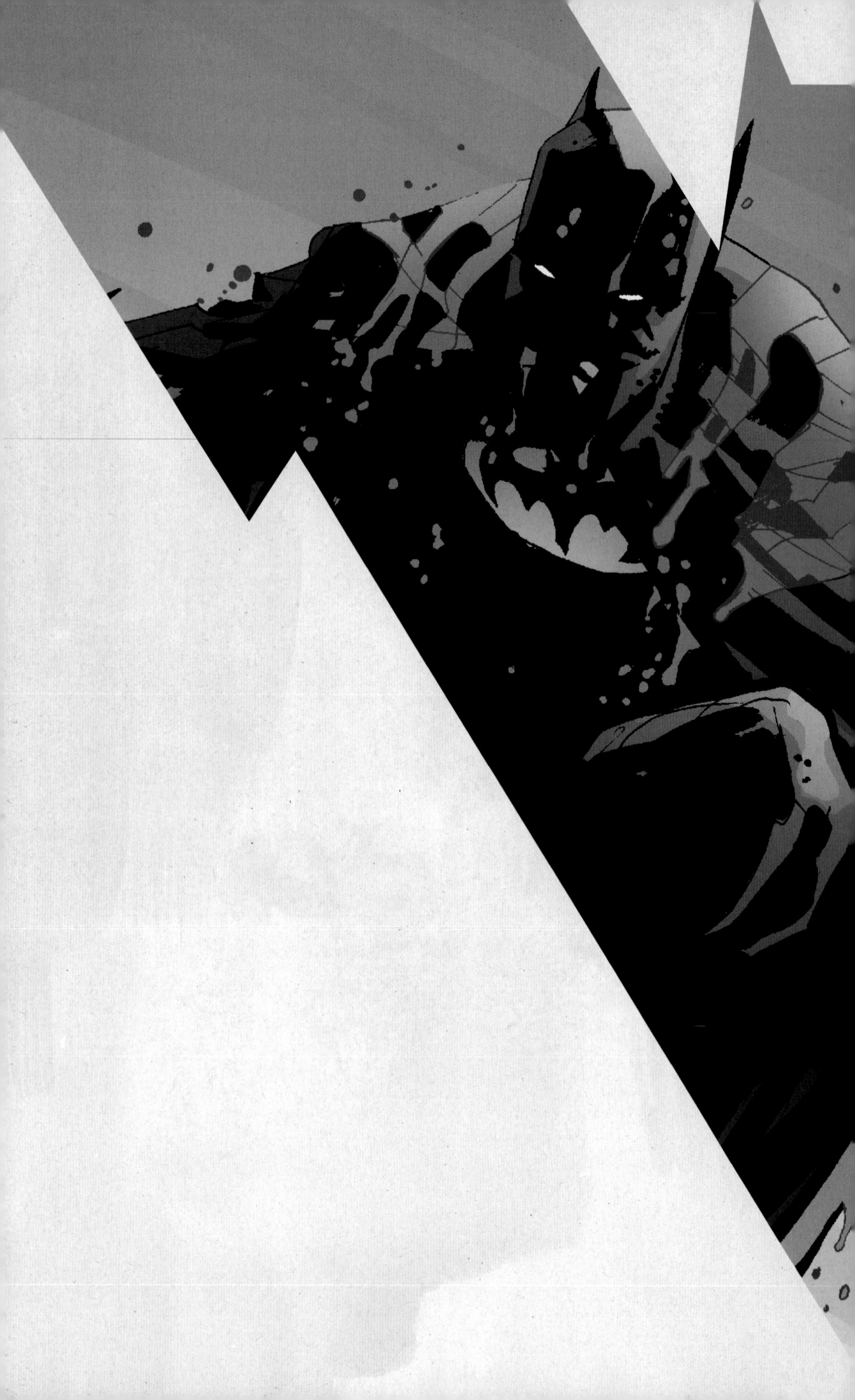

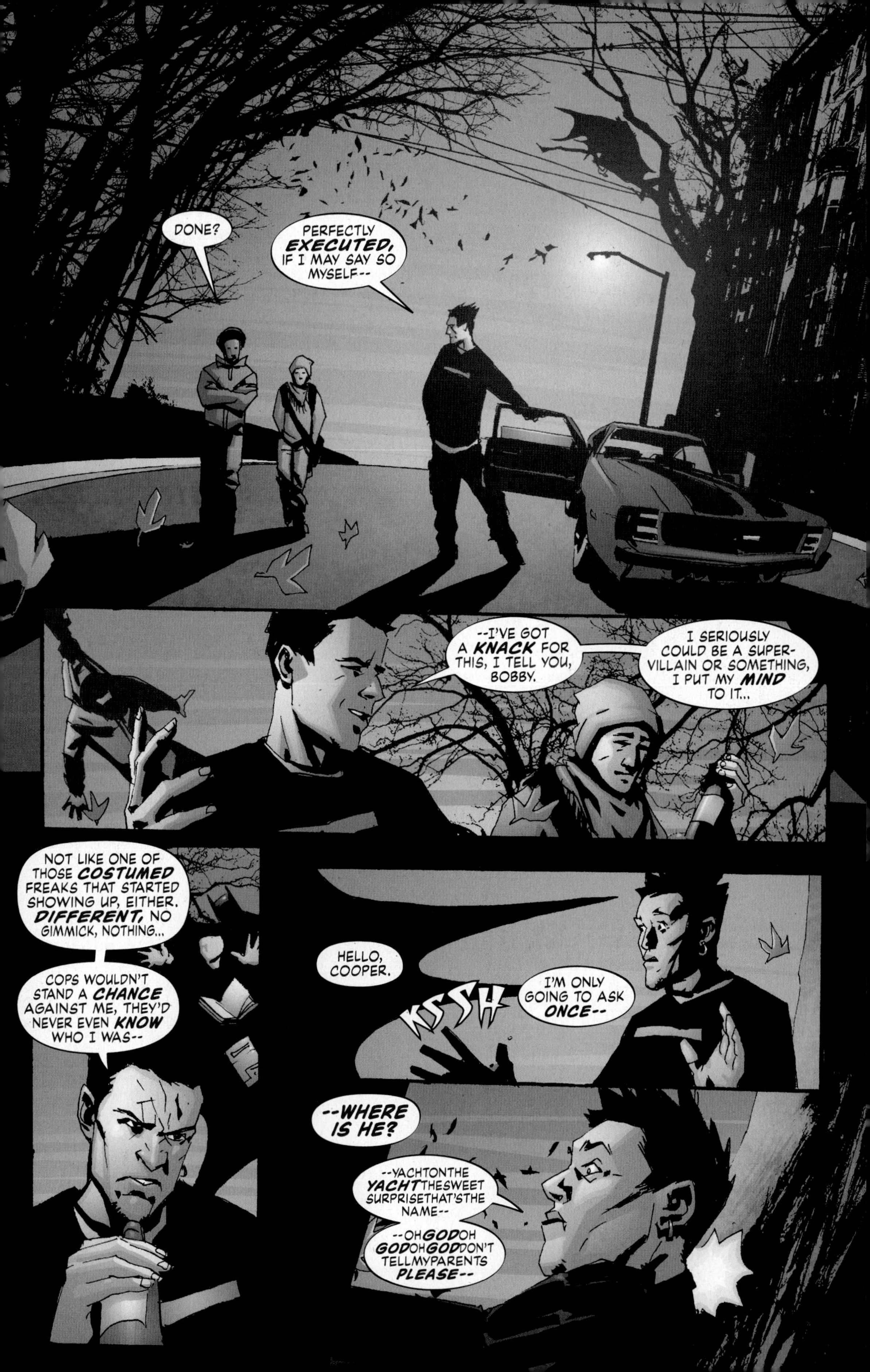
DONE?
PERFECTLY EXECUTED, IF I MAY SAY SO MYSELF--
--I'VE GOT A KNACK FOR THIS, I TELL YOU, BOBBY.
I SERIOUSLY COULD BE A SUPER-VILLAIN OR SOMETHING, I PUT MY MIND TO IT...
NOT LIKE ONE OF THOSE COSTUMED FREAKS THAT STARTED SHOWING UP, EITHER. DIFFERENT, NO GIMMICK, NOTHING...
COPS WOULDN'T STAND A CHANCE AGAINST ME, THEY'D NEVER EVEN KNOW WHO I WAS--
HELLO, COOPER.
KSSH
I'M ONLY GOING TO ASK ONCE--
--WHERE IS HE?
--YACHTONTHE YACHT THESWEET SURPRISETHAT'STHE NAME--
--OHGODOH GODOHGODDON'T TELLMYPARENTS PLEASE--

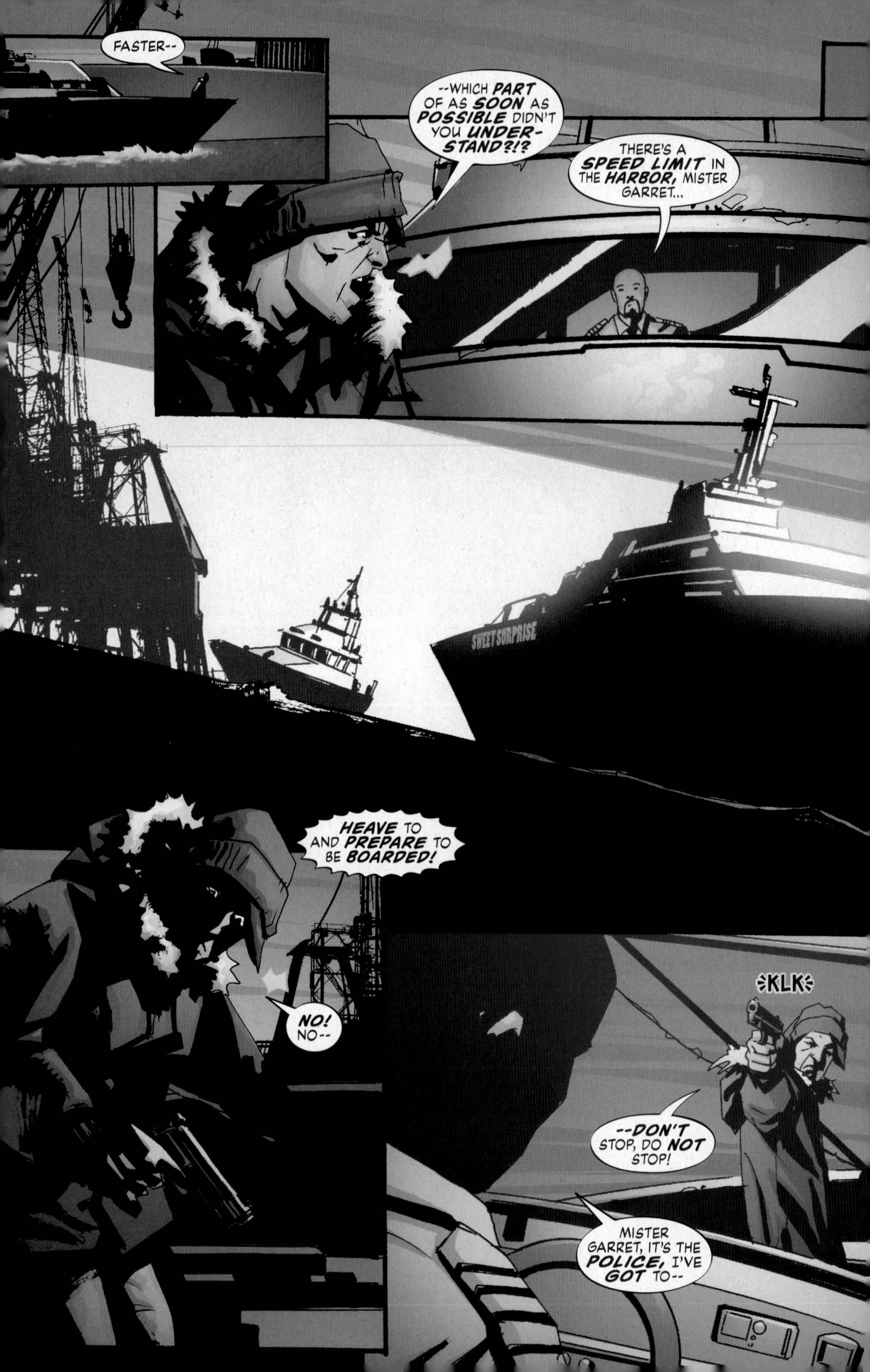
FASTER--
--WHICH PART OF AS SOON AS POSSIBLE DIDN'T YOU UNDER-STAND?!?
THERE'S A SPEED LIMIT IN THE HARBOR, MISTER GARRET...
SWEET SURPRISE
HEAVE TO AND PREPARE TO BE BOARDED!
NO! NO--
KLK
--DON'T STOP, DO NOT STOP!
MISTER GARRET, IT'S THE POLICE, I'VE GOT TO--

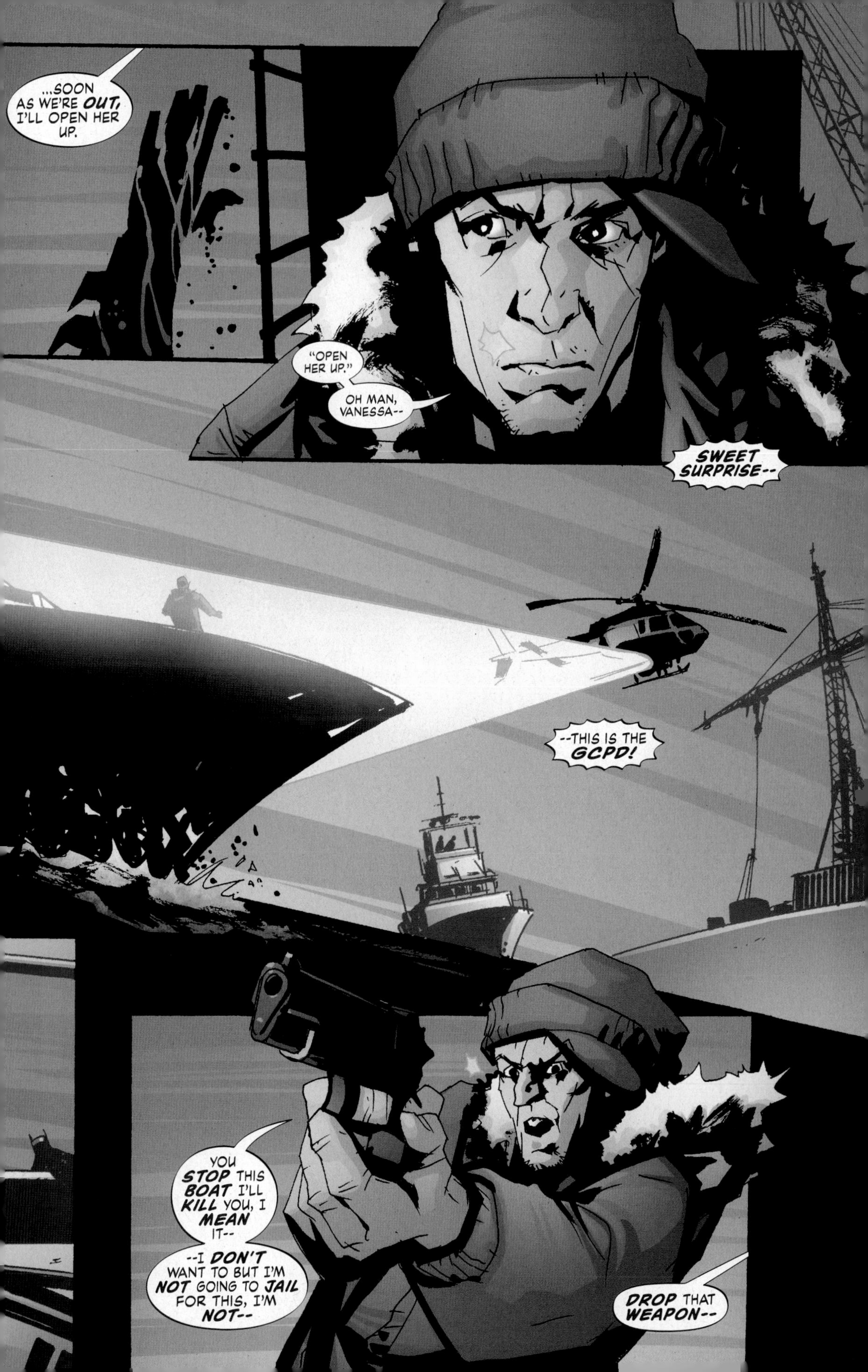
...SOON AS WE'RE OUT, I'LL OPEN HER UP.
"OPEN HER UP."
OH MAN, VANESSA--
SWEET SURPRISE--
--THIS IS THE GCPD!
YOU STOP THIS BOAT I'LL KILL YOU, I MEAN IT--
--I DON'T WANT TO BUT I'M NOT GOING TO JAIL FOR THIS, I'M NOT--
DROP THAT WEAPON--

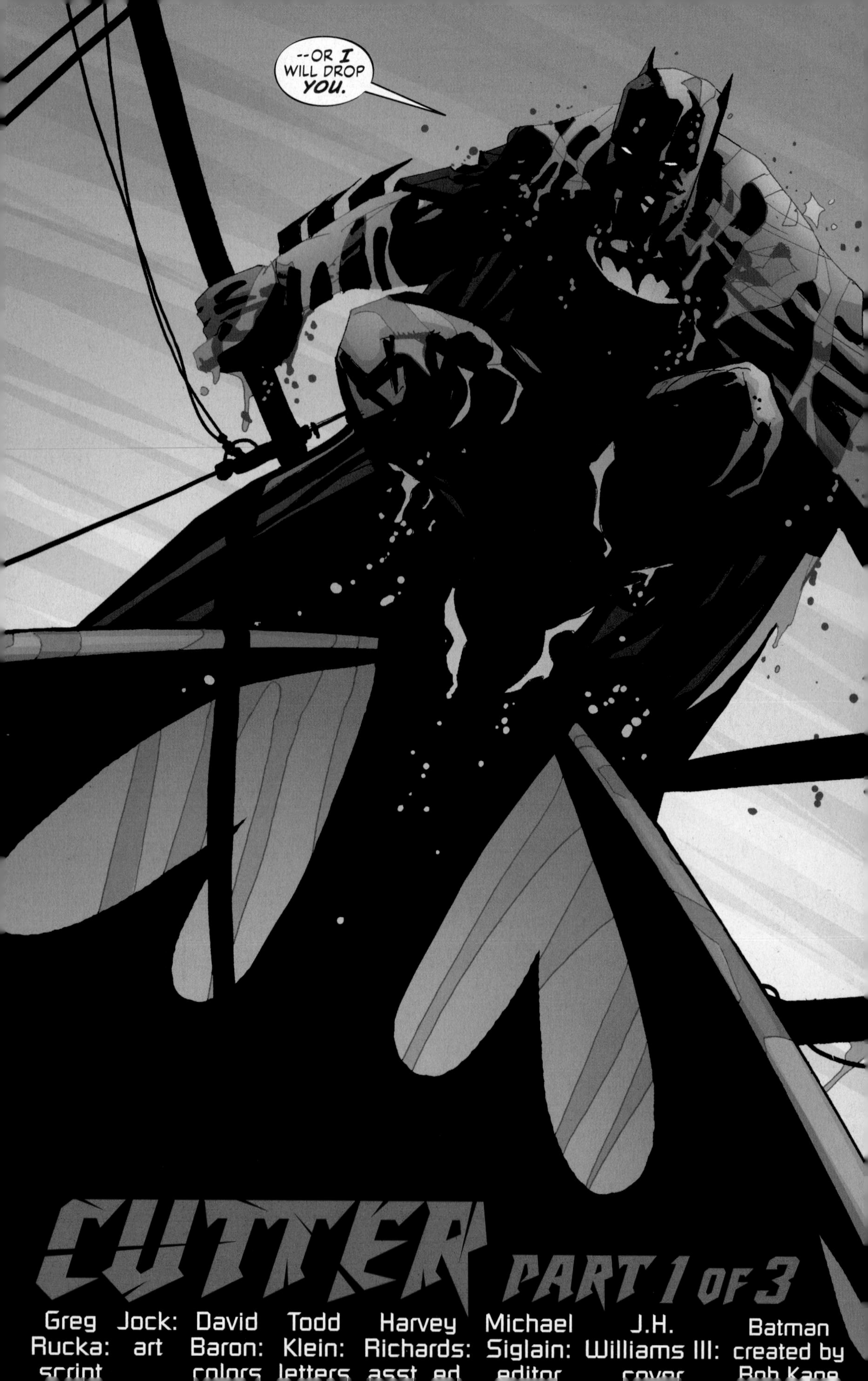
--OR I WILL DROP YOU.
CUTTER PART 1 OF 3
Greg Rucka: script
Jock: art
David Baron: colors
Todd Klein: letters
Harvey Richards: asst. ed.
Michael Siglain: editor
J.H. Williams III: cover
Batman created by Bob Kane

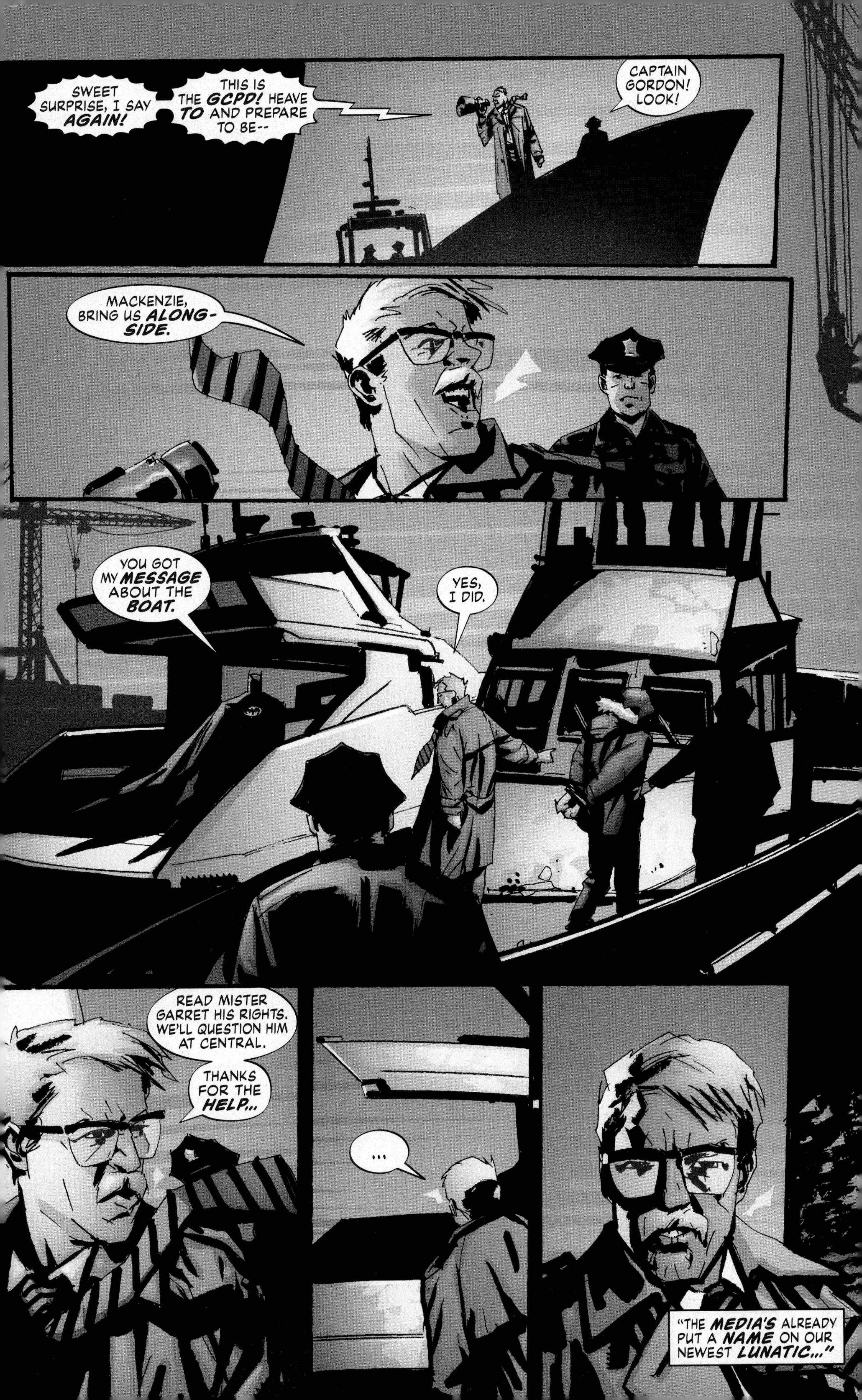
SWEET SURPRISE, I SAY AGAIN!
THIS IS THE GCPD! HEAVE TO AND PREPARE TO BE--
CAPTAIN GORDON! LOOK!
MACKENZIE, BRING US ALONG-SIDE.
YOU GOT MY MESSAGE ABOUT THE BOAT.
YES, I DID.
READ MISTER GARRET HIS RIGHTS. WE'LL QUESTION HIM AT CENTRAL.
THANKS FOR THE HELP...
...
"THE MEDIA'S ALREADY PUT A NAME ON OUR NEWEST LUNATIC..."

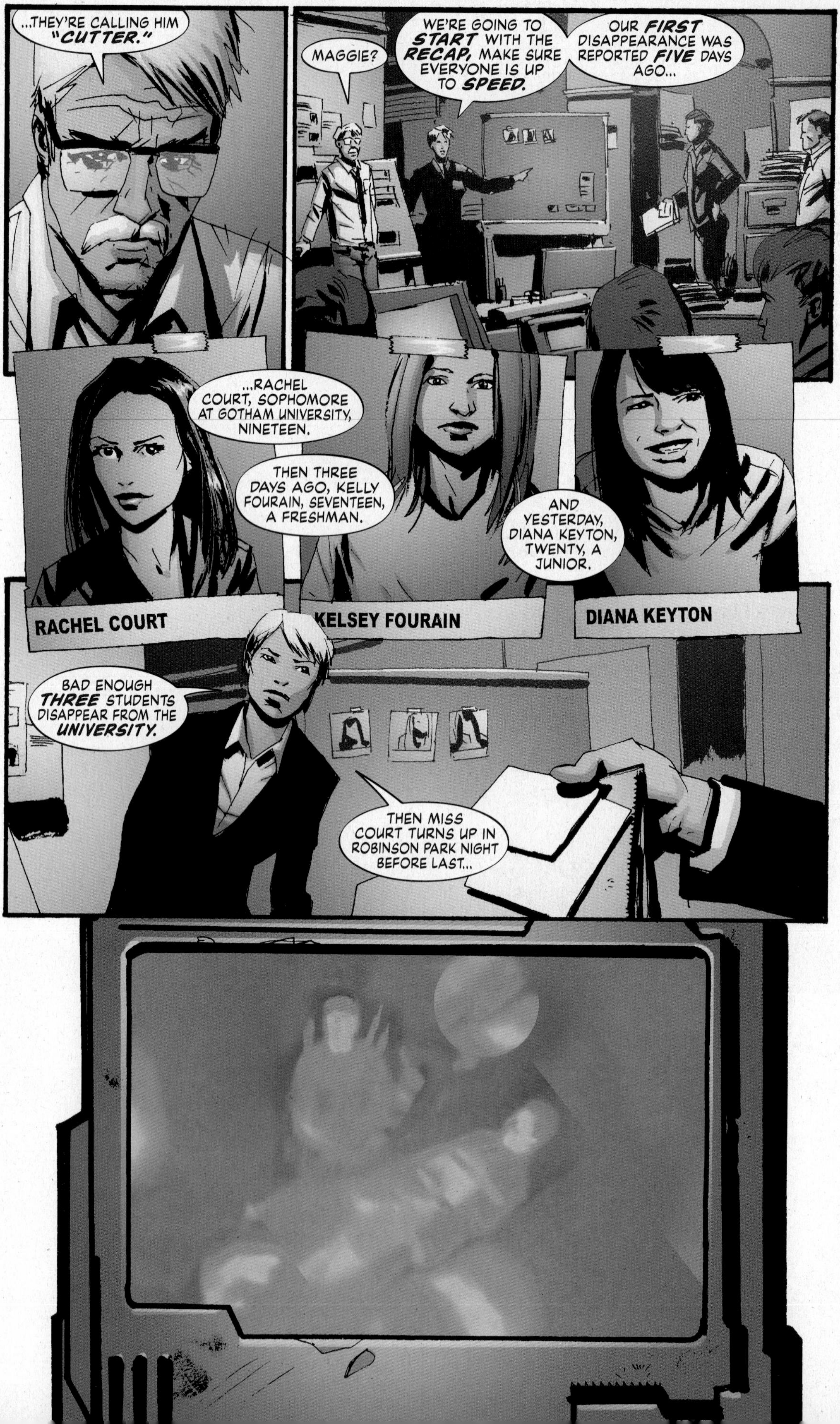
...THEY'RE CALLING HIM "CUTTER."
MAGGIE?
WE'RE GOING TO START WITH THE RECAP, MAKE SURE EVERYONE IS UP TO SPEED.
OUR FIRST DISAPPEARANCE WAS REPORTED FIVE DAYS AGO...
...RACHEL COURT, SOPHOMORE AT GOTHAM UNIVERSITY, NINETEEN.
THEN THREE DAYS AGO, KELLY FOURAIN, SEVENTEEN, A FRESHMAN.
AND YESTERDAY, DIANA KEYTON, TWENTY, A JUNIOR.
RACHEL COURT
KELSEY FOURAIN
DIANA KEYTON
BAD ENOUGH THREE STUDENTS DISAPPEAR FROM THE UNIVERSITY.
THEN MISS COURT TURNS UP IN ROBINSON PARK NIGHT BEFORE LAST...

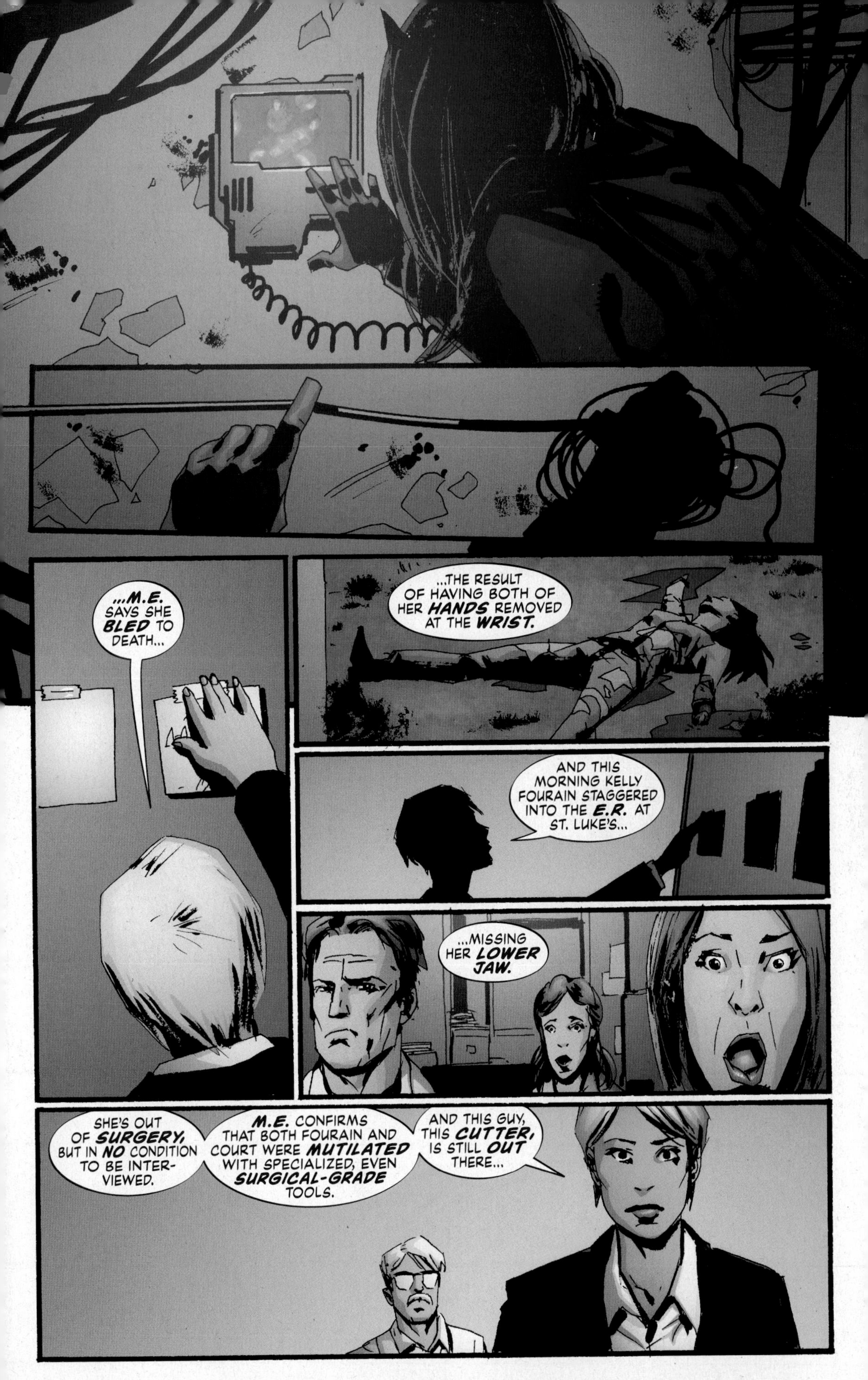
...M.E. SAYS SHE BLED TO DEATH...
...THE RESULT OF HAVING BOTH OF HER HANDS REMOVED AT THE WRIST.
AND THIS MORNING KELLY FOURAIN STAGGERED INTO THE E.R. AT ST. LUKE'S...
...MISSING HER LOWER JAW.
SHE'S OUT OF SURGERY, BUT IN NO CONDITION TO BE INTER-VIEWED.
M.E. CONFIRMS THAT BOTH FOURAIN AND COURT WERE MUTILATED WITH SPECIALIZED, EVEN SURGICAL-GRADE TOOLS.
AND THIS GUY, THIS CUTTER, IS STILL OUT THERE...

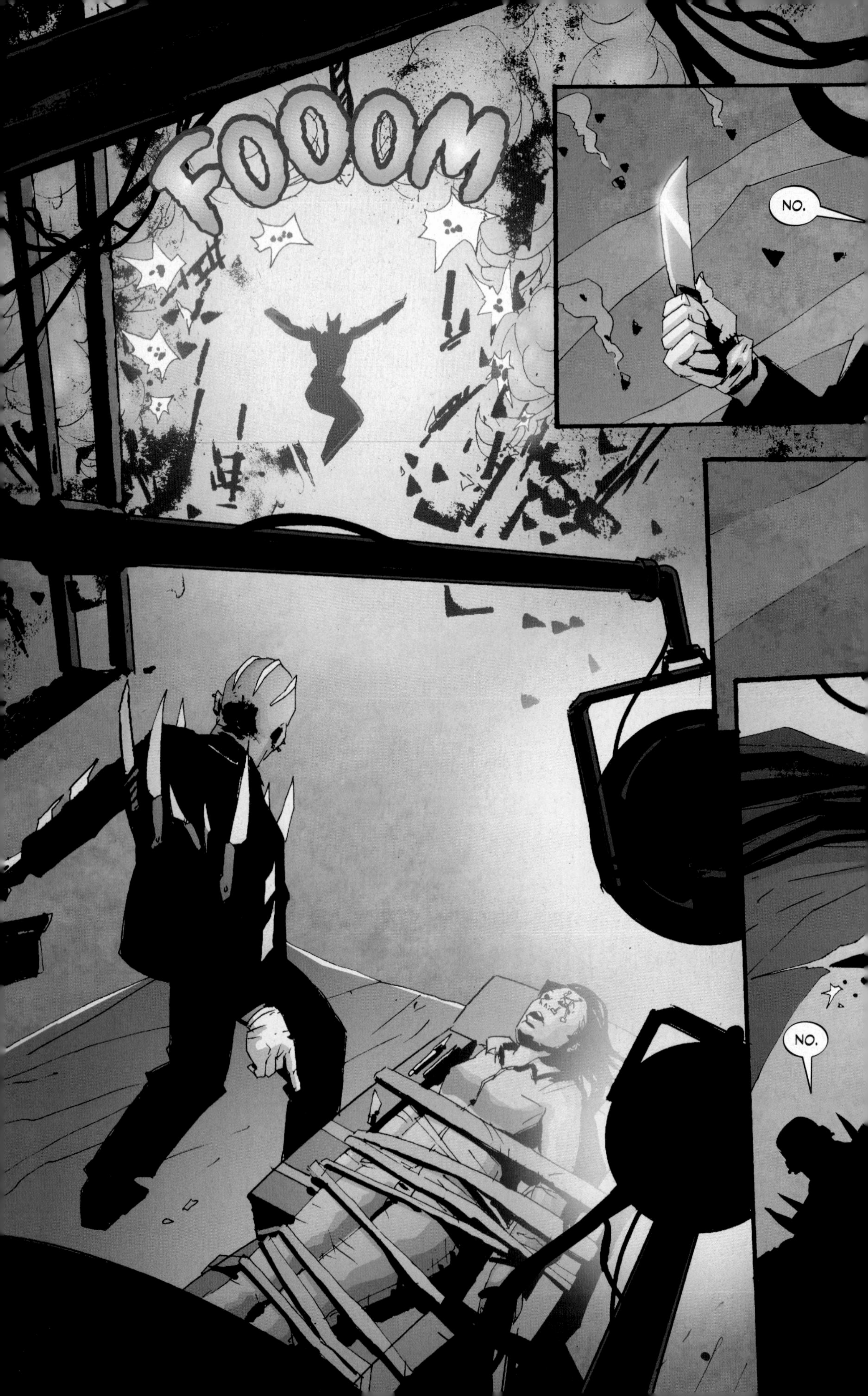
FOOOM
NO.
NO.

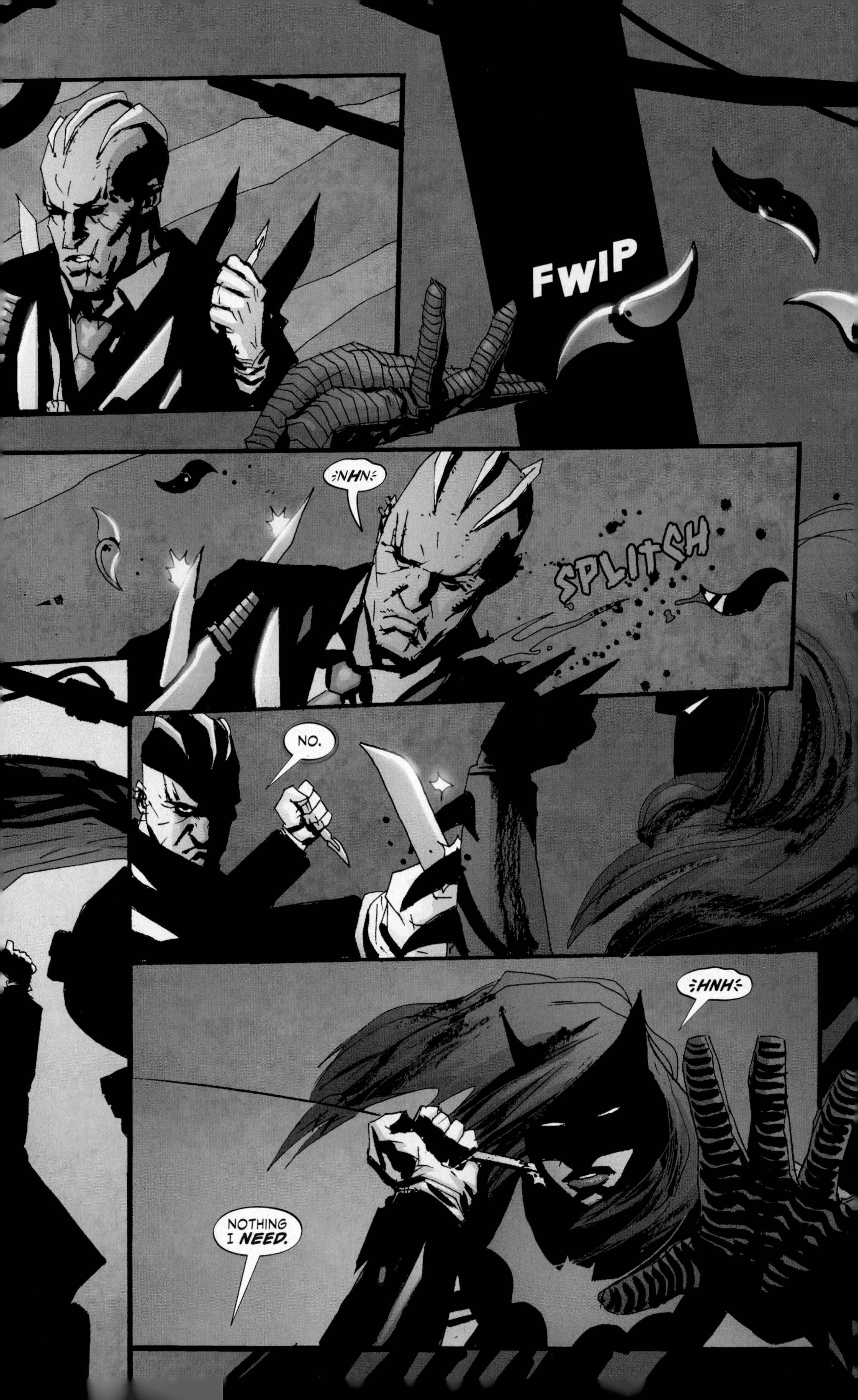
FWIP
NHN
SPLITCH
NO.
HNH
NOTHING I NEED.

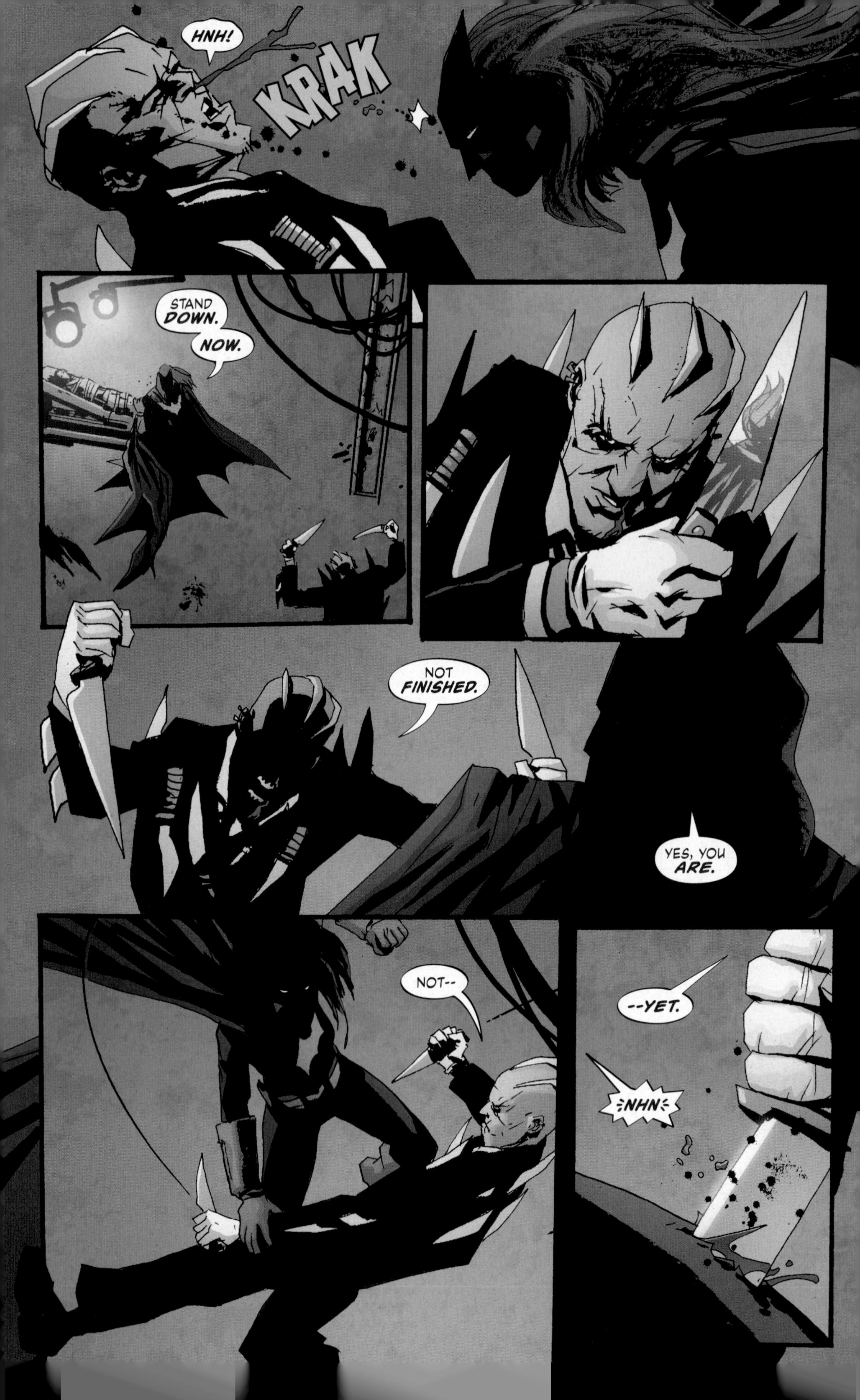
HNH!
KRAK
STAND DOWN.
NOW.
NOT FINISHED.
YES, YOU ARE.
NOT--
--YET.
NHN

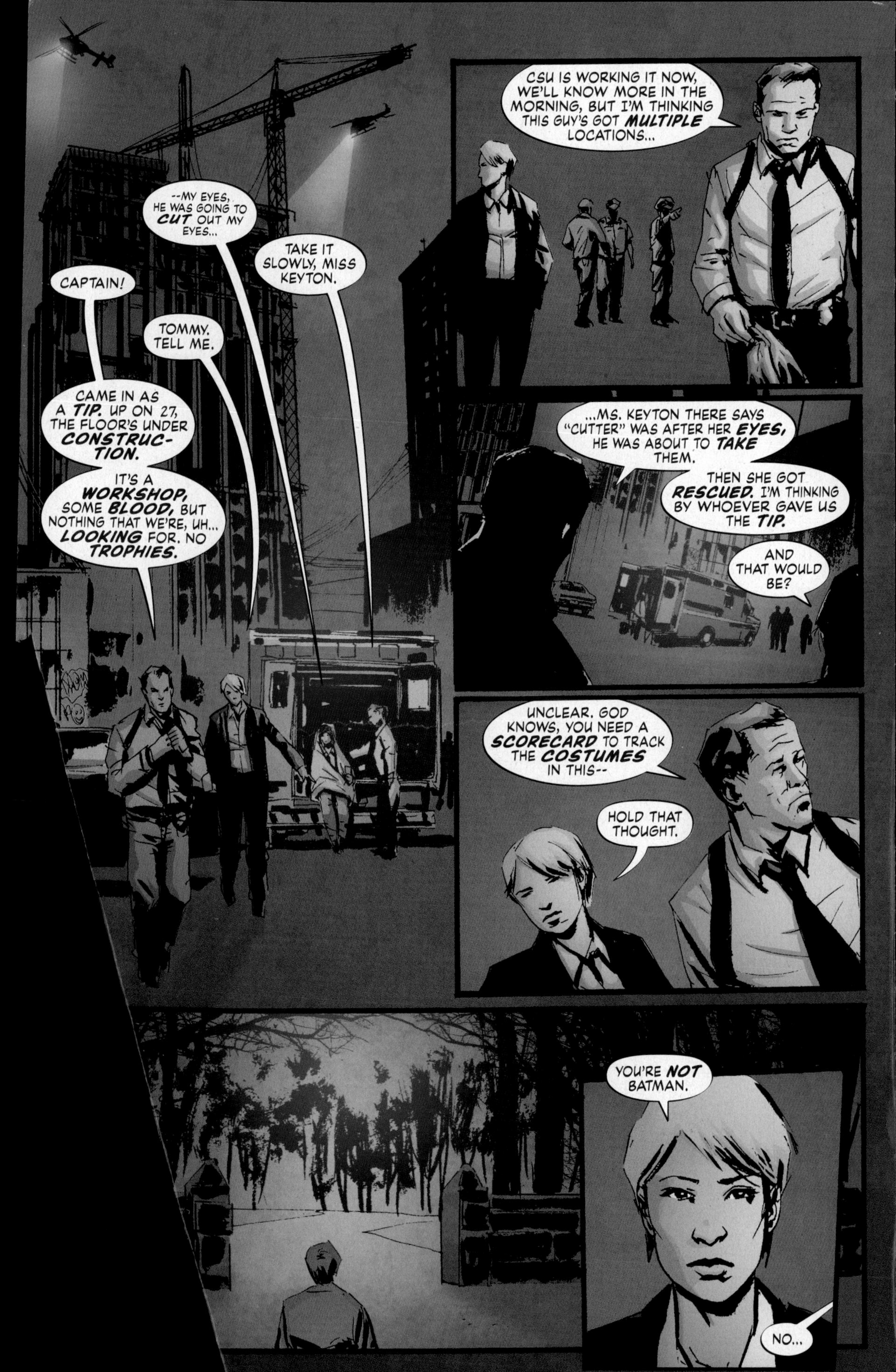
CAPTAIN!
TOMMY. TELL ME.
CAME IN AS A TIP. UP ON 27, THE FLOOR'S UNDER CONSTRUCTION.
IT'S A WORKSHOP, SOME BLOOD, BUT NOTHING THAT WE'RE, UH... LOOKING FOR. NO TROPHIES.
--MY EYES, HE WAS GOING TO CUT OUT MY EYES...
TAKE IT SLOWLY, MISS KEYTON.
CSU IS WORKING IT NOW, WE'LL KNOW MORE IN THE MORNING, BUT I'M THINKING THIS GUY'S GOT MULTIPLE LOCATIONS...
...MS. KEYTON THERE SAYS "CUTTER" WAS AFTER HER EYES, HE WAS ABOUT TO TAKE THEM.
THEN SHE GOT RESCUED. I'M THINKING BY WHOEVER GAVE US THE TIP.
AND THAT WOULD BE?
UNCLEAR. GOD KNOWS, YOU NEED A SCORECARD TO TRACK THE COSTUMES IN THIS--
HOLD THAT THOUGHT.
YOU'RE NOT BATMAN.
NO...

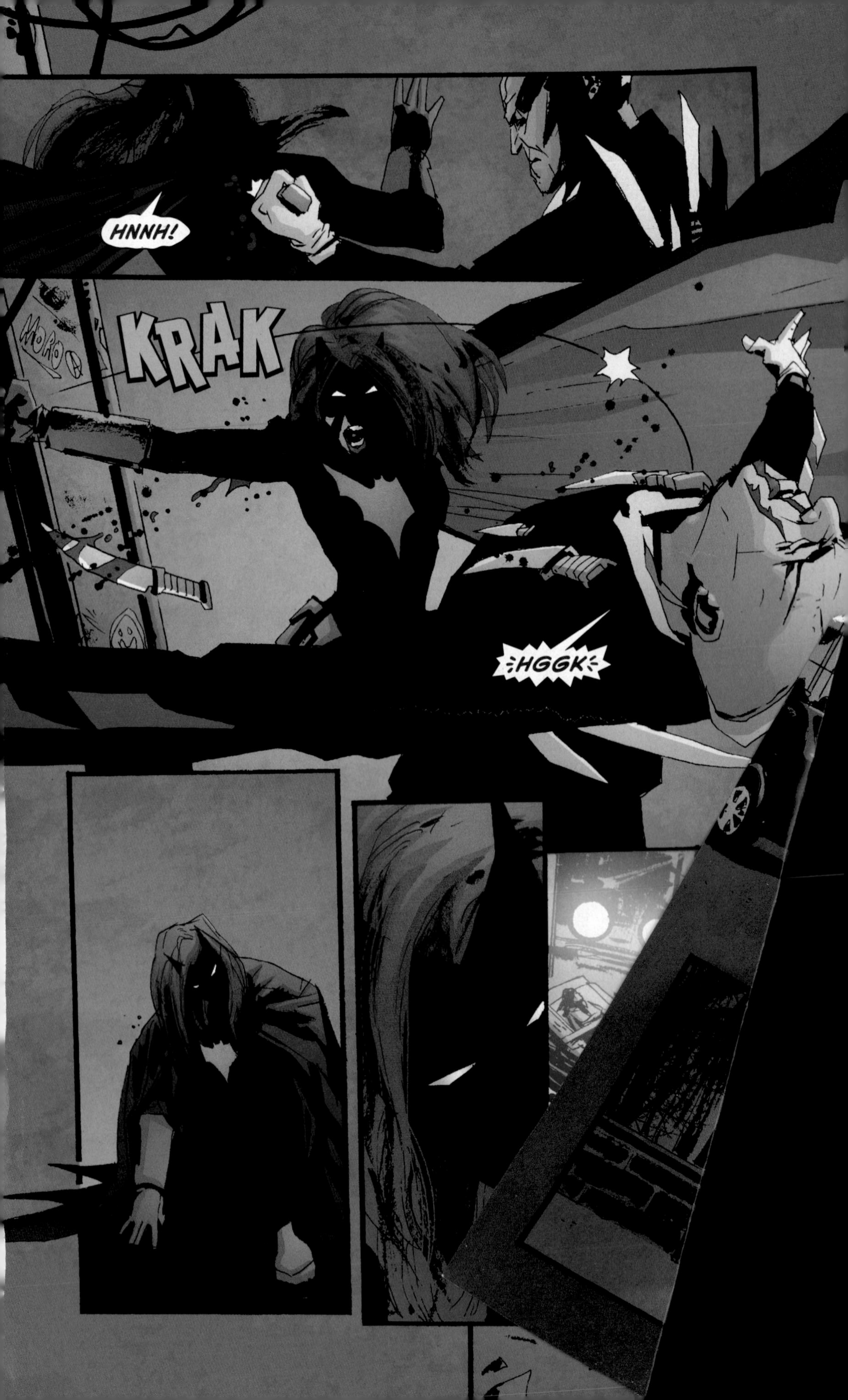
HNNH!
KRAK
MORO
HGGK

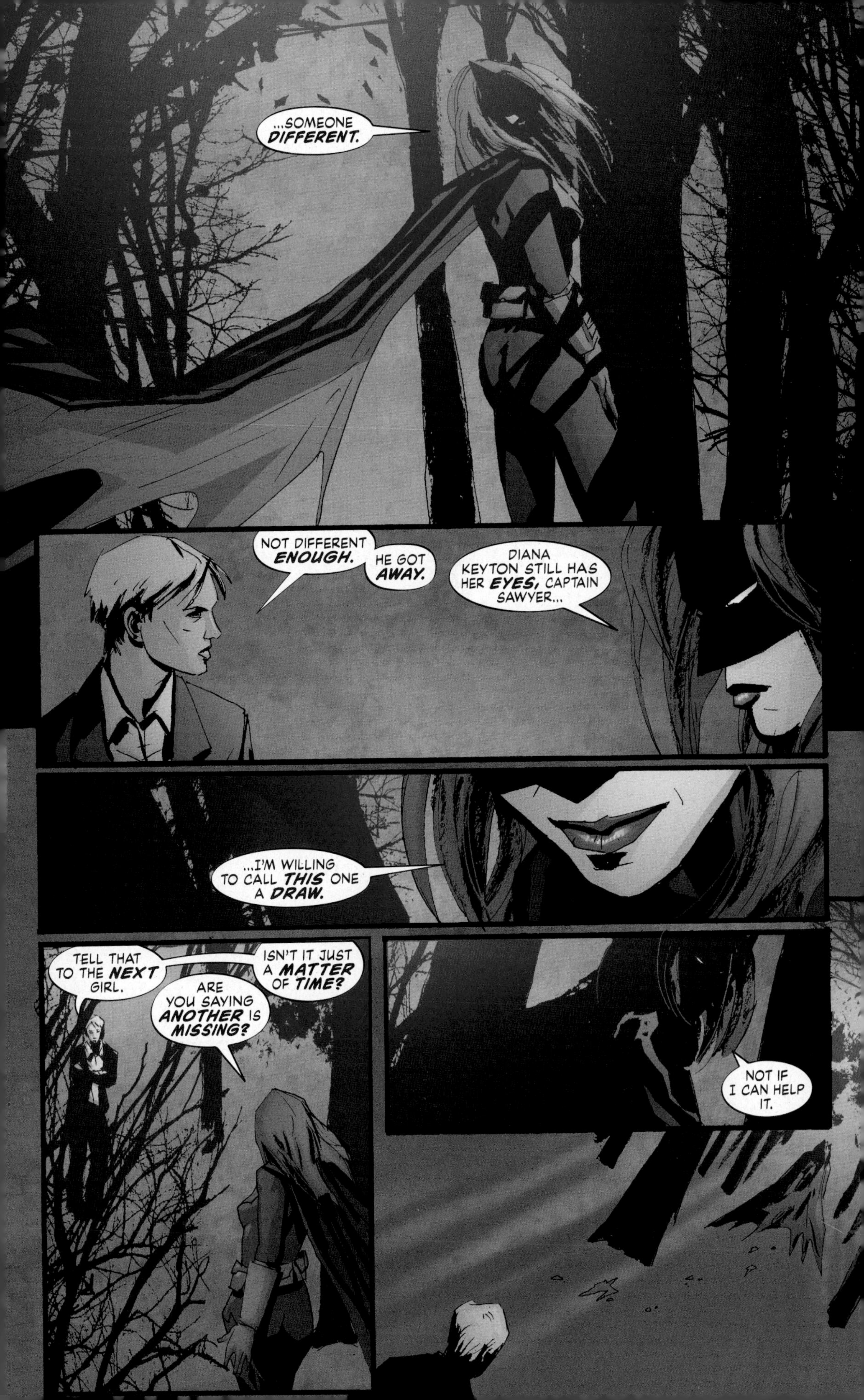
...SOMEONE DIFFERENT.
NOT DIFFERENT ENOUGH.
HE GOT AWAY.
DIANA KEYTON STILL HAS HER EYES, CAPTAIN SAWYER...
...I'M WILLING TO CALL THIS ONE A DRAW.
TELL THAT TO THE NEXT GIRL.
ARE YOU SAYING ANOTHER IS MISSING?
ISN'T IT JUST A MATTER OF TIME?
NOT IF I CAN HELP IT.

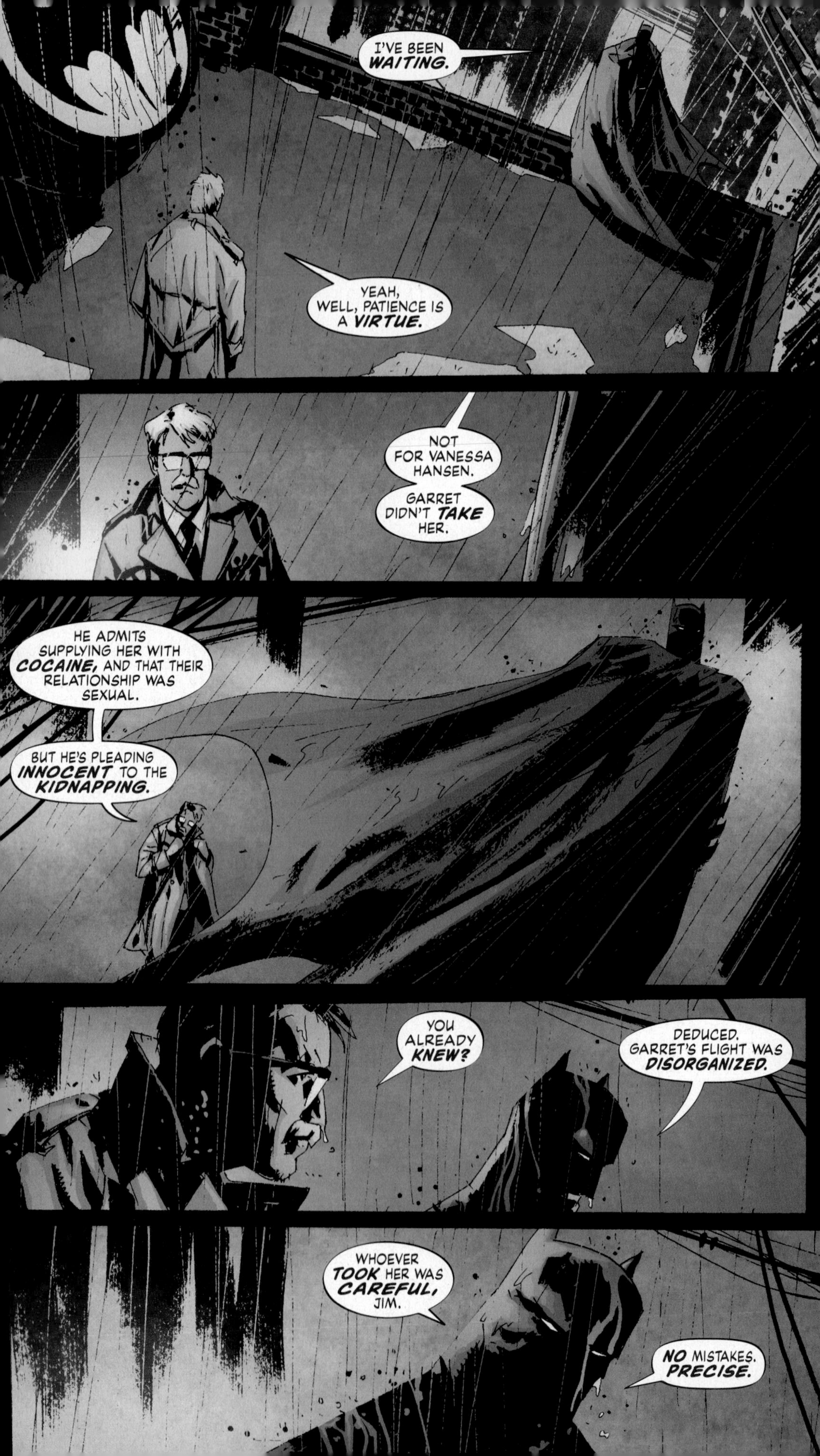

I'VE BEEN WAITING.
YEAH, WELL, PATIENCE IS A VIRTUE.
NOT FOR VANESSA HANSEN.
GARRET DIDN'T TAKE HER.
HE ADMITS SUPPLYING HER WITH COCAINE, AND THAT THEIR RELATIONSHIP WAS SEXUAL.
BUT HE'S PLEADING INNOCENT TO THE KIDNAPPING.
YOU ALREADY KNEW?
DEDUCED. GARRET'S FLIGHT WAS DISORGANIZED.
WHOEVER TOOK HER WAS CAREFUL, JIM.
NO MISTAKES. PRECISE.

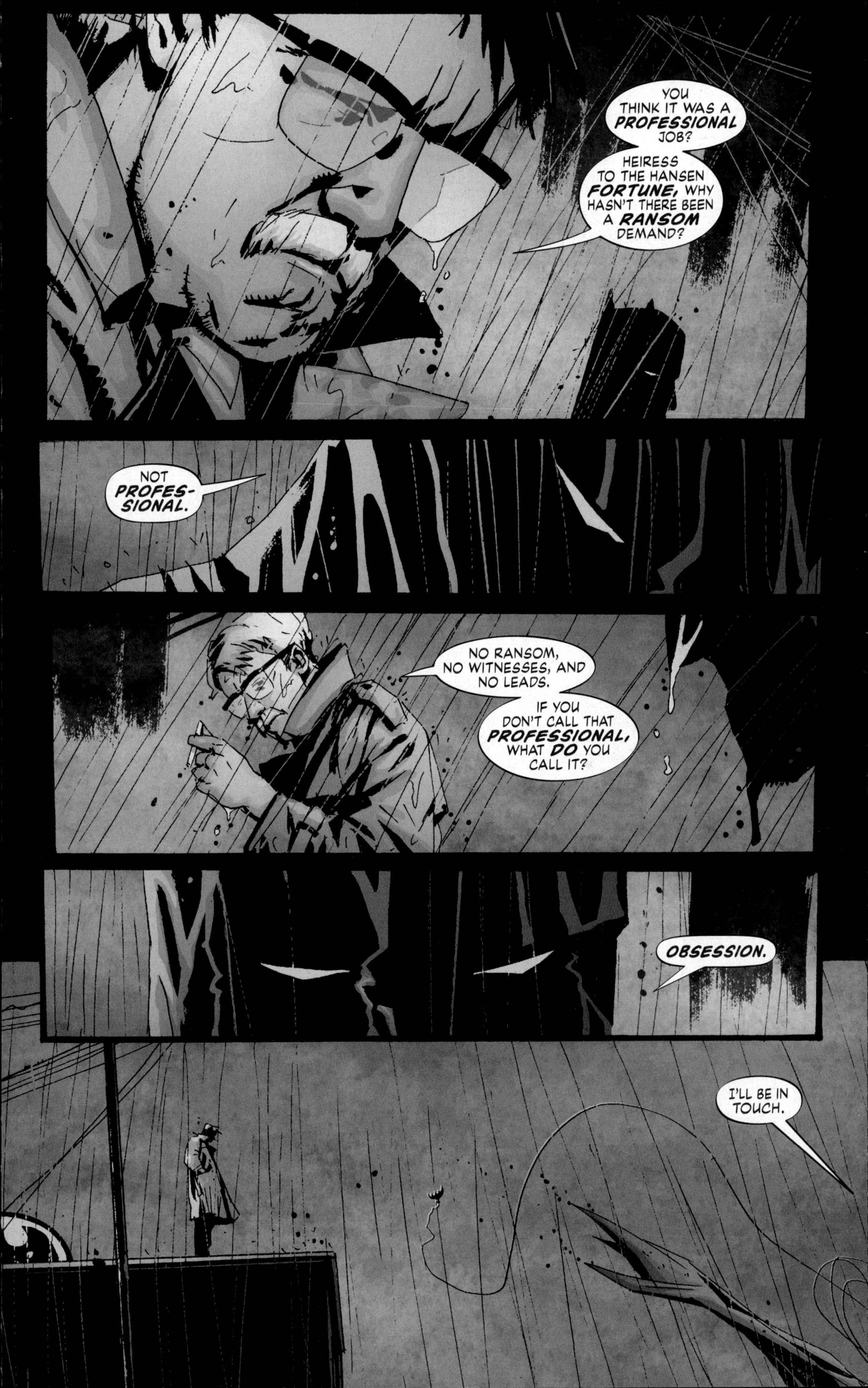
YOU THINK IT WAS A PROFESSIONAL JOB?
HEIRESS TO THE HANSEN FORTUNE, WHY HASN'T THERE BEEN A RANSOM DEMAND?
NOT PROFES-SIONAL.
NO RANSOM, NO WITNESSES, AND NO LEADS.
IF YOU DON'T CALL THAT PROFESSIONAL, WHAT DO YOU CALL IT?
OBSESSION.
I'LL BE IN TOUCH.

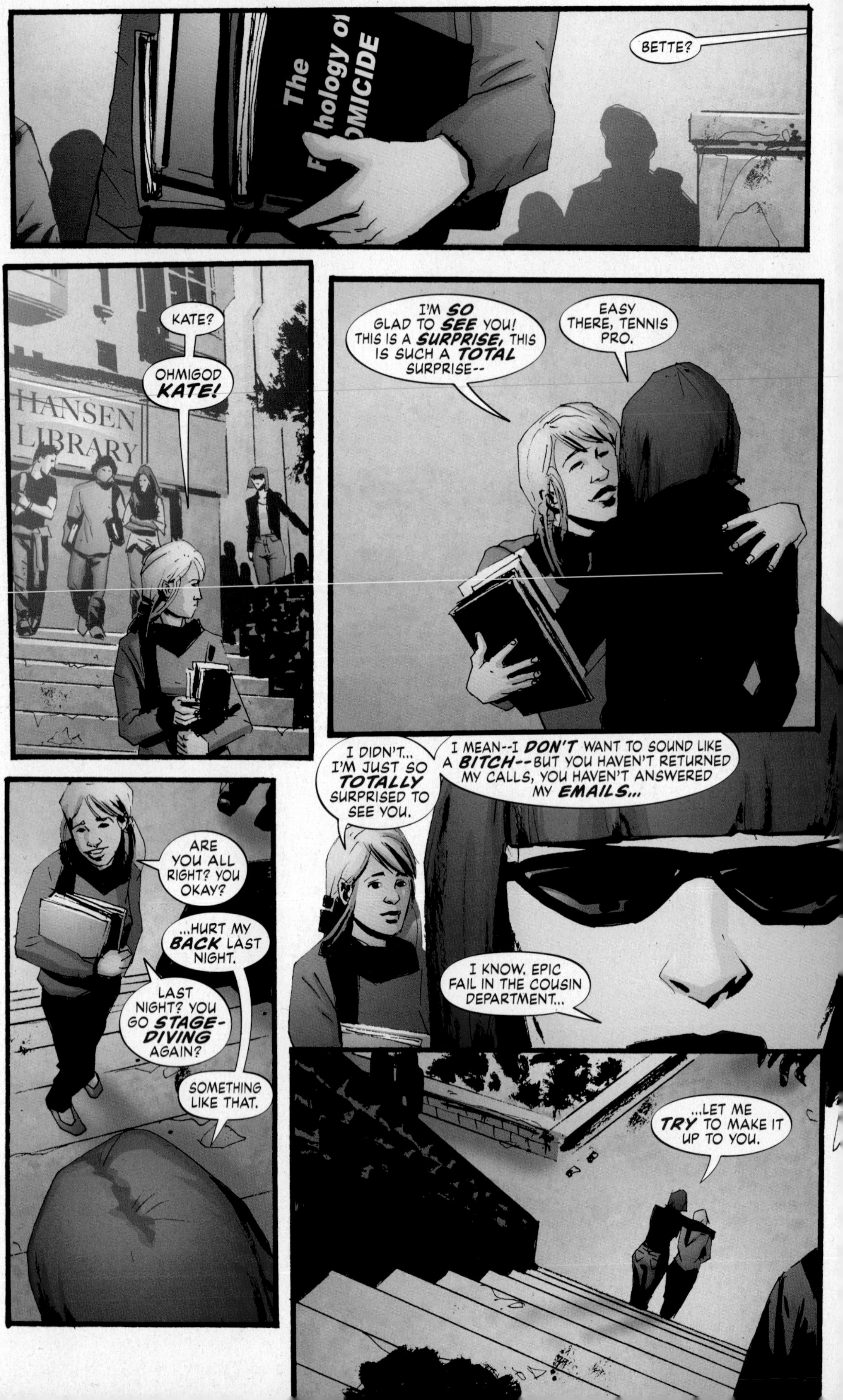

The ...hology of ...OMICIDE
BETTE?
KATE?
OHMIGOD KATE!
HANSEN LIBRARY
I'M SO GLAD TO SEE YOU! THIS IS A SURPRISE, THIS IS SUCH A TOTAL SURPRISE--
EASY THERE, TENNIS PRO.
ARE YOU ALL RIGHT? YOU OKAY?
...HURT MY BACK LAST NIGHT.
LAST NIGHT? YOU GO STAGE-DIVING AGAIN?
SOMETHING LIKE THAT.
I DIDN'T... I'M JUST SO TOTALLY SURPRISED TO SEE YOU.
I MEAN--I DON'T WANT TO SOUND LIKE A BITCH--BUT YOU HAVEN'T RETURNED MY CALLS, YOU HAVEN'T ANSWERED MY EMAILS...
I KNOW. EPIC FAIL IN THE COUSIN DEPARTMENT...
...LET ME TRY TO MAKE IT UP TO YOU.

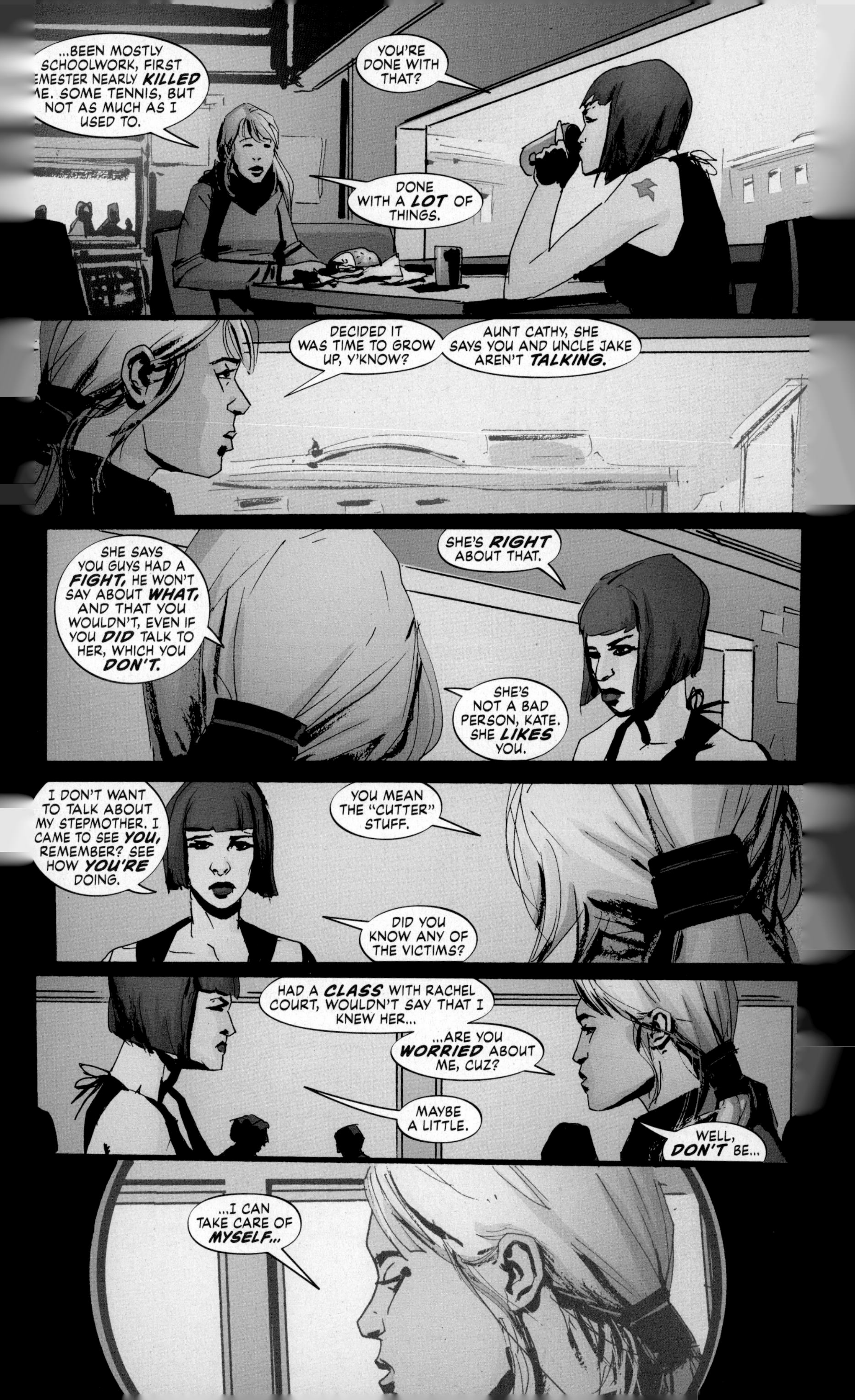

...BEEN MOSTLY SCHOOLWORK, FIRST SEMESTER NEARLY KILLED ME. SOME TENNIS, BUT NOT AS MUCH AS I USED TO.
YOU'RE DONE WITH THAT?
DONE WITH A LOT OF THINGS.
DECIDED IT WAS TIME TO GROW UP, Y'KNOW?
AUNT CATHY, SHE SAYS YOU AND UNCLE JAKE AREN'T TALKING.
SHE SAYS YOU GUYS HAD A FIGHT, HE WON'T SAY ABOUT WHAT, AND THAT YOU WOULDN'T, EVEN IF YOU DID TALK TO HER, WHICH YOU DON'T.
SHE'S RIGHT ABOUT THAT.
SHE'S NOT A BAD PERSON, KATE. SHE LIKES YOU.
I DON'T WANT TO TALK ABOUT MY STEPMOTHER. I CAME TO SEE YOU, REMEMBER? SEE HOW YOU'RE DOING.
YOU MEAN THE "CUTTER" STUFF.
DID YOU KNOW ANY OF THE VICTIMS?
HAD A CLASS WITH RACHEL COURT, WOULDN'T SAY THAT I KNEW HER...
...ARE YOU WORRIED ABOUT ME, CUZ?
MAYBE A LITTLE.
WELL, DON'T BE...
...I CAN TAKE CARE OF MYSELF...

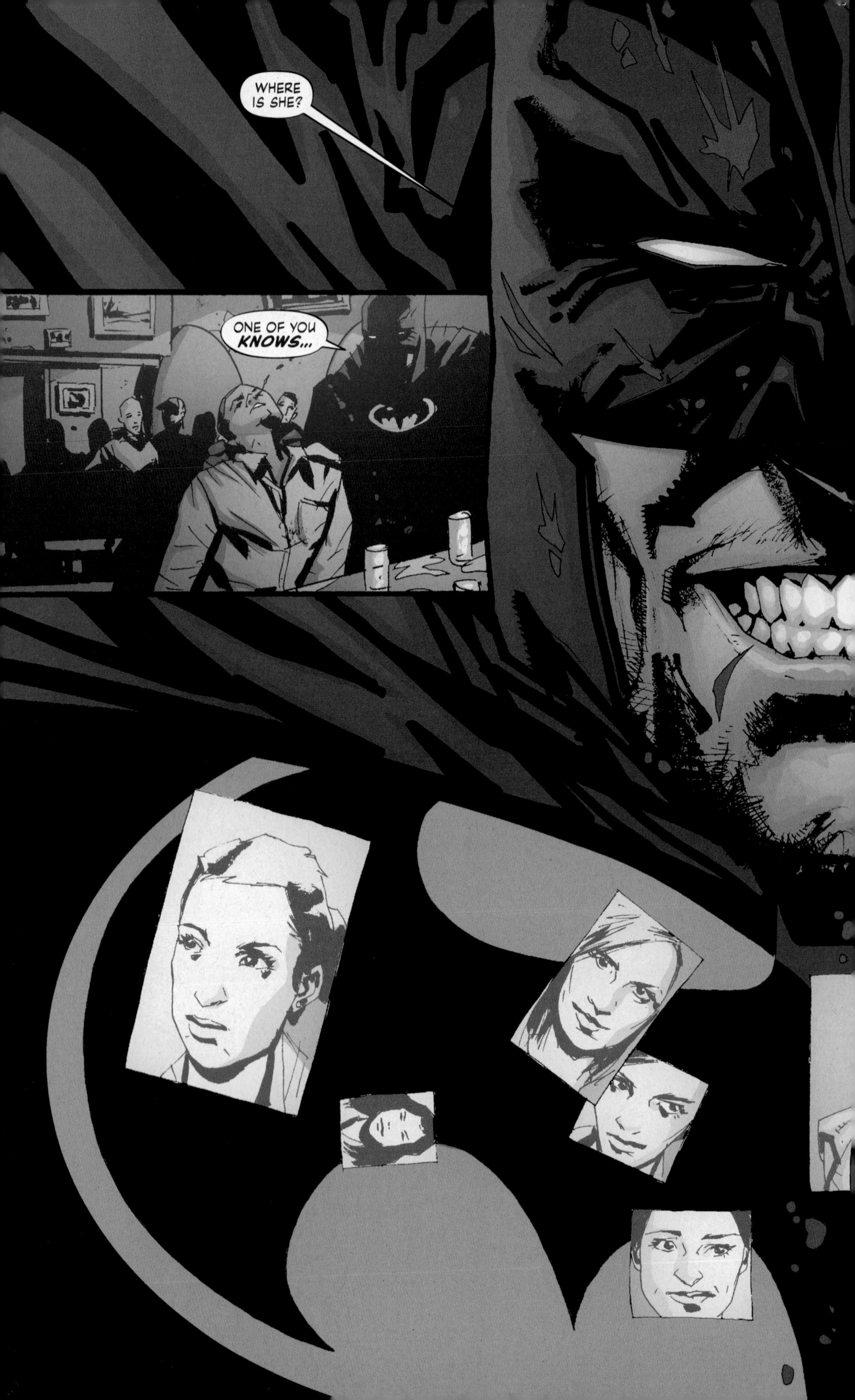
WHERE IS SHE?
ONE OF YOU KNOWS...

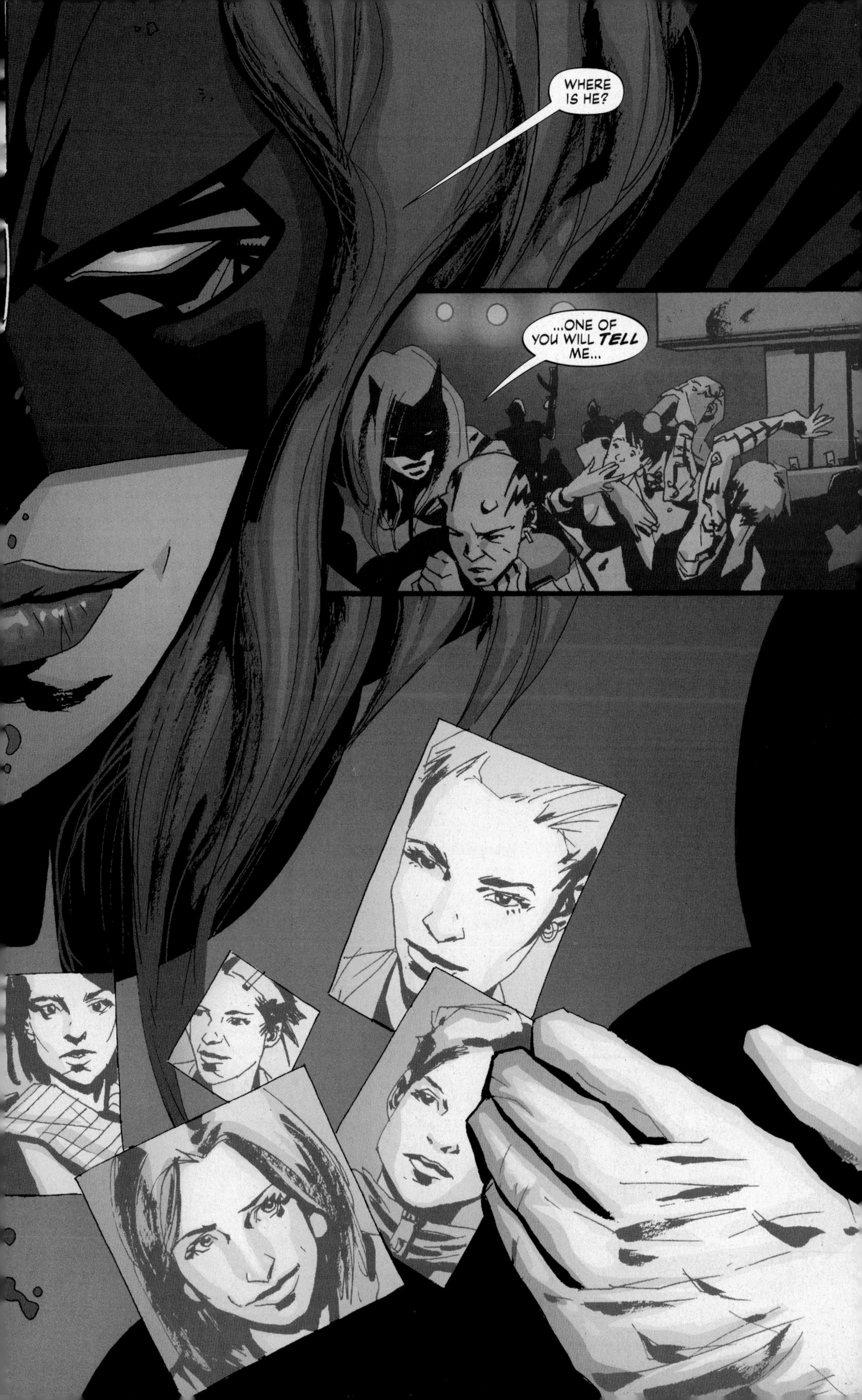
WHERE IS HE?
...ONE OF YOU WILL **TELL** ME...

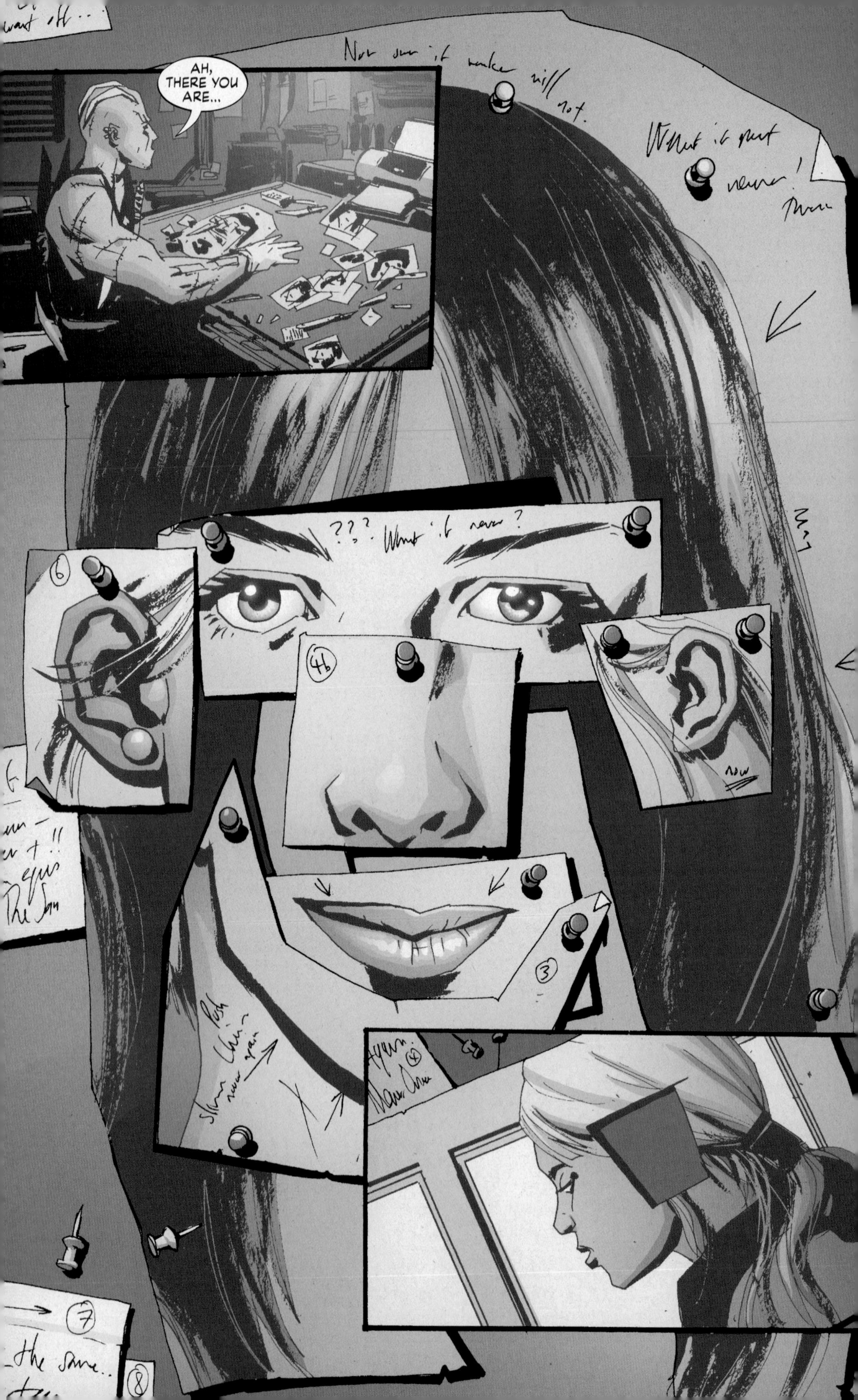
AH, THERE YOU ARE...
??? What if never?

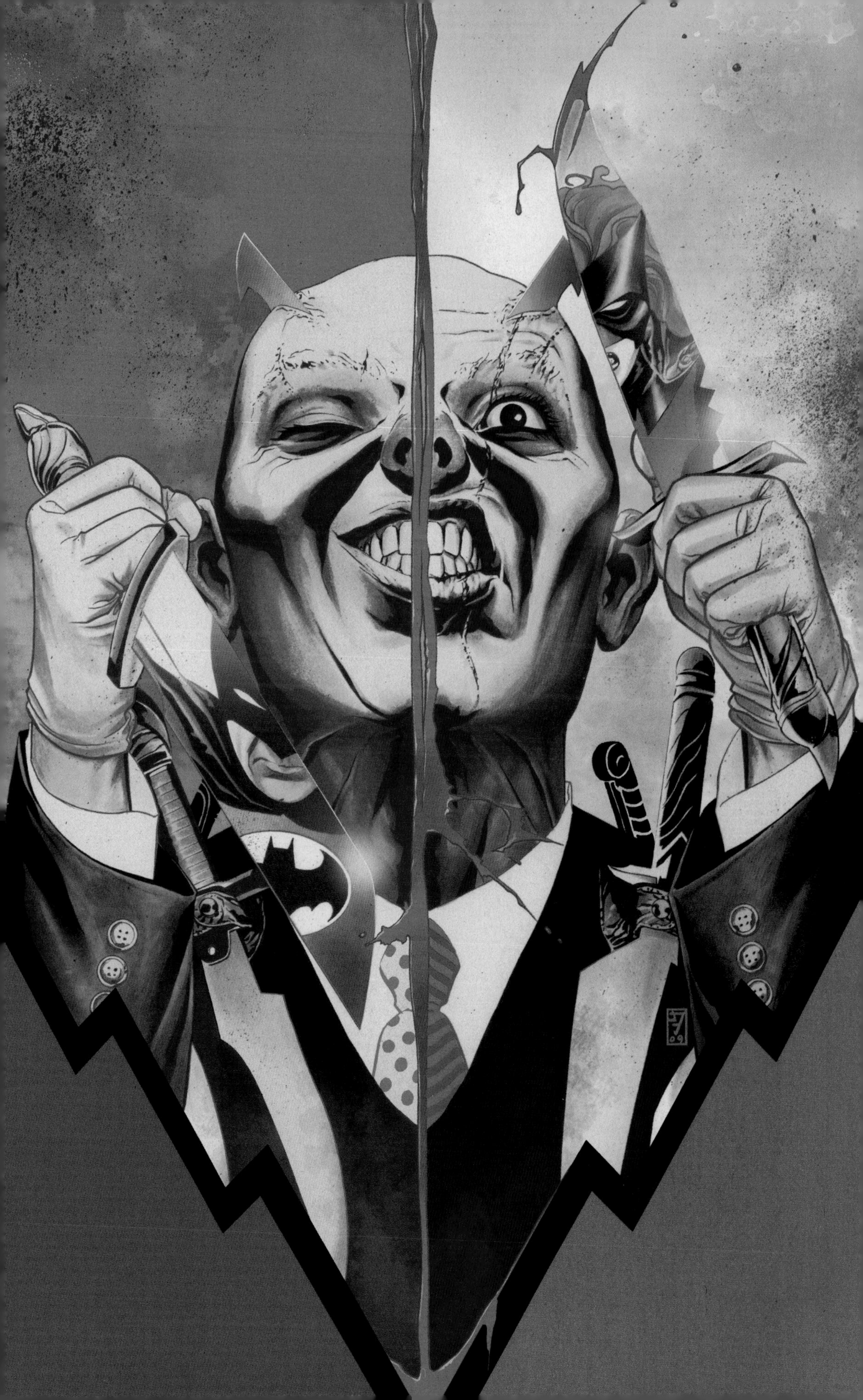

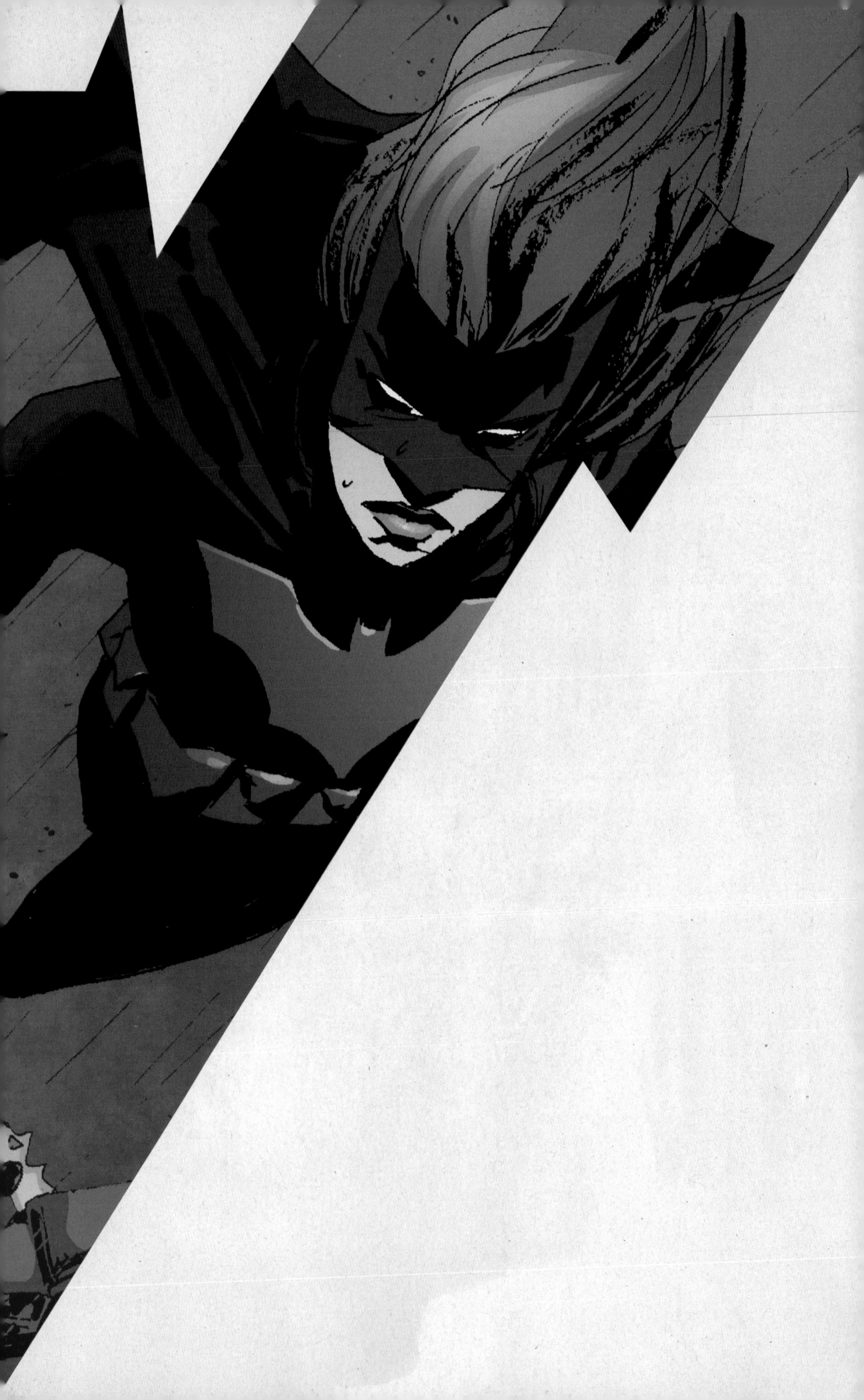

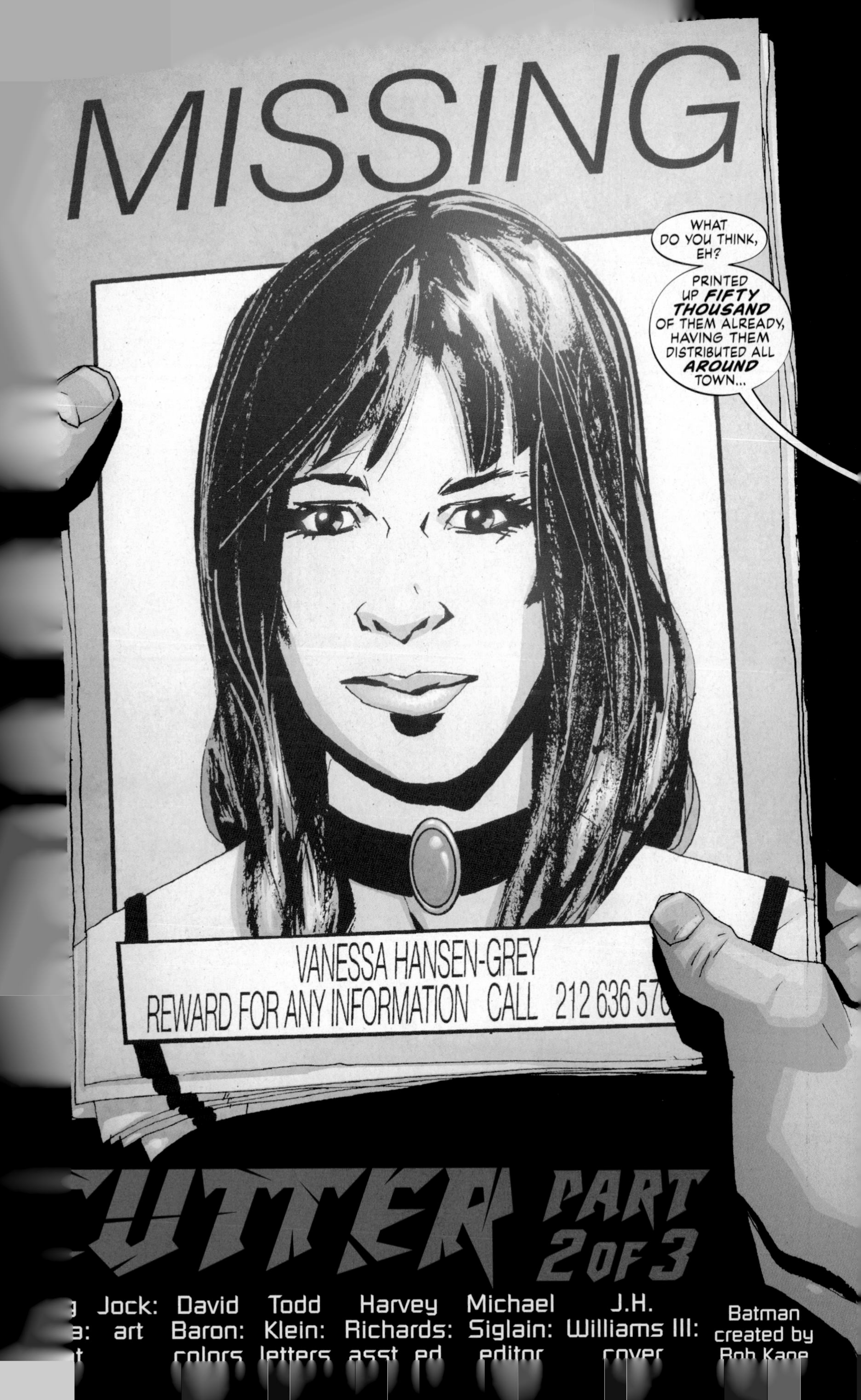
MISSING
WHAT DO YOU THINK, EH?
PRINTED UP FIFTY THOUSAND OF THEM ALREADY, HAVING THEM DISTRIBUTED ALL AROUND TOWN...
VANESSA HANSEN-GREY
REWARD FOR ANY INFORMATION CALL 212 636 57
UTTER PART 2 OF 3
Jock: art
David Baron: colors
Todd Klein: letters
Harvey Richards: asst. ed
Michael Siglain: editor
J.H. Williams III: cover
Batman created by Bob Kane

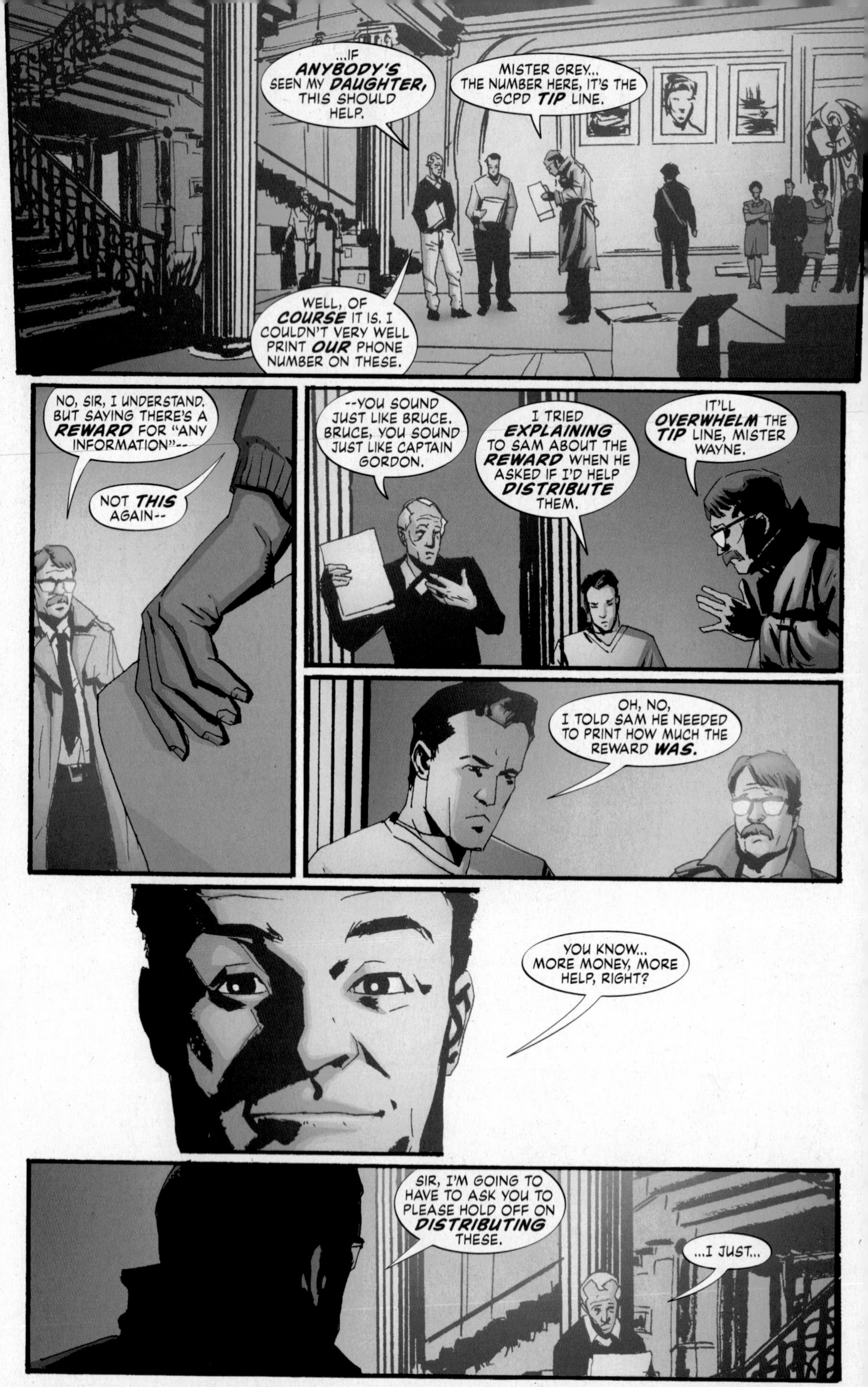
...IF ANYBODY'S SEEN MY DAUGHTER, THIS SHOULD HELP.
MISTER GREY... THE NUMBER HERE, IT'S THE GCPD TIP LINE.
WELL, OF COURSE IT IS. I COULDN'T VERY WELL PRINT OUR PHONE NUMBER ON THESE.
NO, SIR, I UNDERSTAND. BUT SAYING THERE'S A REWARD FOR "ANY INFORMATION"--
NOT THIS AGAIN--
--YOU SOUND JUST LIKE BRUCE. BRUCE, YOU SOUND JUST LIKE CAPTAIN GORDON.
I TRIED EXPLAINING TO SAM ABOUT THE REWARD WHEN HE ASKED IF I'D HELP DISTRIBUTE THEM.
IT'LL OVERWHELM THE TIP LINE, MISTER WAYNE.
OH, NO, I TOLD SAM HE NEEDED TO PRINT HOW MUCH THE REWARD WAS.
YOU KNOW... MORE MONEY, MORE HELP, RIGHT?
SIR, I'M GOING TO HAVE TO ASK YOU TO PLEASE HOLD OFF ON DISTRIBUTING THESE.
...I JUST...

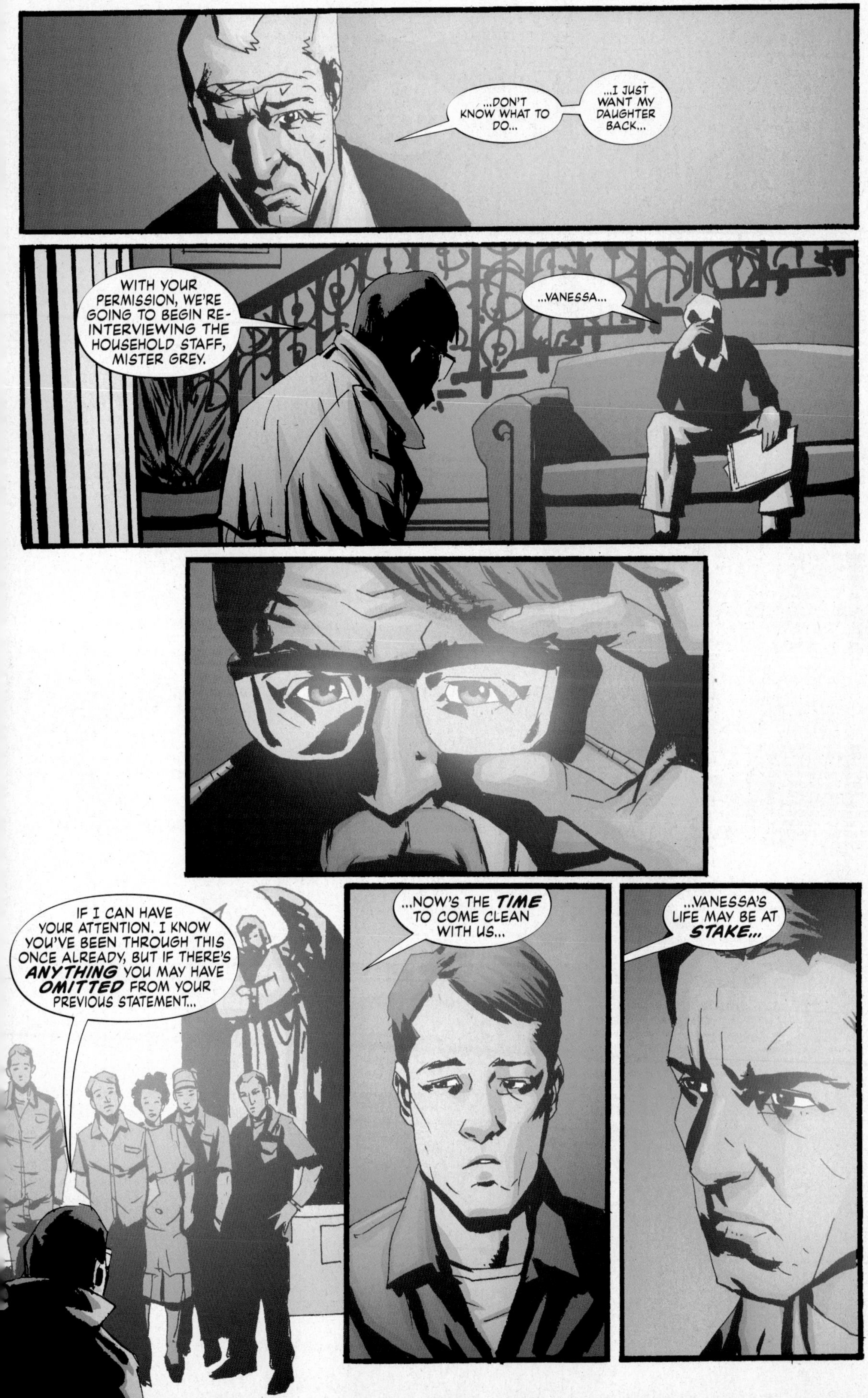
...DON'T KNOW WHAT TO DO...
...I JUST WANT MY DAUGHTER BACK...
WITH YOUR PERMISSION, WE'RE GOING TO BEGIN RE-INTERVIEWING THE HOUSEHOLD STAFF, MISTER GREY.
...VANESSA...
IF I CAN HAVE YOUR ATTENTION. I KNOW YOU'VE BEEN THROUGH THIS ONCE ALREADY, BUT IF THERE'S ANYTHING YOU MAY HAVE OMITTED FROM YOUR PREVIOUS STATEMENT...
...NOW'S THE TIME TO COME CLEAN WITH US...
...VANESSA'S LIFE MAY BE AT STAKE...

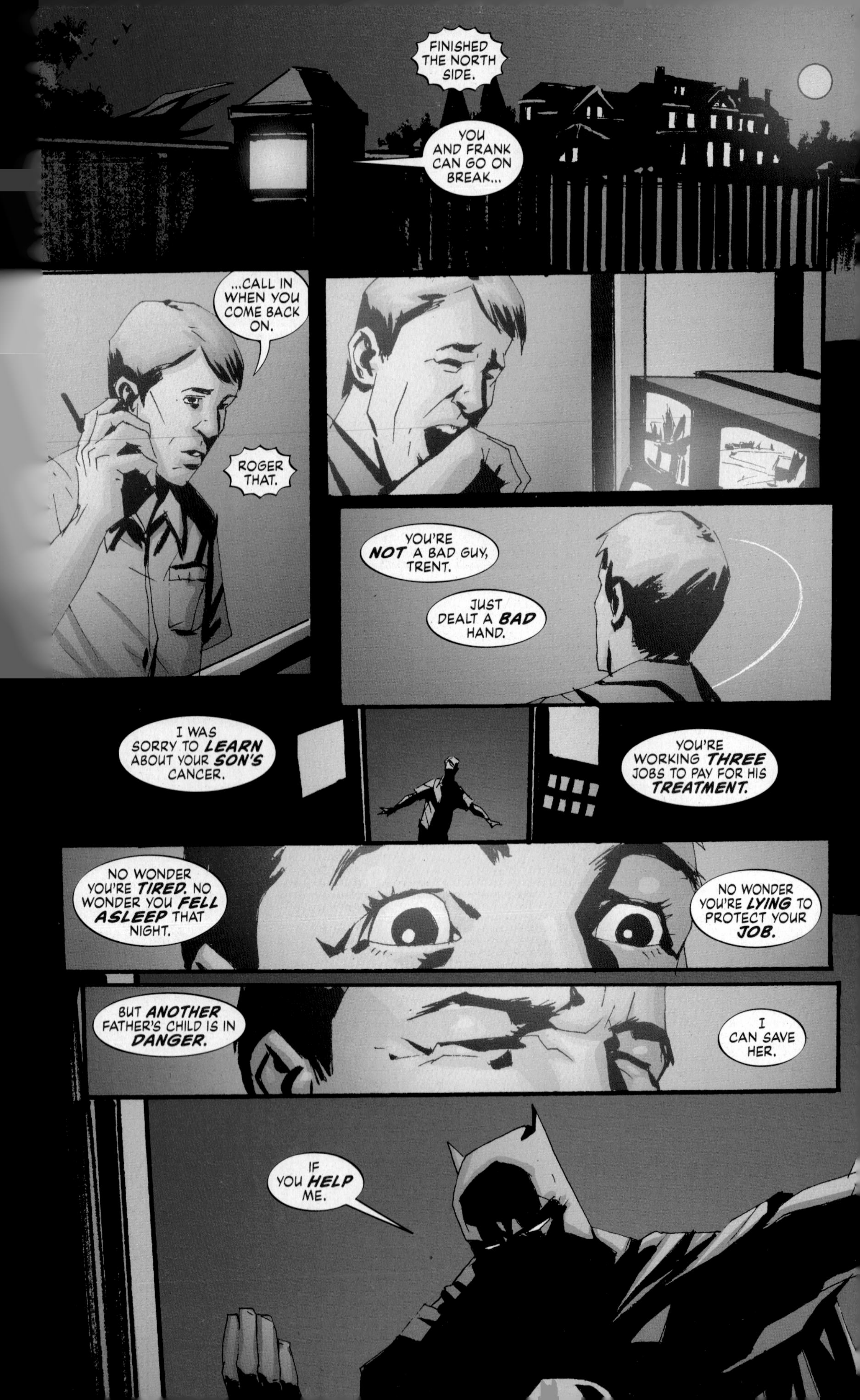
FINISHED THE NORTH SIDE.
YOU AND FRANK CAN GO ON BREAK...
...CALL IN WHEN YOU COME BACK ON.
ROGER THAT.
YOU'RE NOT A BAD GUY, TRENT.
JUST DEALT A BAD HAND.
I WAS SORRY TO LEARN ABOUT YOUR SON'S CANCER.
YOU'RE WORKING THREE JOBS TO PAY FOR HIS TREATMENT.
NO WONDER YOU'RE TIRED. NO WONDER YOU FELL ASLEEP THAT NIGHT.
NO WONDER YOU'RE LYING TO PROTECT YOUR JOB.
BUT ANOTHER FATHER'S CHILD IS IN DANGER.
I CAN SAVE HER.
IF YOU HELP ME.

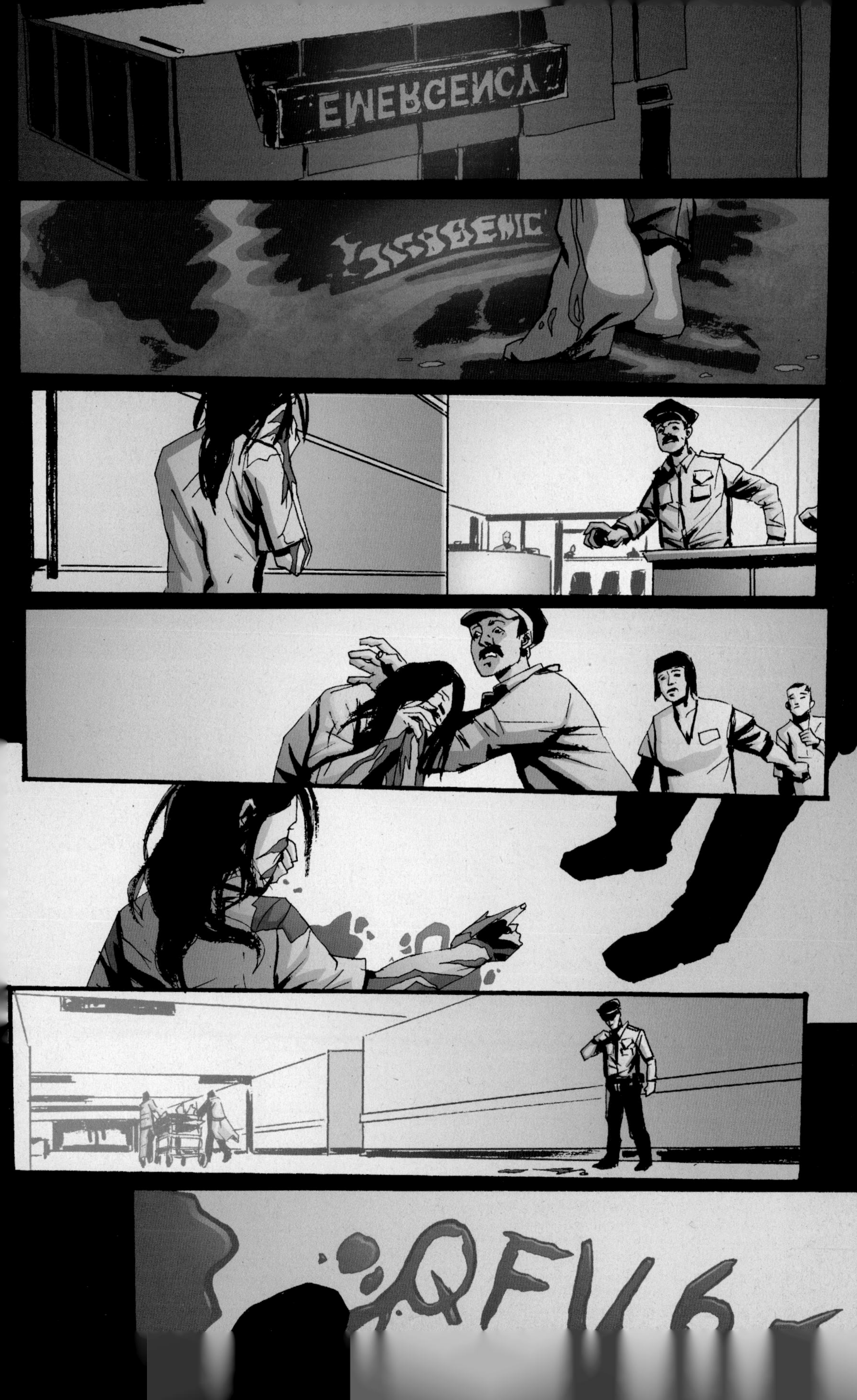
EMERGENCY

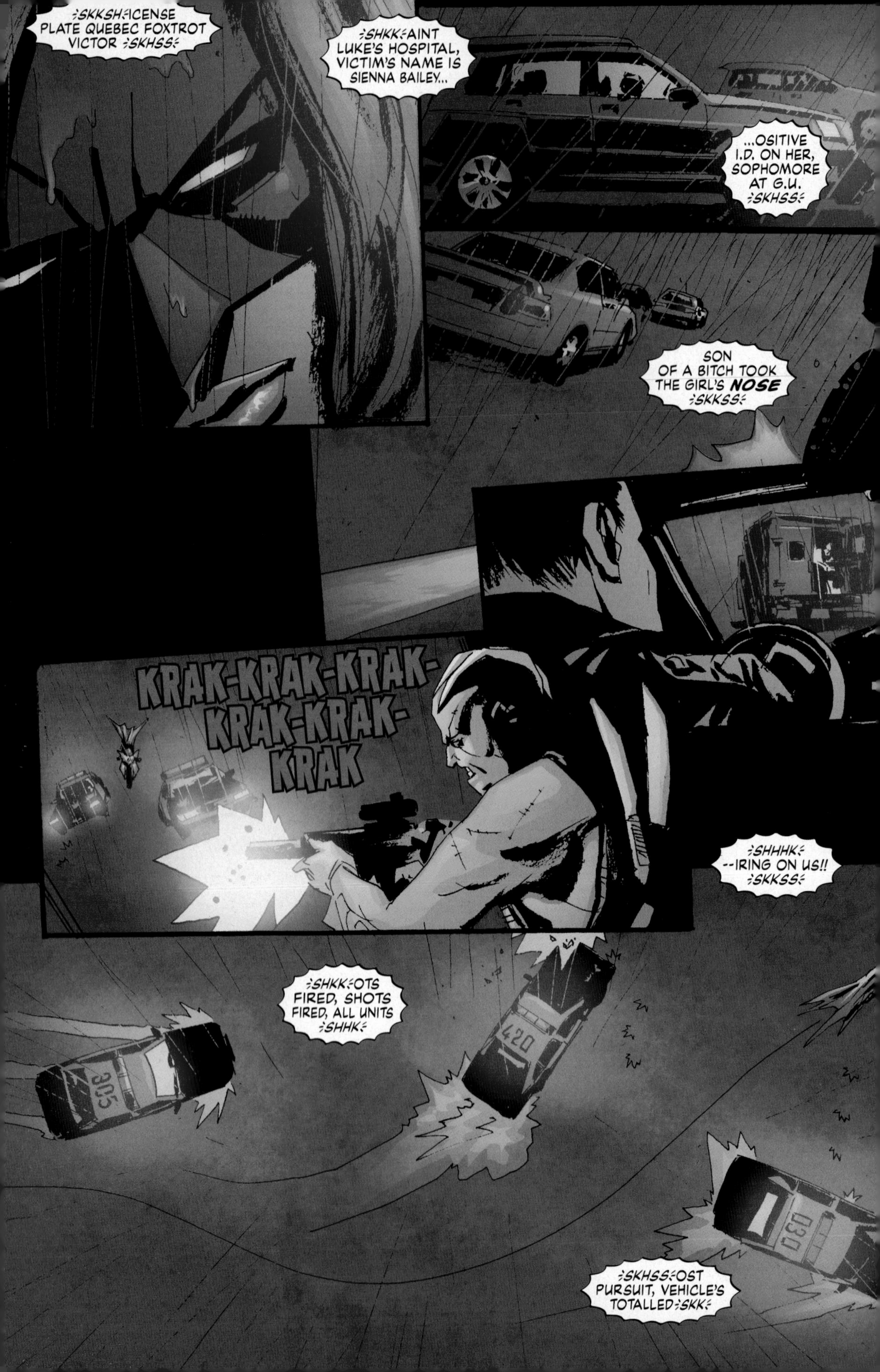
-SKKSH-ICENSE PLATE QUEBEC FOXTROT VICTOR -SKHSS-
-SHKK-AINT LUKE'S HOSPITAL, VICTIM'S NAME IS SIENNA BAILEY...
...OSITIVE I.D. ON HER, SOPHOMORE AT G.U. -SKHSS-
SON OF A BITCH TOOK THE GIRL'S NOSE -SKKSS-
KRAK-KRAK-KRAK-KRAK-KRAK-KRAK
-SHHHK- --IRING ON US!! -SKKSS-
-SHKK-OTS FIRED, SHOTS FIRED, ALL UNITS -SHHK-
305
420
030
-SKHSS-OST PURSUIT, VEHICLE'S TOTALLED-SKK-

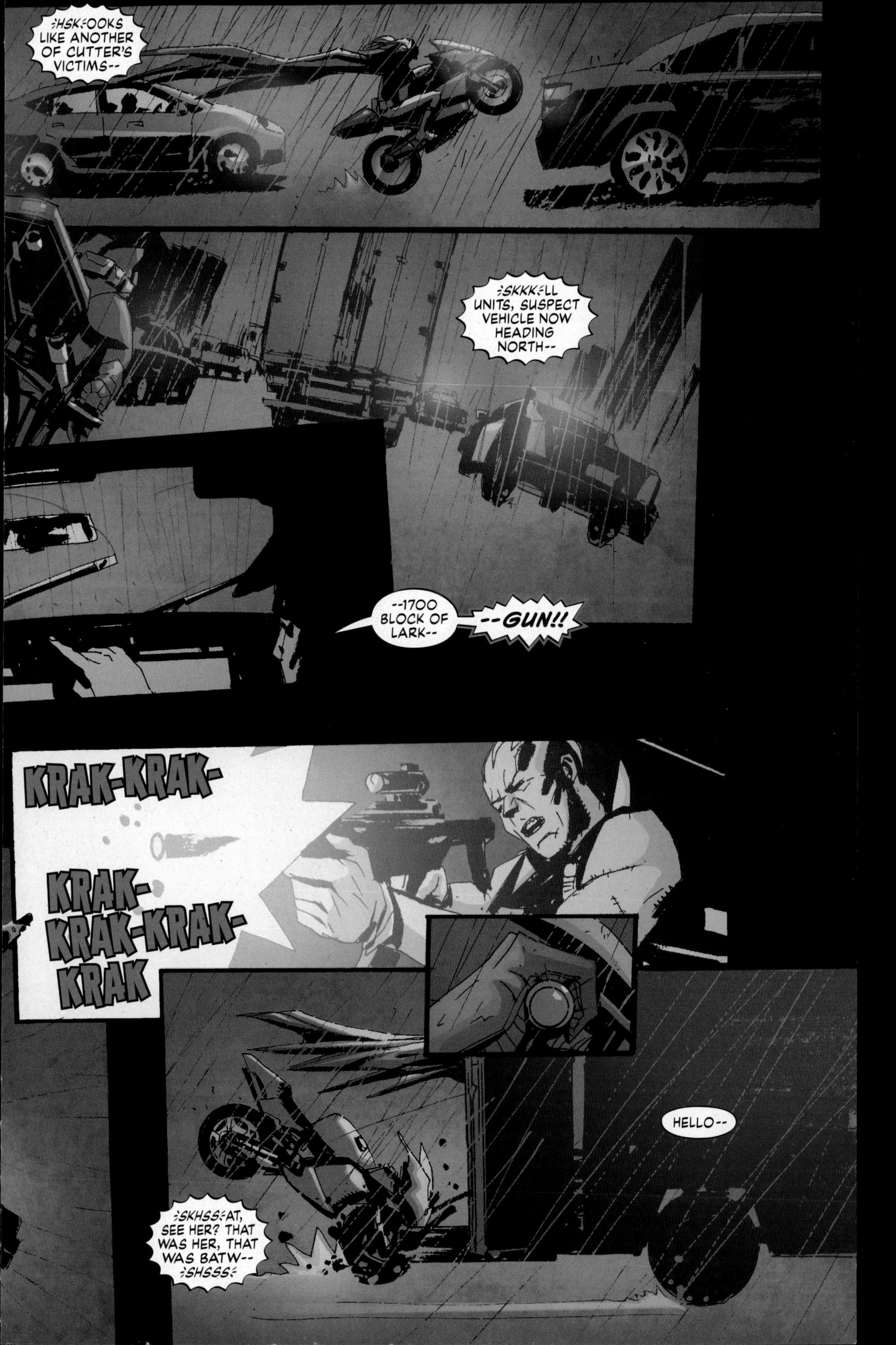

⚡HSK⚡OOKS LIKE ANOTHER OF CUTTER'S VICTIMS--
⚡SKKK⚡LL UNITS, SUSPECT VEHICLE NOW HEADING NORTH--
--1700 BLOCK OF LARK--
--GUN!!
KRAK-KRAK-
KRAK-KRAK-KRAK-KRAK
HELLO--
⚡SKHSS⚡AT, SEE HER? THAT WAS HER, THAT WAS BATW-- ⚡SHSSS⚡

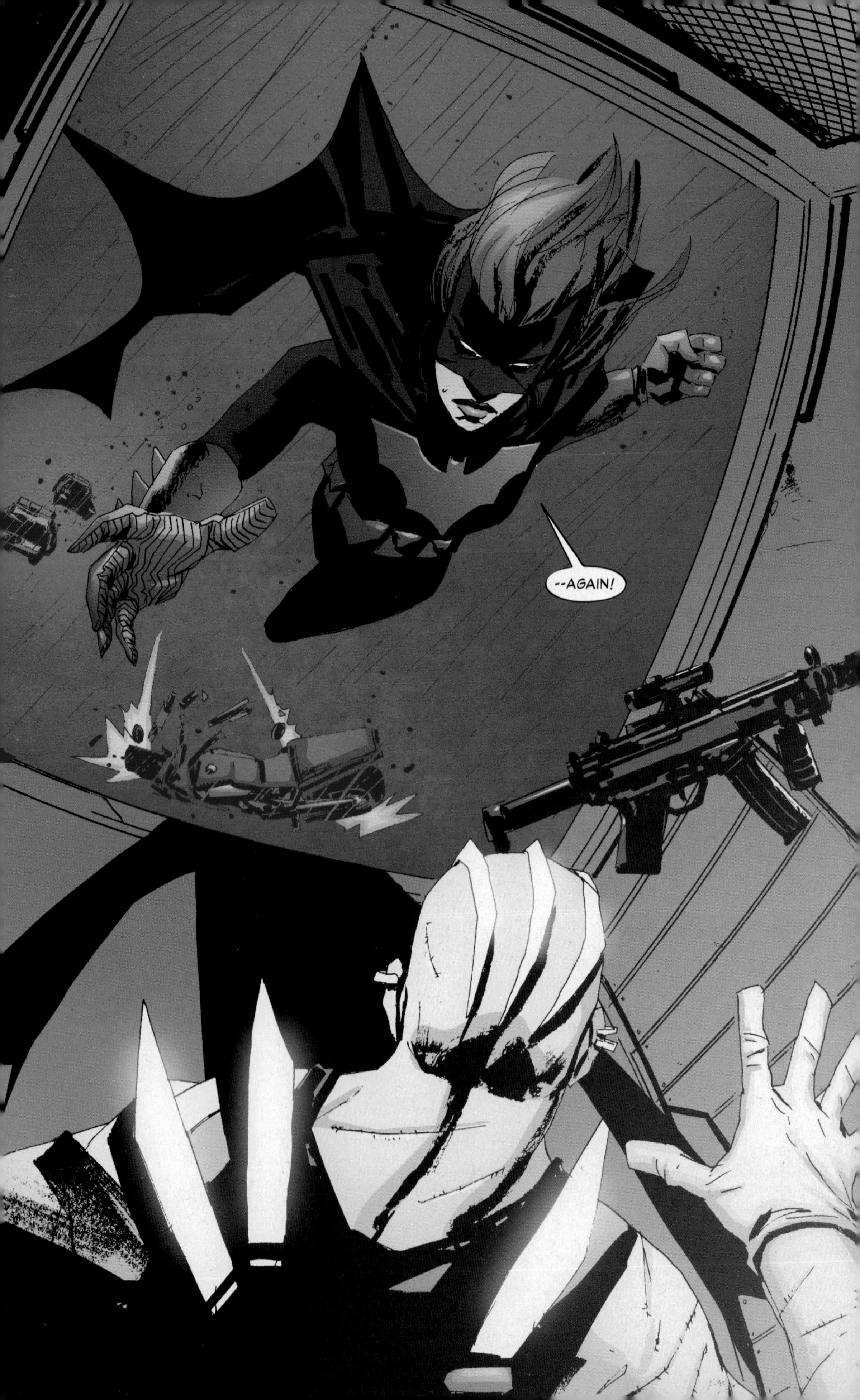
--AGAIN!

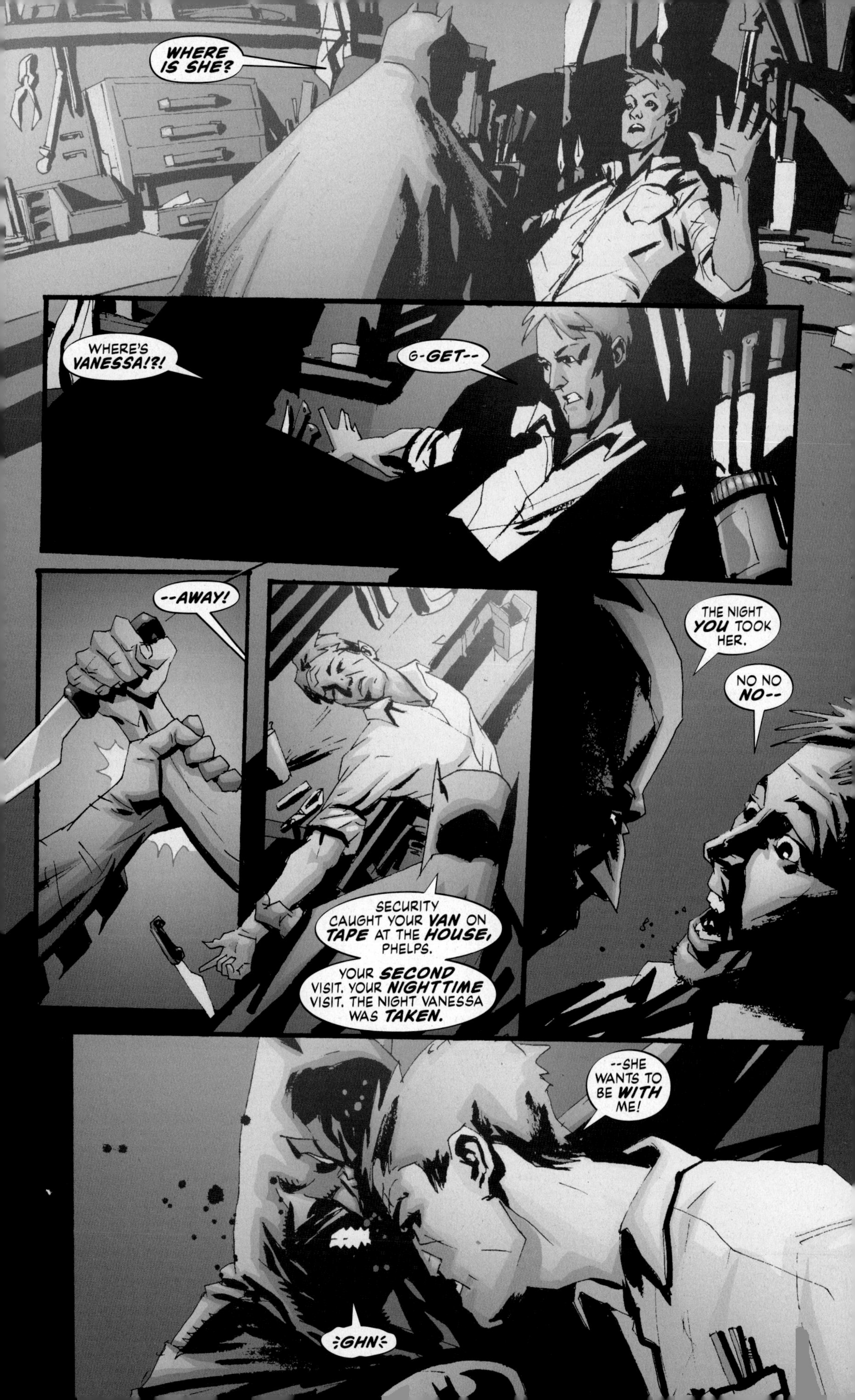
WHERE IS SHE?
WHERE'S VANESSA!?!
G-GET--
--AWAY!
SECURITY CAUGHT YOUR VAN ON TAPE AT THE HOUSE, PHELPS.
YOUR SECOND VISIT. YOUR NIGHTTIME VISIT. THE NIGHT VANESSA WAS TAKEN.
THE NIGHT YOU TOOK HER.
NO NO NO--
--SHE WANTS TO BE WITH ME!
GHN

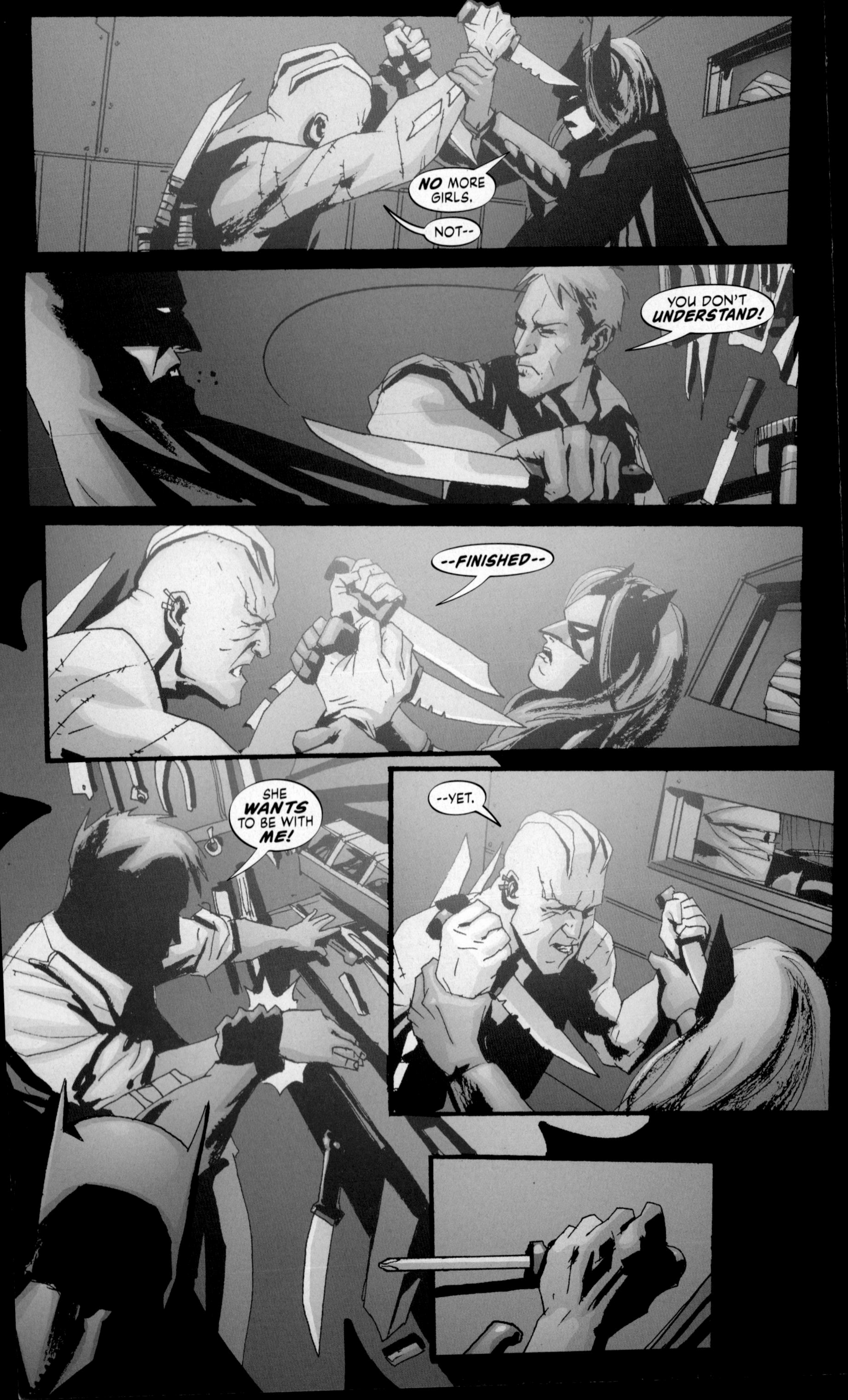
NO MORE GIRLS.
NOT--
YOU DON'T UNDERSTAND!
--FINISHED--
SHE WANTS TO BE WITH ME!
--YET.

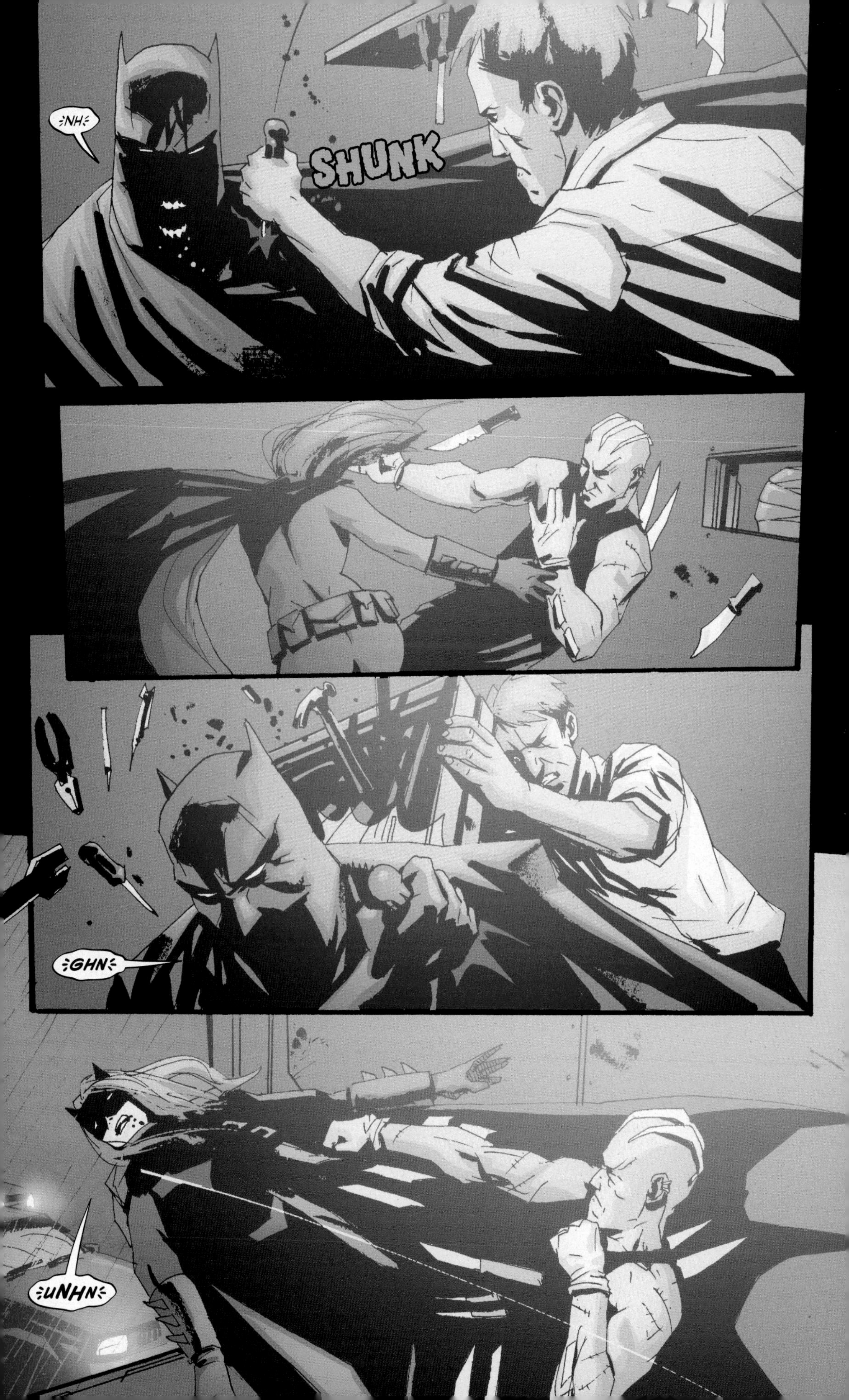
NH
SHUNK
GHN
UNHN

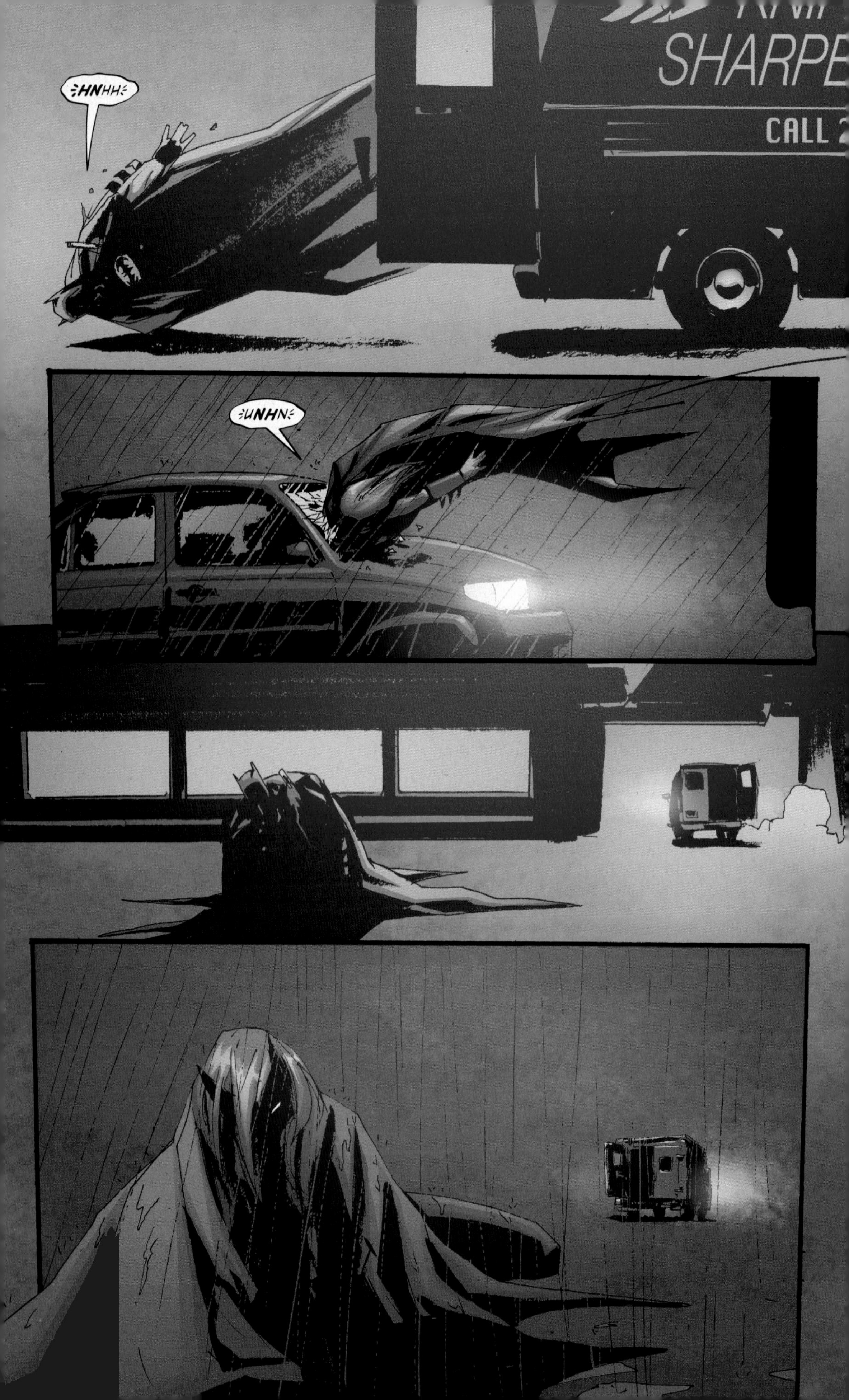
SHARPE
CALL 2
HNHH
UNHN

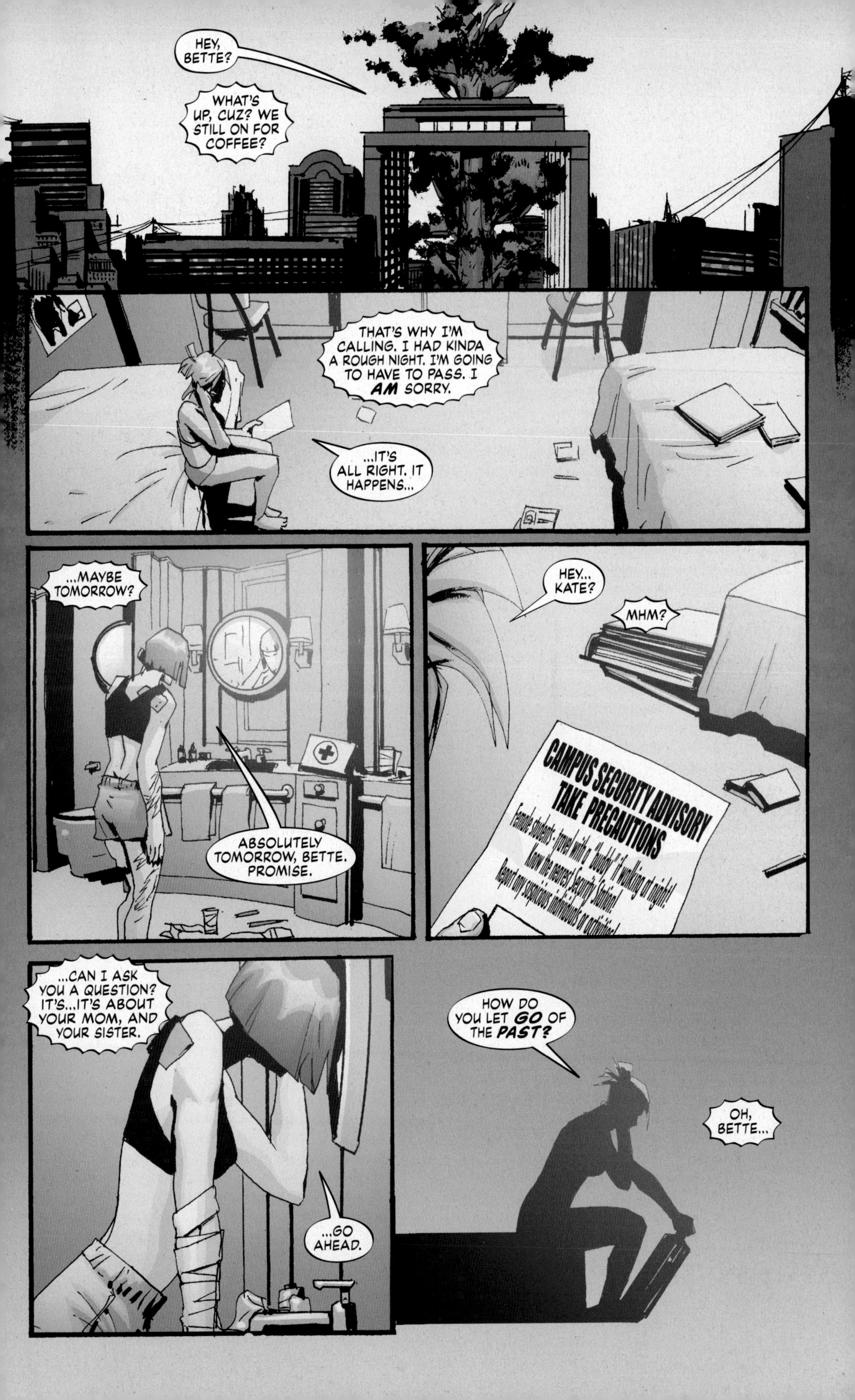

HEY, BETTE?
WHAT'S UP, CUZ? WE STILL ON FOR COFFEE?
THAT'S WHY I'M CALLING. I HAD KINDA A ROUGH NIGHT. I'M GOING TO HAVE TO PASS. I **AM** SORRY.
...IT'S ALL RIGHT. IT HAPPENS...
...MAYBE TOMORROW?
ABSOLUTELY TOMORROW, BETTE. PROMISE.
HEY... KATE?
MHM?
CAMPUS SECURITY ADVISORY
TAKE PRECAUTIONS
Female students - travel with a "buddy" if walking at night!
Know the nearest Security Station!
Report any suspicious individuals or
...CAN I ASK YOU A QUESTION? IT'S...IT'S ABOUT YOUR MOM, AND YOUR SISTER.
...GO AHEAD.
HOW DO YOU LET **GO** OF THE **PAST?**
OH, BETTE...

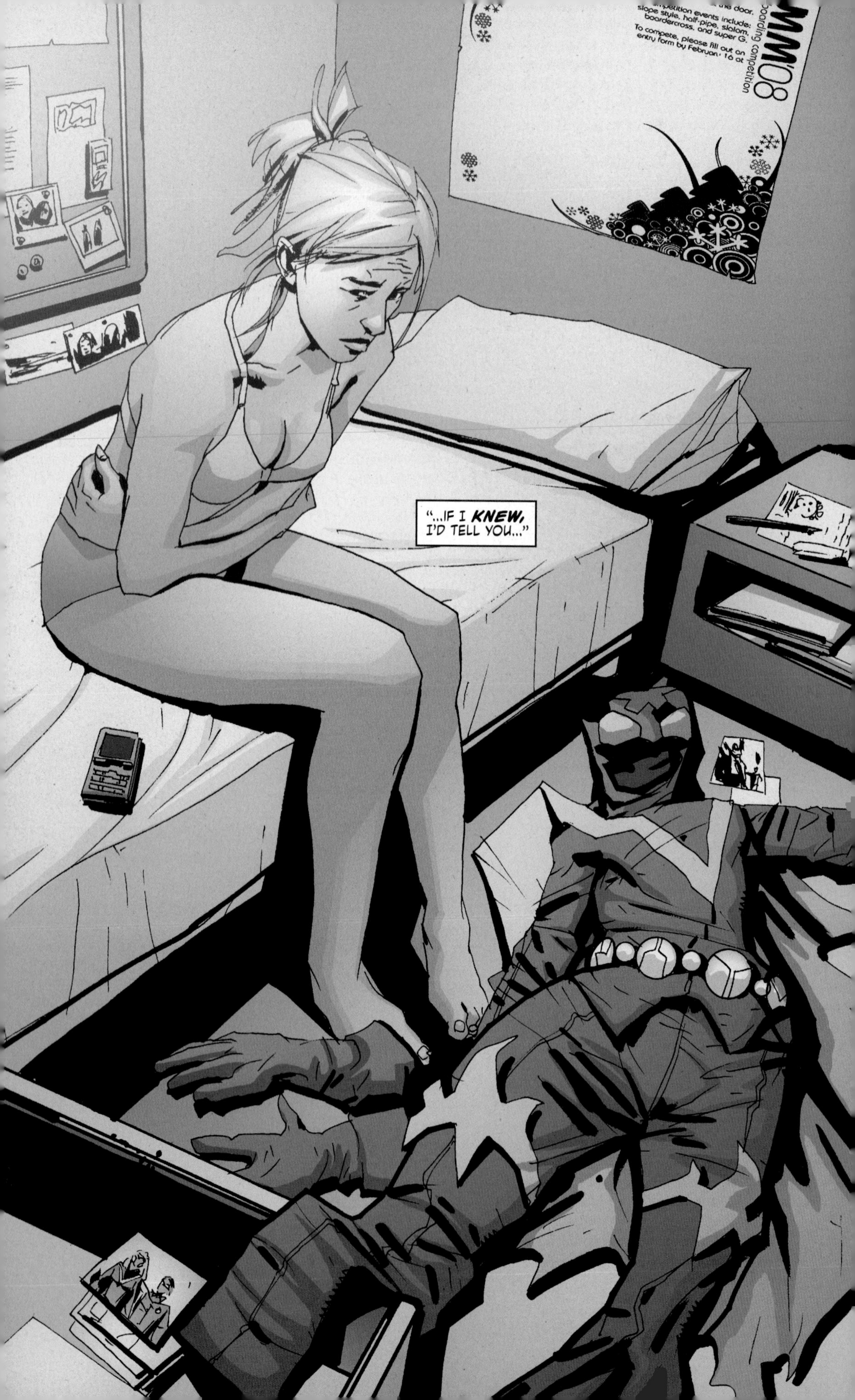
MM'08
boarding competition
slope style, half-pipe, slalom,
boardercross, and super G.
To compete, please fill out an
entry form by Februan' 16 at
"...IF I *KNEW,* I'D TELL YOU..."

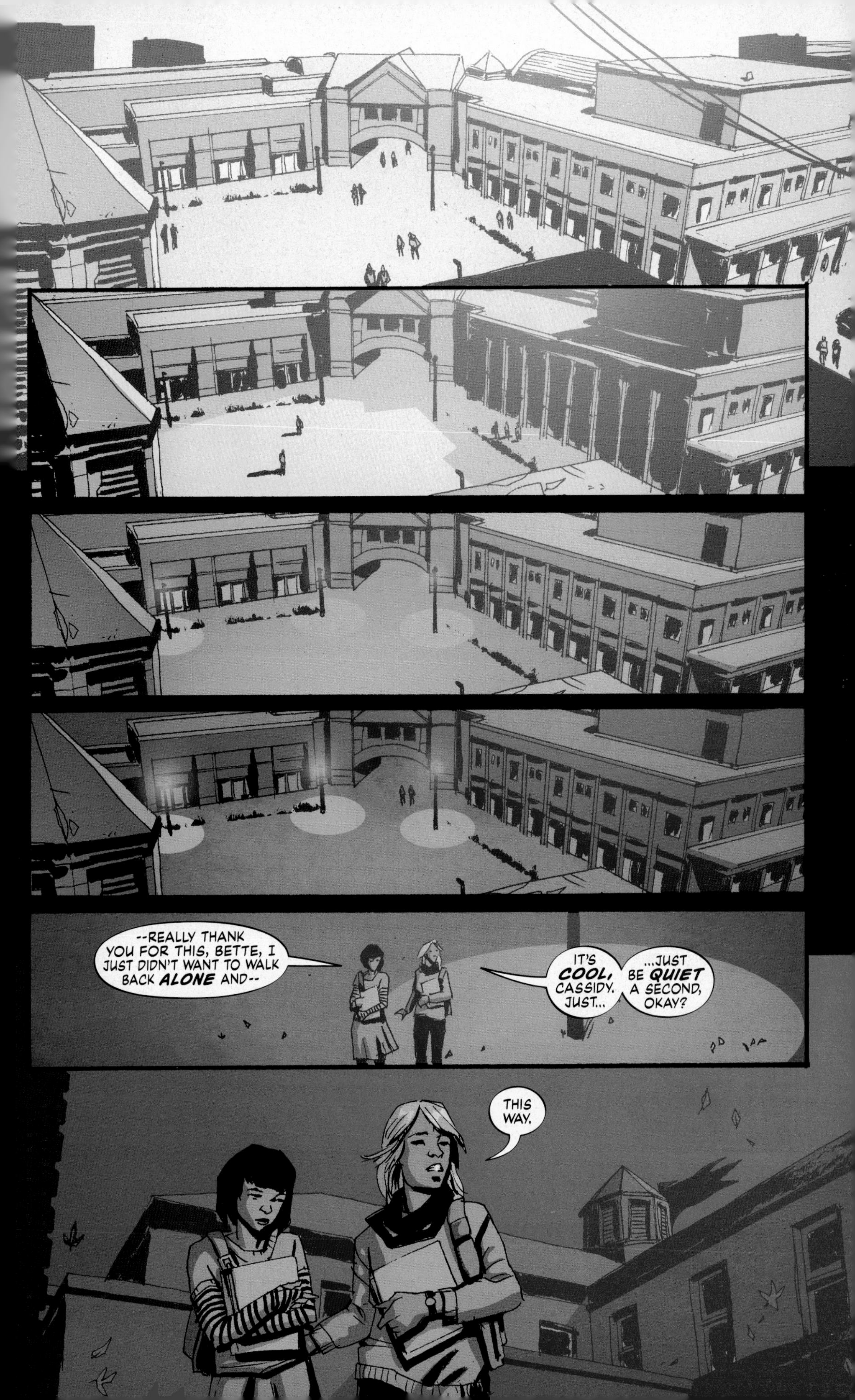
--REALLY THANK YOU FOR THIS, BETTE, I JUST DIDN'T WANT TO WALK BACK ALONE AND--
IT'S COOL, CASSIDY. JUST...
...JUST BE QUIET A SECOND, OKAY?
THIS WAY.

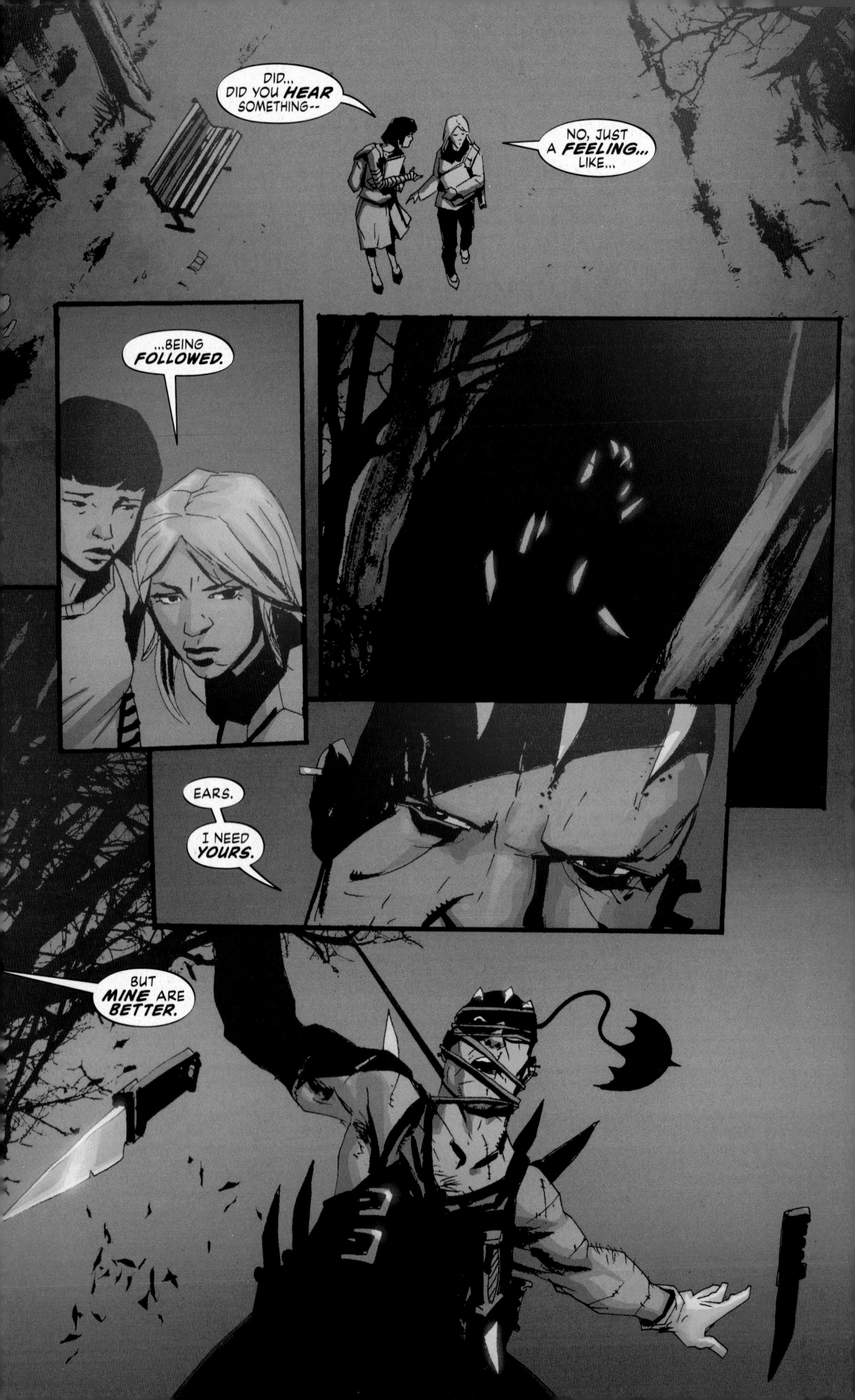
DID... DID YOU HEAR SOMETHING--
NO, JUST A FEELING... LIKE...
...BEING FOLLOWED.
EARS.
I NEED YOURS.
BUT MINE ARE BETTER.

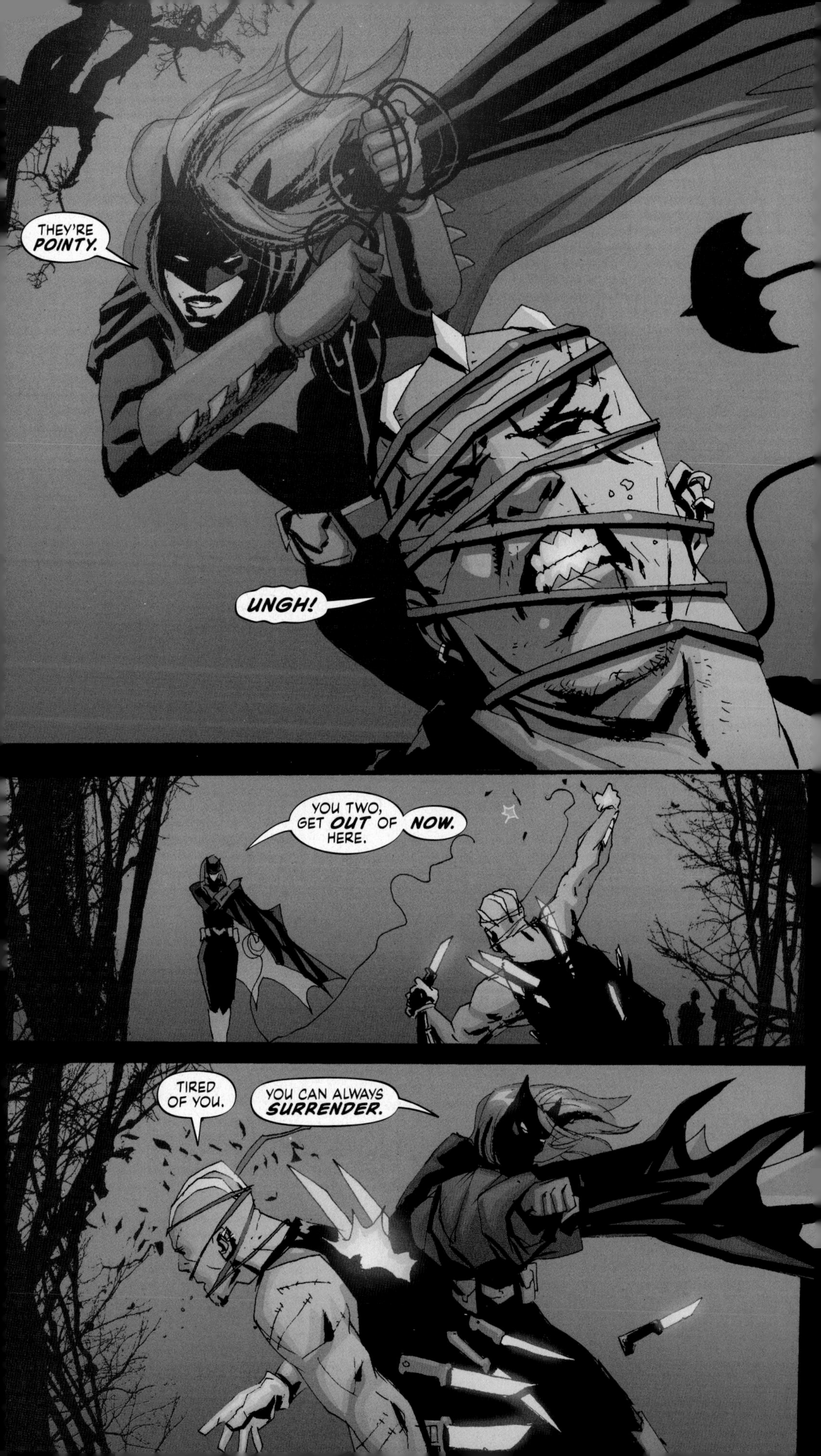

THEY'RE POINTY.
UNGH!
YOU TWO, GET OUT OF HERE.
NOW.
TIRED OF YOU.
YOU CAN ALWAYS SURRENDER.

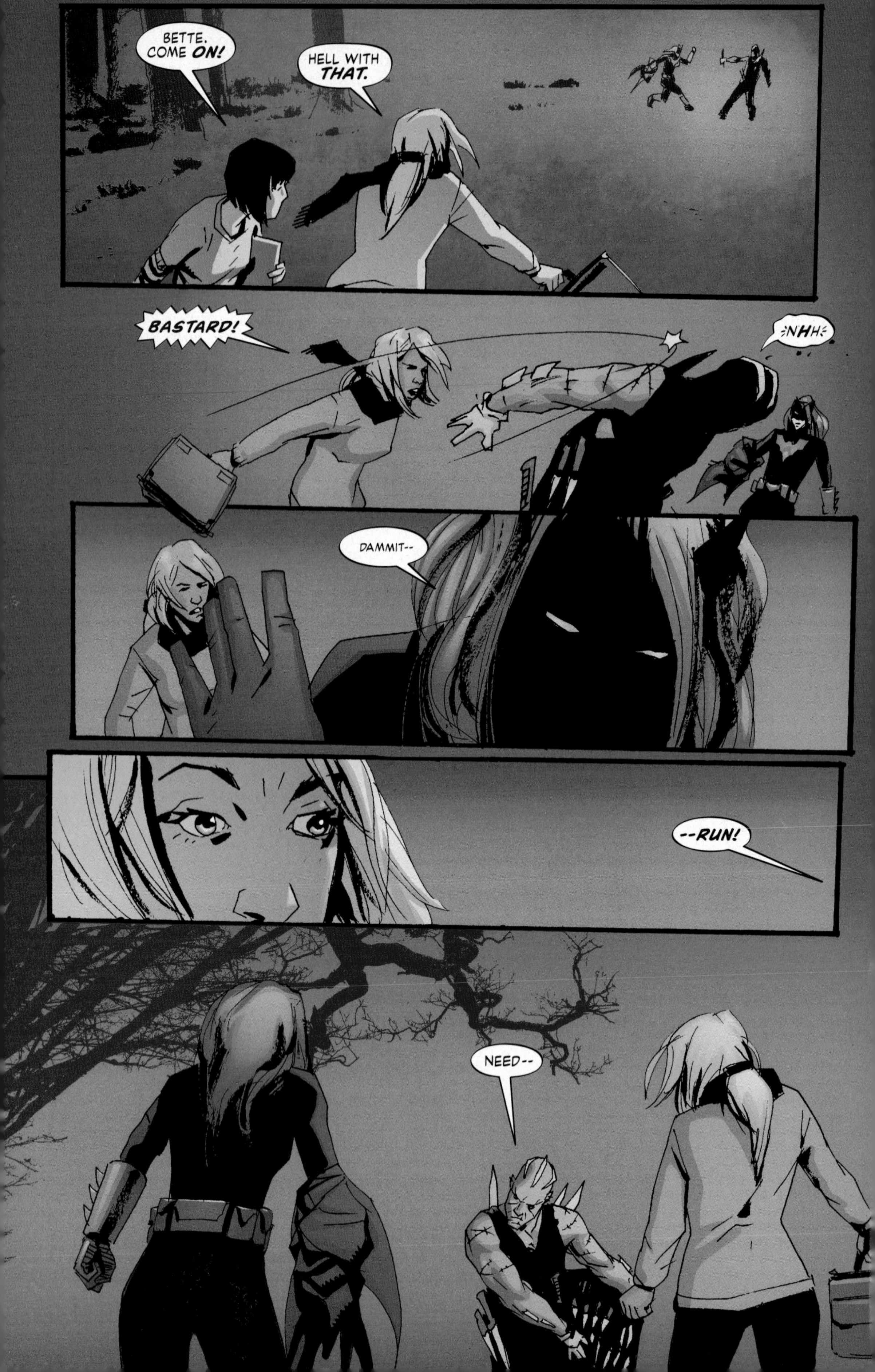
BETTE. COME ON!
HELL WITH THAT.
BASTARD!
NHH
DAMMIT--
--RUN!
NEED--

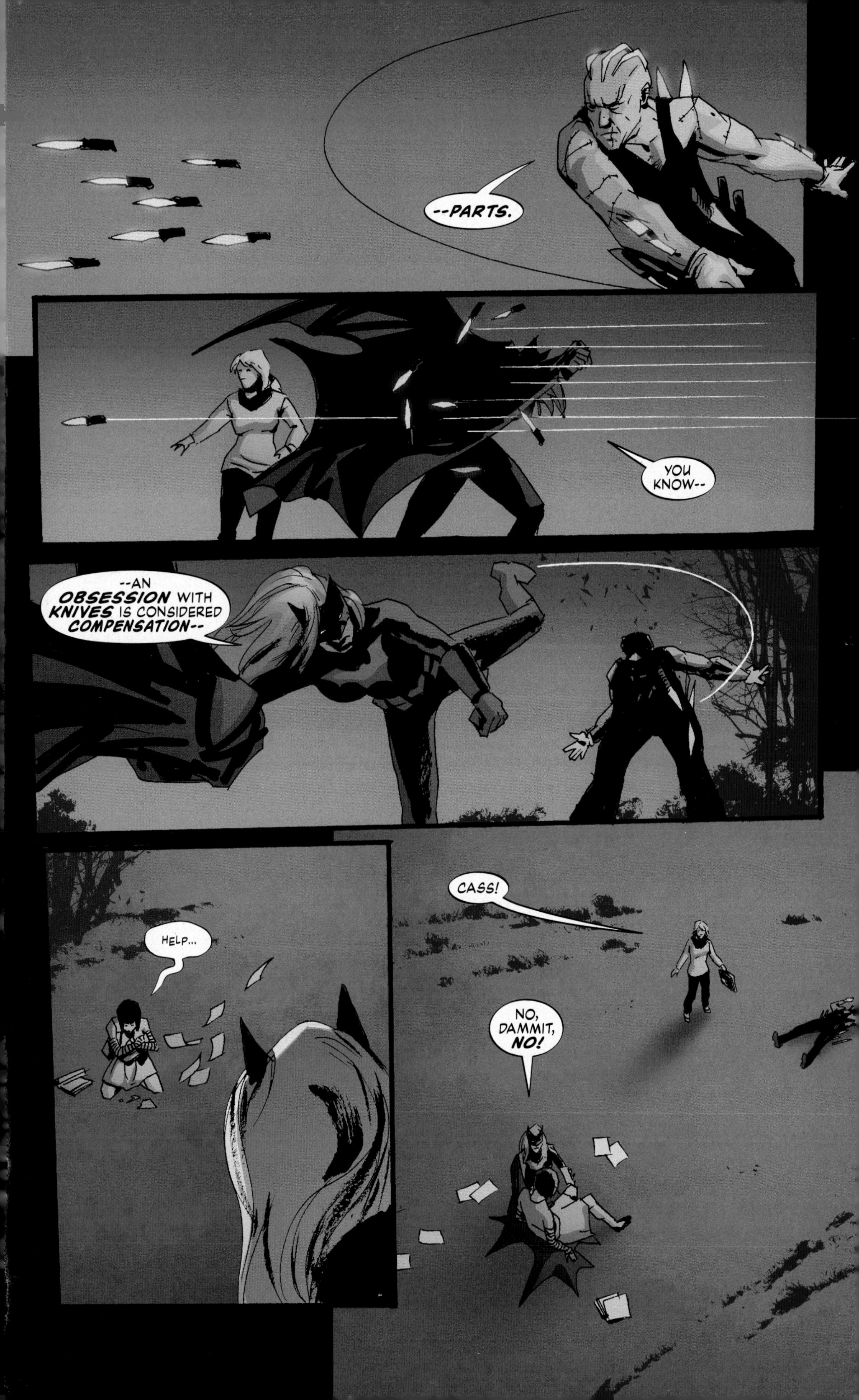
--PARTS.
YOU KNOW--
--AN OBSESSION WITH KNIVES IS CONSIDERED COMPENSATION--
HELP...
CASS!
NO, DAMMIT, NO!

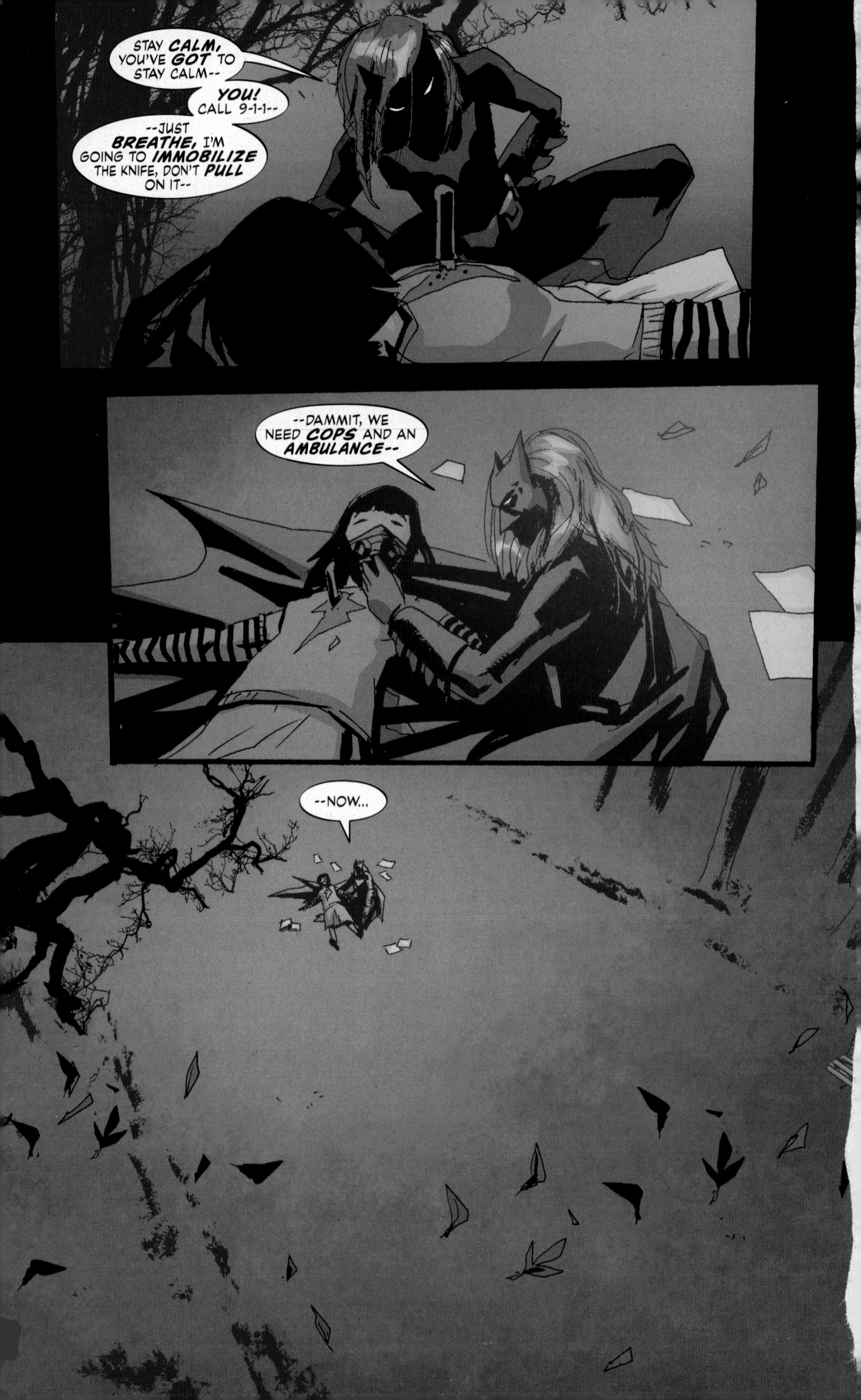
STAY CALM, YOU'VE GOT TO STAY CALM--
YOU! CALL 9-1-1--
--JUST BREATHE, I'M GOING TO IMMOBILIZE THE KNIFE, DON'T PULL ON IT--
--DAMMIT, WE NEED COPS AND AN AMBULANCE--
--NOW...

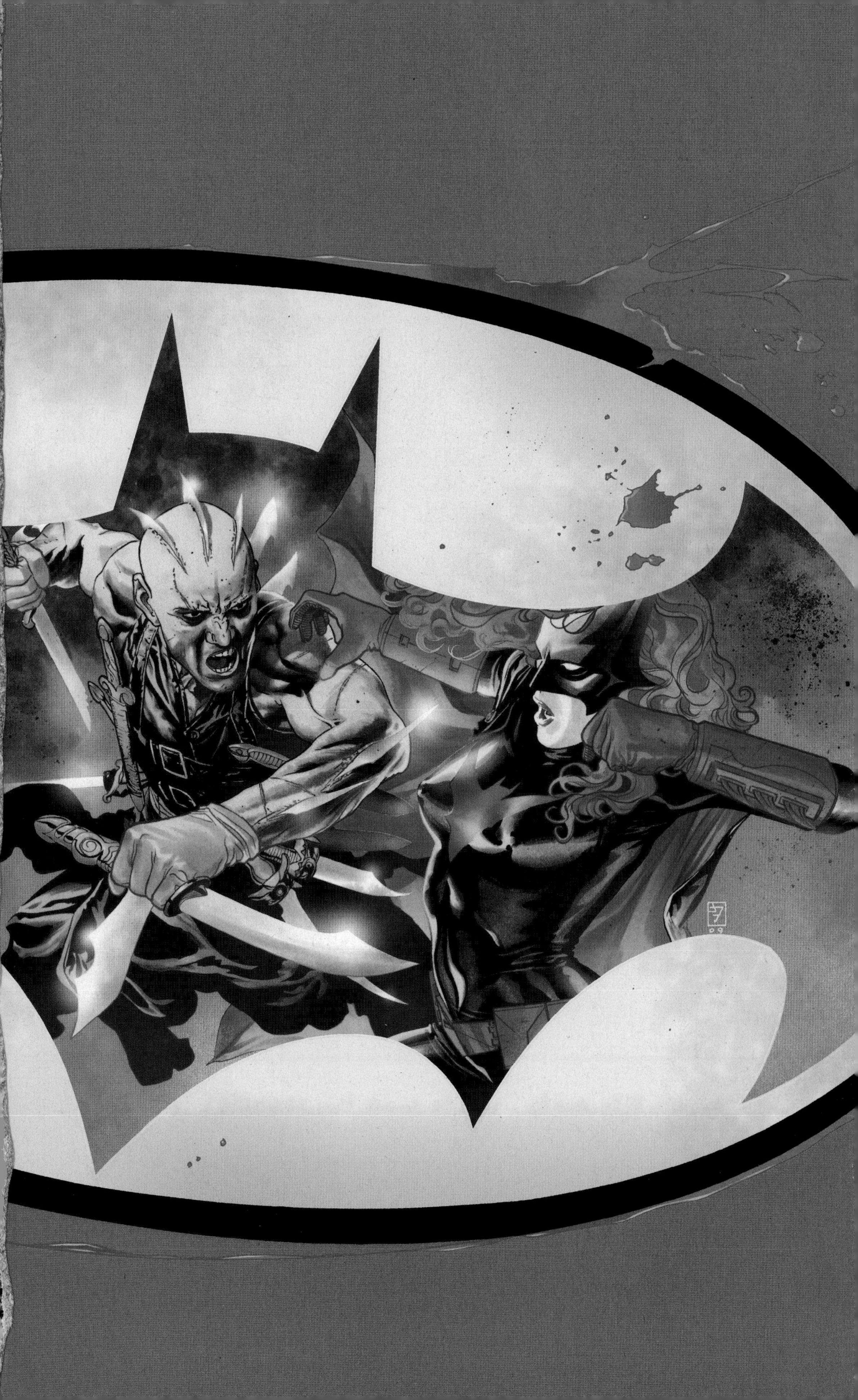

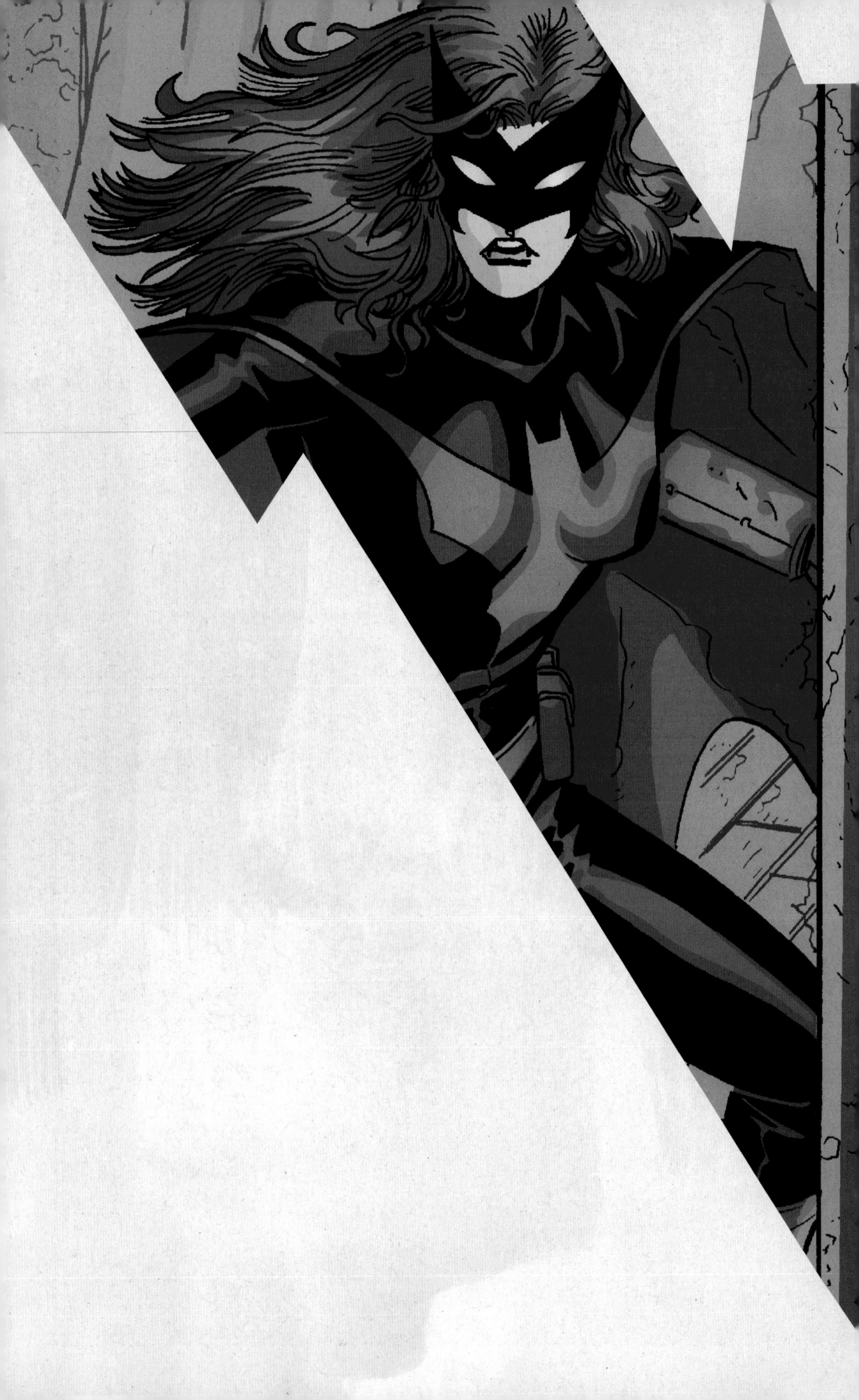

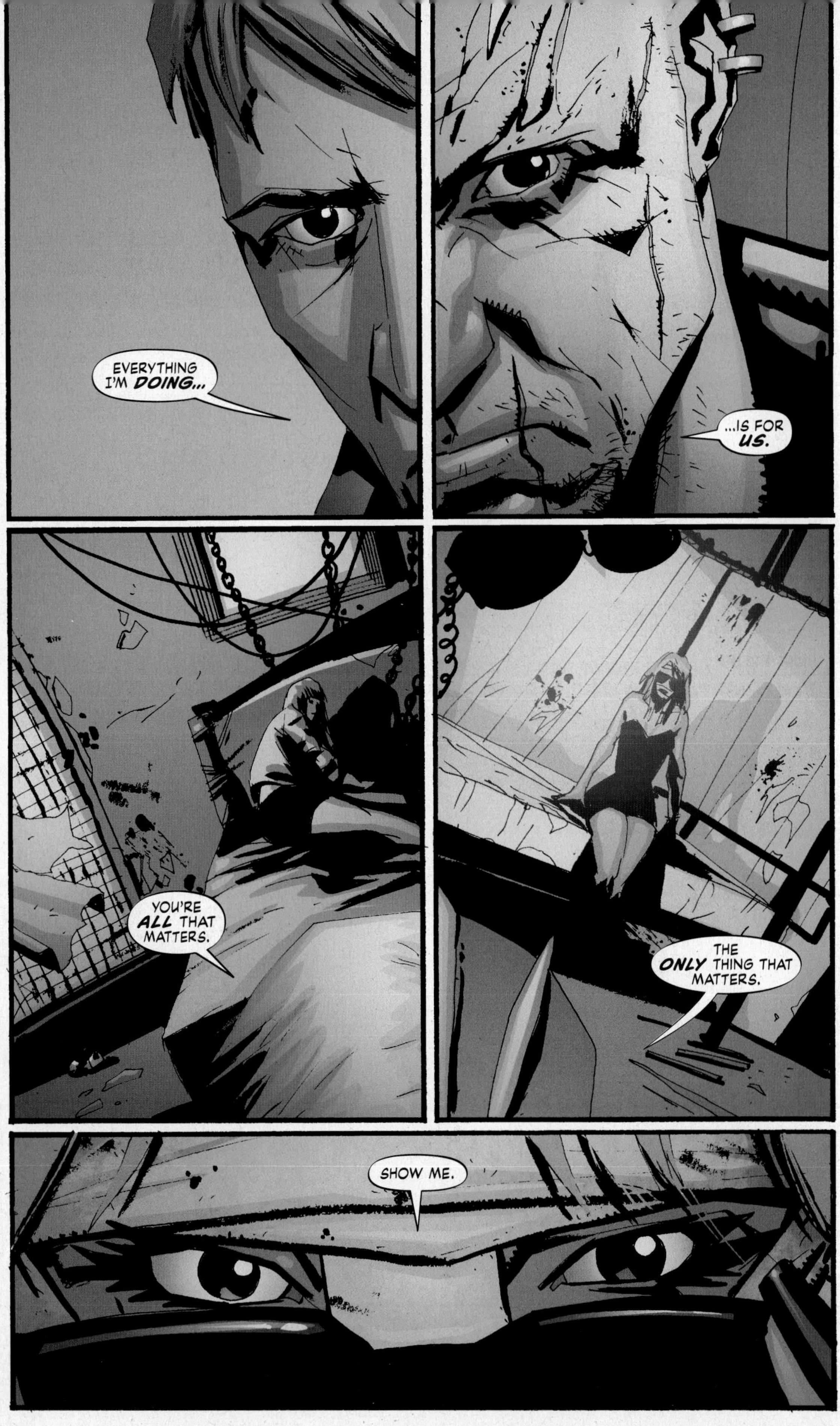
EVERYTHING I'M DOING...
...IS FOR US.
YOU'RE ALL THAT MATTERS.
THE ONLY THING THAT MATTERS.
SHOW ME.

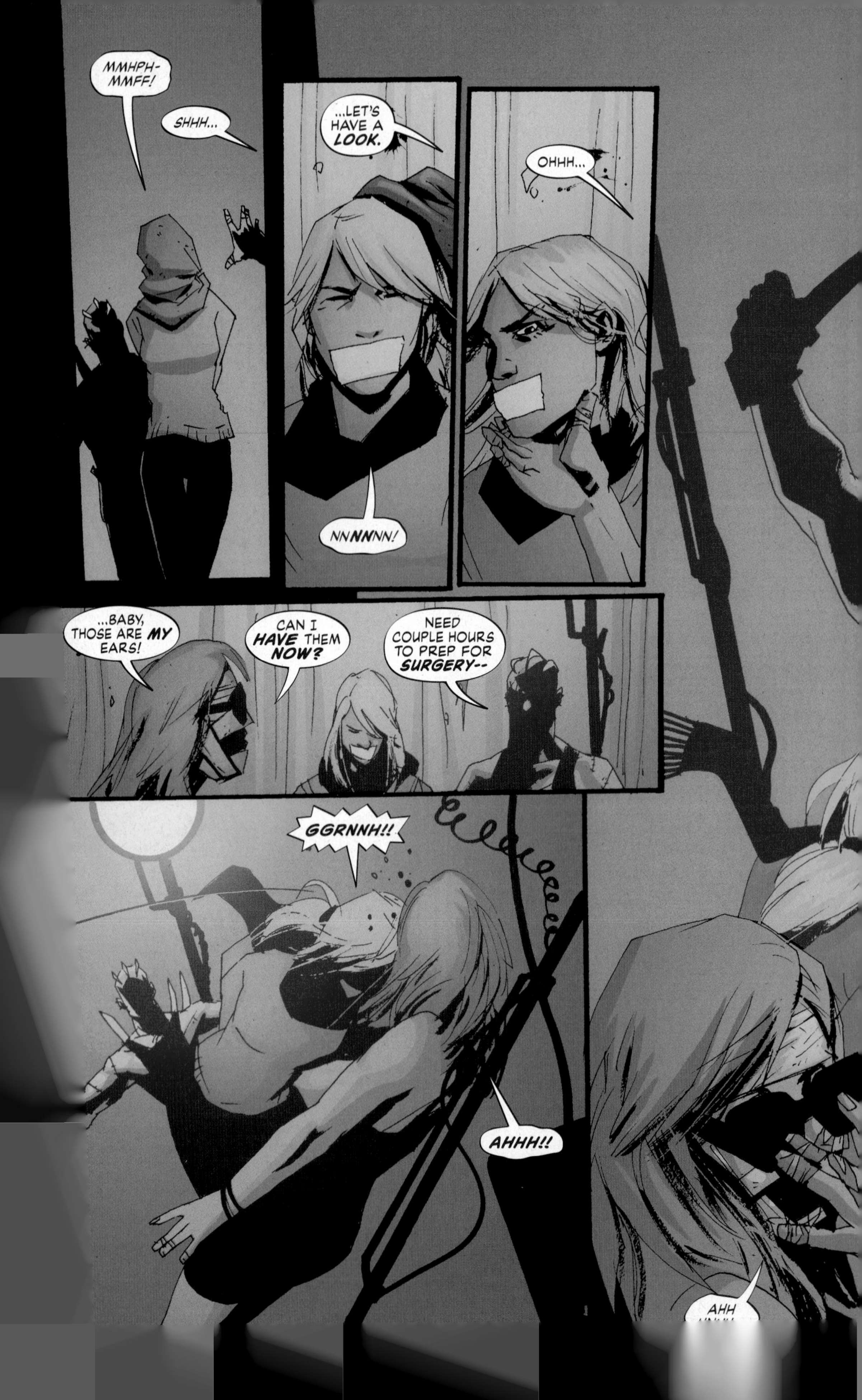
MMHPH-MMFF!
SHHH...
...LET'S HAVE A LOOK.
NNNNNN!
OHHH...
...BABY, THOSE ARE MY EARS!
CAN I HAVE THEM NOW?
NEED COUPLE HOURS TO PREP FOR SURGERY--
GGRNNH!!
AHHH!!
AHH

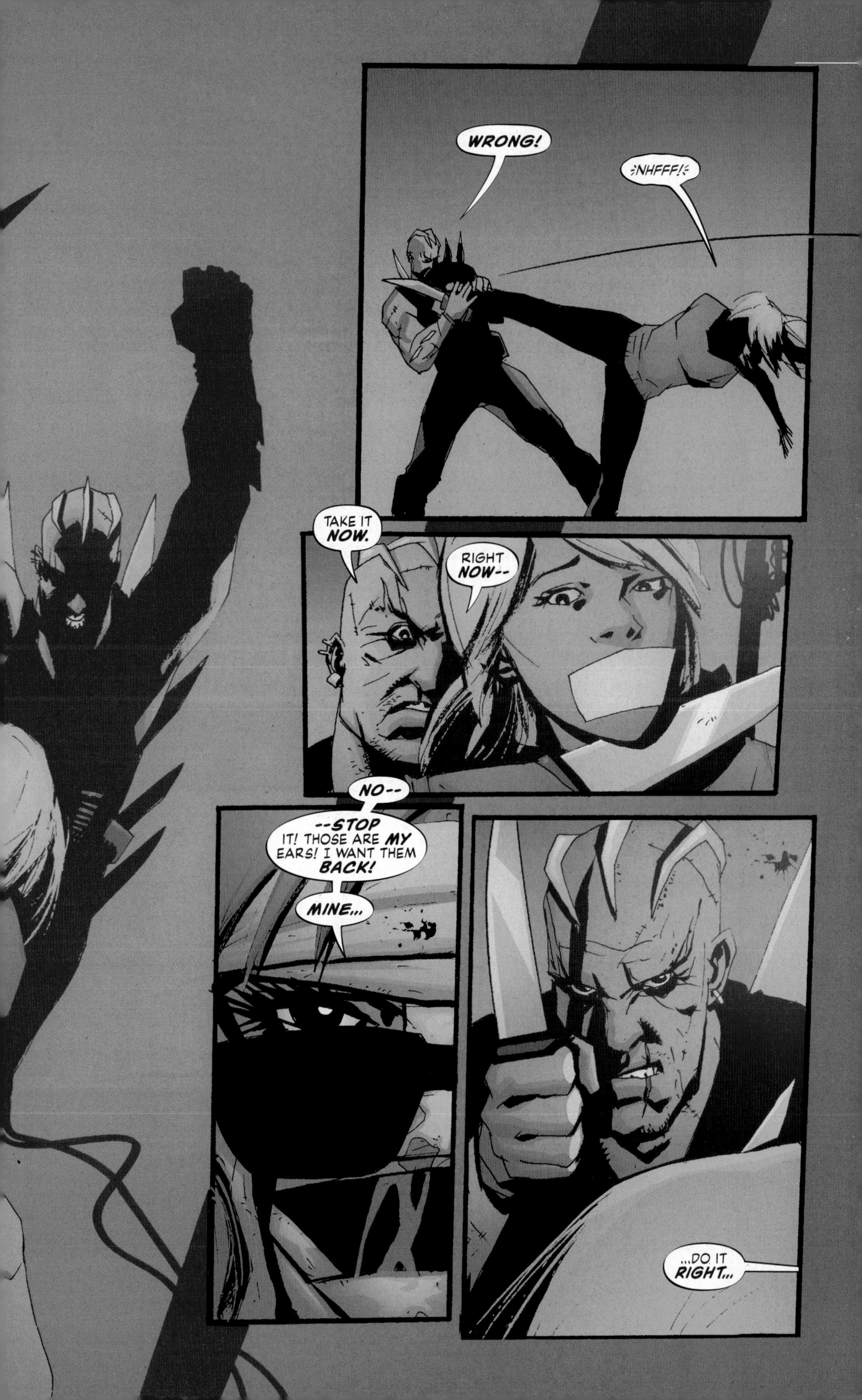
WRONG!
NHFFF!
TAKE IT NOW.
RIGHT NOW--
NO--
--STOP IT! THOSE ARE MY EARS! I WANT THEM BACK!
MINE...
...DO IT RIGHT...

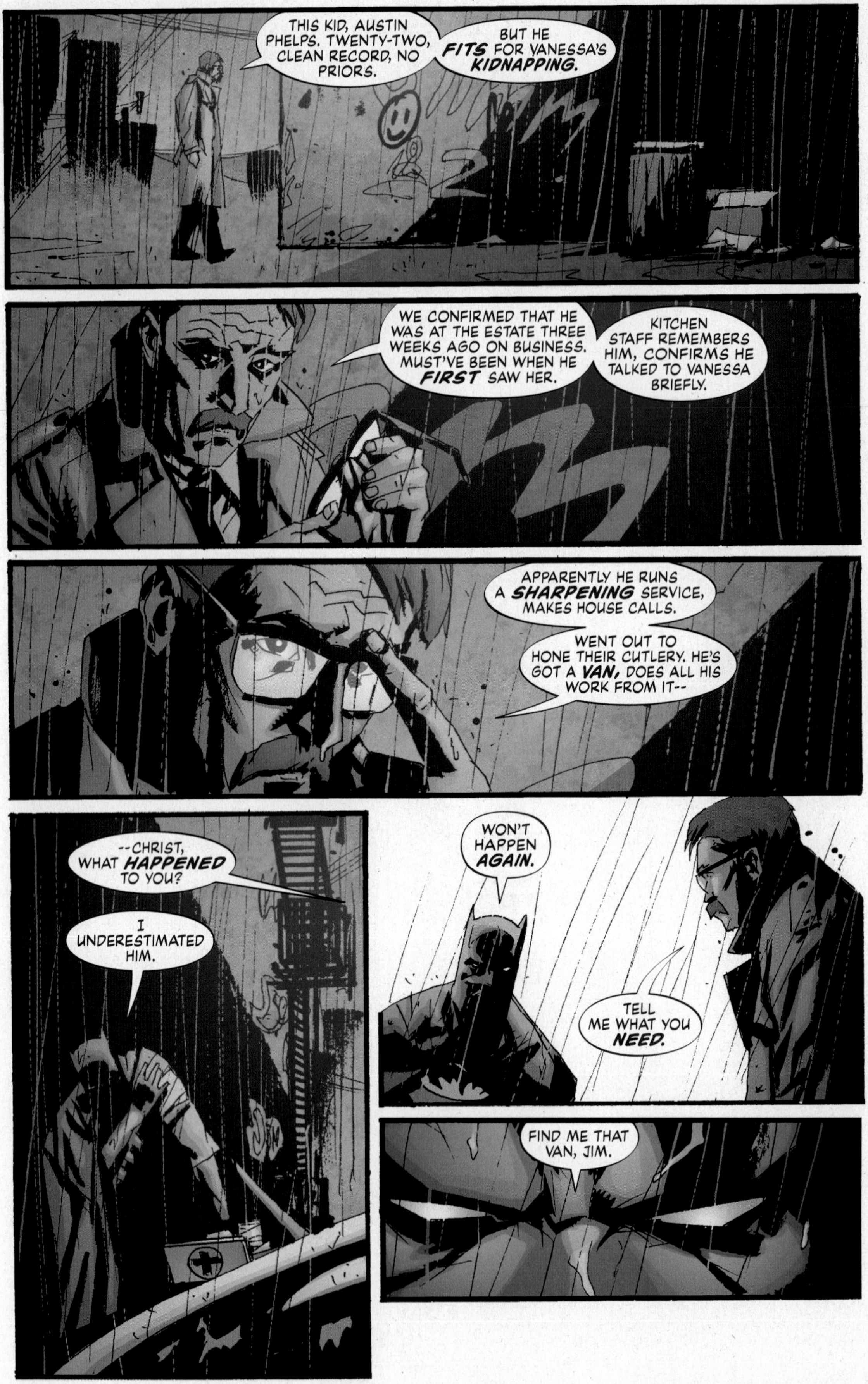
THIS KID, AUSTIN PHELPS. TWENTY-TWO, CLEAN RECORD, NO PRIORS.
BUT HE FITS FOR VANESSA'S KIDNAPPING.
WE CONFIRMED THAT HE WAS AT THE ESTATE THREE WEEKS AGO ON BUSINESS. MUST'VE BEEN WHEN HE FIRST SAW HER.
KITCHEN STAFF REMEMBERS HIM, CONFIRMS HE TALKED TO VANESSA BRIEFLY.
APPARENTLY HE RUNS A SHARPENING SERVICE, MAKES HOUSE CALLS.
WENT OUT TO HONE THEIR CUTLERY. HE'S GOT A VAN, DOES ALL HIS WORK FROM IT--
--CHRIST, WHAT HAPPENED TO YOU?
I UNDERESTIMATED HIM.
WON'T HAPPEN AGAIN.
TELL ME WHAT YOU NEED.
FIND ME THAT VAN, JIM.

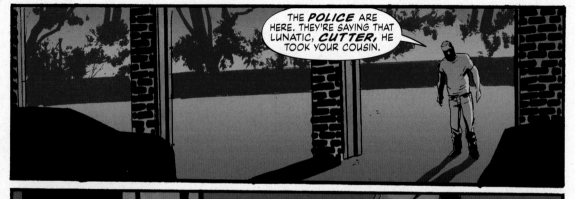

THE *POLICE* ARE HERE. THEY'RE SAYING THAT LUNATIC, *CUTTER,* HE TOOK YOUR COUSIN.

I SAW THE DUCATI ON THE NEWS, SHINY SIDE *DOWN.*

I *KNOW* YOU'RE HERE.

I'M YOUR DAMN *FATHER,* KATE, YOU *DON'T* IGNORE ME.

LET ME *HELP* YOU.

YOU DON'T JUST--

CUTTER'S USING AN *ARMORED CAR,* VIGILANCE MODEL 7, MANUFACTURED BY KORD.

ALL ARMORED CARS THESE DAYS HAVE A GPS TRACKING SYSTEM INSTALLED.

FIND ME THAT CAR, COLONEL.

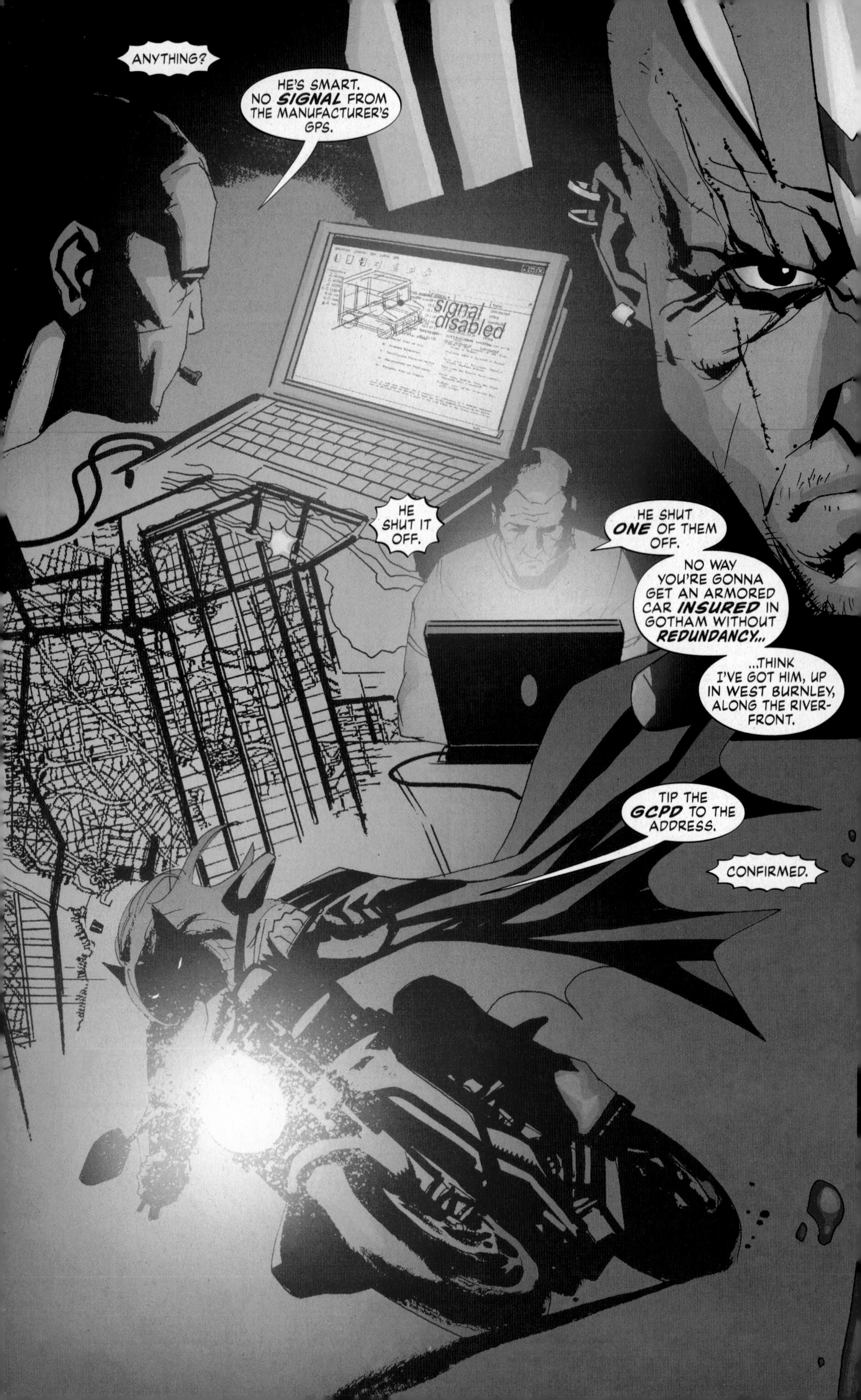
ANYTHING?
HE'S SMART. NO SIGNAL FROM THE MANUFACTURER'S GPS.
signal disabled
HE SHUT IT OFF.
HE SHUT ONE OF THEM OFF.
NO WAY YOU'RE GONNA GET AN ARMORED CAR INSURED IN GOTHAM WITHOUT REDUNDANCY...
...THINK I'VE GOT HIM, UP IN WEST BURNLEY, ALONG THE RIVER-FRONT.
TIP THE GCPD TO THE ADDRESS.
CONFIRMED.

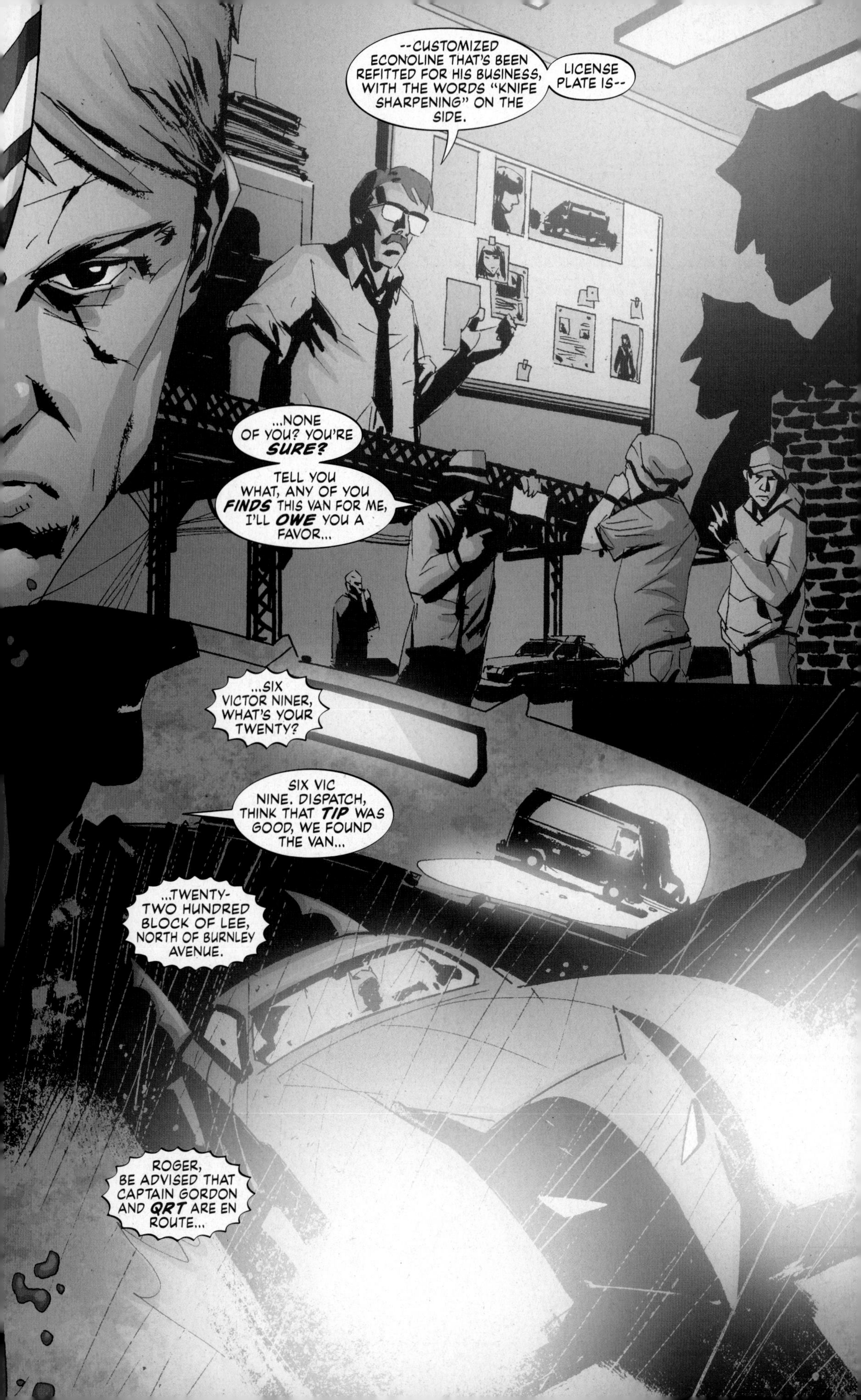
--CUSTOMIZED ECONOLINE THAT'S BEEN REFITTED FOR HIS BUSINESS, WITH THE WORDS "KNIFE SHARPENING" ON THE SIDE.
LICENSE PLATE IS--
...NONE OF YOU? YOU'RE SURE?
TELL YOU WHAT, ANY OF YOU FINDS THIS VAN FOR ME, I'LL OWE YOU A FAVOR...
...SIX VICTOR NINER, WHAT'S YOUR TWENTY?
SIX VIC NINE. DISPATCH, THINK THAT TIP WAS GOOD, WE FOUND THE VAN...
...TWENTY-TWO HUNDRED BLOCK OF LEE, NORTH OF BURNLEY AVENUE.
ROGER, BE ADVISED THAT CAPTAIN GORDON AND QRT ARE EN ROUTE...

WHERE ARE WE?
GOT AS MANY OF THE GUESTS OUT AS WE COULD. PHELPS IS HOLED-UP IN 202, BUT WE CAN'T BE SURE THE GIRL'S WITH HIM...
MOTEL
AND IF SHE IS, QRT IS WORRIED HE MIGHT JUST CUT HER THROAT IF THEY STORM THE LOFT.
SNIPERS HAVE A SHOT?
NO LUCK, NO VISUAL AT ALL ON THE INTERIOR...

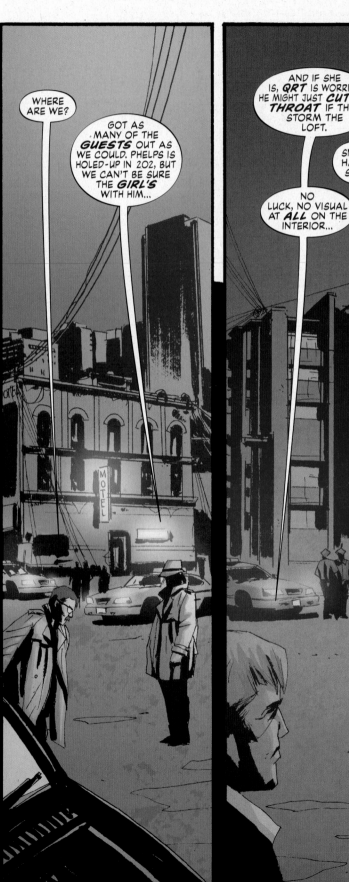

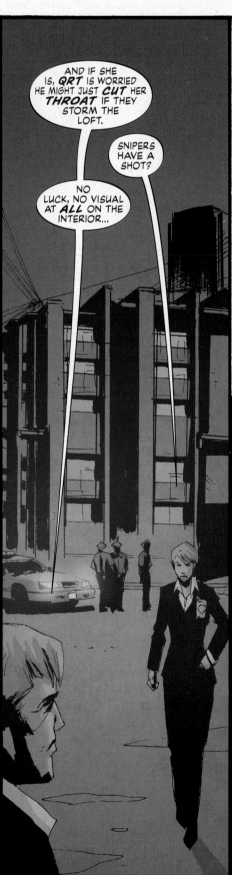

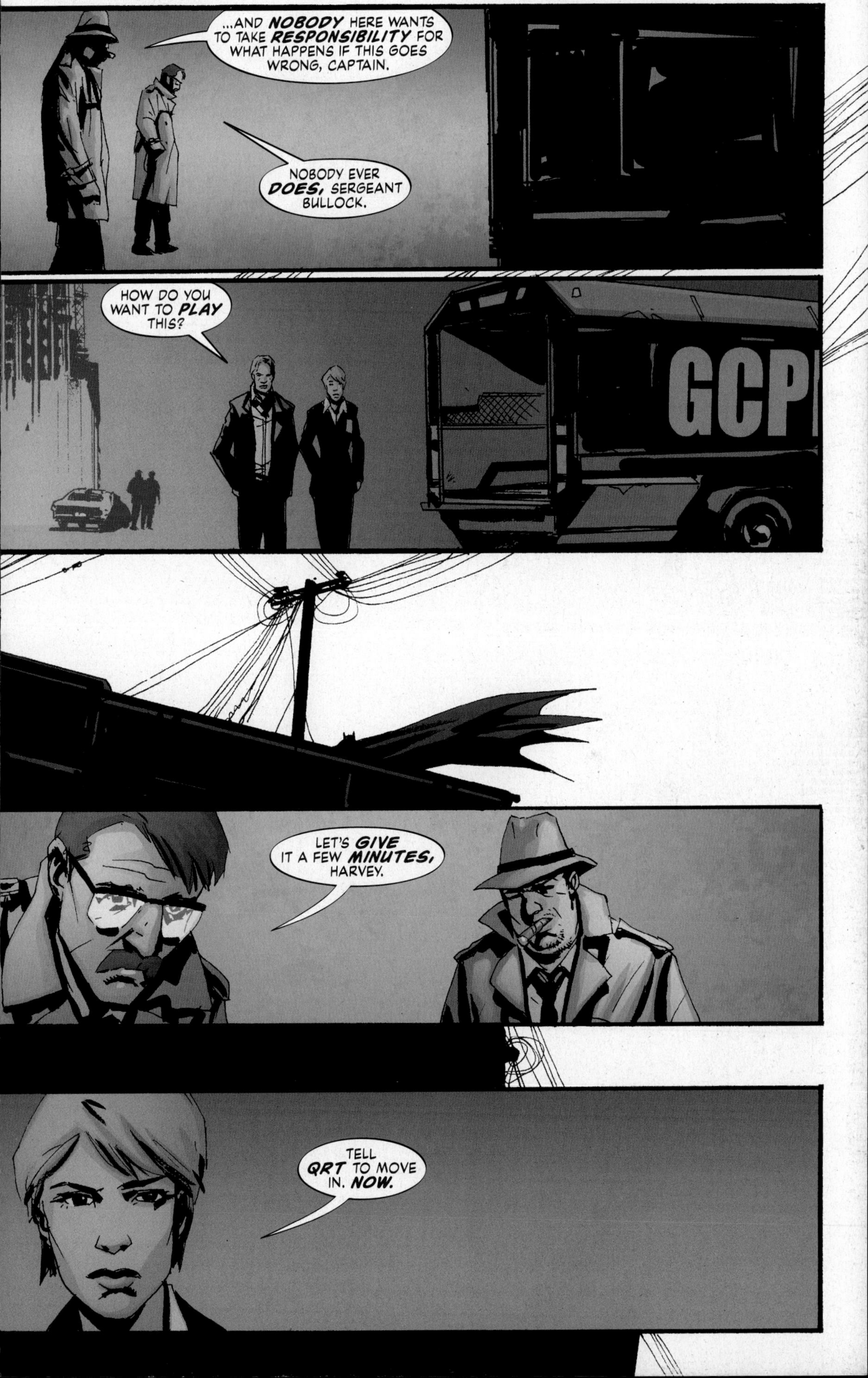
...AND NOBODY HERE WANTS TO TAKE RESPONSIBILITY FOR WHAT HAPPENS IF THIS GOES WRONG, CAPTAIN.
NOBODY EVER DOES, SERGEANT BULLOCK.
HOW DO YOU WANT TO PLAY THIS?
GCP
LET'S GIVE IT A FEW MINUTES, HARVEY.
TELL QRT TO MOVE IN. NOW.

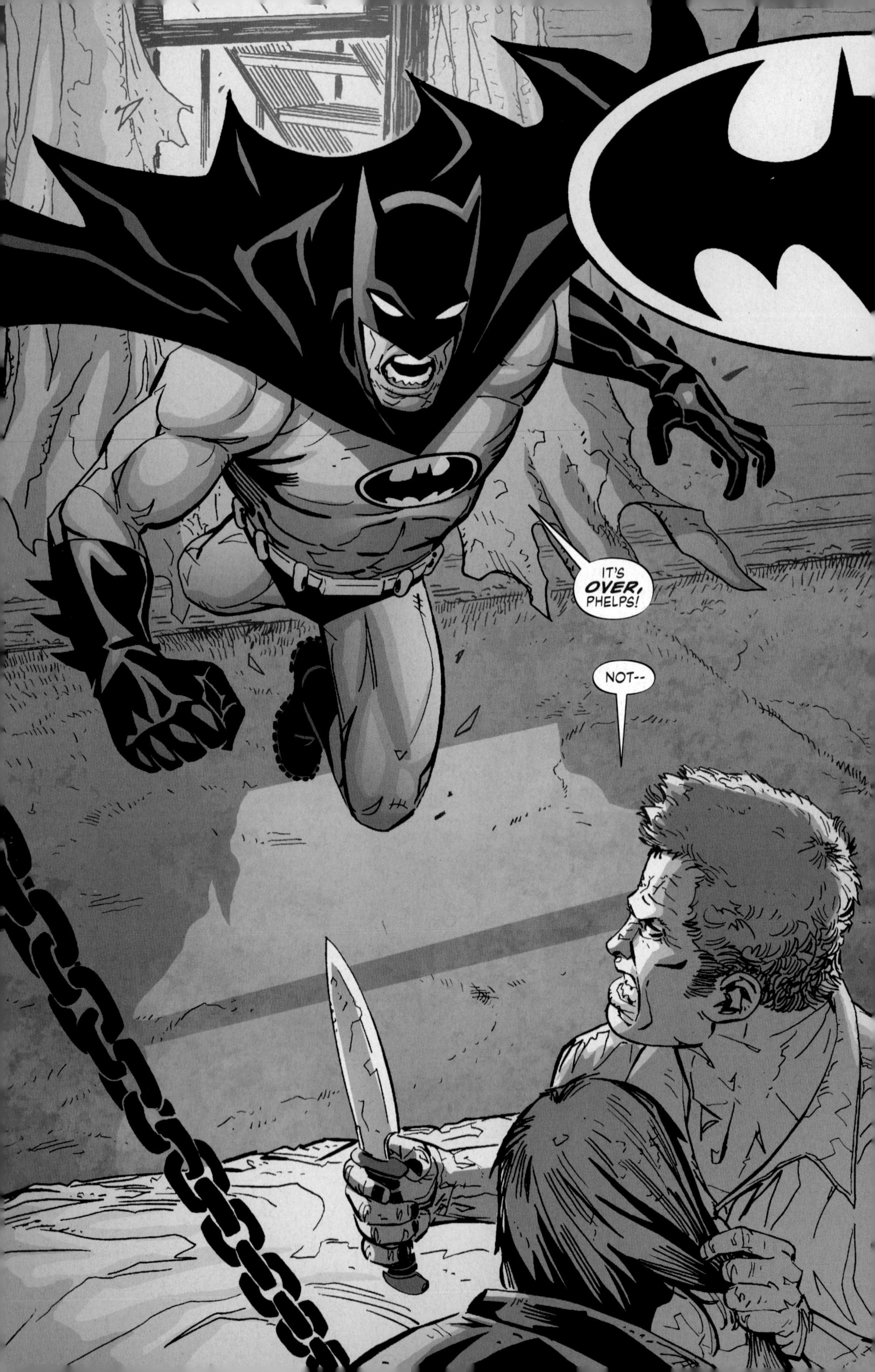
IT'S OVER, PHELPS!
NOT--

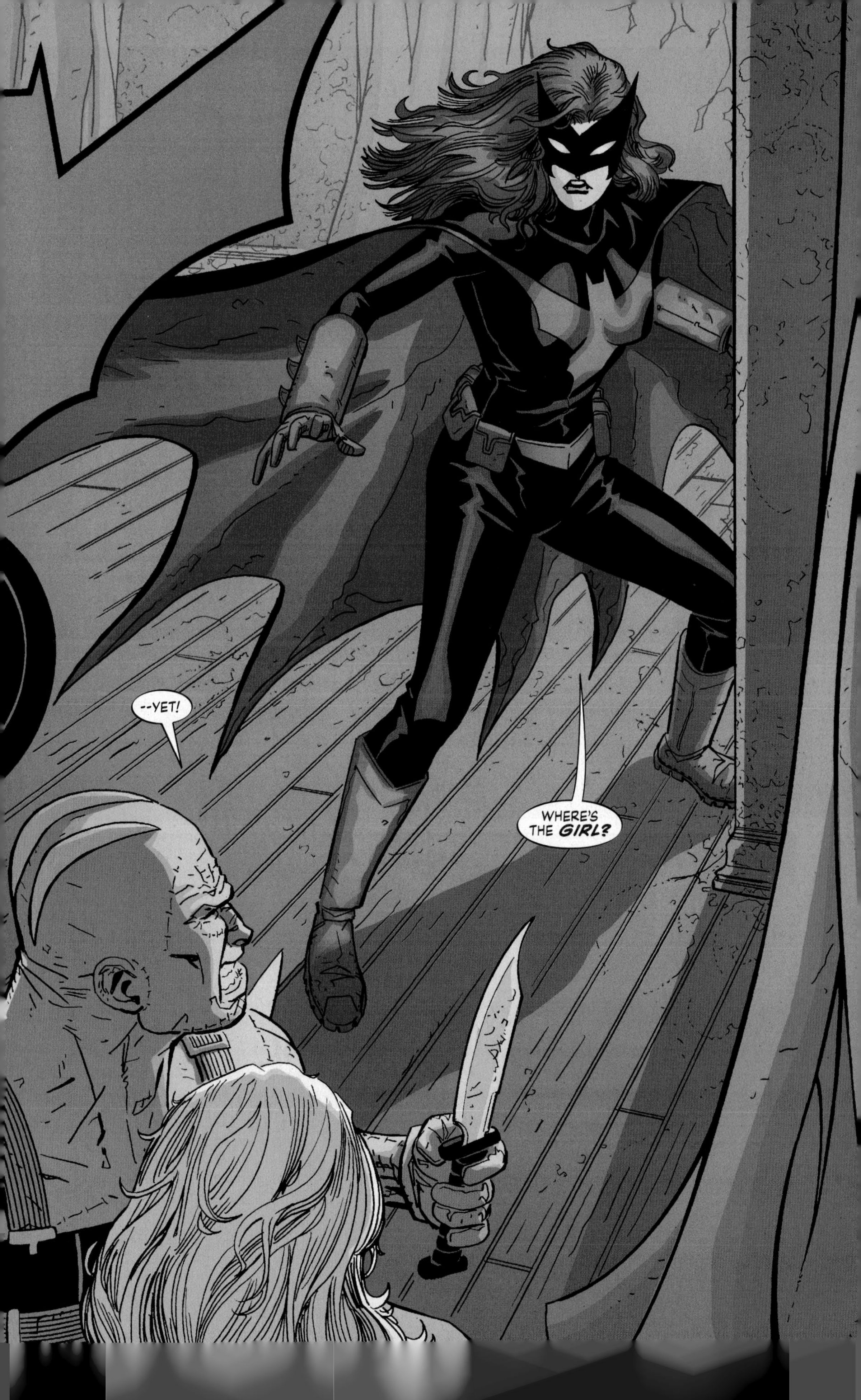
--YET!
WHERE'S THE GIRL?

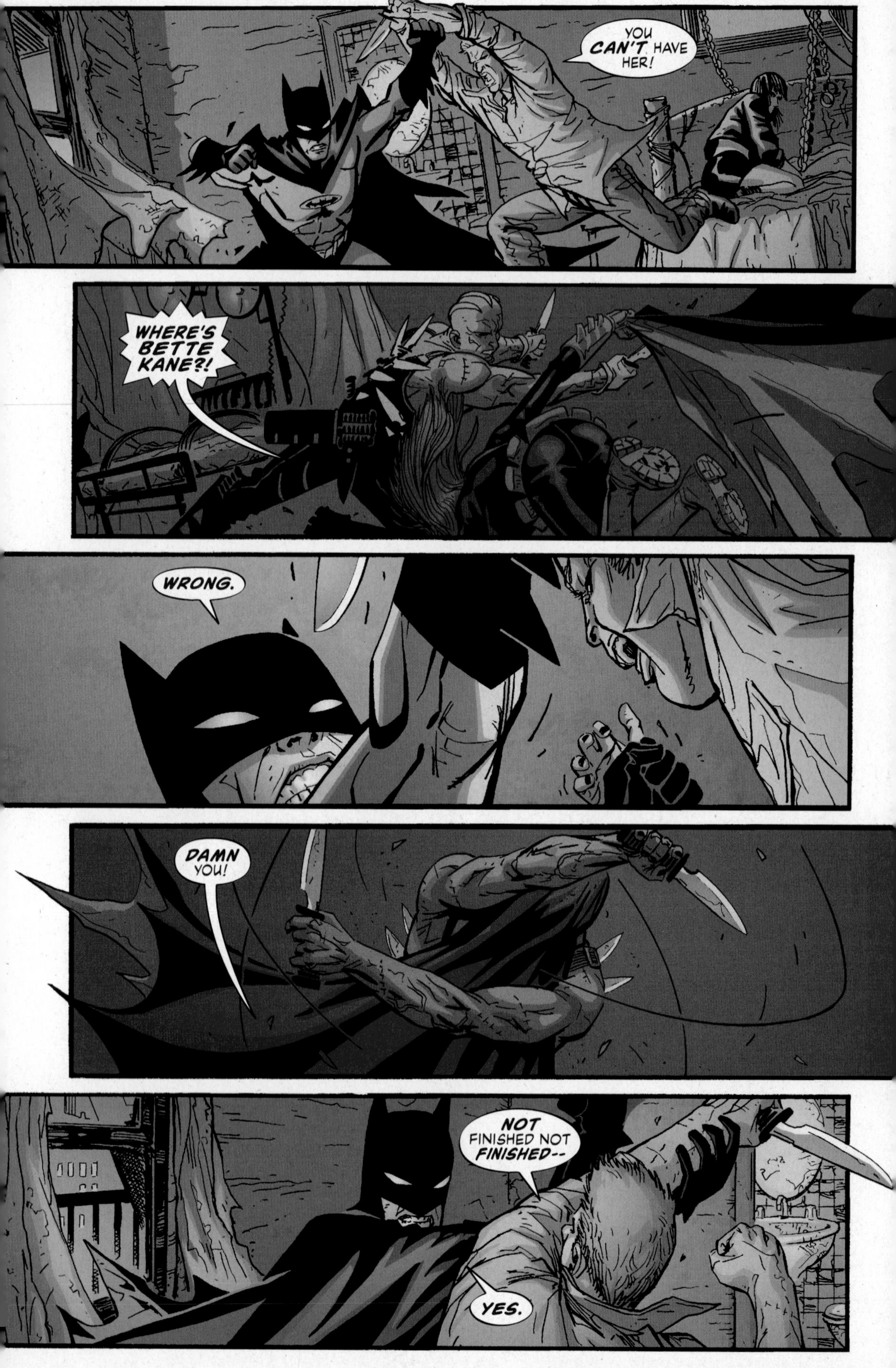
YOU CAN'T HAVE HER!
WHERE'S BETTE KANE?!
WRONG.
DAMN YOU!
NOT FINISHED NOT FINISHED--
YES.

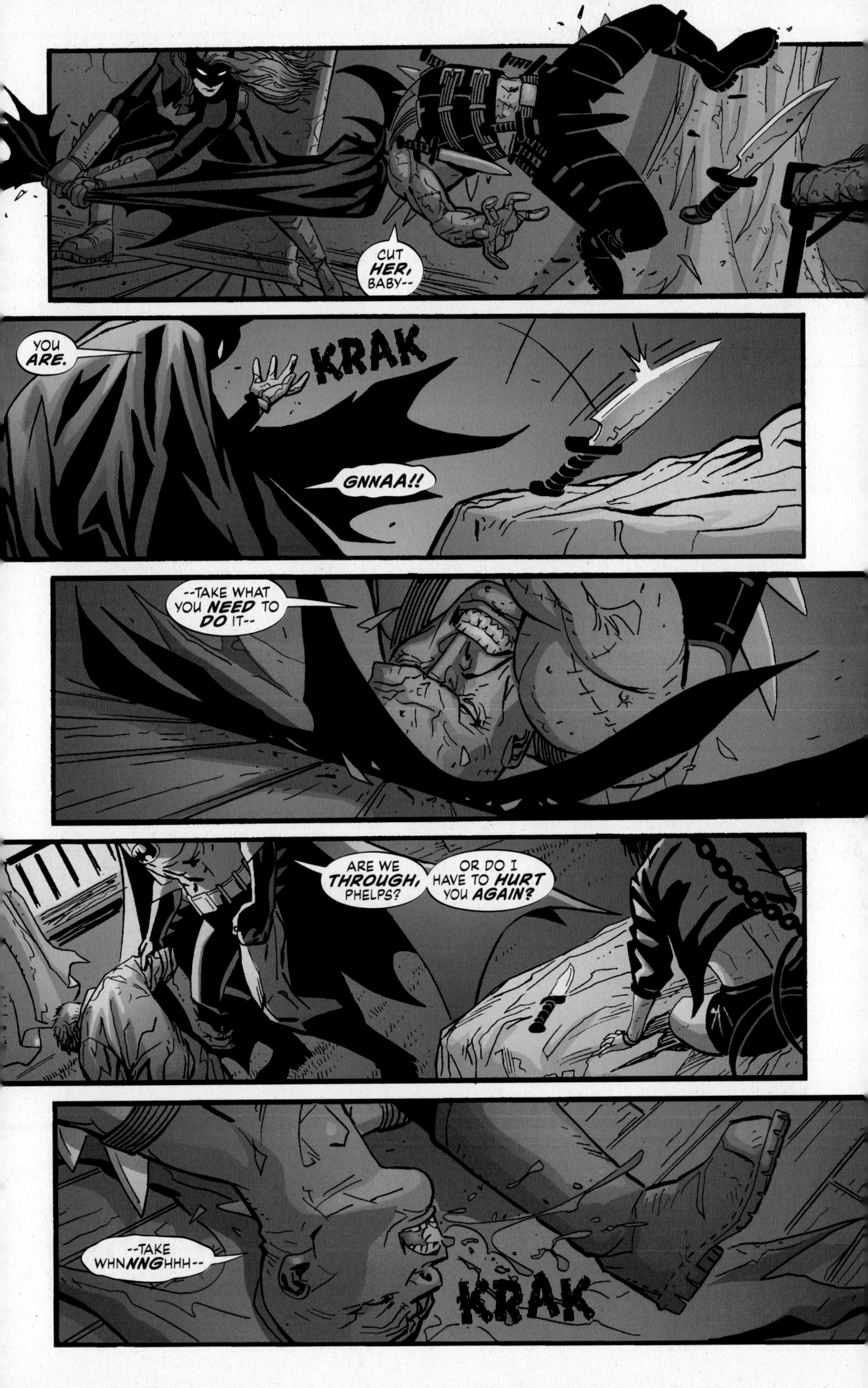
CUT HER, BABY--
YOU ARE.
KRAK
GNNAA!!
--TAKE WHAT YOU NEED TO DO IT--
ARE WE THROUGH, PHELPS?
OR DO I HAVE TO HURT YOU AGAIN?
--TAKE WHNNNGHHH--
KRAK

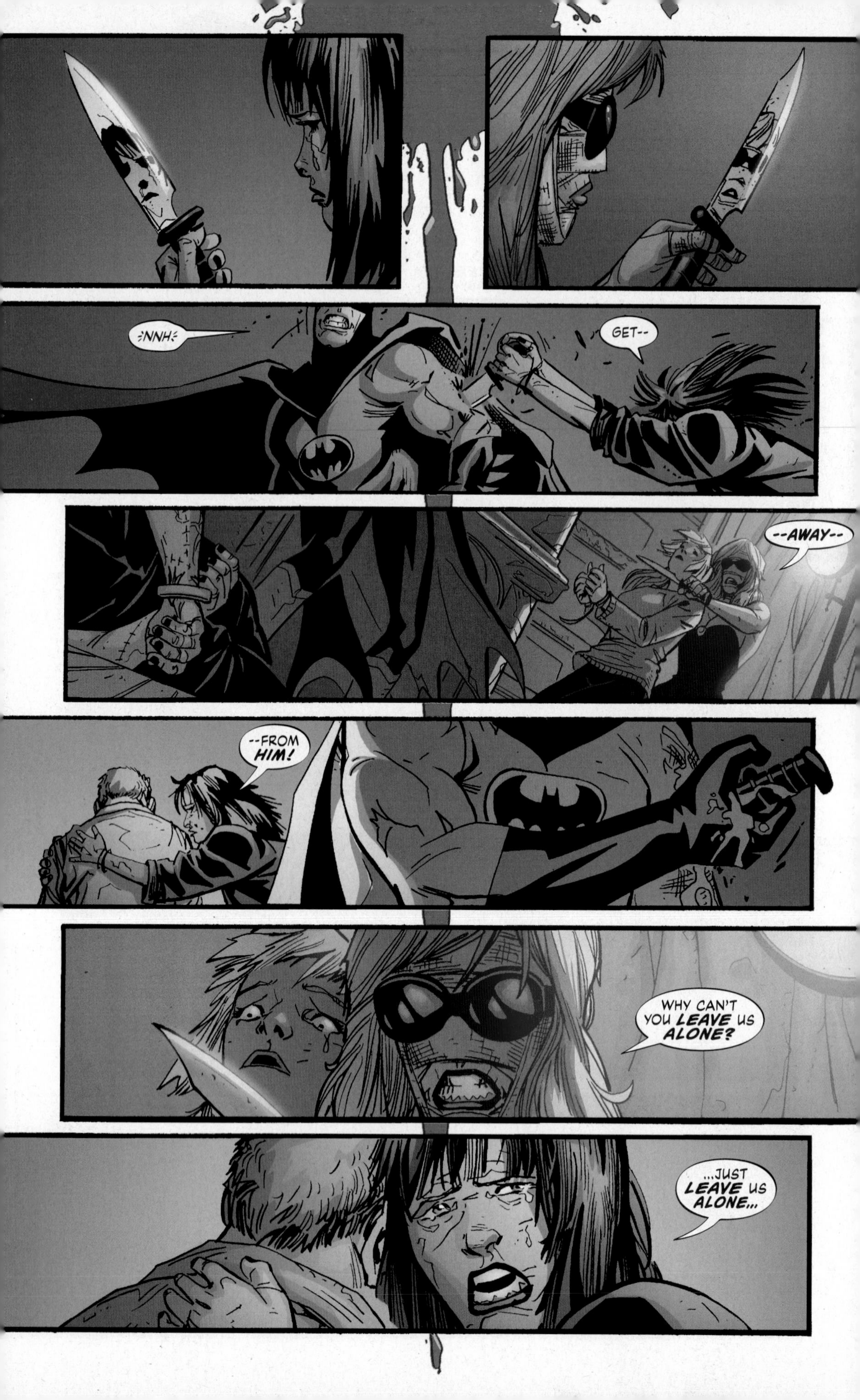
NNH
GET--
--AWAY--
--FROM HIM!
WHY CAN'T YOU LEAVE US ALONE?
...JUST LEAVE US ALONE...

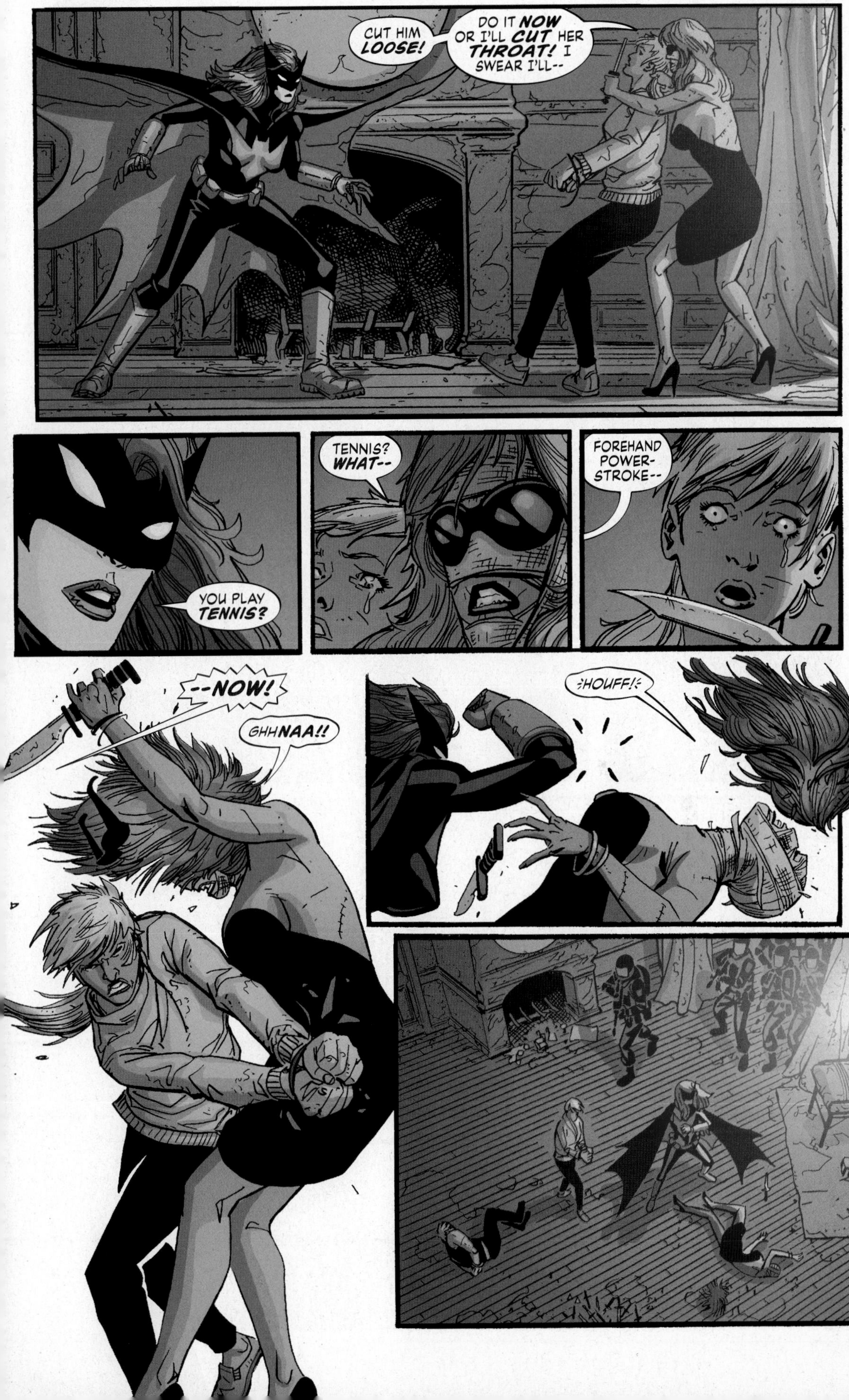
CUT HIM LOOSE!
DO IT NOW OR I'LL CUT HER THROAT! I SWEAR I'LL--
YOU PLAY TENNIS?
TENNIS? WHAT--
FOREHAND POWER-STROKE--
--NOW!
GHHNAA!!
HOUFF!

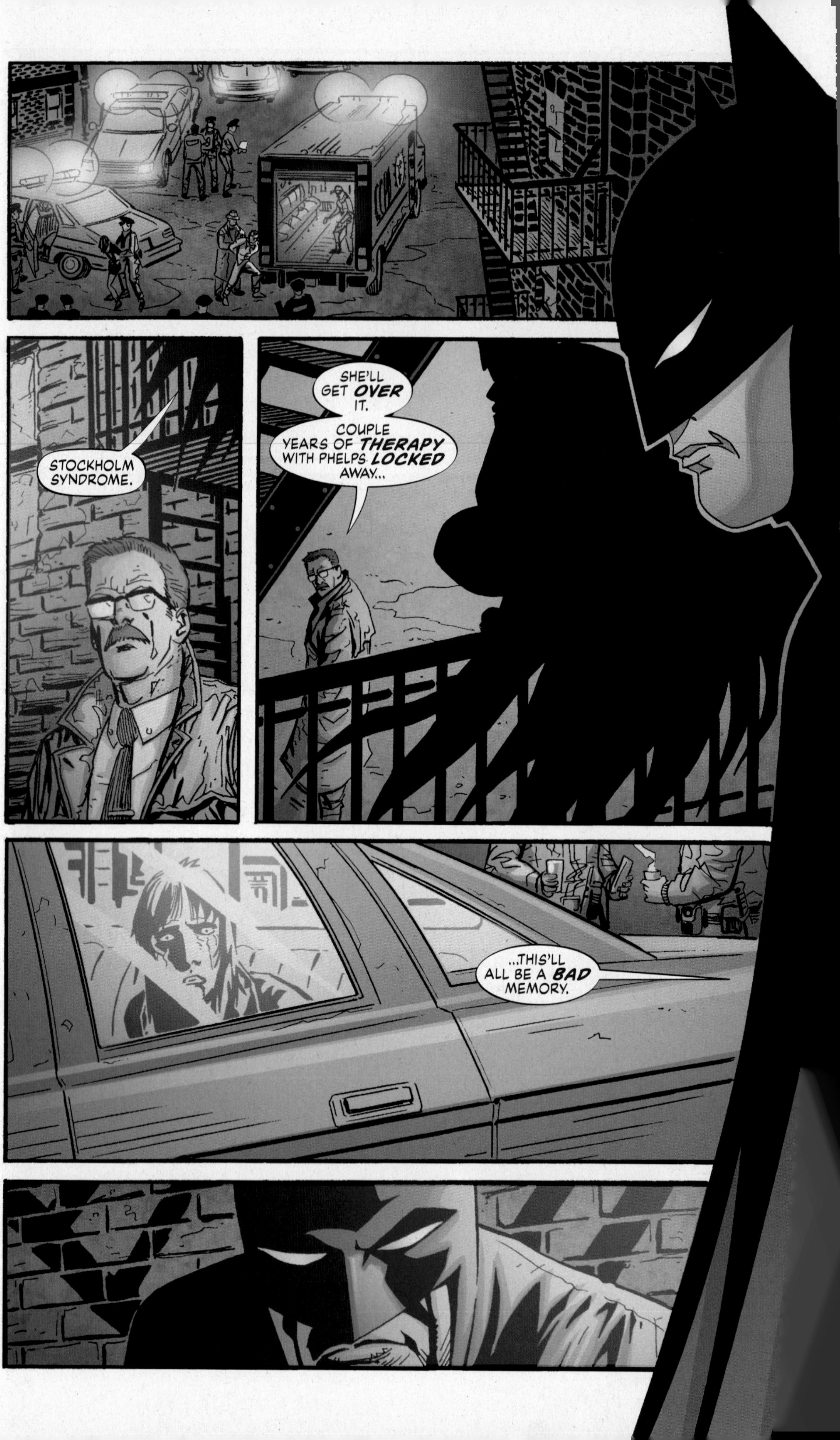
STOCKHOLM SYNDROME.
SHE'LL GET OVER IT.
COUPLE YEARS OF THERAPY WITH PHELPS LOCKED AWAY...
...THIS'LL ALL BE A BAD MEMORY.

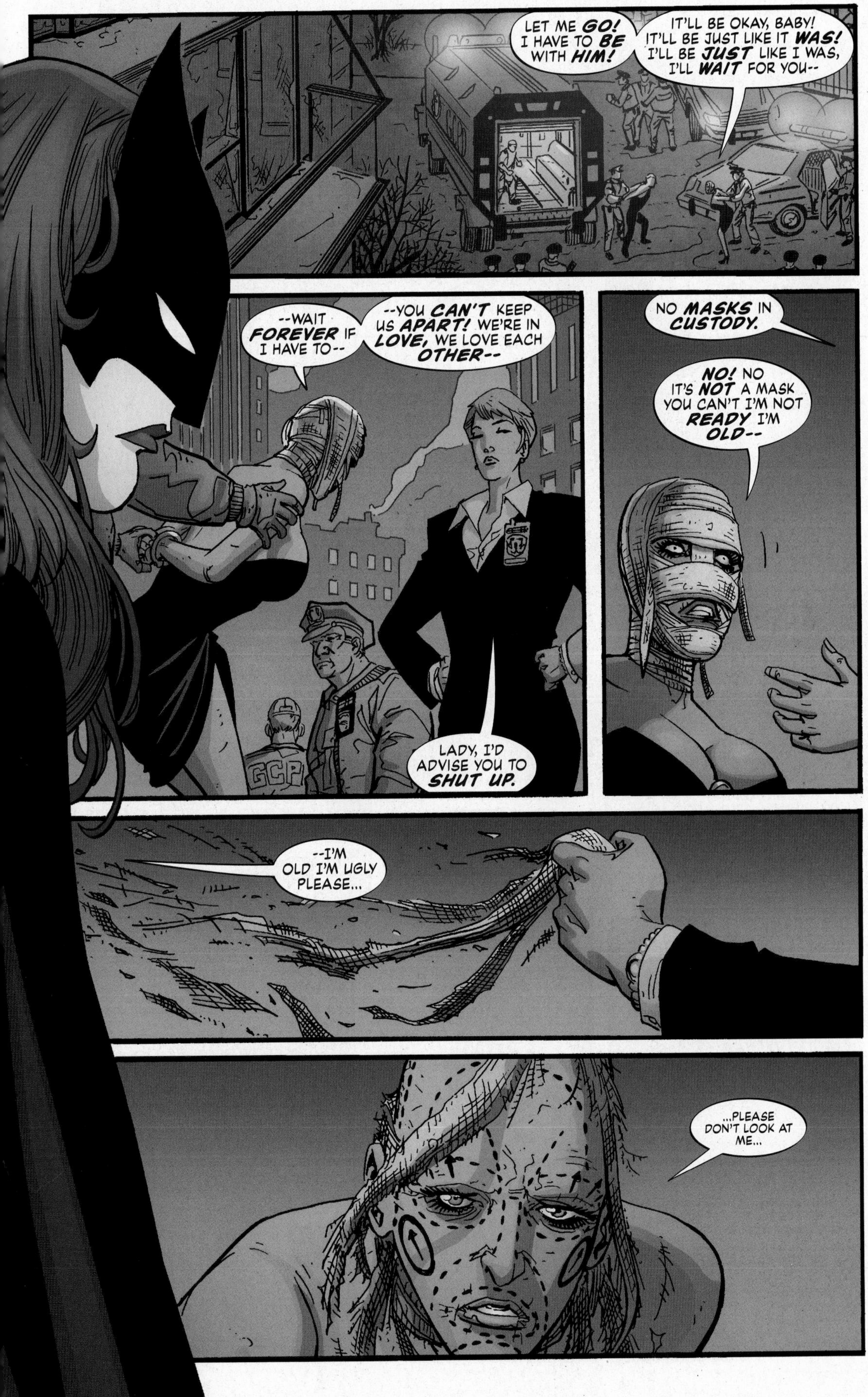
LET ME GO! I HAVE TO BE WITH HIM!
IT'LL BE OKAY, BABY! IT'LL BE JUST LIKE IT WAS! I'LL BE JUST LIKE I WAS, I'LL WAIT FOR YOU--
--WAIT FOREVER IF I HAVE TO--
--YOU CAN'T KEEP US APART! WE'RE IN LOVE, WE LOVE EACH OTHER--
LADY, I'D ADVISE YOU TO SHUT UP.
GCPD
NO MASKS IN CUSTODY.
NO! NO IT'S NOT A MASK YOU CAN'T I'M NOT READY I'M OLD--
--I'M OLD I'M UGLY PLEASE...
...PLEASE DON'T LOOK AT ME...

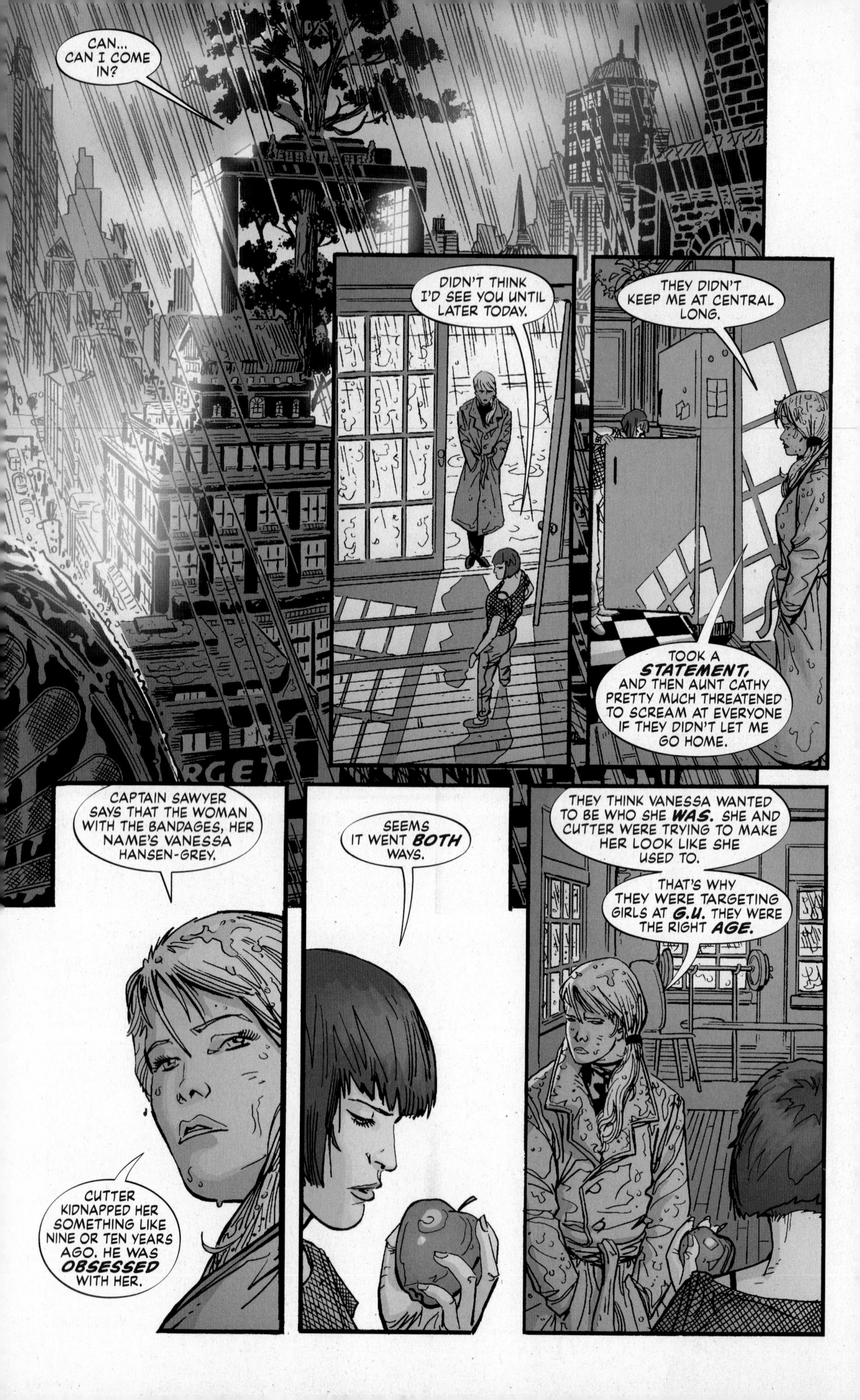
CAN... CAN I COME IN?
DIDN'T THINK I'D SEE YOU UNTIL LATER TODAY.
THEY DIDN'T KEEP ME AT CENTRAL LONG.
TOOK A STATEMENT, AND THEN AUNT CATHY PRETTY MUCH THREATENED TO SCREAM AT EVERYONE IF THEY DIDN'T LET ME GO HOME.
CAPTAIN SAWYER SAYS THAT THE WOMAN WITH THE BANDAGES, HER NAME'S VANESSA HANSEN-GREY.
CUTTER KIDNAPPED HER SOMETHING LIKE NINE OR TEN YEARS AGO. HE WAS OBSESSED WITH HER.
SEEMS IT WENT BOTH WAYS.
THEY THINK VANESSA WANTED TO BE WHO SHE WAS. SHE AND CUTTER WERE TRYING TO MAKE HER LOOK LIKE SHE USED TO.
THAT'S WHY THEY WERE TARGETING GIRLS AT G.U. THEY WERE THE RIGHT AGE.

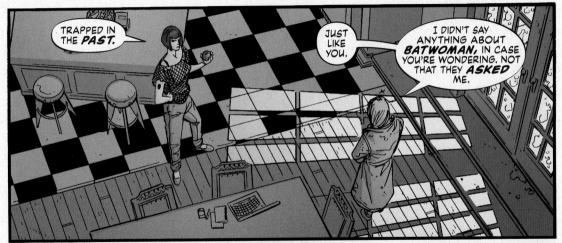

TRAPPED IN THE *PAST.*

JUST LIKE YOU.

I DIDN'T SAY ANYTHING ABOUT *BATWOMAN,* IN CASE YOU'RE WONDERING. NOT THAT THEY *ASKED* ME.

THAT'S WHY YOU *DO* IT, ISN'T IT?

BECAUSE OF WHAT HAPPENED TO YOUR MOTHER AND YOUR SISTER?

IT'S LIKE YOU SAID ABOUT LETTING GO, AND NOT BEING ABLE TO.

IT'S *MORE* COMPLICATED THAN THAT.

I CAN'T DO IT *EITHER,* KATE.

I CAN'T LET THE PAST *GO.*

I TOLD YOU ALREADY, I CAN'T HELP YOU.

I DON'T KNOW WHAT'S *HAUNTING* YOU, BETTE, BUT I CAN'T *HELP.*

YOU CAN.

I *CAN'T!*

DAMMIT, BETTE, WHAT IS IT YOU *WANT* FROM ME?

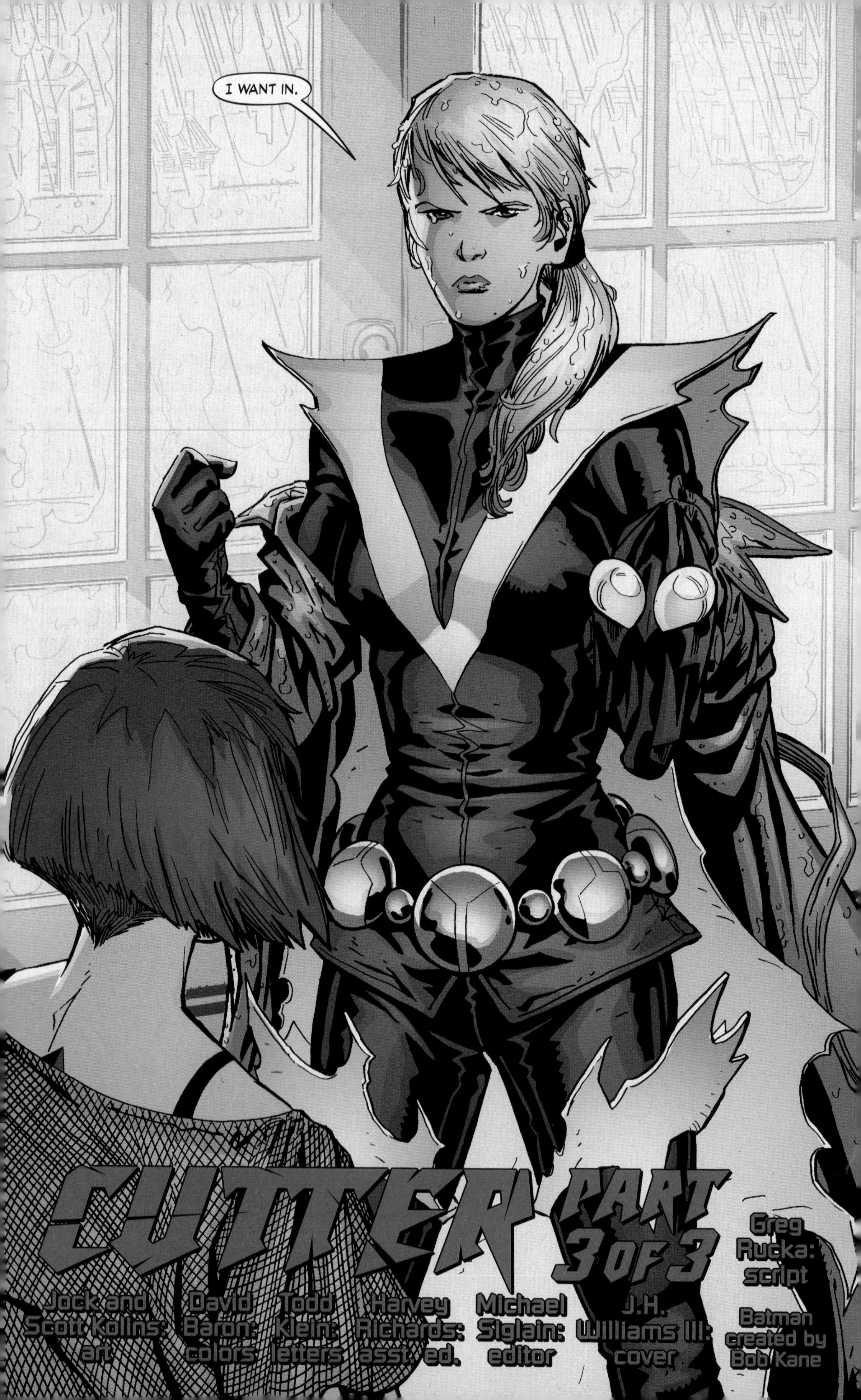
I WANT IN.
CUTTER PART 3 OF 3
Greg Rucka: script
Jock and Scott Kolins: art
David Baron: colors
Todd Klein: letters
Harvey Richards: asst. ed.
Michael Siglain: editor
J.H. Williams III: cover
Batman created by Bob Kane

DETECTIVE COMICS #854 VARIANT COVER BY J.G. JONES

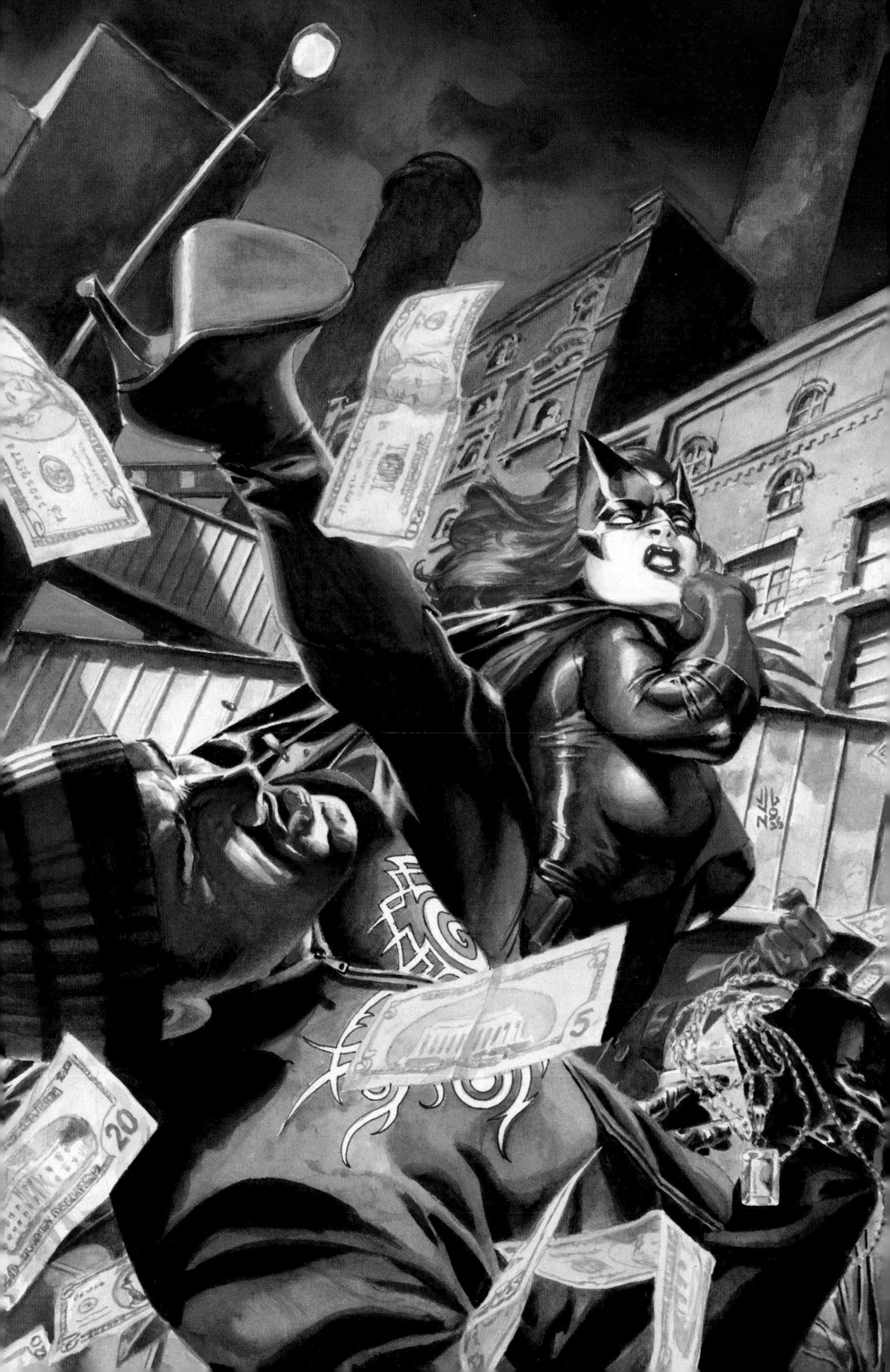
5
20

DETECTIVE COMICS #854 SECOND PRINTING COVER
BY J.H. WILLIAMS III

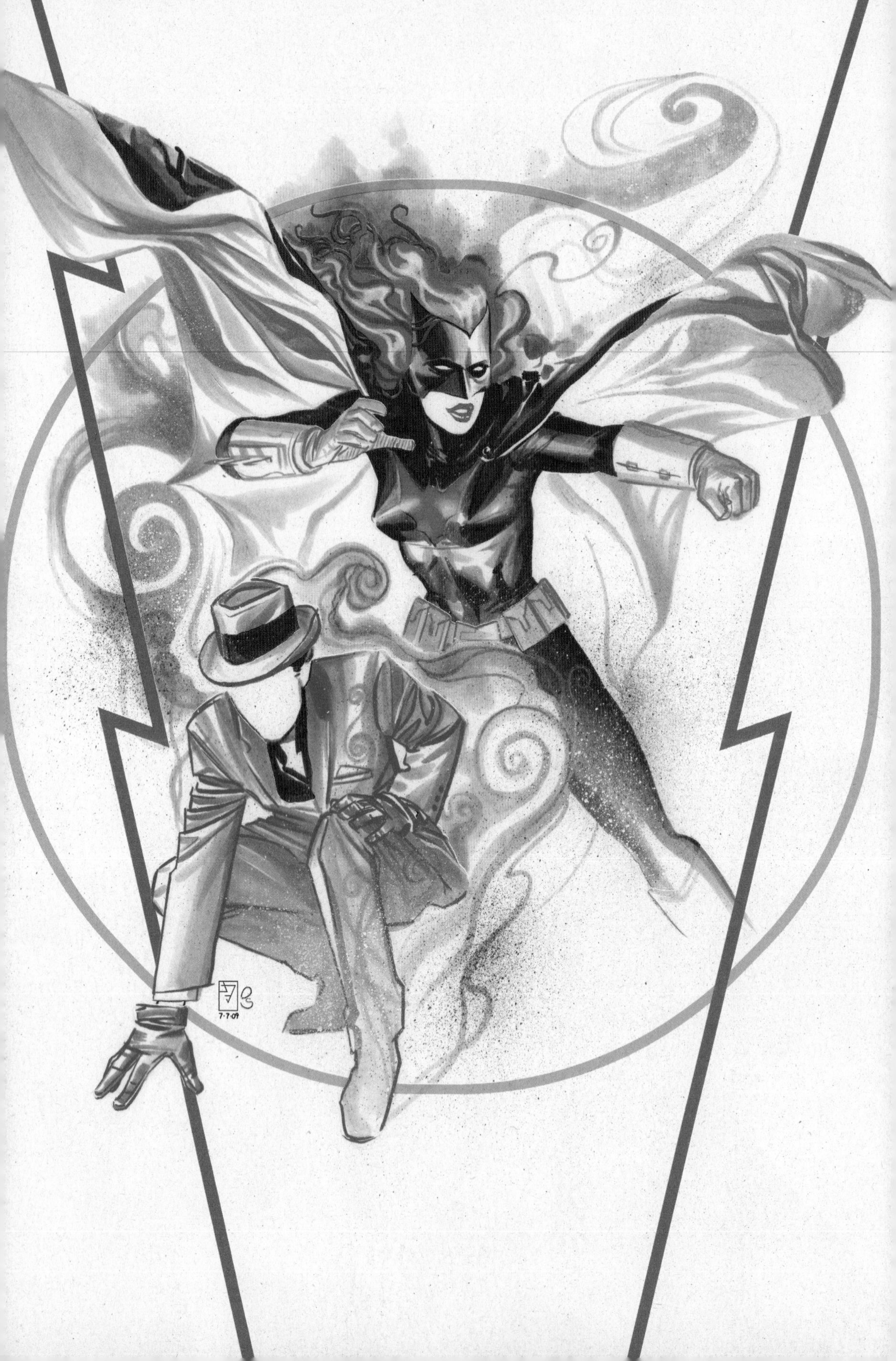

DETECTIVE COMICS #858 VARIANT COVER
BY ADAM HUGHES

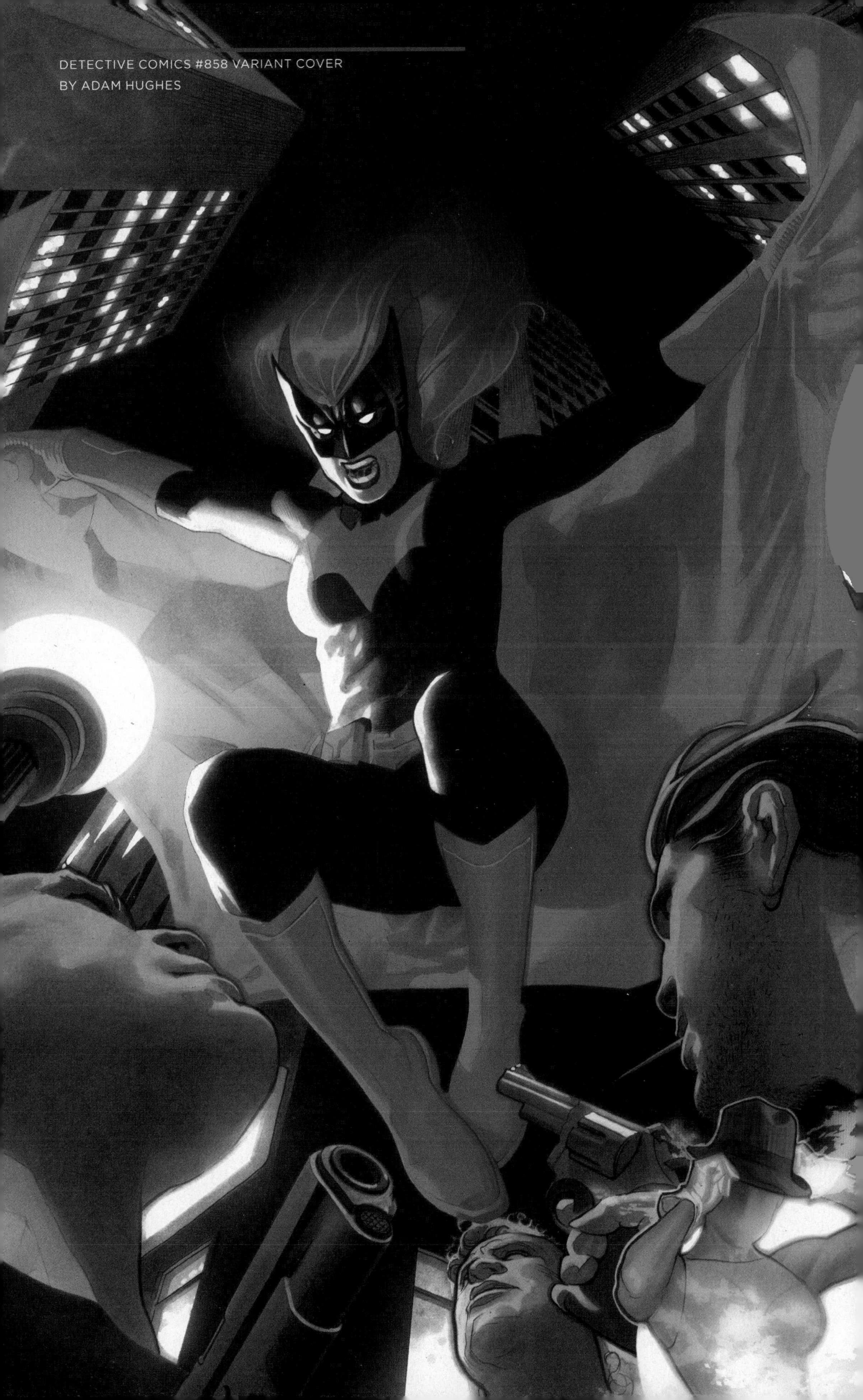

DETECTIVE COMICS #859 VARIANT COVER BY JOCK

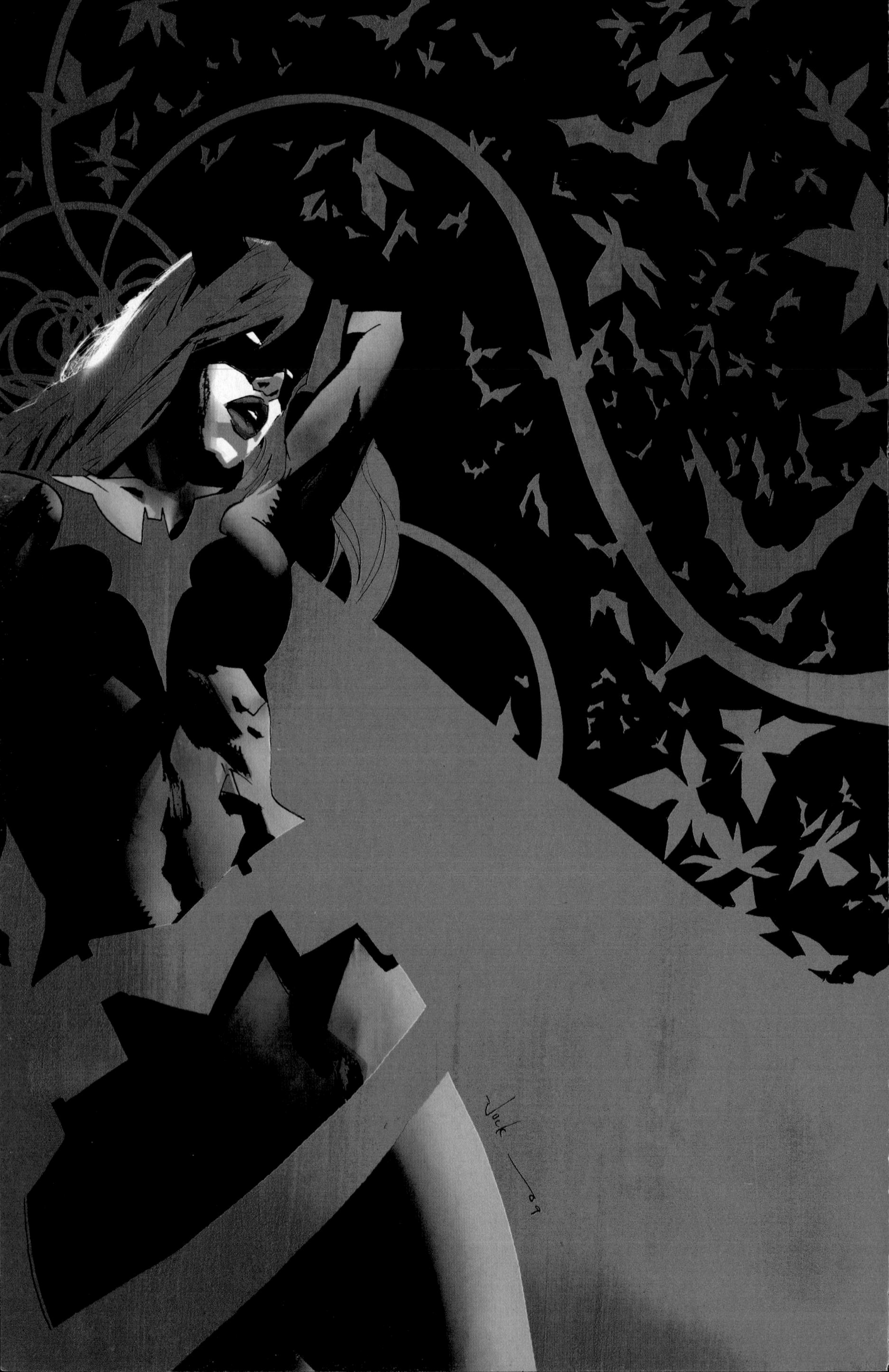
Jock

DETECTIVE COMICS #860 VARIANT COVER BY ALEX ROSS

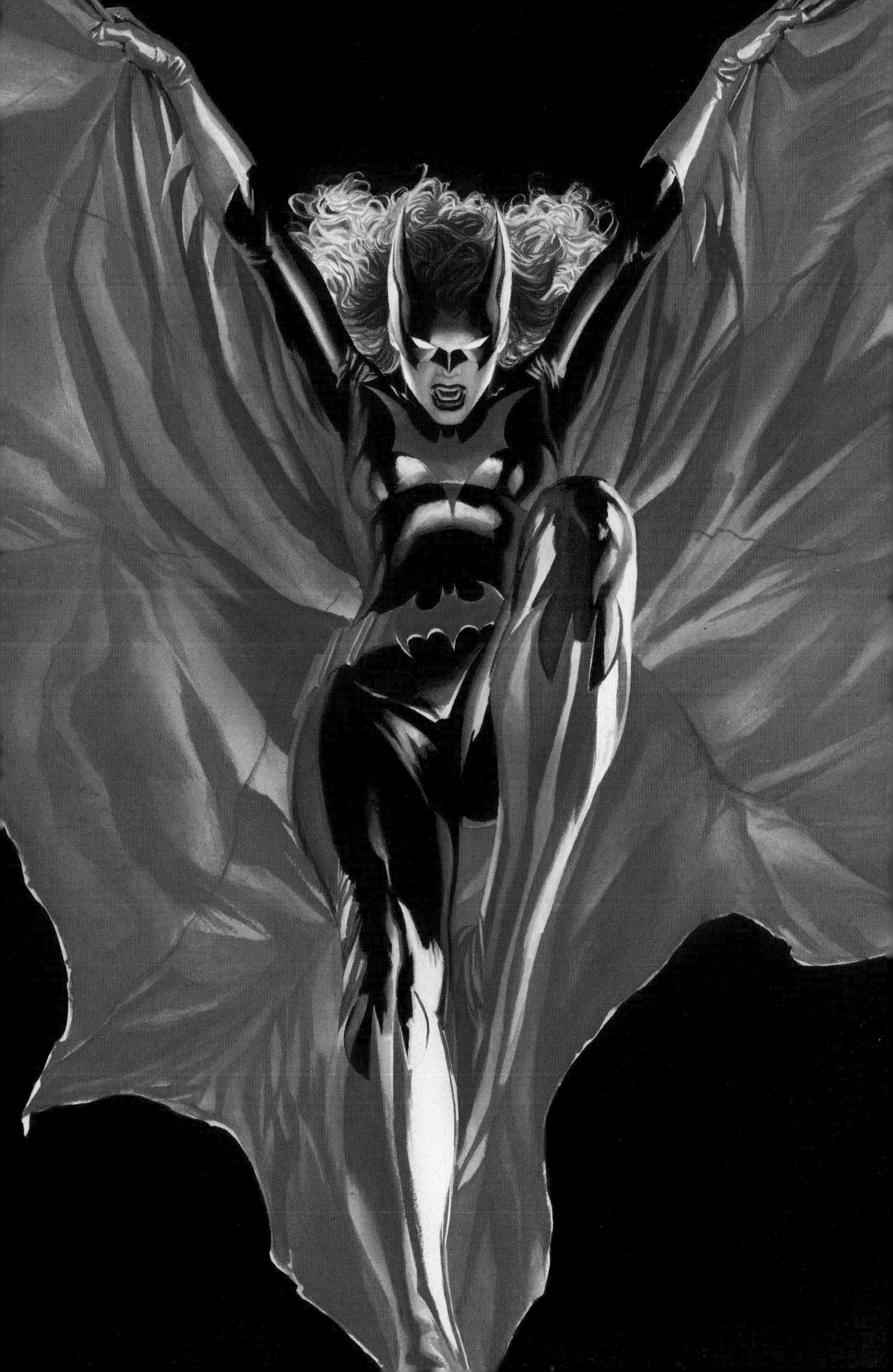

BATWOMAN - CHARACTER SHEET - ROUGHS

THESE CHANGES TO CURRENT COSTUME KEEP THE SAME BASIC LOOK BUT ADD MORE SENSIBILITY AND FUNCTIONALITY

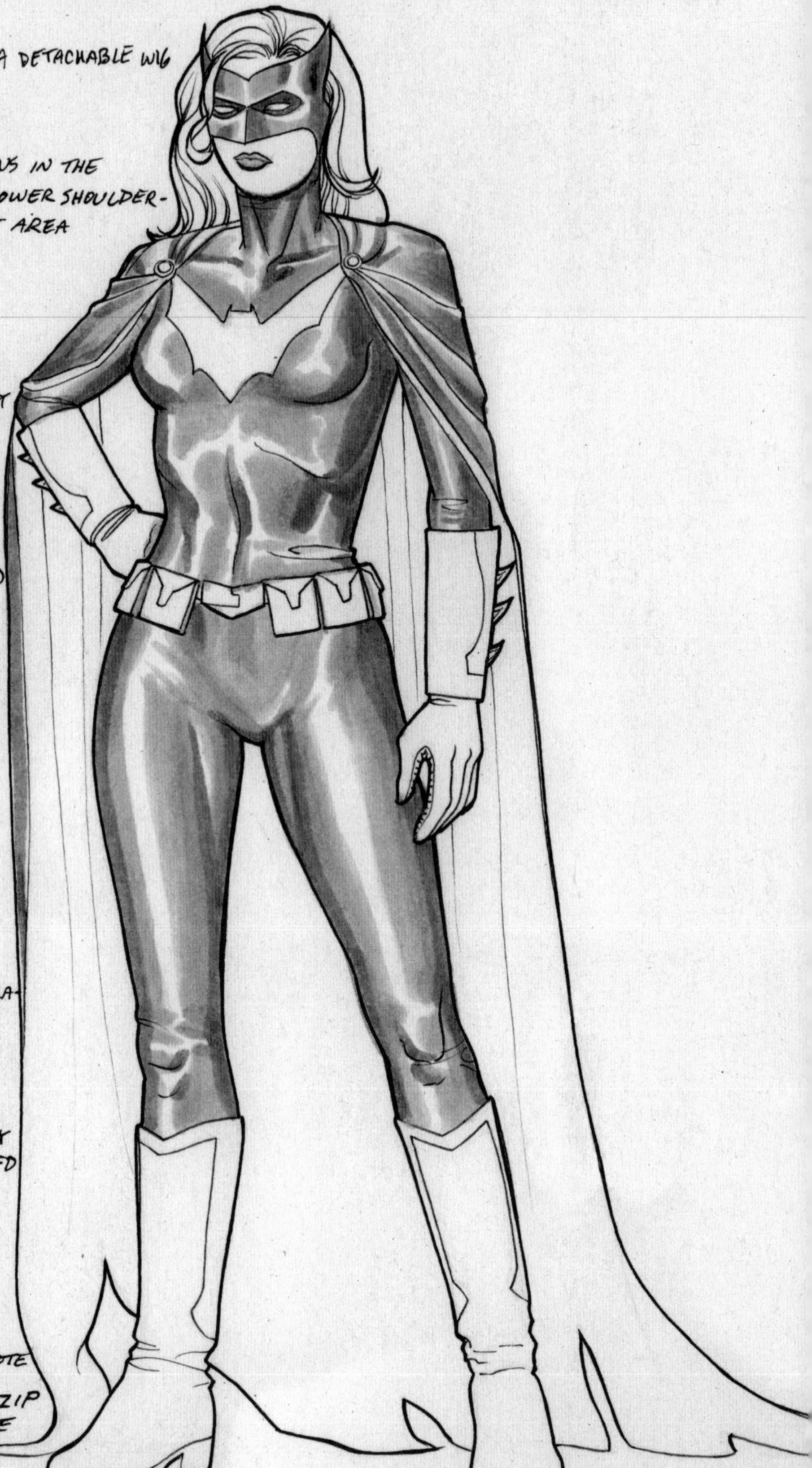

HAIR WILL BE A DETACHABLE WIG
CAPE FASTENS IN THE FRONT TO LOWER SHOULDER-UPPER CHEST AREA
MORE HEAVY ARMORED ARM BRACERS THAT ARE SEPARATE FROM GLOVES - GLOVES TUCK UNDER BRACER AT WRIST -
BELT IS FASTENED AND NO LONGER LOOSE - FITS TIGHTLY
CAPE IS MUCH LONGER - DRACULA-ESQUE
NOTE - THE CAPE ONLY COMES TO FIVE POINTS FORMING A VERY CLEARLY STYLIZED GIANT RED BAT DESIGN WHEN COMPLETELY UNFURLED
BOOTS ARE NOW MORE REALISTIC TO PURPOSE - NOTE ON ADDITIONAL DRAWING THEY ZIP UP ON THE SIDE

MASK IS ACTUALLY A MORE PROTECTIVE
THICK MATERIAL - THAT WRAPS AROUND
LOW UNDER THE HAIR - BIGGEST
CHANGE IS THE NOSE AREA NOW COVERS
HER NOSE MORE PROTECTIVELY THAN
BEFORE - ALSO HAS A MORE SERIOUS
ATTITUDE LOOK EVERYTHING IN THE
MOLDING - NOTE THE SLOTS AROUND
WHERE THE EAR AREA IS - THIS FOR
ENHANCED AUDIO ABILITY

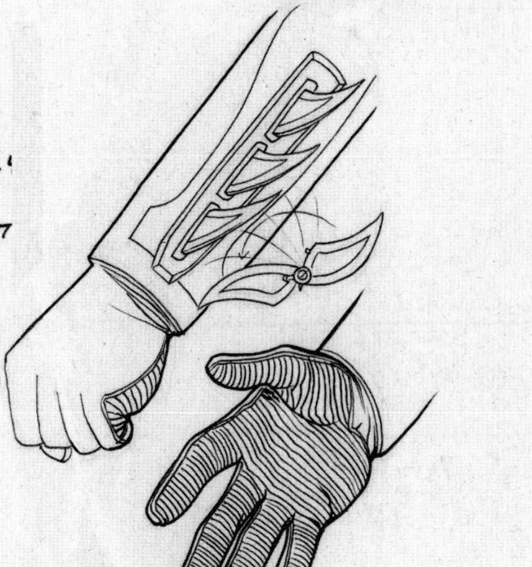

BRACER POINTS ARE DETACHABLE
AND BECOME/TRANSFORM FLIP OUT
THROWING WEAPONS

LARGER POUCH ON BELT
IN BACK - CONCEALED BY CAPE MOSTLY
- FOR LARGER WEAPONS OR
EQUIPMENT

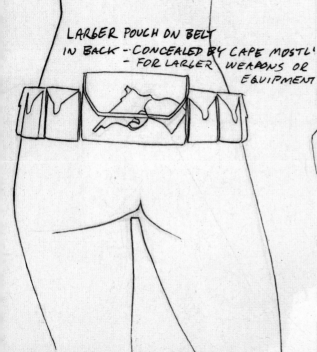

INSIDE PALM AND FINGERS
HAVE TEXTURIZED RIBBING FOR
ENHANCED GRIPPING ABILITY
ON HARD OR SMOOTHER SURFACES
- BETTER THAN ANY TYPICAL GLOVE'S
ABILITY FOR THIS

KATHY KANE - CHARACTER SHEET - ROUGHS
A COMPLETELY DIFFERENT LOOK THAN PREVIOUSLY
MORE DEFINITIVE PERSONALITY - RETRO - ROCKABILLY LOOK
SHE IS REALLY INTO ALTERNATIVE AND EDGY MUSIC -
    A BIT OF PUNK - PSYCHOBILLY - GOTH AND REFLECTS THIS IN HER
    PERSONAL STYLE - THIS LOOK HERE IS JUST ONE ASPECT

HER SKIN IS LITERALLY
VAMPIRE WHITE PORCELAIN
VERY LITTLE COLOR AT
    ALL

BLUE BIRD
TATTOO

EYES ARE GREEN
AND SHE WEARS DARK
    RED LIPSTICK
COOL TONED EYE
SHADOW

LARGE
NAUTICAL STAR
TATTOO

WHITE BOW

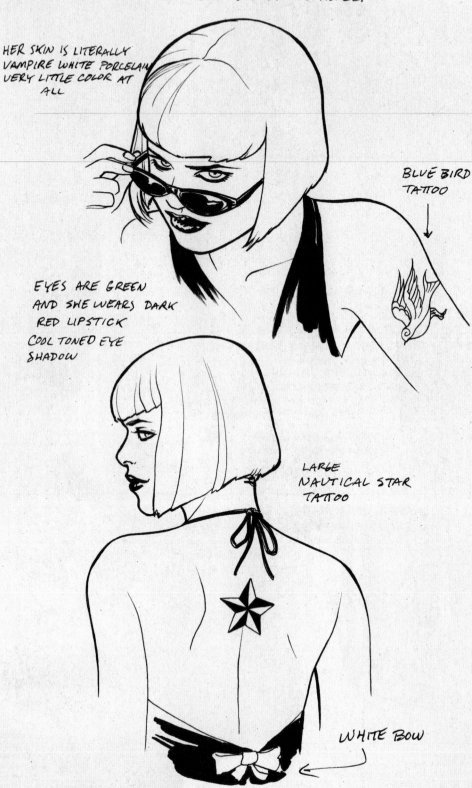

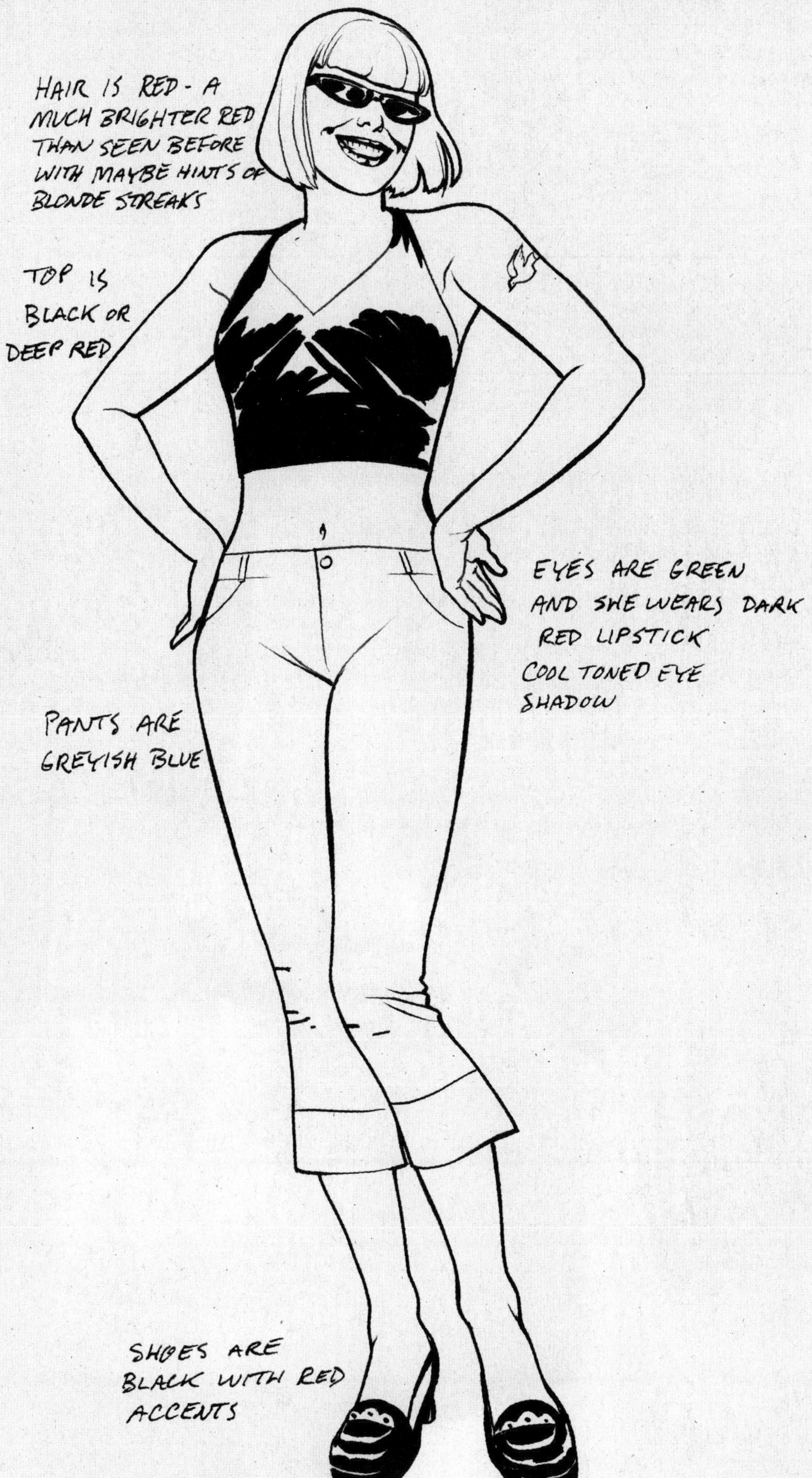
HAIR IS RED - A MUCH BRIGHTER RED THAN SEEN BEFORE WITH MAYBE HINTS OF BLONDE STREAKS
TOP IS BLACK OR DEEP RED
EYES ARE GREEN AND SHE WEARS DARK RED LIPSTICK
COOL TONED EYE SHADOW
PANTS ARE GREYISH BLUE
SHOES ARE BLACK WITH RED ACCENTS

Jim – This is the mirror spread.

ONE:
Full body shot, BATWOMAN. Iconic. More an art element, as discussed, than an actual storytelling panel. This is the mirror to Panel Eight.

NO COPY.

TWO:
Interior of the MAIN COMPARTMENT, as BATWOMAN enters.

ALICE is standing at the PUMP CONTROLS, and she's livid. The ▮▮▮▮ thing's broken! This isn't fair! Nothing's fair!! Maybe she's holding one of the BROKEN WHEELS in one hand.

In her OTHER HAND, she's holding a PISTOL, pointed at BATWOMAN.

1 BATWOMAN:	You're done, High Madame.
2 BATWOMAN:	I **disabled** the pump, you're not killing **anyone** today.

3 ALICE:	I can't **stand** this any **longer**!

THREE:
BATWOMAN shielding herself with her CAPE – covering her head with it – as ALICE empties the GUN at her. The BARRAGE of shots is knocking BATWOMAN to a knee.

ALICE is screaming at BATWOMAN as she fires.

4 ALICE:	And as for you!
5 ALICE:	As for you, I'll shake you into a kitten, that I will!!!

6 SFX:	BLAMMBLAMMBLAMMBLAMMBLAMMBLAMMklk
klkklk	

FOUR:
BATWOMAN, on one knee, lowering the CAPE to look.

ALICE has dropped the gun, already going out the ROOF HATCH. Maybe just her legs visible as she climbs out.

7 BATWOMAN:	Dammit, **stop**!

[continued]

FIVE:
Exterior of the plane, ALICE is pulling herself along the wing on hands and knees to reach one of the CANISTERS, determined to succeed. The WIND whips her hair and clothes violently.

BATWOMAN is just emerging from the HATCH behind her, shouting at her. Her GRAPPLING GUN is in her hand.

8 BATWOMAN: It's **over**, Alice!

SIX:
BATWOMAN fires the GRAPPLING GUN, the line catching ALICE around one ANKLE.

ALICE has grabbed the CANNISTER RIG with one hand, holding on to it, and with the other is pointing her REMAINING PISTOL back at BATWOMAN.

She's crying uncontrollably. She doesn't want to lose. She can't lose. If she loses, who is she?

9 SFX: paff

10 ALICE: The **face** is what one **goes** by, generally.

SEVEN:
ALICE SHOOTS, hitting the GRAPPLING GUN in BATWOMAN'S HAND.

BATWOMAN is losing the GRAPPLING GUN, obviously.

11 SFX: BLAMMM

12 BATWOMAN: ahg!

13 ALICE: Who am **I**, then?

EIGHT:
Full body shot, ALICE, iconic, the mirror image of Panel One.

NO COPY.

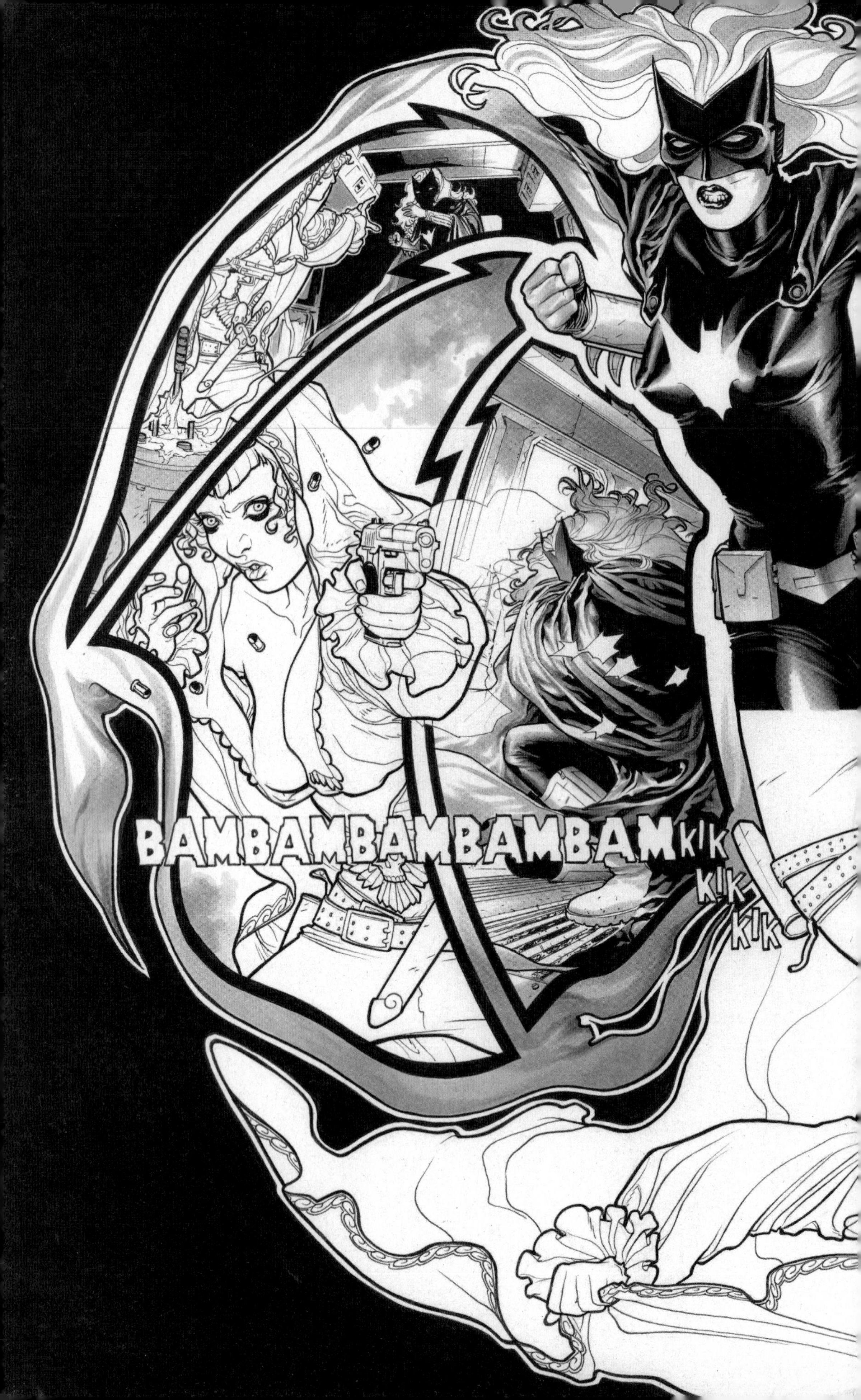
BAMBAMBAMBAMBAMBAM
KIK
KIK
KIK

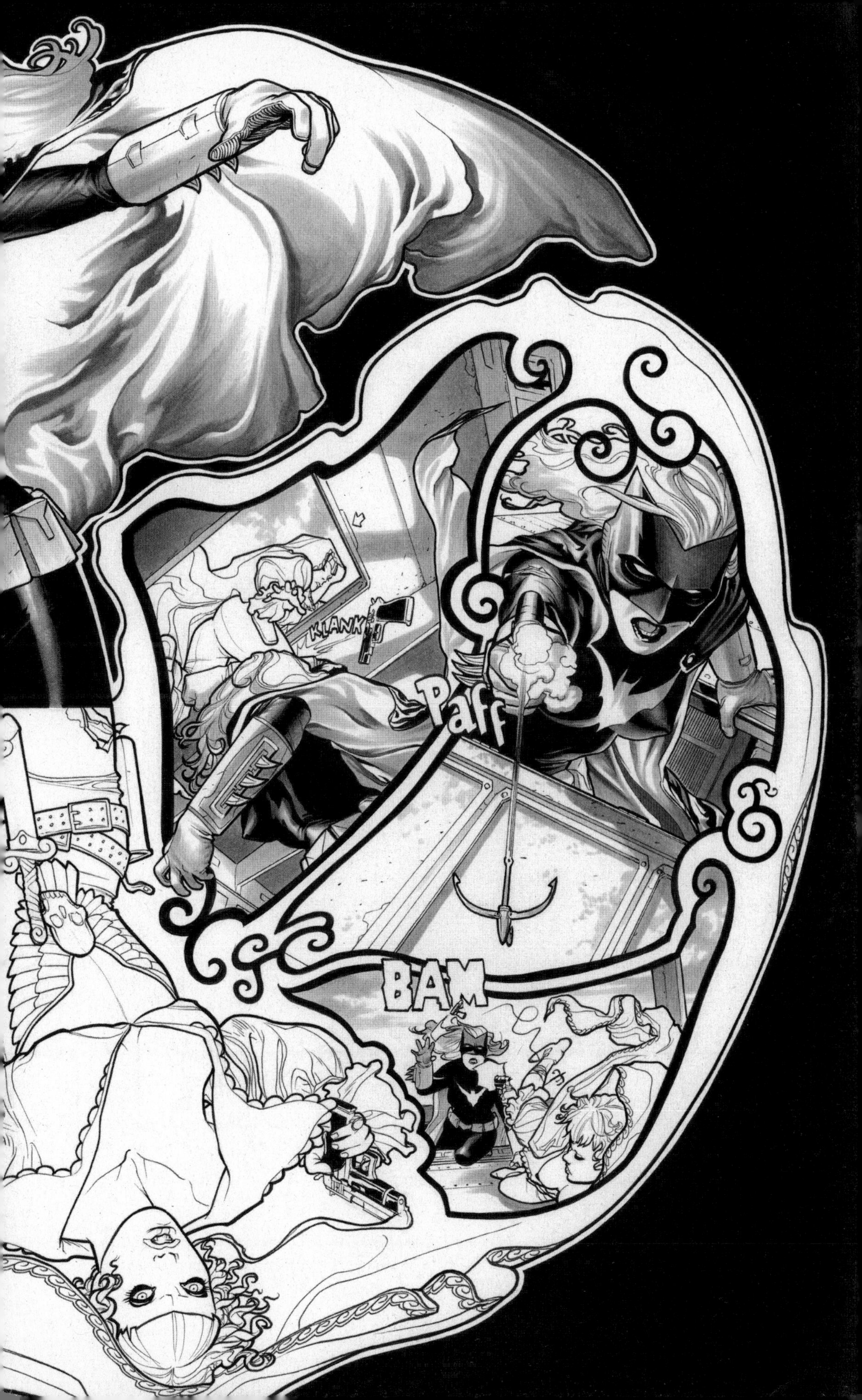
KLANK
Paff
BAM

THESE TWO PAGES REVEAL THE ORIGINAL SCRIPT BY GREG RUCKA FOR *DETECTIVE COMICS #859*, PAGES 8 AND 9 — FOLLOWED BY THE ORIGINAL BLACK-AND-WHITE ART FOR THE PAGES BY J.H. WILLIAMS III, WITHOUT COLORING OR LETTERING.

ONE:
Wash in on the SYMBOL of the Kane Heresy, the Dark Faith's circle emblem, with a CHALICE on its side, spilling WINE or BLOOD.

We *may* be able to see the top of ABBOT'S HEAD in this panel.

For the record, the Heresy is based in the ruins of pre-No Man's Land Gotham, in what was once a small church before the earthquake. The location serves as a combination place of worship, as well as a dormitory/home for those members of the Heresy unable to control their change, i.e., those Monster Men who can't, for whatever reason, revert their forms to "human."

They try to keep it nice, here, but let's face it – it's an old church that was damaged in an earthquake and is buried underground. How nice can that be? Thing to remember is that Alice's Dark Faith has bucks; Abbot's has nada.

1 ABBOT:	My story. Listen, because it is yours, too.
2 ABBOVE:	The prophesy is told in the Blasphemies, in the Book of Lilith.
3 ABBOT:	That on the eighteenth day past the feast of All Saints...

TWO:
Angle, past Doctor MALLORY KIMBALL, as she enters her office at St. Luke's Hospital, in Gotham.

MALLORY has stopped short, reacting to BATWOMAN standing in her office.

Jim, I'd like to play this differently than in a Batman title, if that makes sense – in a Batman book, Mallory would enter the office, and then we'd see Batman come out of the shadows behind her or something like that. I don't want to do that here with Kate; it's against her character, and frankly we've seen it a million times before.

With that in mind, yes, Batwoman has been waiting for Mallory, but she's not trying to scare her or ninja-tactics her. Not sure where this should put her in the room, or what pose she should be in, but she's been waiting.

BATWOMAN still has the injuries she was carrying last issue – the conceit is that all of the "present" stuff is taking place the same night, which is also the same night as the events of issues 3 and 4.

This means BATWOMAN may still be bleeding from one or two of her various wounds – that stab wound that Alice gave her in the arm is particularly nasty.

4 BATWOMAN:	Doctor Kimball.
5 BATWOMAN:	I need a **favor**.

THREE:
Back to ABBOT, panning down a bit, maybe swinging around to look at him, as if he's speaking directly to us. He's wearing his human form.

6 ABBOT:	...the Apostle of the First would come to Gotham...
7 ABBOT:	...and there he would murder the "Twice-Named Daughter of Cain."

FOUR:
BATWOMAN is holding out the TWO SAMPLE TUBES from last issue, offering them to MAL-
LORY. BATWOMAN is doing this with her wounded arm.

MALLORY is reacting to the sight of the STAB WOUND on Batwoman.

8 BATWOMAN:	I need a DNA test run on these samples.
9 BATWOMAN:	I need to confirm they're from **monozygotic** twins.

10 MALLORY:	You're **wounded**.
11 BATWOMAN:	Will you do this for me?

FIVE:
On ABBOT. He's beginning to transform into his WOLFMAN form.

12 ABBOT:	So many times, the High Madame poured these words in my ear.
13 ABBOT:	So many times, it had to be the **truth**.

SIX:
MALLORY has taken the samples in one hand, already setting them aside. With her other hand, she's
taken BATWOMAN'S wounded arm by the WRIST. Mallory is clearly concerned about the wound.

BATWOMAN is still in the same place she was last issue, and she's barely feeling the injury, now.
Focused entirely on Mallory – the injury doesn't matter, what matters is the DNA test, that's the only
thing she cares about right now.

14 MALLORY:	You've been **stabbed**—
15 BATWOMAN:	Doctor Kimball. Mallory. Will you test them for me?
16 MALLORY:	I can have the results by tomorrow night. Now take off your gauntlet, let me take a look at—

SEVEN:
On ABBOT, and he's fully transformed now. Growling out his words.

17 ABBOT:	It rrrr had to be grrr **truth**.

EIGHT:
MALLORY reacting.

BATWOMAN has pulled her hand back, already turning, heading to the window. Business here is
done, time to go.

18 BATWOMAN:	I'll be back tomorrow night.

NINE:
Tight on ABBOT, his WEREWOLF EYES.

19 ABBOT:	It rrrr **wasn't**.

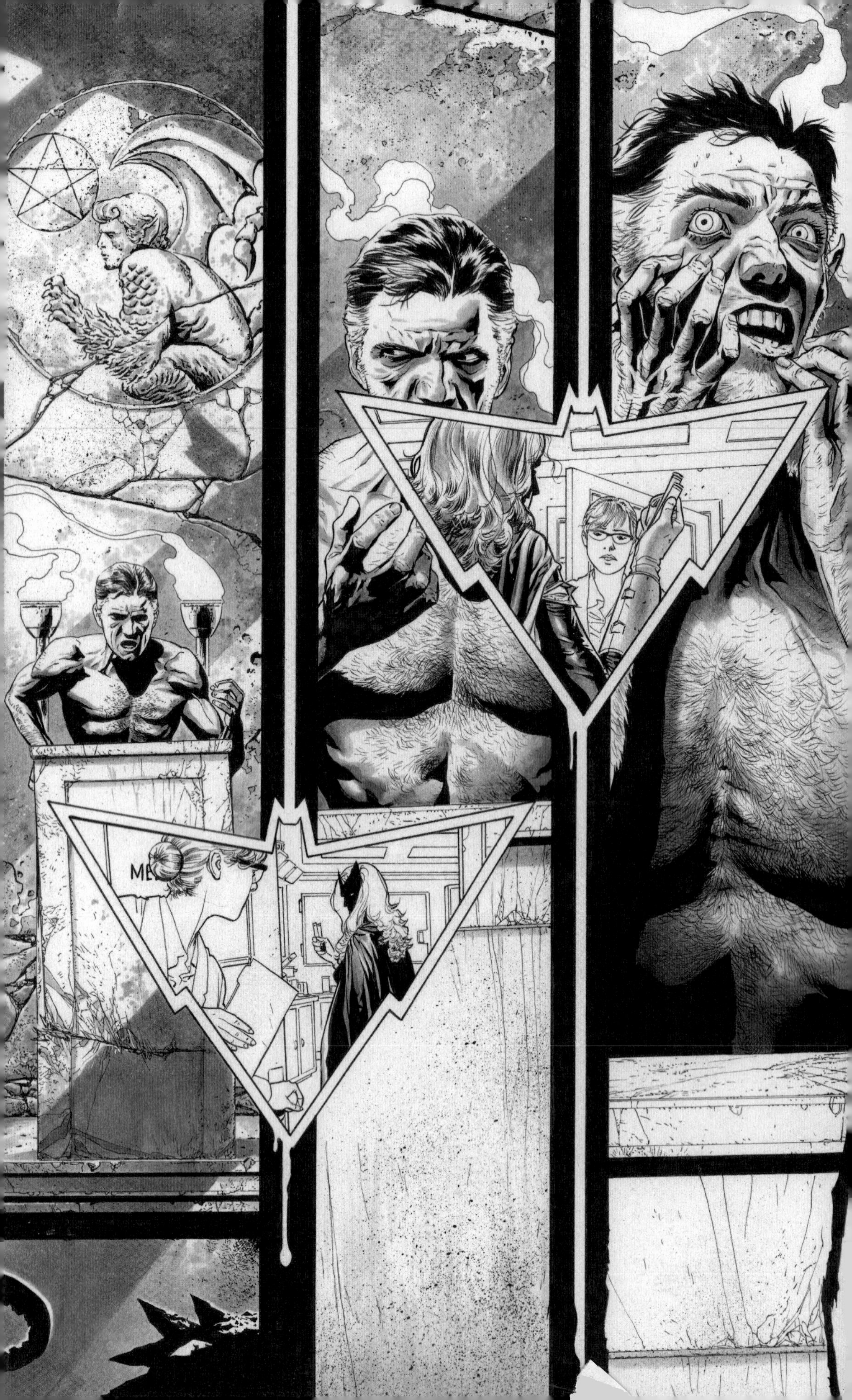